ONCE DELIVERED TO THE SAINTS

AN ORTHODOX APOLOGY
FOR THE NEW MILLENNIUM

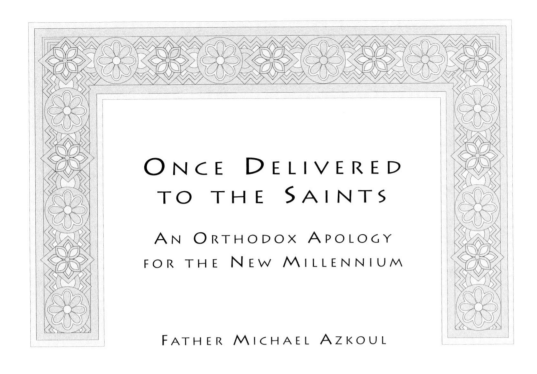

ONCE DELIVERED TO THE SAINTS

AN ORTHODOX APOLOGY FOR THE NEW MILLENNIUM

FATHER MICHAEL AZKOUL

SAINT NECTARIOS PRESS

ONCE DELIVERED TO THE SAINTS

AN ORTHODOX APOLOGY FOR THE NEW MILLENNIUM

BY FATHER MICHAEL AZKOUL

PRINTED IN THE UNITED STATES OF AMERICA

LIBRARY OF CONGRESS CATALOG CARD NUMBER 00–133947

ISBN: 0-913026-84-0

PRINTING: 9 8 7 6 5 4 2 1

DESIGN AND PRODUCTION: FOTI

DECORATIVE BANDS: ® ADAPTED FROM THE SCULPTURE AND MOSAICS
AT SAINT SOPHIA CATHEDRAL, CONSTANTINOPLE

COVER: DEESIS AND SAINTS, HARBAVILLE TRIPTYCH, 10TH CENTURY IVORY,
MUSÉE DU LOUVRE, PARIS. PHOTO © R.M.N. ARNAUDET

SAINT NECTARIOS PRESS
10300 ASHWORTH AVENUE NORTH
SEATTLE, WASHINGTON 98133-9410

E-MAIL: ORDERS@ORTHODOXPRESS.ORG

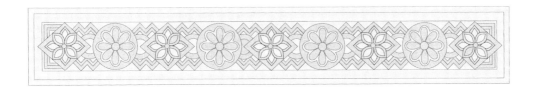

DEDICATION

ΜΕΤΑΒΑΣΙΣ ΕΙΣ ΑΛΛΟ ΓΕΝΟΣ

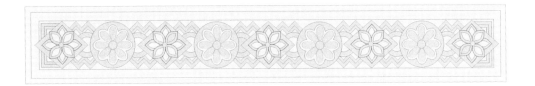

ABOUT THE AUTHOR

Fr Michael Azkoul was born in Grand Rapids, Michigan in 1930. He received a BA in philosophy in 1954 from Calvin College, a BD in theology in 1958 from St Vladimir's Russian Orthodox Seminary, and an MA and a PhD in medieval history from Michigan State University, (1963-1967).

Fr Michael has taught at Michigan State University, Youngstown State University, St Louis University, Washington University, and Seminex Lutheran Seminary. He is the author of *Anti-Christianity: the New Atheism* (1981), *The Teachings of the Holy Orthodox Church* (1986), *The Influence of Augustine of Hippo on the Orthodox Church* (1990), *St Gregory of Nyssa and the Tradition of the Fathers* (1995), and *The Toll-House Myth: the Neo-Gnosticism of Fr Seraphim Rose* (1997). He has written for scholarly journals including *St Vladimir's Theological Quarterly, The Greek Orthodox Theological Review, Theological Studies, The Byzantine and Patristic Review,* along with numerous articles and pamphlets.

Fr Michael was ordained to the diaconate (1956) and to the priesthood (1958) by Archbishop Anthony Bashir of the Antiochian Orthodox Archdiocese in the United States, where he served until, in witness to genuine Orthodox Christianity, he left that Archdiocese over concerns having to do with ecumenism. He became a priest of the Russian Orthodox Church Abroad, and served that Church until the repose of the saintly confessor of the faith, Metropolitan Philaret of New York in 1985. Concerns regarding the direction of that jurisdiction following 1985 led Fr Azkoul to affiliate himself with the Holy Orthodox Church in North America, whose traditional attitude towards the faith and the canons is well-known.

Had Fr. Azkoul espoused contemporary ecumenism, which assumes the branch theory of the Church, his magisterial command of patristic theology would have secured for him a pre-eminent place on one of the major theological faculties associated with the ecumenist patriarchates.

His defense of historic Orthodox Catholic Faith makes him a true modern confessor. He resides in St Louis, Missouri with his wife, Theodora.

TABLE OF CONTENTS

FOREWORD   XIII

PREFACE   1

CHAPTER 1   INTRODUCTION: NEW ASSUMPTIONS   5

1   FAITH AND REASON   6

2   CONSENSUS PATRUM   10

3   THE EUCHARIST DEBATE   15

4   CHRISTUS ARCHETYPUS   18

5   THE GREAT SCHISM   21

CHAPTER 2   THE APOSTOLIC TRADITION   25

1   SAINT BASIL THE GREAT   27

2   THE VINCENTIAN CANON   30

3   THE DEVELOPMENT OF DOCTRINE   36

4   OBSERVATIONS   53

CHAPTER 3   THE GOD OF ABRAHAM   55

1   THE EXISTENCE OF GOD   57

2   HE WHO IS   66

3   FILIOQUE   78

4   IMAGO DEI   90

5   THE BEATIFIC VISION   96

CHAPTER 4   MEGA MYSTERION   101

1   THE WESTERN CHRISTS   102

2   THE CHRIST OF CHALCEDON   114

3   THE LAST ADAM   120

4   PASCHA   127

5   JUSTIFICATION   144

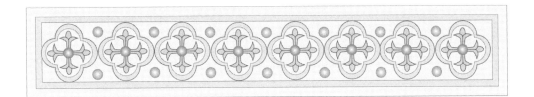

CHAPTER 5 THE BODY OF CHRIST 153

1 THE ONE CHURCH 154

2 THE NEW EVE 164

3 SACRAMENTA FUTURI 174

4 EPISCOPATUS UNUS EST 184

CHAPTER 6 THE EIGHTH DAY 207

1 MEANING IN HISTORY 209

2 MAN AND THE STATE 218

3 MONASTICISM 237

4 THE ICON 250

CHAPTER 7 EPILOGUE: ORTHODOXY AND THE SPIRIT OF ECUMENISM 263

1 THE TWENTIETH CENTURY 263

2 THE OBERLIN STATEMENT 268

3 FR GEORGES FLOROVSKY 270

4 MEGALE IDEA 276

5 SCHISM IN THE SOUL 289

CONCLUSION 305

GLOSSARY 317

LIST OF ABBREVIATIONS 325

BIBLIOGRAPHY 327

INDEX 347

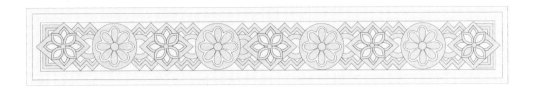

FOREWORD

I am delighted to write the Foreword for the new book *Once Delivered to the Saints: An Orthodox Apology for the New Millennium* by my good friend, Father Michael Azkoul. Father Michael and I were schoolmates and roommates at Holy Cross Orthodox Seminary where we had numerous discussions and often arguments on philosophical and theological issues.

I must confess, in spite of the caustic style (reminiscent of the Patristic method) I find the book speaks the truth and with great depth. Theology for the Orthodox is not an academic discipline nor is it an exercise in philosophical or theological speculation. Theology is not metaphysics. For the Orthodox, theology is a *charisma*, an illumination by the grace of God and a vision of the divine, uncreated light. It is an apologetic for the Incarnate Logos Who leads us to the Father in the Holy Spirit. Theology for us is not abstract but is rather personal, I–Thou relationship. Theology is an expression from the heart of the Church and apologetical in nature. The church Fathers wrote theology not for universities or academic responsibilities to attain tenure but to defend the faith "once delivered to the Saints."

In today's world of cultural pluralism, where everything is relativistic, the theologians must have the courage to speak out about what Orthodoxy has maintained throughout the centuries. Unfortunately Christ has been exiled from our world and the church is turned into a social or cultural society or organization. Through His Church, Christ is extended throughout the ages because the Church is the manifestation and continuation of the Incarnate Word of God. The Church is open to every human being in every generation and in all places. It is also Pentecost because the Holy Spirit, "whom the world cannot receive" (John 14:17), dwells in the members of the Body of Christ. That is those members who undergo glorification (*theosis*). St John Chrysostom states: "if the Spirit had not come, the Church would not have been constituted." It is the Holy Spirit that illuminates and guides the theologian to articulate and defend the faith of the gospel that the Holy Fathers defended and delivered to us.

In a most scholarly manner, Father Michael gives an exposition of the Holy Orthodox Faith and defends its position in the present cultural, relativistic society. He maintains the Patristic spirit of "holding fast" to the uniqueness of Orthodoxy that offers the truth of salvation "only" through Christ. He speaks and analyzes the important topics such as "faith and reason," the "great schism," the "Apostolic Tradition," "the existence" of the God of Abraham, Christ, the Church, eschatology, and a very critical chapter on ecumenism.

Perhaps many of these topics analyzed by Father Michael will clash with the contemporary trends and often will be labeled as "bigoted" and "hateful." I think that all Orthodox "voices" must be heard. This text is indeed a systematic, well-reasoned exposition of the Christian Orthodox message. And I further think that Father Michael has done an excellent "job." It is an exposé of the Orthodox faith that may offend some but the text "speaks the truth in love." I would say that Father Michael does not make any attempt to accommodate the contemporary zeal for "political correctness." This book is an Orthodox apologetic and a critical exposé of modern culture. This is in line with the Patristic tradition that was not absorbed into the philosophic trends of the time but defended the truth of the Incarnate Christ, the Logos.

This important text is one that needs to be studied with care for it contains the "faith of our Fathers."

George C. Papademetriou
Associate Professor of Systematic Theology
Holy Cross Orthodox Theological Seminary
Brookline, Mass

August, 2000

ONCE DELIVERED TO THE SAINTS

AN ORTHODOX APOLOGY
FOR THE NEW MILLENNIUM

PREFACE

Something remarkable has happened to the Orthodox Church in the second half of the twentieth century. The world rediscovered her. In the United States, at least, she attracted a significant number of converts. "Remarkable," I say, because Orthodoxy has had little organized missionary outreach anywhere on the globe since the fall of the Russian monarchy.

American converts—notably ex-Protestant evangelicals—have demonstrated great zeal. They have constructed institutions of learning, founded theological academies, published journals of Orthodox opinion, made public confessions of faith, produced Orthodox study guides and catechisms, and forcefully defended in public debates, lectures and videos their decisions to become "Eastern Orthodox Christians." Others, too, have joined the Church and the battle for the saving truth. They give every indication of competent familiarity with the history and doctrine of the Orthodox Church.

But there is a dark side to these "conversions." First, converts have been rapidly baptized (if at all), without sufficient catechizing which, according to St Hippolytus, is a three-year undertaking before Christian initiation (*Apost. Trad.*, XVII, 1 Dix). Second, they have achieved clerical and lay ministries in "mainstream Orthodoxy" with a celerity contrary to simple prudence, the strictures of the canons, and the counsels of the holy Fathers. Last, too many proselytes are motivated more by the pyschological need for stable doctrine and values, for structure in their worship, for order in their lives—almost lost in Protestantism, and disappearing in post-Vatican II Roman Catholicism– something they claim to have found in the traditionalism of the Orthodox Church, rather than love for the Truth.

In a word, we have every reason to believe that the profession of faith by too many of these converts is not genuine. They seem unacquainted with the truth that the "Christianity" of the post-Orthodox West is both sire to and offspring of a perverse and devolving occidental culture; and, consequently, their conversions to Orthodoxy should have involved (as they usually do not) an explicit rejection of the fundamental symbols, ideals and values of Western life and thought.

1

   As a result, I am not persuaded that recent converts to Orthodoxy recognize her as the New Israel, the Catholic Church, the Ark of salvation, that
is, in "becoming Orthodox," they have been translated to another reality—
μετάβασις εἰς ἄλλο γένος. Support for my brooding suspicion is the demo-
graphic that they have swelled the ranks of the so-called "ecumenist" and
"New Calendar jurisdictions" which consistently exhibit a contempt for the
canonical mandates of the ancient Councils with a cavalier insensitivity
toward canonical church order. They brazenly modify the divine Services
and subvert the Orthodox social ethic with the contemporary "political correctness." This indifference to, if not a disdain for, apostolic doctrine and
piety, is characteristic of the reconstructed vision of a pastel Orthodox, the
implicit denial of τῇ ἅπαξ παραδοθείσῃ τοῖς ἁγοῖς πίστει, "the Faith once delivered to the Saints" (Jude 3).
   In part, this book is addressed to these so-called "evangelical Orthodox"
and to all recent neophytes who, although sincere, are almost always unpre-
pared for the patristic experience and misguided by too many religious and
philosophical misconceptions, by too many false tutors, by the spiritual and
cultural baggage of their former lives. Of course, this book also speaks to the
next generation of Orthodox, the Orthodox of the new millennium; and, for
that matter, to everyone who confesses Christ as God while harboring very
serious doubts about the state of Western religions and culture.
   If nothing else, then, *Once Delivered to the Saints* is a sign against the self-
deception of so-called "ecumenical" Orthodox who, while protesting their
fidelity to her Apostolic Tradition, nonetheless seek in every way to conform
the Church of God to this world. From time to time, they may object to the
social agenda of the World Council of Churches, but they remain within an
organization whose ultimate aim is to incorporate Roman Catholicism, Protestantism, Orientals, Judaism, Islam, Hinduism, etc., and Orthodoxy herself
into a universal religion, contrary to the Christian Revelation which has
established the One, Holy, Catholic and Apostolic Church for the salvation of
the human race.
   Once Delivered to the Saints is no mindless display of partisan intransi-
gence, nor a fanatic and obscurantist manifesto, but a candid introduction to
the immutable Faith of Christ. No doubt this "apology" for historic Orthodoxy will clash with the "spirit of the age." Her claim to exclusivity and infallibility will necessarily carry the perception of "theological arrogance" for a
world whose call for "diversity" and inclusiveness allows no absolutes.

Perhaps, for some who are demanding a serious re-examination of Western life and thought, this work will not prove offensive. It may offer some insight into the direction their lives and their world should take if there is to be any hope for a radical "transvaluation of values." This book will also be a warning to them: salvation, in every sense of that word, has no chance of realization if their method is to rework Western ideas which have been reworked *ad nauseum* for a millennium; nor is the solution a merger with oriental paganism, a syncretism which promises only an experiment in futility. In other words, the ancient Orthodox Faith is their only "living option."

Special attention will been given to those doctrines in the history of Christian theology which explain the religious (and cultural) disposition of the occident, and, consequently, forms the basis of its difference with Orthodoxy. At the same time, no one should assume that *Once Delivered to the Saints* rests on the naive optimism that by sheer force of logical or historical argument the reader will come to share my convictions. What is said here has been said before, ignored and opposed before; nevertheless, it is worth restating, in a new way, to a new generation of searchers who may be willing to listen.

I am grateful to Hieromonk Haralampos of the Holy Transfiguration Monastery of Boston, Fr George Turpa, Assistant presbyter of the St Nektarios Greek Orthodox Cathedral, Toronto, Ontario, and Theodore Williams, Ph.D., Atlanta, Georgia, for their comments and criticism. Likewise, a great debt of gratitude is owed to Fr Neketas Palassis, presbyter of the St Nektarios American Orthodox Church and editor of the *Orthodox Christian Witness*, Seattle, Washington, for publishing this book, motivated only, as usual, by a love of the Savior.

Fr Michael Azkoul
St Louis, May, 2000

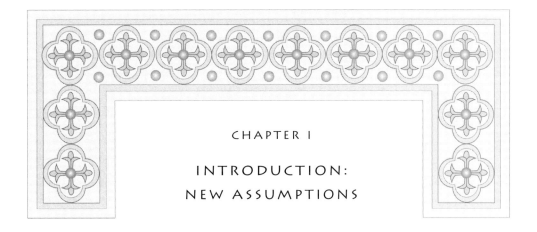

CHAPTER I

INTRODUCTION:

NEW ASSUMPTIONS

Not a few people are fascinated by the "mystical theology of Eastern Church," "the grandeur of her Liturgy," "the richness of her patristic tradition," "the inexplicable persistence of monasticism," "the marvellous aesthetics of her iconography," the "intriguing" concept of salvation, *theosis* (θέωσις)[1]–even the curious attachment of some Orthodox to the Julian Calendar. But to be "strangely attracted" to or fascinated by Orthodoxy is not always to understand her. Understanding must come by faith; indeed, a faith which has been and is being cleansed from pre-judgments, whatever their longevity, whatever their ostensible profundity.

Understanding Orthodoxy is difficult for outsiders. It is impossible for anyone who approaches her invested with a cultural history alien to her mind. As a matter of logical necessity, then, a fruitful knowledge of the Faith requires a new vision of God, of Christ, of the Church and history and, therefore, the adoption of a new set of assumptions. What this means we hope to clarify in the pages that follow.

---

[1]   The Christian Church has always held that salvation consists of becoming a son of God, i.e., the deification (*theosis*) of both body and soul through communion with the Divinity by the grace of the only Savior, Jesus Christ, the Son of God by nature. The saved, the sons of God by grace, become incorruptible and sinless (Rom. 2:2; I Cor. 15:53-54) by being incorporated into the Body of Christ, that is, the Church; they "partake of the divine Nature" (II Pet. 1:4) by sharing in the divine Sonship through the communicable, uncreated divine Energies or Operations of Jesus Christ in the Holy Spirit. This universal teaching on Christian soteriology of the ancient Church and the Fathers has largely been forgotten or misunderstood in the post-Orthodox West.

Deification (*theosis*) is discussed in chapter 4, pp. 135-137; see also I Tim. 6:16; II Tim. 1:10, and Rom. 2:2. Cf. Ps. 82:6; and John 10:34..

1 FAITH AND REASON

There is no assumption more fundamental to human experience than the relation which obtains between "faith" or "revelation" and "reason."[2] There is certainly no more crucial "problem" in the history of Western thought. On their definition and relationship hangs the truth or falsehood of all its philosophies and theologies. Indeed, the concept of "Christian philosophy" (so dear to Roman Catholicism), neither achieved unity in the Middle Ages, nor finds it today—a disunity of thought which explains, among other things, the plurality of religious doctrines in both the Papacy and "the Protestant movement" which emerged in the last days of medieval Scholasticism. There is indeed a common spirit which accounts for the incessant repetition of Western ideas, secular and religious.

A   The nature and possibility of "Christian philosophy," as the post-patristic West has always imagined it to be, depends now, as it always has, on the pre-established harmony between "nature" and "grace," the temporal and the spiritual; that is to say, on the relationship between "faith" or "revelation" and "reason" or "philosophy." In his classical work, *Reason and Revelation in the Middle Ages* (New York, 1938), Professor Etienne Gilson outlines three positions of *faith* and *reason* taken by the Latin Scholastics (impacting inevitably and fundamentally the entire intellectual history of the West): "the primacy of faith," "the primacy of reason" and "the harmony of reason and revelation." The first subordinated reason to faith, denying to philosophy the ability to discover transcendent truth without faith (fideism). In this connection, any conflict that arose between reason and the teachings of revealed religion was always resolved in favor of the latter. Too often, reason became the enemy of faith, as St Paul had already warned, "Beware lest any man cheat you by philosophy, and vain deceit; according to the tradition of men. . .and not according to Christ" (Col. 2:8).

Appeal was often made to Tertullian who had spoken for this point of view in the seventh book of his treatise, *On the Prescription of Heretics,*

> For the province of philosophy is the material of the world's wisdom, the rash interpreter of the nature and dispensation of God. Indeed heresies are themselves instigated by philosophy. The same subject-matter is discussed over and over again by the heretics and

---

2   In the post-Orthodox West, "faith" (*fides*) has two meanings; it refers to the act of believing and to the object of that belief. The first is the act of assenting, the second the object to which the intellect assents. In either case, it is "assent without knowledge." Latin and Protestant, even secular philosophers and theologians, continue to maintain the distinction. "Faith" today is generally equated with subjective religious experience.

the philosophers.... Whence comes evil? Why is it permitted? What is the origin of man? And in what way does he come?... Whence comes God? which Valentinus settles with the answer: from *enthymesis* and *ecktroma*.

Unhappy Aristotle! who invented for these men dialectics, the art of building up and pulling down, an art so far-fetched in its conjectures, so harsh in its arguments, so productive in its contentions—embarrassing even to itself, retracting everything, and really treating of nothing!

The simplest Christian has a "philosophy" by revelation which the professional philosopher by reason can never attain.

Other medieval thinkers held the reverse opinion, or that revelation was given to become rational. The starting point of all inquiry is reason, not faith. Faith is inferior to reason, because the latter offers rational assurance where faith demands only "assent without knowledge." Reason is necessary to make religious doctrine persuasive. Therefore, everything taught by the Church for the belief of her members must be subject to the review and approval of human reason, lest faith become an obstacle to understanding. Some Scholastics followed the thirteenth century Arab philosopher, Averroes (Ibn Rashid), who taught that "there is no wisdom in the world save that which is provided by philosophers." "Nothing is to be believed, save that which is self-evident, or can be deduced from self-evident propositions".[3]

Gilson approved of neither the "Averroists" nor the fideists, whether in spirit or method. In expounding the position of Thomas Aquinas, he elaborates his own: the harmonization of faith and reason, revelation and philosophy: the conciliation of their independent spheres, the rights of critical inquiry and the duty of submission to a revealed order, the integrity of natural values (*ius humanum quod est ex naturali ratione*) and of Christian values which come by grace (*ius divinum quod est ex gratia*). Revelation, Gilson contends further, is self-sufficient and self-contained, a distinctive order of knowing independent from, but not, in principle, opposed to reason or philosophy. They are formally distinct, the Christian revelation is an indispensable auxiliary to reason. Thus, some things are attainable by reason alone, but "with faith as a safe guide to rational truth and an infallible warning against philosophical error."[4] Any conflict between faith and reason, of course, is evidence that reason has erred, for the truths of Christianity are infallible. This canon of judgment applies especially to any philosophy which calls itself Christian.

---

[3]   Quoted, in Gilson, p. 64.

[4]   *Ibid.*, p. 83.

Gilson's summation is interesting not only for what it says, but what it fails to say. There was no unanimity amongst the medieval theologians and philosophers on what wisdom belongs to faith and what wisdom belongs to reason, and he fails to provide us with an explanation for that diversity. He might have admitted that medieval Roman Catholicism, in the process of redefining the Christian Tradition, allowed her intellectuals to experiment with variant perspectives. Although demanding adherence to a set of basic doctrines, ecclesiastical authorities otherwise gave the Schoolman the freedom to organize their social and political thinking in accordance with norms and values not specifically Christian.

One ought not to be surprised, then, that the Scholastics trespassed with regularity the "boundaries" erected by the Fathers. For Gilson, as for Thomas *cum sui*, the Fathers were "shoulders" upon which medieval man sat to look further. It was a terrible legacy for the West, as we shall see, a legacy with enormous philosophical and theological consequences, in particular that metaphysical dualism, inherited from Augustine, which will continue to dominate the Western thinking from the time the Latins separated from Orthodoxy. We need not ask, then, why the relationship between faith and reason became a question at all; or why the Scholastics needed to wrestle with all those complex "problems" related to it, "problems" already resolved by the Fathers.

B   According to Aristotle, "philosophy should be called the (rational) knowledge of truth." The end of rational or "theoretical knowledge" is the truth as opposed to practical knowledge whose purpose is action. Now we do not know a truth without apprehending its cause; but there are many truths, and none so great as the Cause from which all other truths are derived; hence, that Cause which is the principle of eternal things must always be the most true (*Meta. I*, 10, 11 993b 20-28). Here is the definition of "the foreign philosophy" which the Fathers rejected as the way for establishing the truth of the Christian religion. Never have I read anywhere in the writings of the Fathers that the name for "philosopher" is "the absolutely wise man," that is, he who seeks with his reason "the highest causes" (*Meta. I*, 1, 1 981b28-30).

Aquinas, of course, claimed to possess the Christian revelation ("faith") which permitted "the Christian philosopher" to rationally know things about God which have been hidden from the "natural" intellect. For example, faith provides the intellect with the knowledge that God is "triune." Furthermore, although by faith, Thomas said, we know that God transcends whatever man may know about Him by reason, yet we do not conclude that the Christian is forbidden the rational pursuit of "final causes" or "Cause." We are ever confident that "it is impossible that the truths of faith should oppose the principles which human reason knows naturally" (*On the Truth of the Catholic Faith V*, 3; A.C. Pegis, ed.).

The patristic "solution" to the "problem" of faith and reason is soteriological, not "philosophical" (in the ordinary sense). We recall that St Justin Martyr, in his *Dialogue with Trypho*, tells the Jew that the aim of "philosophy" is not the quest for truth, but union with God; and since He is the ultimate object of all Justin's searching and desiring, the Saint called himself a "philosopher" (*Dial. c. Tryp.* II, 6 FC). Later, St Basil the Great, in his *Address to the Young Concerning Worldly Study*, will instruct his monks that learning of any sort has no profit for the Christian unless it contributes to his salvation (*Ad Adol. de Leg. Gen.* II, 6-8 L). There is no discord between what the Christian believes and what he thinks, because what he thinks presupposes what he believes; and what he believes is revealed from God. Thinking is only a reflection on the experience of believing. From a human point of view, an integrated vision of things alone accounts for the saving "knowledge" of God.

Likewise, writes St Gregory the Theologian, it is from the Spirit Who dwells in the Church that "comes our new birth, and the regeneration of the new creation from which arises the spiritual knowledge (ἐπίγνωσις) of the dignity of Him Who has recreated us" (*Ora XXX*, 28 PG 36 165A). St Gregory introduces us to a number of ideas not found in the locutions of the Schoolmen and their successors. He testifies to another understanding of "faith"— "faith" as more than "assent," as a totality of "the substance of things hoped for, the evidence of things not seen" (Heb. 11: 1); and "reason," enlightened by Baptism, regenerated by the Spirit, becomes, for all its limitations, the sentinel of the soul, a discipline for the human spirit in its search for the realities beyond the senses, for its apprehension of noetical things.

Indisputable to the Fathers was that all truth, whether of the Church or of the nations, is revealed, is the work of the divine Logos "Who enlightens every man that comes into the world" (John 1:9); and, to Whom every thought must become captive (II Cor. 10:5)—a belief which explains their attitude towards pagan letters and philosophy. They could justifiably use the truths uncovered by "the natural philosophy of the Greeks," in the cause of Christian apologetics while, at the same time, excoriating Plato and Aristotle and all of Hellenism as "vain," "subtle," "foolish," "contradictory and artificial," to employ some of the vintage adjectives of St Basil (*Hom. in Ps.* XXXIII, 7 PG 29 341A). What the Fathers accepted or rejected was determined by "the Faith," not by some ambition to elevate an ostensibly subjective faith to an ostensibly objective knowledge, the so-called *fides quaerens intellectum*.

Consequently, the title of "Christian philosopher" has a meaning with which students of medieval and modern thought are sorely unfamiliar. His purpose is not to prove by reason what he already believes on faith. He is not impelled by the desire to persuade the unbeliever that Christianity and Christian doctrine are demonstrable. Plato and Aristotle are not his mentors. He is rather a man of Tradition. To quote St Gregory of Sinai,

> . . .a teacher initiated into things divine. . .inspired by the Holy Spirit. . .he interprets what is intelligible [noetical] and invisible in terms of what is sensible and visible. . . . A divine philosopher is he who through ascetic purification and noetic contemplation has achieved a direct union with God, and is a friend of God, in that he esteems and loves the supreme, creative and true wisdom above every other love, wisdom and knowledge. . . . An interpreter of sacred texts adept in the mysteries of the kingdom of God is everyone who after practising the ascetic life devotes himself to contemplation of God and cleaves to stillness. . . (On Commandments and Doctrine, 127, in *Philokalia* [vol. 4]).

The Christian philosopher does not search for the Truth, He already possesses it, having been initiated into it by the Holy Spirit. His ministry is to assimilate and interpret it, to protect and proclaim it. He is an ascetic not an academician.

2 Consensus Patrum

Who are these Church Fathers whose testimony on matters of the Faith (and reason) the Orthodox Church holds as definitive? If we are to believe the modern patrologists, the Fathers were only a stage in the development of Christian doctrine, Hellenizers whose disagreements finally settled into rival theological camps, whose well of creativity finally evaporated in the fourteenth century, and who, in any case, must be seen as ultimately background to Latin Scholasticism. If this conventional picture of the Fathers is true, then, there is surely no justification for viewing them as supreme witnesses to the Christian Faith. The notion of a patristic consensus, on the face of it, is absurd, for the evidence patently demonstrates that there is no agreement among them, neither in what they affirm nor in what they deny. More than this, some of Fathers, like Origen, were condemned by the Church and others, like Augustine, if the Orthodox did not simply ignore them, became sources of controversy.

Such is the indictment of more than five centuries of Western scholarship. Of course, one might legitimately question the scientific tools and the metaphysical principles of that scholarship, especially when it predictably draws conclusions about the theology and spirituality of the Fathers consistent with the demands of its secularity. No matter how serious and fair such scholarship claims to be, it must distort the truth about the Church and her Fathers when the revelation of the Divine in human history is discounted by these purveyors of scientific enlightenment. Since she rejects this "interpretation" of the Fathers, the Orthodox Church bases herself on the revelation of Jesus Christ and the Tradition which originated with Him and the Apostles. The opposition between Orthodoxy and sceptical academia is not one of subjective and arbitrary opinion versus objective and impartial science, but a difference in faith, in the source, goal and content of the faith *once delivered to the Saints*. The Fathers, as members of the Church, as her spokesmen, under the influence of the Holy Spirit, testify to that faith and life.

For this reason alone, the Fathers must be treated as extraordinary men;[5] therefore, any analysis of them which hopes to explain their sermons, commentaries, treatises, canons, icons, hymns and practices as expressions of human ingenuity, must also explain the Church's belief in their literary and spiritual activities as Divine influence. The proclamation of St Gregory the Theologian that the Fathers "philosophized like fishermen, not Aristo-

---

5   The Fathers of the Church are indeed a fraternity. Modern scholarship has not only presumed to fill the patristic roll with their own candidates (including the heretics, Tatian, Tertullian, Origen, Augustine, etc.), but more recently have decided to add women (*matrologia*) despite the mandate of Tradition to the contrary. K. Corrigan includes the names of Christina Mirabills, Marie d'Oignies, Juana Inez, Elizabeth of Spaalbeeck, Hildegard of Bingen, etc; and, of course, St Macrina, the sister of Sts Basil and Gregory, largely on the basis of the dialogue, *On the Soul and the Resurrection*, of which she, he argues, not St Gregory of Nyssa, is the real author. But St Gregory tells us, as Corrigan admits, that St Macrina was educated primarily in the Scriptures, having little proficiency with the profane culture required for authorship of *On the Soul and the Resurrection* (See the introduction to Corrigan's translation to *The Life of St Macrina* by St Gregory, Bishop of Nyssa. Saskatoon, 1987, x).

Jaroslav Pelikan elevates St Macrina to the status of a Church Father, because she is, as he also maintains, the hidden writer of St Gregory of Nyssa's dialogue *On the Soul and the Resurrection*. She ought to be ranked as "the fourth Cappadocian" (*Christianity and Classical Culture: The Metamorphosis of Natural Theology in the Christian Encounter with Hellenism*. New Haven, 1983, p. 8). Nothing in the history of the Orthodox Church accomodates Pelikan's "political correctness." In point of fact, her presence in the dialogue is a literary device for the exposition of St Gregory's doctrine. St Basil was the teacher of all his brothers and sisters—Βασίλειος, ὁ κοινὸς ἡμῶν πατὴρ καὶ διδάσκαλος (*Hom. opf.* PG 44 123B). (See also the Feast of St Gregory of Nyssa (10 Jan), Exapostilarion and Fourth Ode of Matins.) The eleventh century mosaic in Kiev's church of St Sophia pictures three Cappadocians, St Basil the Great, St Gregory the Theologian, St Gregory of Nyssa. Icons, as we shall see, have more than aesthetic value; they are vehicles of dogmatic truth and uncreated grace.

telians"—ἁλιευτικῶς, ἀλλ᾽ οὐκ Ἀριστοτελικῶς (*Hom.* XXIII, 12 PL 35 1164C)—alludes precisely to that fact. Like "fishermen" means with the power of the Holy Spirit. If that is true, then, "philosophizing" here denotes something other than rhetoric, logic and dialectics. "Not Aristotelians" suggests that the Fathers "philosophized" differently from an Aquinas or a Hegel. They spoke according to the Tradition of the Church, for which reason the Orthodox call them "holy Fathers."

"We follow the holy Fathers in everything," wrote St Maximus the Confessor. "They instruct us in the beautiful heritage of our Faith" (*Pyrr.* PG 91 296-297; *Ep. XII* PG 91 465). They are exegetes of Scripture which is a closed book without them. The teachings of the Fathers do in fact not belong to them, but came from the grace which Christ granted them. "Our holy Fathers and Teachers," Maximus said, "owe the truth which they spoke and which was spoken through them to the Holy Spirit." The same power attributed to the Scriptures—"inspired by God" (θεόπνευστος)—is applied to them (*Ambig.*, 42 PG 91 1341).[6] This being true, it would follow that they were not "original thinkers"—not in the sense so much revered by modern intellectuals. Although conceding that the holy Fathers took language and concepts from Plato, Aristotle and Plotinus, we are not obliged to believe that with this "Greek wisdom" they hoped to erect personal systems of theology or to work out philosophical problems like Plotinus or Kant, while drawing on the Scriptures for religious support. Their design was to provide the Church with a means for confuting and communicating with both unbelief and heresy, and even to developing a Christian culture for that purpose.

Furthermore, it may be methodologically useful to classify the Fathers according to Greek philosophers for whom they had some liking; but whatever their esteem for pagan wisdom, we must not understand that affinity as creating a "dependency" on the Greeks. The Fathers had no inclination to

---

[6]   Interesting is the modern evaluation of the Fathers. "Taken together," observes Pelikan, "these inspired and holy fathers of the church catholic, Eastern and Western, were the norm of traditional doctrine and the standard of Christian orthodoxy" (*The Christian Tradition* [vol. 2], p. 20). He apparently believes his own words, having departed the Lutheran confession for the Church which follows the holy Fathers and recognizes them as the "norm" and "standard of Christian orthodoxy"? He must have come to the conclusion that this attitude towards the Fathers does in fact not belong to another time; and that all Christian doctrine has not "developed" beyond the landmarks they erected.

If so, Pelikan must also have concluded that the Lord and His Apostles anticipated no evolution of His teachings beyond what He gave to the Apostles (Matt. 28:20). Pelikan must also have become aware that developing Faith was not the understanding of the primitive Church; nor, judging from the ancient *Lives*, that Christian martyrs died for a religion whose doctrine and piety would be something else tomorrow.

reconstruct the Faith "once delivered to the saints" *à la* Scholasticism; for here there are irreconcilable differences in our understanding of the Christian religion itself. Again, whether by placing the Fathers in various theological schools (Alexandrian, Cappadocian, Antiochian, Latin, Syriac, etc.) according to some scholarly schemes; or, as in most cases, by classifying these patristic schools as rivals in matters of faith—the necessary result of historical prejudices and circumstance—an Orthodox has to consider such schemes as inadmissable. At best, to arrange them according to philosophical predelictions or the theological motifs of Christian schools indicates no more than the way each confronted threats to and the needs of the Church. Unity of faith need not outlaw the variety of expression.

Similarly, no one is obliged to embrace the scholarly opinion that we should look for the roots of Latin, Greek, Syriac and Slavic patristic teachings in something other than the Apostles, Evangelists and the Prophets; and, what is the same thing, that the Fathers built on the achievements of other Fathers, as if the Fathers in one generation, attracted by the power of their thought, became disciples in another generation; or worse, that they deliberately cultivated followers. Put another way, St Basil the Great was not to St Gregory the Wonderworker what Augustine was to Aquinas or Kant to Fichte. Deference to and dependence on the Fathers before them was rather a sign of their reverence for and loyalty to the holy Tradition to which the entire patristic fraternity was tenaciously committed. We must not think that each Father made a new deposit to the evolving "ecclesiastical tradition," but rather affirm that he gave his inspired *witness* to the continuous and unalterable Faith of the Church.[7]

There has been "a cloud of witnesses" to "the Faith once delivered to the saints," but the Church has not placed all on the patristic roll. Sometimes those "witnesses" have been writers of enormous reputation and influence, yet she has not honored them with the title "Father of the Church." She could not, lest the cry of contradiction be raised and, therefore, the idea of a patristic consensus lose all credence; and, of course, any subsequent appeal to the Fathers as inspired becomes a ludicrous fiction. In any case, it is the Church herself who determines which among those "witnesses" are her spokesmen, not the heterodox and the unbeliever with their own biases.

---

[7]   Early patristic history is the history of embattled and persecuted orthodoxy maintaining a long and finally successful struggle against insidious heresy. There was indeed from the outset an immutable Truth of which the Church, with the Holy Spirit, was the guardian (See the valuable article by G.S. Bebis, "The Concept of Tradition in the Fathers of the Church", *The Greek Orthodox Theological Review* XV, 1 (1970), 22-55).

Eliminate Augustine, Origen and Clement of Alexandria, Tertullian, Tatian, Eusebius of Caesarea, Didymus the Blind, Evagrius Ponticus, etc. from the patristic rolls, and the charge of contradiction between the Fathers, quickly loses its cogency.[8] None of these "theologians" has a place on the Orthodox calendar, neither in her hagiographies or *menaia*, none have a cultus.[9] If such writers had not simply apostacized, if they were not anathematized by Church councils, they were deprived of any ecclesial privilege because of their doctrinal errors which were too many and too serious, for too long, or they lacked the piety which Orthodoxy expects of her spokesmen.[10] Some of what these theologians have written is profound and useful, but they nonetheless speak for themselves not for the Church since their opinions derive from personal experience.

The attitude of the Church towards Christian writers has always been dictated by a serious regard for her status as the divine steward on earth. She cannot endorse the position of "critical" historiography which argues that doctrinal innovation and heresy are legitimate forms of dissent, a catalyst by which norms and principles of religious life and thought unfold with the general evolution of human civilization. But the Church, while recognizing the importance of some external changes in her life, even the necessity of them—congruent with her Faith—allows neither political nor social change to direct what she believes. The Holy Spirit will not permit her to err, no matter the perversity of her faithless sons. There will always be a remnant preserved by grace which will protect and proclaim the Faith of the Apostles.

---

8   For example, H.A. Wolfson, *The Philosophy of the Church Fathers* (vol. 1): *Faith, Trinity, Incarnation*. Cambridge (Mass.), 1956.

9   Strange fate for a "genius" that Augustine should find no place in the life of the historic Orthodox Church. For a short while, he became a source of controversy in the East, at the time of the Crusades; and again in the seventeenth century—not without the help of Tsar Peter the Great. In our own day, indifferent to the heterodoxy of Augustine, the State Church of Greece in 1968 abitrarily placed the Bishop of Hippo on the ecclesiastical calendar for 15 June. Various Old Calendar Orthodox Churches happily concurred, likewise promoting the untenable opinion that his writings were altered by redactors (See my *The Influence of Augustine of Hippo on the Orthodox Church*. Lewiston [NY], 1990, pp. 1-11).

10   When reading the Fathers, modern patrologists pay no heed to this idea. They have their own view of the Fathers and church history. Thus Bernard McGinn refers to Origen as "the master of early Christian thought" who also "laid the foundations of Christian mysticism" (*The Foundations of Mysticism* [vol. 1], pp. xvii, 108). What does he mean? Origen's theology was temporarily the theology of the Church? The dominant theology among many rival systems? The Alexandrian heretic best expressed what the Church believed at the time? Why was he displaced? "Doctrinal development"? Why was he finally condemned by the Fifth Ecumenical Council (553)? But Origen claimed loyalty to the Tradition of the Church (*De Princ.* I, 2 ANF).

Thus, too, her Fathers are not "agents of change." Their task has not been, even as it is not now, to propose "creative" solutions for difficult political, social and intellectual problems. They were (are) guardians and expositors of the Christian Faith.[11] As the ancient Fathers refused to substitute Christianity for the spiritually bankrupt Graeco-Roman culture, neither have her modern Fathers conformed Orthodoxy to the spirit of this age. We are reminded of the words of St Leo the Great that God raises up "reverent witness" to "the one Faith which justifies the saints of all ages," "the Faith which is no discovery of earthly wisdom…but rather what was taught by the Only-Begotten Son Himself, and established by the Holy Spirit" (*Serm. LXXVII*, 6 PL 52 415A).

3   THE EUCHARIST DEBATE

If the Fathers of the Church are the supreme witnesses to the Christian Faith delivered in the holy Tradition of the Savior's infallible Church—at the heart of which are the divine and inerrant Scriptures—then, the only conclusion to be drawn with regard to the Scholastics or Schoolmen and Protestant theologians which followed them, is that they could not supercede (nor had superceded) the Fathers, but that necessarily they, and the West instructed by them, radically deviated from "the Faith once delivered to the saints." It is a conclusion worthy of historical consideration if it can be shown why and when such apostasy happened. Was there in fact a single event or idea which explains the departure of the West?

For the answer we turn to events which occurred during the ninth century "Carolingian Renaissance," the "Augustinian revival." This "rebirth" or "revival" initiated a rethinking of the Christian Tradition, whose first major effort is found in the philosophy of Scotus Eriugena (800-877), whom the famous Cardinal Nicholas of Cusa will call "the interpreter and perpetuator of Augustine." His *De divisione naturae* or *Periphyseon* introduced "the principles of dialectics" which, as Eriugena said, mingled nicely with the thought of the Greek Fathers (Sts Gregory of Nyssa, Gregory the Theologian, Maximus the Confessor, and Dionysius the Areopagite). The work of the Scot does in fact mark the transition from the patristic *phronema* to the philosophizing that will characterize the post-Orthodox theologians of the present. Of particular interest to us, however, is Eriugena's application of dialectical analysis to the Eucharist.

He maintained that "there is nothing among visible and corporeal

---

[11]   See the illuminating study by Fr Theodore Stylianopoulos, "Historical Studies and Orthodox Theology or the Problem of History for Orthodoxy," in *The Greek Orthodox Theological Review* XII, 3 (167), 34-41.

things which does not signify something incorporeal and intelligible."
Hence, "this visible Eucharist, which the priests of the church celebrate daily
on the altar...is a type and analogy of spiritual participation in Jesus" (*Peri.* V,
3 PL 122 865-866). In the equivocal language of Augustine, Scotus referred
to the Eucharist as a "truth-bearing sign" in which the Faithful "spiritually
sacrifice (Christ) and eat him not dentally but mentally"—*mente non dente*
(*Exp. Ev. John* I, 31; SC 180; cf. Augustine, *Tract. in Ioan.* LXXX, 3 PL 35 1810)).
To not a few of his critics, it is in his doctrine of the Eucharist that Scotus' heterodoxy first appears; and indeed when the Latin West began to manifest a
new theological disposition.

In the same century, two Gallican monks, Ratramnus and Radbertus of
Corbie, wrote treatises entitled, *De corpore et sanguine Domini liber,* and, while
coming to different conclusions about the subject, both appealed to the
authority of Augustine. Contrary to his opponent, the latter insisted that the
Eucharist was not a memorial, for the bread and wine on the altar signify the
Presence of the Body and Blood of Christ. What is remarkable here is their
understanding of the relationship between physical elements and the spiritual substance of the Sacrament. In neither view were the elements and the
substance conceived as integrated. Both Ratramnus and Radbertus (and
Eriugena) seemed unaware that their dispute—the Eucharist as a "memorial" or a "sign" of the divine Presence—could have been settled in christological terms: as His humanity and Divinity are related "without separation or
confusion," so are the physical and the spiritual in the Eucharist.

In other words, though the antagonists had a knowledge of the Fathers,
especially Radbertus, their dispute showed no appreciation for the patristic
conception of the Sacraments, that is, the christological presuppositions of
mystagogy; or, at least, christology was not the chief component of their
arguments. Ratramnus, so devoted to rational consistency, failed to see that
his conception of this central act of Christian worship carried with it an
implicit rejection of the Incarnation. Radbertus, with whom the idea of
transubstantiation (see glossary) originated, also failed to join the Divine and
the human in the Sacrament. Like Augustine, he defined the Eucharist as a
union, not the integration, of things physical and spiritual "by (created)
grace, not by nature." Neither monk produced a formula of the Eucharist
accepted by the Western Church. The dispute was not resolved.

In the next century, another pair of writers, Adelmann of Liege (c. 1050)
and Hildebertus of Lavardin (c. 1100), attempted to account for "the Real
Presence" in the Eucharist by means of a "communication of properties" in
which Christ's humanity, though limited in itself, gains a certain mutuality
with the Divine.

By the eleventh century, the medieval theologians, unaware of or indifferent to the insights of Adelmann and Hildebertus concerning Christ and

the Eucharist, continued in the current practice of searching (guided by the ideology of Augustine) for a formula that would clairfy the distinction between Christ's "physical body" and His "mystical body."[12]

In yet another treatise with the familiar title, *De corpore et sanguine Domini liber*, Lanfranc of Bec reported that Berengar of Tours (d. 1088), whom some believe to have been the father of the Scholastic method of dialectic disputation, hoped by means of that method to settle the issue left unresolved by the Corbie controversy and other writers. His solution was to expound all church doctrine, not only the Eucharist, by logic or "reason"—*rationibus omnia velle comprehendre*—leaving nothing to sacred authority or "faith"—*relictis sacris auctoritatibus* (*De corp. et sang. Dom.*, 17 PL 150 427). He played an important role "in the formation of a technical philosophical language. . . thus 'substance,' 'accident' and 'transubstantiation' crystallized as technical terms with a fixed meaning in the stress of the Eucharistic controversy."[13]

Despite the plague of new concepts, a few theologians showed a cognizance of christology as the principle of the Eucharist and *vice versa*. For example, the *De sacramento corporis et sanguinis dominici* of Alger of Liege (d. 1131) seemed, however tenuously, to arrive at precisely that determination. Yet, he could not carry his theory to its logical conclusion. Apparently, he did not recognize the importance of Chalcedon to his argument; or, perhaps, Alger's mind-set simply caused him to repeat the old error that the physical elements of the Eucharist are "sacred signs" of a "sacred reality," thus demonstrating once more the crucial role Augustinian sacramental ideology continued to play in Latin theology.

There is no better example of Augustinian dominance than Peter the Lombard (c. 1150). When he defined the Eucharist as "sacramental sign," a *signum* of the divine Presence, he only reaffirmed Augustinian dualism, that is, the bread and wine of the Sacrament merely signify the presence of Christ. The Eucharist is the visible sign of God's grace (*signum gratiae Dei*). In other words, the matter and spirit of the Mystery do not intertwine, they are not united "without confusion or separation." Here is a theory concerning the central act of Christian worship with immense relevance to the understanding of Christ, the Church, of cosmology and the Christian vision of history[14] with which the Latin West was slowly loosing touch.

---

12   See E. Mersch, *The Whole Christ: The Historical Development of the Doctrine of the Mystical Body in Scripture and Tradition*. Trans. by J.R. Kelly. London, 1956, p. 441f. Neither the Scriptures nor the Fathers referred to the Church as "the mystical Body," but merely the Body of Christ (I Cor. 12). "Mystical Body" is reserved for the Eucharist, "the Mystical Supper."

13   Knowles, D., *The Evolution of Medieval Thought*. New York, 162, pp. 5-6

14   See St Gregory of Nyssa, *Adv. Apol.* PG 45 1152C; St Leo the Great, *Serm. I in Nat.*, 1 54 11A.

If the Eucharist is merely the sign of the divine Presence in bread and wine, that is, merely a "trans-substantiation" (Aquinas) or a "con-substantiation" (Luther), like water in a glass; and, therefore, not a true unity of the physical and the spiritual, then, what is said of the Eucharist is applicable to Christ. If the two dimensions of the Eucharist are not mystically "co-inherent," then, neither are the two natures of Christ; and, it follows that the Church as the Body of Christ is no unity of the Divine and the human; and, in cosmological terms, the Infinite has not mingled intimately with the finite. The medieval dualism is the Nestorianesque bifurcation of "form" (μορφή) or "attributes" and "matter" (ὕλη) or "substance" which externally joins the Divine and the human. But such a shadowy union negates an Incarnation into which the baptized are incorporated or "assumed" and, therefore, outlaws the possibility of deification. Salvation hinges upon the union of the uncreated divine Nature with the created human Nature without "confusion or separation."

Whatever its historical dimensions, whatever its form, this dualism of the Middle Ages is another "assumption" of post-patristic or post-Orthodox Western thinking which must be displaced if the true Faith is to have any relevance for it. We will see its significance in our examination of apostolic christology, for, after all, it is Christ Whom the Fathers describe as "the Archetype" of all things; and it is by virtue of the mysterious relationship of His two Natures that the members of His Church "partake of the divine Nature" (II Pet. 1:4). It is because these two Natures are joined in the union καθ᾽ ὑπόστασιν that Christians eat and drink "the Body and Blood of God," that we are incorporated into Him through Baptism; and that all the Mysteries and rites of the Church sanctify those who belong to Christ and His Bride.

4 CHRISTUS ARCHETYPUS

Augustine's postulate, God and the soul ("I")[15] as the two poles of reality, is the first principle of medieval and modern philosophy and theology. It is an idea borrowed from Greek philosophy by the Bishop of Hippo and adapted to his own "Christian philosophy," a duality which became a permanent feature of post-Orthodox Western culture, settling in the medieval world as the unconscious basis of all its theology, philosophy and life. There was nothing

---

15 Friedrich Heer calls Augustine "the real founder of Western Christianity." His *per Christum hominum ad Christum Deum* is a denial of "the Eucharist-centered cosmos" (*The Intellectual History of Europe.* Trans. by J. Steinberg. Cleveland, 1966 pp. 21, 128).

Valuable, too, are the comments of C. Yannaras who believes that the West, through the Franks, inherited the Augustinian mentality which involves more than some "heretical deviations" or "the legal mentality accompanying (his) rationalism." "There exists, from all that, something much more drastic in the Augustinian teaching: the preponder-

more significant about it, however, than this duality as the presupposition of Augustine's christology, a Nestorian christology—perhaps as the result of reading Theodore of Mopsuestia.[16] To be sure, neither Augustine's christology nor the future generations which it poisoned seemed conscious of the mischief his theorizing had wrought. The tragedy of his tradition has been its rationalism, a mentality which has blocked the christological interpretation of the Christian world-view.

By the twelfth century, Western theology had ceased to have any direct connection to traditional christology. The Schoolmen, consciously or not, developed their theories in terms of the Augustinian duality of the Divine and human. Instead of the patristic witness to the christological unity of things visible and the invisible "without confusion or separation," the Scholastics came to think of reality in terms of the parallel dimensions of nature and supernature, nature and grace, the finite and the Infinite or, as one historian expresses it, with "the result that an iron law of spiritual dialectic was to bind Europe in the tension of spirit and matter for the next thousand years," and to "dominate the construction of late medieval christologies."[17]

Whatever the relationship between the Divine and the human recognized by medieval theologies/philosophies, this spiritual dialectic allowed Greek philosophy to dictate their cognition. Nothing escaped their curiosity and imagination. From one point of view, the entire Christian heritage was subject to argument with the result that solutions to the "problems" came not

---

ance of the religious element over the ecclesial element. Sharing in the truth of the Church presupposes the renunciation of individuality of the ego, the transformation of life into a loving communion, in accordance with the triadic original of true life... Augustine conceived of and preached the Church as a religion, something which convinces the human understanding rationally, which aids in the individual self-possession and morality, and which offers the individual the protection and assurance of higher authority" (*Elements of Faith: An Introduction to Orthodox Theology.* Trans. by K. Schram. Edinburgh, 1991, p. 156).

16   On Augustine and christological dualism, see J. McWilliam-Dewart, "The Influence of Theodore of Mopsuestia on Augustine's Letter 187," *Augustinian Studies* X (1979), 113-132. Fr Florovsky speaks of "an endemic Latin tendency to Nestorianize, a tendency perpetuated, indeed aggravated in Protestantism." He also recognizes in Protestantism "a revival of monophysite tendencies in theology and religion where man is reduced to complete passivity and is allowed only to listen and to hope" (See G.H. Williams, "Georges Vasilievich Florovsky: His American Career (148-165), *The Greek Orthodox Theological Review* XI, 1 [165], 66). But Protestantism is indebted to Augustine for these "monophysite tendencies," that is, a monergism which rises from Augustine's doctrines of irresistible grace and predestination. Although both the Papacy and Protestantism exhibit such "tendencies," they are not conscious delineations of the heresies they express. Chalcedonian christology as the first principle of the Christian world-view has long been lost in the West.

17   Heer, p. 220

by the "authority" of the Scripture and the Fathers, but by theories such as the so-called "problem of universals" or "Platonic Ideas" (about which more will be said). Philosophical schools eventually formed on account of the positions taken on the "universals controversy"—the "realist" holding that between thought and being or spirit and matter there was a direct and onto-logical correspondance; while the "nominalist" insisted that inasmuch as "universals" were the creations of language, a gulf exists between the world inside and around the mind. Thus, for example, the schools understood the Eucharist differently, depending on whether they explained it philosophical-ly or theologically; and whether they considered any but a theological analy-sis as justifiable. The "realists" maintained that the link between spirit and matter permitted the nature of the Eucharist to be understood in terms of both reaon and faith. The "nominalists" insisted that reason could not bridge the difference between spirit and matter and, therefore, the truth of the Eucharist is better left to faith. By virtue of such disputes medieval philoso-phy and theology developed the language and concepts which became the alchemy of all future discussions on such matters for centuries to come. Thus, on the eve of the Reformation, nominalism was the prevailing philos-ophy in Western Europe. It established the individual as the "real," describ-ing anything generic or collective as a semantic generalization. Moreover, the "truths of faith" lay outside the "truths of reason"—hence, the nominalist "twofold theory of truth"—which freed the latter, philosophy and science, to go wherever the ego would take it. And, to be sure, it is not difficult to rec-ognize in such things the nestorian (perhaps, docetic) christology—admit-tedly, a perspective with little or no meaning for that era—which the philos-ophy of nominalism presupposed. At the same time, an autonomous theolo-gy was naturally free to develop other strategies for its encounter with the Divine.

The nominalists had defined all rational knowledge as the result of sense-data presented to the faculty of cognition. There were people, then as now, who believed that knowledge was not limited to the conversion of the raw material from sensuous impressions into a knowledge of objects; and it was nominalism which indirectly promoted the belief—with the idea that religious knowledge was independent of philosophy and science—that the individual soul by "intuition" and "inspiration" could find another reality, a spiritual realm. The period before and following the Reformation had more than its share of "radicals," "enthusiasts," "mystics" and "apocalypsists" who claimed to have transcended the strictures of logic and dogma.

In this way did nominalism play an essential role in the development of occidental individualism, whether of the "mystical" or "rationalist" type, an essential component in the emergence of "the Protestant Reform" which understood Christianity as ultimately a personal relationship between Christ and the individual soul. The historical Church, therefore, was not conceived as a living organism, but as the spiritual collocation of believers, of individuals possessing a common faith. The true Church is unseen, and knowledge of her membership belongs to the soul whose certainty of salvation came by faith, born of grace, manifested in righteousness, and guaranteed by God from all eternity.

What the Reformation did for the religious soul, the Cartesian Revolution will do for the secular self. The Augustinian ("nestorian") polarity of God and man—"If I am deceived, I am" (*De Civ. Dei*, XI, 63 MD) and "Not to believe is not to understand" (*De Trin.* XV, ii, 2 FC)—was essential to both, however it may have been modulated. *Credo* will grant the individual sovereignty over the realm of the spirit as *Cogito* will grant it sovereignty over the realm of the time and space. The total secularization of the West had become predictable, when the exterior side of religion and society had no other end than the interior life of the individual. We need only to observe developments in the twentieth century: the supernatural obfuscated, religious faith subjectified, morality relativized, the arts bullied by the physical sciences, and history as the obsequious servant of evolution.

5 THE GREAT SCHISM

The conventional date for "the great Schism" of the Eastern and Western Churches is 1054 A.D. In point of fact, it occurred gradually and piece-meal, beginning with the ninth century controversy between Constantinople and the Carolingians over the *filioque* clause and sealed in the eleventh century by the mutual excommunications of "Old" and "New Rome." It is curious that despite all the polemical literature of the period historians continue to insist that the "division" of East and West was a "division" within the one Church for basically "non-theological" reasons, nowithstanding the doctrinal differences.

However, the events of the time do not permit us to ignore serious theological differences in favor of a disputable historical theory and ecumenist sentiment. Thus, when examining St Photius' opposition to the Latin heresy of the *filioque*, we ought not view his actions as a jealous defense of "the Greek people."[18] Pope Nicholas I (858-867) saw in "the Greek revolt" a rejection of his divinely ordained headship, whatever else may have been the

---

18 J. Hergenroether characterized Photius' "polemics" as an outburst of Greek national pride. See his *Photius Patriarch von Konstantinopel: Sein Schriften und das Griechische Schisma* [bd. 3]. Darmstadt, 1966.

pontiff's motivation for his excoriation. The Patriarch Michael Cerularius (1043-1058) had no tolerance for Papal aspirations to universal jurisdiction. His justification for the excommunication of "the Pope and his followers" did not include, whether before or after the concurrence of the Eastern Patriarchs, a defense of Greek culture. Pope Pascal II (1099-1118) accused "the Greek heretics of plotting schemes to crush and humiliate the holy Catholic Church." Pope Innocent III (1198-1216) hoped to compel the submission of "the Greeks" to his authority by the violence of the Fourth Crusade (1204). All the "councils of union" would have been pointless without the resolution of religious doctrine and custom.

In every case, such attitudes presupposed a conception of the Church and her unity. The Papacy claimed a "universal ordinary," a government over the entire Church, an ecclesiology which, in time, developed into a theory of the earthly Church as one enormous organism, a legal institution, with a single visible head, the Pope, whose connection with the invisible or heavenly Church was indirect, as grace to nature. Later, Protestantism will declare the earthly Church shattered, with an invisible unity only found in the Mind of God, of which the broken and groping earthly denominations are but a pale reflection.

The Orthodox teach that the universal, visible Church on earth is composed of many "local churches" with their succession of bishops, all possessing the same Faith, the same law, a common love; indeed, it is an invisible or charismatic unity, but also a visible and temporal one by virtue of their intercommunion and the historical identity and continuity of their institutions. But, also, she perceives that everything physical about her is united to everything invisible about her, which includes heavenly things, joined without "separation or confusion." Unlike Protestantism, therefore, the Orthodox believe the "communion of the saints" to encompass not only the Faithful on earth but the Faithful or Saints in the heavenly realm; and, unlike Rome, Orthodoxy holds that the unity of the Church depends on no external authority, but rather on deifying Grace—the power of her Mysteries, her life of mutual love and the voluntary obedience of her sons and daughters.

Nevertheless, histories of the Christian Church pay little or no attention to these ecclesial differences, at least, not insofar as determining who has the right to bear the name Christian.[19] Historians generally argue that the his-

---

[19] Bishop Kallistos (Timothy Ware) takes a curious position on the question of "the great schism." While he concedes that disparity of doctrine is central to it, he does not believe that the separation of East and West is any more than a schism. He also makes the remarkable statement that "on the human level it [the Church] has been grievously impoverished by the separation. The Greek east and the Latin west needed and still need one another" (*The Orthodox Church*. Harmondsworth [Eng.], 1964, p. 70.

torical Church offers no demonstration of "one Lord, one Faith, one Baptism"; and, where they do not openly state it, church histories take for granted that the Christian Church continues to develop with "division" as something natural and expected. It would seem that no matter what their doctrine and spirituality, any sect claiming to be Christian is identified by the experts as part of the Church. Because historians are unwilling to admit the existence of one true Church (in the name of scholarly objectivity), they write and rewrite the history of Christianity as if all the conflicting doctrines and spiritualities were the result of historical circumstance and, to be sure, human genius and folly.

Consciously or not, historians begin writing their histories of the Church with certain assumptions, not the least of which is the treatment of history as neutral ground, without the necessity of any reference to the "supernatural" (revelation)—a very unscientific thing to do, considering that if the supernatural does exist and is part of history, to ignore it is necessarily to offer an incomplete, if not a perverted, historical record of the human experience. Clearly, once the historian admits the presence of a divine Providence and the revelation of the incarnate God, he is bound to reconsider the idea of one universal and infallible Church. He is then obliged, also, to question the theory of doctrinal development and to reexamine its ontological and epistemological presuppositions. In other words, modern scholarship would be required to break new ground, to abandon many of its old attitudes in the search for new assumptions, a proper search that would demand a reassessment of the holy Fathers and the discovery of the christological category.

"The faith once delivered to the saints" (Jude 3) is the Scriptural definition of the Apostolic Tradition. "The faith" is "the faith of Jesus Christ," "the faith in Jesus Christ," "the faith" which is received because it is taught by One in whom we believe. Christ "delivered" (παραδοθείσῃ) it "once" (ἅπαξ, *semel*) to His Apostles (Matt. 28: 19-20). Thus, it is called "the Apostolic Tradition" or, more precisely, "the Tradition of Christ": He "delivered" His words to His Apostles to be "handed over" to His Church and through her to all the nations. In the words of Tertullian, *In ea regula incedimus quam Ecclesia ab Apostolis, Apostoli a Christo, Christo de tradidit* (*de Praes.*, 37 PL 2 50B).

Tradition, which exists only within the Church, contains everything she must profess. Whatever is necessary to believe for salvation is found in her. Whatever is necessary for salvation is found in her—whether it takes the form of theology, or spirituality, or custom, or law or art or music. All is bestowed by God, given not only for the spiritual redemption of individual members, but for the transformation of the culture and history of the nation which has embraced her. If there are new, but not novel, doctrinal and liturgical forms, they appear according to the challenges she faces. From time to time, then, she has reluctantly placed "the faith of Christ" into doctrinal, ethical, liturgical, canonical, or iconographical formulae and images. The sacred content of Tradition is changed neither by what the Fathers have written, nor by the customs of the local Church, nor by the composition of Creeds by the universal Church. These are all witnesses to the immutable Tradition which they expound and defend.

All definitions of Faith have ceased with seven Ecumenical Councils of the Church, as *The Patriarchal Enyclical Epistle of 1848* proclaimed, "the Faith has long ago been sealed in completeness, admitting neither diminution or increase, or any change whatsoever."[1] Of the continuous and immutable

---

[1] Paragraph 20 of *The Encyclical Epistle of the One Holy Catholic and Apostolic church to the Faithful Everywhere, dated 6 January 1848, being A Reply to the Epistle* (continued)

Tradition, then, only some aspects of it have been reverently formulated. No differently inspired than the Scriptures, the words which the Councils employed to express "the faith once delivered to the saints" were ordained by the Holy Spirit, and none, not even another Ecumenical Council, may amend, subtract from or add to what has been received.

Yet, Orthodoxy admits external change sometimes prior to conciliar decree (in things relative to the "economy" or governance of her churches), such as local statutes and customs, canons and ritual symbols, even doctrinal language. All these things manifest "the faith once delivered to the saints." Regarding the content of that Faith, however, there has not been, nor can their be, "development"—not of her Scriptures, αἱ Γραφαί (the records of both covenants), nor any part of the Tradition which originally was transmitted orally (Rom. 10: 14-18)—*auditus fidei*, i.e., through the sacramental rites of the Church. The Holy Spirit Who dwells in her will not permit it.

In this chapter there will be no need to repeat all the evidence, patristic and Scriptural, which demonstrate the existence of a single and unbroken "tradition" of the Church[2] originating with the Apostles. The fact that it has two dimensions does not suggest two sources of revelation—the written Scriptures *and* oral Tradition—which is a medieval Latin invention. Our purpose here is to describe the Christian concept of Tradition, falsely reconstructed by Roman Catholicism, falsely calumniated by Protestantism. To St Basil the Great (a Greek Father) and St Vincent of Lerins (a Latin Father), we have turned for the phenomenology of it. If we have properly understood them, the idea of "doctrinal development" is, as all other heresies, a product of "the foreign philosophy," *externa sapientia*.

(cont'd.) of *Pope Pius IX, To the Easterns.* Published in English at Constantinople, 1863. Reprinted by the Orthodox Book Center. Hialeah, Fla., 1958. Local synods and the Canons of the Fathers were ratified by Canon 2 of the Fifth Ecumenical Council (553) and also have universal validity.

2 According to the famous sixteenth century Lutheran theologian, Martin Chemnitz, the word "tradition" was employed in at least eight different ways by "the ancients"; but "the papalists sophistically mix together such testimonies without discrimination and, as the saying goes, whitewash all tradition in one pot in order that they may disguise them under the pretext and appearancae of antiquity" (*Examination of the Council of Trent* [pt. 1]. trans by F. Kramer. St Louis, 1971, p. 220). With special regard to the Fathers, Chemnitz "loves and praises the testimonies of the fathers which agree with Scripture", but he found no *consensus patrum* (*ibid.*, p. 256).

His critique of the Council of Trent and its medieval predecessors may well have been appropriate, considering the "development" of "papalists" doctrine; but we are not thereby compelled to agree with what emerged from Chemnitz's research, not on "tradition" nor the Fathers. His *Examination* shows little knowledge of "the Greek Church."

For an introduction to her conception of "tradition, See Fr George Florovsky, "The Function of Tradition in the Ancient Church," *The Greek Orthodox Theological Review* IX, 2

1   SAINT BASIL THE GREAT

Allusions to Tradition are everywhere in St Basil's writings, but none with more clarity than in his *On The Holy Spirit*. It is significant that his discussion of Tradition (which he began to detail in section 53) is part of his *apologia* for the Christian doctrine of the Holy Spirit. Indeed, the two are related, since Tradition is the vehicle of her doctrine. In addition, his task required him to distinguish true and false Tradition, that is, between true and false religion. The latter, he says, is the invention of those who "have been led into error by their close study of heathen writers...the students of vain philosophy"—τὴν ματαίαν φιλοσοφίαν ἐσχολάκοτες (*De Sp. Sanct.* II, 5 PG 32 76A).

Consistent with the other Fathers, Basil blames the existence of false pneumatology on the influence of pagan philosophy.[3] He is convinced that the aim of "our opponents" (the Arians), "the enemies of 'sound doctrine' (I Tim. 1:10), is to bring down the foundation of the Faith, the Faith of Christ, by leveling the Apostolic Tradition ... They clamor for written proof, and reject as worthless the unwritten tradition of the Fathers, but we shall not as cowards abandon the fight against those who oppose the saving and necessary doctrine which the Lord delivered to us, that the Holy Spirit is equal to the Father..." (X, 25 112C).

The remarks of St Basil raise several interesting questions. The Arians "clamor for written proof," presumably the Scriptures. By directing them to "the unwritten tradition of the Fathers," was St Basil opposing the "written" to the "unwritten word"? Were the Arians ignorant of the Church's *disciplina arcani*, given to the catechumens before and after their Baptism? To the first question "no," because the Saint knew that the Arians had their own version of the Scriptures, with an interpretation of them which suited their doctrine. Second, both Basil and the Arians knew that the Scriptures presupposed "oral tradition"; and since many of "our opponents" were baptized originally in the Orthodox Church, they were also inculcated *en mysterio* (ἐν

(1963-64), 181-200; G.S. Bebis, "The Concept of Tradtion in the Fathers of the Church," *The Greek Orthodox Theological Review* XV, 1 (1970), 22-55; and G.W.H. Lampe, "Scripture and Tradition in the Early Church," in *Scripture and Tradition*. Ed. by F.W. Dillstone. Greenwich, 1955, 23-52.

3   See my "The Greek Fathers: Polis and Paidea," *St Vladimir's Theological Quarterly* XXIII, 1 & 2 (1979), 3-21; 67-86.

4   *En mysterio* is often translated wrongly as "in secret" or "in silence." There is some truth in these renditions, because ecclesial "dogmata" are the privilege of the initiated, the baptized, "the enlightened," those eligible to participate in the Liturgy of the Faithful, the *missa fidelium*. These teachings were kept unwritten and private in order to safeguard them from heretics, Jews and pagans whose unbelief profaned the Christian Truth; hence, the sixth canon of the Synod of Laodicea (364) forbidding the presence of heretics in "the house of God" during the time of worship.   *(continued on next page)*

μυστηρίω)[4] as was every catechumen. Thus, the call for "written proof" was a subterfuge by which to set aside the evidence mounted against them.[5]

St Basil's defense of the "oral tradition" rests on the fact that too much of what the Orthodox Church believes is inexplicable without it::

> Among the dogmas and the proclamation preserved by the Church, we have some teachings which derive from written documents, while from the tradition of the Apostles others which have been delivered to us in the Mystery. In relation to true piety, both have equal force.... Were we to reject such customs on the grounds that they have no written authority, or because they seem to be less important, the result would be to unintentionally violate the very spirit of the Gospel itself; and, indeed, diminish the power of the Christian proclamation.

(cont'd.)   In addition, the exclamation, "Catechumens, depart!" during the divine Liturgy, requires the unbaptized believers to leave "the house of God." As "unenlightened" or "uninitiated" they are "unworthy" to participate in Mystery of the Eucharist which culminates in Holy Communion. "Take care not to betray the holy of holies," writes St Dionyius the Areopagite. "...Keep these things of God unshared and undefiled by the uninitiated: only by way of sacred enlightenement for 'the holy' let it be done" (Eccl. Hier. I, 1 PG 3 372A). Hence, the words of the Byzantine Liturgy prior to the communion, "Holy things for the holy."

Therefore, the accurate translation of en mysterio is "by way of the mysteries," that is, "under the form of rites and (liturgical) usages or 'habits'," asserts Fr Florovksy. "St Basil is referring here to what is now denoted as disciplina arcani" ("The Function of Tradition in the Ancient Church," 194, 195).

[5]   R.P.C. Hanson reviles St Basil's review of the Church's oral tradition as "a disasterously uncritical excursus into history." Basil holds the "unreflecting assumption that all existing custom has always been there, a status de fide..." Basil, he writes, had no support from the Scriptures or anything else, "so he falls back upon declaring that his customs are the apostolic ones. This is the only way that he can devise an authority for his customs... Behind this unfortunate and totally unjustifiable claim for a genuine apostolic origin for liturgical and customary practice of the contemporary Church, lies an uncertainty about how to use biblical material..."

St Basil searched the Bible for "oracles to justify contemporary ecclesiastical practices," Hanson continues, "and had the insight and honesty to see that there was none there. The Bible was not a manual of liturgy nor a code of ecclesiastical law. Therefore, a legend of apostolic origin for rite and custom must be invented and tradition, instead of being left to describe doctrinal development and exploration in continuity with the orignal Gospel, becomes a historical fiction" (Tradition in the Early Church. London, 1962, p. 184).

Hanson's critique of St Basil invites a few comments. The Saint had "no support from the Scriptures"; he searched them for "oracles to justify the practices he favored"; he "had the insight and honesty to see that there was none," aware that "the Bible was not a manual of liturgy nor a code of ecclesiastical law"; and, also, behind Basil's "disasterously uncritical excursus into history...lies an uncertainty about how to use biblical material..." Apart from Hanson's priggish condescension, perhaps it is he and not St Basil who is "unreflective."

Hanson trusts in the methods of modern historiography. He is a true believer in

For instance…where is it written that we bless ourselves with the sign of the cross …or turn to the East in prayer…invoke the Holy Spirit at the time of the consecration, etc.? The validity of these practices is derived from unwritten teachings and transmitted in the Mystery, not the gospels or epistles.…

Are we not indebted to our Fathers who guarded these unpublished and secret teachings from the curious and inquisitive? The teachings forbidden to the uninitiated are unlikely to be displayed in writings for everyone to see.…

Why did mighty Moses not make all parts of the altar public? Why were the profane placed outside the sacred precincts of the Tent…? He knew what contempt attaches to the familiar and what interest is naturally associated with the unusual. In the same manner, the Apostles and the Fathers legislated from the beginning the treatment of holy things in the Church. These aweful Mysteries were guarded in silence and in secrecy in order to prevent the debasing of Christian dogma through familiarity with the unwritten tradition which express them… (66, 188A-189A).

A careful reading of St Basil's discussion about Tradition is surely contrary to the conventional Western misrepresentation of it. It is not a coercive authority, nor mindless habit; and certainly it is not data or a resource which the inquisitive may question and rewrite.

Moreover, holy Tradition is not only a body of truths and practices, but also the means of their transmission, as St Basil observed. Scriptures are a vehicle; likewise the place where they are read and sermonized is the

---

"doctrinal development and exploration" as the only way to understand Church history. Thus it is inconceivable to him that St Basil and the Fathers were in possession of knowledge whose "source" was not, whose ultimate "authority" was not, the Bible. Hanson presumes that the Saint was "uncertain" about the use of Biblical material, that is, he did not know and therefore could not have applied modern methods of Biblical criticism. Why is it implausible to Professor Hanson that the Fathers had an understanding of Scriptural interpretation which was given to the Church by Christ Himself (Luke 24: 26-27)?

In fact much of what St Basil believed came to him by way of oral tradition (*disciplina arcani*), and the theological controversies in which he was embroiled implicated the customs and practices which he personally observed in Cappadocia, in Greece, and Syria, Egypt and Palestine. Therefore, there is solid ground on which to argue that these customs were not inventions. Indeed, Hanson is not justified in describing this holy man as a a procurer of "legend" and a fabricator of history.

Why does Hanson's call St Basil an "honest" and "insightful" man when he gives every indication that the Saint was trying to deceive St Amphiliochius, for whom he wrote *On The Holy Spirit*? Did St Basil think to fool his readers, especially his enemies, by merely asserting that such liturgical practicies were apostolic? Did Hanson compare Basil's list with those of other churches? other Fathers? Why does he arbitrarily dismiss *disciplina arcani* as the source of these customs? What does he think that St Basil hoped to accomplish with "historical fiction"? Support the Church's pneumatology with dissimulation? Why did the Church canonize a liar? Why call him "the Great"?

Church's worship—*lex credendi est lex orandi*—essential to which is the Eucharist, the ritualization of the *mysterion*, "the mystery hidden before the ages, but now made manifest unto the saints" (Col. 1:26). The Eucharist carries, then, a double meaning, even as Christ Himself: the communication of the God-Man and the institution by which His revealed truth is communicated to the initiated. Thus, the Eucharist is "the Mystery of Mysteries," that of which all other Mysteries or Sacraments are aspects and to which, then, they are all ordained as to their end. Tradition, then, is both what is transmitted and the means by which it is transmitted or delivered, including the word of the Scriptures.

The catechumenate is the first level of oral instruction, followed with greater knowledge after initiation (Baptism/Chrismation); and so it is with participation in the other Sacraments or Mysteries. This form of spiritual inculcation was called "the hidden discipline" *(disciplina arcani)*. It was hidden from the profane eyes and ears of the unbeliever; hence, St Cyril of Jerusalem's command that initiates not write down or rehearse the Nicene Creed nor share it with the "unenlightened" (*Procat.* 12 PG 33 521A). The Symbol or Creed, even as the Scriptures, are wrongly misunderstood by them, and would become the object of endless mockery and quarrel.

Thus, "in learning the Faith we profess," Cyril further cautioned the Catechumens, "acquire only what has been delivered (παραδιδόμενος) to you by the Church, and what has been formed by her from all the Scriptures" (520A). To be sure, some of what the Church teaches is publically proclaimed (κήρυγμα), some is not (δόγμα), and what is not, is commonly handed down in the Church orally. "This is the kind of divine enlightenment into which we have been initiated by the hidden tradition through our inspired teachers," St Dionysius the Areopagite will declare, "a tradition united with the Scriptures" (*Div. Nom.* I, 4 PG 3 592B). Tradition, then, has a historical or public aspect as well as a charismatic and private aspect, a fact that should not be forgotten as we review the Vincentian Canon.

2   THE VINCENTIAN CANON

In the second chapter of the *Commonitorium*, St Vincent of Lerins proposed "a fixed, general and guiding principle for distinguishing the true Catholic Faith from the degraded falsehoods of heresy." He answers the objection— "such a principle is really superfluous since the holy Scriptures are available for that purpose"—with the argument that "all men do not place one identical interpretation upon the Scriptures. The statements of the same writer are explained by various men in different ways, so much so that it seems almost possible to extract from it as many opinions as there are men. Novatian expounded Scripture in one way, Sabellius in another, Donatus in another,

Arius, Eunomius, etc. another. Thus…there is a great need for laying down a clear rule for the exposition of the prophets and apostles in accordance with the exegetical standard of the Catholic Church" (II, 2).

This "rule" (the Vincentian Canon, as it is known) will be a guide in distinguishing true and false Christian tradition. "We shall hold to this rule if we follow universality, antiquity and consent. We follow 'universality' if we acknowledge one Faith to be true which the whole Church throughout the world confesses; 'antiquity,' if we in no wise depart from those interpretations which it is patent our ancestors and fathers proclaimed; and 'consent,' if in antiquity itself we follow the definitions and opinions of all, or nearly all, bishops and doctors alike" (II, 3).

In a word, the Catholic Church has one Faith, while all else is heretical perversion. There is a timeless *standard* by which to recognize the difference—a standard or principle which is available to all and to which believers may always appeal—lest the purpose of the *Commonitorium* be pointless. The truth, then, is universal, but also ancient, an antiquity which palpably "cannot now be led astray by any deceit of novelty." Yet, "what if in antiquity itself, someone may ask, two or three men, or it may be a city, even a whole province be detected in error? Then we take the greatest care to prefer the decrees of the ancient General Councils, if there are such, to the irresponsible ignorance of a few men."

"But what if some error arise which has no precedent? Then we must do our best to compare the opinions of the Fathers and inquire their meaning, always recognizing that they, though belonging to diverse times and places, nonetheless continued in the faith and communion of the one Catholic Church; and let them be teachers appoved and preeminent. And whatever we shall find to be have been held, approved and taught, not by one or two only but by all equally and with one consent, openly, frequently, and persistently…" (III, 4). In other words, St Vincent maintains there is a visible, continuous and unbroken Tradition to which the believer may turn for verification of the Church's teachings. He summarizes his argument in the famous dictum—"to believe as true what is held everywhere, always, by all" (*quod ubique, quod semper, quod ab omnibus creditum est*).[6]

---

6   Vladimir Lossky states that the Vincentian Canon could not have extended to the New Testament Scriptures, "for they were neither 'always,' nor 'everywhere,' nor 'received by all' before the establishment of the Scriptural canon" ("Tradition and Traditions," in *In the Image and Likeness of God*. Ed. by J.H. Erickson & T.E. Bird. New York, 1974, p. 159). Lossky makes a serious mistake. He treats the New Testament Scriptures as a doctrinal source alongside Tradition, rather than a partial transcription of it. The NT Scriptures are a divine authority precisely because they were composed by and for the Church, whether by the Apostles themselves or their disciples. As Luke confesses, "Forasmuch as many have taken in hand to set forth in order a   *(continued on next page)*

Criticism of St Vincent's rule or standard comes from an unexpected source. In more than one article, the prominent Orthodox historian, Fr Georges Florovsky, criticizes "the inadequacy of the Vincentian Canon." He is not certain whether the Canon is an empirical criterion or not. Of what *omnes* is St Vincent speaking, asks Fr Georges? Is it a demand for the universal questioning of all the Faithful? "Very often the measure of truth is the witness of the minority—and not the *omnes*," Florovsky argues. "It may happen, too, that the heretics spread everywhere, *ubique*, and that the Church is relegated to the background of history, that it will retire into the desert. . ." Again, how do *semper* and *ubique* apply? "Is it the experience of faith or the definitions of faith to which they refer?"

In fact, Florovsky contends, there is no evidence which satisfies the demand of Vincent's *semper*. Nor were "the experience of faith or the definitions of faith" "everywhere" known. "Universal consent" is useless as a method of proving the Christian Truth. The antiquity of "consent" is not relevant to the argument, Fr Georges insists, because the beliefs of antiquity were not "everywhere" and for "all"; neither must we think that the Church is limited "to the dead letter of Apostolic writings." In truth, no "formal criterion of catholicity" is adequate; but there is a hidden "charismatic tradition" which is truly universal, although it is not seen by everyone who examines the history of Christian doctrine.

One needs to take great exception to Florovsky's analysis of the Vincentian Canon. First, granted that it is not wholly an "empirical criterion," it is also not entirely "charismatic," inasmuch as the Tradition which St Vincent delineates in his Canon is a constituent of the Church which is the body of the historical and suprahistorical Christ. Second, Fr Georges is surely disingenuous when asking whether "universality" would seem to require the questioning of all the Faithful. St Vincent suggests the answer to this criticism with regular allusions to the bishop as "head of the Church" and teacher of the Faith. In other words, nothing more is necessary to fulfill this note of the Vincentian Canon than the knowledge of what the bishop expounds "bare-headed" in his church. It is the episcopacy to which we turn in order to find "universality," as St Irenaeus told the Gnostics (*Adv. Haer.* IV, xxvi, 2).

Third, Florovsky's objection that "very often the measure of truth is the witness of the minority" (and, therefore, not "all") is misleading. St Vincent's *omnes* does not refer to every baptized member of the Church, but to "the

---

(cont'd.)   declaration of those things surely believed among us, even as they delivered (παρέδωσαν, *tradiderunt*) unto us from those who from the beginning were eye-witness and ministers of the word" (Lk. 1:1-2). Hence, the Faith of the New Testament Scriptures was "always," "everywhere" and "received by all," and despite Lossky's unsubstantial assertion, does meet the criteria of the Vincentian Canon.

definitions and opinions of all or nearly all, bishops and doctors alike" who, incidentally, were always in the "minority." In any case, whether "the faith once delivered to the saints" was or shall be held by a "minority" is irrelevant. The Christian Truth, written or unwritten, was delivered to the Fathers and Councils, evidence of what had been taught and preached "always" to "all," "everywhere." Whether it was believed "always," by "all," "everywhere" is not the pertinent point. Some day the Church shall be reduced to a precious few ("When the Son of Man comes, shall he find the Faith on the earth?" [Luke 18:8]), and the Faithful who have persevered will possess the Truth by which men are saved, even to the end of world.

Fourth, one may agree with Florovsky that, for example, all conciliar definitions of the Faith did not exist from the beginning, nor indeed were they known as they were defined, and perhaps not everyone knew them after they were published. Yet, the Truth of all Christian doctrine, whether formulated by Councils or delineated by the Fathers, was known and borne by the Church from the beginning, long before any heresy occasioned the necessity of their verbalization. Florovsky is making argument in the name of "objectivity"; but he fails, because he generally takes seriously the theological idiom dictated by the academic "history of doctrine."

Finally, Florovsky's objection that "antiquity" offers no criterion for the substantiation of the Christian Tradition—since the past has no promise of *ubique, semper, omnibus*—simply misses the point. Fr Georges' reproach that the Vincentian Canon presupposes the Apostolic writings as a "dead letter" is gratuitous. The Saint appealed to "antiquity" not because it was "dead," but because it could no longer be altered by mortal hand. It is where the immutable Christian Tradition began, and, therefore, the measure of all that follows. What existed in the beginning will remain until "the end of the age." What was believed by the first Christians will be believed by the last.

Again, St Vincent never expected *antiquitas* to stand alone. He made it clear that not every theological opinion received by the Church in the past was part of the Apostolic Tradition. It is not to be inferred, of course, that he included every religious writer of Christian antiquity among his authorities.[7] For example, Origen trusted in "the splendor of his learning, and of his

---

7   If the argument that there is a single, unchanged and unchangeable Apostolic Tradition is to have any cogency, new habits of thought are necessary. First, one may no longer assume the existence of two theologies, Latin and Greek. Diversity of form does not necessitate diversity of substance. The same Tradition was sometimes approached differently. Secondly, the idea that the Latin and Greek Fathers do not testify to a single body of truth is also false. That they sometimes attacked the same problems with variant words and style does not constitute the formation of peculiar traditions. Thirdly, we must no longer place the Latin or West Roman Fathers in orbit around the religion of Augustine of Hippo, as if they were all his predecessors or   (continued on next page)

erudition" (*Comm.* XVII, 43), "rashly following the bent of his own genius and placing too much confidence in himself, making light of the ancient simplicity of the Christian religion; and presuming also that he knew more than all the world, despising the Tradition of the Church and the decisions of the ancient Fathers, interpreting as a consequence certain passages of Scriptures in a novel way, whereby he earned the reproach of the Church of God..." (*Comm.* XVII, 44).

Likewise, "Tertullian who, as Origen[8] held the first place among the Greeks, held the first place among the Latins...comprehended all philosophy and had a knowledge of all the schools of philosophers, and was acquainted with all their rules and observances, and with their many histories and studies" (*Comm.* XVII, 46), but eventually apostacized. St Vincent might also have chosen to openly rebuke Augustine of Hippo, had there not been an encyclical by St Celestine, Bishop of Rome, expressly forbidding attacks upon him.[9] The Saint knew that Augustine had often differed with the Fathers. The Bishop of Hippo read these "other authors," as he called them, "not as if their works necessarily contained the truth, but to familiarize myself with their thoughts and writings which are the result of holiness and learning" (*Ep.* LXXXII, 1 PL 33 277).

(*cont'd.*) beneficiaries. And, finally, if we may repeat: not everyone on the scholar's list of Fathers may be found on the Church calendar, especially Augustine—whatever his magic relevance for the religious, philosophical and political history of the medieval and modern West. There is much fundamentally wrong with his teachings, beginning with his treatment of pagan philosophy. He was in large measure responsible for the development of a new theological tradition and for "schism" of East and West.

   8   I am unaware of one modern patrology which does not refer to Origen and Tertullian as "fathers of the Church." Which ancient or medieval authority so honors them? On what church calendar are they found? In what *menaion?* (See above, Chap. I, 5).

   9   The *Commonitorium* was in fact an indirect attack upon Augustine. St Vincent never mentions his name; but he also does not place him on the list of Fathers (XXX. 39) who championed the cause of the Council of Ephesus (431). He seems either not to have known or not to have cared that Augustine received an imperial invitation to attend Ephesus (See G. Weigel, *Faustus of Riez.* Philadelphia, 1938, p. 49f & note 77). Owen Chadwick observes that judged by St Vincent's famous Canon, *quod ubique, quod semper, quod omnibus*, "Augustine's theology falls to the ground" (*John Cassian*, Cambridge [Eng.], 1968, p. 120).

   Perhaps here is the unspoken reason for Gerhard Ladner's evaluation. St Vincent's opposition to "the Augustinian explication of implicit dogma makes him adhere rigidly to conceptual categories which significantly evoke Greek patristic ideologies of identity between 'end' and 'beginning' of reform as the return to paradise, progress as purification." Ladner emphatically takes him to task for failing to define "the progress of dogma as change from the implicit to the explicit" (*The Idea of Reform: Its Impact in the Age of the Fathers.* Cambridge [Mass.], 1959, p. 411f.). Ladner's views of the Greek Father is stereotypical. With Vincent he associates a conception of Tradition which surely reduces the *Commonitorium* to absurdity.

Thus, "concerning the Holy Spirit," Augustine wrote (*De fid. et symbol.* IX, 19 PL 40 191), "learned and distinguished exegetes of the Scriptures have not offered a complete and careful examination of the subject, an intelligent discourse which allows us to clearly determine His special individuality...." He thought to improve on the work of his predecessors as if they had discoursed on theological subjects to satisfy themselves, to make personal contributions to the Christian Tradition. In a word, Augustine was suggesting that Tradition "developed" in the hands of the right man.

Later in the *Commonitorium*, St Vincent answered the question about "progress" in theology (which Florovsky neglects to mention), a question propounded, if not in opposition to Augustine's daring speculations, then, in response to the curiosity of friends. "Shall there, then, be no progress in Christ's Church? Certainly, all possible progress..., yet on the condition that it is real progress, not an alteration of the Faith...greater clarity within its own kind, that is to say, understanding a doctrine in the same sense and treating it in the same way." In other words, the Saint distinguished between necessary "clarification" (*profectus*) or fruitful "amplification" (*amplificatio*) and forbidden "change" (*permutatio*) (XXIII, 54).

For Vincent, "progress" implied no abandonment of his Canon. If there is to be a "husbandry of God's Church, let her children cultivate and nurture what has been given to us by them" (the Fathers). "For it is only right that those ancient doctrines of heavenly philosophy should, as time passes, be guarded, smoothed and polished, without being changed, maimed or mutilated." Let "the ancient doctrines of the heavenly philosophy" receive "proof, illustration, defining while retaining their integrity, completeness and special properties" (XXIII, 57).

Altering Church teachings, even the least of them, Vincent warns, invites further tampering and, in the course of time, discarding them; while, introducing foreign elements into "the ancient Tradition," is the augur of interminable innovation, until finally "nothing will be certain, nothing unadulterated, nothing sound, nothing pure" (XXIII, 58). "But the Church of Christ is the careful and diligent guardian of the doctrines deposited to her care." Thus, she "never changes anything in them, never diminishing nor adding, nor subtracting what is necessary, nor inviting what is superfluous, never loosing what is her own, never appropriating what belongs to another."

According to St Vincent, then, "the decrees of the Church's Councils," what has been "committed to our trust by the holy Fathers," signifies the condemnation of all "profane novelties, the *anathemata* of anyone who preaches another doctrine than what we have received" (Gal. 1:9). He insisted that the Scriptures which have been left to us by our ancestors, must be interpreted "according to the traditions of the universal Church and, in keeping with the rules of Catholic doctrine...following 'universality,' 'antiquity' and 'consent.'

In other terms, St Vincent allowed that in antiquity some Christian teachings have been "left shapeless and rudimentary," hence the Church "fashions and polishes" them, while what has been given form by proper explication, the Church "consolidates and strengthens; and if anything has been defined, she keeps and guards it" (XXIII, 59).

The preservation of the Faith, however, did not always entail rigid conformity in matters of ecclesiastical customs. Vincent recognized a diversity of customs throughout the history of the Church. For instance, he encouraged his contemporaries to revive lawful practices neglected in the past and enforce them "with great zeal," providing, of course, that they did not involve "novelty" or an offense to Catholic doctrine (XXIII, 59). Neither should we be surprised if he found diversity in the writings of the Fathers, in their styles of writing, languages and interests, in their solutions to various moral and political problems, etc.

The *Commonitorium* displays no uncertainty concerning the unanimous witness of the Fathers to the Apostolic Tradition. It was chiefly in them, as we said, that he looked for *quod ubique, quod semper, quod ab omnibus*. This "rule" was a reflection upon the Apostolic Faith which recent events had brought him to undertake. The challenge did not lead him to impose his personal views on the Church. To look upon his Canon in this way requires a conception of Tradition which is no part of St Vincent's thinking.

3   THE DEVELOPMENT OF DOCTRINE

Heinrich Klee (1800-1840) was not the only nineteenth century church historian to mistakenly think that "the theory of the development of doctrine" is possible only from a Protestant point of view.[10] *Ecclesia semper reformanda* is the only justification for the theory's existence. Protestants are not alone in the opinion that the church in her doctrine and mission has periodically suffered from worldly diversion and, therefore, requires renovation. To be sure, the roots of the idea of "church reform" may be legitimately traced to the Latin Middle Ages, probably with Alcuin and the Carolingians.[11]

---

[10]   Klee was the successor to J.A. Moehler at the University of Munich. In his two volume *Lehrbuch der Dogmengeschichte* (Mainz, 1837-1838), he argued that the substance of dogma was unchanging. Khomiakov was fond of Moehler.

[11]   I refer not only to the triadology of Alcuin and the *Libri Carolini* taken directly from Augustine, but also to the Frankish repudiation of II Nicea (787) and its reaffirmation of traditional iconology. Interesting, too, is the fact that the Carolingian Empire encompassed many of the nations that were Arian in faith. Platonists, the Arians were no friend to art. Nevertheless, Augustine's philosophy is largely to blame for the Carolingian attitude towards Christian art (See H. Liebschutz, "Development of Thought

A   As we have said, this early medieval period was also the time of the first
Augustinian revival. His authority and example provided the Carolingains
with the opportunity to challenge, even if inadvertently, the tradition of the
Fathers. The Bishop of Hippo, the Carolingians discovered, had read "other
authors" critically but with respect, not deeming "anything in their works to
be true merely because they thought and wrote them, whatever may have
been their holiness and learning" (*Ep.* LXXXII, 1 PL 33 277). Indeed, he
believed himself not to be changing but to be refining the works of his predecessors. Judging from the results, he exceeded his own expectations.

Augustine provided his immediate disciples and future admirers with
opinions found nowhere in patristic literature. We need only mention the
doctrine of "original sin" formulated by him. "Neither Greeks nor Latins
held the doctrine of imputation," as Cardinal Newman remarked. "Nor does
it appear in the Apostle's nor the Nicene Creed."[12] There was much more to
his legacy, everything from Augustine's new paradigm of the Trinity to his
unique predestinarian soteriology, from his identification of God with being
to a Nestorian ecclesiology, his adaptation of the Platonic Ideas to his unusual theory of Baptism and the Eucharist.

There is certainly nothing of greater historical consequence than Augustine's "subjectivism," particularly his configuration of the Trinity linked with
the analysis of the human soul. On account of this, Augustine placed extraordinary emphasis upon the Christian's inner life. At this point, at least, he
abandoned Plotinus and sought for the "way back" to God within the intimate depths of his own soul where he was free from the distractions of the
senses and the anguish of his mortality. This experiment in spirituality,
reduced external objects to the mere occasion for the soul's enrichment.
Within, he discovered not only the power of God's irresistible grace, but also
the site where the soul encountered God Himself—irrespective of the order
or law of nature, an opposition which set the soul against everything exteri-
or to it. By this route, he came to foster, for himself, his Scholastic posterity,
and Western Reform movements in general, the distinction between grace
and nature, far different in their conception from anything held by the
Fathers.

---

in the Carolingian Empire," in *The Cambridge History of Later Greek and Medieval Philo-
sophy.* Ed. by A.H. Armstrong. Cambridge (Eng.), 1967, pp. 567-570; A. Freeman,
"Theodulf of Orleans and the *Libri Carolini*," *Speculum* XXXII, 4 (1957), 696f.; K. Flasch, "Le
Conflit d'Augustine" (Trans. by A. de Libera), in *Saint Augustine*. Paris, 1973, pp. 40-51.

12 *An Essay on the Development of Christian Doctrine*. Ed. with intro. by J.M.
Cameron. Hammondsworth, 1973, p. 83 (1845 edition). How else to explain the disparity between Augustine and the doctrinal tradition of the Church save by the notion of
doctrinal development? More will be said about Newman's theory.

Without that precedent, there would have been no Anselm of Canterbury (1033-1109). "Although what ought to be sufficient has been said by the
holy Fathers and their successors," he wrote, "yet will I take pains to disclose
to inquirers what God has seen fit to lay open to me" (*Cur Deus Homo* I, 2 PL
158 362). Anselm and his disciples were famous for their reckless use of reason in the "demonstration" of divine truths. No better example of this ambition was his treatment of the Atonement "by reason alone." He discarded
"the Ransom doctrine" which had existed in the Church for a thousand years
in favor of "the Latin theory" (see chapter IV). Anselm was the first great representative of Scholastic Realism.

Peter Abelard (1079-1142), *l'enfant terrible* of the Schools, knew Anselm's
work, and not without sympathy for his desire to elevate faith into knowledge—*credo ut intelligam*—yet, his interest lies rather with the contemporary
sprachlogik, the conviction that all speculation was impossible without words
and images, including the "speculative theology" of the Fathers. In his
methodology Peter marked an epoch with his *Sic et non*, where he developed
a *problema dialecticum*, "a literature of questions" (Vignaux), a reaction to the
traditional teachings of his day. Question by question *Sic et non* arranges the
dicta sanctorum, challenging the opinions of the Fathers with the express purpose of showing that "by doubting we come to questioning, and by questioning we perceive the truth," as he wrote in the prologue.

Abelard's design was to reconstruct "the basis of faith in the likeness of
human reason" (*Hist. Calam.* IX PL 178 140-141), an addiction that will only
develop in him, and those like him, who have a distaste for mystery. To
obtain meaning, he stated, the dogmas of faith must become comparable to
something we know. He therefore drew analogies from human experience
to make dogma amenable to reason. The result of this procedure was to set
"authority" or "faith"—the Scriptures and the Fathers—against "reason"—
philosophy—which would allow him to profess the teachings of the Church
while pursuing his intellectual aims without her interference.

Abelard admitted that "logic has made me odious to the world"—
odiosum me mundo reddidit logica—perhaps, a veiled reference to the Cistercian monk, Bernard of Clairvaux (d. 1153), who despised his rationalism
and, consequently, roused ecclesiastical authorities against him. He had
written a letter to the Cardinal of Ivo that "Master Peter had exceeded the
limits set by the Fathers"—*Transgreditur terminos quos posuerunt patres nostri*
(*Ep.* CXXXIX PL 193 359B). He places too much trust in human reason and
thinks rational knowledge superior to living faith. Nevertheless, Bernard
was himself a speculative theologian of wide reading and great intellectual
cunning, gifts he employed to insure the condemnation of Abelard at the
Synod of Sens (1140).

Somewhere between Bernard and Abelard stood Hugh of St Victor (1178-1141) who was called "the new Augustine." *De sacramentis christiane fidei* was the first attempt to provide the reader with a comprehensive view of theology and its branches, including a discussion of "universals" (Platonic Ideas). Hugh defined faith as "the will to assent to things of the soul with a certitude greater than that of opinion but less than that of science—*Fides est certitudo quedam animi de rebus absentibus supra opinionem et infra scientiam constitua* (PL 176 330). Although the soul enjoyed direct contact with God—in the words of Augustine, *nulla natura interposita*—yet, reason is not without value in the acquisition of truth.

Since Hugh believed that the rational understanding of Christianity was ever increasing, like so many of his times, he viewed "the way of modernity" to be superior to "the way of the Fathers." The latter, he insisted, failed to embrace "the totality of sacred knowledge," to multiply the "talents" which the Lord had given them; nor did they supply it with "an internal order which would generate a higher intelligibility," a criticism of the Fathers which seems not to have involved Augustine. His systematic theology anticipated what not long after him would be known as *summa*.[13] Some scholars believe that Hugh of St Victor was in fact the first to compose a medieval *summa*.

The facts, however, seem to favor Peter Lombard's *Libri senteniarum* as the initiator of the whole movement toward systematic theology. His book contained hundreds of quotations from Augustine—nine-tenths of all his patristic references. Lombard (1100-1160) also cited Sts Hilary and Ambrose almost thirty times. Among the Greek Fathers none is mentioned more than St John Chrysostom, with some twenty occurrences. The Cappadocian Fathers appear rarely, less than Origen. There is an allusion to St John of Damascus whose *De fidei Orthodoxia* had just recently been translated into Latin by the Masters of Paris. A few "modern" teachers are quoted, especially his own. Yet, it seems that "his patristic quotations do not rest upon a thorough perusal of the Fathers, but on previous compilations and anthologies, some of which can be identified, and a few manuscripts..."[14]

After Lombard, there was a proliferation of *summae*, none so formidable as the volumes of Thomas Aquinas (1224-1272). His desire was to put new order into the sprawling theology dominated by Lombard's *Sentences*, and

---

[13] M.D. Chenu, *Nature, Man, and Society in the Twelfth Century.* Trans. by J. Taylor & L.K. Little. Chicago, 1968, p. 288; also, J. Pieper, *Scholasticism: Personalities and Problems of Medieval Philosophy.* Trans. by R. & C. Winston. New York, 1960, p. 64.

[14] Knowles, D., *The Evolution of Medieval Thought.* New York, 1964, p. 180f.

also to legitimatize the idea of organic "progress" in theology. As part of his program, Aquinas tried to define the place of the Fathers, the *sancti*, as they were sometimes designated. To distinguish them from later theologians, he described them as orthodox in doctrine, with holiness of life, notable members of the ancient Church, who had received ecclesiastical approbation as teachers of the Faith. The leading figures among them (e.g., Augustine), Thomas anointed *doctores ecclesia*.

Whatever his reverence for them, the Fathers, Latin or Greek, never achieved in the writings of Aquinas (or any Scholastic) the stature they have always possessed in the Orthodox Church. "The authority of the canonical Scriptures offers us the proper and necessary arguments (*proprie et ex necessitate argumentando*)," he said, "while the authority of the fathers and doctors of the Church provide us with undoubtedly proper, though not apodeictic, but only probable arguments (*arguendo ex propriis sed probablia*); and, finally, philosophers give us only external and probable arguments (*externa argumenta et probablia*). Again, it is far more important "to abide by the authority of the church than of Augustine or Jerome or any doctor whatever" (*S. T.* I, q. 1. a. 8 ad 2; q. 10 a. 12 ad 1).

In other terms, "it is necessary for us to believe the words of the canonical Scriptures, and not the expositors of Scriptures"—*dicta expositorum necessitatem non inducant quod necesse sit eiscredere, sed solum Scriptura canonica* (*Quaes. disp. et quaest. quodl.* XII, 17 a. 1). The Scriptures are infallible. "Accordingly, that certain doctors seem to have differed in matters the holding of which is this or that way; it is of little consequence so far as the faith is concerned, or even in matters of faith, which were not yet defined by the Church," exclaimed "the angelic doctor." "Although if anyone were obstinately to deny them after they been defined by the authority of the Church, he would be deemed a heretic" (*S. T.* II q. a 2 ad 3).

His statements suggest that a doctrine is heretical or true only after its definition by the Church—which, of course, allowed Aquinas to freely speculate theologically and philosophically on any subject upon which the Pope and the Church had not yet officially spoken.[15] If he were right, Arianism, for example, would not have been a heresy before the Council of Nicea. Reading his philosophical theology, one is left with the very distinct impression that he viewed the history of Christian doctrine as the accumulation of new knowledge by superior ratiocination—no doubt inspired by God. The Fathers, essential as they may be to the growth of such knowledge, belong to a lower plateau of it.

---

[15] B.J.F. Lonergan, *Grace and Freedom: Operative Grace in the Thought of Thomas Aquinas.* New York, 1971, p. 139.

Thomas' subordination of the patristic tradition to the authority of the Scriptures—surely a failure to understand both—is symptomatic of the gradual reconception of Holy Tradition *in toto*. For Thomas to have advised others to judge the teachings of the Fathers by the Scriptures is a failure to understand their role in the life of the Church as the expositors of Holy Writ. How simple, then, to comprehend that setting Scripture outside of Tradition, as Thomas did, would eventually lead to putting Scripture against Tradition, especially when the interpretation of Scriptures has no authoritative direction, but is left to the individual conscience, as it will be, or to the "burning in the heart" as the sign of the Spirit's presence—*testimonium spiritus sancti internum.*

Aquinas' treatment of Scripture and Tradition which will eventually devolve into Protestant bibliolatry has a history which paradoxically begins with the development of medieval Latin ecclesiology, that is, with the aspirations of Pope Nicholas I. His desire for papal monarchy will culminate in the canonical reforms of Pope Gregory VII. According to his *Dictatus Papae* of 1075 all previous political and and legal orders were declared null and void. The Pope was "the sole judge of all" who alone possesses the power "to make new laws that meet the needs of the time." From an ecclesial point of view, the canons of the Seven Ecumenical Councils were no longer binding on Latin Christendom and the Pope; rather they were subject to his judgment as the head of the universal Church. The living Pope threatened to replace the Scriptures and all "traditions"—in the plural, a term which arose about this time.

"The Papal Revolution," as H.J. Berman calls it, would not have been possible without a revision of Tradition, a revision which included, as we have already seen, a reduction of the "ancient Fathers" to one of many authorities. Quotations were taken from their writings to be used in the endless *argumenta* of the Scholastic Masters. The Fathers were also incorporated into a higher body of truth, the so-called *authentica*, which included all "post-apostolic revelations." Hence, the commingling of papal decrees and encyclicals, canon law, the philosophcial theories of the Scholastic Masters, the continuous growth of doctrinal innovation, all for the sake of "the papal revolution," only served to obscure the true nature of the Apostolic Tradition.

There was yet another consequence to the new idea of Tradition. The academizing and periodizing of the Fathers, the transformation of "received tradition" by the *authentica*, the placing of Scriptures along side of it, left the believer "without any clear knowledge as to what was of immemorial Tradition in the Church and what was the speculation of recent schoolmen or the claim of papal propagandists." Here were the initial steps taken in "the reduction of revealed doctrine to the message of Scripture alone," a "step" publically taken first by the Englishman, John Wyclif (d. 1349), and his followers.[16] He was the first Protestant, arguing that the Church was composed of the elect, and the Scriptures their only law.

B   One idea persisted into the Protestant Reformation: the conviction that a "pure doctrine" existed somewhere in a single authoritative system of faith. According to A.C. Outler, some scholars call this belief "classical consciousness."[17] For Roman Catholicism of the sixteenth century, "pure doctrine" was lodged in the Scriptures, creeds, dogmas, canons and cultus as well as in the "fathers" and papal declarations, all preserved and inculcated by the teaching magisterium of the Church. Protestantism found "pure doctrine" in the Scriptures alone which, of course, needed exposition. Rejecting the authority of "Catholic traditions," and without any ecclesiastical direction, the Reform movement, initiated by Luther, was almost from the beginning a number of rival confessions, each confident that it possessed the "pure doctrine."[18]

The Protestant versions of "classical consciousness" rested on the motto—*sola scriptura, sola fide*. Faith in Christ, welcomed into the heart by "the testimony of the Holy Spirit" Who, through the Scriptures and "the preaching of the word," justified and illuminated the believer. In this way, "the absolute authority of the Church," writes Emil Brunner, "had been replaced by the absolute authority of a Book."[19] But there is more. Not without irony, each sect claiming to have drawn all its doctrine from "the Book" also summarized the results of their peculiar exegesis as obligatory "confessions," such as *Confession of the Brethren* (1526), *The Augsburg Confession* (1530), *The Confession of Magdeburg* (1550), *Thirty-Nine Articles* (1571), *Confessio Belgica* (1603), etc. In a word, every sect in modern Christendom has its own *traditio*.

---

[16]   H. Meyer, *The Philosophy of Thomas Aquinas*. Trans. by F. Eickhoff. St Louis, 1944, p. 23.

[17]   Knowles, p. 332.

[18]   "The Idea of 'Development' in the History of Christian Doctrine: A Comment," in *Schools of Thought*. Ed. by P. Henry. Philadelphia, 1984, p. 8. J.M. Headly equates "classical consciousness" with the "substantialistic" view of history, i.e., the belief in a reality outside any historical process, basically unaffected by the accidents of time. This is a Platonic conception of time adopted by St Vincent for his idea of Tradition which all Christians even into the Reformation accepted." The "substantialistic" view of Tradition "denies any critical review, private investigation or rational verification; consequently, it is opposed to the historical consciousness" (*Luther's View of Church History*. New Haven, 1963, p. 57).

[19]   *Reason and Revelation: the Christian Doctrine of Faith and Knowledge*. Trans. by O. Wyon. Philadephia, 1946, p. 11.

The Reformers may have claimed that their doctrines originated "in the word of God"—"Scripture interpreting Scripture"—but the truth of the matter is that *ab intio* Protestantism took theological positions which were "antipapist," demi-Augustinian, metaphysically Nominalist, historically eschatological, and epistemologically gnostic; that is to say, positions born of all those historical forces which characterized the late culture of the Latin Middle Ages, an indebtedness it has generally been reluctant to admit; neither does Protestantism confess this, nor the crucial role it has played in the history of modern philosophy.[20]

Protestantism stridently claimed to have recovered ("re-formed") the ancient purity of the Church, a Church which has no necessary unity save in heaven. Some members of the earthly Church—the Christian denomination has no relevance—belongs to the heavenly Church by virtue of divine justification which comes by faith alone in Christ alone. Their faith comes by grace, grace to the "elect," chosen by the secret Counsel of God before the foundation of the world. They are "concealed saints in the hidden Church" (*abscondita est ecclesia, latent sancti*), as Luther said. They must have been unaware that such a Church, without a succession of bishops, without Tradition, had soaring implications for christology.

Moreover, Protestant inquiries into the Christian past, not unlike those of Latin theologians, was little more than a search for confirmation of their Scriptural interpretations, that is to say, their inchoate traditions. The Reformers, whatever their knowledge and use of the Church Fathers, had little use for them other than to demonstrate the Protestant dogma of the primacy and sufficiency of Scriptures. Yet, they could not be faulted entirely for their disdain of what they called "the traditions of men," since by the end of the fifteenth century the Latin distortion of the Christian Economy and the Apostolic Tradition had risen to "a supreme crisis." In fact, the principal works of Luther and the other Reformers "may be appreciated only in the context of this increasing obscurity of the original tradition amidst a labyrinth of rival authorities."[21]

---

20 See Fr Florovsky's "Die Krise de Deutschen Idealimus (II): Die Krise des Idealismus als die Krise der Reformation" (ubersetzt v. E. Luther), in *Orient und Occident* XII, 2-12.

21 J.M. Headly ,*ibid.* p. 78. Augustine's contribution to the Protestant Reformers was his Nestorian dualism, clearly seen in their ecclesiology (see chapters V-VI). Luther, for example, began with the questions that Augustine left unanswered: is the Church a communion of the Spirit, created soley by God for those whom He elects? Is she a soteric and visible organism governed by bishops who instructed their flocks in infallible dogma and nourished them with the Sacraments? Luther instinctively perceived the problem: the oneness of the Church rests not in the unity and   *(continued on next page)*

Perhaps, not so curious, then, is the fact that, during the two centuries following the Reformation and Counter-Reformation (especially after Trent), Protestants and Roman Catholics "hotly debated" the relationship between the "ancient Fathers" and pagan philosophy.[22] The latter, far from dismayed by Augustine's Platonism, for example, seized upon this fact as a sign of harmony between the Christian revelation and natural reason. Although the first Reformers considered Augustine as "father of fathers,"[23] the sustained controversy weakened his authority and generally marginalized the force of any appeal to the Church Fathers. If their theology was not "too pagan" for the Protestants, it was "too dogmatic" for humanists, and not "sufficiently philosophical" for the Roman Catholics.[24]

A benefit of the debate, nevertheless, was the growth of patrological collections, often spurred by the discovery of tampering with the literature of the Fathers;[25] but there was another, far more distressing consequence of the controversy: a steady loss of faith in all religious authority, in the supernat-

---

(cont'd.) succession of bishops, as Augustine sometimes implied, but "in the hidden and uninterrupted continuity of believers, the *successio fidelium* ..." (H. Bornkamp, *Luther's World of Thought*. Trans. by H.M. Bertram. St Louis, Mo., 1958, p. 143).

To the school of Ockham in general and to the "empirical individualism" of Gabriel Biel (1425-1495) in particular, Luther owed his understanding of a human society: the assembly of individual beings (*Encyc. Brit.* [vol. 3]. New York, 1911, p. 920). Thus, the members of the fallible and divided earthly Church are saved not by ecclesial *koinonia*, true Faith and the Mysteries, but by personal "faith alone through grace." Such an ecclesiology was seen as a positive and organic development of Augustine's doctrine of the Church (See E. Wolf, *Peregrinatio: Studien zur reformatorischen Theologie und Kirchen Problem*. Muenchen, 1962).

[22] O. Chadwick, *From Bossuet to Newman: The Idea of Doctrinal Development*. Cambridge (Eng.), 1957, p. 58.

[23] As Martin Luther said, "When Augustine is eliminated from the list of the Fathers, the others are not worth much." ("On the Councils of the Church," in *Luther's Works* [vol. 41]. Ed by J. Pelikan, etc. St Louis, 1966, p. 27).

[24] Chadwick, *op. lit.*

[25] Of particular interest to Orthodox is the *filioque*. The Lutheran convert to Orthodoxy, Adam Zernicavius, in his *Tractus de processione Spiritus Sancti* (written in Latin), (1795-1796; translated into Greek by E. Bulgaris, Archbishop of Cherson (1776); and into Russian at the beginning of the twentieth century, uncovered numerous forgeries in the writings of the Fathers. For example, he examined the original MSS of the Venerable Bede and found that the phrase *Spiritus sanctus ex Filio procedat* and other words which accomodate the Latin heresy are interpolations. St Bede's record of the Synod of Hatfield (679) decrees—"the Holy Spirit ineffably proceeding from the Father and the Son as proclaimed by the holy Apostles" (*A History of the English Church and People*. bk. IV, chap. 17)—in the Latin text refers to the temporal mission of the Spirit (See P. Ranson, "The Filioque: the Vital Orthodox Understanding of the Procession of the Holy Spirit," in *Orthodox Light* VII, 1 [1995], 1-16); and C. Lampryllos, *La Mystification fatale: Étude orthodoxe sur le Filioque*. Lausanne, 1987. On the corruption of the writings of the Latin Fathers in particular, see pages 117-120.

ural and the miraculous, a skepticism which turned post-medieval thought inward in matters of religion, and outward in matters of knowledge, driven by the *sentiment* that whatever was understandable the self could find. Thus, the Reformation, by stressing the singularity and sovereignty of the individual conscience and "renewing the Augustinian iron law of dialectic between spirit and matter," only contributed to the new secularism and humanism wrought by the Renaissance: man's innate goodness and his capacity to find the truth by thinking and personal initiative. Here is "the basic principle of all modern philosophy."[26]

By the end of the eighteenth century the desacralization of the West seemed a foregone conclusion. Regicide and the spread of democracy—for which the new philosophies and religious ideologies were largely responsible—secured the expulsion of God from his cosmos.[27] By the nineteenth century, all hope of reconciling traditional values and the new secular vision had vanished. A profoundly radical critique of religion proclaimed an earthly destiny for the human race.

C   Georg Hegel engineered the demise of the "classical consciousness" and the shift to something new—a "historical consciousness."[28] As the eighteenth century had repudiated "dogma," "orthodoxy," and "tradition," the next century conjured the hope that history would uncover, among other things, the essence of true religion—a task undertaken not only by the Hegelians of the Right, the idealists, but by the Hegelians of the Left, the materialists. The former saw the evolution of the Church as part of the cosmic unfolding of the World-Spirit; and, the latter interpreted the existence and history of the Church as part of the universal class struggle.

The holy Fathers, as an episode in the development of the "classical consciousness," were necessarily obfuscated by the Hegelian "positivity of the Christian religion." Church history, he explained, should be studied as an example of "how simple and fundamental truths became gradually overlaid with a heap of errors, owing to passion and ignorance; and to prove that, in this centuries-long and gradual process of defining the several dogmas, the Fathers were not always led by knowledge, moderation and reason; that

---

26   E. Frank, *Philosophical Undertanding and Religious Truth*.New York, 1956, p. 6.

27   In the West, the expulsion of God from the universe does not always mean the denial of His Existence. Eighteenth century Deism simply rejects the idea of Providence and special revelations, such as miracles. But the conscious detachment from supernatural religion often becomes a rebellion against God and all religion. "Whenever modern man speaks about progress in history," says Frank, "he actually means advancement towards enlightenment and rationalization which has finally led to a determined revolt against God" (*Ibid.*, p. 130).

28   Outler, p. 9.

even in the original reception of Christianity, what was operative was not simply a pure love of truth, but, at least, to some extent, very mixed motives, very unholy considerations, impure passions. . ."[29]

Above all, the Fathers were blamed for originating the distortion of the Biblical message—for an *ersatzchristentum*, a "dogmatic" Christianity which, with the assistance of Greek philosophy, through the centuries has obscured the genuine portrait of the historical Jesus and His "primal Gospel." Given the distinction between the historical truth and ecclesiastical novelties, Hegel's disciples (Baur, Strauss, Feuerbach, etc.) created a "new discipline"—*dogmengeschichte* or "the history of dogma"—whose purpose was to distinguish between "history" and "myth." The "crowning glory" of this enterprise was Adolph von Harnack's *Lehrbuch* which, together with his *Das Wesen des Christentums*, are histories about Christianity which exemplified the new "consciousness" by the application of the critical principles of historical inquiry (See Chap. VI).

Harnack (1859-1930) set for himself the task of identifying the origin of dogmas and portraying their development. He began with the assumption that "progress" was a necessary attribute of history and Christianity was an inherently historical religion. When applied to church history, then, the idea of "progress" allows the historian, said Harnack, "to appreciate it in all its phenomena as the history of the spirit."[30] The Christianity of the Fathers and the Schoolmen, he described as "dogmatic Christianity," stages in the development of the Church, which stood between the religion of the Gospel and the religion of *cultus* (rites, icons, etc.), that is, of "superstition."[31] Harnack explained the distortions of "dogmatic Christianity" with the famous phrase, "Dogma in its conception and development is a work of the Greek spirit on Christian soil."[32]

Furthermore, Harnack said, the Protestant Reformation, the beginning of the third stage of doctrinal development, did in fact not essentially alter the character of the previous two stages of Christianity. The "old dogma remained powerfully within it, because of its tendency to look back and to seek for authority in the past (especially Augustine), partly in the original and unmodified form."[33] Not until the nineteenth century did that "spiritual revolution" start, "which must in every respect be regarded as a reaction against the efforts of the rationalistic epochs, changing thereby the conceptions of the Christian religion and its history."[34] How curious that Harnack spoke of modernity's *höhere selbstbewusstsein* as a reaction to rationalism. *Superbia congnescendi* was the very insignia of the ninenteenth century.

---

[29] *Early Theological Writings*. Trans. by T.M. Knox. Chicago, 1948, pp. 172-173.

[30] *History of Dogmas* (vol. 1). Trans. by J. Millar. London, 1905, p. 33.

[31] *Ibid.*, p. 16.   [32] *Ibid.*, p. 17.   [33] *Ibid.*, p. 19.   [34] *Ibid.*, p. 32.

England's Oxford Movement pretended to challenge the "the spirit of the times." It boasted a conscious return to "the ancient Catholic Tradition," especially those "great landmarks" of church history, such as the Nicene Creed, which bear directly on the understanding of the great mysteries of the gospel."[35] But despite the efforts to demonstrate the organic continuity of Christian beliefs, the Oxfordians could not entirely escape the power of the new "historical consciousness." The assumptions of their investigations were not christological. The patristic *"mind"* (φϱόνημα) had long departed the West, whatever the considerable love and knowledge of the Oxfordians for ancient and medieval literature.

The idea of "development" was now the key to any understanding of history, and most assuredly church history and doctrine; indeed, it was the dominant feature of all knowledge, whether biology, physics, geology and, in short, metamorphizing the modern view of every science. One of the Oxford Movement's most celebrated figures, John Henry Newman (1801-1890), was in 1845 received into the Roman church, on the eve of which he wrote, *An Essay on the Development of Christian Doctrine.* His writings dealt with Christianity as a historical religion, an effort where by treating "development" as "a hypothesis," he could show the correspondence between the early Christianity and the modern Church and explain away the doctrinal "difficulties" commonly found in the study of church history. His approach, as well as his conclusions, mark him as "a fashioner of the *zeitgeist*," as much as Hegel or Darwin, Marx or Mill, for his *Essay* "would not have been written, and would not have been thought to be required fifty years before."[36]

The Oxfordian Newman seems to have been a man of "classical consciousness" judging by his 1835 sermon, "The Patristical Idea of Antichrist" in which he affirmed his devotion to the holy Fathers. "When they speak of doctrines," he said, "they speak of them as being universally held. They are witnesses to the fact of these doctrines having been received, not here or there, but everywhere. We receive those doctrines which bear witness that all Christians everywhere held them... They do not speak of their own private opinion. . . ," but of what "has ever been held by all the churches down to our time without interruption ever since the Apostles..."[37] His confession was reminiscent of the Vincentian Canon—*quod ubique, quod semper, quod omnibus creditum est*—a "rule" he will reject not ten years later.

In his *Essay*, now critical of the Canon, Newman asked, how must we understand that the Church holds only what has been taught "always"? Every century, every year, every month? Does "everywhere" mean in every

---

35   Fairweather, E.R., ed., *The Oxford Movement.* New York, 1964, p. 78f.

36   J.M. Cameron, Intro. to Newman's *Essay,* p. 43.

37   *Discussions and Arguments.* London, 1972, pp. 24-47.

country or every diocese? Nothing proves that the Christian truth was held by "all." He also attacked St Vincent's "the consent of the Fathers" as something essential to our understanding of Tradition. Does "consent" require us "to produce the direct testimony of everyone of them?" "How many Fathers, how many places, how many instances constitute a fulfillment of the test proposed?" In other words, from the very nature of the case, St Vincent proposes a condition which can never be fulfilled. The Canon cannot be applied uniformly and it is inadequate to cover every exception and all the explication of implicit doctrine, such as Augustine's "original sin."[38]

What advantage, then, does "development" have over the Vincentian Canon? "I saw that the principle of development not only accounted for certain facts, but was itself a remarkable philosophical phenomena, giving character to the course of Christian thought."[39] Newman believed the science of doctrine to be true science. He, therefore, compared the theory of doctrinal development to the rise of the other branches of learning—social, political, mathematical, physical, etc. Thus, just as there may be false sciences, there is also, he warned, "a false or unfaithful development which is called a corruption."[40]

How do we distinguish them? True development is always in conformity to the eternal "idea"[41] which, according to Newman, is the only representation of a truth deposited in the Church by God from the beginning. The "idea" is both permanent and changing; it never loses its identity while ever in a state of germination.[42] Thus, any "development" is "to be considered a corruption which obscures or prejudices its essential idea, or which disturbs the laws of development which compose its organization, or which reverses its course..."[43] "A development which is faithful," he continued, "must retain both the doctrine and the principles with which it started. Doctrine without its correspondent principles remains barren, if not lifeless, of which the Greek church seems an instance..."[44]

True development has numerous characteristics: preservation of the ideas or deposit of doctrines, continuity of principles, the power of assimilation or natural growth, early and definite anticipation or the seminal presence of the future developments, evolution of the original idea in a gradual and orderly fashion, "preservative additions" or augmentation which saves the previous stage, and finally, "chronic continuance" or "duration" in oppo-

38 *An Essay on the Development of Christian Doctrine*, p. 76.
39 *Apologia Pro Vita Sua.* Garden City (NY), 1956, p. 287.
40 *Essay*, p. 105.
41 The "idea" (or "form") here is immanent, something akin to Aristotle's *entelechy*.
42 *Ibid.*, p. 99.   43 *Ibid.*, p. 121.   44 *Ibid.*, p. 129.

sition to heresy which must inevitably evaporate.[45] In other words, the "idea" is a revealed truth established from the beginning but only in time coming to total fruition, like the acorn which becomes an oak.

Newman's theory conceives the development of doctrine as a "coincidence of opposites" (*coincidenta oppositorum*). He, like Hegel, was a modern heir of Aristotle. He was not indifferent to the Church Fathers, to be sure; but they are, however important, merely a component of the process. Tradition would not be what it is without them. Neither would it be what it is without the Schoolmen. As Thomas Aquinas said before him, "whatever they believed who lived later, was contained, albeit implicitly, in the faith of the Fathers who preceded them. But there was an increase in the number of the articles of faith believed explicitly, since to those who lived in later times some things were known explicitly which were also known implicitly by those who lived prior to them" (*S. T.* II q. 1 a. 7).

D   The present writing of church histories and the renewed interest in patristic studies are endowed with an "ecumenical consciousness." Pope Leo XIII in the bull *Aeterni Patris* (1879) enjoined students of theology to study Thomas Aquinas which necessarily led them to an inquiry into the teachings of the Fathers, for three reasons: no doubt because Thomas had cited them as authorities, but also because, as the patristic period was seen as part of history's greater complexity, Roman Catholic scholars were given the task of reconciling their discoveries with their church's conservatism; and, finally, because the pride of the Orthodox Church was her loyalty to the Fathers, a knowledge of the patristic doctrine was imperative for any hope of "reunion" between them (and the rest of Christendom).

Among the Protestants, the liberal influence of Baur, Schleiermacher, Ritschl, and Harnack had begun to recede. The psychological, sociological, and phenomenological approaches to the patristic period became less frequent. The old animosities and polemics were generally missing from church histories and the comparison of doctrines. Albeit anti-supernaturalism was no longer understood as necessary to the theory of doctrinal development, it continued to influence historiographical methods. In most quarters of academia, the theory settled in quietly as a venerable principle of scientific thought. It was too much a part of modern Western culture to disappear completely.

A perfect illustration of the new "ecumenical consciousness" is the five volume work by the Lutheran church historian, Jaroslav Pelikan, *The Christian Tradition: A History of the Development of Doctrine* (The University of

---

45   *Ibid.*, pp. 136-145.

Chicago Press, Chicago, 1971-1989). The first volume opens with two Latin quotes—Harnack's motto, *Veni Creatur Spiritus*, and Newman's coat-of-arms, *Cor ad cor loquitur*. They suggest that Pelikan has taken a position midway between them. He rejects the naked "liberalism" of the first and the ostensible "conservatism" of the second. Pelikan argues that there is a subtle dialectic between permanence and historical process. The Gospel message never changes or, more precisely, is continuous while "doctrine has not always been the same, not even formally."[46]

Pelikan makes the predictable Protestant comparison between dogma as "the normative statements of the Christian belief adopted by various ecclesiastical authorities and enforced as the official teaching of the Church" with the Scriptural doctrine of Christ and the Apostles. What the historical Church understands by the Lord's teachings is "an ongoing process rather than a given product."[47] Professor Pelikan cannot believe in the existence of changeless and historical Christian truth, for such an "assumption" carried to its logical conclusion, would "of course, preclude the writing of a history of doctrine in our sense of the word 'history,' which is based on the assumption that the study of a development in chronological sequences helps to make the past intelligible."[48]

His remarks are interesting from several points of view. To reject the "assumption" that the Christian past must be unintelligible if it possesses changeless truths places the Church's most elementary teachings in jeopardy, either by the incessant recycling of theological language or by new cultural ideas and values which reform and relativize the achievements of the past. Again, his not uncommon distinction between the teachings of the Church and the teachings of Christ and His Apostles is historically indemonstrable, even if it did not presuppose Pelikan's personal understanding of the divine Economy.

Not unlike so many of his contemporaries, Pelikan envisions neither the Church nor history in christological terms. If he did, he would also recognize the necessity of a "chalcedonian" interpretation of both history and dogma; and, therefore, the presence of the transcendent God in history, the future in the present, which unconfusedly and inseparably unites the spiritual and physical dimensions of reality. Moreover, Pelikan's *History*

---

46 *The Emergence of the Catholic Tradition, 100-600* (vol. 1). Chicago, 1971, p. 3.

47 *Ibid.*, p. 4, 6.

48 Not "timidity," but in the words of Feast of the Three Hierarchs on January 30, "By the word of understanding. . .the simple words of the fishermen. . .the Power of the Spirit" did the 318 Fathers compose "the simple content of our Faith." See also Antony Khrapovitsky, "The First Ecumenical Council," in *Orthodox Life* XXXIV, 6 (1984), 9-14.

embodies all those unexamined assumptions of Western historical thinking which, throughout the West's post-Orthodox history, have fired the ontological tensions which have defined its existence since the Middle Ages. Above all, Pelikan deceives himself if he thinks his *magnum opus* was written "christologically" neutral.

The premises of *History* predetermine the conclusions of an otherwise well-written study of church history. His treatment of the Fathers, for example, is not unsympathetic, but Pelikan will not countenance their belief in doctrine as changeless or eternal truths. He finds no doctrinal unity anywhere in the history of the Church, no *consensus* among the Fathers of the ecumenical Church, an argument he illustrates with the composition of the Nicene Creed (325). Pelikan insists that it initially had no universal approval. The idea that the Fathers of the Council gave no thought to winning a consensus seems not to have occurred to him. He implies that a Creed for the universal Church requires the approval of all, and since unity of Faith could not be found anywhere in the fourth century, a consensus was impossible to achieve. He suggests, therefore, that the Creed was imposed upon the Church with imperial support.

But, then, Pelikan's whole critique is meaningless if the Creed is in fact the verbalization of an uninterrupted and infallible Tradition. The assembled bishops believed themselves already in possession of such a Tradition. Nicea was not a parliament, but a φροντιστήριον, as St Gregory the Theologian called it, where the doctrine of the Trinity was put into words (*De vita sui* PG 37 1148A). The chief preoccupation of the Council Fathers was to find suitable words to express it, a clear and accurate formula which would safeguard "the faith once delivered to the saints"; and, of course, to establish a boundary between the Church and heresy.

One need not wonder why the Creed or "Symbol" of Nicea became part of the Baptismal rite, nor the reason that the Nicene Creed, like so much else surrounding the Mysteries, was hidden from the uninitiated in the Mysteries of the Church. As the Creed was a "definition" of the "unproclaimed" truths of revelation, it also became a part of the Church's worship. Pelikan is aware of the Creed's history, but he interprets its liturgical status as the means of propagandizing the decisions of the Council, as the vehicle of spreading its version of the Christian Faith to the masses. He would not consider the actions of the Council as "deliverance from error and the preservation of the Faith from every pollution" (Aposticha of the Vespers, July Feast of the Holy Fathers).

But there is more to Professor Pelikan's opinions on the formation of the Nicene Creed. He is alarmed that Nicea (and the Council of Constantinople which completed it) "left certain fundamental doctrinal questions unanswered and certain lingering suspicions unallayed." Unwilling to believe that the Creed is a "formulation" of things already held by the Church from the beginning, he is bewildered by the "dangerous" lack of system and completion, especially the doctrine of the Trinity. He is uncomfortable with the Council's treatment of the Holy Spirit, which declared no more than—*And [we believe] in the Holy Spirit, the Giver of Life, Who proceeds from the Father; Who together with the Father and the Son is worshiped and glorified; Who spake by the prophets....*

Pelikan considers the Council's adoption of philosophical terms—οὐσία and ὑπόστασις—to describe the unity and plurality in God as poor solution to the theoretical problems it faced. He prefers the Augustinian triadology which eventually took root early in the Latin Middle Ages and did much to shape its language and life. Yet, other than Augustine and his school, Pelikan is unable to find anyone earlier than Alcuin—"the Holy Spirit proceeds completely from the Father and completely from the Son" (*De Trin.* II, 19 PL 101 25)—and a handful of Frankish theologians, in particular the *libri Carolini*, who adopted Augustine's model of the Trinity and the heretical *filioque* necessary to it. Professor Pelikan, it would seem, considers the Augustinian triadology and the subsequent Western theological speculation on it as an advance over the "timidity" of Nicea.[49]

Nicea and its defenders, Pelikan observes, really settled very little. Having disposed of "the problem of the Holy Spirit with a formula which said everything and nothing," and introducing the idea of *homoousios* (ὁμοούσιος)—"same essence" of the Three Persons in one God—"the question of the One" was left unanswered and the Creed neglected to codify a term for "the Three." His analysis implies, of course, that the Fathers of the Council borrowed language from Aristotle in order to resolve theological questions philosophically, as the medieval Schoolmen were wont to do, as is the addiction of modernity. But the Council and the Church Fathers were not wrestling with great metaphysical issues, such as "the one and the many," "permanence and change," etc. Nor was the distinction between "nature" and "person" limited to a refutation of Arianism in particular, nor Hellenizers in general. The purpose of the Council was ultimately the reaffirmation of "the faith once delivered to the saints."

Pelikan was disconcerted by Nicea's "combination of philosophical terminology for the relation of One and Three with a refusal to go all the way toward a genuinely speculative solution," a "timidity" not only typical of the Cappadocians, the earliest apologists of the Creed, but of all subsequent

---

[49]   *The Spirit of Eastern Christendom*, 600-1700 (vol. 1), pp. 217-223.

patristic triadology. Curious, then, is his appreciation of the Fathers' respect for "the mystery of Faith." One is compelled to ask, why, considering his professed admiration for the Fathers, Pelikan fails to connect their "timidity" with their respect for "the mystery of Faith"? Making such a connection could have assuaged his annoyance at their refusal "to go all the way toward a genuinely speculative solution" with regard to the triadology of the Creed. To frustrate the demands of reason is nothing less than overturning the theory of "doctrinal development" which is such an important part of his faith. Pelikan's *History*, and all books like it, are based on fallacious principles because they are based first on an erroneous faith.

4   OBSERVATIONS

One may trace the antecedents of the modern theory of doctrinal development to the Gnostics, Augustine, Aquinas, to Joachim of Fiore, and even to the Renaissance (see chapter VI). We may insist that it is the Reformation that unleashed the intellectual forces that prepared the way for the "historical consciousness" of the nineteenth century. However examined, this theory is ultimately a product of philosophy—the philosophy of post-Orthodox European culture: Greek philosophy adapted and revised first by the Schoolmen (with Augustine as their prototype), extended and refined by modernity, methods and mentalities which for a millennium has generated a "science" hostile to the Fathers, indifferent to the *skandalon* of the Gospel.

The theory of doctrinal development, whether in its methods or objectives, is *de facto* not a science, but a faith, an aspiration; it is not a device for uncovering the facts of history, but a violation of them, a rationalism which compels history to answer only the questions put to it. "Development" serves the purpose of its advocates, confirming their presuppositions and the conclusions which their mind and method demand, with the result that history surrenders no certainty, and offers no vision, no hope.

This is not the only objection to the theory of "doctrinal development." It is contemptuous of the Scriptural declaration, "the faith once delivered (traditioned) to the saints" (Jude 3). The advocates of the theory do not begin their examination of Christian doctrine with the imperatives of the divine Revelation; and, of course, "historians of dogma" generally discount the experience of the Church Fathers without whom there is no Tradition and the Scriptures remain closed. Candor admits that in the theory of doctrinal development the Church is confronted with a rival world-view, a hostile credo, and not, as some would like to believe, rational science versus irrational faith. We could say here is the clash between two faiths. That the person who espouses the theory is Christian or not, religious or not, educated or not, does not alter the facts.

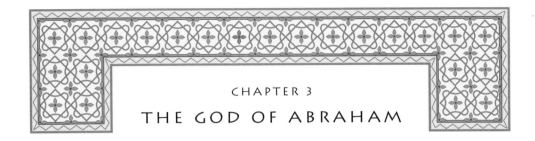

CHAPTER 3

THE GOD OF ABRAHAM

The God of Abraham, Isaac and Jacob is the Creator of the heavens and the earth. He made all things from absolutely nothing (οὔκ ὄν), not pre-existent, co-eternal matter (μή ὤν). The Faith teaches us that, like the Incarnation, creation was an act of divine Condescension. Creation is not a *tour de force*, a demonstration of divine Omnipotence; on the contrary, the existence of the world is declaration of His Self-limitation, of humility. The God of Genesis adds no glory to Himself by the exercise of His Uncreated Energies through which the Sovereign Lord is also related to His creation. We may believe that He created from divine Love (ἀγάπη), if such a motive does not imply necessity. Neither may we hope to find in Trinitarian theology a solution to the philosophical problems of Immanence and Transcendence, the Finite and the Infinite, the Many and the One, which so tormented the Greeks. Without "revelation" God remains utterly unknowable to the creature.

Therefore, when the holy Fathers, from time to time, recycle Plato and Aristotle's "proofs" for the Existence of God, they do not thereby equate the God of Abraham with the "God" of the philosophers, as the medieval Schoolmen did. If it is true that God's Existence and Essence are the same, then, it is impossible to know God at all, because, as the Fathers assert, the Essence of God is forever unknowable. The medieval exegesis of Exodus 3:14 ("I am that I am") is a revelation of God as being, which has no place in the patristic tradition. The object of "knowledge" is being while God transcends all created existences, physical, human or noetical. Indeed, God does not "exist"— not as created things. Reason alone cannot "know" what or even that He "is." Here is the "pious agnosticism" of all the Fathers and of the Orthodox Church.

Of what value, then, are the "proofs" which are sometimes found in patristic literature? They stand to reconfirm what God has written in the "heart," to reignite the spark of "knowledge" choked by sin; and, surely, to strengthen the hand of the believer with the atheist and agnostic. In no case, however, may such knowledge constitute the first principle of a "scientific theology"—which also has no place in Orthodoxy. Contrary to Aquinas *cum sui*, "the knowledge of God" is not "like other truths which may be known by natural reason...preambles to the articles of faith; for faith presupposes natural knowledge, even as grace presupposes nature and perfection" (*S.T.* Ia, q. 2. a. 2). There is no "natural knowledge" of God, because, as the Fathers declare, man's condition is very unnatural after the Fall. "Natural" is better understood as the condition from which humanity fell in Adam and to which Grace returns to us in Christ. The logical inference is that the theologies of the post-Orthodox West—and, for that matter, of the Nestorian and Monophysitic creeds—do not originate with Revelation. Where their doctrine approximates the Faith of the Church, one recognizes only remnants of a Christian past. In the particular case of European religions, their doctrinal innovations explain the existence of a mentality which has severed them from that past. Such innovations are ultimately the result of the supercilious ambition of the medieval intelligentsia to prove the dogma of the Trinity by *natural* reason, along with whatever else attracted their interest. This attempt, among other things, brought "the method of theology to the center of attention, including its relation to (pagan) philosophy." The search for a valid method of stating theological opinion was part of a greater cultural enterprise which aspired to "the reintegration of the entire Christian Tradition through the repossession of the church fathers, especially of Augustine."[1]

In truth, all modern Western thought, even the sciences, as Alfred North Whitehead once observed, is greatly indebted to its medieval period for the basic principles and questions (and many of its answers) of its disciplines—such as the categories of thought (cause, effect, space, time, etc.)—albeit reworked to suit subsequent generations. Over the entire course of its development hangs the "grey eminence" of the celebrated fifth century ecclesiastical writer, Augustine of Hippo (354-431). To many occidental theologians and historians, he is the apex of patristic theology, the only "Father" with whom they need to deal in order to understand the history of early Christian thought.

The purpose of this chapter is, of course, to argue that erring in one point of religious doctrine is to err in all; but primarily to present the traditional theology (triadology) of the Orthodox Church, reaffirming the patristic distinction between the "transcendent" and "economic Trinity." In the former, the unoriginate *hypostasis*, God the Father, is identified as the only "source" (ἀρχή, πηγή) of God the Son, and God the Holy Spirit, the second

---

[1]   Pelikan, J., *The Christian Tradition* (vol. 3): *The Growth of Medieval Theology (600-1300)*, p. 284.

hypostasis begotten of Him and the third *hypostasis* proceeding from Him. With regard also to the divine Economy, the Son, emptying Himself of His heavenly Glory, submits Himself to the Father, while the Holy Spirit, "the Spirit of Christ," is "sent" by the Father to man through the Son for his sanctification and salvation (Matt. 10:20; Luke 24: 49; John 15:26; Acts 2:33; I Cor. 2:11; Phil 1:19; Tit. 3:6, etc.).

Thus, when speaking of the uncreated Trinity, the distinction is to be made between "the incommunicable Essence" and "the communicable Energies" of God"—explicit in the teachings of the East Roman Fathers, implicit in the West Roman Fathers, and lost in the heretical West with the ascendancy of Augustine's rationalism.[2]

1   THE EXISTENCE OF GOD

The ancient Greeks extended the reason of sinful man to the limits of its powers. Naturally, then, all philosophies, medieval or modern—to the consternation of Western thinkers—are nothing but "the restatements of ancient positions."[3] The Christian Revelation, however, is super-philosophical and non-rational. In the common understanding of the word, philosophy is the product of reason, the rational enterprise of a fallen human nature. Thus, the attempt to reconcile the Christian Revelation with the philosophy of Middle Platonism, as Origen did, or with Neo-Plotinism, as Augustine did, or with Aristotle, as Aquinas did, denatures both Greek philosophy and the Gospel, as the history of the Latin Middle Ages and the modern West, in general, demonstrates.

To be sure, Greek philosophy achieved some truth, truth which God had left in Nature (John 1:9) by His Providence, and which subsequently proved useful to the Church in her delineation and communication of the Christian

---

2   The "post-patristic" era of the West begins with the Augustinian revival of the Carolingian *renovatio.* Augustine's *De Doctrina Christiana* became the agenda of Frankish learning (See R. W. Southern, *The Making of the Middle Ages.* New Haven, 1959, pp. 170-218). Charlemange slept with a copy of *The City of God* under his pillow. Alcuin of York, his minister of education, wrote the Augustinesque *De fides Trinitate* which, along with the books of the African bishop himself, were the theological arsenal for the *libri Carolini* in their debate with St Photius and the Byzantines over the *filioque.*

3   "For Western philosophers are constantly bedeviled by the discovery that they *cannot* think outside certain well-worn ruts—that however hard they may try, their 'new' philosophies turn out to be restatements of ancient positions, monist or pluralist, realist or nominalist, vitalist or mechanist," writes Alan Watts. "This is because these are the only alternatives which the conventions of thought can present, and they cannot discuss anything else without presenting it in their own terms" (*The Way of Zen.* New York, 1957, p. 39). It is a fruitful insight, but Watts does not go far enough in his analysis of Western philosophies; and we did not expect that he would.

Faith; but which, incidentally, did not provide Christians with a license to pursue and study philosophy as an independent "order of discourse,"[4] presuming it to be a knowledge which in and of itself contributes to our salvation. Neither does the Church permit her members to mingle philosophy and Christianity for the purpose of creating a "Christian philosophy," that is, a rational version of revealed Faith, whether the Faith is the ground of that philosophy or not.

A   Nothing better illustrates the false attitude towards both "faith" and "reason" in the history of post-Orthodox Western theology than the so-called arguments for the Existence of God. The epistemological dualist almost always denies their validity; the epistemological realist generally appreciates the "arguments" or "proofs"; or, as in the case of some monists, mystics and pantheists, they are ordinarily treated with the greatest indifference, since their idea and experience of God and the universe are ultimately the same.

The controversial Ontological Argument devised by the English Scholastic Anselm of Canterbury (1033-1109), and a criticism of it nearly eight hundred years later by the German philosopher Immanuel Kant (1724-1804), is an illustration of the perfect continuity of Western thought. Thus, the God whose Existence Anselm sought to prove, a proof which Kant will reject, is nevertheless the Deity of Western philosophy, "the absolutely necessary being" (*ens realissimum*)—Kant's *eines notwendigen Wesens*.[5] The latter was a medieval "realist"—metaphysics is a true wisdom: the ontological archetypes of created things are "real," thought communes directly with being without recourse to the senses—and, therefore, he held with logical conviction that human reason can apprehend the truth (*esse in intellectu*); it does not apprehend a likeness of the object, but encounters it directly. Therefore, when the clever Archbishop of Canterbury delineated the Ontological Argument in his *Proslogium* and *Monologium*, he took Augustine's advice and entered "the inner chamber" of his mind, seeking there the Face of God and

4   E. Gilson, *The Spirit of Medieval Philosophy.* Trans. by A.H. C. Downes. New York, 1940, p. 37; and his *Reason and Revelation in the Middle Ages.* New York, 1938.

5   To be historically accurate, the so-called "Ontological Argument" is a title applied by modern writers to Anselm's *a priori* "proof." It was Kant who described the Argument as "independent of experience" (*erfarhung*). Kant also referred to it as *kartesianischen*, "the celebrated demonstration of Descartes." He did not mention Anselm in his criticism (*The Critique of Pure Reason.* Trans. by J.M.D. Mecklejohn. London, 1950. the Transcendental Dialectic, ch. III, sec. 5). He may not have read Anselm's works. No doubt, like Descartes, Kant conceived the "proof" in terms of the duality of subject (*res cogitans*) and object (*res extensa) i.e., vernunft* and *gegenstand* (See A. Koyré, *L'idée de Dieu dans le philosophie de S. Anselm* [Paris, 1923], 231-234; D. Knolls, *The Evolution of Medieval Thought,* p. 102).

praying, "Come Thou now, O Lord my God, teach my heart where and how it may seek Thee, where and how it may find Thee" (*Pros.*, ch. 1).[6] He had every certainty that God would bless him in his quest to prove the Existence of "the most real Being."[7]

God can be conceived not to exist, Anselm said, only if we do not grasp what the word "God" signifies; but once understood, "God is that which a greater cannot be conceived," as the good bishop declared in the fourth chapter of the *Proslogium.* "And he who thoroughly comprehends this, assuredly knows that this being so truly exists, that not even in a concept can it be nonexistent." But for a moment, requested Anslem, let us suppose that the idea of His Existence resides in the mind alone, and not in reality; then, the idea of God is not "something than which nothing greater can be conceived."[8] Any inferior idea (a house, a cow, etc.) which has a corresponding reality or object, is greater than the idea of God which has no matching object, and the highest idea is therefore inferior to any lesser idea with a complimentary object. Thus, the mortal mind cannot conceive a being greater than God, lest "the creature rises above the Creator" (*Pros.* ch. 3).

A quick response came from Guanilo, a monk of the Convent of Marmoutier near Tours (France). He anticipated the objections of Kant with his emphasis on the disparity between thought and being, pointing out that the divinity of whom Anselm speaks, although conceivable, may in fact not exist. Moreover, the word "God" does not mean the same to everyone, aside from the fact that "existence" itself is not a concept. Throughout the Middle Ages some agreed with Anslem, others with Guanilo; likewise during the Renaissance, Reformation and into the present. Immanuel Kant's "refutation" seems to have become generally decisive for modernity.[9]

According to Kant, "philosophers have always talked about an absolute-

---

6   Translated by S.N. Dean. Iassie (Ill.), 1951.

7   All the arguments for the Existence of God, whether in their Greek, medieval or modern form, are ultimately "sound and fury signifying nothing." Not because such arguments are without utility, but because the God they demonstrate—"the Western God"—is no God. A false God is the work of the imagination. The history of debates over the validity of Anselm's proof is a history of intellectual futility and spiritual blindness (See my "The Western God," *Saint Nectarios Orthodox Conference* [22-25 July]. Seattle, 1980, pp. 13-24).

8   The Latin is *id quo (aliud quo) melius nequit cogitari* or *cogitari non potest.* The wording differs in Anselm's various essays. The source of this formula is Augustine—*quo esse aut cog-itari melius nihil possit* (*De mori. mani.* II, 11, 24 PL 32 1355). See Karl Barth's "A Presupposition of the Proof: The Name of God," in *The Many-Faced Argument: Recent Studies on the Ontological Argument for the Existence of God.* Ed. by J. Hick & A.C. McGill. New York, 1967, pp. 119-134.

9   See A. Runze, *Der ontologische Gottesbeweis, kritische Darstellung seiner Geschichte seit Anselm bis auf die Gegenwart.* Halle, 1882.

ly necessary Being, but have never taken the trouble to prove that such a Being is cogitable, much less that its existence is truly demonstrable." "By cogitating a thing," he continued, "I do not in the least augment the object of my conception with the addition of a statement concerning its existence"— *Denn sonst wuerde nicht eben dasselbe, sondern mehr existieren, als ich im Begriffe gedacht hatte, und ich koennte nicht sagen, dass gerade der Gegenstand meines Begriffs existiere.*[10] In other terms, every deduction from a premise is hypothetically true, that is, on the assumption that the subject of the syllogism is real. But the truth of a definition is not established by its assumptions.

As we have already suggested, Kant's criticism of the Ontological Argument is only "conclusive" from a certain point of view—if there is no direct contact between reason and its object, if there is no match between God and the idea of Him, if God has not stamped the knowledge of His Existence on the human mind. Anselm's logic is irrefutable if a concept and its object are the same, especially God, since indeed there can be no conception higher than the conception of God Who is a being greater than any other being which exists. Given this identity of thought and being, then, the idea of "the perfect and necessary Being" contains no contradiction, and God must exist, "since 'a merely possible necessary Being' is an absurdity, a contradiction in terms."[11]

Paul Tillich furnishes an opinion which he hopes will put an end to this interminable debate over the "proofs" of the divine Existence. He maintains that it is the result of a conflict between two kinds of religious philosophy—the supreme example of "the ontological type" is Augustine of Hippo, and "the architect of the cosmological type" is Thomas Aquinas. "The Augustinian tradition can rightly be called 'mystical,'" Tillich states, "if mysticism is defined as the experience of the identity of subject and object in relation to Being itself." In other words, "the nerve of the ontological argument is that God is the presupposition of all thought." For Thomas, the rational way to God is mediated—hence, "there is no logical transition from the necessity of being itself to a highest being, from a principle which is beyond essence and existence to something that exists."[12] Some medieval philosophers, usually nominalists (of which Kant was a modern representative), will go much further than Aquinas, denying any contact with *transcendentalia* (truth, good-

---

[10] *Kritik der Reinen Vernunft.* Leipzig, 1920, 460-465 (Zweiten auflage).

[11] Copeleston, F., *A History of Philosophy* (vol. 2): *Medieval Philosophy* (pt. 1): *Augustine to Bonaventure.* Garden City, 1962, p. 185.

[12] *The Theology of Culture.* New York, 1959, pp. 13-15. Tillich is not entirely fair. Aquinas may have rejected Anslem's proof for the Existence of God, but like him identified God as being, i.e., as the object of rational knowledge, enhanced though it might have been by Grace. For Thomas, God is precisely *ens realissimum*: His Existence is His Essence, His Essence and Being are the same (*S. T.* I, q. 3 art. 4).

ness, beauty, etc.), save through the experience of faith. The Existence of God may be a moral postulate, useful in the fulfillment of our duties, but such an affirmation in no way extends to fact.

B   Only the "fool" denies the Existence of God (Ps. 14:1). He is a fool because he denies what is written in his heart; or, as St John of Damascus insisted, "the knowledge of the existence of God is implanted in us by nature" (*De Fid. Orth.* I, 3 NPNF). Why atheism, then? Because "the wickedness of the evil one has prevailed so mightily against man's nature, as even to drive some into denying the existence of God..." (*op. cit.*). Thereafter, St John expounded a number of reasoned arguments against the "fool's" denial—the Existence of God from "design" ("The heavens declare the glory of God..."), "contingency" ("Everything has a beginning...") and "causality" ("There is a first Cause..."). St John's motive is to draw the atheist out of the depths of ignorance to the light of the spiritual or gnostic knowledge of God (θεογνωσία). He appeals, then, not to discursive reason, but to the inner man ("heart" or "spirit") where the embers of that "knowledge" continue to simmer, however meagre the glow.

Thus, in the writings of the Church Fathers, the question of the knowledge of God (θεογνωσία) is not fundamentally an intellectual matter; it is part of their soteriological vision, that is, faith ("the Faith") and worship. Patristic commentaries, for instance, on Romans 1:20 ("For the invisible things of Him from the creation...") clearly have that purpose. "By day and by night His voice is heard," writes St Leo the Great, "and the beauty of the things made by the operations of the one true God, a beauty which never fails to instruct the ears of the heart with the teachings of reason, so that 'the invisible things of Him may be perceived through the things that are made,' whereby we may serve the Creator rather than the creature" (*Serm.* XIX, 2 PG 52 187A).[13]

The remarks of St Leo are pertinent testimony to a living Tradition on the matter of God's Existence and the manner of His apprehension. Dealing

---

[13]   See also St Ambrose, *De Sp. Sanc.* II, 12, 142; and St John Chrysostom, *Ep. ad Rom.* III, 1 PG 60 412-413; St Gregory the Theologian, *Ora* XXVIII, 6 PG 35 32C. "The distinguished philosophers among the Gentiles," Augustine maintained,"...perceived that the invisible things of God were understood by the things that were made, yet the whole truth was held back from them on account of their wickedness, because they philosophized without...Christ" (*De Trin.* XIII, 19, 25 PL 42 1034). Said Thomas Aquinas, "'The invisible things of Him...' But this would not be unless the existence of God could be demonstrated..." (*S. T.* Ia, q. 2 art. 2).

In his *Lecture on Romans*, Luther declared, *...certe oftenderunt se notionem divinitas in corde habuisse* (*Werke.* Weimarer Ausgabe [bd. 56]. 1983. s. 176); and Calvin's *Commentary on the Romans*, "'Since the invisible things of Him...' This world is a mirror, or the representation of invisible things. He does not mention all the particulars which may be thought to belong to God; but Paul states that we can arrive at   (continued on next page)

specifically with this aspect of the question, St Basil the Great spoke for the entire patristic fraternity when he warned that the quest for the "knowledge" of God must eschew "the mischief of dialectics," exhorting the Christian to "reverent judgment." Without piety, the mind, misdirected by demons, finds only idols.[14] In other words, God remains hidden from those who will not seek Him, for He is "seen" with "the noetic eyes of the my heart." Purity of heart finds God, while Aristotle's logic is powerless to affirm or deny Him.

C   According to St Isaac the Syrian, without the Holy Spirit there is no "knowledge" of God. His Grace is the only strength by which mortals may climb the ladder of virtues to meet Him. The greater our sanctity the greater our *knowledge*. "For a soul to suppose that by its own strength it can produce a sufficiency and certitude of knowledge," he writes, "is a sign of spiritual delusion."[15] The ascent to God is not the reward of education, but the gift of sanctification, which comes to the purified soul which has brought the flesh into submission to the divine Will. By itself reason (διάνοια, *ratio*) cannot escape the "weight" of the senses, nor hope to enjoy the experience which comes to the spiritual man (I Cor. 2: 10-16) whose "heart" (καρδία, *spiritus*), whose inner being, receives the Spirit's gift of *gnosis*[16] whereby it may comprehend things noetical.

St Isaac *(Homily* 52 HTM) expounds three degrees of knowledge corresponding to the three aspects of man: of the body or the sense, of the soul or

---

(contd.)   the knowledge of eternal power and Divinity, for He, as the Framer of all things, must necessarily be without beginning and end.... When we arrive at this point, the Divinity becomes known to us, which cannot exist except accompanied with all the attributes of God, since they are included under that idea" (Trans. by J. Owen. Grand Rapids, 1948, p. 70).

[14] *Ep. ad Amph* CCXXXIII, 369. Loeb Classical Library (vol. 3), with Greek text. Translated by R.J. Deferrari. London, 1938 (L).   Jaroslav Pelikan interprets the Cappadocians, for instance, as viewing the proofs for the Existence of God in purely epistemological terms, that is, under the aspect of natural theology (*Christianity and Classical Culture: The Metamorphosis of Natural Theology in the Christian Encounter with Hellenism.* New Haven, 1993, pp. 57-73). Pelikan pays no attention to the role of the Uncreated Energies as the revelation of God in nature. He assumes this doctrine belongs to another time, having developed with the "growth" of Byzantine theology, largely the work of St Gregory Palamas; but even in his brief discussion of Gregory he shows little appreciation for the Energies (*The Christian Tradition: A History of the Development of Doctrine* (vol. 2): *The Spirit of Eastern Christendom (600-1700)*, pp. 265-270).

[15] *Homily* 52, in *The Ascetical Homilies of St Isaac the Syrian.* Trans. by the Holy Transfiguration Monastery. Boston, 1984 (HTM).

[16] The Biblical word, *gnosis* or *epignosis* (or St John's variant, γιγνόσκω) owes nothing to Greek philosophy, such as the "Know thyself" (γνῶθι σ'αύτον), the self-reflection to which the Delphic Oracle exhorted Socrates. *Gnosis* (the translation of the Hebrew

reason, of the spirit. Adam possessed all three levels of knowledge. They functioned perfectly, each according to design. Rational and sensual knowledge acted together, limited to temporal things, albeit the faculty of reason scanned realities ideal and invisible, while the knowledge of the spirit, *gnosis*, communicated with the Divine. With the fall of man, the ailing senses lost their dependability, darkened reason was harassed by delusion, and the passions afflicted the spirit or mind of Adam and those born of his substance. The divine Economy, St Isaac tells us, included a plan for the restoration of human nature and its powers of knowing.

The Saint describes the new process of knowing. The unregenerate must be satisfied with the first degree, with what St Isaac calls "contranatural knowledge": the information of the senses and reason greatly diminished by the Fall. Without spiritual rebirth, man functions satisfactorily at the common level of commerce, art, science, etc., something available to everyone. Often he experiences the conflict between senses and the results of rational activity, and surely of the restless spirit. It is a condition of which unregenerate man is aware, as his literature and philosophy reveal, but a frustration he seems unable to resolve. In the post-Orthodox West, it is a frustration assuaged only by the arbitrary, if not presumptuous, faith that the sublime end of man's temporal journey is the totality of knowledge, the unity of the ideal, empirical or intuitive form. That is, one day all that can be known shall be known; but, until that moment, we must be content with *"trial and error."* The author of this optimism is Augustine. "Whatever things are known," the Bishop of Hippo asserts, "are known to us, and certainly are true; otherwise they would not be known. For no one knows false things,

---

dahat) is the knowledge of God and the Christian *mysterion;* including, in the manner of the rabbinical *halakah*, the knowledge of Scriptures and its ethical implications. It is also required for contemplation. St Clement of Rome (*I Clem.* XXXIV, 2 FC) describes it as "immortal gnosis" (ἀθάνατος γνῶσις), since it is the knowledge of the new man, the man oriented toward "the Age to Come" (αἰὼν τοῦ μέλλοντος). Also, *Gnosis* is the highest form of knowledge, the knowledge of things noetical and holy. Such a knowledge does not exclude the cooperation of the senses and reason; but it is not given without "faith" (πίστις, *fide*)—"faith" as personal conviction, as experience of the inexplicable, as well as "the Faith" or teachings which Christ bequeathed to His Church.

Significant, too, is the absence of the idea of *gnosis* or some equivalent in Augustine's writings. He uses "wisdom" (*sapientia*), for the knowledge of God which differs from *gnosis* by its "psychological reflexive orientation; it is not the mystery of God in Christ that it has directly in view," explains Louis Bouyer, "but the mystery of ourselves, which God aids us to unravel." Thus, "anthropocentrism. . .psychocentrism has been introduced. Its emergence will trace out the main line of progressive alienation of the Latin West with regard to the ancient tradition" (*A History of Christian Spirituality* (vol. 1): *The Spirituality of the New Testament and the Fathers.* Trans. by M.P Ryan. New York, 1960, pp. 15-20, 182f., 237-255, 493f.).

except when he knows them to be false and if he knows this, then he knows the truth, for it is true that they are false" (*De Trin.* XV, 10, 17 1070).

The Socratic epistemology of Augustine finds no resonance in the thinking of St Isaac the Syrian who declares human knowledge limited not only by man's finite nature, but by his sin, if not demonic persuasion. In the Orthodox world, only the true Faith promises escape from the lure of the senses and the treadmill of reason. Hence, the second degree of knowledge to which St Isaac refers is the "natural" level as opposed to the "contranatural or "unnatural" cognition of the sinful man.[17] Achieving this plateau of knowing, the Christian has regained a level comparable to Adam in Paradise. His heart is "warmed" as it progresses towards "the sufficiency and certitude" engendered by his "natural" faith. "Natural knowledge. . .makes straight the pathways of the heart which lead to (greater) faith." It belongs to the soul purified or being purified, the senses returning to focus, elevated by and collaborating with the Spirit, as much as it is possible. Thus, as the "mind" or "heart" or "spirit" (highest part or crown of the soul) presses forward to spiritual perfection, its comprehension grows and becomes increasingly independent of its temporal ground. Finally, the "natural" man finds himself at "the threshold of the knowledge of God," a "threshold" which is abruptly lost if the passions regain their power. "They pull the mind or spirit back to earth."[18]

The *third and highest degree of knowledge is the degree of perfection*, that level of the spiritual life in which the passions have been expunged or, at least, fatally weakened. *Gnosis*, out of which *theoria* is born, is the instrument of comprehension. Here the Faith by which we are saved wins absolute "sufficiency and certitude," because the Christian, having won dispassion (ἀπά-θεια), enjoys the "mystical" experience of his spirit. The rectified senses and reason collaborate with the spirit in its ascent to the noetic realm. The Christian Faith has transformed his "natural knowledge"; it is wholly supra-sensible and suprarational, declares St Isaac, affording the human spirit with the ability "to see the mysteries of the Age to Come." "Contemplation" or *theoria* has taken the mind beyond its mortal limits, apprehending the ineffable

---

[17] See C. Cavarnos, "The Nature and Uses of Reason According to the Greek Orthodox Tradition," *The Greek Orthodox Theological Review* I, 1 (1954), 30-37; and St Justin Popovich, *"The Theory of Knowledge of Saint Isaac the Syrian,"* in *Orthodox Faith and Life in Christ.* Trans. by A. Gerostergios. Belmont (Mass.), 1994, pp. 117-168.

[18] "Not to everyone, my friends, does it belong to philosophize about God," warns St Gregory the Theologian, "not to everyone—the subject is not so cheap...Not for everyone...only those who have been purified in soul and body, or at the very least are being purified. For the impure to touch the pure is, we may surely say, unsafe..." (*Theol. Ora.* I, 3 NPNF).

things of "the innermost depths of the soul itself, immaterially, suddenly, spontaneously and unexpectedly, since, according to the words of Christ, *the Kingdom of God is within you* (Luke 19:21); it is revealed without thought" *(Homily* 49 HTM).

The third degree of knowledge is "supranatural." The condition of human knowledge at this level has been transfigured by man's encounter with things divine—now far superior to the conviction with which the believer first committed himself to Christ as God the Son and Savior of the world—and a new outpouring of "the light of Grace," the uncreated Energy (as the agent of deification, θέωσις) almost completely permeates the perfect. Furthermore, all members of the temporal Church have available to them the same means for transcending the senses and the dictates of reason. In this world, however, only a few Christians have reached the degree of perfection which allows them a glimpse of the eternal Glory. And, not so incidentally, St Isaac ends his discourse with the observation that, at the level of *theoria*, the objections of secular wisdom are pointless, neither able to refute nor confirm the suprarational or supranatural vision and assurance.

D   Whether in this life or the next, whether inundated by Grace and deified, whether with the eyes of a resurrected body, or the eyes of the pure soul, or even with the reason purged of darkness nor with holy *gnosis*—no creature ever attain to a knowledge or vision of the Essence of God, which is radically incommensurate with anything He has made. "For Him there is no name, no word, formed in the soul or uttered by the tongue, whether in this world or the Age to Come," exclaims St Gregory Palamas. "There can be no sensible or noetical contact with Him. We may not represent to ourselves by the slightest imagery or word the nature or existence of God, save that He is totally inapprehensible, a truth at which we arrive by negation, that is, He is comparable to nothing which exists. Therefore, it is not permitted even to call Him an 'essence' or 'nature,' if these terms are understood in the ordinary sense" *(Theop.* PG 150 937A).

The heretic Eunomius was probably the first to argue that if His Essence is unknown, the creature is forever ignorant of God (see St Basil, *Ep ad. Amphil.* [234], 372 LC). Augustine held a similar opinion. "We cannot rightly say that anything is known while we are ignorant of its substance"—*nullo modo autem recte dicitur sciri aliqua res, dum eius ignoratum substantia (De Trin.* X, 10, 16 981). He, like the Arians, equated the divine Attributes with His Substance. Whether Augustine read Eunomius, we cannot say; but one thing is certain, they both drank deeply at the well of Hellenism which is the probable source of this opinion.[19]   That the Bishop of Hippo qualified his assertion *(ib.,* I, 1, 3 821)—*"to consider and know completely is difficult"* (*intueri et plene nosse difficile est)*—does not mitigate his rationalism. Eunomius, too, may have subsequently modified his theology; but, according to the evidence, he made no statement to the effect, as Augustine had, that his doctrine came "through His own secret inspiration (*per occultas inspirationes*) and admonitions, by His manifest words, or through conversation with my brethren" (*ib.*, I, 3, 5 823).

There is some irony in Augustine's understanding of philosophical enlightenment, since he believed that from the beginning of the human race, God has made Himself known in diverse ways to numerous persons—including "noble pagans" to whom He revealed Himself by a special "enlightenment" (John 1:9) and by the things that are made, "even His eternal power and Godhead" (Rom. 1:20). St Paul was referring to a higher "order of discourse." Augustine's boast was the boast of a gnostic—*ad occultas inspirationes*—thus, in a very real sense, placing himself beyond any rational opposition as well as above the Christian Tradition whose defender he claimed to be.

2   HE WHO IS

The accusation of St Hippolytus of Rome that the origin of heresy was "the wisdom of the Greeks" (*Ref. omn. haer*, I, proem. ANF), was not peculiar to him; it was an attitude common to all the Fathers that a pretentious reason accounted for the heretical ambition to rewrite the Apostolic Tradition, whatever the pretense for altering it. The heretic, affirms St Ambrose, reaches his conclusions (e.g., "the Son is unlike the Father") "by the force of subtle disputation" and "dialectics," whereas the Scriptures admonish us, *'Take heed that no man spoil you by philosophy and vain deceit...'"* (*De Fide*. I, 5, 41-42 FC). The patristic admonition was finally inscribed in the eleventh century *Synodicon* of Orthodoxy:

> Anathema to those who who devote themselves to Greek studies and instead of merely employing them as part of their education, adopt the foolish doctrines of the ancients and accept them as truth. Anathema to those who firmly believe such doctrines and commend them to others, both secretly and overtly.

Put another way, heresy is the falsification of Christianity which, according to the *Synodicon* (itself a summary of patristic thinking), originates with the

---

[19] See the valuable discussion in J.S. Romanides, "Notes on the Palamite Controversy and Related Topics," *The Greek Orthodox Theological Review* VI, 2 (1960-1961), 196-205. The opinion of Fr John Meyendorff that the philosophical disputes in fourteenth century East Rome were "a domestic quarrel between Byzantine humanists and monks" (*Introduction to the Study of Gregory Palamas*. Trans. by T. Lawrence. New York, 1963, pp. 52-53) is a dubious assessment of the Byzantine situtation. The evidence suggests rather a clash between Scholastic and Orthodox theology.

adoption of "the foolish doctrines of the ancients and accepting them as truth." The heretics apostacize to form an extra-Christian sect which, in the course of time, may or may not disappear. Historically, these sects have developed their own theologies, beginning with their peculiar ideas of God. "The foolish doctrines of the ancients" are woven into the fabric of their world-view.

A   Knowledge for the medieval thinker was always the knowledge of being which is perceived to be the condition of all human knowledge, the very first object grasped by the intellect. "Being" is the common denominator of all existence, including the Divine (*analogia entis*). Whatever the differences between things, all are being. There is in fact a hierarchy of being—reaching from the most inanimate to the very pinnacle of being, the divine Nature itself. The station of something on the scale of being determines its character and the extent of our possible knowledge concerning it. Thus, if one believes that God is being, He is conceived as "the supreme Being," that is, both total being (*totum esse*) and true being (*verum esse*), and everything else, whether spiritual or physical being, is gradually less comparable to Him. The unique disparity between God and all else is His eternity and plenitude of being. Whatever exists outside of Him, according to medieval philosophers and theologians, is created, contingent and imperfect.

At the same time, not all medieval thinkers agreed on the relation of created being to the Creator, as the Universals controversy showed. To take one example, Essence and Being are the same in God for Thomas Aquinas. He did not choose to call Him "God" or "Being" for want of a better word, as the Fathers did. He contended that we know what the Deity is by His "effects," that is, other beings or essences, which resemble Him—*omne agens agit sibi simile* (*analogia entis*). God is "the first Mover, and moves all other beings toward their perfection," Thomas asserts, "all perfections [attributes] found in things must pre-exist in Him superabundantly" (*Comp. Theol.*, 20; CV). "God is the first and most perfect Being. Therefore, He must be the cause of being in all things that have being...God is existence itself; hence existence belongs to Him by virtue of His essence, while it pertains to all other things only by way of participation" (*ibid.*, 68).

God is "self-existing being," simple and unique, while the things He has created are composite, such as man who is a mixture of the spiritual and the material. "Therefore, all beings other than God are not their own being, but are beings by participation." "It must be, then, that all things which are differentiated by the diverse participation of being, so as to be more or less perfect, are caused by one First Being, Who possesses being most perfectly" (*S. T.* I, q. 44, a. 1) . Created being is being by similitude or analogy. The fundamental difference between God and His creatures, to repeat, is that the

Substance or Essence of God is identical with His Being or Existence. There are three reasons that the Essence of God is His Existence. If His Being and Essence differed, then He would be caused by another—hence, not be the First Cause—which is impossible for Him. Again, "being is the actuality of every form or nature." But if the Essence of God is distinct from His Being, "it is distinct from it as actuality is to potentiality." In God, however, there is no potentiality; He is perfect, *actus*. He cannot become other than what He is. He is what He is, having neither beginning nor end. Therefore, "His Essence is His Being." Finally, if God's Being or Existence and Essence are not the same, "He is being by participation in another and, consequently, He would not be first being—which is absurd. Therefore, God is His own being and not merely His own essence" (*S. T.* Ia, q. 3. a. 1).

If the Being and Essence of God, the supreme Being, are identical, and "the first principle of knowledge" is the knowledge of being, the natural inquiry becomes—and Thomas replies to it (*S. T.* Ia, q. 12, a. 1)—"whether any created intellect can see the essence of God?" With his usual subtlety, Aquinas finessed the negative theology of Sts John Chrysostom (*In Ioann*, hom. XV PG 59 98) and Dionysius the Areopagite (*De Div. Nom.* I, 5 PG 3 593), arguing from I John 3:2, *We shall see Him as He is*, in the Age to Come. The fact that God is infinite and transcendent does not imply, Aquinas explained, that He cannot be known at all, merely that He cannot be known as He knows Himself (q. 12, a. 8). In a word, God is "supremely knowable" by Grace.

The vision of God, *visio beata*, Thomas insisted, is "the highest operation of the (created) intellect" and, therefore, its beatitude. Although the apprehension of the divine Essence in this life is improbable, "God can be known in this life by natural [according to nature] reason," even without virtue and Grace. Thomas appealed to Romans 1:19, *"That which is known of God*, namely, what can be known by natural reason, *is manifest in them"* (q. 12, a. 12). Natural human reason can know God because He is being (*ens*). The "natural man" can know, at least, *that* He exists, while His "effects" (created being) may suggest to those who search for Him *what* He is. In point of fact, if we follow the logic of Thomas—if the Essence and Existence of God is the same—then, to "know" (by reason) *that* He is, is to know *what* He is.

In truth, the logical, rational God, the *ens summum*, the *primum movens*, "the Supreme Being" of theological philosophy, the God of the proofs is nothing but a "dead thing," as Miguel de Unamuno called "the God-idea." But it is a "dead thing" for reasons of which the Spanish philosopher himself was unaware, that is, "the God-idea" is "the Western God," the Augustino-Scholastic God, a deity with no reality, a *simulacrum*. As a philosophical enterprise, therefore, the search for "proofs" is futile, not only from the epistemological but from the theological point of view. The Bishop of Hippo's

connivance with Neo-Platonism and the Scholastic *misalliance* with the spirit of Augustine provided the West with a heavy dosage of false theology
which ever since has been its fatal heritage. There is no better evidence of
pseudo-God than the conversion of a mystery to the first principle of
"Christian phil-osophy." Recognizing no distinction between Essence and
Energy in God, none between the transcendent and economic Trinity, the
God of Exodus—"I AM THAT I AM" (Ex. 3:14)—necessarily becomes a
"being" whose Existence and Essence are the same: He is *ens* in both His
"existence" and His "essence" and, therefore, to know the one is to know the
other. This accounts for the Western idea of salvation as the vision of God's
Essence, which some might argue should be available in this life.

But God is incomprehensible, precisely because His Essence is His Existence; and that identity is the death of the "natural theology" which pretends
to demonstrate the knowability of God by reason alone. But, as we have
seen, mortals "know" that God "exists" only because He has put the "knowledge" of Himself in them; and has otherwise revealed Himself to a Moses, to
the Prophets, even to "the noble Gentiles" in preparation for His divine
Economy through which He was incarnate of the Virgin Mary. It is in terms
of these facts that the theology of the Fathers is, on the one hand, "negative"
and, on the other, justifies their discourses on the Activity of God in the creation; and, to be sure, it permitted the circumspect use of Greek philosophy
to the Fathers in their elaboration of Christian doctrine.

B   Everywhere in patristic literature, God is described as καθ᾽ ἑαυτοῦ, the
"hidden God," *Deus Absconditus*, the Σιγή or "silence" of St Ignatius of Antioch, He Whose knowledge can be attained neither through the study of the
visible world nor by even the profoundest speculation. He is not "being," not
essentia, not οὐσία, but ὑπερούσιος. In the words of St John Chrysostom, "He
transcends the grasp of mortal thought; inaccessible to the angels, unbeheld
by the Seraphim, unimagined by the Cherubim, invisible to Principalities,
Authorities, and Powers; and in a word, to all creation" (*De Incomp. Dei* III, 1
PG 48 720).[20] Thus, even the "names" of God describe only His Energies and
not His Essence, nor even the Persons of the Trinity.

How does the patristic "theology of names" compare with the opinions
of Master Thomas? "We can give a name to anything in as far as we can
understand it," he maintained. "...in this life we cannot see the essence of

---

[20] "Dionysius affirms," says St Maximus the Confessor, "that no one has seen or
will ever see the hidden reality, i.e., God's Essence... none can or will be able to place into
thought or express in words what God is in Himself" (*Schol. on Cel. Hier.* IV, 3 PG 4 55).
See also St Cyril of Jerusalem, *Catech.* VI, 11 PG 33 617A; St Leo the Great, *Serm.* LXXVII,
4 PL 52 413B; St Gregory Palamas, *Cap. phys., theol., etc.,* 78 PG 150 1176B; St Gregory of
Nyssa, *De Vita Moy.* PG 44 377B; St Gregory the Great, *Hom. Ezek.,* VIII, 16 PL 861A, etc.

God; but we can know God from creatures as their cause, and also by way of excellence and remotion"—that is, He has the perfection of being "eminently" (excellence), by the removal of everything from the concept of God which is known not to belong to Him. "In this way, therefore, He can be named by us from His creatures, yet not so that the name which signifies Him expresses the divine essence in itself or in the way that the name 'man' expresses the essence of man in himself, since it signifies the definition which manifests his essence. For the idea expressed by the name is the definition" (*S. T.* Ia, q. 13, a. 1). But if God's Existence and Essence are the same, to know the one is to know the other, even if imperfectly. The divine "name" must, to some extent, manifest the Essence of God, which Thomas denies. If they do not, the "names" are meaningless, for they identify nothing. Again, the "names" cannot apply to the "effects" of God, because they are created.

Thomas could not escape the contradiction because his theology was lacking the critical distinction between the Essence of God and His Uncreated Energies which also would have called upon him to concede His transcendence to all being. The holy Fathers, far more concerned with Tradition than logic, refused to envelop God in the category of being; therefore, any "name" (or attribute) is inapplicable to God essentially; He is beyond knowledge, for being is the condition of human knowledge; and a "name" always has some relevance to the idea or thing to which it applies; and which, in this case, is God *qua* His Energies. In Christian theology, what we know of God comes by way of divine Condescension—not by "common sense" nor "mystical intuition," nor psychedelic experience, not by some astute analysis of being, and not, indeed, by virtue of Plato's eternal Ideas concerning which Augustine (*Lib. 83 Quaest.*, q. 46 PL 40 30) and Aquinas (*S. T.* Ia, q. 15, a. 3) and other thinkers have sometimes inferred His Existence. They believed that the Ideas, the eternal prototypes of the created things, are stamped by God on the mind of man as the regulative principle of his knowledge. Yet, the human intellect can only apprehend these eternal principles in themselves when Divinely illumined.

C   Not without good reason, then, did St Gregory the Theologian exhort, Βάλλε μοι Πλάτωνος τὰς ἰδέας, "Attack the Platonic Ideas" (*Ora.* XXVIII, 10 PG 36 24B), and so voiced the judgment of the Fathers and the Church for all time. Nevertheless, after what St Gregory urged in his *Theological Orations*, there are some historians who mine the writings of the Fathers to uncover appeals to the Platonic Ideas (Forms, Archetypes, Exemplars) in their articulation of the Christian cosmogony. No doubt, St Basil made reference to the "archetypes" which are discerned now "contemplatively" and in the Age to Come "distinctly"—καὶ ἄφθαρτον ἐπενδυσάμενοι καὶ ἀθάνατον, τούτων τὰ ἀρχέτυπα κατοψόμεθα (*Ep.* VIII, 12 PG 32 265C); but the "forms" with which

God made the cosmos are themselves created, the tools of His Uncreated Energies (*Hex.* II, 2 PG 29 32B). "God created all the heavens and all the earth, erecting the essence (οὐσίαν) with the form" (εἴδει) (*ibid.*, 3 33B). In other words, a careful reading of the first homily of Saint Basil's *Hexaemeron*, with its statement of purpose—both a defense of Christian eschatology and a polemic against pagan cosmogony (i.e., theology)—provides us with considerable evidence that patristic cosmology is no captive of Platonism.

But even more, the Fathers already possessed the answer to the "problem" of God's relation to the creation: the Uncreated Energies. The use of "archetypes" or "forms" to describe an aspect of the divine Activity is a detail of little consequence in comparison with the great cosmological themes which dominated their thinking. In addition, Plato the dualist would have approved neither St Basil's radical alteration of his theory, nor an ontology which joins created matter (ὕλη) and eidetic form, the finite and the Infinite "without separation or confusion" (Cf. St Gregory of Nyssa, *Con. Eun.* V PG 45 705B-708A). Plato would have been further confounded by the patristic teaching that the principles of the world's origination and government were immanent (St Dionysius the Areopagite, St Maximus the Confessor), temporary, and the creative instruments of the divine Will.

D   A fundamental difference between the Fathers, and the Augustinian-Thomist tradition is precisely the doctrine of creation. According to the Fathers the cosmos exists by virtue of His Energies, while the latter insist that the material and spiritual worlds receive their being (*esse*) through participation in the divine Ideas which subsist in the Mind of the Creator and necessarily share in His Attributes (love, goodness, justice, etc.)—inasmuch as God is His own Attributes. By means of these Ideas, God participates in the existence of all things, that is, all elements of the creation have their eternal duplicate in the Mind of God or, more precisely, in God the Son Who created everything by these "exemplars." Although the distance between Creator and creature is infinite, they are analogous. Also, the multiplicity of the divine Ideas, we are told, do not derogate the divine unity, for God's way of knowing is not a series of distinct acts, but "one eternal and ineffable vision" (*De Trin.* XV, 7, 13 1067).

The theory of Ideas (exemplarism) passed to the Latin Middle Ages from Augustine. He had no more fervent protégé than Thomas Aquinas, the Dominican monk who had every reason to believe that there must be Ideas in the divine Mind—*necesse est ponere in mente divina ideas* (*S.T.* Ia, q. 15, a. 1). God is good and has not created things by chance, but intelligently, according to a plan, with order and harmony. Therefore, God loves and wills His Essence–the Essence inhabited by the Ideas. Consequently, He "wills things to be multiplied, inasmuch as He wills and loves His own perfection,"

Thomas declares. "Moreover, in willing Himself, God wills all the things which are in Himself, for all things, in a certain manner, pre-exist in God by their *rationes*. In willing Himself, then, he [freely] wills [the existence of] things (*Contra Gent.* I, 75 Pe).

The theory of Ideas has several problems. Augustine was aware of them, but it was for the Middle Ages to attempt their solution. They seem to introduce multiplicity into the divine Essence, because every created thing has its own exemplar. Thomas argued, with little satisfaction, that there is only one Idea in the kaleidoscopic Mind of God, one Idea with many faces: the Idea takes the image of the object it is creating. His adaptation of the Platonic and Augustinian theories spawned other logical difficulties which palpably threatened the divine Freedom and Simplicity. One *Idea* may be the exemplar for all that exists, but the Idea must nonetheless change for each creature. Also, God is good and therefore would need to erect "the best possible of all worlds," to quote Leibnitz. But this would pose the danger of necessity in God. Thus, Thomas distinguished between absolute and hypothetical necessity: the Will of God, though it always chooses the good, nevertheless chooses it "as appropriate to its own goodness, not as necessary to it" (*Contra Gent.* I, 81 Pe). This answer was not persuasive, but Thomas the Schoolman typically lived by dialectic and was certain that he would be saved by it.

Mental *legerdemain* did not rescue Aquinas. The divine Ideas (κόσμος νοητός) are the creature of Greek philosophy—*scientiam speculativam*, as the Scholastics liked to say—the cosmetic of a false concept of God. The problems incurred by philosophical theology—in this case, to reconcile the Simplicity, Unity and Liberty of God with myriad Ideas placed into His Essence—are self-inflicted. They are the consequence of self-evolving cataphatic theology which presupposes the proportional participation of all beings in the Supreme Being (*analogia entis*). Perhaps, Thomas adopted the Ideas as an act of loyalty to Augustine, since in fact his system does not require them. Aristotle had no use for them. The Ideas were part of his scheme to demonstrate the philosophical nature of Christianity. *Fides quaerens intellectum* is a labyrinth of intellectual *malfaisance* and of spiritual delusion. The need to elevate subjective "faith" into objective or cognitive "knowledge" has its roots deep in the psyche of a culture estranged from its Christian source.

E   The Church views God under three aspects: the eternal and Uncreated Essence, the eternal and Uncreated Persons, and the eternal and Uncreated Energies or Operations or Powers—knowledge of the divine Life which God has revealed in Christ. When the theology of the Church came under attack in the fourteenth century, St Gregory Palamas came to its defense, the occasion being not a quarrel between Byzantine schools of philosophy, as some historians think, but between Christian spirituality, hesychasm, and a "foreign wisdom." Ultimately, of course, the "controversy" had far wider implications than a difference of pieties.

Barlaam of Calabria[21] and others, stressed the philosophical notion of the divine Simplicity—axiomatic to Scholastic theology and philosophy[22] inherited from Augustine (*De Trin*. VI, 6 PL 42 928)—which disallowed any distinctions in God, for which reason Barlaam attacked the patristic differentiation between incommunicable Essence and communicable Energies. St Gregory Palamas replied that to deny this distinction would mean the total devastation of the Church's teaching on the triune God as Creator, Providence, and Savior. In fact, the denial of the distinction was tantamount to atheism *(Triads* III, iii, 6 NG). The Energies involve no violation of the divine Essence, since They involve no division in His unoriginate and unknowable Essence. The distinction between Essence and Energy is an apostolic inheritance, a mystery which admits no scrutiny. Barlaam's agitation, Palamas observed, is the result of a theology which conceives God in terms of being, a theology which, introducing such a distinction, would establish an intolerable contradiction; indeed, an impossibility for people who, as St Gregory noted, "believe that the Divinity is altogether comprehensible" (*Theoph*. PG 150 929C).

---

21   Why Barlaam, the Greek monk and teacher of the Italian humanist, Petrarch, went to Constantinople from Italy (1330), is not entirely clear. On arriving in the East, he engaged the eminent Byzantine scholar, Nicephorus Gregorias, in a quarrel. A wounded Barlaam limped to Thessalonica, and from there to Mount Athos where he became acquainted with practice of hesychasm, the ancient ascetical method of inner quiet. Being an Augustinian, he condemned its advocates for pretending to see "with their physical eyes the divine and uncreated glory of God" in this life. St Gregory Palamas rushed to their defense; hence, the debate over the Uncreated Energies of God. With no immediate resolution, the matter was finally decided in Palamas' favor by two local synods held in June and August of 1341 (See J. Meyendorff, *St Gregorie Palamas et la mystique orthodoxe*. Paris, 1959, 88-110). Barlaam returned to Italy and was awarded a bishopric.

22   The medieval Latin "process theologians," such as Meister Eckhart, Nicholas of Cusa, or Raymond of Lull, and later the philosophy of Jacob Boehme and the Romantic ontologies which it spawned, recognized a distinction in God—the unchangeable and simple *Gottheit, Deitas,* Θεότης and the changeable *Gott, Deus,* Θεός—in order to reconcile the immutability of God with His ostensible mutability as Creator. If we may believe Nicholas Berdiaev, this distinction is the explicit denial of "the immutability and inertia of God and the Absolute" (*The Divine and the Human*. Trans. by R.M. French. London, 1949, pp. 22-48); and also that the mysterious bifurcation between "God" and "the Absolute" no less than the Crucifixion was a "tragedy experienced by the divine life" (*The Meaning of History*. Trans. by G. Reavey. London, 1949, p. 47f). Berdiaev consciously allied himself with the Monophysite christology of "the Divine and human dialectic" of German Idealism, a "dialectic" which his fellow expatriate, Fr Sergius Bulgakov, Dean of the Russian Orthodox Theological Academy in Paris, forcefully described in his *Die Tragoedie der Philosophie* (Uebers. V.A. Kresling. Darmstadt, 1927).

They seem to have lost sight of St Gregory's words that "if the divine Energy is in no way differentiated from the divine Essence, then the act of creation is indistinguishable from generation and procession; and then the creature also will be confused with Him Who is begotten and Him Who proceeds. . . and so the Son of God and the Holy Spirit will not be differentiated from the creature which will likewise be generated by and proceed from God the Father; thus, will the creation be confounded with God and God numbered among His creatures" (*Theol. Cap.* 96 PG 150 1189B). To put it another way, if the Uncreated Energies are not differentiated from the Essence of God, then, man and the cosmos cannot "partake of the divine nature" (II Pet. 2:4), for if they did "partake," if they were "assumed"—inasmuch as the creation's union with God through Grace defines our salvation—the consequence would be the degradation of the divine Persons or, what is the same thing, the monophysitic absorption of the creature by the Creator.

Moreover, the failure to make the distinction between Essence and Energy must lead to a whole series of other absurd conclusions, such as the denial of the divine Foreknowledge. If the Essence and Will and Knowledge are the same in the Trinity, then, "the divine Energies are in no way distinct from the divine Essence, neither will they be distinct from each other; thus, the Will of God will not be distinct from His Foreknowledge which means that either God does not foreknow all things, because He does not will all that occurs, or else He wills evil also, because He foreknows it" (*Theol. Cap.* 100 1189D). From these remarks, we are not free to conclude that St Gregory knew about the Augustinian idea of Predestination;[23] although, he may have had some knowledge because of his debate with Barlaam on the nature of theology, particularly on the idea of the divine Simplicity.

Also, if one denies any distinction between God's incommunicable Essence and His communicable Energies, in favor of rationalist theology,

---

[23] Predestination, the soteriology which had so much influence on the medieval and Reform theology, stems from Augustine of Hippo. Given his penchant for elevating "faith" to "knowledge," it was inevitable that he should develop such an idea. He maintained, of course, that the Fathers who wrote before the Pelagian heresy touched only incidentally upon the "problem" of Predestination (See the discussion in R. Garrigou-Lagrange, *Predestination.* Trans. by B. Rose. St Louis, 1953, pp. 39-54). But no matter how vigorously his disciples have tried to defend him, they could find not a single Church Father who taught that God has from all eternity arbitrarily predetermined some to blessedness and others to damnation. Neither in the Scriptures nor the Fathers is Grace presented as compulsory or irresistible.

Although the Lutheran *mantra*—"Justified (or saved) by faith alone, through grace alone, in Christ alone"—is not found in Augustine, his doctrine of predestination accounts for it. Excluding Pelagianism as a Christian soteriology, we have two choices: synergy or predestination, i.e., either a man contributes to his salvation or he is saved by God alone, meaning that God predetermines the moment and the occasion of his conversion. If, however, the individual is able to accept or reject the gift of the Grace by

then, we must of necessity equate Them, as St Gregory has already indicated; thus the divine Essence is somehow the Cause of all things outside Itself—and everything contingent is what Aquinas called the "created effects" of the divine Mind. St Gregory confronted the opponents of Orthodox theology with two choices: either admit the distinction between Essence and Energy or Operation or Power (call it what we will), and, contrary to Augustine and the Scholastics, abandon the philosophical idea of the divine Simplicity which necessarily reckons divine Grace and Light to be Uncreated; or else deny categorically the distinction between Essence and Energy thereby insuring either that any communion between Creator and creature is wholly external; or concede that any direct intimacy with God is pantheistic absorption, that is, the creature's loss of freedom and identity. In which case deification in the Christian sense is mere tautology.

There is yet one more implication to the theology of "divine Simplicity." Augustine developed a theory of God's Providence in which the divine theophanies (e.g., God in Paradise, the Angels of Abraham's hospitality, the Burning Bush, the Angel of Great Counsel, the Transfiguration, etc.) cannot be genuine manifestations of the Divine. Augustine taught that "the corporeal form of these things came into being for a purpose: to signify something and then pass away"—*ut aliquid significaret atque praeteriret* (*De Trin.* II, vi, 11 853). These theophanies, as Palamas' Scholastic opponents will later say, are a form (μορφή) or figure (τύπος), a material sign of the Divinity's Presence *a la* Augustine. In part, his reasoning rested on the idea of divine Simplicity, that is, God's immateriality and lack of distinctions, such as the "economic" and "transcendent Trinity"; and, in part, presupposes his "Nestorian" dualism, which suggested no immediate contact between the Divine and things created and material (cf. *De Trin.* II, v, 10 PL 42 851).

---

which the saving faith comes to the elect, then Christianity is not entirely the work of God and the individual has some role to play in his fate. This has sometimes been called "semi-Pelagianism"; but, more accurately, it is "synergy" (cooperation).

Speaking for the Orthodox Church, St John of Damascus stated, "Predestination is the work of the divine Command based on foreknowledge...God predetermines those things which are not within our power and according to His prescience...without His help and cooperation, we cannot will or do any good. We have it in our power either to abide in virtue and follow God...or to stray from it..." (*De Fid. Orth.* I, 30 NPNF). He confirmed the words already spoken by St Pope Gregory the Great, "God names them as the elect because He perceives that they persist in faith and doing good"—*Quos et lectos nominat, quia cernit quod in fide et bono opere persistant* (*Hom. in Ezek.* IX, 8 PL 77 873C); and St Ambrose, "*Whom He did foreknow, He also did predestinate* (Rom. 8:29). He did not predestinate them before He knew them, but He did reward them whose merits He foreknew"—*non enim ante praedestinavit, quam praesciret: sed quorum merita praescivit eorum praemis predestinavit* (*De Fid.* VI, vi, 82 PL 16 692D-693A); and St Hilary, *quia quos et praescivit, hos et praedestinavit* (*Tract. Ps. LXVII*, 10 PL 9 449B-450B); cf. St Jerome, *Dial. c. Pel.* III, 6 PL 23 602B.

F   Palamas' Western critics were certain that the doctrine of Uncreated Energies, with a few minor exceptions, had no patristic antecedents, that is, little is found in the Greek Fathers, nothing in the Latin Fathers—the latter whom Barlaam quoted extensively in his writings. But, then, he and his associates, were also at variance with St Gregory about the nature of the Christian Tradition. They, not unlike most of the modern non-Orthodox "experts" of St Gregory (Jugie, Guichardan, Meyer, Rahner, etc.), viewed "Palamism" as the final stage in the development in "Greek theology," an innovation which, if not a futile attempt to emulate Scholasticism, was the final episode in its long alliance with Hellenism.

Barlaam, Nicephoras Gregorias, *et. alii* interpreted the general "silence" of Sts Cyprian, Hilary of Poitiers, Paulinus of Nola, Gregory the Great, etc., on the Uncreated Energies as proof of their critical evaluation of "Palamite theology." Necessarily, then, such "anti-Palamite" writers were ready with a definition of the word "operation" whenever it appeared in the sermons and treatises of the West Roman Fathers. Barlaam, etc., took for granted that the understanding of *substantia et operatio* in their writings always bore Augustinian and Scholastic stamp, that is, the simple Substance acting outwardly (*ab extra*) created the world. But if the Greek and Latin Fathers shared a common Tradition, then, it is unimaginable that the latter were ignorant of the distinction between God's Essence and Energy.

Admittedly, the Latin Fathers had little to say about the Uncreated Energies or Operations, but we may not then suppose that they had no knowledge of them. There are any number of reasons to explain the paucity of discussion in Latin patristic literature about the Energies, not the least of which is the lack of pastoral need for their theological delineation. Also, silence was the best strategy during the Arian controversy which might otherwise have raised the charge of polytheism against the Orthodox Church.

Nevertheless, public statements about "the Operations of God" in the writings of the Latin or West Roman Fathers are present and, on occasion, their remarks are more than a passing allusion. We are already acquainted with the opinion of St Leo the Great. In addition, there is St Ambrose who stated that "the Son says He can do nothing of Himself, because His operation cannot be separated from the Father. In a like manner, the operation of

---

24   The Greek Fathers are not alone in distinguishing "essence" and "energy." They do not always use same words to describe the concepts. In the case, of the Latin Fathers, they generally employ "substance" and "operation." For example, St Ambrose writes, "there is no discrepancy in Divinity or in operation"—*nulla est discrepantia divinitatis aut operis* (*Hex.* VII, 41 PL 14 273D); and, "Well is painted the soul in which shines the copy of the divine operation" —*Illa anima bene picta est, in qua elucet divinae operationis effigies* (273D); and "she who was destined to bring forth redemption must not be excluded from the divine operations"—*tamen redemptionem sibi paritura non debuit ab usus divinae operationis excludi* (*Parad.* X, 47, 315A).

the Holy Spirit is inseparable. Thus, the things of which He speaks He declares to have been heard from the Father"—*Similiter et Spiritus sancto operatio non decernitur. Unde etiam in quae loquitur, audire a Patre dicitur (De Spir. Sanct. II, xii, 136 PL 14 803D-804A).* St Gregory the Great said, "No man has ever possessed simultaneously all the operations save the Mediator between God and man, Whose Spirit proceeds from the Father before all ages"— *Nullus vero homo operationes Sancti Spiritus omnes habuit, nisi solus mediator Dei et hominum cuis est, idem Spiritus quo de Patre ante saecula procedit (Moralia XXIX, 74 PL 76 519B).*

According to St Hilary of Poitiers, the Incarnation was the result, to use his expression, of the "powers of God. . .powers which our reason cannot comprehend, but of which our faith, on the sure evidence of His activity, is convinced" (*De Trin.* III, 4-5 NPNF). But so did St Dionysius and St Gregory Palamas. Other Fathers chose *operatio*; hence, St Irenaeus, "God. . .is shown forth through all these operations: the Spirit also working indeed, and the Son ministering, while the Father was approving and man's salvation accomplished" (*Adv. Haer.* IV, xx, 6 ANF); and others, preferred, *dynamis* (δύναμις), *thelema* (θέλημα), *pronoia* (πρόνοια), etc. (St Maximus the Confessor) to *energeia* (St John Chrysostom, St Cyril of Alexandria, etc.). Ignoring the distinction between incommunicable Essence and the communicable Energies, Western scholarship converts "operations" or "powers," etc. into God's Activity or His Attributes, or even the Platonic Ideas or Forms.

The metaphysical bias of post-Orthodox West alone explains its inability to recognize the existence of a monotheism other than its own. It seems never to have occurred to it that the distinction between "essence" and "uncreated energy" is not a metaphysical proposition that salvation might be more than "the remission of sins," and "everlasting happiness"; it might be, as the Fathers taught, deification, *theosis;* and that deification is participation in the divine Nature, the very Life of God, which requires a Grace which is an extension of that Nature, a Grace which is an Uncreated Energy of God. A "created grace" can deify nothing; and "participation" according to the mode of our likeness to the divine essence—*secundum quod alique modo participat divine essentiae similitudinem,* to quote Thomas Aquinas (*S. T.* Ia q. 15, a. 2)—is not deification. Nothing transforms the creature save his participation (μετοχή) in the Uncreated Glory of God: human mortality becomes human immortality only by "union" in Him Who alone is the Immortal One —θεὸς μόνος ἔχων ἀθανασίαν (Tim. 6:16).

Reading St Gregory Palamas, it is obvious that the theology of the Uncreated Energies has a long and evident literary tradition among the Greek Fathers. We should not doubt that the Latin Fathers were advocates of that theology despite their reluctance to discuss it. In any case, we should be persuaded that inasmuch as all the Fathers viewed salvation as deification, they understood that participation in the divine Nature would not involve the confusion of the Divine and human substances. Grace was the only means to their union. They recognized, too, that a created Grace could not deify. In other words, only the distinction between the divine Essence and the Uncreated Energies (Grace, in this instance) could explain the possibility of salvation.

3   THE FILIOQUE

Vladimir Lossky is right that "the *filioque* was the sole ground for the separation of the Eastern and Western Churches,"[25] if he means that from a false theology emerges a false christology, ecclesiology, etc. The *filioque* cannot be examined apart from the doctrine of the Trinity itself. Thus, if it is wrong that the Holy Spirit "proceeds from the Father and the Son," whether in time and/or eternity, then, the idea of God which it presupposes is false. Either we hold with Thomas Aquinas, "This name 'person' in God signifies a relation(s) subsisting in the divine nature" (*S. T.* Ia, q. 33, a. 2); or, with St Photius that the Son and the Spirit issue from the Father "not by reason of nature, but hypostases" (*Discourse on the Mystagogy of the Holy Spirit*, 16).[26]

No doubt, both St Photius the Great, Patriarch of Constantinople and the Dominican monk believed his triadology to have been delivered to the Church by the Lord, while any other doctrine of God was of human invention. Both claimed to "follow the holy Fathers."[27] And both held a different conception of Tradition. In truth, the *filioque,* an Augustinian legacy, may not be discovered in Christian antiquity prior to the fifth century. Furthermore, whatever the triadological models of the Latin Fathers, none of them con-

---

[25] "The Procession of the Holy Spirit in Orthodox Triadology" (trans. by E. Every), in *The Eastern Churches Quarterly* VII, 2 (1948, the Supplementary Issue), 31. There is no evidence to suggest that the *filioque* was the theology of the Latin Church from the beginning. Nothing in the writings of the Latin Fathers (including Pope St Gregory the Great) persuades me that they advocated the Augustinian paradigm of the Trinity, or that they neglected to distinguish between the transcendent and economic Trinity. Prosper of Aquitaine, Fulgentius of Ruspe, Caesarius of Arles, Alcuin of York and the Carolingians adopted the heresy on the authority of Augustine. In this matter, however, the universal Church was unanimous. Pelikan is right to call it "the notorious issue of the Filioque, the medieval Western doctrine..." (*Christianity and Classical Culture*, p. 239).

[26] Λόγος περὶ τῆς τοῦ ἁγίου πνεύματος μυσταγωγίας. Translated by the Holy Transfiguration Monastery, (with Greek text) as *On the Mystagogy of the Holy Spirit,* Studion Publishers, New York, 1983.

[27] It is worth reminding the reader that the patristic roll is not the same in both Orthodoxy and the heterodox West, especially with regard to writers who associated themselves with the doctrines of Augustine, none of whom were placed on the Church calendar until our "ecumenical era."

structed a "theology of relations." Nothing in their sermons or treatises may be found, whether before or after Augustine, which approximates his trinitarianism, nor resembles the modifications which his theology underwent during the late Middle Ages.

A   Many of the differences in the Augustinian tradition and "the tradition of the Fathers" contain subtleties which by modern standards seem frivolous, especially with regard to the Trinity. Yet, one thing ought to be clear: if the Carolingians were not persuaded by the arguments of St Photius, and *vice versa*, it was not for the want of cogent argument, but rather the mentalities which predisposed them to their peculiar positions. They were captivated by Augustine's way of thinking, *modus et forma* which came to characterize all subsequent Roman Catholic theology–"an abiding trust in logic,"[28] a trust in the logician who "embraces all things in his dialectic, and that being is common to all things" (*Meta*. IV, 2 1004b20). The history of post-Orthodox theology in the West would not have disappointed the Philosopher.
        One is apt to wonder why the Carolingians, the Scholastics, the Reformers were dissatisfied with the patristic affirmations about the Trinity, while, at the same time claiming to "follow" them. As we have seen, the intellectual climate bred a new understanding of Tradition which, among other things, opposed the Scriptures to the Fathers; and, in part, revised the list of Fathers by a special reading of them. The medieval and modern West has always been strongly inclined to the position that the Latin Fathers, and some of the Greek Fathers, prepared the ground for Augustine's triadology.[29] Finally, the history of "Christian doctrine" since the late Middle Ages, secular and ecclesiastical, has upheld the unexamined assumption that all the Fathers shared with Augustine the common dream of elevating faith to knowledge.
        "The Greeks"—as Westerners referred to the Christians of the East—had every reason to resent the abuse of Tradition by the "schismatic Latins," whether it took the form of the *filioque* or some other heresy. At the same time, "the Greeks" had little knowledge of the extent to which so much of the West had deviated from Tradition. St Photius was not the only Orthodox theologian to believe, mistakenly, that "Saint" Augustine's works had been corrupted by medieval redactors. His protest rested on his confidence in an unchanging Tradition and in the Bishop of Hippo's fidelity to it. "The Greeks" learned of their error from the gradual translation of Augustine's works into their language, and from the debates which transpired during the

---

[28] Remarks in Appendix 8 of Dom Velecky's translation to *The Summa Theologiae of St Thomas Aquinas* (vol. 6). London, 1965, pp. 149f (with Latin text).
[29] *Ibid*., Appendix 9, pp. 151-153.

Council of Lyons (1274) and Florence (1439). Before that time very little was known of him in the East. Perhaps, too, like the Patriarch, St Gennadius II (1405-1472), the former crypto-Thomist, many Byzantines came to know the "real" Augustine. The humanists, on the other hand, approved his eagerness to surpass "those who before us disputed these matters" (*De Trin.*, I, 3, 5 PL 42 823), his ambition to be a philosopher in the classical sense.[30]

Unlike the Scholastics and the humanists of the Renaissance, even some of the Protestant Reformers, the Orthodox have never approved theological experimentation. Whatever the attitude of Luther, Calvin, Zwingli, etc., towards Augustine's theology *in toto*, their ecclesiology would not have been what it was without him, that is, recognizing a sharp division between the visible and the elect Christian, between the historical Church and "the true Church," a distinction which depends as much upon Platonism, the unspoken truth of Protestantism,[31] as their misreading of the Scriptures. Likewise, they were indebted to Augustine for his theory of predestination, irresistible and created grace, a crypto-nestorian christology, and the *filioque*. The Reformation was the tail of a tradition which runs perceptibly from fifth century

---

[30] Adolf von Harnack insisted that Augustine deserves to be called a "philosopher," because he "brought to an end the development of ancient philosophy by completing the process" and "making the inner life of man the starting-point of reflection on the world" (*The History of Dogma* [vol. 5]. Trans. by J. Miller. London, 1898, p. 107).

[31] Luther claimed to ignore Aristotle in his delineation of the "coming forth of the Son and Holy Spirit from the Father." In 1514, he delivered a sermon in which he described an eternal motion in God which does not alter His Nature: the Father is mobile (*res mobiles*), the Son is the "movement" (*motus rei*) of God, the Spirit His repose (*quies motus*). In another sermon, several years earlier, Luther openly approved Augustine's theory of the soul as the image of the Trinity. He referred to the analogy as "a datum of faith." Perhaps, with greater honesty, he recognized that, given that analogy, "we cannot truly distinguish the Persons of the Trinity"—*Audio unam essentiam et tres personae esse, Wie es zugehe, nescio credam* (*Werke* [bd. 39]. Weimar Aus., ss. 8-10). Luther seems to have overlooked Augustine's Platonism without which there would have been no conception of the analogy between the soul to God (See the discussion in P. Vignaux, *Luther, Commentateur des Sentences.* Paris, 1935, p. 29f).

Theologically, modern Protestant theologians continue to share the same position with their medieval predecessors. According to Karl Barth, "It is the Father and the Son together who fix the unity a third time in the Holy Spirit (*welche die Einheit Gottes ein drittes mal befestigen im Heligen Geist*). God the Father and God the Son are together the origin of the Holy Spirit: *qui procedit a Patre Filioque*. It is this which the poor folk of the Eastern Church have failed to understand" (*Dogmatik im Grundriss.* Stuttgart, 1947, s. 55). Yet, Barth offers no appraisal of the philosophical presuppositions of the filioquist triadology. The same spiritual myopia led him to call for a revision of the "traditional" formula, that is, for a new formula of "one God in Three persons." He opted for "one God in three modes of the divine Being" (*Dogmatik* [bd.I, 1]. Zurich, 1947, s. 378). His reasons are philosophical. The "poor folk of the Eastern Church" unphilosophically sometimes describe the Persons of the Trinity as "the modes of subsistence"—ἤτοι τὸν τῆς ὑπάρξεως τρόπον τὴν διαφορὰν ἐνοοῦμεν (St John of Damascus, *De Fid. Orth.* 1, 8 PG 94 828D).

Africa to sixteenth century Europe. No wonder the narrow and parochial intellectualism of the West has been convinced for so long that the God of Augustine is the God of Christianity.[32]

B   Unfortunately, patristic theology is treated as if anyone were entitled to discourse on it, as if the subject were so "cheap and low" that it is available to "every audience, at all times, on all points" (St Gregory the Theologian). Theology is not the province of dialectics, not amenable to free speculation, not subject to neat systematization. The right theology is not always the most logical, nor the most satisfying to reason. The truth of Christian theology is revealed.[33] Theology has its own kind of *knowledge*: spiritual knowledge (γνῶσις), which along with contemplation (θεωρία) and holiness (ἁγιασμός) are the ineluctable conditions of theologizing. It cannot be disassociated from the whole body of Church doctrine or, as St Dionysius the Areopagite declared, "only those fully initiated into our theological tradition" may become theologians (*Div. Nom.* II, 4 PG 3 640D). Not without reason, then, did St Photius entitle his treatise, *Discourse on the Mystagogy of the Holy Spirit*.

---

32   To my knowledge, there is not one modern thinker in the West, whatever his attitude towards the Trinity, who has not merely assumed that the Augustinian triadology is the traditional Christian position. For example, the German philosopher, Georg Hegel (1770-1830), developed a theodicy by adapting Augustinian Trinitarians (including the *filioque*) to his own ontology (dialectic), and without even citing the Latin doctor's works. "Here is the truth towards which the Hegelian 'representation' is pointing," asserts the Roman Catholic theologian, B. Margerie, "according to which 'the moments' of the (Trinitarian) Concepts are organized with reference to their final unity in the Spirit" (*The Christian Trinity in History.* Trans. by E.J. Fortman. Hill River [Mass.], 1982, p. 261f.). In other terms, centuries of christological speculation in the West has produced "a metaphysical tradition that, from Augustine to Hegel, interpreted the Trinity as the most profound of all the mysteries of being" (Pelikan, *Jesus Through the Centuries*, p. 5).

33   Western rationalism has effected members of the Orthodox Church who should know better. For example, a Russian bishop, V. Rodzianko, asserts that "the filioque clause in the West and the failure to treat it theologically in the East were both due to... a strange non-patristic idea..." ("'Filioque' in Patristic Thought," in *Studia Patristica* [vol. 2, pt. 2]. Ed. by K. Aland & F.L. Cross. Oxford, 1955, 296). Vladika apparently has a Western notion of "theology" as a discursive science. Theology was a "theoretic" wisdom which the holy Fathers never treated as the opportunity for private speculation. The perimeters to the subject had been set by Tradition.
      Contrary to the Papacy, no Father, Latin or Greek, advocated the *filioque* (cf. J.Gill, "Filioque," in *The New Catholic Encyclopedia* [vol. 5]. New York, 1967, 913-914). Which Latin Father was an "Augustinian"?—Cyprian? Ambrose? Hilary of Poitiers? Paulinus of Nola? Neketas of Remesiana? Zeno of Verona? Faustus of Riez? Peter of Ravenna? Maxim of Turin? Gregory the Great, etc.? Since the Greek and Latin Fathers were members of the same Church it is impossible that they would have expounded Christian theology in opposition to each other and the Apostolic Tradition.

Theological truth is not, in the first instance, a product of personal inquiry, neither is it the result of historical circumstance.[34] Theology comes to the Church from God, a part of the original deposit, included in the teachings of the Lord to His Apostles, "handed over" to every generation of Orthodox in "the Faith once delivered to the Saints." Theology does not develop with or like the sciences and, therefore, none may claim a new "knowledge" greater than "those who disputed this matter before us." There is no new Christian doctrine, only new forms and formulations of ancient truth. The study of the Trinity begins with personal and living faith, a disposition of the soul which presupposes the Faith of the Church, "the Faith of the Fathers."

Reading St Photius' *Discourse on the Mystagogy of the Holy Spirit*[35] is not the same thing as reading Augustine's *De Trinitate*. They have different "minds." Not by accident, then, did the former choose the word "mystagogy" ("to initiate into the mysteries") for his work on the Third Person; and not by chance is the concept missing entirely from Augustine's book. If, then, St Photius and the other Fathers are right about "the procession of the Holy Spirit," it is not by the weight of superior logic and research, but because the Orthodox Church is right about it, and right because her Faith is right, and her Faith is right because her Tradition is right and her Tradition is right, because it originated with the Apostles, and right because the Holy Spirit preserves and guides it. If Augustine and those who follow him are wrong about the *filioque*, it is because their theology and tradition is wrong, and it is wrong because the Apostles are not the source of it, and the Holy Spirit dwells only where the Church is.

St Photius was not only defending Orthodox pneumatology, but Christianity itself. Thus, *Mystagogy* opens with a solemn declaration that "a pronouncement of the Lord opposes them…the Son Himself delivers His mystical teaching that the Spirit proceeds from the Father." The proponents of the *filioque*, he called "impious" (*Myst.*, 2). The sharp rebuke is not name-calling, but a reminder to his opponents that heresy is a spiritual condition, not faulty syllogism. The "pure of heart" abide in the Scriptures, the Fathers, and in each of the seven Ecumenical Council "through which is seen the open

---

[34] Augustine's was "a Neo-Platonist reflecting on the word of God," writes Margerie. His doctrine of the Spirit as the reciprocal love of the Father and the Son, and "the filioque as both a condition and cause of this" depended on bishop "Augustine's intuition." "It is not at all astonishing that the Church had to wait until the end of the fourth century to begin to suspect that the doctrine pertained to the deposit of Revelation…" (*The Christian Trinity in History*, pp. 121 [n. 14], 320).

[35] On the *Mystagogy* and its place in the history of the debate between St Photius, and the Carolingians, see the Intro. to the HTM translation pp. 3-27.

and clear proclamation of piety and of the doctrine that the Spirit proceeds from the Father and not from the Son. What godless herd taught you otherwise? Who of those that contravene the Master's ordinances has led you to fall into such lawless beliefs?" *(Myst.,* 5).

Judging by the *Mystagogy,* the Patriarch seems not even to have heard or, perhaps, not examined the theory of "the relation of opposites"; and surely had not understood the immense influence of pagan Greek thought on its construction. St Photius was innocent philosophically, and he made no direct response to Augustinian "Platonism" in the *Mystagogy.* Not that one of the most learned men of his time was ignorant of the classics, but rather that his theological convictions were derived not from the force of his reasoning, but from that Tradition which included "those sacred and blessed high priests of Rome initiated into the knowledge of truth...those sacred and blessed high priests of Rome who both believed and taught this throughout their lives, and remained in the same confession until they passed from this perishable life" *(Myst.,* 89).[36]

C   What was the reaction of his opponents to the "mystical teaching" of St Photius, and the support he claimed from the Scriptures, the Fathers and "those sacred and blessed high priests of Rome"? The response of the Carolingian theologians may be read in the literature of the era. They zealously defended the *filioque* with no little reliance on the arguments of Augustine. Thereafter medieval writers hurled the necessary invective against the "heresy of the Greeks" without much analysis. With the development of the *medieval summae* the question of the *filioque* was treated in systematic detail. With Augustine in hand,[37] Thomas Aquinas wrote at some length on the subject. He was compelled to admit that the *filioque* is not "verbally expressed" in the holy Scriptures, but rather is inferred from various statements of the Old and New Testaments. Moreover, Thomas could not deny

---

36   Among "the sacred choir of Primates" *(Myst.,* 86), Photius included Sts Celestine (78), Leo the Great (79), Vigilius (82), Agatho (83), Gregory the Great, Zacharias (84), Leo III (87), Benedict (88), and Adrian (89). With a poor knowledge of Western church history, the Saint has no suspicion that Augustine, whose writings he had not read, was the author of the *filioque*. The Patriarch argued that this heresy was not "plainly taught" (περιφανῶς δογματίζεται) by him or the "other" Latin Fathers. Photius insisted that their writings were "maliciously altered" (71). He was not entirely comfortable with that defense and, therefore, made some clumsy excuse that anyone can err, especially in the heat of battle with heretics (72).

37   Part I, Question 36 of the *Summa Theologicae* is devoted to "The Person of the Holy Spirit." Other than Augustine, Thomas cites only St John of Damascus and St Hilary of Poitiers in favor of the *filioque*. But book I, chapter 8 of John's *De Fidei Orthodoxia*, gives him no solace, neither in language nor concepts—"We believe   (continued on next page)

that the "clause" was added to the Nicene Creed, but he justified the innovation with the argument that "during the time of the ancient councils the error of those who say that the Holy Spirit did not proceed from the Son had not yet arisen; it was not necessary to make an explicit declaration on that point. Later, when certain errors rose up, in another council assembled in the West, the matter was explicitly defined by the authority of the Roman Pontiff [sic], the authority by which the ancient councils were summoned and confirmed.[38] Nevertheless, the truth was contained implicitly in the belief that the Holy Spirit proceeds from the Father" (*S. T.* Ia, q. 36 a. 2).

D   Question 36 of the *Summa Theologiae* makes clear his meaning. Thomas reaffirmed the procession of the Holy Spirit from the Father and the Son as from one principle. As Augustine said, "We must confess that the Father and the Son are the Principle of the Holy Spirit, but not two Principles" (*De Trin.* V, 14, 15 PL 42 921). Taking up the cause of the new triadology, Aquinas turned to the fifth chapter of Aristotle's *Metaphysics.* "The Greeks use the words 'cause' and 'principle' differently when speaking of God," Thomas observed. "Whereas the Latin Doctors do not use the word 'cause,' but only 'principle.' The reason is that 'principle' is a wider term than 'cause,' just as

---

(contd.)   also in the Holy Spirit, the Lord, the Giver of Life, Who proceeds from the Father and rests in the Son." St Hilary provides even less support: *Qui Patre et Filio acutoribus confitendus est* (*De Trin.* II, 29 PL 10 69) which is sometimes translated, "We are bound to confess Him (Holy Spirit) proceeding from the Father and the Son"; but which is more accurately rendered, "Who is confessed on the authority (or "testimony") of the Father and the Son." Elsewhere, St Hilary stated, "The Advocate shall come and the Son shall send Him from the Father, for He is the Spirit of Truth Who proceeds from the Father" (VIII, 19 NPNF); and, "Accordingly, He receives from the Son, Who is both sent by Him and proceeds from the Father" (VIII, 20); and, lastly, "For the Spirit proceeds from the Father and is sent from the Father by (or through) the Son" (*ib.*).

[38]   The Emperors called the Ecumenical or General Councils of the ancient Church, not the Popes. As *primus inter pares*, the Patriarch or Archbishop of Rome confirmed the decisions of all such Councils; but the other Patriarchs also gave their approval. Thomas passed over in silence the Orthodox Popes who "remained in the same confession until they passed from this perishable life." He also contradicted himself. Aquinas maintained that no heresy had arisen which made "any necessary declaration on that point"; then, he said that the fourth century Nestorians were "the first to introduce the error that the Holy Spirit did not proceed from the Son" (*S. T.* Ia q. 36 a. 2). But the Church had no reason to argue "the double procession," since the Nicene Creed had already decreed that the Holy Spirit *proceeds from the Father* alone.

Margerie makes an important comment. With the elevation of the *filioque* to a matter of faith (see Pius XXII, *Mystici Corpus, Acta Apostolica Sedes* [vol. 35]. Rome, 1943, 227), there also comes "the full emergence of the infallible primacy of the Roman Pontiff as the dogmatically recognized guide in matters of dogmatic expression. Formerly, this primacy was already at work, but it had not yet become the object of dogmatic definition" (*The Christian Trinity...*, pp. 167f.).

'cause' is more common than 'element.'[39] For the first term of a thing, as also the first part, is called the 'principle,' but not the cause...'cause' seems to mean diversity of substance and dependence of one on the other; which is not implied in the term 'principle'" (*S. T.* Ia, q. 33, a. 1).

His error was to let the terminology of Aristotle define his subject, rather than, as the Fathers[40] had done, to choose words which best expressed the divine Truth, inadequate as they might be. For the Fathers, such words as "cause"—*causa* (Lat.), αἰτία or πηγή, πηγαία θεότης (Grk.)—described God the Father as "source" and "unity" of the Son and the Spirit, so as not only to avoid the error of a "diversity of substance" (which so terrified Augustine and Thomas), but also to protect the Trinity against a Sabellian reduction. Or, to use the phrase of St Photius, "Sabellius, or rather some other semi-Sabellian monster, would again sprout up among us" with the *filioque* (*Myst.*,9). Aquinas either misunderstood or merely dismissed the argument of "the Greeks." His preoccupation was the divine Simplicity—*Idipsum*, Augustine called It (*Ps.* CXXI, 3 PL 37 1621)—a false premise which led him to an equally false conclusion. That is, Aquinas believed that the error of equating the Person of God the Father with "cause"—or, for that matter, the Person of the Son with generation, and the Person of the Spirit with spiration—produced "the diversity of substance" in the divine Nature. Thomas was committed to the notion that God's Simplicity requires the identity of Person and Essence.

Asking "whether in God the Essence is the same as the Person?" (*S.T* Ia, q. 39, a. 1), Thomas cited Augustine: "When we say the Person of the Father,

---

39   According to Aristotle, 'cause" has several meanings: (1) that from which a thing comes into being; (2) the form or pattern, i.e., the definition of the essence which include this, and the parts included in the definition; (3) that from which change or the resting from change begins; (4) the end, i.e., that for the sake of which a thing exists (*Meta.* bk. V, ch. 1 1013a20-2 35). "Element" apparently has only two senses: (1) the primary component of a thing, "indivisible into other kinds"; and (2) something small and single which may be used in many ways, because "it is present in a plurality of things" (*ib.*, ch. 3 1014a25-1014b15). We cannot be certain what Augustine utilized from among these definitions, but, then, his inclination was always towards the idiom of Platonism.

40   "It is the custom with the Greeks to say that the Son and the Holy Spirit are principled [by the Father]," Thomas mentions. "This is not, however, the custom of our Doctors" (*S. T.* Ia, q. 36, a. 2). As we have seen, medieval theologians often counted the eminent "masters" of recent times as "our doctors." Of the "ancient doctors" or Fathers, he mentioned only St Hilary in this Article, whom he misquoted (see footnote 37). Nothing is more replete with dubious citations from the Fathers than his polemic, *Contra Errores Graecorum*. His basic source for them was Urban IV who, in his desire to convert the Orthodox by any means, directed the Vatican *ateliers*, to edit patristic documents (See C. Lampryllos, *La Mystification Fatale*, 98-101; and Fr P. Ranson, "Le Filioque: Importance vitale de la compréhension orthodoxe de la Procession du Saint Esprit," in *La Lumière du Thabor* [vol. 24]. Paris, 1989, 40f.).

we mean nothing else but the Essence of the Father"—*cum dicimus personam Patris, aliud dicimus quam substantiam Patris* (*De Trin*. VII, 6, 11 943). In the same place, Augustine averred that inasmuch as Essence or Substance is the same in each Person of the Trinity, to define each Person according to His Properties is to divide the Essence of God. What is a "Person" in the Trinity? Thomas relied on the school of Augustine, and specifically his disciple Boethius (480-524), for his understanding of the word. "The category of Essence preserves the unity, the category of relation multiplies the Persons"—*Ita igitur substantia continet unitatem, relatio multiplicat trinitatem* (*De Trin*. VI, 5-10 PL 64 255). "Relation," not properties, distinguishes the Persons.

If we listen to the Fathers, God has disclosed the antinomy of "essence" or "substance" and of "persons." Revelation has yielded nothing more than that the enigmatic Persons are distinguished by their properties—the Father: "cause," the Son: "generation," the Holy Spirit: "spiration." Thomas allowed that "paternity" distinguished the Person of the Father from the Son and the Spirit; but the Father is also the "principle" of the Trinity—and here the trouble begins—a "principle" He shares with the Son. Nothing had outraged St Photius and "the Greeks" more than this equation made by the Carolingians (i.e., Augustine). One Person of the Trinity cannot borrow from or share in the property or character of the Other. So, if "causality" (principle) belongs to both the Father and the Son, it must also belong to the Holy Spirit, for what is possessed by two must be possessed by three and,[41] consequently, referred to the divine Nature. Depriving the Spirit of "causality," as the Augustinians prescribed, signified the subordination of the third Person (*Myst.*, 19, 32).

As the holy Fathers teach, the unity of the Persons is found not only in Their common Nature or Essence, but in the Father (monarchy) Who is Their

---

41 The Fathers made no place for "dyad" in the Trinity. "Where the Trinity is concerned," Lossky wrote, "we are confronted with the Three or with the One, but never with Two." The Person of the Father is the only "source" or "cause" of the Trinity. The diversity of Persons is absolute. The property of one Person cannot be shared by another. "There is no question here of a simple essence, self-enclosed, upon which a 'relation of opposites' has been superimposed in order to validate philosophical speculation as a complement to the Christian Revelation." Augustinian triadology is a version of Pythagorean theology, that is, the opposition between Monad (God) and the Dyad which arose from It ("The Procession of the Holy Spirit in Orthodox Triadology," 42-45). See St Dionysius the Areopagite, *De div. Nom.* 13 PG 3 980D-981A.

Ernst Kantorwicz makes a curious observation about the Trinity, albeit incidentally. "It would appear from biblical passages…that the 'Lord' who dwells in the king…is God the Father rather than the Son, although admittedly in the later Middle Ages it become increasingly difficult," he writes, "to distinguish clearly between the first and second persons of the Trinity" (*The King's Two Bodies: A Study in Mediaeval Political Theology*. Princeton, 1981, p. 153).

only "Cause." If, on the other hand, He is not the unique "Principle" of the other Persons, and the Spirit proceeds from both the Father and the Son, then, either the Father and the Son form One Person or "the Person of the Son has subsumed some part of the Father's *hypostasis*" *(Myst.,* 16), and the hypostatical properties, which alone differentiate the Persons of the Trinity, have vanished; *ergo,* Sabellianism. If, on the other hand, the "causality" of the Son is opposed to the "causality" of the Father, the balance of Essence and Persons is destroyed by two "causes" in God *(Myst.,* 35). And to conclude that the Spirit proceeds from the impersonal unity composed of Father and Son is to destroy, if nothing else, the equality of the Persons *(Myst.,* 19, 32).

E   Photius warned his readers not to be confused by the Scriptural phrase "the Spirit of Christ," because it alludes to His "temporal mission" not His eternal origin *(Myst.,* 64, 94). The distinction between the "transcendent" and "economic Trinity" is lacking in the Augustinian triadology. "But the Holy Spirit does not proceed from the Father into the Son, and only subsequently from the Son in order to sanctify the creature," declared Augus-tine, "but He proceeds from Both at the same time, although the Father has given this to the Son, that just as the Holy Spirit proceeds from Himself, so He also proceeds from Him" *(De Trin.* XV, 16, 29 921). Augustine, well aware of the traditional doctrine of "the monarchy of the Father," was self-conscious about his changes. The Bishop of Hippo, therefore, allowed that "He has given this to the Son, that just as the Holy Spirit proceeds from Himself, so He also proceeds from Him"—*quamvis hoc Pater Filio dederit, ut quemadmodum de se, ita de illo quoque procedat (ib.* XV, 27, 48 1095-1096). Augustine's concession to Tradition was disingenuous.

He may have acknowledged that the Father is the ultimate "origin" of the Third Person, but, as we have seen, he does not define "causality" as the singular property of the Father's Person. Somehow He "gave" *(dederit)* to the Son a share in it, in His very Paternity. One may query, how does one Person of the Trinity surrender His identity to another? Augustine never answered the question, probably because he never asked it. Instead he hoped to serve Tradition with an artificial distinction between "the principle procession" *(principaliter)* of the Holy Spirit from the Father, and His secondary "procession" from the Son *(De Trin.* XV, 16, 29 1081). To the end of his life, he made no retraction concerning the unity of the Father and the Son as the condition for the Spirit's procession.

Augustine's position demanded that he abandon the so-called "Nicene model" of the Trinity, perhaps thinking to avoid, among other things, the dispute with Arians over the question of divine Generation which consumed so much of the Greek Fathers' time. He bypassed the controversy over "passion" in the Father, which even the Arians recognized was incompatible with the traditional idea of God. He did not want to busy himself with the dispute over "passion" in the Fathers as necessary for the generation of the Son, a "passion" without which, as the heretics argued, the Son could not be generated from the Substance of the Father. Since there is no "passion" in the Father, the Son must be a created being or the lesser deity (Λόγος) of Philo and the Greeks. Employing the same Platonic concept of the divine Simplicity adopted by the Arians, Augustine hoped to put an end to the Arian contagion. His solution involved a modification of the Trinitarian orthodoxy. He dismissed the traditional antinomy between "essence" and "*hypostasis*" in favor of the "relation of opposites."[42] In this philosophical reconstruction of the Trinity, he offered a new explanation for the relationship of the Son and the Spirit to each other and to the Father.

Augustine insisted that if the Father is the single Principle in the Trinity, there is no recognizable distinction between the other Persons (*De Trin.* V, 12, 13 919-920). He changed the Father from being the "principle" of the Trinity, to being the supreme Cause in a series of effects: the Son issues from Him alone, while the Holy Spirit is the result of the common Love between Himself and the Son, a mutual "Gift" (*donum*). "When therefore we speak of gift and the giver of a gift," asserted Augustine, "we are clearly expressing their mutual relationship; hence, the Holy Spirit is in a certain sense the ineffable communion of the Father and the Son"—*Ergo Spiritus sanctus ineffabilis est quaedam Patis Filiique communio* (*ib.*, V, 11, 12 919). In other words, the Father and the Son love each Other by means of Him Who is Their common Love, the Holy Spirit. He is the One by Whom the Two are joined—*quo uterque conjugitur*. He is the relation between the Father and the Son. "Love" is another name for God the Holy Spirit (*ib.*, XV, 17, 27 1079).

But if "God is Love" (I John 4:8, 16) and each Person of the Trinity is God, then, as Augustine had to concede, each Person of the Trinity is Love. But what belongs to all Three in their transcendence, runs the patristic maxim, belongs to the Essence and is not peculiar to One Person, something Augus-

---

42 The inability, if not the unwillingness, of Orthodox ecumenists to understand the errors of Augustinian trinitarianism, with all its philosophical assumptions and implications, only underscores their loss of fidelity to the Tradition of the Church. Looking for equivalent theological language in the Greek and Latin Fathers, or to argue that ἐκπορεύεται has been wrongly translated as "proceed" (passive) rather than "to go out" (active), etc., is not only futile but places in doubt the infallibility of the Apostolic Tradition which is the source of Orthodox teachings. Bishop Rodzianko offers this irenic definition of the "double procession": "I believe in the Holy Ghost, the Lord and Giver of life, Who, shining forth from the only-begotten Son—Whose only Spirit He is, and from whose generation He has everything—makes Himself to go out from the Father" ("Filioque in Pat. Th.", 308).

tine could not admit. Why does he refer to a single *hypostasis* as Love? Because "God is Love" and it is the nature of Love to unite; while the unity of God is found in His impersonal (simple) Essence; and, therefore, the difference between the Persons must exist outside the Essence. His logic compelled Augustine to define the Father as the Principle of the Trinity, the Son as "begotten" from Him, and the Holy Spirit as "proceeding" from Both (*filioque*), the Love of the Father for the Son and the Son for the Father.

Augustine might have avoided this triadological logomachy had he ignored the *analogia entis* or positive theology of Greek philosophy, and clung vigorously to the revealed and apophatic theology of the Church. He might also have developed instead a Christian theology of the Uncreated Energies. If Love is an Energy or Operation of each of the three Persons or, more precisely, the impact of Their acts, Augustine's entire scheme collapses under the weight of its superfluity. Lacking the theology of the Uncreated Energies, however, and approaching triadology from a philosophical perspective, "the relation of opposites," the choice of the Holy Spirit as the bond of Love between the Father and the Son and His procession from Both, would seem to be an unavoidable conclusion of his postulations.

F   With a few refinements, Aquinas repeats the same doctrine and exhibits the same logic as Augustine (*Summa Theologiae* Ia, q. 36. a. 2). Hence, the question, "Whether the Holy Spirit proceeds from the Son?" to which he answered "that the Holy Spirit is from the Son, for if He were not from Him, He could in no wise be personally distinguished from Him." Moreover, "it cannot be said that the divine Persons are distinguished from each other in any absolute sense; for it would then follow that there would not be one essence of the Three Persons." *Ergo*, "the Son and the Holy Ghost must be related to each other by opposite relations. Now there cannot be in God any relations opposed to each other, except relations of origin (q. 28, a. 4). But "relations opposed to each other by origins" are "to be understood as of a *principle*, and of what is *from the principle*." Also, Thomas observed, "it is necessary to say that either the Son is from the Holy Spirit, which no one says; or that the Holy Spirit is from the Son, as we confess."

This conclusion is the result of Aquinas' faith, not his logic, for he had not demonstrated that the Son could not proceed from the Holy Spirit. He is conscious of this theoretical possibility; thus, he argues that as "love must proceed from a word," so the Holy Spirit as Love must proceed from the Word. "For we do not love anything unless we apprehend it by a mental conception"—an interesting idea from several points of view. With Augustine, he held that nothing can be known unless its essence is known which is the same as saying that nothing may be loved of which we have no "mental conception." We have seen that the Fathers describe the Essence of God as forever beyond the ken of the created intellect, whereas for Aquinas the appre-hension of the divine Essence by the created intellect is man's beatitude, an experience normally reserved for eternity (*S.T.* Ia, q. 12, a. 1).

One would be safe to argue that the difference between the Fathers and "the Augustinian tradition" is much more than the *filioque*; it is in fact the philosophical deity of Augustine and the post-Orthodox Western theologies born of it. There is a certain irony here: the spiritually myopic Thomas was blinded to his error, in part, by a search in the history of the Church for con-firmation of his own doctrine and the source of "the Greek error." He claimed to find it among the Nestorians "who were the first to introduce the error that the Holy Spirit did not proceed from the Son. This error was embraced by Theodoric the Nestorian, and several others after him, among whom was also (John) Damascene" (q. 36, a. 2).

Thomas was right that St John (*De Fid. Orth.* I, 8 PG 94 832f.) was a pro-ponent of "the Greek error," but not for the reasons expounded by Aquinas. It never occurred to this Scholastic (or any other) that this eighth century Greek Father, as all the others before and after him, professed "the Greek error" about God and "the doctrine of the Holy Spirit" on the basis of holy Tradition, not philosophy. Had Aquinas studied carefully the works of St John, he might have concluded that, although they both had an affinity for Aristotle, the influence of the Philosopher on himself was not as it was on the Damascene for whom a synthesis between the Christian Faith and Greek philosophy was unthinkable. If, also, Thomas had examined the writings of St John and the Fathers in general, for their truth rather than as a resource for his own theology, he might have compelled "the foreign philosophy" to ser-vice of the Church; and, perhaps, too, he may have discovered that the *fil-ioque* was a figment of the philosophical imagination.

4   IMAGO DEI

Augustine viewed the Trinity from two points of view: God as eternal Being, and God in His relationship to the creation, especially the human soul which, like Himself, is pure spirit. The soul of man was created in the image of the Trinity. Thus, the knowledge of the soul leads to the knowledge of God. Augustine took the advise of Socrates, *"Know thyself"* (Γνῶθε σ'αὐτόν). His anthropology was revolutionary.

A   Augustine was indebted to the "Christian Neo-Platonism" of Marius Victorinus (4th c. AD) with whose philosophy he became familiar while a student in Rome (383), where he had also read Victorinus' translation of Plotinus' *Enneads*. With it Augustine's fertile mind formed a theological sys-tem unprecedented in the history of Christian thought, beginning with his exegesis of Gen. 1:26 ("Let us make man according to our image...") by which he was able to view the human soul as a reflection of the Trinity. Here, for the first time in the history of the early Church, the image of God (*imago Dei*) in man was understood as the image of all three divine Persons. Traditionally, it was equated with Him Who is the very *Imago Dei*, the divine Logos (II Cor. 4:4); or, more exactly, "the Image of the Father" ("Let us make man after our own Image..."), for "the Son is the Image of the Father," as St Hilary of Poitiers said (*De Trin.* V, 8 NPNF). Also, novel was the attempt to demonstrate Christian triadology from the nature of the soul. Augustine looked "inward" for the solution to a question he should not have asked. He might have been dissuaded from the theological experimentation had he taken seriously the words of St Hilary that "no human research will ever find an analogy for this (triune) condition of the divine Existence" (*Ib.*, III, 1).

Nonetheless, Augustine borrowed his comparison between the "inward man" or soul to "the Triad on High" from Victorinus. The latter described "the simplicity of the triadic soul" as "to be," "to live" and "to understand," all united in one essence (ὁμοουσία),[43] but "individuated in their own substance without separation, division, overflowing, extension or reproduction; but they are always three, each existing in the reality in the other which truly and subtantially exist. Therefore, the soul is 'according to the image'" (*Adv. Ar.* I, 63 PL 8 1087D). The Father, said Marius, is "the great Divinity" of the Trinity," He Who is differentiated from the other Persons by His activity.[44] The Son is other than the Father "in that He moves Himself and acts for the sake of manifestation." The Spirit differs "from the Father and the Son" as *vivicatio*

---

[43] "It is strange that nowhere in the *De Trinitate* does Augustine refer to *homoousion* (consubstantial)," remarks Stephen McKenna in the Introduction to his translation of Augustine's *The Trinity*. It was "the key-word of the Council of Nicea (325) against the Arians" (FC [vol. 45]. Washington, DC, 1963, x, n. 19). Not so strange when one considers that, as Paul Henry writes, he owed almost nothing to the Greek Fathers or "to his Latin forerunners, Tertullian and Hilary of Poitiers, both of whom were concerned with upholding materially the doctrine of the Scripture and Tradition than with trying to express it systematically in terms of modern thought" ("The *Adversus Arium* of Marius Victorinus: The First Systematic Exposition of the Trinity," in *Journal of Theological Studies* I [1950], 42).

Henry might also have included St Ambrose among the "Latin forerunners" ignored by Augustine. They had very little in common, however much Roman Catholic scholars trumpet their affinity. In the matter of pneumatology, observes H. Reuter (*Augustinische Studien*. Aalen, 1967, 192), Augustine consulted neither *De Fide* or *De Spiritu Sancto* of St Ambrose, who was committed to apophaticism and the language of antinomy. For the Bishop of Hippo, "negative theology was educational, not dogmatic" (See I.V. Popov, *The Personality and Teachings of the Blessed Augustine* [vol. I, pt 2]. Trans. by A. Lisenko. Sergiev Posad, 1916, pp. 362-365).

[44] *Letter to Candidus the Arian* V, 2, 30 (*in Marius Victorinus: Theological Treatises on the Trinity*. Trans. by M.T. Clark for FC (vol. 69). Washington D.C., 1981).

in motu. "The three are, therefore, *homoousioi,* and on that account all three are one God" (*Adv. Ar.* I, 8 1044D). Both are manifestations of the Father, but the Spirit is manifested so as to distinguish Him from the Father and the Son, that is, by proceeding from Both. In other words, the simplicity and multiplicity in God are reconciled, as the soul itself indicates, by the conversion of the three hypostatic characteristics (paternity, generation, procession) into relationships (cf. Plotinus, fifth *Ennead*). To know oneself metaphysically, then, is to possess, however imperfectly, a knowledge of the Trinity.

Augustine made a few adjustments in the theory, such as replacing Victorinus' "to live," "to be," and "to understand" with "to remember," "to understand" and "to will" (*De Trin.* X, 9, 19 983). There is, as not a few writers have pointed out, a major flaw in this theory, whether Victorinus' or Augustine's version. God and the soul are pure spirit (albeit the one is created and the other uncreated being); therefore, along with the angels the soul is ontologically kin to God. If, indeed, this kinship or analogy were true, and the idea of their likeness is strictly applied, Augustinian (and Victorinian) anthropology ("psychology") has transformed Christian triadology into a form of Sabellianism,[45] inasmuch as the faculties of the soul (memory, intellect, and will) are in fact non-hypostatic dimensions of it. That is, they are merely three faculties of the soul. But the Persons of the Trinity, although sharing one Essence, are three individual realities in God, not triple manifestations of God. Even if it were true that the Spirit proceeds from the Father and the Son, some other method would have to be found to explain the Trinity in order to avoid this modalist heresy. Deserting the Greek *analogia entis* would need to be the first step.

---

[45] The Sabellians taught that the Father, Son and Holy Spirit are one and the same being, that is, three names or titles for the same Substance. Here was a careless attempt to safeguard the unity of God. Sabellius used analogies to explain his theology, e.g., sun (Father), light (Son), heat (Holy Spirit), that is, a single source with two emissions. God is not three hypostases (Persons) who share a common Essence (See *Documents of the Christian Church.* Selected and edited. by H. Bettenson. New York, 1947, pp. 54-58).

"Sabellius, who did not know how to maintain this antinomy, seeing above all the unity of substance," Vladimir Lossky concurs, "lost the notion of the Trinity of Persons and replaced the living God of the Christians with the divine essence of the pagan philosophers" ("The Theology of Light in the Thought of St. Gregory Palamas," in *In the Image and Likeness of God.* New York, 1974, p. 52). M. Nedoncelle observes that, "The comparison of the three faculties is wanting, because it does not express the diversity of persons" ("L'intersubjectivite humain est-elle pour saint Augustine: un image de la Trinité?" *Augustinus Magister* [vol. 5]. Paris, 1954, 600-601). *"Les relations intratrinitaires qui ont remplace, pour ces théologiens, la distinction selon l'hypostase, resemblent étrangement aux 'noms'*

B   The human philosophy of the Greeks amalgamated with the revealed
wisdom of the Church must necessarily compromise both. Reconciliation of
"faith" and "reason" demands the modification of all principles. Thus, when
Genesis announces, "Let us make man in our image," one may be curious
why Augustine replaced the traditional concept of the *imago Dei* in man as
"the image of the Image of God"(the Son) with the soul as the analogy of the
Trinity. We have every right to suspect that the thinking of Augustine was
influenced by philosophy. It is not really important whether Augustine
deduced the soul from the Trinity or the Trinity from the soul. Neither his triadology or nor his idea of the soul is grounded in Tradition.

Cardinal Newman, as he tells us in his *Essay*, justified this "insight" of
Augustine about God and the soul by their understanding of the Christian
theological tradition, that is, by "doctrinal development." It is clear that
Augustine (and Newman) did not find his opinions in this matter among the
Fathers. According to the Fathers, the divine Logos, God the Son, "the Image
of God," is the Creator. He stamped the "image of God," of Himself, on man;
thus, man is "the image of the Image of God." "The phrase 'after His image,'"
wrote St John of Damascus, "palpably refers to the side of man's nature
which consists of mind and free will, whereas 'after His likeness' means similarity in virtue so far as that is possible" (*De Fid. Orth*. II, 12 NPNF). To be
sure, that God the Son is the Creator and the image of man is the Image of
God, does not exclude the Father and the Spirit from Christian anthropology, as Cyril of Alexandria observed. Inasmuch as the Persons of the Trinity
are one God, "the marks of the whole consubstantial Trinity" are present in
Adam, that is, he received the Spirit in order to become divine; he was identified with the Son that he might become a son of God (*Doctrinal Questions
and Answers* IX, 2; Wickham).

More than one modern patrologist has noted the differences between
Augustine and "the other Fathers" on this matter. Not a few have spurned
the latter as unoriginal compared to the "creative ingenuity" of Augustine.

C   There is something historically more interesting about Orthodox triadology than her conception of the Trinity, a position consistent with Tradition.
God is always worshiped as He is revealed. In this way, whatever the Fathers
may have said in defense of this Tradition, whatever concepts or language

---

interchangeables dans l'herésie de Sabellius," observes Fr Ranson. *"C'est pour cette raison que
l'Église Orthodoxe a toujours considére le Filioque comme une forme de sabellianisme"* ("Le
Filioque...," 45).

they have used to rationally strengthen and communicate the Faith, that Faith remains unaltered. In the post-Orthodox West there has occurred a curious theological development—to believe in God without, at the same time, believing in the Trinity, or linking Him necessarily to the Incarnation and the Church. How is this dichotomy to be understood? We need to look more deeply into the history of Western religious thought.[46]

The gradual "marginalization" of the Trinity began already in the Latin Middle Ages with the philosophical distinction between *de Deo uno* and *de Deo Trino*. The latter is a mystery of the Faith, while the "one God"—accessible to reason— belonged to "natural theology." Aquinas, for instance, discussed this "natural theology" at the beginning of his *Summa Theologiae*, particularly in his five demonstrations for the Existence of God. The Protestant Reformation reinforced the distinction between the God of reason and the Trinity of faith. In Luther's writings, the Trinity regularly served as a way of pointing to the God of Grace Who is known only through the divine gift of faith in Christ, contrasted by the sterile effort of sinful man to cogitate God by his "darkened" reason. Furthermore, the Reformers commonly identified "the Word of God" with the Scriptures rather than with Christ. No wonder Luther and the other Reformers placed the sermon at the center of their liturgies, and the pulpit was situated higher than the altar in their temples. Thus, Calvin declared that "the Church is born from the Word of God" (*Ecclesia nata est ex Dei verbo*), meaning from the writings of the Old and New Testament Scriptures rather than of the Eucharist, the Body and Blood of the Incarnate Logos or *Word* born of the Virgin Mary.

By the seventeenth century, any opportunity for the Trinity to play the major role in Christian apologetics was lost. Using the same metaphysics as the Protestants and the Roman Catholics, Deists (e.g., Newton, Clarke, Browne, Herbert of Cherbury, John Locke, etc.) were able to present arguments which denied the Trinity.[47] Most of their critics merely denounced the Deists as heretics. In his *Vindication of the Holy and Blessed Trinity* (1690), the Anglican, William Sherlock, tried to show the contradictions in the opinions of Unitarians and atheists. The Trinity, he said, is a "thinking Substance" with both Intellect and Spirit, as any other living being. He was repeating Augustine's triadology. Sherlock should be given credit, nevertheless, for taking the Trinity seriously and for trying to lead others of his generation to do the same; yet, as so many before and after him, he could not demonstrate

---

46 Placher, W.C., *The Domestication of Transcendence*. Louisville, 1996, p. 164f.

47 See B. Willey, *The Seventeenth Century Background*. Garden City (NY), 1953.

the identity of God as Trinity nor any necessary connection between the idea of the Trinity and the Christian Economy. According to Michael Buckley, "In the absence of a rich and comprehensive christology and pneumatology of religious experience, Christianity entered into the defense of the Christian God without an appeal to anything Christian."[48]

Perhaps aware of the futility of discussing God in Biblical terms with the concepts of the Christian revelation, in a culture perceived as hostile to the language and experience of faith, Roman Catholics could do little more than Sherlock. They seemed to have lost faith in talking philosophically about the Trinity as the identity of God. If they had any doubts about the spirit of the times, the famous seventeenth century Jesuit theologian, Leonard Lessius, pretending to refute atheism in his *De Providentia Numinis et Anime immortalitate* (1613), puts an end to them. He treated atheism as a philosophical rather than a religious issue; and, therefore, took arguments for the Existence of God from the ancient Greek philosophers when he might have depicted atheism as a rebellion against Christianity and the true God. If nothing else, the effect of his work was to eliminate from theological discourse any appeal to christology in fixing the reality of God. Lessius became a model for other Latin theologians who likewise excluded from their theological apologetics any discussion of Christ. Eventually the disappearance of christology from such writings was so commonplace that it did not occur to theologians to include it.

What are we to conclude? With the centuries of cataphatic theology "the chickens had finally come home to roost." The Christianity of the West was in full retreat before the growing secularism of its culture. Rather than the Trinity as central to Protestant hermeneutics and apologetics, it stressed a personal relationship between the believer and Jesus Christ, the authority of the Scripture and "the inner testimony of the Holy Spirit." The Roman Catholics continued to equate the God of Abraham with the God of the philosophers without also making argument for the finality of His revelation in Christ and the Church. In both cases, the marginalization of the holy Trinity went hand in hand with the obfuscation of the Christian Faith, with no little assistance from the developments in modern philosophy which reduced the traditional duality between God and the soul to the self and the world.

---

48   *At the Origins of Modern Atheism.* New Haven, 1987, p. 67. In fact, there has always been a christology and pneumatology, conventional and unconscious. Their development, whether by the Latins or the Protestants, has made little difference in the course of Western theology.

5   The Beatific Vision

A discussion of salvation as the supernatural act of the created intellect whereby the beatified soul enjoys a direct, intuitive and clear knowledge of the Triune God as He is in Himself[49] is better placed in a chapter on the doctrine of God. Roman Catholicism claims that the beatific vision is divinely revealed and they appeal to the Fathers and the Scriptures to show it. In point of fact, the so-called vision "face to face" (I Cor. 13:12) is a logically necessary conclusion from the Scholastic idea of God (and man), and not a revealed truth. To describe it, as some do, as the full and definitive experience of the direct self-communication of God Himself to the individual human being when by (created) Grace God's Will has achieved full realization, is to do no more than conceal the intrinsically philosophical nature of the theory in theological rhetoric.[50] The beatific vision has in fact no basis in the Apostolic Tradition, however the evidence may be construed.

A   According to traditional Roman Catholic thinking, every creature possesses an innate and indelible orientation towards its perfection to which it is brought by its own proper good. But that good cannot be something imperfect and temporary, for then there remains something to be desired. Its end must be complete and infinite if the creature is to achieve perfection. Since only God is the complete and infinite Good, He alone fits the description of the creature's necessary end. God is the eternal Good, the *terminus ad quem* of all creatures, the Mover Who draws all things to Himself, as Aristotle said. But, then, a problem arises. If it is the end of man to apprehend the universal Good by his intellect—the Good not circumscribed by space and time nor subject either to corruption or to change—how is this end to be realized? The Scriptures expressly declare that no man can see God, nor may anyone see His face and live (John 1:18; I John 4:12; I Tim. 6:16; Ex. 33:20); while, at the same time, St John the Theologian states, "We know that when He shall appear, we shall be like Him, and we shall see Him as He is" (I John 3:2).

Here is a paragraph from his *Summa Theologica*, awash with Aristotelian principles, which promises a solution:

> I answer that, Since everything is knowable according as it is actual, God, Who is pure act without any admixture of potentiality, is in Himself supremely knowable. But what is supremely knowable in itself may be knowable to a particular intellect, because of the excess

---

[49]   Pope Benedict XII describes the beatific vision as *visio intuitiva et facialis* of God's Essence (*Benedictus Deus*, 1336). He lent this doctrine the full force of his "apostolic authority," intimating that the beatific vision is a revelation of the Holy Spirit (see 5B).

[50]   See K. Rahner, "Beatific Vision," in *Sacramentum mundi* (vol. 1). Ed. by K. Rahner, etc. New York, 1986, p. 151.

of the intelligible object above the intellect; as, for example, the sun, which is supremely visible, cannot be seen by the eye by reason of the excessive light. Therefore, some who admit this hold that no created intellect can see the essence of God. This opinion, however, is not tenable. For the ultimate beatitude of man consists in the use of his highest function, which is the operation of the intellect. Hence, if we suppose that a created intellect could never see God, it would either never attain to its beatitude, or its beatitude would consist of something beside God; which is opposed to faith. For the ultimate perfection of the rational creature is to be found in what which is the source of its being; since a thing is perfect so far as it attains to its source. Further, the contrary opinion is also against reason. For there resides in every man a natural desire to know the cause of any effect which he sees. Thence arises wonder in men. But if the intellect of the rational creature could not attain to the first cause of things, the natural desire would remain in vain. Hence, it must be granted absolutely that the blessed see the essence of God (*S.T.* Ia q. 12. a. 1).

The key phrase is "the blessed." "None may see God as He is either in this life, or in the angelic life, in the manner that visible things are seen by corporeal vision," explains Augustine (*Ep.* CXLVII, 11 PL 33 609). The creature cannot see God "as He is" with the eyes of the flesh or the natural powers of the intellect which depend upon them. But if, in the next world, the powers of the intellect are enhanced by Grace, and "the blessed" have become like Him, then, man shall behold God. "To see the essence of God is possible to the created intellect by grace, not by nature" (*S.T.* Ia q. 12 a. 4).

The logic is flawless, given the principles with which Aquinas (and Augustine[51] before him) had to work; but the sight of God's Essence depends upon the concept of God as being, and therefore analogous to the creature which seeks to gaze upon It. However, the argument falls to the ground if God is "superessential," and if Grace, according to this world-view, is created. In other words, there can be no "participation" in the eternal Good, God, and therefore no beatific vision, where there can be no unity between the knower (man) and the Known (God). Participation in the divine Nature is possible only if Grace is uncreated, only if the creature is deified; but not even uncreated Grace permits the creature, angelic or human, to behold the unspeakable and unapproachable Essence of God.

---

51   Augustine is the author of the beatific vision doctrine. He is the first to interpret John 17:3 as the face to face apprehension of God. "And what is 'life eternal'? That they may know Thee the only true God and Jesus Christ Whom Thou has sent.' Not, indeed, as those will know Him who, although impure of heart, yet will be able to see Him as He sits in Judgment, in His glorified servant-form; but as He is to be known by the 'pure of heart,' as the only true God, the Son along with the Father and the Holy Spirit, because the Trinity is the only true God" (*In Evang. John*, tract. CXI, 5; and XXXIV, 9; LIII, 2, etc. FC).

B   On the third Sunday of Advent 1329, and afterwards in public consisto-
ry, Pope John XXIII (1316-1334) preached that the souls which have died in a
state of grace go into Abraham's bosom, *sub altari Dei*, and do not enjoy the
beatific vision (*visio facie ad faciem*) of the Lord until after the Last Judgment
and the Resurrection; and he even instructed his secretary to collect passages
from the Fathers which favored his teaching. The uproar which followed led
King Philip VI (France) to finally refer the question to the Paris faculty of theology (1333), which concluded that the souls of the blessed behold the God
immediately after death. John refused to retract his doctrine. He might have
been tried by a general council for heresy, had he not been stricken by a fatal
illness. On his deathbed, the Pope confessed that the purified souls of the
just do see the divine Essence of God so far as the state and condition of a
separated soul allows him.

Pope John's confession did not quell the controversy. For the peace of
the Faithful, his successor, Pope Benedict XII, issued the decree, *Benedictus
Deus* (1336), proclaiming that all the blessed, after the Ascension of Christ
into heaven, do behold the divine Essence "with an intuitive and face-to-face
vision, with no creature mediating in the manner of natural knowing; but
rather that the divine essence immediately showing itself to them without
covering, openly and clearly; and that when they see in this way they have
full enjoyment of that same divine essence." More than a hundred years
passed before the words of Pope Benedict were reaffirmed. During the
Council of Florence (1439), Pope Eugenius IV published the bull, *Laetenur
coeli*, as part of the *Decree for the Greeks*. It implies that "the Greeks" failed to
espouse the doctrine of beatific vision. There is also an allusion to purgatory in this statement. "The souls of those who after the reception of Baptism
have incurred no stain of sin at all, and also those which after the contraction
of sin have been purged, whether in their bodies or when delivered from
their bodies," it maintained, "these are immediately received into heaven and
see clearly the one and Triune God, just as He is, yet one person more perfectly than another, in proportion to the diversity of merits."

Not thirty years later an English artist illustrated a copy of the papal
decree with an "icon" of God. The icon was divided into three levels. On the
bottom were two people kneeling on either side of "the earthly spheres,"
representing the Christian faithful who believe even though they cannot see
the object of their adoration. A few rays of Divinity are visible to them, but
they are not connected directly to those emanating from the higher levels or
spheres above them. On the platform above them, are two saints, mediators
between heaven and earth, St Benedict and St Paul, who themselves experience "the light of God." In the topmost register the immense disembodied
head of the Deity represents the direct "face to face" vision. This Gothic
image of God as the divine Essence simultaneously offers something to per-

ceive and also retracts it, presenting a picture of something that the viewer will eventually see only after death. One may suppose that if God may be pictured as a glittering globe, there is no reason that Michaelangelo could not paint the Creator as a Greek athlete on the ceiling of the Sistine Chapel. In either case, this blasphemous "theology in color" violates, among other things, the patristic dictum that what has not been seen—what has not been "circumscribed"—cannot be depicted.

In this entire episode, there is something unexpected, a truth uttered by Pope John XXIII. With a few exceptions, he said, the souls of those who have fallen asleep in the Lord are in fact not immediately elevated to heaven, any-more than the souls of the reprobate are cast into hell (*gehenna*). Such things must await the Age to Come, even as Augustine said (*Evang. in John*, tract CI, 5). In this, he approached the Orthodox teaching on the Particular Judg-ment, that the saved are consoled in "Abraham's bosom," paradise, and the damned are consigned to "place of torment," hades. There is something else of importance, generally ignored in this medieval controversy: if the soul were to enjoy a beatific vision, it could not do so alone; it must encounter the Essence of God with the body which, in this present life, it practiced the good and committed evil. In his oration at the funeral of his brother, Caesarius, St Gregory the Theologian mused, "And, as it shared the hard-ships of the body through a common life, so also is bestowed upon the body the joys of the soul hereafter, gathering it up into itself, and becoming with it one in spirit and mind in God" (*Ora. VII*, 21 PG 35 781BC).

C   The witness of the Fathers is clear.[52] Beatitude, they tell us, is achieved only in the Age to Come, when, after the Resurrection of the body and Judgment of the Church and the entire human race, the saved are deified as citizens of God's eternal Kingdom. At that moment, writes St Gregory the Theologian, "we shall come together in a common life to commonly discern the holy and blessed Trinity, with hearts most pure and perfect"—ὡς ἂν ἀλλήλοις συζῶντες, καὶ συνεποπτεύοντες τὴν καὶ μακαρίαν Τριάδα, καθαρώτερόν τε καὶ τελεώτερον (*Ora. XLIV*, 82 PG 36 604D-605A). St Basil the Great main-tains that it is man's "end" (*telos*) and "final beatitude" to contemplate God without a "mirror," but "face to face"[53] when "our mind is arisen and awak-ened to that blessed summit as it contemplates the 'oneness' and 'aloneness' of the Word"—καὶ πρὸς ὕψος μακάριον διεγείρεται, ὁπηνίκα ἂν θεωρήσῃ τὴν ἑνάδα καὶ μονάδα τοῦ Λόγου (*Ep. VIII*, 7 PG 32 257C).

---

52   All our patristic citations on theory of the beatific vision are also quoted in M.J. Redle's article, "Beatific Vision," in *The Catholic Encyclopedia* (vol., 2). Washington D.C., 1967, 186-193. We have allowed the holy Fathers to speak for themselves. It will be apparent that they do not understand the vision "face to face" of the blessed as the direct and intuitive apprehension of the divine Essence.

"The reward of the righteous," St Ambrose of Milan affirms, "is to see the face of God, 'the light that enlightens every man' (John 1:9)." We see Him now "only through a mirror darkly, but then face to face." In the Age to Come, "we will be allowed to look upon the glory of God, and His face shall be revealed" (*De bono mortis*, 2 PL 14 562D-563A). St Leo states that God has already revealed His Glory in Jesus Christ. At the Mount of the Transfiguration, certain of His disciples previewed the Son of Man coming into His Kingdom. They beheld "in the kingly brilliance which, as specially belonging to the nature of His assumed Manhood...the unspeakable and inaccessible vision of the Godhead Itself, which is reserved until eternal life for the pure in heart, something which they could not otherwise see while surrounded by mortal flesh"—*Nam illam ipsius Deitatis ineffabilem et inaccessibilem visionem, quae in aeternam vitam mundis corde servatur, nullo modo mortali adhuc carne circumdati intuerei poterant et videre* (*Sermo LI*, 2 PG 54 310B).

In the Age to Come, St John Chrysostom informs us, we shall indeed see God "face to face," as the Apostle says. But, clearly, Paul's words are not to be taken literally, because God has no face. "We shall not know Him as He is" (οὐχ ὅτι οὕτως αὐτὸν εἰσόμεθα), but as He makes Himself known. The expression "face to face" means that we shall behold Him with "greater clarity and distinctness." "Even as He comes to us now, so then we shall cleave to Him, enjoying His most blessed society and wisdom, and shall therefore know many things formerly hidden"—καὶ πολλὰ τῶν νῦν ἀπορρήτων εἰσόμεθα, καὶ τῆς μακαριοτάτης ἐκείνης ἀπολαύσομεν ὁμιλίας καὶ σοφίας (*In Ep. I Cor.*, XXXIV, 2 287). In a word, the Fathers testify that no creature, mortal or deified, may behold the divine Essence. "The blessed" shall gaze upon the Uncreated Energies, none more clearly or distinctly than "the unapproachable Light" in which, forever joined to His "assumed Humanity," the glorified and enthroned Christ dwells with the Father and the Spirit. Body and soul we shall look upon Jesus' countenance "face to face" in the Kingdom of our God. Such is the "beatific vision," the face of our incarnate Lord.

---

53   The editors of St Basil's letters in volume thirteen of *Fathers of the Church* have permitted πρόσωπον πρὸς πρόσωπον to be rendered not "face to face," but as "beatific vision" (p. 31). They have not so much translated St Basil as interpreted him.

CHAPTER 4

MEGA MYSTERION

The *mega mysterion* is Christ—"Even the mystery which hath been hidden from eternity and from generations, but is now manifested to His saints: to whom God has made known the riches of the glory of this mystery among the Gentiles; which is Christ in you, the hope of glory" (Col. 1:26-27). He is "the mystery of godliness: God manifested in the flesh, justified in the Spirit, seen of angels, preached unto the Gentiles, believed on in the world, received up into glory" (I Tim. 3:16). "Who is so dull that he cannot understand that 'the mystery of godliness' (I Tim. 3:16) is simply the dispensation of the flesh assumed by the Lord," wrote St Hilary of Poitiers, "the mystery of great godliness, and a mystery no longer kept from our eyes, but 'manifested in the flesh'...this is the whole system of the faith set forth by the Apostles in its proper order... His assumption of the flesh is therefore also the mystery of great godliness, for through the assumption of the flesh the mystery is manifested in the flesh..." (*De Trin.* XI, 9 NPNF).

The "mystery of godliness" is more than "the enfleshment of the Logos," to borrow St Cyril of Alexandria's phrase; it is the revelation in and through Christ of God's Plan for the salvation of His creation—"the mystery of His Will...That in the dispensation (οἰκονομίαν) of the fullness of times (καιρῶν), He might gather into one all things in Christ, both which are in the heavens, and which are on earth" (Eph. 1:9-10). Hence, St Paul's reference to "the mystery of the gospel" (Eph. 5:19), "the mystery of the Kingdom of God" (Eph. 4:11) and, to "the mystery of the Church" as the *mega mysterion* (Eph. 5:32)— "His body, the fullness of Him that fills all in all" (Eph. 1:23). With good reason the Fathers used the words "Incarnation" and "Economy" interchangeably.

Leaving the role of the Church in God's Plan for another chapter, we give our attention here to the Person and Work of Jesus Christ or, more precisely, the significance of the relationship between His Humanity and Divinity, a relationship which determines every other aspect of the divine Economy—of the "great mystery"—of Christ as the Conqueror of death, the Mediator, the Last Adam, the one Man, the new Beginning, the Angel of Great Counsel, Messiah, the Father of the Age to Come.

1   The Western Christs

If Western christologies of the last millennium have not clung to the dogma of "the 630 God-inspired fathers" of the Fourth Ecumenical Council of Chalcedon (451), we may reasonably infer from their writings that the thinking of Western theologians and philosophers has been conditioned by the idea of history as evolutionary change; hence, Chalcedon is viewed as a stage, however important, in the development of Christian dogma. The Latins claimed loyalty to the Council, but it is a misleading protest in view of its understanding of holy Tradition. Indeed, theologians of the post-Orthodox West, from Anselm to Thomas, Duns Scotus to John Calvin, Eckhart to Suarez, Schleiermacher to Barth, consciously or not, have contributed to a new conception of the Incarnate Logos. To believe, for example, that the Atonement did not involve a "chalcedonian" relationship between the Divine and the human is not consistent with the Scriptural and Patristic teaching.

An elementary study of Western thought reveals three general models of christology which not only have their prototypes in Christian antiquity but which have been repeated under different forms throughout occidental history. First there is the "traditional" dualism or crypto-Nestorian christology of Augustine; hence, Protestantism and Roman Catholicism. Second, is the monophysitic christology of Romanticism whose Deity is the "two-Gods-in-One" of Plato; and, third, is the Christ of atheistic materialism, the neo-Pelagianism of modern monotheletic (autosoteric) humanism which pictures the Savior not so much as a man but as a symbol, possessed of a kind of "delegated divinity," living an exemplary moral life.

A   Augustine's teachings initiated a new theological tradition—to which every other Western idea of God (and, therefore, Christ) has been a reaction or reaffirmation. His rationalism, when it finally triumphed, gave the West a new direction. From Neo-Platonism, the Bishop of Hippo took his basic metaphysical principles: duality and dialectic between the Divine and the human, which is nowhere better illustrated than in his christology, his unsuccessful attempt to explain the presence of these two poles of reality in the single Person of Christ.

It is characteristic of Augustine that, while never denying that Christ is God and man, he was never able to fuse the two natures, despite the use of such words as *commixtus* to define Their relationship. His reluctance may have been grounded in the desire to protect the Divinity of the Word; but the influence of the Platonic (and Manichean) teaching of the spirit/matter antithesis seemed finally to settle the issue. He resorted to metaphors in order to illustrate, as he saw it, the unity of the human and the Divine in Christ, such as his favorite: the union of body and soul.[1] None of them were convincing.

His trouble began with adoption of the Platonic definition of the human soul—"a reasonable soul, using a terrestrial and mortal body," "a reasonable soul possessing a body," "the soul...a spiritual substance, endowed with reason, adapted to rule the body."[2] Augustine depicted man as an immaterial soul, a complete entity, which was only accidentally united to a body. "The Augustinian definition of the soul," asserted Etienne Gilson, "is identical with the Augustine definition of man."[3] Inasmuch as Augustine identified the personhood of a man with his soul, wrote Harnack, he naturally constructed the God-man from the Logos and the soul, although "his highest interest belonged to the soul of Jesus."[4]

Augustine's conception of human nature explains his Nestorian christology. "By the Grace of God, a man without antecedent merits, at the very inception of his existence," he wrote, "so allied that nature to the one person of God the Word that the very same Son of God was Son of man, and vice-versa"—*gratiam Dei qua homo nullis praecedentibus meritis, in ipso exordio naturae suae quo esse ceopit, Verbo Deo copularetur in tantam personae unitatem, ut idem ipse esset filius Dei qui filius hominis, et filius hominis qui filius Dei* (*Ench.* I, 4 PL 40 252). As he says elsewhere, Christ was "the Word of God having the man"—*habens hominem* (*In John Evang.* XIX, 15 FC)–not one Person known in two unconfused but inseparable natures, but the Son of God taking a man to Himself. Augustine hesitates to allow that humanity to merge essentially with His Divinity (*de Agon. Chr.* XI, 12; XVIII, 20). In this way, Christ could suffer in the flesh without "any change in or destruction of His Divinity (*ib.*, XXIII, 25). In other words, while speaking expressly of the union of God and man, Augustine understood that union to mean "mutually present, but distinct."[5]

---

[1] Augustine defined the soul as "a special substance endowed with reason, adapted to rule the body"—*esse substantia quaedam rationis particeps, regendo corpori accomodata.* He was eager to demonstrate the substantial unity of body and soul, observes J.M. Colleran, "but his inability to settle the problem of the nature of the union of spiritual soul and material body prevented him from giving an entirely satisfactory definition of the soul itself." He did indeed insist upon the body as part of human nature, but "this does not warrant the conclusion that in the course of time he abandoned the Platonic concept of the soul utterly and completely" (*The Greatness of the Soul and the Teacher*, in *Ancient Christian Writers* [vol., 9]. Westminster, 1950, p. 201, 219).

[2] *In John Evang.* XIX, 5, 15; *The Greatness of the Soul*, XIII, 22. ACW

[3] *The Spirit of Medieval Philosophy*. Trans. by A.H.C. Downes. New York, 1940, p. 174.

[4] *...von der menchlichen Person (Seele) aus konstruiert Augustin den Gottmenchen...dass sein hoechstes Interesse den menschlichen Seele Jesu gehoert...* (*Lehrbuch der Dogmengeschichte* [bd. 3]. Leipzig, 1910, 120.

[5] McWilliam-Dewart, J., "The Influence of Theodore of Mopsuestia on Augustine's Letter 187", *Augustinian Studies* X (1979), 116. Interesting is the reaction of some church historians to the "Nestorianizing tendency" in Roman Catholicism to the *Tome* of the Orthodox St Leo the Great, the purported source of Papist   *(continued on next page)*

In his doctrine of Christ, Augustine may well have come under the influence of Theodore of Mopsuestia. Not that the reading of him alone persuaded the Bishop of Hippo to mutilate the Orthodox christology; but rather he found in Theodore new ideas applicable to a position he had already taken. Theodore held that the union of the Logos with the human personality (the soul) was "according to Grace" (κατὰ χάριν)—created Grace?—and, not as the Fathers taught, an "essential" unity (κατ' οὐσίαν).[6] Thus, the humanity and Divinity are "mated" by Grace, meaning that the Virgin Mary did not beget a human nature "intertwined" with God the Son. It is only because the soul is immaterial like God that "the Godhead and the soul are directly united in Him," A. Grillmeier asserts, "and man is only joined to the Godhead by the mediation of the soul"—*Verbum particeps carnis effectum est rationalis anima mediante* (*Ep. CXL ad Hon.* IV, 12 PL 33 542)[7]—and not the body, because matter and spirit are opposed.

(cont'd.)   christology. Fr John Meyendorff suggests that the Saint never "digested Cyrillian theology" ("Papers and Discussions of the Bristol Consultation" [25-29 July 1967], *The Greek Orthodox Theological Review* XIII, 2 [1968], 308).

In truth, St Leo stressed the two natures of Christ against Monophysitism; but this accent did conflict with St Cyril's christology. "This is the Faith of the Fathers, the Faith of the Apostles!" proclaimed the Council of Chalcedon. "We believe as all Orthodox believe! Anathema to those who believe otherwise. Peter has spoken through Leo! So have the Apostles taught as the God-blessed Leo rightly taught, even as St Cyril taught. Eternal be the memory of Leo and Cyril who taught the same!" (Mansi [vol. 6], 971). Better to look to the crypto-Nestorianism of Augustine and the medieval Schoolmen for the christology of Roman Catholicism (and Protestantism).

6   Patristic christology demands an essential union between the humanity and the Divinity in Christ. "...we do not hold that each nature is separate and by itself, but that they are united to each other in one subsistence," wrote St John of Damascus. "For we look upon the union as essential, that is, as true and not imaginary. We say that it is essential, moreover, not in the sense of two natures resulting in one compound nature, but in the sense of a true union of them in one compound subsistence of the Son of God ..." (*De fid. Orth.*, III, 3). Cf. St Gregory the Theologian, *Ep.* CI PG 37 180B.

Some scholarship is convinced that Augustine's christology was strongly influenced by Theodore of Mopsuestia, whom the Nestorians called "the Interpreter." He was translated into Latin and his writings distributed in the anthologies of Eastern theologians. Although the two bishops disagreed on the role of Christ's human will (and, therefore, man's will in his salvation), "they were in full agreement on the importance and the unique quality of the grace given to Christ," writes McWilliam-Dewart (*ib.*, 131), "and they rose to the same note: 'that singular grace' (*singularis gratia*): O grace which is above all and was given to Jesus! O grace which overcomes all nature!—*O gratia quae super omnia data est Jesu! O gratia superavit omnium naturam!* (*Ench.* IX, 36 PL 40 250; *De Civ. Dei* X, xxix, 1 PL 41 308). Both conceived the Incarnation in terms of "a union of grace," i.e., the human nature of Christ "belonging to the person of the Word through free will sustained by grace" (*l.c.*). See also R.A. Greer, "The Analogy of Grace in Theodore of Mopsuestia's Christology," in *The Journal of Theological Studies* XXXIV, 1 (1983), 1-23.

7   *Christ in the Christian Tradition.* Trans. by J.S. Bowden. New York, 1965, p. 325. Theodore of Mopsuestia shared the body-soul dichotomy, a Platonic legacy, in common with Augustine. We must not be surprised that, along with Augustine, Theodore held

Is *anima mediante* symptomatic of Augustine's revulsion for the flesh? He had very definite views about sex, insisting that by the sexual act "original sin" was transmitted from parents to child (*C. Faust.* XXIV 1 PL 42 274), a theory which has induced many to believe that he never completely escaped his Manichean past. And, then, we have these calamitous remarks, "How much less, then, could a female body pollute the Word of God—who is neither corporeal nor visible—when He took flesh from her (Virgin Mary) along with a soul and spirit through the incoming of which the majesty of the Word dwells in less immediate conjunction with the frailty of the human body." The Word "can in no way have been defiled by a human body, in which the human soul remains undefiled, so long as it rules and vivifies the body; and if the soul abstains from carnal things" (*De Fid. et Symb.*, IV, 10 PL 40 187).

His christological speculations finally brought Augustine to the conundrum expressed in *De Trinitate* (I, x, 20 834-835), "Wherefore, since the Son is both God and man, the manhood in the Son is more another substance than the Son in the Father (*alia substantia homo potius in Filio quam Filius in Patre*)," he exclaimed awkwardly, "just as the flesh of my soul is more another substance than my soul—although one person—than is the soul of another man to my soul." The opening statement, "Wherefore, since the Son is both God and man..." is clearly heretical, for if Augustine is right, then "the concrete man-being, the *homo* in Christ, is nothing other than the God-Son Himself while the Son is not personally identified with the Father, but is rather opposed to Him as a different Person."[8] He has thrown doubt on the consubstantiality of the Son with both man and God.

A host of verbal errors, as many have characterized his theory, do not explain the image of Christ he reorganized; nor, indeed, do they justify a philosophical mind, which ignores the Christian Tradition for the ideal by which Augustine hoped to understand whatever he believed. But even worse, his independent theorizing opened the door to further deviation from holy Tradition, and for greater dependence on pagan philosophy, which only lent itself to a further distortion of Christianity. The inevitable redefinition of the Faith, as history relates, has finally brought the West to the secularism

---

that the soul is the human *persona* (christologically translated as two Sons or natures in Christ); and "therefore, it was not a body which the Son had to assume, but an immortal and rational soul." The body is "healed" only by virtue of its association with its soul (see the discussion in R.A. Norris, *Manhood and Christ: A Study in the Christology of Theodore Mopsuestia.* Oxford, 1963, chaps. 10, 15-16). Some of the Fathers also concluded that the Word joined Himself to a human nature "from the side of" the soul in opposition to Apollinarianism; and, of course, on account of the soul's superiority to the body. But Christ's Divinity, nevertheless, penetrated His complete humanity.

8 Ternus, J., "*Das Seelen-un Berwussteseinleben Jesus*," in Das *Konzil von Chalkedon: Geschichte und Gegenwart* [bd. 3]. hrsg. A. Grillmeier & H. Bacht. Wuerzburg, 1959-1961, 209-210; and the discussion in Grillmeier, *Christ in Christian Tradition*, pp. 319-328.

now consuming the twentieth century. This devolution is the result of a false conception of both the Divine and the human which has become a fundamental assumption of the West's life and thought.

B   Augustine's reformulation of the traditional christology—and theology in general—was not without a history after his death, for his adherents managed, among other things, to influence the decisions of the second Council of Orange (529) regarding Grace and predestination. His patrimony must wait to fructify until the Latin Middle Ages where it was defended, expanded and adapted to the spirit of the age. The Latin world-view did not fundamentally change during the Renaissance nor did its Augustinian christology. The Protestant Reformers and their successors, while adapting the "traditional" christology to its doctrines of the Church (and justification), otherwise made no serious alterations. Augustine was amenable to both Protestant and Roman Catholic as well as to philosophical and theosophical interpretation.

A notable example of the latter was the German Lutheran, Jacob Boehme (1575-1624), the lonely cobbler of Goelitz, whose place in the dechristianization of the Western culture is palpable to any student of its eighteenth and nineteenth century thought. The apex of a long line of European Gnostics, which included Raymond of Lull, Nicholas of Cusa, Meister Eckhart, Paracelsus, Sebastian Frank, Angelus Silesius, etc., Boehme was christologially a Monophysite (pantheist), who powerfully impacted not only modern philosophy, from the *Sturm und Drang*, Goethe and the Romantics, Hegel and Schelling, etc. to the Russian Sophiologists (Soloviev, Berdiaev, Florensky, etc.), but also Quietism, Pietism, and the history of English theosophy. The contemporary New Age movement has also been influenced by him.

There are numerous reasons for calling Boehme a Gnostic, not the least of which was his claim to having thrice received sudden divine illuminations (characteristic of all Western "mystics," including Augustine) of intensifying brilliance, the "illumination of the Holy Spirit which instructs aright in all things, and searches τὰ βάθη τοῦ Θεοῦ, the depths of God" (I Cor. 2:10).[9] The "light" gave him access to "the great Mystery," *magnum mysterium*, the Absolute, which lay behind Nature, the visible symbol of Its reality, an immaterial reality which pierces the shell of time to bathe Nature with a fierce and transcendent beauty, and history with meaning and direction. His revelations allowed Boehme to answer the traditional Gnostic questions: "Whence the origin of the cosmos?" or what is the same thing, "Whence the birth of God?" "Why something, why not nothing?"[10] They are questions

[9]   *The Signature of All Things with Other Writings.* Trans. by W. Law, with Intro. by C. Bax. New York, n.d., I, 3.

[10] See E.B. Koenker, "Potentiality in God: Grund und Ungrund in Jacob Boehme," *Philosophy Today* XV, 1/4 (1971), 45f.

which "take greater account of the irrational and mysterious nature of things divine," Berdiaev tells us, "and allows more freely the possibility of infinite evolution in the knowledge of these mysteries, while rejecting, on the other hand, conceptual knowledge."[11]

Boehme claimed that divine illumination gave him a "sight" of the ultimate incomprehensible, immutable reality, "a stillness without being; there is nothing which gives rise to anything: It is an eternal rest which has no parallel, a groundlessness without beginning or end." We may not yet refer to It as "God," for nothing exists, not good or evil, not time or matter, only the "eternal rest" of that "Nature" (if the word is applicable) of which we shall never have knowledge—the Absolute, the *En Soph* of the Jewish Kabbalah, the *Nihil* of Cusa, the *Abgrund* of Eckhart; and, in some respects, even the *To Hen* of Plotinus—the *Ungrund* of Berdiaev from whence all things spring, including evil and the Trinity Itself.

How does the Absolute, *Gottheit*, *Urgott*, this impersonal Nothing (*Nichts*) become Something (*Etwas*)? How is that possible if, as Boehme stated, the Absolute is unchangeable, without desire, without consciousness? How, too, can the Absolute emit the Trinity, or experience anything which, by definition, It has never known or done before?[12] Even more, It is "not called God or known as God, for there is in it neither good nor evil." The *Ungrund* is like an "Eye" (Αὐγή), a mirror to Itself. It is the repository of all the creative possibilities of the Absolute. Its own reflection rouses desire in It, that is, for Itself. This "desiring Will" is the beginning of all Absolute's activity and, likewise, Its end, since there is nothing greater to desire. Hence, the "desiring Will" is a drawing-in, albeit "there is nothing yet to be drawn, save the Will which draws Itself. In this way it represents to Itself what It is; and this representative image is the mirror (*Spiegel*) in which the Will apprehends Itself, for the *Ungrund* is a likeness of the Will."

Boehme referred to this "mirror" as "the eternal Wisdom" (Σοφία), the feminine element of the Absolute, which resides in the "bosom of the Godhead" as His Essence, a resonance of the Absolute in which She loves Herself. Wisdom is passive, a "virgin matrix" in which the Absolute reveals Itself..."[13] In other words, Wisdom or Sophia "plays" before the Eternal as Its "pure imagination," that is, the κόσμος νοητός (Plato's World of Ideas) by which It realizes the divine Plan (*Vorsatz*) for everything that will eventually exit "beyond" It.

---

[11]   Introductory Essay to Jacob Boehme's *Six Theosophic Points and Other Writings.* Trans. by J.R. Earle. Ann Arbor, 1970, xv.

[12]   Augustine may have been the first Christian theologian to raise the question of novelty in God (*De Civ. Dei* XII, 20-21), as Koenker observes ("Potentiality in God...," 50).

[13]   *The Aurora.* Trans. by J. Sparrow, London, 1960, VI, 5-6.

The first emanation of the Absolute is the Holy Trinity, "God," the three-fold "distinction" whose emergence was excited by the divine Sophia; also described by Boehme as the "house" of the Father, the Son and the Holy Spirit "Who proceeds from the Father and the Son" (*Ex. Six Myst. Pts.*, IV, 4). Sophia is Their common Substance. Each shares in Sophia with no loss of the properties peculiar to each Person (*Six Theol. Pts.* I, 3). *God* now exists (θεο-γονία). Being now exists: the cosmos unfolds (κοσμογονία) with God Whom the Absolute ejected for that purpose.

The "birth" of the Trinity follows the scheme of thesis, antithesis and synthesis.[14] In "the threefold Will" of the Absolute, the Father is the initial "outgoing Will" from the Abyss;[15] the Son is the derived "ingoing" or "recon-ceived Will," as Boehme sometimes called it; and the Holy Spirit is the activity resulting from this turning of the Will on Itself.

He is the "outgoing Will of the Father" and the "ingoing Will of the Son."[16] The Spirit is their unity. Here is the paradigm of the *coincidentia oppositorum* so fundamental to Romantic and Hegelian thought.[17]

Boehme proclaimed Sophia to be the instrumentality of God's birth (θεογενεσία, *Gottesgeburt*), that is, she, as *kosmos noetos*, brought the Absolute to the consciousness of things temporal and spatial. She accounts for movement in the Divine, that is, God: the Father Who plans, the Son Who executes, the Holy Spirit Who, proceeding from the Father and the Son, vivifies the cosmos and all that it contains. They are not only the Absolute's revelation but Its Self-realization: the creation is the unfolding of the Absolute as "God," as nature and history (including later the redemption of man in Christ) according to Sophia's Ideas.

Thus, the birth of God or the Trinity is the beginning (*principium*) of the world-process: theogony is cosmogony, *deus explicitus*. To use the words of

    [14]   Brinton, H.H., *The Mystic Will: Based on a Study of the Philosophy of Jacob Boehme.* New York, 1930, p. 181.

    [15]   Because the Father rises from the *Ungrund*, argues J.J. Stoudt, Boehme is saved from pantheism (*Jacob Boehme: His Life and Thought.* New York, 1968, p. 216). He may be right, but a logical problem persists: if the Father, along with the other Persons of the Trinity, came out of the Absolute, it would seem that They have the same "substance" as the Absolute (likewise Sophia) unless Stoudt (and Boehme) is willing to admit the existence of a foreign element within the Absolute, an eternal companion, so to speak; in which case, It is not Absolute. No matter, there is a single determinative Will which controls reality—for all of Boehme's talk of "freedom"—since everything proceeds from the Absolute as everything must return to It.

    [16]   *Of the Incarnation of Jesus Christ.* Trans. by J.R. Earle. London, 1934, I, 16.

    [17]   See the discussion in A. Koyre, *La Philosophie de Jacob Boehme.* Paris, 1968, 317f.

Schelling, "The philosophy of Nature is the science of the eternal transformation of God into the world"[18]—and, for that matter, the reverse is also true. Boehme, of course, denied *creatio ex nihilo*. We cannot believe, he said, that God created the world from nothing, for "nothing" has no meaning outside the Absolute: not even God is nothing. If, as the traditional cosmogony proclaims, the universe was created out of "nothing" (οὐκ ὄν), then, the stuff of it must have come from beyond the Absolute—which is impossible—beyond Its powers and, to be sure, the powers of God.

Thus, all things, in one form or another, directly or indirectly, are created from the substance of God; and, therefore, the Absolute. The supreme image of the Trinity is man. He is quite literally, *kleiner Gott*, the complete image of God, or of "the Being of all beings" (*ib*. I, 6). No creature is more like God than he. Adam was neither male nor female, an androgynous being, the image (ἔκτυπος) of God and Sophia, their Substance and creative Energy. Adam was placed in Paradise, a "spiritual" and "sophianic" world—"the whole" filled with "the heavenly essence," "the Light-breath" or "divine Vitality," "the Breath of the Holy Spirit."

Becoming weary of his unity with God, Adam slept and lost cognizance of Him. The result was the "original sin"—an idea first proposed by Origen and the ancient Gnostics. While he slept, he succumbed to "the satanic darkness" (Boehme subscribed to the "myth" of a pre-cosmic fall of Lucifer), by which he lost the divine Power and Light. God removed Eve from his side and the sexual element was born (*Six Theo. Pts*. IV, 19). Adam and Eve were expelled from Paradise and into "the present world of time and necessity." (The world of eternity and freedom is another world reached only by the spirit). They became the objects of God's "grim wrath" and their souls became "half devil" and "half animal."

Their "original sin" determined "the scope of death which opened the gates of hell, and for which reason God became man: that He might destroy death, change hell into great love, and smash the Devil's vanity" (*ibid*., 19-23). Boehme's Christ is the incarnate "eternal speaking Logos" which had created all things according to His "highest, deepest Love and Humility" (*ib*. III, 7). He was born of the Virgin Mary—"magically, as all mortals would have been born had Eve not been seduced by the devil"—and subsequently "drowning" our infirmity and death on the Cross, after which He descended into Hell (not Hades) where He encountered and assuaged God's wrath and abolished the devil's Kingdom.

---

[18] *Lehrbuch der Naturphilosophie*, in *Werke* (bd. 1). hrsg. von A. Weiss (1907), 4.

On account of Christ's redemption, the contradictions within human nature are resolved and the human race is restored to the divine Harmony. Man will become once more what he was before the fall, when he was neither man nor woman, "the masculine Virgin," as was Jesus the Christ Himself, the "second Adam" (*Myst. Magn.* IV, 20). In other words, the Logos became "man" in order to "regenerate" or, more exactly, to "reintegrate" man, whereby He might return him, as part of the world-process, to God. In fact, Christ is "the Moment" in which the theogonic-cosmogonic process begins the journey back to the Absolute (cyclicism).

But the return was impossible unless the division caused by Lucifer was abrogated. Christ initiated the reunification of humanity by His conquest of the evil and thereby resolving the dialectic between "life" (*Ja*) and "death" (*Nein*), commencing with the reuniting of man and woman. Unlike Adam's sleep induced by the devil, Christ's sleep on the Cross was not a "sleep of vanity." Vanquishing the evil one, He re-forms man and woman, returning our first-parents to "the angelic image" they once shared. We shall become the complements which God wanted for them. "For man ("fire") must rule," concludes Boehme, "and the woman ("light") must soften his fire, and bring it unto a gentle image of God" (*On the Incarn.*, I, viii, 13). Christ as Redeemer, as the Second Adam, restored man's original image, to the condition the first Adam enjoyed before his apostasy.

If nothing else this process of "re-androgynization" is contrary to the Orthodox teaching that Christ revealed Himself "to be of the male sex when He opened the Virgin's womb" (Canon of Pascha, Troparion, Ode 4). Here is an indication of everything else that is wrong in Boehme's pantheistic system, not the least of which are his expostulations about the division of reality into the Absolute and the God which reveals Himself as the unfolding cosmos. From the Christian perspective, when Boehme declares, "Life's wheel shall revolve. To live in Love is to live in eternity, to live in eternity is to dwell in God... a true rest, a Sabbath, beyond selfhood's evil and worldly evil" (*Myst. Magn.* XI, 31), means that "salvation" is the return of all things, including the Trinity and the cosmos, to the Abyss from which all things first emerged.

The Gnosticism of Jacob Boehme is sometimes complex, requiring for most a new vocabulary and way of thinking. If nothing else, his theosophy is the restatement of a vision of things that refuse to die; it is sufficient for our purpose to understand that, not unlike so many ideas eroding the culture of the West, his theosophy (his religion) represents a system of thought which rises from the very history of thought of which it is a natural but deleterious product. Reading Boehme should also alert us to the importance of Augustine to the entire post-Orthodox Western Christian-Hellenic experiment, including Boehme's Gnosticism.

C   Ludwig Feuerbach, like virtually all the German thinkers of the nineteenth century, began his philosophical reflections with Lutheran (i.e., a neo-Augustinian) theology. He was filled with the spirit of the times, an era of European history consumed with the hope of reconstituting "the ideals of Western culture on a radically secular and humanistic, that is to say, a radically non-Christian basis."[19] The occasion for Feuerbach's statements on the nature of religion was his revulsion for the philosophy of Hegel, formerly his teacher.

Contrary to Hegel, Feuerbach refused to believe that Christianity was "the absolute religion." Hegel had aspired to do for Lutheranism what Aquinas had done for Roman Catholicism, albeit his first principle was not the *summum bonum*, but "the dialectical identity of philosophy and theology, thought and being." Feuerbach fiercely reproached Hegel for his ambition "to reestablish a lost and defeated Christianity by means of philosophy," a futile enterprise which only perpetuated the basic error of all modern philosophy since Descartes, a system he described as nothing else than medieval theology "broken up and transformed into philosophy."[20]

True philosophy, Feuerbach argued, begins not with the postulation of God or the infinite or the useless effort to deduce the mortal from the immortal, the contingent from the absolute, the definite from the indefinite; rather the truth of religion will emerge from the analysis of man himself, that is to say, on the "sensuous basis" of one's own experience, which discovers the truth of things in one's own body, where the spirit merges with corporeality. There is no independent soul, of which the mind is the uppermost part. In other words, the "I" is not, as Descartes believed, a neutral "it," but something personal, "a masculine and feminine experience."

The individual is fated to be a social being, that is, the coming to self-awareness is linked to his association with others, all of whom share a common material nature and physical environment. The encounter of one human being with another accounts for both personal and social consciousness. "I and thou," social cohesion, is the *raison d'être* of human existence. Their unity through love produces the family, the family the city, the city the state; in a word, man is a political being. Not without reason, then, did Feuerbach declare that "the fellowship of worship must be replaced by the fellowship of work," "politics must become our religion"[21] and "man must become the god for man—*homo homini Deus est.*"[22]

---

[19]   Aiken, H.D., Introduction to *The Ages of Ideology.* New York, 1960, p. 25.

[20]   Loewith, K., *From Hegel to Nietzsche: the Revolution in Nineteenth Century Thought.* Trans. by D.E. Green. London, 1965, p. 74.

[21]   Kierkegaard explained in *Angriff au die Christenheit* the   (continued on next page)

There is no "God" but man, no "superhuman being," which in fact is "nothing else than a product and reflex of the human mind." "God is what the understanding thinks is the highest. . .the *ens realissimum*, the most real being, of the old onto-theology" (*EC*, p. 38). He is merely a construction of the human mind, a creature of the understanding. Moreover, the idea of God as "a morally perfect being is nothing less than the realized idea, the fulfilled law of morality, the moral nature of man posited as the absolute being; man's own nature, for to be moral God requires man to be as he himself is." The divine is "the perfection of the moral will" (*ib.*, 46-48).

What, then, is the Trinity? It is "man's consciousness of himself in his totality. . .the mystery of the Trinity is the mystery of participated, social life—the mystery of I and thou" (*ib.*, p. 293). How did it arise? God *qua* God (Father), as a simple and solitary being, begets another. There is a need for duality, of love and community, "of the real completed self-consciousness, of the *alter ego*." Hence, a second divine being (Son) is set along side Him, different from him in personality but identical with him in essence. "God as Father is *I*, God the Son, *thou*. The '*I*' is understanding, the '*thou*' love." The holy Spirit is not a person. The "third person" is nothing more than the love of the divine Persons for each other (*ib.*, 67).[23]

What, then, is the Incarnation? The answer is found in Feuerbach's enigmatic aphorism, "the secret of theology is anthropology" (*ibid.*, p. 270). "God, says religion, made himself human that he might make man divine—*Deus homo factus est, ut homo Deus fieret* (Augustine, *Serm. ad Pop.* CCCLVXXI, 1)." Hence, the Incarnation is simply "the human *form* of a God already in man's nature, who in the profoundest depths of his soul is a merciful and therefore a human God" (*ib.*, p. 51). When pondering the Incarnation, Feuerbach cautioned, we must not think metaphysically. "We have reduced the apparently supernatural and super-rational mystery to a simple truth inherent in human nature," he boasted, "a truth which does not belong to the Christian religion alone, but which, implicitly at least, belongs more or less to every religion as such" (*ib.*, p. 54). "The Incarnation, the mystery of the 'God-man,' is therefore no mysterious composition of contraries, not a synthetic fact as

---

(cont'd.)   resurgence of politics in Western culture is the result of the dissolution of the Christian Faith. Feuerbach wanted to convert all theologians to politicians. This ideal brought Loewith (p. 81) to the conclusion that the modern Western state is the result of "faith in man as the god to man."

22   Feuerbach, L., *The Essence of Christianity*. Trans. by G. Eliot. 1957, p. 271.

23   Feuerbach adapted Augustine's model of the Trinity, including the *filioque*. He maintained that the Holy Spirit is the mutual love of the Father and the Son (He by Whom God loves man), and, therefore, "proceeds" from the Father and the Son. Feuerbach considered the "personality" of the Spirit to be "too vague and precarious to serve as a third complementary being" (*EC*, p. 76).

it is regarded by the speculative religious philosophy," but rather "it is an analytic fact—a human word with a human meaning" (*ib.*, p. 56).

Who, then, was Jesus Christ? He was the "miraculous Redeemer," the living symbol of that "feeling to be free of the law's morality, i.e., from the conditions to which virtue is united in the natural course of things" (*ib.*, 143). But more than this, Jesus was proof that "God is a human being, God is man" (*ib.*, 145). Thus, the Incarnation is a process, a principle of future realization. If, therefore, God is man's destiny, man is the object of himself. The content of the divine nature is the human nature. The "Son" becoming man is not the descent of an "extra-mundane being" into the world, but the ultimate unification and reconciliation of the entire human species.

As Karl Barth observed, man, for Feuerbach, "is the beginning, the middle and the end of religion." He believed that theology had become anthropology long ago, but never so clearly as since the Reformation, especially with Luther who emphatically shifted the interest from Who God is to what God is for man.[24] It was now the time for a "new philosophy," a philosophy which converts "the friends of God into the friends of man, believers into thinkers, worshippers into workers,[25] candidates for the other world into students of this world, Christians, who by their own confession are half-animal, half-angel, into men, whole men." Feuerbach wanted men and women of the future to become "anthropolitans, not theologians. . .to change from religious and political footmen of a terrestrial monarchy and aristocracy into free, self-reliant citizens of earth."[26]

Feuerbach's subjected all "supernaturalism" to this kind of scrutiny, converting everything divine into something human. If he believed in the superiority of the Christianity he knew, it was precisely because he conceived it as something more open to such secular reductions than the religions of the East. Ludwig Feuerbach was part of that school of historical thought which, therefore, not only advocated a distinction between "the Christ of history" and "the Christ of Faith," but abolished the first while changing the second into an allegory of his materialistic philosophy.

---

24   Introduction to *The Essence of Christianity*, xix.

25   The use of "worker" ("proletariat") is significant, especially for those seeking the historical roots of Marxism. According to G. Masaryk, "the atheist humanism of Feuerbach constitutes the spirit of Marxist socialism" (*Die philosophischen und sociologischen Grundlagen des Marxismus*. Vienna, 1889, 17). According to Fr Sergius Bulgakov, "Feuerbach is Marx's untold secret...the rejection of theanthropism in the name of anthropotheism; it is theomachistical, militant atheism." To be sure, "Marx somewhat changed and completed his teacher's doctrine" (*Karl Marx as A Religious Type: His Relation to the Religious Anthropotheism of L. Feuerbach*. Trans. by L. Barna. Belmont [Mass.], 1979, pp. 22, 79).

26   *Principles of the Philosophy of the Future*. Trans. by M.H. Vogel. New York, 1966, no. 54.

Finally, we must recognize a certain irony in the philosophy of Ludwig Feuerbach, an irony which he shared with others of his stripe: christology is indeed the other side of soteriology. His Christ is the "the highest triumph of the heart," "savior," the "supreme being," the revelation of "the mystery." We may also agree with Feuerbach that it is "perverse to attempt to deduce the Incarnation from purely speculative, i.e., metaphysical, abstract grounds" (*EC*, p. 52). He insisted that the world will finally come to understand this truth as history provides the human race with greater enlightenment.

2   THE CHRIST OF CHALCEDON

The Fourth Ecumenical Council of the Orthodox Church, assembled by the Emperor Marcian at the Anatolian city of Chalcedon (451), dogmatized the ancient Faith of Church concerning the Person of Jesus Christ. As the Council stated, the christology which it defined (ὄρος)[27] was only the formulation of the Catholic Faith which the previous generations of Christians had delivered to it—*hoc Catholica fides tradit*. They verbalized the prevision of the Prophets, the assertions of the Lord Himself, the preaching of the Apostles, the expositions of the holy Fathers.

Thus, Chalcedon the "God-inspired" Council, reacting apologetically to the needs of the Church—under circumstances which dictated the language[28] and conceptual framework of its definition—produced a dogma engineered, among other things, to refute the christological heresies of the fifth century. Critical to the Council's deliberations was the *Tome* (451) of

---

[27]   As the fifth session of Chalcedon declared: *Therefore, following the holy Fathers, we all with one accord teach men to acknowledge one and the same Son, our Lord Jesus Christ, at once complete in Godhead and complete in manhood, truly God and truly man, consisting also of a rational soul and body; of one essence with the Father as regards his Divinity, of one essence with us as regards his manhood; like us in all respects, apart from sin; hence, as regards his Divinity, He was begotten of the Father before the ages, as regards his manhood, it was begotten, for us men and our salvation, of Mary the Virgin, Theotokos; one and the same Christ, Son, Lord, Only-begotten, recognized in two natures, without confusion, without change, without division, without separation, the distinction of the natures in no way annulled by their union; but rather the properties of each nature preserved and joining to form one person and subsistence, not as parted or separated in two persons, but one and the same Only-begotten God the Word, Lord Jesus Christ; even as the prophets from earliest times spoke of Him, as our Lord Jesus Christ Himself taught, and the Creed of the Fathers delivered to us* (Mansi [vol. VII], 116f).

[28]   The "Oriental Orthodox" or "non-Chalcedonians" insist that their objection to Chalcedon was its "political" inspiration, rather than its christology with which they fundamentally agree; also, their difference with "the Eastern Orthodox" is more terminological than substantive (See "The Minutes and Papers of Aarhus Consultation" [11-15 August 1964], *The Greek Orthodox Theological Review* X, 2 [1964-1965]; and "Papers and Discussions of the Bristol Consultation" (already cited). They insist that the history of their synods shows their christology to be perfectly traditional. Whose "tradition"? The Apostolic Tradition of which there can only be one? The Orientals reject the last four

Pope St Leo the Great and the *Anathemata* (431) of Pope St Cyril of Alex-andria. Architects of the Chalcedonian dogma, Leo and Cyril, held that "the mystery of the Incarnation" which they "rightly and unswervingly" expounded, was "in every way the confession and doctrines of the holy Fathers" (St Cyril, *Ep. LV* 293C); and, of course, this was ultimately a defense of the Christian Economy.[29] The Pope of Rome approached "the mystery of Christ" from the side of His two natures, the Pope of Alexandria from the side of His divine Personality.

A   It is a mistake to think that St Leo taught two independent but coordi-nated natures in Christ, a mere coincidence of the Divine and human. Such an interpretation of St Leo's *Tome* (read during and confirmed by the Council of Chalcedon) is false. But it is precisely the position taken by the modern Coptic theologian, V.C. Samuel, who argues that St Leo's "great error" was the proposition—"each nature performs what is proper to it in communion with the other, the Word, for instance, performing what is proper to the Word and the flesh carrying out what is proper to the flesh." "A teaching of this kind does not affirm Christ's personal unity," Samuel contends, "but regards the natures as two persons. The phrase 'in two natures' defined by the coun-cil of Chalcedon must have meant the same teaching as that of Bishop Leo, so it cannot be accepted."[30]

But neither St Leo nor the Council used the expression "two Persons," except as a reproach of the Nestorian doctrine; and their "one Person recog-nized in two natures"—μία ὑπόστασις ἐν δυσί φύσεσιν—intimated no such christology. When the Nestorians and the Monophysites equated "person," "nature," and "subsistence," it was inevitable that they should misconstrue "two natures" as "two persons." The Monophysite appeal to St Cyril of Alex-

Ecumenical Councils (implicitly denying the infallibility of the Orthodox Church) and their dyotheletism.

In recent Consultations, the Orientals have resorted to the language of tolerance. "Some of us affirm two natures, wills and energies. . . Some of us affirm one united divine-human nature, will and energy in the same Christ..." (CopNet: "Recent Efforts For Unity Between the Two Families of the Orthodox Church," p. 13). At the same time, they call upon Orthodoxy to recognize as Saints those whom she has anathematized as heretics—a brazen form of "ecumenical relativism." The "Chalcedonian" Patriarch of Antioch is now in full communion with the Oriental heretics.

29   Strange is the absence from both the Consultations of Aarhus and Bristol of any discussion of the relationship between christology and soteriology, i.e., deification. The participants were wrong to assume that the resolution of their differences would be determined by the right christological *formula*. Also, the opinion of Rev Vitaly Borovy (Aarhus, *Grk. Orth. Theol. Rev.* X, 2, 33) that the Orthodox Church is not "bound" to coun-cilior and patristic declarations is utterly heterodox.

30   *Ibid*, 50.

andria was misconceived; he clearly agreed with St Leo, as Chalcedon proclaimed;[31] and their agreement was not the result of common logic, but of
common Faith.

Thus, wrote St Leo in his *Tomos*, "the unity of Person is understood in
both natures"—*unitatem personae in utraque natura intelligendam* (*Ep. XXVIII
ad Flav.*, 5 PL 54 771A). Put another way, "the unity does not introduce confusion, nor do the individual properties destroy unity"—*nec infert unitas con-
fusionem nec dirimit proprietas unitatem* (*Pasch. Serm* LIV, 1 PL 54 319B). As St
Cyril stated before him, "one Person is the bearer of both natures," these
being "neither confused, nor divided," that is, they are joined in such a way
that there is no confusion, mixture, change, assimilation, or transition of the
one into the other nature"—οὐχ ὡς τῆς τῶν φύσεων διαφορᾶς ἀνῃρημένης διὰ
τὴν ἕνωσιν (*Ep. IV ad Nest.* PG 77 45C).

Why is the right understanding of the relationship between "person"
and "natures" so crucial? In his letter to St Flavian, Archbishop of Constantinople, St Leo astutely placed the question of christology in soteriological
perspective. "The Nativity which occurred in time," he wrote, "took nothing
from nor added anything to Christ's divine and eternal Birth, but expended
itself wholly for the restoration of man who had been deceived: in order that
He might both vanquish death and overthrow by His strength the devil who
possessed the kingdom of death. For we should not now be able to overcome the author of sin and death if God had not assumed our nature and
made it His own, a nature which sin could not contaminate nor death detain"
(*ib.*, 2 759A). For this victory to be accomplished, it was necessary that "the
properties of both natures and their substances have come together in one
Person" (*ib.*, 3 759A).

St Cyril said nothing else. "When Christ had completed the Economy
with us, trampled on the devil, thrown down all his might, and destroyed
the 'power of death' itself, He restored for us a new and living way by having ascended 'into the heavens' and 'having appeared before the Face of God
the Father on our behalf', as it is written. He is seated with Him even in the

---

[31] "One God-Logos incarnate" or "one is Christ, the Logos from the Father, with
His own flesh" (*Ep.* XL PG 77 192f) is the way that St Cyril of Alexandria expressed the
relation of God the Son to His human nature. ". . .one being is distinct from the other,
together they form the one and only Christ. . .union does not mean the coming together
of one thing, but of two or more things which are intrinsically different," he wrote in
another letter (*Ep. XLIV* PG 77 225). "When we say 'union', we confess the union of the
flesh, which has a soul, and the Logos...what has been united cannot be divided. On the
contrary, the Son is one, His nature one, as that of the incarnate Logos. . .neither was the
nature of the Logos transformed into flesh, nor flesh into the Logos. Each nature is
understood as remaining itself...." Nowhere in his writings does St Cyril hold that after
the Incarnation the Logos became one nature with His humanity and that Christ exercised only a single Will (See J. Karmiris, Aarhus, 69; P.C. Tsonievsky, Bristol, 172).

flesh, not as a man considered separately and a different Son besides the Word, not as a man indwelt (ἔνοικος) by Him, but as the Son, truly the one and only-begotten Son even when He became man. Accordingly, He is seated with Him as God with God, Lord with Lord, as true Son of His Father, being thus by nature even though in the flesh"—φύσει τοῦτο ὑπάρχων, κἂν νοοῖτο μετὰ σαρκός (*Ep.* L PG 77 268A).

Clearly, the divine Plan of salvation presupposes a true christology. Unless Christ is one divine Person "recognized" in two complete natures the Incarnation[32] has no soteric value. Unless He is man, man has no means of access to God; unless He is God, no one can be saved or deified. Obviously, no human being can "save" or "heal" himself, that is, acquire the immortality, incorruption, and sinlessness (which by nature belong to God alone) and are communicated by Uncreated Grace to the creature. Only a God Who is completely and genuinely human, with two natures truly and permanently and mutually penetrated (*communicatio idiomatum*), can that end be achieved: God, in order to deify; man, in order to be deified.

On the other hand, there is no purpose in Christ's "assumption" of man if between His humanity and Divinity there is no essential connection. The Church as the Body of Christ—that into which the baptized are incorporated—is impotent as the instrument of man's rebirth, if she is not united to the Divinity of the Savior; or, if, as the Nestorians say, the Divinity passes through Christ's humanity "as water through a pipe." But, on the other hand, if the Divinity and humanity of Christ are confused, if they become one Nature and equated with one Person, unity in Christ must involve the dissolution of the creature's identity and freedom. Man, then, is not a "partaker of God" by Uncreated Grace, but is absorbed by the Divine.

B   If the Incarnation is understood in terms of the divine Person of the Son known in two natures; and if salvation demands that relationship between Person and nature, then, not only is the Incarnation the presupposition of soteriology, but of any other correlative matter. As it is necessary for our salvation that the Person/Nature of God the Son is united with a total human being, so must we admit, as St John of Damascus stated, that He possesses "two natural Wills" and "two natural Energies" (*De Fid. Orth.* III, 14). In other words, He has the Will (and Uncreated Energies of God), and likewise, having becoming man, He is in possession of a human will and energy, save, of course, that the Savior was a man "like as we are in all points yet without sin" (Heb. 4:15).

---

32   The Fathers used the words *Incarnatio* (Lat.) or Ἐνσάρκωσις (Grk.) and *Dispensatio* (Lat.) or Οἰκονομία (Grk.) to describe the divine Plan of salvation. The words are synonyms.

Furthermore, as Christ had two "natural Wills," elaborates the Damascene, so each Will has a corresponding Energy, i.e., "the efficient (δραστική) and essential activity of nature" (*ib.*, III, 15), or "movements in harmony with nature" (*ib.*, III, 22). The Energies, like the Wills, belong to one Person of Christ and, therefore, involve a mutual exchange arising from "the ineffable union" of His natures. Also, the Energies are not independent and arbitrary. They do not act separately, but conjointly one with the other (συνέργεια). The humanity of Christ does not "energize" in isolation from His Divinity, nor does His divine Nature "energize" as God alone, but they act together theandrically.[33] The name "Christ" signifies the unity of the Divine and the human.

Thus, Christ's Energies, His Divine and human Wills, are the Wills of His Person, that is, a Will natural to His *divine Hypostasis* as God the Son and a human Will which belongs to Jesus as the Son of Man, functioning together as from one Person by virtue of Their union. The divine Will is "superessential" and beyond all human understanding. It mysteriously acts upon the human Will of the God-Man, a created Will which has both the Energy and the Freedom to do what It has chosen; but, as St Maximus the Confessor stated, God moves His human Will "by impulsion, not compulsion" (*Ad Marn.*, 9 PG 91 81D).

The Fathers defined the free will as self-determination, "a freedom which exists in all men...man by nature possesses the faculty of will" (*Disp. c. Pyr.*, 61). Thus, He went voluntarily to the Cross (Phil. 2:8), a demonstration not only of His obedience to the Father, but of His freedom to obey. Although "neither obedience nor disobedience are proper to Deity," to be true man Christ possessed the power to choose between them. He had the ability to choose between opposites, but never chose the option to do evil.

In the language of soteriology, if Christ had "assumed" no human will, then, St Maximus concludes, man's will could not have been set free from sin, for "what has not been assumed is not healed" (*ib.* 139). At the same time, we must not think that because the human Will of Christ was free it was therefore "*gnomic*"—(ἡ γνώμη, the human "way of knowing," "judgment," "deliberation," "opinion," "purpose"). He had a human will, but, as He was an extraordinary man (Heb. 1:9), so likewise His Will was extraordinary. "He did not deliberate in an ordinary way, hampered by ignorance, doubt, opposition, contradiction. . ." Such are the impediments of sinful men, whose knowledge is imperfect and uncertain, and whose employment of the will, on the basis of that knowledge, is also marred by the passions of our fallen

---

[33] On the soteriological implications of theandry and theanthropy, see J. Popovich, "L'Homme et le Dieu-Homme," *Études de Théologie Orthodoxe*. Trad. Jean-Louis Palierne. Paris, n.d., 1-29.

nature (*ib.*, 87, 95). Therefore, the term "gnomic" (γνωμικός) applies to the decisions of the will rather than to the nature of it; but, the sinless Christ had a human Will without "gnomic" fault or limitations.

There is nothing in the Fathers which argues that, as a man, Christ had no liberty by virtue of the ontological union (συνάφεια) between His human and divine Wills. Indeed, in the history of the patristic literature there is everywhere agreement with the conclusions St Sophronius of Jerusalem's *Epistola Synodica* (634): Christ is "one in two," one divine Person in two natures (μία ὑπόστασις ἐν δυσὶ φύσεσιν) and, consequently, two Wills with Their corresponding Energies. "So He voluntarily manifested His humble humanity as *physikos*, yet remaining God. He was for Himself ruler over His human sufferings and actions... Therefore, was His humanity superior to ordinary men, not as if His nature was not human, but that in voluntarily becoming man, He undertook sufferings without compulsion nor of necessity, neither against His human Will (as in the case with us), but when and to what extent He willed" (Mansi [vol. XI], 484f.).[34]

St Sophronius upheld the necessity of free choice in the Lord's human nature, lest the Incarnation appear to be a sham. He took a position which "opposes Nestorianism" and "sets aside Eutychianism." To be candid, Nestorianism is less troublesome relative to Christ's human freedom than either Orthodoxy or Monophysitism. The Nestorian heresy, admitting two Persons, a separate Divine and human *hypostasis* in Christ, united only by "mutual engagement" or "God's good Favor" (κατ᾽ εὐδοκίαν), a moral union; hence, the Divine does not interfere with the human choices and actions of the Savior; but Nestorian christology negates all hope of salvation, since the humanity is not assumed by the Divinity. On the other hand, christological monergism or Monophysitism, the Eutychian heresy, while insuring "salvation" (ἀποθέωσις) of man also denies to Him choice and thereby suppresses genuine humanity in Him.

The "royal way" between the heresies is the signature of the Fathers: Christ "the one Person of God the Logos incarnate"—μία φύσις τοῦ Θεοῦ Λόγου σεσαρκωμένη (St Cyril of Alexandria). The paradoxical union of the two natures in no way prohibits to His humanity freedom of choice. What Jesus Christ did, and continues to do, as God is beyond all human and angelic comprehension; and, ultimately, so were His earthly miracles and suffering. When Messiah cured the ruler's son, although absent from him, He acted as God. When He wept for Lazarus, He behaved as man; but, in restoring the blind man's sight by His touch, the Savior acted as God-Man, by a

---

34 See C.J. Hefele's discussion of the Council of Jerusalem (634) and Monotheletism, *A History of the Councils of the Church* (vol. 5). Trans. by W.R.Clark. Edinburgh, 1896, pp. 41-61.

"theandric Energy," as St Dionysius referred to It (PG Vol. 3, 1072B, Letter IV).

The resurrected ascended human nature is deified and forever bound to His Divinity and Its actions, but what Jesus did while on earth, He chose to do, without having to do it.[35] He did not sin, because He was not subject to death, since, like Adam in Paradise, Christ, "the Second" or "Last Adam" was able not to die as He was able not to sin. When Adam sinned, he died, and his race shares in his mortal substance; but Christ, on account of His unique Birth, did not inherit "Adam's curse." His Death was voluntary, and not "the wages of sin." After the Resurrection, the deified Christ was unable to die, unable to sin, unable to experience pain or aging; and, so shall be the condition of His "brethren" in the Age to Come. His race has acquired the eternal life He won for it on the Cross.

3 THE LAST ADAM

Christ and Adam are the founders of two races, while Adam was also "the type of Him Who was to come"—Ἀδὰμ ὅς ἐστιν τύπος τοῦ μέλλοντος (Rom. 5:14).[36] "The first man Adam was made a living soul, the last Adam (Christ) was made a quickening spirit.... The first man is from the earth, earthy; but the second man is the Lord from heaven..." (I Cor. 15:45, 47). Adam was created in "the image and likeness of God." Christ, by Whom the ages were made, is "the brightness of His Glory, the express Image of His Person" (Heb. 1:2-3). He Who was the Incarnate Image of God, Jesus Christ, is the father of a new race, even as Adam was the original ancestor, the progenitor of the humanity which sprang from him.[37]

---

[35] For Roman Catholic dogmaticians, the "problem" of free will in Christ is *una ex gravissimis theologiae*. As they see it, if Christ, in suffering for us, did not act "of His own free choice...if He was not free, His Passion lacked meritoriousness and therefore had no power to redeem us. If He was free, He was able to rebel against the commandment (*mandatum*) of the Father.... Consequently, it is necessary to deny either." (J. Pohle & A. Preuss, *Christology: A Dogmatic Treatise on the Incarnation.* St. Louis, 1952, p. 218.)

[36] A "type" or "figure" is a historical person or event in sacred history which points to another person or event in the future, such as Adam to Christ, Eve to Mary, Israel to the Church, the Jordan to Baptism, etc. Modern scholarship often treats typology as a form of allegory. The Fathers use different words—*sacramenta* (St Hilary of Poitiers) or *mystikoi* (St Gregory of Nyssa)—to describe both typological and allegorical subjects. An allegorical interpretation discovers hidden moral and spiritual meanings in the Scriptures.

[37] "*Adam wird als Typus des kommenden (Messias) bezeichnet,*" P. Lengsfeld maintains. *Paulus vergleicht Christ Gnadentat zum Heil mit Unheilstat des ersten Menchen, um an den umfassenden Unheils der Adamstat die Unveriversalitaet des heilschaffenden Tuns Christi zu veranschaulichen* (*Adam und Christus.* Essen, 1965, 29-30). Lengsfeld has properly identified the motive for *die Adam-Christus-Typologie im NT*, but, as so many of his contempo-

A   "From this earth, while it was still virgin," wrote St Irenaeus, "God took dust and fashioned the man, Adam, the beginning of humanity" (*Proof of Ap. Preach.*, 32 ACW). "Christ was begotten of the Virgin Mary. . .of the Holy Spirit," explains St Maximus of Turin. "Each comes forth from God as a father. . .each had a virgin mother, each. . .is a son of God, Adam a creature, Christ of the divine Substance" (*Serm.* L, 2 ACW). Adam was formed out of "virgin earth" on the sixth day ("Friday") of the old creation, Christ, his descendent, was "born of a (virgin) woman,"[38] during the sixth age of history (see Chap. VI).

Generally, the Fathers (Sts Theophilus of Antioch, Ephraim the Syrian, Hilary of Poitiers, Maximus the Confessor, etc.) state unequivocally that the first *Adam* was made "neither mortal nor immortal." Immortality would have been his reward for obedience. He was sinless, but not perfect, that is, able to sin; not immortal, but able not to die, possessing the ability to obey or disobey, and, consequently, open to the possibility of temptation to which he (and Eve) did in fact succumb. The object of temptation was the fruit from the tree of the knowledge (γνωστόν) of good and evil (Gen. 2:9). The devil tempted Adam, and succeeded; as he will attempt but fail to seduce Christ (Mark 1:10-13; Luke 4:1-13). The "fault" of "our first parent" brought death, wrote St Peter Chyrsologus, the grace of "our new parent. . .restored us from this punishment (death) to life" (*Sermon* CXI FC).

B   The first head of the human race, Adam, was tempted in "the garden of Eden" (ὁ παράδεισος)[39] where God had situated him. That a tree was at the center of the cosmic drama is not without eminent typological significance.

---

raries, he treats the subject "scientifically" and interprets the Apostle's witness in terms of its so-called Hellenistic-Gnostic and Jewish background. He displays no knowledge of the Fathers, His free-will or His impeccability" (J. Pohle & A. Preuss, *Christology: A Dogmatic Treatise on the Incarnation.* St Louis, 1952, p. 218).

38   According to the Fathers, Christ was a "virgin," not only as to His moral state, but as "the new beginning." Adam was also a virgin. If, then, He had any ties of Adam, it was that He might also save ("recapitulate") Adam's righteous offspring before the Incarnation. This truth is illustrated by the Orthodox liturgical celebration of Old Testament Saints. His Virgin Birth has no connection with Augustinian theory of "original sin" (see note 40), a doctrinal fiction which compelled Scholasticism into a series of theological innovations, such as, Christ was "born of a virgin" to avoid the "taint" of "original sin" (A. Pohle, *Christology*, p. 210). For the same reason, medieval theology eventually developed the theory of "the Immaculate Conception" of the Virgin Mary (eventually dogmatized by Pope Pius IX in 1854). There was also some attempt, very limited to be sure, to protect the Mother of God from the guilt of "original sin" by also exempting her mother, St Anne, from it (See Chap. 5).

39   "Some, indeed, have pictured Paradise as a geographical place, and others, as a noetical realm," observed St John of Damascus. "But it seems to me that, just as man is a creature in whom we find both sense and mind blended together,   *(continued on next page)*

His willful sin of disobedience was the result of encouragement from "the woman" (taken from his side as he slept) and Satan's deception (Gen. 3:1-25). Adam and Eve were removed from Paradise where they could no longer dwell by virtue of the mortality wrought by the "ancestral transgression" (προπατορικὸν ἁμάρτημα).[40] They could no longer remain in a state uncongenial to them. But, contrary to the conventional notion, the exile of Adam and Eve from Paradise was more an act of "divine mercy and guardianship than indignation," as St John Chrysostom observed. To have remained in Paradise, sinful and mortal, would only have extended their fallen state endlessly (*Comm. on Gen.* XVIII, 3 PG 53 151).

From the Genesis narrative several important conclusions emerge. First, the consequences of Adam's Fall on creation. Adam lost more by his disobedience, and Christ recovered more by His obedience, than a state of privilege for him. The first man was the head of the creation; thus, what befell him, likewise befell his domain. Both humanity and the cosmos were now under the control of death through Adam's sin, as God warned (Gen. 2:17); that is, under "the power of the devil who is," "the author of death," as St Valerian of Cimiez referred to him (*Hom.* I, 5; *Hom.* XI, 1 FC). Although "death passed to all men" (Rom. 5:12) on account of Adam, yet, St Peter Chrysologus cautions, "do not think it unjust...that all men have their existence through this one" (*ib.*). The human race inherited the mortality of its first parents, not the guilt of their folly.

Not only do the Scriptures and the Fathers speak of death as the fruit of Adam's sin, but also the loss of man's "likeness" to God and the "cracking" of

---

(*cont'd.*) in like manner this most holy temple of man combines the properties of both sense and mind..." (*De Fid. Orth.* II, 11 PG 94 916BC). "Paradise" is not mythical. As with all creation itself, it was a spatio-temporal site, although an environment different from and higher than the world in which fallen man lives.

[40] The Orthodox use the expression "ancestral transgression" in place of "original sin" is not primarily a polemical tactic. The very concept is foreign to the Apostolic Tradition. In point of fact, man stands in the midst of a spiritual collision between God and the evil one—not as the object of the divine Wrath on account of an "original sin" inherited from Adam. The evil one is the central figure in this cosmic tragedy; hence, the Cross (Heb:2:14). The devil's victories, therefore, come by the clever strategy of deception and temptation, the manipulation of the passions born when man became corrupt through his mortality. The divine Plan was a Plan for his rescue: Uncreated Grace in Christ by which the creature through the Holy Spirit is given a share in the divine Life which alone is invulnerable to the devil's machinations. In a word, "original sin" is not required to explain evil in the world. (See J. Romanides, "Original Sin According to St Paul," *St Vladimir's Seminary Quarterly* IV, 1-2 (1955-56), 5-28; and 216; and St Cyril of Alexandria, *Doct. Quaest.*, 6, in *Selected Letters* [Greek text]. Trans. & ed. by L.R. Wickham. Oxford, 1983, pp. 201, 203).

the *imago Dei* which resulted in the "shattering" of the human race by virtue of the lost communion with God, who is the source of human unity and harmony. In addition, Adam's shame brought corruption not only upon himself and his descendants but the creation over which he was to have mastery; consequently, "the creation groans and travails in pain together until now" (Rom. 9:22). Conversely, as St Irenaeus testifies, Christ's Redemption has established Him as the new "head" (κεφαλή, *caput*) of a "new creation" (II Cor. 5:17). The restoration of mankind to communion with God through the Church came as the direct result of the Incarnation (*Adv. Haer.*, IV, xxxviii, 1 ANF). In truth, "God the Son became man in order to regather in Himself the ancient creation, so that He might slay sin and destroy the power of death, and give life to all men" (*Adv. Haer.* III, xix, 6 ANF).[41] In this, he follows St Paul—ἀνακεφαλαιώσασθαι (Eph. 1:10). Christ has commenced the reversal of all that befell the creation because of man's disobedience.

Second, the Genesis typology prefigures the manner in which God will recover the creation from death, sin and all evil, thereby returning it to fellowship with the Trinity in Jesus Christ. "For if through the offense of one [man] [the] many [all] are dead, much more the Grace of God and the gift by Grace, which is by one man, Jesus Christ, hath abounded to many" (Rom. 5: 15). "For since by one man came death, by man came also the resurrection of the dead. For as in Adam all die, even so in Christ shall all be made alive" (I Cor. 15:21-23). To the Colossians, St Paul wrote, the Father, "having made peace through the blood of the Cross, by Him to reconcile all things (τὰ πάντα) unto Himself; by Him, I say, whether things in earth or things in the heavens" (1:20).

At the heart of this contrast between the cosmic Christ (Archetype of creation) and the microcosmic Adam (the mirror of creation) is the question of "life" and "death" raised by the figure of "the tree," the anti-type of the Cross. "And being found in the fashion of a man," writes St Paul, "He humbled

---

41   Contrary to H. Rashdall, the doctrine of Recapitulation is not a theory borrowed by St Paul from Gnosticism (*The Idea of Atonement in Christian Theology.* London, 1925, p. 237). St Paul offers no "theories" in his epistles and Gnosticism was a heresy which the Apostle condemned (I Tim. 6:20), and Sts Irenaeus and Hippolytus refuted. To "recapitulate all things in Christ" (Eph. 1:10; Col. 1:15) is perfectly consistent with Paul's doctrine, as the Fathers testify (See V. Lossky, "Redemption and Deification," in *In the Image and Likeness of God.* New York, 1974, pp. 97-110). It refers to ἀνακαίνωσις or "renewal" (II Cor. 5:17) of creation and, therefore, to deification ("what is assumed is healed"). Creation, angelic and human, animal and physical, is already Christ's dominion—as the expression "the Last Adam" implies—a Lordship completely realized in the Kingdom. Then will He be "the head over all things to the Church, which is His Body, the fullness of Him that fills all in all" (Eph.1: 22-23).

Himself and became obedient, even to the death of the Cross" (Phil. 2:8). To which St Peter adds, "Who of His own self bare our sins in his own body on the tree" (I Pet. 2:24). Thus, the Apostles (I Pet. 2:24) drew a parallel not only between Christ and Adam, but the tree of Paradise and the Tree or Cross of Calvary. "Instead of 'the tree of the knowledge of good and evil'," St John Chrysostom said, "we have the Tree of the Cross. Instead of the death of Adam, we have the death of Christ" (*De Coem.*, 2 PG 49 396). "A tree caught Adam for me," exclaimed St Ephraim the Syrian, "blessed be the Cross which has caught for me the Son of God" (*Nisibene Hymns* XLI, 13 NPNF). "Tree against tree...hands against hands," echoes St Gregory the Theologian, "one tree expels Adam, the other (Cross) reconciles the ends of the earth" (*Apol.*, 25 PG 35 433C).

Again, the Paradise lost by Adam through the "tree" was recovered by Christ through the "tree" of the Cross, beginning with His agony in the "garden" of Gethsamene. "In paradise was the fall," instructs St Cyril of Jerusalem, "and in a garden was our salvation. From the tree came sin, and until the Tree it remained" (*Catech.* XIX PG 33 769A). Not by inadvertence, then, did Christ promise to "the thief" crucified with Him, "To-day you shall be with me in Paradise" (Luke 23:43). In the eloquence of the *Octoechos*, "Verily, because of a tree Adam was estranged from paradise. Because the tree of the Cross, the thief came to reside in paradise" (Beatitudes, Tone 4).[42]

Salvation is, indeed, a return to Paradise, an idea, however, which, needs some clarification. When St Gregory of Nyssa and other Fathers spoke of "the return to the original splendor," they did not mean to the pristine Eden of our first-parents, but rather to the state of fellowship with God or, to quote St Basil the Great, "The economy of our Savior, Jesus Christ, is a recall from our fallen state to intimacy with God previously destroyed as the result of Adam's disobedience" (*De Sp. Sanc.* XV, 35 PG 32 128C). There is no Greek cyclicism at work here.

---

42. The subject of "the last things" (eschatology) will be discussed in another chapter. As already mentioned (chap. 3), the world which the soul encounters after its separation from the body (death) is the state of the Particular Judgment (with exceptions, e.g., the Theotokos, assumed bodily into heaven). The soul must be judged with the body and, therefore, it cannot immediately ascend to heaven or fall into hell. Rather the saved anticipate eternal joy with God ("Abraham's Bosom," "Paradise"), while the damned endure the misery of "outermost hades," foretasting the torments of hell (cf. Luke 16:20-31; cf. II Cor. 12:4). These states of the departed soul bear no resemblance to Purgatory nor the Gnostic Toll-House Myth (See e.g., St Gregory the Theologian, *Ora* VII, 21 PG 35 781BC; St John Chrysostom, *Comm. on Matt.* XXVIII, 3 PG 57 373-374). Consult also the rites for the Burial of the Dead, Parting of the Soul from Body (*Service Book of the Orthodox Church*. Hapgood trans. Englewood, 1975); and Lev Puhalo (Archbishop Lazar), *The Soul, the Body and Death*. Chiliwack (BC), n.d.

C   The return to Paradise is the reacquisition of a promised Glory (δόξα, *kabod* in Hebrew) lost to the creature by sin and death. Thus, when Moses writes that Adam was created "in the image and likeness of God" (Gen. 1:26) and St Paul declares that he created "in the image and glory of God" (I Cor. 11:7), the allusion to man's "likeness" to His Creator is evident. Likewise, the absence of his "likeness" to God indicates the absence of the Glory in which and for which Adam and Eve were made. As St Macarius of Egypt tells us, "When, using the woman as his accomplice, the devil deceived Adam, he divested him of the Glory which enveloped him" (*Hom. III*, 37 Ph).[43]

In Christ that Glory is restored to man and the creation, for Christ is the Glory of God (II Cor. 3:18). But God the Son is also "the Image of God" (II Cor. 4:4) which clearly suggests that not only was man deprived of the glory (δόξα), but the *imago Dei*, although not effaced, was defiled, lacking now its original lustre. Man's reason is proud and dark, his will rebellious which, in part, describes the unbelief of "them who are lost," mortals governed by "the god of the age [who] has blinded the minds of them which believe not, lest the light of the glorious gospel of Christ, Who is the image of God, should shine unto them" (II Cor. 4:4). Victims of "the ancestral transgression," "their minds (i.e., the image) are corrupted by the subtlety of the "serpent" who diverts them from "the simplicity that is in Christ" (II Cor. 11:3).

The return to Paradise is the "renewal" of the image of God in man, freedom from the devil and the resuscitation of the "likeness" suffocated by his disobedience. In this way, the "mind" or spirit of man acquires "a clear vision of the glory of the gift it has received, regains it former nobility and restores to its Creator His own image pure and unalloyed," exults Nikitas Stithatos. "And it continues to add to its labors until it has cleansed itself of every stain and impurity and is privileged [once more] to comtemplate and commune with God" (*On the Inner Nature of Things*, 86 Ph). St Macarius the Great adds, the "inner being" of believers "who through perfect faith are born of the Spirit, 'shall reflect as in a mirror the Glory of the Lord, and are transfigured into the same image from Glory to Glory' (II Cor. 3:18)." The truly believing soul will enjoy "spiritual light and mystery while still in the flesh" and be invested later with "deathless and incorruptible Glory" (*ib.*, 137, 142 Ph).

The Glory which the "new man" (Col. 3:10) enjoys is the Uncreated Light[44] which God eternally inhabits (I Tim. 6:16). It is the Light from eter-

---

43   *The Philokalia* (vol. 3). Trans. by G.E.H. Palmer, etc. Boston, 1984 (Ph).

44   The Light of which the Fathers speak, says Fr J. Romanides, "is not the created light, the *lumen gloria* of Latin theology 'by which' or 'in which' the elect will see the divine essence, and the uncreated glory which is the very same divine essence." Neither Augustine nor any of his successors believed that "the Light of   (continued on next page)

nity; indeed, from the Age to Come: it is the Light of future Glory, of the Kingdom. God is this Light (I John 1:5), the Logos is this Light (John 12:6), "Light from Light," as the Nicean Creed declares. The Spirit is Light. In a word, the Light of the Trinity is the Uncreated Energy. It is the very Light which Adam knew in Paradise, and which, as St Macarius (*ib*. III, 36) reminds us, frightened the evil one when he saw It on the face of Moses (Ex. 34:30-31), at the Transfiguration of the Lord on Mt. Tabor, accessible to the Saints as "the uncreated and divine effulgence" about which St Gregory Palamas discoursed so profoundly.[45]

The Incarnation was an invitation to the human race (and, consequently, all of creation of which man is the crown and custodian) to participation in the eternal Light of God. In the Risen Christ that Light has been made present; it is the sign that God has begun His recovery of the world from the darkness into which it fell. The Savior, then, is ὁ ἔσχατος ἄνθρωπος, the first installment of God's promise. He is "the firstborn among many brethren (Rom. 8:29), "the firstborn of every creature" (Col. 1: 15), "the firstborn from the dead" (Col. 1:18). Christ is our type and precursor and, therefore, what He is, the saved shall become. He was the first man to receive Glory, for His body was "raised in Glory" (I Cor. 15:43). When His Own, who have already received "an eternal weight of Glory" shall be raised, "He will change our lowly body to be like His glorious Body" (Phil. 3:21).

A glorified human nature which has been "recapitulated" in Him, in His risen Body, shall become a "new creature"—a process which has begun already for them who have been incorporated into His Body: a humanity which is "sown in corruption, raised in incorruption...sown in dishonor, but is raised in Glory..." (I Cor. 15: 42-43). The members of the Christian race have already begun to be "conformed to the image of the Son of God"— συμμόρφους τῆς εἰκόνος τοῦ υἱοῦ αὐτοῦ (Rom. 8:29)—by their faith and ascetical struggle, transformed by the Uncreated Grace of the Holy Spirit, and, as in the case of numerous Saints experiencing that Light (e.g., St Symeon the New Theologian) who are witnesses to the presence of the Uncreated Light of the holy Trinity in the Church.

(*cont'd.*) Glory" revealed to the prophets and the saints was "a deifying gift" (θεοποιὸν δῶρον). ("Notes on the Palamite Controversy and Related Topics," in *The Greek Orthodox Theological Review* VI, 2 [1960-1961], 194, 198). The Latins advocate the existence of two glories, the uncreated and incommunicable Light of God, and the created light for the creature.

[45] See the valuable discussion in B. Krivosheine, *The Ascetic and Theological Teaching of Gregory Palamas* (Reprint from The Eastern Churches Quarterly, 4). London, 1938. More will be said on this topic.

3   PASCHA[46]

We have learned what God has done (i.e., the divine Economy, the Incarnation) to recover His creation from sin, death and the devil, but the question remains, how did He accomplish His purpose? According to St Justin Martyr, the answer was given already in prophecy. "Those who were saved in Egypt, were saved by the blood of the Paschal lamb, with which they painted the doorposts and lintels of their dwellings. For the Lamb was Christ, Who was later sacrificed. Thus, as the blood of the paschal lamb preserved those in Egypt, so the blood of Christ was to save those who believed on Him" (*Dial. CXI*, 4 FC).

Why the references to "blood"? Justin only reaffirms the words of St Paul, "In Whom we have redemption through His (Christ) blood" (Eph. 1:7), His "precious blood" (I Pet. 1:18). Without the shedding of blood, there is no "remission of sins," as the Law declares (Heb. 9:22). Without blood there is no life—"For the life of the flesh is its blood, inasmuch as it is life; and I have given to you on the altar to make expiation for the soul" (Lev. 17:11). Blood is the seal of the covenant between God and His People (Ex. 24:8). In the case of the new covenant, the slaughtered Lamb of the ancient Passover is the type of Him Whom St John the Baptizer called "the Lamb of God which taketh away the sin of the world" (John 1: 29). Hence, the Lord spoke of His "blood of the new testament (covenant), which is shed for the many"—τὸ ἐκχυνόμενον ὑπὲρ πολλῶν (Mark 14:24), that is, the Savior died for "*the* many" ("all"). On the Cross, His Blood became the source of life for mankind, not only by erasing our sins but by destroying death of which sin is the "sting" (I Cor. 15:56).

A   How did the Crucifixion produce new and eternal life and, indeed, a new relationship with God? How did the Cross give humanity access to the divine Nature? "The Son of Man came not to be ministered unto, but to minister and to give His life a ransom (λύτρον) for the many" (Matt. 20:28; Mark 10:45; I Tim. 2:6; and Esa. 43:3). With whom did He exchange His Life for

---

46   "Easter" is the common name in America and Great Britain for the feast observed throughout Christendom in commemoration of the Resurrection. The word "Easter" (German, *Ostern*) is a survival of Teutonic mythology. The word is derived from *Eostre*, or *Ostara*, the Anglo-Saxon goddess of spring, to whom the month answering to our April, was dedicated. The name of the feast in other languages (*paques*, French; *pasqua*, Ital.; *pascua*, Sp.; *paaske*, Dan.; *paasch*, Dutch; *pasg*, Welch) is derived from the Latin *pasch* and the Greek πάσχα—"passed over"—in memory of the great deliverance from the destroying angel which "passed over the houses of the children of Israel in Egypt when he smote the Egyptians" (Ex. 12:27), a type of Christ's Redemption. The feast of Pascha includes not only the Resurrection but the Good Friday and Great and Holy Sabbath following it (See T.M. Fallow, "Easter," *Encyc. Brit.* [vol. 7-8]. New York, 1911, 828-829).

ours? To whom did He pay the "ransom"? To that which had carried the human race into captivity. To death, the grave, *sheol, hades* as the Lord revealed to the Prophet, "I will ransom them from the power of the grave; I will redeem them from death" (Hos. 13:14). "The ransom was offered to death on behalf of all," exclaimed St Athanasius, "so that by it He once more opened the way to the heavens"—ὡς γὰρ ὑπὲρ πάντων αὐτὸ προσήνεγκε τῷ θανάτῳ· οὕτω δι' αὐτοῦ πάλιν ὡδοποίησε τὴν εἰς οὐρανοὺς ἄνοδον (*De Incar. Verbi Dei*, 25 PG 25 140C).[47]

If Christ is the ransom "offered to death," it is because Christ is "our Passover" (I Cor. 5:8). By the blood of the sacrificed Lamb shed on the Cross, the "curse" of death ("the wages of sin") and the "curse" of the unfulfillable Law inherited by Adam's posterity, is annulled. "But look at it in this manner," urges St Gregory the Theologian, "that as for my sake He was called a 'curse' (Gal. 3:13), Who destroyed my curse; and 'sin' (I Cor. 15:45), Who removes the sin of the world; and because, He is a new Adam (II Cor. 5:21) to replace the old, just so He makes my disobedience His own as Head of the whole body"—Ἀλλ' οὕτω σκόπει· ὅτι ὥσπερ κατάρα ἤκουσε δι' ἐμὲ, ὁ τὴν ἐμὴν λύων κατάραν· καὶ ἁμαρτία, ὁ αἴρων τὴν ἁμαρτίαν τοῦ κόσμου· καὶ Ἀδὰμ ἀντὶ τοῦ παλαιοῦ γίνεται νέος· οὕτω καὶ τὸ ἐμὸν ἀνυπότακτον ἑαυτοῦ ποιεῖται, ὡς κεφαλὴ τοῦ παντὸς σώματος (*Ora.* XXX, 5 PG 36 108CD).[48]

---

[47] G. Aulen describes "the ransom doctrine" as the "classical" and "dominant" Christian teaching on the Redemption. It was universally held by the Fathers; it is Biblical. "In spite of all the diversities of the different Fathers," he writes, "the general agreement between them on the subject is such that it is possible to treat them together in a single comprehensive statement" (*Christus Victor: An Historical Study of the Three Main Types of the Idea of Atonement*. Trans. by A.G. Herbert. New York, 1956, pp. 36, 39). Even heretics, such as Origen and Tertullian, identified the Atonement with Ransom (S. Lyonnet & L., Sabourin, *Sin, Redemption and Sacrifice: A Biblical and Patristic Study*. Rome, 1970, p. 210f.).

Aulen's reference to the "diversity" among the Fathers concerning "ransom," especially when heretics are included among its supporters is misleading. Some Fathers stated that it was paid to the devil, others to the grave; and others, such as St Gregory the Theologian, to God the Father. Later, Gregory seems to have corrected himself, saying that Christ's Death was a ransom paid to the grave (e.g., *De vita sui* PG PG 37 1141A). For St Ephraim, it was a ransom to the devil ("lord of the grave") or to the grave (his "kinsman") (*Nis. Hymns XLI*, 15).

Ransom paid to the devil (or, what is the same thing, to the grave) is the only doctrine of Redemption mentioned in Orthodox liturgical texts (see footnote 52), relying on St Paul— "He (Christ) also Himself took part of the same; that through death He might destroy him that had the power of death, that is, the devil" (Heb. 2:14). Golgotha is a cosmic drama in which "the power of evil ultimately overreaches itself when it clashes with the power of good, with God Himself. It loses the battle at the moment when it seems to be victorious" (Aulen, p. 55).

[48] The reference here is to the Church, "the Christian race" as the Fathers and Orthodox Service Books calls her. Contemporary racism has no place in Orthodoxy. God sees mankind divided into the "race of Adam" and the "race of Christ."

Commenting on the Gospel of John 1:29, St Cyril of Alexandria maintained that a new race of men was *in* Christ (as the fallen race had been *in* Adam) when He gave His Life on the Cross (as Adam had lost the life of the world by a tree) a ransom for all. "As we were in many sins, subject thereby to death and corruption, the Father gave up His Son as a ransom (ἀντίλυτρον) for us. One for all, because all are in Him and He is better than all: one died for all, so that all might live in Him. For we were all in Christ, Who because (διά) of us and for our sake (ὑπέρ) died and rose again..." (*Exp. in Joan Evang.* II PG 73 102). Here, then, was the reason for the Incarnation. As St Leo the Great confirms, "you who were made in the image of God, albeit corrupted in Adam, you were refashioned in Christ"—*Recordare te factum ad imaginem Dei [Gen. 1:26]; quae, etsi in Adam corrupta, in Christo tamen est reformata* (*Serm.* XXVII, 6 PL 54 220B).

B To be "refashioned" means to become immortal and incorrupt; and to become immortal and incorrupt requires that we die to these evils which defile and mortify us. But sinful created beings have no such power. We must share in the Passion of Christ. Thus, the Savior went to His voluntary Death not in stead of but "in behalf of us" (ὑπὲρ ἡμῶν),[49] that He might redeem (λυτρώσεται ἡμᾶς) us from all iniquity, and purify us unto Himself a peculiar People..." (Tit. 2:14). Not so incidentally, this verse suggests that "expiation" and "propitiation" (commonly associated with Christ's sacrificial Death) are words all too often misunderstood. They are ordinarily and falsely rendered "to placate the Wrath of God" by "paying the penalty" for the sins of men.[50]

49 The idea of the "vicarious atonement of Christ" is common in late medieval and modern theological literature (See the discussion in H. Rashdall, pp. 93-98). It means that Christ died in man's place, paying the penalty he could not pay, that is, the Savior "makes up for" or "makes amends," "atones" for human sins. But the early Church developed no such doctrine. St Paul declared that Christ died on our behalf (ὑπέρ) and not instead or in place of (ἀντί) of man (e.g., I Thess. 5:10; and Gal. 1:4).

50 The word "expiation" or "propitiation" (ἱλαστήριον, ἱλάσκομαι, ἱλασμός in Grk.; *kippur* in Hebrew) is closely related to the idea of "sacrifice" (Rom. 3:25; Heb. 2:17; I John 2:2; 4:10; and Lev. 16:16, 20). "Sacrifice" connotes "intercession," "mediation." In the Septuagint "expiation" implies "to have mercy" or "to hear favorably." Sometimes, it is rendered "to propitiate the face of the Lord"—ἱλάσασθαι τὸ πρόσωπον Κυρίου (Zech. 8:22-23 LXX); hence, "praying," "entreating" or "beseeching" or "asking God." It also has the meaning "to purify" or "to cleanse," καθαρίζειν (Ex. 29:26 LXX), a deliverance from sins (Lyonnet & Sabourin, p. 145f.). Applying these things to Christ, we conclude that the Cross was not an attempt to appease or placate an angry God. Rather Christ, as the representative of the human race, conquered death on the Cross, recovered the creation from the devil, cleansed the human race from sin, all a "sacrifice of praise" to God. Those who have "put on Christ" share in His Death and Resurrection and become part of His offering to the Father.

The purpose of the Crucifixion was indeed "the remission of sins," "the death of death," the overthrow of the devil, but also "a sacrifice of praise" (Ps. 49:14, 23; Jerm. 33:11; and Heb. 13:15), a "praise" allowed even to those in hades ("the abode of the dead"). Christ descended into "the grave," spreading the Love and Mercy of God even "unto the spirits in prison" (I Pet. 3:19), where the martyred St John the Baptizer had previously proclaimed to its inhabitants His Coming (Beheading, Troparion, Tone 2). Those in the "darkness" who believed on Him, St Aphrahat exclaimed, "He brings forth...by His Power and they shall go forth to see the Light" (*Sel. Dem.* XXII, 4 NPNF). "Thus, after He had liberated those who had been bound for ages," said St John of Damascus, "He immediately rose from the dead, showing us the way of resurrection" (*De Fid. Orth.* III, 29).

Christ's victory over "the grave" is now, today (σήμερον, *hodie*) as the Feast of Pascha ecstatically proclaims. He is already "the firstfruits" of the Age to Come, the first man of the new creation. "The last enemy (ἔσχατος ἐχθρός)," death, is already destroyed (I Cor. 15: 26).[51] The creation is already offered and accepted by God the Father as "as a sacrifice to God for a sweet smelling savor" (Eph. 5:2), meaning that "the remission of sins" has been achieved, the regenerated creation has been offered to the Father, and the risen Lord, re-presenting mankind, ascends to the Right Hand of Majesty. Finally, the Holy Spirit is sent by Christ to His People. "The Church is the Age to Come," St John Chrysostom said. Nothing any longer impedes the *koinonia* between the Creator and the creature, save disbelief.

C   This "classical idea" of Ransom stood for one thousand years as the teaching of the Church, as the understanding of His Redemption with which the Lord provided her. The complete break with the Apostolic Tradition came with the work of Anselm and Abelard.[52] Indeed, neither, while devel-

---

[51] There are two Greek words which, if misunderstood, lead to endless confusion about the Christian Faith—*telos* (end, finished) and *eschatos* (last). When the curtain falls, the play is over (τέλος). The season's last *(ἔσχατος)* harvest of grapes does not shut down the farm. Christ is "the last man" (ὁ ἔσχατος ἄνθρωπος) or "the last Adam" (ὁ ἔσχατος Ἀδάμ). He is the pattern of all who belong to Him. He is the type of the saved. The risen Lord is the Man of the future, of the end-time *(ἔσχατος)*. Together, He and His new humanity, shall enter the Kingdom of God. Thus, Jesus is the beginning and the end, "the alpha and the omega" (Rev. 1:8).

[52] Rashdall, *The Idea of the Atonement*, p. 350. Also, J. E. L. Oulton, who views this "grotesque theory" as a product of its time (*The Mystery of the Cross.* Greenwich, 1957, p. 20); and G. Aulen who considers Anselm's *Cur Deus Homo* "a great advance on the early church," surpassing "the idea of a transaction with the devil, as well as the grotesque idea of a deception of the devil" (*Christus Victor*, p. 47). These writers, objecting to a "theory" of the Fathers, do therefore disdain a teaching of the Orthodox Church. She affirms that "he who by the tree did deceive the first Adam was himself deceived by the Cross" (Elevation of the Cross, Vespers, Glory). Also, the proclamation of the Vespers: "By Thy

oping Atonement theories *a priori,* appealed to ancient doctrine.[53]   H. J. Berman refers to Anselm's work in particular as a "revolution in theology."[54] This "revolution in theology" had its antecedents in the labors of Augustine, even though there seems very little in the theories of Augustine and Anselm's on the Atonement to connect them directly.   What the Archbishop of

Cross, O Christ our Savior, the dominion of death hath been destroyed, and the deception of the devil hath been abolished; and the race of man, having been saved by the Faith, doth ever offer praise to Thee" (Stichera of the Third Tone); "By Thy precious Cross, O Christ, Thou hast put the devil to shame; and by Thy resurrection, Thou hast blunted the sting of sin; and Thou hast saved us from the gates of death. We glorify Thee, O Only-begotten One" (of the Fifth Tone). The devil was deceived by his own ignorance and pride.

If the Fathers sometimes employed melodramatic imagery in describing the Crucifixion scenario—"hook" (St Gregory of Nyssa), "snare" (St Gregory the Theologian)—they were taking poetic license to provide a mystery with some understanding. Even Augustine pictured the Cross as a "mousetrap." According to St John of Damascus, it was death which approached, "and swallowing up the body as a bait is transfixed on the hook of Divinity, and after tasting a sinless and life-giving body, perishes and disgorges all that he had swallowed" (*De Fid. Orth.* III, 27 PG 94 1096C-1097A). One way or the other, it was the devil who was defeated on the Cross, having lost the power of death by which he dominated men through the passions which came by death or, more accurately, corruption.

Rashdall, Oulton and Aulen are firmly rooted in the theory of doctrinal development without which it would be impossible for them to justify the doctrinal innovations to which they adhere. Even more, how else to explain their admission that "the ransom theory" is Apostolic, universally held by the early Church, or that the Lord Himself referred more than once to His Sacrifice as "ransom," yet is to be considered as unworthy of belief? Again, why do they deny that God would have any dealing with the devil (cf. Job 1:6-12), an element so important to the "the ransom theory"? To accept only what is palatable to reason, we call rationalism.

[53] Anselm's nod to the past with the remark, "what ought to be sufficient has been said by the holy fathers and their successors" (*CDH*, I, 1 SND), has a hollow ring. His purpose, according to Paul Tillich, was to determine the "rational adequacy of the substitutional suffering of Christ in the work of salvation." Intriguing, too, is Tillich's explanation for the West's unwillingness to dogmatize Anselm's theory of the Atonement. "It has wisely restricted itself from doing so, because there is no absolute theory of the atonement. Abelard. . .and Origen as well as others have had different theories of the atonement." Nevertheless, "the Church" seems to have preferred Anselm's theory, "most probably because it has the deepest psychological roots...the feeling that a price must be paid for our guilt, and that since we cannot pay it, God must" (*A History of Christian Thought*. Ed. by C.E. Braaten. New York, 1968, p. 166). There is the confident assumption here that the history of evolving doctrines promises no "orthodoxy," and, that Anselm's is to be congratulated dor taking that history to a higher stage. Is there to be another?

[54] Anselm's "revolution in theology" was accompanied by a "revolution in legal science" which rested on the analytic division between faith and reason, Berman comments, and particularly on the belief that it was possible to demonstrate by reason alone what had been delivered by divine Revelation (*Law and Revolution: The Formation of the Western Legal Tradition*, pp. 174-198). Anselm's "new theology" was greatly inspired by his devotion to Augustine (See R.W. Southern, *Saint Anselm: A Portrait in a Landscape.* Cambridge [Eng.], 1990, pp. 71-87).

Canterbury acquired from the Bishop of Hippo was the spirit of theological experimentation, a method, and not a few important concepts, such as "all sin is injustice," "limited atonement,"[55] etc. Also, it was Augustine who refocused his thinking about the devil, leading to the conclusion that, as man is guilty of offending the Justice of God, so Christ was punished on the Cross in our place to assuage the Wrath of God.

With that mentality, the great *desideratum* became the question of "the necessity and efficacy" of the Redemption: "how God ought to or could have condescended to those things which we affirm" (*CDH*. I, 4). Anselm might have found the answer in the patristic tradition which both he and Augustine presumed to revise and augment. But why did he replace the ancient belief that the Cross as Christ's conquest of death and the devil with the Atonement as "satisfaction" or "reparation" to God the Father? Why, too, after the laborious discourse on the Atonement in these legal terms,[56] did Anselm unexpectedly turn to the idea of "merit"? (*CDH*, II, 19)? No doubt, he loved the logic of the satisfaction theory, but he must have been impelled by another argument. With the idea of satisfaction, he was unable to reach the idea of the Church, that is to say, Anselm could not show any immediate connection between the Cross and the role of the Church in man's redemption.

If Christ made satisfaction on the Cross for a community of believers, then, nothing was required of them who were guilty of both actual and original sin. The Church must be redefined, unless we argue that only members of the Church contribute in some way to their own salvation, that is, by "merit." On account of good works or "works of merit," the satisfaction of the Cross is imputed to those who belong to Him.[57] If nothing else, Anselm's ambivalence alerted the West to the nexus between "satisfaction" and "merit"[58] and, to concepts which have no place in the classical doctrine of

---

[55] The expression "limited atonement" is Calvinist, an idea the Reformer may have drawn from Augustine comments concerning election. "...the whole mass of the human race is condemned," asserted Augustine; "for he (Adam) who at first gave entrance to sin has been punished with all his posterity who were in him as in a root, so that no one is exempt from this just and due punishment, unless delivered by mercy and undeserved Grace; and the human race is so apportioned that in some is displayed the efficacy of merciful Grace, in the rest the efficacy of just retribution. For both could not be displayed in all; for if all had remained under the punishment of just condemnation, there would have been seen in no one the mercy of redeeming Grace. And, on the other hand, if all had been transferred from darkness to light, the severity of retribution would have been manifested in none. But many more are left under punishment than are delivered from it, in order that it may thus be shown what was due to all" (*De Civ. Dei*. XXI, 12 MD).

[56] See Berman, *Law and Revolution*, pp. 595-598.

[57] Ritschl, A. B., *A Critical History of the Christian Doctrine of Justification and Reconciliation*. Trans. by J. Black, Edinburgh, 1872, p. 68f.

[58] *Ibid.*, pp. 32-40.

Atonement. The price the Scholastic West had to pay was a break with ancient Tradition, a break which involved not only the introduction of law into soteriology ("justice"), but *a fortiori* the integration of philosophical and anthropological ideas necessary in the formation of a doctrine which not only denied the devil center-stage in the great Work of Christ's Work, but also in some quarters, reduced the Atonement to a moral drama.[59]

D   According to Anselm, "there is nothing more just than supreme justice, which maintains God's honor in the arrangement of things, and which is nothing other than God Himself." He upholds nothing with more justice than the honor of His own dignity. He who seeks to defraud Him must expect to receive punishment or pay what is due Him—*poena aut satisfactio*, according to the Germanic legal maxim. His lost honor must be recompensed or punishment must follow, lest He be unjust to Himself, or be accused of weakness, "which is impossible" (*CDH* I, 13). The "satisfaction" (restitution, reparation, retribution) the Lord demands is usurious, insists Anselm, always "something greater than the amount of the obligation" (*ib.*, I, 21).

Such is the case of man's sin against God. If he hopes to regain the right relationship with the Supreme Being, he must return everything to God which he took from Him and more—"it is fitting" (*rectitudo*), to use Anselm's favorite expression. "It is fitting" or "right" that the honor due to Him is restored unto surfeit. As God suffered loss by him, His Justice demands a return of the violated moral order to the condition in which God created it. But man cannot repay Him, since the Fall corrupted not only Adam, but the entire human race. He must expect the Wrath of God, His "desire to punish" (I, 6), because the unjust cannot "merit" the justice owed to God, "and a sinner cannot justify a sinner" (I, 23). No member of Adam's race can restore the honor of God and satisfy His Justice. "None but God can make it, but none but man ought to make it," therefore, "it is necessary for the God-man to make it" (II, 6). Because He was sinless, His own death was not required; but if not required, then, it was voluntary; and if voluntary, the Sacrifice of Christ was meritorious and to excess; hence, His merit was counted by the Father as payment (lest He appear unjust) for the debt of all men's sins.[60]

---

[59] Rashdall, *The Idea of the Atonement*, p. 351.

[60] Vladimir Lossky describes Anselm's *Cur Deus Homo* as "the first attempt to develop the dogma of redemption apart from the rest of Christian teaching." He summarizes Anselm's theory as "a drama played between God, who is infinitely offended by sin, and man, who is unable to satisfy the impossible demands of a vindictive justice... the Son of God, Who has...become man in order to substitute Himself for us and to pay our debt to the divine justice" ("Redemption and Deification," p. 99). Lossky is mistaken on several counts.

First, although "the dogma of redemption" was *examined* by   (continued on next page)

Anselm's understanding of "redemption" followed naturally from his theology, a theology which, incidentally, will continue to influence, in this and other matters, Latin and Protestant doctrines. Like Anselm, Christ's Atonement for them has never ceased to orbit about the concept of *iustitia Dei*.[61] The idea of "justice" had changed from the time that Plato and Cicero first tried to decipher it, a change which was a reflection of their cultures. In the theology of the Latin Middle Ages and beyond, *iustitia* was a juridical category.[62] Therefore, *Cur Deus Homo*[63] was implicitly as much a disquisition on the nature of law as it was on soteriology. No wonder that the Archbishop of Canterbury argued that if God acted by His Compassion only the divine Justice would be canceled, for Compassion alone must treat "the guilty and the not guilty alike" (I, 13)—a conclusion which Anselm reached on the basis of human logic, or, more precisely, on the basis of a Germanic understanding of justice. Therefore, "the divine Honor" with Its demand for satisfaction is the imposition of "the feudal ethic" upon the divine Economy.

The false idea of the Redemption falls with the fallacious idea of God it presupposes; and a fallacious idea of God leads to an erroneous christology, to "a Nestorian diremption" of His Personhood.[64] Anselm cannot conceive of God Himself laying upon the Cross—especially since it is man who must pay the penalty—not even to saying that God "suffered in the flesh, not through the flesh." He preferred, "the life of *that man* (my italics) Jesus is more precious than everything that is not God"; and, "*that man* did not succumb to any compelling force..."; "the Father by His command did not com-

---

(cont'd.) Anselm apart from the rest of Christian teaching, it was nevertheless "developed" consistent with the spirit and doctrine of the new Latin theology. Second, the God of Anselm is not "vindictive." His justice is retributive. Out of His Mercy, He sent His Son to die voluntarily for Adam and his offspring, "to free us from our sins, from His own Wrath, from hell, and from the power of the devil" (*CDH* I, 6, 8).

61 McGrath, A. E., *Justitia Dei: A History of the Christian Doctrine of Justification* (vol. 1): *From the Beginnings to 1500*. Cambridge (Eng.), 1986, pp. 51-70.

62 *Ibid.*, p. 53f.

63 J. McIntyre (*St Anselm and his Critics: A Reinterpretation of the Cur Deus Homo*. Edinburgh, 1954) insists that anything of importance in Anselm's argument can survive the removal of every trace of feudal imagery and the supposed contamination of his Atonement theory by elements of German law. "The *Cur Deus Homo*," writes R.W. Southern, "was the product of a feudal and monastic world on the eve of a great transformation" (*St Anselm...*, p. 222).

64 "Anselm wished to trace back everything to satisfaction, and adhered strictly to the Augustinian theory that it was the man Jesus alone who lay on the Cross," wrote Adolph von Harnack. "Yet, Anselm could not reconcile such a notion with the doctrine of the two natures: Christ is the *man* whose life has infinite value... When Anselm now continues to use the two-nature doctrine as a hallowed tradition, a quite Nestorian dirimention of the Person is the result..." (*History of Dogma* [vol. 6]. Trans. by W. M. Gilchrist. Oxford, 1899, p. 74).

pel *that man* to die..."; "*that man* redeemed all other men when what He freely gave to God, God reckoned for the debt they owed."[65] If there is no mention here of deification as the end of Redemption, it is because Anselm's christology makes no place for it.

The Augustinian "Christ" of Anselm is not the Christ Who became man that man might become a God. He is the God-man Who for "necessary reasons" was part of a legal transaction by which Christ as sinful man's Surrogate was punished on the Cross to restore the offended honor of God. There is no talk of the devil, the grave or deification, only satisfying the divine Justice for man or "paying the price for" him (vicarius atonement). The benefit to man is the restoration of the promises God made to Adam, that is, to be rational and holy that man might enjoy God forever (*CDH* II, 1). On the contrary, the Fathers teach that the purpose of Christ's Redemption is deification; His "ransom" was an act of Love and Mercy; indeed, of condescension. Christ went to His voluntary death to "conquer death" and negate the obstacle to man's and the whole creation's becoming "partakers of the divine nature"(II Pet. 1:4). By Grace, the creature becomes immortal as the Creator is Immortal, sinless as He is Sinless, incorrupt in body and soul as He is Incorruptible.

This universal teaching of the ancient Church on Christian soteriology has largely been forgotten or misunderstood by the post-Orthodox West. Salvation is deification (*theosis*), "to partake of the divine Nature" (II Pet. 1:4), that is, a "participation" in an immortality which is the property of God alone (I Tim. 6:16); and comes to man through Christ alone (II Tim. 1:10). In Christ, the Son of God by nature, the saved become incorruptible and sinless, fundamental characteristics of immortality (Rom. 2:2; I Cor. 15:53-54). If immortality (hence, eternal life) belongs to God alone, how does man inherit it? The creature cannot obtain from the Creator what is peculiar to His Nature.

The Fathers give the answer: the divine Energies or Operations.[66] The uncreated and incommunicable Essence of God remains forever beyond any human or angelic knowledge or direct experience, but His Energies are com-

---

[65] "A Meditation on Human Redemption," in *Anselm of Canterbury* (vol. 1). Ed. & trans. by J. Hopkins and H. Richardson. New York, 1974, pp. 137-144.

[66] See St Irenaeus, *Adv. Haer.* V, pref. PG 7 1120; St Hippolytus of Rome, *Ref. Omn. Haer.* X, 2-30 PG 16 3442C-3445A; St Athanasius, *De Incarn. Verbi*, 54 PG 25 12B; St Gregory of Nyssa, *Ora. Cat.* XXV PG 45 65D; St Gregory the Theologian, *Ep. CI Cled.* PG 37 184A; St John Chrysostom, *Comm. on Rom.*, hom. XV (8:28); St Cyril of Alexandria, *Ep. I Monach. Aeg.* PG 77 21A; St Maximus the Confessor, *Ad Thal.*, 60 PG 0 21Ab; St Hilary of Poitier, *De Trin.* II, 24 PL 10 66B; St Ambrose of Milan, *De Sacr. Incar. Dom.*, IV, 23 PL 85B; St Peter Chrysologus, *Serm. LXVII* PL 52 81AB; St Maxim of Turin, *Serm. C1*, 3 ACW; St Leo the Great, *Serm. XXV*, 5 PL 54 211C; St Ephraim the Syrian, *Paradise Hymns* XII, 15-18, etc.; also Tertullian, *Adv. Marcion* II, 27. Cf. Ps. 82:6; and John 10:34.

municable. Man shares in the divine Immortality by the Grace of Jesus Christ in the Holy Spirit. They receive this Grace who have been incorporated into Christ, that is, the Church, thus becoming sons of God by grace.[67]

Deification is an historical process which began in the Church, the Body of Christ, with the coming of the Holy Spirit. The ascended Christ, His humanity deified, is the prototype of the saved. With His return, all things, which have not been consigned to hell, shall enter wholly into the Divine Life. In the Age to Come, the Church shall have evolved into the eternal Kingdom, with Christ as King. Grace will not merely perfect nature, it will transfigure it. Through His Uncreated Energies, God shall absorb the creature as "the sponge soaks up water" (St John Kronstadt).

In this world, Baptism is the initiation into the Divine Life, the Life of the Spirit Who dwells in the Orthodox Church. She is filled with His Grace, which is acquired by the individual through the true Faith, the Mysteries (especially, the Eucharist), struggle with the passions, and the whole life of piety. "The end of the life of virtue is to become like God," writes St Gregory of Nyssa (Beat. 1 PG 44 1200C). Necessarily, then, monasticism, is the surest way to that end. In a word, the Orthodox Church defines salvation as deification.

The change in this basic understanding of Christian soteriology began with Augustine, although early in his career he had followed the Tradition of the Church. "Christ," he said, "was first made a partaker of our mortality. However, He was made mortal, not of His Substance, but of ours. Thus, we are made immortal, not of our substance but of His. . ." (*Ennar. in Ps. CXLVI,* 11 PL 106-107). Later, he modified his view, declaring that "we are made gods by [created] grace, not of God's Substance" (*ibid.,* XLIX, 2 565). As the term "adoption" was commonly associated with the idea of salvation in Augustine's works, many historians hold that he had always understood deification to mean simply "the fully realized images of the Trinity in us through our bond with the God-man."[68]

Augustine, writes J. Burnaby, shrinks from using the language of deification, despite his Neo-Platonism. His idea of it was no more than the "cleaving to the eternal Creator whereby we shall be invested (*officiamur*) with eternity." "The superiority of his understanding lies in the conviction, first that 'cleaving to God' must be the personal union of love, and, second, that the union of love is neither the cause nor effect of a transformation of

67 A. Kalomiros, "The River of Fire," in *Saint Nectarios Orthodox Conference* [22-25 July 180]. Seattle, 103-134.

68 B. McGinn, *The Foundations of Mysticism [vol. 1]: The Presence of God: A History of Western Christian Mysticism.* New York, 11, p. 251.

human nature but is itself that transformation."[69] Yet others maintain that Augustine held a doctrine of deification in common with the Fathers.[70]

Numerous quotes can be drawn from his writings, as Bonner does, to prove his contention, but Augustine's idea of deification gradually became ambiguous, and almost superfluous in the last decade of his life. He left for the Latin Middle Ages the problem of created grace in relation to uncreated grace, especially in connection with deification. Obviously, a created grace cannot deify; but, if salvation is deification, of what ultimate purpose is created grace (*gratia creata*) in the divine Economy? And if, as Augustine and his tradition see it, uncreated grace (*gratia uncreata*) is incommunicable, how is man saved? These questions generated a number of interesting answers, especially among medieval mystics. To this day, Protestantism[71] is silent, having developed its own "Biblical" soteriology, while Roman Catholic theology has been unable to resolve the issue.[72]

E   Peter Abelard's version of medieval Nestorianism, more radical than his predecessor, had similar consequences.[73] He took the Anselmian "revolution" in another direction. By offering medieval theology an alternative to the Archbishop's "objective view" of Christ's Death, he described the subjective and moral effects of the Cross. He replaced the theory of satisfaction with the notion of human merit as the necessary component in salvation. His christology, of course, determined his view of the Redemption; or, per-

---

[69] *Amor Dei.* New York, 138, p. 17.

[70] G. Bonner, "Augustine's Conception of Deification," *The Journal of Theological Studies* XXXVII, 2 (186), 36-386).

[71] E. Huenemann, Foreward to J.J. Allen's *Inner Way: Eastern Christian Spiritual Direction*. Grand Rapids, 14, xiv. See also "Grace" in *Sacramenti Mundi* [vol. 2]. Ed. by K. Rahner. New York, 1968, 409-424).

[72] Christos Yannaras observes that the "problem" of deification in Roman Catholic Theology could be solved with the distinction between the divine Essence and Uncreated Energies. Clinging to its theology of the "divine Simplicity," however, there is no place for deification. At least, from the time of Aquinas, Roman Catholicism has explained God's relation to the world in terms of His "active essence" which means that either deification must be viewed as participation in the divine Essence (which it cannot do) or it must provide a new and innovative definition (which it has attempted) of deification ("The Distinction Between Essence and Energies and Its Importance for Theology," *St Vladimir's Theological Quarterly* XIX, 4 [1975], 232-245).

[73] "When he (Abelard) speaks of the Trinity," maintained Bernard of Clairvaux, "he sounds like Arius, of Grace like Pelagius, of the Person of Christ he writes like Nestorius"—*cum de Trinitate loquitur, saput Arium; cum de gratia, saput Pelagium, cum de de persona Christi scripsit Nestorium* (*Ep.* CXCII PL 182 358D-359A). As an historical note, it is not surprising that the Ecumenical Council of Ephesus, recognizing their kinship, condemned both Pelagianism and Nestorianism.

haps, the reverse is true. In any case, he denied both the "ransom" and the "satisfaction theories," as Rashdall remarks, because he saw them as "unintelligible, arbitrary, illogical, and immoral."[74] First, he adamantly rejected the idea that "the doctrines of faith" could be established in the way promoted by Anselm, that is, by reason constructing the "objective necessity" of Christ's Death. He refused to believe that the true God is either "deceptive" or "vengeful." Instead, he nominated Love as the sole motive for the Atonement; and, therefore, "merit" as the only human response to the divine overture.

Abelard supposed that the purpose and cause of the Incarnation to be the illumination of the world with God's Wisdom to the end that humanity would love Him and be saved. For this reason, too, Christ mounted the Cross, that is, not in order to release the believer from sin and the devil, but as the exemplary of love whereby our response in love and faith warrants "the adoption as a son of God," "the possession of liberty," and "redirection of the will."[75] To be justified by Christ's Blood means, then, to become loving. He died to display His Love for us. The efficacy of Christ's Death, then, is explained entirely by its subjective influence upon the soul of the sinner.

Abelard, as we have already implied, came to this vision of the Redemption or Atonement largely at the expense of traditional christology.[76] True, he affirmed that none could be reconciled to God without Christ; and he claimed to uphold the doctrine that the Savior consisted of two Natures and one Person, yet beyond these concessions his conception of the Atonement had no basis in Tradition. He set forth his teachings with a number of metaphors which confirmed not Abelard's "orthodoxy," but an essentially flawed "Nestorian" christology; for example, the Divinity of Christ is joined to His humanity like "a sprig from an oak tree" or "the branch of a fig tree"; or Christ's humanity as a "covering" in which the Son of God is clothed, a "tabernacle" which the Divinity inhabits.

Like Augustine, he commonly testified to Christ as a man *assumptus a Deo*, although, again, with slightly different results from the same premise. Abelard was reluctant to speak boldly and clearly of the humanity of God

---

[74] Rashall, *The Idea of Antonement...*, p. 360.

[75] See P.L. Williams, *The Moral Philosophy of Peter Abelard*. Lanham (Md.), 1980, pp. 163-169.

[76] Abelard "stressed the exemplary purpose of the Incarnation and Crucifixion at the expense of the redemptive," David Knowles insists, "and minimized the conception of original sin, regarding it as a penalty rather than a stain; and regarding Grace as an assistance rather than as an enablement. He claimed to react against all legalistic interpretations, such as the opinion that the Blood of Christ was a discharge of the rights of the devil over mankind" (*The Evolution of Medieval Thought*, p. 127). See also, A.V. Murray, *Abelard and St Bernard: A Study in Twelfth Century Modernism*. New York, 1967, pp. 61-70.

the Son, even less than Augustine. "He was born of the flesh in such a way that He was ignorant of the flesh's weakness," Abelard remarked; "and so He was in the flesh as if not in it, as if dead in it while totally in the spirit. . ." —*quasi in caro; et tanquam mortua in carne, et tota vivens in spiritu* (*Serm.* II PL 178 390A). "It is fitting," he said, that the divine Logos, in Whom are situated the Ideas by which He created the world, should don human flesh like a garment in order to manifest His Wisdom to men. Since men learn through the senses, "it is fitting that Christ became visible to them. And He became man and thereby illuminates our dark shadows and exhibits by word and example the fullness of all virtues"—*nostras illuminans tenebras tam verbis quam exemplis, omnium nobis plenitudem virtutum exhiberet* (*Serm.* II 396B).

F   After Anselm and Abelard, neither the Schoolmen nor the Reformers introduced anything substantially new into "the theology of the Atonement."[77] The theory of the Crucifixion as "satisfaction," however, passed into the history of dogma together with the idea of "substitutionary atonement," that is, the doctrine that Christ "endured for us those sufferings which we deserved to suffer in consequence of the sin of our first parents," as Thomas Aquinas wrote in chapter 228 of his *Compendium of Theology*. He accepted "without any fault of His own the punishment charged against us." Thomas, however, listed "satisfaction" as one of many reasons for Christ's Sacrifice on the Cross (cf. ch. 231). "By His Passion," he wrote, "Christ not only made sufficient but also superabundant satisfaction for the sins of the human race"—*et ideo passio Christi non solum sufficiens, sed etiam superabundans satisfactio fuit pro peccatis humani generis* (*S. T.* IIIa, q. 48 a. 1).

But Thomas was not entirely comfortable with Anselm's explanation. He fully admitted that giving satisfaction to God by the death of Christ is the most suitable course (*condigna*), but one which required further elucidation. He was annoyed by the supposition that the Atonement was the arbitrary Will of God, as a perspective from which the whole value of Christ's sacrifice on the Cross ought to be regarded. According to Anselm, as we saw, satisfaction was understood as a condition for the forgiveness of sins, a condition which, on account of the nature of God, produces infinite consequences and, therefore, demands that reparation to divine Honor must be infinite, a payment finite man must but cannot make; hence the Incarnation.

---

[77] The Reformers argued for a direct relationship between the Atonement and St Paul's doctrine of Justification (See Rashdall, *ib.*, p. 397f); and A.C., Clifford, *Atonement and Justification: English Evangelical Theology, 1640-1790: An Evaluation.* Oxford, 1990; and H. Anderson, ed., *Justification By Faith: Luthern and Catholics in Dialogue VII.* Minneapolis, 1985; C.B. Moss, *The Christian Faith: An Introduction to Dogmatic Theology.* London, 1954, pp. 179-203. See the next chapter.

Thomas contended that even if the offense of man were infinite in its magnitude, it could not fit the description of an infinite crime; and, therefore, God is wholly within His rights to overlook it, or even to demand a satisfaction appointed by Himself rather than some law of parity which even the Divine ought to follow. Aquinas nevertheless agreed with Anselm that satisfaction should be "acceptable" to God; hence, the Incarnation (*S.T.* IIIa. q. 48 a. 2). But Thomas wanted to show a necessary connection (as Anselm failed to do) between the God-Man as One Who gave satisfaction while, simultaneously involving man in his own redemption (II Cor. 5:14), particularly the Church of which He is the Head (q. 49 a. 1).

In other terms, God the Son, freely condescending to put on flesh, to voluntarily endure the Cross, to satisfy the offended Majesty of God, acquired merit for Himself as one Man Who died for all. "If anyone," Thomas asserted, "out of a just will deprive himself of what he was naturally entitled to possess, he then deserves that something should be superadded to him as the reward of his voluntary sacrifice. But Christ, in His Passion, humbled Himself beneath His dignity, whereby by His Passion He merited exaltation" (*ib.*, a. 6). In addition, Christ received Grace not merely as an individual, but as Head of the Church, whereby grace might be imputed to His Own. He merited salvation for them. United to Jesus Christ Who fulfilled the demands of "absolute justice" (*simpliciter iustitia*), His members are raised to a certain parity with God by virtue of which suitable reward follows the merit (*meritum de condigno*).

As Thomas was dissatisfied with speculations of Anselm and Abelard, so were other Schoolmen dissatisfied with them all. Like Thomas, Duns Scotus (1265-1308) designated the free choice of God as cause in the saving work of the Cross; but he also found in his predecessors, among other things, a lack of precision. Aquinas allowed that sin is a turning away from the eternal to a changeable good, which, as an act of the creature, is necessarily finite. This was the major flaw in the doctrine of satisfaction of which Thomas failed to divest himself: he was willing to admit that in sin an injury was done to the divine Honor which gave to it a certain infinitude. Dun Scotus rejected the idea of sin as infinite in its consequences: "If you say that sin is infinite, and intend thereby to maintain that evil, according to the very idea of it, is intrinsically infinite, then, that is untrue; for in such a case, it would be necessary to assume a supreme evil and a Manichean God" (*Comm. in Sent.* III, dist. xix, q. 1, sec. 13 OO). Indeed, sin against God is graver than sin against any other being, but we may not infer, as Anselm said, that man's sin against God necessitates infinite reparation (*ib.*, sec. 14).

Duns Scotus chose to look at The Atonement with an unusual view of merit. Thomas had conceived of the essence of merit as marked by spontaneity and with the specific intention of honoring God which led to a legally produced objective equity between the Divine and the human. Against this conception of merit, however, Scotus set the moral subjective standard—*Meritum est alquid acceptum* (sec. 4). God accepts as meritorious any ethical act which has the intention of honoring Him. Thus, adding the standard of merit to the idea of sin as finite, Duns Scotus' could hold the opinion that the merit of Christ itself was finite, that is, His Passion was restricted entirely to His human nature. Therefore, if "the merit of Christ" is finite, it depends essentially on a principle which is finite, lest there be no merit at all; for merit can be attributed only to the created will, not the uncreated Will of God the Son.

If so, of what value was Christ's merit in respect to its sufficiency? How does a finite merit extend to all the elect, everywhere and always? Duns Scotus maintained that relative to His suffering and meriting, and with a reasonable regard to the God-Man Himself, God was able to accept His sacrifice as infinite, and He applied it to a finite number of persons. "But as is the number of those on behalf of whom God chose to accept that Passion, so great is the number of those for whom it is sufficient. Yet, according to the idea of the thing to be accepted, when regarded in itself, the work of Christ does not admit to being accepted by God on behalf of an infinite number, as it was not in itself infinite" (*Dist.* xix, q. 1 sec. 7). Scotus made his position clear that just as Christ's merit is limited in its effect, so must the efficacy of the Cross be limited as judgment upon sin and death.

Faithful to his premises, Duns carries his logic to its necessary conclusion: the Incarnation is restricted to the Church of the elect, i.e., composed of that number which God had predetermined from the first would be the recipients of Christ's merit. "As the election of the predestined before the Passion of Christ is foreseen as a means of saving them after their fall into sin, it follows that the whole Trinity chose the elect unto Grace and blessedness in view of the execution of this degree even prior to His prevision of the Passion as a means of salvation that was to be accepted on behalf of the elect who fell through Adam. . . . Wherefore, so far as the efficacy of His merit is concerned, Christ earned initial grace only for those who are predestined to eternal blessedness" (sec. 6).

ᕼ   In the Latin Middle Ages, a Christ born to die, sacrificing Himself to satisfy the demands of God's Justice and Honor, the Saviour was not always treated in an objective way. The Reformers, while accepting medieval ideas of the Atonement, were far more concerned with the effect of Christ's sacrifice on the individual believer. For Luther the Cross was a demonstration of God's Wrath on humanity: "All men are under God's Wrath and subject to eternal damnation." "God has found a remedy for this evil. He determined to send His Son into the world, that He might become a sacrifice for us and make satisfaction for our sins by the shedding of His Blood and death, thereby removing from us the Wrath which no creature could assuage" (WA [bd. XXI], 358, 34). "He had to take our place and become a sacrifice for us, bearing and placating the Wrath under which we had fallen. Christ "appeased God's anger and made payment for us...a satisfaction for our sins" (*ib.*, 363, 14).[78] His merits are then imputed to the predestined.

According to Martin Luther, Christ is the Mediator between God and man—although he rarely delineates the christological reasoning which qualifies the Lord for this role—which means that He is One Who has "canceled all of God's Wrath and Displeasure, making our hearts sure of His Paternal Grace and Love. For how could He still be angry with us and wish to damn us when He has given His only Son so earnest a command to empty Himself of all His divine Glory and Power, and for our sakes to cast them under the feet of the devil and death" (XXI, 477, 25). Recalling the rest of Luther's theology, we are reminded that the divine Mercy is ultimately restricted to the "elect," those Christians who are forensically justified by (subjective) faith and Grace alone, that is, those Who by His Secret Counsel God has predestined from all eternity to salvation.

Luther's idea of salvation as the one-sided and gratuitous act of the Father (monergistic) was translated by Calvin into his central doctrine: God's absolute Sovereignty and, therefore, the "absolute necessity" of the Cross whose effects flow to the saved (*Inst. Chr. Rel.* II, xii, 1 B). Although Luther seems to have held that Christ died for the world (rescuing only a few), Calvin, with greater consistency, maintained that He suffered for those predestined to Glory: salvation is "limited" to those Whom God has "unconditionally" elected, the "saints" whose "perseverance" in faith to the end of their lives is guaranteed by God's "irresistible grace," that is, those whom God by His inscrutable and just decree has chosen from all eternity for everlasting joy. The God of Calvin (and Luther) is Augustine's God "Whose will of necessity must come to pass, as those things which He has foreseen will surely come to pass" (*ib.*, IV, xxiii, 8; Cf. Augustine, *De corr. et grat.*, XI, 14 PL 44 924), even as those who have been predestined to damnation.

Calvin and Luther differ with some of their Protestant contemporaries—and many of the second generation Reformers—on the question of predestination (among other things), but there seems to be little disagreement among them on the nature of the Atonement as a divine act of retributive jus-

---

[78] Anselm's concept of *iustitia Dei*, upon which his theory of the Atonement was built, is rooted in the theology of Augustine. Likewise, Luther described himself as an Augustinian and heir of a dogmatic tradition in which "a strict idea of *iustitia Dei* was paramount." Luther seems to have gone "far beyond Anslem; yet, they have Augustine in common relative to 'the Justice of God'" (I.D.K., Siggins, *Martin Luther's Doctrine of Christ.* New Haven, 1970, p. 134).

tice.[79] From all that has been said, therefore, we may legitimately speak of a continuity in the historical development of Atonement ideology, whether in its Anselmian, Abelardian, Thomistic or Scotist form. For all their talk about "re-forming" the Church by rediscovering the pure Gospel, Luther, Calvin and Zwingli were the theological progeny of the Middle Ages. If they differed in any way from their medieval benefactors, they were far more concerned with the subjective dimensions—albeit far less with the moral aspect—of the Redemption, a concern which demanded a new ecclesiology.

H   Metropolitan Anthony Khrapovitsky, the modern Russian Orthodox spokesman, opposed the heterodox theory of the Atonement (and its implications) for sundry and fundamental reasons. From a strictly historical point of view, the theory is not traditional. The ideas of "satisfaction" and "merit" are found neither in the Scriptures nor among the Fathers, but belong to "feudal ethics," he writes, such as the "satisfaction" paid to a knight for his injured honor. Again, the notion that "the Son of God obtained mankind's forgiveness from the wrathful Creator Who received satisfaction from the shedding of the Blood and the Death of His Son...is the most unpersuasive sophism, a mere juggling of words."[80] St Anthony might have called such a doctrine of the Redemption "grotesque."

Moreover, the Crucifixion as vicarious punishment has no support from Scriptural typology, argued Metropolitan Anthony. If the animal sacrifices of Old Israel are types of Christ's Sacrifice on the Cross, as indeed they are, there is no evidence that the animal victims were punished. Rather they provided a meal, which explains the addition of flour, oil and salt to it. "They were sacrifices for sin, but the immolation of the animal here was the same as that which accompanied all priestly actions, as in a peace-offering, although there were also some completely bloodless sacrifices of various grains. It follows," he concludes, "that in the eyes of the people of the Old Testament a sacrifice meant a contribution..."; so was it with the Passion of Christ. His Blood was a pure gift to God, not the result of punishment, nor a "sacrifice to justice."[81] In other words, the Savior was not our substitute for the Cross, He was not punished in man's place to appease the Vengeance of God, nor was He the Mediator of merit. Christ on the Cross was the representative of the human race before the Father, offering Him a new and purified humanity and cosmos by His Sacrifice.

---

79   The Reformers, if not Western Christendom as a whole, regarded God as a Judge; in fact, His "primary attribute" seems to have been "retributive justice" (Aulen, *Christus Victor*, p. 127).

80   Rashdall, *ibid.*, pp. 438-443.

81   *The Dogma of Redemption*. Trans. by Holy Transfiguration Monastery. Montreal, 1979, p. 6.

5   J<small>USTIFICATION</small>

Given this testimony about the Cross, we must expect a radically different understanding of justification and sanctification in the christology of the Fathers than is found in the heretical West.

Baptism is the Mystery of Justification (δικαιοσύνη).[82] The Mystery is the remission of sins and rebirth, among other things: the water of redemption, the water of sanctification, the purification of flesh and spirit, the loosing of bonds, the remission of sins, the illumination of the soul, the laver of regeneration, the renewal of the spirit, the gift of adoption to sonship, the garment of incorruption, the fountain of life.

Thus, the declaration of the bishop or presbyter after the anointing with chrism of the newly-Baptized,

> Thou art justified. Thou art illumined. Thou art sanctified. Thou art washed in the Name of the Father, and of the Son, and of the Holy Spirit (Cf. I Cor. 6:11).

Chrismation, the second stage in our regeneration, is the reception of the Holy Spirit, the beginning to the process of holiness or sanctification (ἁγιωσύνη) whose end is perfection or, more precisely, deification.[83] In other words, baptized into Christ, the image in which Adam was created is revitalized. Human nature, in body, soul and spirit, is reclaimed from the devil. The same image in which man was created, is now recreated. So, as Adam received the Holy Spirit and became a "living soul" (Gen. 2:7 LXX), He returns to us (having once been lost by the sin of Adam) in the Mystery of Chrismation. He dwells in the Savior as in a Temple; and he who is incorporated into the Church, the Body of Christ, hears the same words spoken to the Apostles, "Receive the Holy Spirit" (John 20:22); mayhaps, words heard by Adam. In other terms, justification comes by union with Christ, with His Body, the visible, historical Church, through which God is realizing a New Covenant with His People.

---

82 For example, this illustrative passage from St Paul: "Therefore by the deeds of the Law there shall no flesh be justified (δικαιωθήσεται) in His sight, for the Law is the knowledge of sin. But now the Righteousness of God (δικαιοσύνης Θεοῦ) without the Law is manifested, being witnessed by the Law and the Prophets; even the Righteousness (δικαιοσύνη) of God which is by the Faith of Jesus Christ to all who believe; for there is no difference: all have sinned and come short of the glory of God. Being justified by the gift of Grace through the Redemption that is Christ Jesus Whom God hath set forth to be a propitiation through the Faith in His Blood, to declare His Righteousness (δικαιοσύνη)..." (Rom. 3:20-25)

83 McGrath comes to an interesting conclusion relative to justification. "The Orthodox stress on the immediacy of the divine, and the direct encounter of man with the Holy Spirit, naturally leads to this encounter being expressed in terms of deification" (*Iustitia Dei* [vol. 1], p. 3).

Luther's description of "justification" as "the article by which the Church stands or falls"—*articulus stantis et cadentis ecclesia*—fatally distorts the Biblical teaching of justification, with his suggestion that it does not bring the Christian a real participation in Christ, but rather only through "faith" places him in an juridical relationship by which God declares him to be "innocent."[84] The Reformer was wrong to separate spiritual renewal from regeneration in the life of the Church and, therefore, equally wrong to deny that Baptism (and Chrismation) to be the theanthropic vehicle of his transference in the Spirit from the state of sin to the state of righteousness.

A   For Luther and the other Reformers, justification is a legal or forensic idea, wherein God forgives the believer in Christ despite the inexpungible nature of sin. Metropolitan Anthony Khrapovitsky maintained that the Protestant view of justification is nowhere to be found in the epistles of St Paul. The Apostle does not conceive it as denoting merely "a state in which one is released from the curse laid upon Adam," nor does it carry the implication "that personal sanctity will not bring a man to the Kingdom of Heaven… .In the New Testament, and especially in Saint Paul, the term 'justification' does not have such a specific meaning [as the Protestants give it]; it means rather 'righteousness,' that is, blamelessness, dispassion, virtue. This is the translation of the Greek δικαιοσύνη…has in every instance a moral, not a juridical signification, the latter being expressed by the word, δίκη."[85]

The Saint's argument presupposes what we have already said about the initiatory rites of the Church. Her doctrine is corroborated by the holy Scriptures. The oldest meaning of the word justification or righteousness (*sedaqa* in Hebrew) bears the connotation of "victory" (Judges 5:1-31). Ancient Juda-

---

[84]   "Forensic imputation" is a legal concept. "To impute" is a translation of the Greek λογίζεσθαι which means the mercy of God which allows, as Gerhard Kittel states, to the righteous "the full achievement of right in faith" ("*Dikaiosyne*", *Theological Dictionary of the New Testament* [vol. 2]. Trans. & ed. by G.W. Bromiley. Grand Rapids, 1973, p. 207). Justification or righteousness (δικαιοσύνη) is the Grace which is imputed; but, as Gerhard Kittel observed, both "to impute" (λογίζεσθαι) and "to justify" in the epistles of St Paul are "only figures for being righteous before God." The forensic (therefore, the legal) element ought not to be pressed. "We are not now in the sphere of human jurisprudence. The legal aspect must be transposed at once into a divine key," he emphasizes. Paul's use of the legal concepts introduces the truth that God acts not capriciously, but according to "His holy norms, with the covenant and with the true right" (*Ib.*, p. 205).

[85]   *The Dogma of Redemption*, p. 43. The fact that *dikaiosyne*. (δικαιοσύνη) was first used by Aristotle in reference to the Greek *political community* (πόλις) before its appropriation by the Septuagint translators, is not evidence, as McGrath suggests, that "the sphere of *dikaiosyne*..has no immediate practical significance" for "the righteousness of God" (*Iustitia Dei* [vol. 1], p. 10); and, therefore, none to "the City of God," the Church. But the word would seem to fit their purpose exactly.

ism associated God's Righteousness with defense of Israel; hence, the word falls within the framework of "covenant"; or indeed in the context of marriage: when God and Israel mutually fulfill their covenant obligations to each other, a state of Righteousness is said to exist. Israel's conquest in war was a manifestation of their mutual fidelity. God delivers an obedient people from its plight. In a word, righteousness or *sedaqa* (impossible to translate as "justice," as some would like) has strong "soteriological overtones."[86] In some Old Testament verses, "righteousness" and "salvation" are equated. "I will bring my *sedaqa* (δικαιοσύνη) near; it is not far away. And my salvation (σωτηρία) shall not be delayed (Is. 46:15; 56:1 LXX). The two terms, then, are premised on a covenant relationship (Ex. 19:5-6; I Pet. 2:5-10) which patently suggests that human righteousness or justification is collective.

To be a righteous man (*hasdiq* in Hebrew, δίκαιος in Greek), then, requires *koinonia* or fellowship with God the Son under the Old Covenant, and with Christ, the Incarnate Lord, in the New Covenant: the *communio sanctorum*. To be justified, then, is union with Christ and his covenanted People. They have a common destiny with Him by virtue of their identification with the Lord's Passion and Resurrection acquired through incorporation into the very Body which suffered on the Cross and rose from the dead.

Some non-Orthodox Biblical scholars are willing to describe the union of Christ and His People as "mystical," a relationship, they say, is clearly shown in St Paul (Gal. 2:16-21; 3:26-29). Others insist that the "mystical imagery" of St Paul, like the "legal imagery" linked with it, was merely his way to express the activity of the Holy Spirit in fulfilling the work of justification.[87] Their interpretation of the Apostle's words depends on their understanding of Christ (and the Church), His nature and mission, something nowhere better manifested than in the Nestorian ecclesiology of the Reformers.

B   The Protestant theory of justification is taken not from the Scriptures, but from the discussion of the topic in the late Middle Ages, a milieu in

---

86   McGrath, *ib.*, p. 8. Luther identified justification with salvation. He conceived it as "an act of Christ. . . He, or God through Him, makes righteous. Justification by faith alone is the same as by Grace alone, by God's *agape* alone. The Christ who justifies is the risen and living Lord. He acts through the means of Grace, the Word and the Sacraments" (G. Aulen, *Reformation and Catholicity*. Trans. by E.H. Wahlstrom. Philadelphia, 1961, p. 60). One may wonder how a Nestorian Christ justifies (and, therefore, saves) with a subjective faith, created grace, an invisible Church with "Sacraments" consecrated without a historical priesthood. On the christological implications of Lutheran ecclesiology, see T. Sartory, *Die oikumenische Bewegung und die Einheit der Kirche*. Augsburg, 1955; and Y. Congar, *Vraie et fausse réforme dans l Église*. Paris, 1950).

87   Kittel (vol. 2), *ib.*, p. 209f.

which the thinking of theologians and philosophers was characterized by dialectic and disputation. In some respects, they were able to draw upon the works of Augustine (in this case, his anthropology), the single greatest authority on all religious matters in the post-Orthodox West. Of particular interest to both the Schoolmen and Reformers, was the Bishop's reaction to the idea of "free will" (*liberum arbitrium*, αὐτεξουσία) as employed by the British heretic, Pelagius.[88] He and his disciples held that man is essentially good; in fact, he believed that the individual could be sinless—*Ego dico posse esse hominem sine peccato* (in Augustine, *De nat. et grat.*, 8 PL 44 251). If man is unable to freely acquire perfection, he said, all the commandments which God has given to that end are pointless. And if he has not the liberty to realize this imperative, all human actions are emptied of moral purpose. Therefore, all men, believers or not, have the power of choice or free will.[89]

Pelagius had thus set the tone of the debate. Augustine replied that men are sinners, corrupted by original and actual sin, without the free will to choose between good and evil unless our nature was first healed by Grace. His reflections on the book of Romans led the Bishop of Hippo to the conclusion that Grace reestablishes free will. To the believer, faith is given, along with the Grace which draws him irresistibly to Christ and to the freedom which that relationship affords. Thus, all human righteousness, all the good works which emerge from it, are but the power of divine Grace on human choice and action, a theory summarized in Augustine's famous maxim, "when God crowns our merits, He crowns nothing but His own gifts"—*cum Deus coronat merita nostra, nihil aliud coronat quam munera sua* (*Ep.* 194, v, 19 PL 33 830).

---

[88] McGrath argues that if the Fathers before Augustine had little to say about justification, they had even less interest, little understanding, of matters such as predestination, Grace and free will, and subjects directly related to it. He explains the lack of interest and understanding on the part of the early Fathers as the consequence of "their neglect of Pauline writings which may reflect uncertainty concerning the extent of the NT canon" (*loc. cit.*). McGrath's theorizing shows a deplorable ignorance of the Fathers. There was no official canon until the fourth century. The letters of St Ignatius of Antioch, for example, have much in common with the writings of St Paul.

[89] Augustine was the first Christian writer to limit genuine free will to the elect. "The pre-Augustinian theological tradition is practically of one voice in asserting the freedom of the human will," writes McGrath (*Iustitia Dei* [vol. 1], p. 20). He adds that it is "with the Latin Fathers that we observe the beginnings of speculation on the nature and origin of sin and corruption, and the implications which this may have for man's moral faculties" (*Ib.*, p. 19). McGarth does not mention a single Latin Church Father. In any case, there is universal consensus in the Church on the nature and origin of sin and corruption, from the very beginning. (See my *The Influence of Augustine of Hippo...*, pp. 73-127).

In other words, man has no freedom to independently "initiate faith" (*initium fidei*), nor make any appeal to God for Grace, nor to contribute anything to his salvation. God alone justifies or elects the individual who then is able to cooperate with God in the process of his sanctification. (Here Calvin agrees with Augustine, while Luther does not.) "Prevenient Grace" or the Grace by which God prepares man's will for the reception of faith and justification, according to the Bishop of Hippo, involves Baptism. Most Reformers denied that the Sacrament incorporates the believer into the Church, erasing the original and all other sins, and reviled the notion that Baptism leads to his sanctification through the other Sacraments of the Church, especially the Eucharist. The Reformers disagreed, because nothing of the visible Church guarantees salvation. As Luther insisted, justification (God's imputation of "innocence") is the only certainty. Differing with this theory, Calvin described the Grace of "sanctification" and "perseverance of the saints" as the only promise of election. In any case, for Luther or Calvin, predestination finally is the cause of salvation. If the individual contributes nothing to his salvation, there is single will (monergism, monotheletism) that accounts for it, the divine Will.

⊂   The Latin Fathers condemned Pelagius for his reduction of salvation to self-justification and Grace to an external moral influence. They opposed Augustine who offered no role to man's will in the destiny of both those who will suffer damnation and those who shall enjoy the eternal blessings of salvation. The Latin Fathers (Sts John Cassian, Vincent of Lerins, Faustus of Riez, Gennadius of Marseilles, Jerome, Gregory of Tours, etc.) had no sympathy with Augustinianism, finding in his theology, as N.P. Williams noted, that God "not merely provides the opportunity of starting us on the road to salvation, but operates in man the very willingness to accept the opportunity, so that not the faintest and most elementary beginning of man's Godward aspiration rises from himself, nor any other source except the arbitrarily bestowed and irresistible Grace of God."[90]

In deliberate opposition to Augustine, John Cassian wrote that "these two, namely, Grace and free will, although seemingly in conflict, in fact are complementary, something which may be concluded from the very nature of rational piety. Were we to draw one way or the other, we would appear to abandon the Faith of the Church" (*Concl.* XIII, 1 NPNF). Prosper of Aquitaine characterized St John and the other Fathers as "the remains of Pelagianism" (*reliquiae Pelagianorum*), for two reasons: believing that the individual, corrupt and rebellious, was capable of taking the initiative in his own

---

[90]   *The Grace of God*. London, 1930, p. 49.

salvation; and also for repudiating Augustine's doctrine of predestination which, of course, is unavoidable when man is saved by irresistible Grace alone. Not until the sixteenth century will these antagonists of Augustine be called "semi-Pelagians." The subsequent victory of Augustine over his opponents was initially the successful campaign by his African, Spanish and Frankish disciples. They circulated his works, lobbied to put his name onto the local ecclesiastical calendar, and erected several frescoes in his honor.

On account of their efforts, one would suspect that the history of Augustinianism had an easy launching; it did not, especially not his theory of "justification." A number of factors conspired to generate considerable confusion about it. First, the West was slow to surrender its "semi-Pelagian" soteriology. Second, as the history of doctrine shows, no council, not even Orange II (529) nor Valence (530) which endorsed Augustine's "predestination to glory," provided subsequent medieval theology with a clear and definitive statement concerning his teaching on justification. Thirdly, many pseudo-Augustinian treatises were circulated with ideas which had more in common with the "semi-Pelagianism" of St Jerome and St Faustus of Riez than with monergism of Augustine. Finally, Pelagius' works were sometimes attributed to the Bishop of Hippo, such as the *Libellus fide* which contained the popular maxim, "If you are not predestined, endeavor to be predestined"—*si non es praedestinatus, fac ut praedestineris*.

D An important controversy over predestination (hence, justification) erupted during the Carolingian era. Gottschalk of Obrais championed Augustine's doctrine of double predestination (*praedestinatio gemina)*, the logical consequence, he argued, of Augustine's theory of Grace. His interpretation was challenged by John Scotus Eriugena, Prudentius of Troyes, and by Gottschalk's most implacable enemy, the remarkable Hincmar, Bishop of Rheims, who found most offensive his notion that "the necessity of salvation has been imposed upon those who have been saved, and the necessity of damnation upon those who perish" (*De praed.*, 26 PL 125 270B). Such a soteriology blatantly denied the reality of human free will, which Hincmar asserted to be real, even if weakened by the Fall. Gottschalk's heresy, he said, amounted to a contradiction of Augustine's genuine teaching in which predestination and foreknowledge are distinguished, so that "the Blood of Christ redeemed the whole world"—*Sanguis Christi est redemptio totius mundi* (*ib.*, 32 309B)—not merely the elect. But Gottschalk replied that it was Hincmar (who on this point did, in fact, cite the pseudo-Augustinian treatise, *Hypognosticum*), that had misrepresented Augustine.

For some reason, the debate on predestination and its relation to justification was not continued into the next centuries. The statement of Pope Leo

IX (1049-1054) seemed to have settled the matter—"I believe and profess that the Grace of God precedes and follows the free will of the rational creature without compromising it"—*Gratiam Dei prevenire et subsequi credo et profiteor, ita tamen ut liberatum arbitrium creaturae non denigem.*[91] The formula was Augustinian with its reference to prevenient grace and a rehabilitated free will which now freely cooperates with sanctifying grace of God. Curiously, the Pope did not employ the word predestination; although, it may have been presupposed.

With no indifference or defiance intended toward the Pope's declaration, Anselm undertook to reconcile the opposition between predestination and free will. In his *De concordia Praescientiae et Praedestinationis et Gratiae Dei cum Libero Arbitrio*, he argued no contradiction exists between predestination and free will. The human will is relatively free even before it came under the influence of Grace. Man, though fallen, had not lost completely the power to choose the good; however, this remnant of Edenic freedom did not provide him with the ability to achieve his spiritual ends or attain salvation. Faith and Grace are required: God alone justifies through Christ, that is to say, only God has the power to restore man to his proper place in the created hierarchy of being, thereby recovering the Justice of the divine order which had been lost to a rebellious humanity.

Not everyone was consoled by Anselm's treatment of justification. Not only did he fail to pay sufficient attention to its ethical dimensions, as Abelard complained, but Anselm was not systematic. He left too many questions unanswered about the human complement, such as the broader and more general problems about the connection between justification and the Church, or justification and the Sacrament. Also unanswered are the very practical issues about Baptism and Penance in their relation to justification, especially with regard to infants. Incapable of rational acts, how can they participate in the Sacrament? Thus, if Bernard of Clairvaux is right that infants are justified by the faith of Mother Church—*iustitia fidei matris ecclesiae* (*Trac. de bapt.* II, 9 PL 182 1037D)—there remains the puzzle of the effect of the Sacraments on those who, like children, have no faith.

The response of the twelfth century theologian, Alan of Lille was not uncommon: children are infused with grace by their Baptism (*virtus fidei in habitu*), which will be manifested (*virtus fidei in actu*) when the infant reaches maturity and is capable of rational choice.[92] Important to the understanding of this distinction was the introduction of the Aristotelian concept of *habitus*, a concept which foreshadowed the dominance of "the Philoso-

---

[91] Quoted in McGrath, p. 211.

[92] *Ibid.*, pp. 92f.

pher" in medieval thought. As *habitus* referred to a condition of the soul, it became an idea which provoked new interest in the subjective appropriation of justification which the theory of infused Grace had raised.

Justification was seen as the change in the believer from what he was into what God actualizes in him. It was generally described as the "initial grace" through which man is translated (*potentia*) from a corrupt *nature* to a condition of habitual *Grace* which neatly corresponded to his crucial distinction between the natural virtue of justice and the supernatural justice infused by God as the basis on which man is justified. In this process, Duns Scotus showed more interest in the purpose of the human will than did Aquinas. Duns was a voluntarist, that is, "the will, by commanding the intellect, is a superior cause in respect of its act."[93] Justification, then, begins with the will which, after all, is primarily responsible for sin and, when revitalized by Grace, plays the principal part in the final beatitude of the elect for whom alone Christ died.

Scotus' voluntarism sparked the thinking of the Nominalist, William of Occam—the teacher of Gabriel Biel, the teacher of Luther. Justification, in the view of Occam and his school, centered on the connection between Grace and merit. Occam saw no conflict in the proposition that good works merit eternal life if wrought by the cooperation of the human will with Grace, a union which brings it into full accordance with the Justice of God. Such a scheme was not inconsistent with Occam's doctrine that the divine Freedom and Sovereignty is the criterion of all righteousness,[94] the Power by which He wills and performs everything righteously. For the omnipotent divine Will, being bound by nothing, is the Good which determines the nature of all good.

E   In part, the Protestant Reformation was a reaction to the medieval theories of justification; and, in part, the movement was the heir to Latin Catholicism, using Scholastic concepts, language and its principles of Biblical exegesis. The Reformers hoped to establish their soteriology on the wholly Augustinian premise that the justified person does not owe his position before God to, nor receive assurance of salvation from, good works. Justification comes by the absolute gratuity of divine Grace through faith alone which, like Grace, is given by God completely on the basis of His ineffable decision to save in Christ those persons whom He has elected from all

---

93   Copelston, F., *A History of Philosophy* (vol. 2 , pt. 2): *Albert the Great to Duns Scotus.* Garden City (NY), 1962, p. 263.

94   The theological question was asked in the Middle Ages, whether something was good because God ordained it, or did God ordain it because it was good? Voluntarists, such as Scotus and Occam, favored the former.

eternity.[95] Yet no matter how they conceived justification and its relation to sanctification, merit or "works righteousness," the result of human cooperation with the Divine, was always proclaimed alien to the Biblical soteriology. The elect are justified by Christ's Righteousness and not by the "church" or sacraments or indulgences, not by the works of the Law, "for by the works of the law shall no flesh be justified" (Rom. 3:20).

It was surely the position of the Reformers, conscious or not, that Christ died only for the elect, for the predestined, who belong to "the true Church" (*abscondita ecclesia*) hidden within the manifold of historical denominations. The elect, scattered among them, are justified by the Righteousness of Christ imputed to them by God; and, in the case of Calvinism, they are justified by the sanctification which comes to the elect by virtue of their predestination to Christ, a relationship through which man's faith is effectual unto good works. Yet, whatever the Reform sect, the word "relationship" by Grace and/or by faith is never clearly defined, save as something which relies wholly on God's arbitrary selection.

It is a doctrine based on a crucial error, whether in classical monergistic Protestantism or in its Pelagian liberal form: an erroneous christology[96] which is inferred from its false doctrine of the Church. An ecclesiology which denies the visible, organic continuity of the earthly Church is, at best Nestorian, at worse, docetic. Necessarily, then, salvation is salvation of the individual whose election requires no necessary connection with the historical ecclesial community. The Grace by which he is saved comes to him directly, a gift of faith. The faith comes to the Christian from God without human cooperation. He has no role to play in the divine Economy. Obedience to the Law cannot save him, neither good works achieved through Grace. The Holy Spirit unconditionally produces justification and sanctification in him who is compelled to believe.

---

[95] See Ritschl, *A Critical History...*, p. 92f.

[96] Gustave Aulen says that Luther never made any statement to the effect that Christ's humanity had "a secondary significance" (*Reformation...*, p. 69); but if he is silent on this matter, the rest of his theology speaks loudly enough, especially Luther's denial of the true Church as temporal and visible.

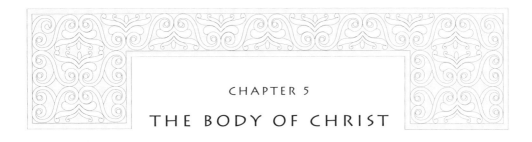

CHAPTER 5

THE BODY OF CHRIST

The Christian Church was founded by Jesus Christ, in the city of Jerusalem, during the third decade of the common era. Christianity is a "new covenant" or "testament" (διαθήκη) between God and the People called by His Name. This "covenant" or "pact" was realized not through the blood of lambs and goats, but on Calvary's Cross. Moreover, the Church was never a Jewish sect, a theory propagated by some modern theologians and historians. Her connection with Judaism was as shadow to reality. "For Christianity did not believe on Judaism," announced St Ignatius of Antioch, "but Judaism on Christianity" (*Ad Magn.*, 10 FC). The *raison d'être* of God's old testament People was the preparation of the world for the coming of the Messiah, "the Son of Man" Who was born of them. The destruction of Jerusalem and its Temple by the Roman legions (70 AD) marked the historic end of the old covenant.

Christianity was not the privilege of a single nation, but divinely and uniquely revealed to become the religion of both Jews and Gentiles, of every nationality and race. As the Lord said to the Apostles, "Go ye therefore, and teach all nations, baptizing them in the Name of the Father, and of the Son and of the Holy Spirit: teaching them to observe all things whatsoever I have commanded you; and lo I am with you even to end of the age. Amen"— πορευθέντες οὖν μαθητεύσατε πάντα τὰ ἔθνη, βαπτίζοντες αὐτοὺς εἰς τὸ ὄνομα τοῦ Πατρὸς καὶ τοῦ Υἱοῦ καὶ τοῦ Ἁγίου Πνεύματος, διδάσκοντες αὐτοὺς τηρεῖν πάντα ὅσα ἐνετειλάμην ὑμῖν; καὶ ἰδοὺ, ἐγὼ μεθ᾽ ὑμῶν εἰμι πάσας τὰς ἡμέρας ἕως τῆς συντελίας τοῦ αἰῶνος. Ἀμήν. (Matt. 28: 19-20).

This commission of the Lord, among other things, authorized the Apostles to continue His ministry, to spread His Gospel to "all nations." When their time was fulfilled, the Apostles left their work to appointed successors whose task was the same—to permeate the world with the Gospel, with the "good news" of the "new covenant": the inauguration of a heavenly Kingdom established in His Body and Blood, a People or Church to which the Apostles (and the Prophets) are the "foundation," "Jesus Christ Himself the chief cornerstone" (Matt. 16:18; Eph. 2:20; 3:5; Rev. 18:20).

As the Lord's command implies, the great "mysteries" of Baptism and of the Trinity are basic to the divine message. Baptism, because it is the beginning of a new Life, the formation of the "new creature," fit for the life of the eternal Kingdom; citizenship papers, as it were, for the divine Life with God, the holy Trinity, which is the Life in Christ in His risen Body, the Church. She is the beginning of God's Kingdom, in which, for which and by which the "new covenant" was effectuated. She is, therefore, the organic union of those who "call upon the Name of the Lord" in "spirit and in truth" (John 4:23; Acts 2:21; Rom. 10:13; 4:24-25). It was to her "saints" that the saving Faith was once delivered. To cite St Peter Chrysologus, "He believes God who professes the Holy Church unto God" (*Sermo* LVII PL 52 360C).

In other terms, if the God of Abraham is the one true God, if He became incarnate to reconcile the creation to Him through the "new covenant" of His Body, there is only "one Faith, one Lord, one Baptism" of the one Church. Not a single "jot or title" of what He revealed to her through the Apostles is subject to alteration, indifference or rejection. Error in the teachings which Christ "traditioned" to her is an act of infidelity, a form of idolatry, a negation of the "new covenant," a perversion of the "gospel" preached to us, worthy of *anathema* (Gal. 1:8); a violation of the immutable Truth, a negation, perversion and violation called "heresy" by the Scriptures and the Fathers. The true Faith is a confession of the true God, a witness to the presence of the Holy Spirit in Christ's Church, to the Scriptures He inspired, to the Mysteries which He perfects, to the inspired wisdom of the Fathers, to the authority of the Canons, to the promises of the Age to Come.

1   THE ONE CHURCH

"There is one body, and one Spirit, even as you are called in one hope of your calling," St Paul declares, "one Lord, one Faith, one Baptism, one God and Father of all, Who is above all, through all, and in you all" (Eph. 4:4-6). From this and other verses in the Scriptures, from the Fathers and the Creed, it is evident that Christ established one Church. Although this Ephesian verse does not use of the word "Church," but rather "body," it points unmistakably to "the Body of Christ" which is the Church, His only Spouse (Eph. 5:31-32). "For the husband is the head of the wife, even as Christ is the head of the Church; and He is the Savior of the Body" (Eph. 5:23).

Christ is "joined" ("adheres," "clings" or "sticks to" = προσκολληθήσεται) to her as if they were "one flesh."[1] He is the Bridegroom, the Head, she the

---

[1]   Eph. 1:32. The Church is described everywhere in the Scriptures in candidly physical terms—"body," "temple," "woman," "city," etc., but also with Greek prepositions as prefixes, such as σύν (con, in Latin) e.g, *"I am co-crucified with Christ"*—Χριστῷ συνεσταύρωμαι *(Gal. 2:20); "we are co-heirs with Christ"*—συγκληρονόμοι δὲ Χριστοῦ *(Rom.*

Bride, the pneumo-physical Body. Their unity is such, to use the words of St John Chrysostom, that "where the head (ἡ κεφαλή) is, there is the body (τὸ σῶμα). No interval divides them; for were there any separation, then, there is no longer a head, no longer a body" (*In Ep. ad Eph.* III, 1 PG 62 26). They are "one Man" (Rom. 5:15) and, consequently, the Church is, as Christ Himself, τὸ μυστήριον μέγα, *sacramentum magnum* (Eph. 5:32), the "complement" (πλήρωμα)[2] or "the many" gathered under His Headship (ἀνακεφαλαιώσασθαι). She is the very augmentation of His humanity to which His Divinity is united. Inasmuch as Christ has re-collected all things to Himself, whether in the heavens or on earth, His Headship extends to everything visible and invisible.

Moreover, His Headship is not limited to the present, for the Savior is "Alpha and Omega, the first and the last, the beginning and the ending, saith the Lord, which is, and which was and which is come, the Almighty" (Rev. 1:8). As Maker, He created everything good; as Savior, He recreates them for the everlasting Good, for all existence has been put under His feet, given to Him "to be the head over all things to the Church, which is His Body, the fullness of Him that fills all in all"—καὶ αὐτὸν ἔδωκε κεφαλὴν ὑπὲρ πάντα τῇ ἐκκλησίᾳ, ἥτις ἐστί τὸ σῶμα αὐτοῦ, τὸ πλήρωμα τοῦ τὰ πάντα ἐν πᾶσι πληρουμένου (Eph. 1:22-23). To be sure, He is not only Head of the human race, but of the angels, "of all principality and power" (Col. 2: 10), and all creation for the Church (1:16).

Thus, "the holy Church," as St Gregory the Great observed, "has two lives: one in time and the other in eternity" (*In Ezech.* II, 10 PL 76 1060). Yet, her existence antedates the creation of the visible world, "an assembly of angels" her first members. With the formation of Adam, the Church entered the history of the world through Paradise; and, even with the fall of man, St John Chrysostom remarked, the life of the Church was extended though God's covenant with Abraham and later with Moses and the Chosen People; and finally she was incarnate in Christ Jesus (*Ep. ad Eph.* X, 1 PG 62 75), for which reason the Church is much more than "the sign and instrument of the Lord's saving activity" (Vatican II, *Lumen Gentium*, 48 [26 Nov 64]). As the

---

8:17), etc; or in Latin, *Christo confixus...coheredes autem Christi*. Such language would be nonsense if the Church were not visible. What, indeed, is an invisible body? See E. Mersch, *The Whole Christ*. Trans. by J.R. Kelly. London, 1956, pp. 128-131, 309-313.

2   A troublesome word, τὸ πλήρωμα ("completion," "complement," "fullness") refers to the Church, and therefore to Christ Himself with Whom she is forever united. But the Church involves more than Christ and his human members, as Fr Florovsky stated ("The Catholicity of the Church," in *Bible, Church, Tradition: An Eastern Orthodox View* [vol. 1]. Belmont [Mass.], 1972, pp. 37-55). She encompasses the angels and the seven heavens which God created. The *to pleroma* is growing even now, wholly realized only in the Age to Come (See St Gregory of Nyssa, *In illud: Tunc ipse Fil. subj.* PG 44 1317D-1320A).

theanthropic society, she is the ontological epiphany in the present of the
past and for the future.

But the future is *now*, the Age to Come has invaded the present course
of time in the Church and her Mysteries. She is, as St Gregory the Theologian testifies, "a single race of angels and men" (*Ora*. XXXI, 13 PG 36 229).
She is already "the city of the living God, the heavenly Jerusalem, and to an
innumerable company of angels, to the general assembly and church of the
firstborn" (Heb. 12:22-23). The Orthodox Church is "the abiding city" (Heb.
13:14) which her children possess and continue to seek. As St John Chrysostom said, "The Church is the heavenly Jerusalem, our Mother" (*Ep. ad Gal.*
IV, 4 PG 61 662).

This mystery of the Church presupposes a christology of no lesser paradox. If God became Man to regain what was lost by Adam, to "recapitulate"
Adam's progeny, as St Paul and the Fathers tell us, then, He is not only "one"
but "many." He is the Church, His Body, into which the "many" have been
incorporated. Members of the Church are of His human Substance, even as
the progeny of Adam spring from his loins. Thus, the Protestant dictum, "the
Church is born of the word of God" (*Ecclesia nata est ex Dei verbo*) is correct if
verbo is the divine Truth; and if "the word is born of the Church" (*verbo nata
est ex ecclesia*), that is, if the written or spoken word of Truth exists for the
Church, for everyone born of and for the Word, the Incarnate Lord, becoming a little "word" in Him, born of "Spirit and the water" (Jn. 3:5), of Baptism.

A   The Church is one *ecclesia de Christo*, as we have seen, but also *ecclesia de
Trinitate*. She is an image of the Triune God. As St Cyril of Alexandria says,

"Since we all receive within us the one Spirit, the Holy Spirit, so
we are 'mingled,' as it were, with one another in God, even as the
Persons of the Father, Son and Holy Spirit, individually indwell the
Other. For, although each member of the Church is distinct from one
another, yet the Spirit, one and indivisible, joins our many distinct
spirits into His own unity...one body and one Spirit, as also you were
called in one hope of your calling: one Lord, one Faith, one Baptism:
one God and father of all, Who is above all and through all (Eph. 4:3-
6). And, truly, if the one Spirit abides in all of us, then the one Father
of all will be God within us, and through Christ He willing brings into
a permanent unity all those who are partakers of His Spirit" (*Com. in
John*. XI, 11 PG 74 561).

Commenting on the same subject, St Anthony (Khrapovitsky) writes that the
life of the Church—hidden from a world divided by sin, only "prefigured by
the Old Testament"—is an icon of the divine Unity. Father, Son and Holy
Spirit are Three Persons in one Essence, "so that there are not three Gods, but
a single God, living a single life." She is, therefore, "a likeness of the Trinitarian existence, a likeness in which many personalities become a single exis-

tence."[3] In other terms, as the Trinity has many Persons, but is one God, so the Church, to use the words of St Paul, "is one, and hath many members, and all the members of that one body, being many, are one body; so also is Christ" (I Cor. 12:12).

B   Roman Catholicism seems not to have developed the ecclesiological implication of the *filioque*. Perhaps, so fundamental is this doctrine to its theology that it never occurred to the heterodox that its triadology demanded ecclesiological justification. The heresy of the *filioque*, nevertheless, is a necessary component of any doctrine of the Roman Church, that is, as the Spirit proceeds from the Son, and the Pope is the "living image of Christ," so He must proceed from the Pope into the Church, the Body of Christ—in a sense, the Pontiff's body—the laity becoming the *so-called catholica passiva*. The people receives the Spirit and His *charismata* from the *catholica activa*, the Pope and the priestly magisterium which are his tentacles. In Orthodoxy, the Spirit, "blowing where it lists" (Jn 3:8), descends upon the whole People of God, sent by Christ to indwell the Temple of His Body, not merely the teaching office, as implied by the *filioque*. He may be acquired by all, whether bishop or presbyter, lay or monastic, male or female, for all are the sons and daughters of the Father through the regeneration of Baptism.

This active role of the Orthodox layman is, of course, not the laicism of classical Protestantism in which each person, is his own "pope," his own "Spirit-bearer," as the result of his denial of the organic visibility of the true Church. Protestantism, therefore, views the peregrinations of the Spirit in this world only in terms of His personal relationship to individual believers or, more exactly, to the "saved," the "elect," those who by "faith in Christ" have been passively justified[4] by the Holy Spirit *sola* (monergism), passively receiving from Him Grace *sola*, passively guided in his understanding of the Scriptures by the Spirit *sola—testimonium spiritus sancti internim*—for the invisible Church *sola*. Thus, does the docetic Protestant idea of "the priesthood of believers" express not only a heretical ecclesiology, but also its theology of the *filioque* relative to its idea of the Church.

But this ecclesiology has not only triadological, but christological implication. Denying the visibility of the historical Church is a denial of the Incarnation, for the Church is His Body; but also its view of salvation by the divine Will alone is a form of monotheletism. An important proof-text of Protestant apologetics is Romans 8:28-29—"And we know that all things work together (πάντα συνέργει) for good to them that love God, to them who

---

3   "The Moral Aspect of the Dogma of the Church," trans. by V. Novakshonoff, in *Synaxis: Orthodox Christian Theology in the Twentieth Century*. Chilliwack (BC), 1976, pp. 8-10.

4   See Chapter IV, sec. 5.

are called according to *His* purpose (κατὰ πρόθεσιν). For whom He did fore-know, He also did predestinate *to be* confirmed to the image of His Son." We know that Augustine made these verses an argument for predestination (*Contra Jul.* V, iv 14 PL 44 792-793). In chapters eight of their commentaries on the book of Romans, both Calvin and Luther, reaffirm the Bishop of Hippo's belief in "election" as "the certainty of salvation," that is, predestination.

Like Augustine, they argue that the phrase "according to (His) purpose," has no other meaning, to use the words of Calvin, than "to distinctly exclude" anything men imagine they could contribute to their salvation, a false pride that would void the Biblical doctrine of "our election. . .by the secret good pleasure of God." "Who are called according to His purpose," Luther concurs, refers only to God's purpose, to "His predestination, or His free election, or His eternal counsel" to save some and reprobate others, as in the case of Isaac and Ishmael, Jacob and Essau (Rom. 9:8-15). They have no doubt that the Scriptures everywhere certify God's "eternal election" and anyone who opposes the doctrine revolts against the truth. Those who oppose predestination possess a "wisdom of the flesh."

Such a reproach must fall on the Fathers whose exegesis of Romans has little in common with the thinking of the Reformers. As we have seen already, they understand predestination, whether to eternal life or condemnation, in terms of individual cooperation with God's Grace. The phrase κατὰ πρόθεσιν was translated by the Reformers "according to *His* (God's) purpose." The Fathers understood and interpreted the text without interpolating *His*. The "purpose" here, as is clear from the context is our salvation. A man's destiny depends upon his "purpose," whether he identifies it with the divine Purpose (synergy). As St Cyril of Alexandria asserts, "The elect are chosen according to purpose, the purpose of Him Who calls as well as he who is called" (*Comm. in Ep. ad Rom.* VIII PG 74 829B; cf. St John Chrysostom, *Comm. in Ep. ad Rom.* XV, 1 PG 60 541).

The "purpose" of God is to save the world by joining all creatures to Christ where men receive the Holy Spirit. The "purpose" of men is to be renewed and transformed by the Third Person of the holy Trinity. "This means," St Seraphim of Sarov tells N. A. Motovilov, "that the Grace of the Holy Spirit which is granted at Baptism in the Name of the Father and the Son and the Holy Spirit, in spite of the fall of men into sin, in spite of the darkness surrounding our souls, nevertheless shines in the heart with the divine Light. . .which after the sinner's conversion to the path of repentance completely effaces any trace of past sin and clothes the former sinner once more with the robe of incorruption spun from the Grace of the Holy Spirit whose acquisition is the very aim of the Christian life."[5]

---

5   *Conversation of St Seraphim of Sarov with N.A. Motovilov.* Jordanville (NY). 1962, p. 17.

Salvation is not solitary, not without the Spirit and not without other members of the Church. The Church is a society, "the communion of the saints." He who is saved is saved with those who have the same "purpose," who share the same theanthropic life. They are united to God the Father in Christ through the Holy Spirit. God's design is to bring human race back into fellowship with Himself, not merely as individuals but as His family. "The adoption of sons" is the result of incorporation into the Son of God. Oneness with Christ is accomplished by Baptism (Rom. 6:3-12) whereby the Spirit is "sent forth into your hearts, crying, Abba Father. So that you are no longer a slave (δοῦλος), but a son, and if a son, then, an heir of God through Christ" (Gal. 4:4-8); or, as St Paul wrote elsewhere, the baptized are "children of God...heirs of God, and joint-heirs (συνκληρονόμοι) with Christ, that the Faithful might suffer with Him (συμπάσχομεν) and so be glorified together (συνδοξασθῶμεν) with Him" (Rom. 8:17).

Thus, God is inseparable from His Church now and in the Age to Come. To be outside the indivisible Church, the historico-eternal Body of Christ, is to be without the "adoption of sons," spiritual rebirth, new creaturehood, the "acquisition of the Spirit," without any possibility of deification, predestined to eternal darkness without light. Such is the meaning of the famous expression, *Extra ecclesiam nulla salus.* There is no salvation outside the Church of Christ, "because the Church is salvation."[6]

C   The Church is "one," "holy," "catholic" and "apostolic." We know that she is "one" and "holy" for reasons to which we have already alluded. Her oneness is the oneness in the Faith, of the Apostolic Tradition. She is the icon of the Trinity. The Spirit is the unique Source of her unity. On account of all these things, we may add that her unity is an organic or substantial unity— *homoousios*—not a mere *esprit de corps*, nor a simple moral union. Moreover, she is holy because the Spirit of God inhabits the Body of Christ; in a word, she is the work of God and "the Lord is holy in all His works" (Ps. 144:17). She exists for "the perfecting of the saints" or "holy ones" (Eph. 4: 12-13).[7] She is a "holy nation" (Ex. 19:6; II Pet. 2:9), whatever may be the sins of her earthly children.

---

6   Florovsky, "The Catholicity of the Church," pp. 37-38.

7   The "saints" (ἅγιοι, *sancti*) are all the members of the Church here and beyond. They form one community, for which reason the Church is sometimes called "the communion of the saints" (*communio sanctorum*, κοινονία ἁγίων). A "saint" is someone who is "called out" (from the verb ἐκκαλέω=ἐκκλησία) to be "holy" and "perfect." Therefore, the word does not carry an exclusively moral sense. In the divine Liturgy, the priest exclaims, "holy things (τὰ ἅγια, *sancta*) to the holy ones (τοῖς ἁγίοις, *sancti*)," that is, to the baptized, to those eligible for Holy Communion, as St Neketas of Remesiana explains (*Expl. of Creed*, 10 PL 51 771). The Saints (capital S) are extraordinary Christians.

The Church is "catholic," because Her Head is God Incarnate. The religion of God is the religion to which every man ought to adhere, for God is the Creator of all, the One to Whom each human being owes obedience and worship. Necessarily, then, "she is spread throughout the world, from one end to the other," St Cyril of Jerusalem exclaims, "...and she teaches universally and completely all the doctrines which mankind ought to know concerning things visible and invisible, heavenly and earthly...she subjects all men to piety...and because she comprehensively treats and heals every kind of sin committed by soul or body, while possessing in herself every virtue which may be named, whether of deed or word, and of every kind of spiritual gift" (*Catech*. XVIII, 23 PG 33 1044B).

Finally, the Orthodox Church is "apostolic," precisely because Christ is ὁ ἀπόστολος—and, indeed, the Holy Spirit is ὁ ἀπόστολος—that is, "the One sent" from God the Father; even as the Lord sent the Twelve and the Seventy Apostles (Jn. 20:21). "The Apostles received the Gospel for us from the Lord Jesus Christ," St Clement of Rome affirmed. "He was sent from God. Christ, therefore, is from God and the Apostles are from Christ" (*Ep. I ad Cor.*, 26 FC). Thus, the Faith of the Apostles is "sent" into the world with the Church, into the diversity of cultures, languages and races, carrying with her the command of the Lord Jesus, abiding always in the "the doctrine and *koinonia* of the Apostles" (Acts 2:42), under the guidance of the Holy Spirit. Thus, she is "apostolic," as we know, because the Church is "the household of God, built on the foundation of the apostles and prophets, Jesus Christ Himself the chief cornerstone" (Eph. 2:20). This one Church is "the Church of the living God, the pillar and ground of the truth" (I Tim. 3:15). She continues the work of the Apostles, a work that will only be completed when her Lord returns.

The Apostolic Faith she offers is "the doctrine of Christ" (Tit. 2:10). Nowhere in her life does she permit "anything contrary to sound doctrine" (I Tim. 1:10), lest "the Faith once delivered to the saints" (Jude 3) be lost, the world deceived, and mankind is once more "tossed to and fro, carried about with every wind of doctrine by the sleight of men" (Eph. 4:14). Since, as her Lord Himself, the Church is also "the way the life and the truth" (John 14:6), so is the Faith she teaches; and, since her Lord is "the same yesterday, today and forever" (Heb. 13:8), so is she, so is the Faith she teaches. She cannot be "carried about with diverse and strange doctrines" (Heb. 13:9).

The Faith of the one, holy, catholic and apostolic Church, the Orthodox Church is infallible. To quote St John of Damascus, "It is disastrous to suppose that the Church does not know God as He really is; that she has degenerated into idolatry, for if she declined one iota from perfection, it would be a blot on her unblemished Faith, destroying the beauty of the whole with that single wrinkle. Nothing is trivial when it leads to something great;

neither is it a small thing to overthrow any detail which belongs to ancient Tradition of the Church, which they defended who came before us. Let us rather imitate their way of life and observe the faith which they professed" (*De Imag.* I, 2 PG 94 1233B). In the words of the nineteenth century Russian Orthodox lay theologian, Alexei Khomiakov, "It is impossible that there should have been a time when she received error into her bosom" (*The Church Is One.* Seattle, 1979, p. 22).

Because "the Church is formed of one Faith, established by the one and only Holy Spirit," as St Epiphanius of Salamis declared (*Adv. Haer.* III, 11, 6 PG 42 781D), she is not only infallible but indefectible—"the gates of hades cannot prevail against her" (Matt. 16:18). She is the Body of Christ, uniting all creation, al things visible and invisible. Whatever her temporal imperfections, they are found among her earthly members who must be "sanctified in the truth" (John 17:17), acquire "the love born of God" (I John 4:7), overcome "the passions of the flesh which wage war against the soul" (I Pet. 2:11), whereby a steadfast Faithful "confirm their call and election" (II Pet. 2:11).

D   When St Paul proclaimed, "one Lord, one Faith, one Baptism, one God and Father of all"—εἷς Κύριος, μία πίστις, ἓν Βάπτισμα, εἷς θεὸς καὶ πατὴρ πάντων (Eph. 4:5-6)—he offered an ecclesiological formula whose elements are not only unalterable, interdependent, but unthinkable one without the other. Beneath the formula was the great Pauline theme of "the mystery of the Faith" (I Tim. 3:9), the ground from which the formula itself emerged and without which nothing else mattered, inasmuch as the participation in the "mystery" is the *sine qua non* of eternal life (Roman 10:9; I Tim. 3:16). Moreover, the Faith to which he refers is not merely "faith" as a subjective trust or commitment, but "the Faith once delivered to the saints," *the Faith* described in the gospels and epistles, elaborated by the hieratic and monastic Fathers; hence, not only a faith *in* Christ, but the Faith *of* Christ.

E   According to most modern historians and theologians, we have thus far drawn an ideal picture of the Church and her life. To the contrary, they insist that church history shows no unity of Faith, nothing but a divided Church which has augmented or depleted its stockpile of doctrine, laws and customs according to its need. History gives ample testimony to a Church torn by heresies and schisms, the incessant emergence of new sects and theologies, opposition between mysticism and dogmatism, and everywhere the naked tension between "tradition and progress." But more than this, it is argued, the Church as a temporal institution is part of history, and history demands that she must grow or perish, and, if Kenneth Scott Latourette is right, the Orthodox Church seems to have preferred the latter.

There is some truth in these objections. The Church has experienced tribulation and challenge, and she has changed externally—her rites, customs, missions, language, even the formulation of her dogma and Canons—but her Faith and spirituality cannot; for it is a condition which follows from the nature of the Incarnation which, although not opposed to the dynamics of history, supersedes them—as well as the foibles and ambition of men. The Church is, to be sure, a "coincidence of opposites" and will remain so until she enters the Age to Come when the Plan of God is fully and finally realized. Even heresies are necessary to that end (I Cor. 11:19; Gal. 5:20; II Pet. 2:1). The Church, in every age, must expect to confront evil in all its guises. Yet, it does not follow that the nature and mission of the Church will change or evil becomes part of the ecclesial fabric.

If St Paul is correct, if there is something which must be "approved," it is the divinely revealed Gospel which the Church is obligated to defend against the doubts of heretics and unbelievers. If, then, there is heterodoxy, there must be orthodoxy: the one is proof of the other. If the orthodoxy of the Church is not perpetual, her existence is meaningless; and if she is not infallible, it is pointless. Thus, St Cyprian of Carthage's description of the Church—"God is one, Christ is one, and His Church is one, and the Faith is one (*Deus unus est, et Christus unus, et una Ecclesia eius, et fides una*)—and the People are united in a substantial unity of body by the cement of concord. Unity cannot be severed; nor can one body be separated by a division of its structure. . ." (*De eccl. unit.*, 23 PL 4 534A). It follows that, "The spouse of Christ cannot be adulterous; she is uncorrupted and pure" (*ib.*, 6 519A).

We come to the conclusion, therefore, that the heretic or heterodox is outside the Church, either as one who has fallen away or avoids her unity. No one can belong invisibly who does not belong to Her visibly, because the Church is the Body of Christ, the extension of the Incarnation, in which the Divinity and humanity of the Lord Jesus is joined "without confusion or separation." There is no access to God save through the Humanity of Christ, His Orthodox Church. Salvation, or deification, occurs only in and through His theanthropic activity in cooperation with man's life of repentance. Only a Nestorian christology allows for a parallel between an infallible spiritual Church with no direct correspondence to a fallible visible Church.[8]

---

8   Augustine was the first great expositor of Nestorian ecclesiology in the West. As Harnack observed, for Augustine "the church is a concept narrower than Christianity." Holding this opinion, one could be in agreement with the aims of the Church while remaining outside of her (*The History of Dogma* [vol. 5], p. 166). To be sure, Augustine conceived the "will's accord" (*consensio volentatem*) with her as indispensable to salvation (ib., IV, xii, 17-24 170); but his "concord of the will" is, in truth, an "abstract thesis," says Archbishop Hilarion (Troitsky). Outside the "visible precincts" of the Church there are no Sacraments and "no salvation" which is not the position of Augustine (*Christianity or the Church*. Trans. by L. Puhalo & V. Navokshanoff. Jordanville [NY], 1971, p. 25).

With all confidence, it may be said that the Spirit-guided Church is ontologically one, visible, and indivisible. All heresy is alienation from the Spirit. "Within the Church, that is to say, within her members," writes Khomiakov, "false doctrine may be engendered, but then the infected members fall away, constituting a heresy or schism, and no longer defiles the sanctity of the Church" (*The Church Is One*, p. 20). Undoubtedly, none may pretend that all the Orthodox Faithful are cognizant of every doctrine and decision of the Fathers and Councils. But, on the one hand, membership in Christ is possible without overt faith (as in the case of infants); and, on the other, it is essential for adults to make a personal commitment to Orthodoxy with every intention to hold all the doctrines within her Tradition, despite their innocent ignorance, and whether they have the competence to explain or defend them.[9]

To hold the true Faith without belonging to Christ and His Church is meaningless, since the act of believing and the espousal of the Faith in which we are to believe has no efficacy outside the unity in Christ. So the contention "that both East and West have the same Scriptures, the same Fathers, the same tradition, and more recently, the same tools of historical research" is ecumenist reverie. The "real tragedy" is not the ostensible similarity between Orthodoxy and the sectarians, nor that from "this immense treasure of scriptural, traditional and sacramental realities, which we have in common, we draw conclusions that still clearly separate us,"[10] but that this irrelevance has so much currency. It is an idea which has foolishly drawn Orthodoxy and heterodoxy together.

St John Chrysostom reminds us of a simple truth. "For if...those men possess doctrine contrary to ours, on account of which we must not mix with them... If their Faith is the same as ours, why are they not with us? There is 'one Lord, one faith, one baptism.' If their cause is right (καλῶς), we are wrong (κακῶς); if we are right, they are wrong... In vain, then, has their altar been raised" (*In Ep. ad Eph.* IV, xi, 5 PG 62 86). As St Cyprian of Carthage declared, "Whoever is separated from the Church is joined to an adulteress and is separated from the promises of the Church. Neither can he who forsakes the Church of Christ attain to the rewards of Christ. He is a stranger; he is profane; he is an enemy. He can no longer have God as His Father, who has not the Church as his mother" (*De unit. Eccl.*, 6 PL 4 531A).

---

9   By virtue of the ecclesiastical "economy," any member of the Church, save children, may baptize an adult or infant in time of emergency. If there is no water, then, soil or air may be used. Martyrs are sometimes baptized in their own blood, or by desire. The classical case is the baptism by desire of the Emperor Valentinian II, the young pupil of St Ambrose, who was murdered before he came to the font (392).

10   J. Meyendorff, "Vatican II and Orthodox Theology in America," in *Vatican II: An Inter-faith Appraisal* (International Theological Conference. University of Notre Dame: 20-26 March 1966). Notre Dame, 1966, 611-612.

2   THE NEW EVE

The "old man," Adam, was fashioned on the sixth day of creation. But it was not until his expulsion from Paradise that the history of our world begins (see chapter 6). The Genesis narrative is also the promise of man's restoration to fellowship with God. The fulfillment of God's promise is foretold in types.

A   There is more to the Genesis typology than Christ as the "second Adam," the "tree" and the Cross. There is also a very important comparison between Eve and Mary. As the virgin Eve was born from Adam's side, so the Church was born from the side of the crucified Christ. "It is from His side, therefore, that Christ formed the Church, even as He formed Eve from the side of Adam...," wrote St John Chrysostom. "And so Moses, too, in his account of the first man, Adam, says: *Bone of my bone and flesh of my flesh* (Gen. 2:23), alluding to the Master's side. Just as God took the rib from Adam while he slept, so now He gave us blood and water after His Death... what was Adam's deep slumber was Christ's death, so that we may know that death is henceforth only a sleep" (*Bapt. Instr.* III, 17-18 ACW).

But there is something yet more interesting about the Genesis history, especially as the Fathers draw out the soteriological implications of its mariology. The Fathers contrast "the virgin Eve"—the first mother of the human race and wife of the first Adam—with the Virgin Mary, the progenitor of the second Adam, He Who was Himself the Creator of our first-parents. St Justin Martyr[11] observes "that He [Christ] was born of the Virgin so that the disobedience caused by the serpent might be destroyed in the same manner that it had originated. For Eve, an undefiled virgin, conceived the word of the serpent, and brought forth disobedience and death; but the Virgin Mary, filled with faith and joy, when the angel Gabriel announced to her the good tidings that the Spirit of the Lord would come upon her, and *the Power of the Most High would overshadow her*, and, therefore, the Holy One born of her would be the Son of God, replied: *Be it done to me according to thy word*" (*Dial. c Tryp.*, 100 PG 6 709D-712A).

---

[11]   The Greek Orthodox theologian, C.N. Tsirpanlis, echoes the usual scholarly opinion that the Eve/Mary typology "was introduced by Justin Martyr, and developed by Irenaeus..." (*Introduction to Eastern Patristic Thought and Orthodox Theology*. Collegeville [Minn.], 1991, p. 53). Tsirpanlis admits that this typology contains "profound soteriological significance," but wants us to believe that the primitive Church had to wait more than a hundred years to reach the same conclusion; or that the Lord (Luke 24:44) failed to instruct the Apostles in a doctrine with such "profound soteriology significance" (See J. Karmiris, "The Ecclesiology of the Three Hierarchs." Trans. by C. Cavarnos, *The Greek Orthodox Theological Review* VI, 2 [1960-61], 135-185).

The disobedient Eve, adds St Irenaeus, was deceived by a (fallen) angel, the obedient Mary "by angelic communication received the glad tidings of God to her who had exhibited obedience. Unlike Eve who was disobedient, the Virgin Mary was obedient that she might become the advocate for the virgin Eve. And thus, as the human race fell into death's bondage by means of one virgin, it was rescued by another" (*Adv. Haer.* V, xix, 1 PG 7 [2] 117B-1176A; cf. III, xxii, 4 PG 7 [1] 958N-960A). Also, opposing the virgins Eve and Mary, St Photius the Great commented, "Adam's daughter, having retrieved the transgression of the first mother, Eve, cleansing herself from the stain that emanated thence, fair and beautiful in the eyes of the Creator, pledges salvation to the human race" (*Hom. on Ann.* VII, 3; Mango).

B   Eve was the spouse of Adam and the mother of the human race, and the "woman" whose progeny was born under the curse of death. The Church is the spouse of Christ and mother of a new humanity, the "woman" whose progeny are born into the blessing of new life. To use another analogy, the Church is the new mother of mankind; indeed, "the Ark of salvation."[12] Not by accident, then, did St Cyprian proclaim, "He no longer has God as his father who has not the Church as his mother. As no one escaped the flood who was outside the Ark of Noah, so also none may escape [death] who is outside the Church"—*Habere iam non ptest Deum Patrem, qui Ecclesiam non habet matrem. Si potuit evadere quisquam qui extra arcam Noe fuit, et qui extra Ecclesiam foris fuerit evadit* (*De unit. Eccl.*, 6 531A).

The Ark of the Covenant is also the type of the Virgin Mary. The Orthodox Church praises her as "the Ark of God" during the Vespers of the Feast of the Falling Asleep of the Theotokos (Lity, Tone 5); and later in the Aposticha (Stichos, Tone 4) as "the Ark whom Thou hath sanctified." No wonder St Ambrose of Milan declared, "How beautiful are those things which have been prophesied of Mary under the figure of the Church"— *Quam pulchra etiam illa quae in figura Ecclesia de Maria propheta sunt* (*De Inst. Virg.* XIV, 89 PL 16 341B). If this true, if the Church is our mother, then, as St Cyril of Alexandria states, "The Ever-Virgin Mary is palpably the holy Church"—τὴν ἀειπάρθενον Μαρίαν, δηλονότι τὴν ἁγίαν Ἐκκλησίαν (*Hom. Div.* IV PG 77 996C).

---

12   St Peter was the first to use the typology of the Ark. "...the longsuffering of God waited until the days of Noah, while the ark was being fitted, wherein few, that is, eight souls (ὀκτὼ ψυχαί), were saved by water, the same antitype wherein now baptism saves us..." (I Pet. 3:20); and, "...spared not the old world, but saved (with seven others) Noah the eighth (ὄγδοον)..." (II Pet. 2:5). The Apostle links Noah (Christ), the ark (Church), water (Baptism), and "the mystical eight," as the Fathers call it, to denote salvation. "The economy of the Ark clearly typifies the saving eight," remarked St Irenaeus (*Adv. Haer.* I, xviii, 3 PG 7 [1] 645B).

Not without paradox, then, the Virgin Mother of Jesus is the Mother of God, *theotokos*;[13] but also as His Mother she is the Mother of all the Faithful, for He is "the first-born of many brethren"; and, they who have Christ as their Brother have Mary as their Mother. Through Baptism we join the divine fellowship, "the Virgin Church," our Mother. In the most explicit terms, St Ambrose asserts that Mary is "a type of the Church which, although wed, is immaculate, conceiving virginally [baptizes] by the Holy Spirit, begetting [sons] without travail"—*Bene deponsata, sed virgo, quia est Ecclesia typus, quae est immaculata, sed nupta. Concepit nos virgo de Spiritu, parit nos virgo sine gemitu* (*Exp. in Luc.* II, 7 PL 15 1635D-1636A).

Furthermore, as "the Second Eve" the Mother of God is the Church—hence, the new Israel; but she has other surprising titles. As St Ephraim the Syrian wrote,

> How shall I (Mary) call Thee a stranger to us, Who art from us? Should I call Thee Son? Should I call The Brother? Husband should I call Thee? Lord, should I call Thee, O Child that didst give Thy Mother a second birth from the waters? For I am your Sister, of the house of David, the father of us Both. Again, I am Thy Mother because of Thy conception, and Thy Bride[14] am I because of Thy sanctification, Thy Handmaid and Thy Daughter, from Thy Blood and Water wherewith Thou hast purchased me and baptized me.

> The Son of the Most High came and dwelt in me, and I became His Mother and by a second birth, I brought Him forth, so did He bring me forth by a second baptism. . . ."(*Hymns on the Nativity* XI NPNF).

C   The Scriptures of the Old Testament have numerous types which allude as much to the Mother of God as to the Church, which implies their identity. Thus, she has a connection with the ancient Patriarchs; for instance, Jacob is a figure of Christ and "Jacob's Ladder" (Gen. 28:11-17) is a type of the Virgin Mary through which God the Son descended to earth. "This (the Virgin Birth) is the descent of God. Wherefore, as is meet, thou dost hear, Rejoice, O full of Grace," the Church chants during the Matins in the feast of

---

[13] "It is truly meet to call holy Mary the Mother of God," affirms St John of Damascus. "For this name embraces the whole mystery of the economy. If she who bore Him is the Mother of God, assuredly He Who was born of her is God as well as man"—Ὅθεν δικαίως καὶ ἀληθῶς Θεοτόκον τὴν ἁγίαν Μαρίαν ὀνομάζομεν· τοῦτο γὰρ τὸ ὄνομα ἅπαν τὸ μυστήριον τῆς οἰκονομίας συνίστησι. Εἰ γὰρ Θεοτόκος ἡ γεννήσασα, πάντως Θεὸς ὁ ἐξ αὐτῆς γεννηθείς, πάντως δὲ καὶ ἄνθρωπος (*De Fid. Orth.* III, 12 PG 94 1029C).

[14] Further evidence that the Latin and Greek Fathers shared the same Tradition can be seen, for instance, in the doctrine of St Paulinus of Nola. "What a great mystery," he exclaimed, "that the Church is at once the Lord's bride and sister" (*Poems* XXV, 187 ACW).

the Annunciation (Ode 9). Likewise in the same Ode, her birth-giving of the Savior is typified in burning bush. "The burning bush did reveal to God-beholding Moses a wonderful miracle. And seeking the fufilment thereof with the passing of time, he cried, saying, I shall behold her who is a spot-less Maiden, who shall be addressed with rejoicing as the Theotokos. Rejoice, O full of Grace, the Lord is with thee."

At the same time, she is foreseen as the New Israel in the dream of Joseph the All-comely (Gen. 37:9) wherein the sun, the moon and eleven stars bow before him. This, of course, is a type of Christ Who will reconstitute Israel with twelve Apostles; but also a figure of the Church (hence, the Virgin Mary) which St John the Theologian sketches in the twelfth chapter of Revelation—the portent of "a woman clothed with the sun, with the moon under her feet and a crown of twelve stars on her head."[15] The reason for equating the Theotokos with the New Israel follows naturally from the Presence of God in Old Israel, albeit He dwelt within her in a far more intimate way. His presence in the Ever-Virgin Mary is prefigured by God's presence "in the womb, in thine inward parts" (*bekrebek*, Heb.), "in the midst (*bekribah*) of the temple" of Israel, as Zephaniah announces; while Zecheriah exults, "Sing and rejoice, O daughter of Zion; for lo, I come and I will dwell (*shakan*) in the midst of thee, says the Lord...Be silent all flesh before the Lord, for He has roused Himself from His holy dwelling" (Zeph. 3:15, 17; Zech. 2:10, 13; and Joel 2:27; 2:14, 17). "Shout and sing for joy, O inhabitants of Zion," Isaiah exhorted the People, "for great in your midst is the Holy One of Israel" (Isa. 12:6).

Israel is not only female, a "virgin" and "mother" (Lam. 1:13; 3:13; Jer. 4:31; 18:13; Micah 4:10), "the wife of Yahweh," "the daughter of Zion" (Isa. 62:11; Zeph. 3:14; Zech. 2:10), but male (Ps. 129:8 LXX). There is a special prophecy to this effect, a prophecy concerning the Messiah Whom Israel will produce, a reference to the Incarnation. Moses describes the Presence of God the Spirit as hanging over the Tent of Meeting as a luminous Cloud (Ex. 40:34-48), the *Shekinah*, a Hebrew word formed on the root of *shakhan* ("to live as in a tent"), which indicates the habitation of God's Glory, His coming among His People.[16] *Shekinah* is translated into the Greek as ἐσκήνωσεν (from σκήνη = tent): "And the Word became flesh and dwelt (ἐσκήνωσεν = "set up a tent," "tabernacled") among us" (John 1:14). We recall also that Jesus astonished the Jews with the declaration, "Before Abraham was, *I am*" (8:58)—*I am*,

---

[15] See St Andrew of Caesarea, *Comm. on Apoc.*, 12 PG 106 320A; and St Berenguard, *In Apoc.* PL 17 874-878). See also Venerable Bede, *Expl. Apocalypsis* II, 12 PL 93 163D-169A.

[16] J. Abelson, *Immanence of God in Rabbinical Literature*. London, 1912; and L. Bouyer, *The Meaning of Sacred Scripture*. Trans. by M.P. Ryan. Notre Dame, 1958, ch. 10.

the Name of God revealed to Moses—an allusion not only to His Divinity, but to His identity as the God of ancient Israel; and most certainly to His Enfleshment.

Thus, the Lord declared to the Jews, "Destroy this Temple, and I will raise it up in three days," to which the Evangelist adds, "But He spoke of the temple of His Body" (John 2: 19, 21), that is, "the Temple of God" in which the Holy Spirit dwells (I Cor. 3:16). But if the Body of Christ is the Temple and the dwelling-place of the Holy Spirit, the Church is His Temple; that is to say, He inhabits the Theotokos. She is the Temple as she is "the Tent," "the Ark," "the Tabernacle" of God, and, of course, "the Spouse" of Christ, His Body, the Church, an equation which explains the Church's teaching on her bodily assumption into heaven after her "falling asleep."[17]

D   Not this doctrine, therefore, nor anything else which the Church teaches concerning the role of Mary may be ascribed to legend. The fact that some of what the Church believes about the Mother of God (e.g., the Entrance of the Theo-tokos into the Temple, etc.) is also found in the uncanonical books, such as the *Protoevangel of St James,* does not imply that mariology belongs to that part of church history which many scholars call "apocryphal."[18] Is it inconceivable to them that the writers of the "pseudo-evangels," often apostates, may themselves have tapped into the Apostolic Tradition, a plagarism which only confirms much of what the Church believes?

If nothing else, the facts teach that the Virgin Mary, as the Mother of God, is also the Church; and as His "daughter," she is His/her first and principle member. Mary is, therefore, the necessary link between the Church and the Incarnation. She anchors the christology, demonstrating the humanity and historicity of the Savior not only against the Gnostics and the Docetists–

---

17   The Feast of the Dormition (15 August) is the commemoration of her "falling asleep" in which, as Orthodox icons show, she is carried away by Christ into Glory. The Orthodox Church, therefore, does not agree with the "theology" of Pius XII's *Munificentissimus Deus.* St Theodore the Studite describes her death as "an ineffable mystery" at which the twelve Apostles were present together with Enoch and Elias (*Ora V.,* 2-3 PG 99 721A-724A). Her assumption was not a "prerogative," nor "done because it was possible and fitting," but because Christ ascended in His Body. The Theotokos as the Church is His Body. She is the type of that perfect (deified) humanity which inherits the Kingdom of God in the Age to Come. She is the "earnest," proof of the *eschaton* made present (See St John Maximovitch, *The Orthodox Veneration of the Mother of God.* Platina [Ca.], 1978; and Fr Michael Pomazansky, *Orthodox Dogmatic Theology: A Concise Exposition.* Trans. by S. Rose. Platina, 1984, pp. 187-195).

18   This finally is the point of Jaroslav Pelikan's *Mary Through the Centuries.* New Haven, 1966.

the former who deny that He is the Creator and the latter who deny the reality of His flesh–; but also against heretics who would turn the historical Christ into a myth. She guarantees as *Theotokos* that He is not only "the Christ of Faith," but "the Christ of history."

Indeed, the Theotokos is part of "the great Mystery" as Mother of the Incarnate Lord, as being intrinsic to prophecy (Isa. 7:14, etc.), as filled with the Grace or Uncreated Energy of the Holy Spirit (Luke 1:35; Ex. 40:35), as *mater ecclesia*. Her perpetual virginity silences all those questions about the infallibility of the Church; or, perhaps, it is the other way around. One need not wonder at the Protestant denial of both. A docetic ecclesiology which negates the visibility of the true Church, also has no place for the Ever-Virgin Mary. She, like the historical Church, is immaculate; or, perhaps, the Church as the Theotokos is immaculate.

E   It is understandable that Protestantism gives no credence to the notion that Christian mariology (and ecclesiology) originates with Jesus Christ and the Apostles whom He chose to spread His doctrine, attributing it rather to "the evolving traditions of the priestly church. " For example, in his *The Virgin Mary in Evangelical Perspective* (Philadelphia, 1971), the Protestant theologian, H.O. Oberman, offers a not uncommon theory concerning "the growth of mariological cultus" in the early Church. Omnipresent Platonism, he opines, begat the Christian asceticism which begat the ideals of virginity which "is the cradle of true Marian devotion" (p. 14). In the wake of the fourth century monastic movement (about which more will be said) came the identification of sexuality with sin and, consequently, the Church's "moralizing elevation of the Virgin which finds its clearest expression in the *semper virgo* [ever-virgin] doctrine, Mary's virginity *ante-*, *post-partum* and even *in partu*" (p. 18).

Oberman's first error is the place he gives to Platonism in the thinking of the Orthodox Church. The second is a fatal ignorance concerning the nature and purpose of Christian asceticism and monasticism. He compounds his errors by lumping virginity together with the "monastic contempt" for marriage and sex—not an unpredictable error considering the medieval view of concupiscence to which the modern world is heir. Oberman had to assume, also, that all the patristic *de virginibus* are deliberate distortions of the Gospel message, that the ideal of virginity (which the Lord Himself practiced) is extra-Biblical, the false piety of subsequent generations which had forgotten the simple message of Jesus; and, finally, that Oberman holds it as impossible, if not unnecessary, to seek "Christian perfection" in this world.

F   The Western "puritanical" ideal of sexuality must be traced ultimately to
Augustine who taught that the "original sin" was transmitted to "the damned
lump of humanity" (*totius humani generis massa damnata*) through the act of
procreation, "the concupiscence...the law of sin which remains in the members of this body of death" (*De pecca. merit.* I, xi, 13 PL 44 116). "But the commingling of the sexes which, after the sin of our first parent, cannot take
place without lust, transmits original sin to the offspring," Aquinas will
repeat (*Comp. Theol.*, 224).   He seems also to have agreed with Augustine
that, because the Mother of God inherited Adamic "concupiscence," the Holy
Spirit carefully protected "the Word of God" in His Incarnation from the "pollution" (Augustine's word) of her female body.

     The Bishop of Hippo left a "mariological problem" for the post-patristic
Latin Middle Ages. Here is where Oberman's "evangelical" criticism ought to
have begun, not with some fiction about monastic (patristic) sexuality. His
objections to what is in fact the Latin profile of the Virgin Mary are not entirely without merit. At the same time, while his discourse shows an awareness
of the mariology of the Fathers, he clearly does not understand them. The
author is also under the predictable and misguided assumption that an
appeal to Augustine is necessarily an appeal to the Fathers, which is also the
common mistake of too many medieval theologians. Thus, he argues that
medieval speculations on mariology bear "patrological" antecedents and is,
therefore, part of the catholic tradition. Thus, the latter teach that to be a
"pure creature" (*pura creatura*) or "pure man" (*homo purus*) is to be "pure" in
the perfection of her humanity. She is, therefore, associated with Christ Who
as "God-man" (*homo deus*) did not wholly belong to mankind. Hence, the
"pure nature" of the Virgin Mary serves as the basis for a bridge between
Christ and the human race: "the foundation for man's *fiducia*, his confident
hope for eternal life..." (*ib.* p. 20). With such opinions clouding the true mariology, no wonder the Reformers and their offspring discarded "the medieval
cultus of the Mary," including the heresy of the Immaculate Conception
which likewise has no place in the Orthodox Church.

G   "For the Byzantine Church had for several centuries before this (twelfth
century) celebrated a feast in honor of Mary's conception," writes E.D.
O'Connor. "It was precisely a celebration of the Immaculate Conception (it
seems to have originated in imitation of the earlier feast of the Conception of
St John the Baptist); but in view of the general Christian conviction about
Mary's sinlessness, it was bound to suggest the idea that, even in her conception, she had been born free from sin. In the East, this idea had been
accepted without difficulty; in the West, however, it would have to overcome

resistance."[19] In fact, neither the Latin nor Greek Fathers taught "this idea." It belongs rather to the Latin Middle Ages whose controversies, as so many others, would have taken a different turn without Augustine's "original sin." There would have been no teaching or papal dogma of the Immaculate Conception, nor any need to find elaborate and complex theories to support "this idea."

When the theory of the Immaculate Conception was first introduced in the twelfth century, it was immediately rejected by some of the most eminent theologians of Latin Christendom, such as Bernard of Clairvaux, Peter of Troyes, Maurice de Sulli, William de Seignali, William Durand, even Thomas Aquinas. Although confessing Mary's sanctification in the womb of St Anne, they labeled the theory of anyone (save Christ) born without "original sin" a novelty. "The Church knows nothing of it," argued Bernard of Clairvaux. "Reason does not establish it nor is there any ancient tradition to recommend it. Are we more learned or more devout than our fathers?"—*quam non ritus ecclesiae, non probat ratione, non commendat antiqua traditio. Numquid Patribus doctiores, aut devotiores sumus* (*Ep.* 174).

Although many defended the innovation, such as Peter Lombard, Bishop Arnold of Lisieux, and later the famous Bonaventura of Bagnorea, it was not until the fourteenth century that the tide begin to turn in its favor. John Dun Scotus (d. 1308) provided the new mariology with its rationale, insisting that Christ could have no relationship with the Blessed Virgin Mary unless she were preserved from original sin—*Sed hoc non esset, nisi meruiset eam praeservari a peccato originalis.* To suggest, he said, that the Immaculate Conception would place her outside Christ's Redemption is nonsense. She was indeed an heir of Adam's disobedience, but that the Savior Himself preserved her from its consequences. In other words, since the "original sin" would have been erased by the Sacrament of Baptism, nothing prevents God from accomplishing the same deed at the instant of her conception rather than later (*Comm. in Quat. Lib. Sent.* III, 3 q. 1, iv).

In 1314, William DeChanac, doctor of Civil Law at the University of Paris, where Scotus had formerly taught, collected the opinions of forty authorities in his book entitled, *Of the Actual Purity of the Mother of God*, in

---

[19] Introduction to *The Dogma of the Immaculate Conception*. Notre Dame, 1958, xii. Here is the dogma to which O'Connor refers: *We define the doctrine which declares that the most Blessed Virgin Mary at the first instant of her conception, by a singular grace and privilege, granted her by Almighty God, through the merits of Christ Jesus, Savior of mankind, was preserved from all stain of sin, is a doctrine revealed by God and this must be held firmly and constantly by all faithful Christians* (Pius IX, *Ineffabilis Deus* [8 Dec 1854]).

order to show the absurdity of the Scotian position.[20] His scholarship went
for naught. The theory of the Immaculate Conception was approved by the
Council of Basel (1439) as "a pious doctrine in conformity with the worship
of the Church, the Catholic Faith, right reason, and Holy Scripture." Not
until much later, however, were several "miracles" to attest its veracity: the
seventeenth century discovery of the so-called treatises of St Caecilius in
Granada, Spain; and later the appearance of the Virgin Mary to a nun, Cath-
erine Laboure (1830), in Paris; to two children at La Salette in the French Alps
near Grenoble (1846); the eighteen visions of "our Lady" vouchsafed to
Bernadette Soubrious near Lourdes (1858); and at Fatima, Portugal (1917).

Other than their "miraculous" nature, there is something culturally significant about these apparitions. They reflect the popular Latin piety of the
day, which was inspired, among other things, by a new religious art, such as
the seventeenth century paintings of Diego Velazquez and Bartolome Mur-
illo who posed "the Blessed Virgin Mary" as a perfect (not deified) human
being ascending alone through clouds into heaven. There is no iconographic suggestion that her divine Maternity was relevant to her glorification.
Naturalistic and stereotypical features, with varying details, fit the description of "the Lady" which appeared to almost a dozen people between 1531
and 1933. Thus, the image, if not the doctrine and cultus of the Christ's
Mother, evolved with theology of the papacy—from the *imperius nostra regi-
na* of Chartres to the proleterian Virgin of the hospital chapel.

H   The apparitions of the Blessed Virgin provided the Papacy with the
"proof" needed to confidently dogmatize the Immaculate Conception, seemingly unaware of its implications. Aside from the fact that the "dogma" reaffirms the Augustinian "original sin"—it necessarily recasts the nature of
Christ's Economy.[21] Thus, if the Mother of God is without "original sin," she

---

[20] DeChanac had anticipated the labors of Ludovico Antonio Muratori (1672-1750)
who authored several treatises in which he showed the unanimous testimony of the
Fathers against the Immaculate Conception (See H. Graef, *The Devotion to Our Lady*. New
York, 1963). The Roman Catholic response to the evidence is generally as prolix as the
theory itself. "All the dogmas, defined or yet to be defined, were known by the Apostles
immediately, formally and explicitly, not merely mediately, virtually or implicitly," writes
A.B. Wolters. "The explicit knowledge was not passed on to the Church, however, except
by way of general principles, written or oral, so that the Church had to rediscover
through the aid of the Holy Spirit what is implicitly contained in these revealed principles" ("The Theology of the Immaculate Conception in the Light of *Ineffabilis Deus*,"
Marian Studies V [1954], p. 38). On the history of the dogma of the Immaculate
Conception, see E. Preuss, *The Romanish Doctrine of the Immaculate Conception*. Edinburgh,
1867.

[21] An Orthodox can only be dismayed by the remarks of Vladimir Lossky that "the
Holy Virgin was born under the law of original sin, sharing with all the same common

becomes radically different from other human beings, including the people of Old Israel whose "recapitulation," in part, motivated the Birth of Christ from "a woman, under the Law." But she is also "the second Eve," the representative of all humanity, a role of which she is deprived by this privilege. Finally, if the "original" sin was at the heart of the Lord's Redemption— rather than the conquest of the devil, the destruction of death and purging of creation from evil—then, for the Savior to have cleansed Mary from the "original sin" (which lies at the root of all other sins), she could not have died, for "the wages of sin is death" (Rom. 6:23). In any case, the argument that the Savior miraculously blocked the "original sin" in her nature is dangerous sophistry, with no patristic or Scriptual basis.

In truth, there is no "original sin" as the inheritance of Adam's guilt; and, therefore, the Immaculate Conception is just another episode in a comedy of Latin errors. It is a dogma signifying nothing. Mary, not unlike every child of Adam, was the victim of his mortality. She was assumed into heaven not because she was free of "original sin" or that she was a perfect human being, but because she is the Church, the deified humanity of Christ who sits at the Foot of Her Savior and Son in heaven. For that reason, also, she is "All-Holy" (Παναγία) and "Ever-Virgin" (Ἀειπάρθενος). Whatever her personal holiness, her divine privileges came to her on account of her role as "the Mother of my Lord" (Luke 1:43), as the Mother of God (Θεοτόκος).

In that role, the All-holy, Ever-Virgin Mother of God, Mary is "the fountainhead of our salvation and the manifestation of the mystery which was from eternity" (Troparion, Feast of the Annunciation, Tone 4). The "second Eve," she is the new humanity, even as the "first Eve" was, "the Mother of all the living" (Gen. 3:21). As the Mother of God, she is the highest of the Trinity's creatures. Therefore, as St Gregory Palamas exclaims, "she is the frontier between created and uncreated nature, and there is no man that shall come to God except he is truly illumined through her, that Lamp truly radi-

---

responsibility for the Fall. But never could sin become actual in her person; the sinful heritage of the Fall had no mastery over her right will" ("Panagia," *In the Image and Likeness*, p. 204). Lossky is joined by Bishop Kallistos (Timothy Ware). "The Orthodox Church has never in fact made any formal and definitive pronouncement on the matter." "In the past many Orthodox Christians have believed in the Immaculate Conception." Thus, "from the Orthodox point of view…the whole question belongs to the realm of theological opinion." His Grace wants us to "suspend judgment on the matter" (*The Orthodox Church*. Baltimore, 1964, p. 264). Whether "some" Orthodox Christians have (or do) "believed" is irrelevant. No member of the Church may hold any "opinion" contrary to the Apostolic Tradition (See S.C., Gulovich, "The Immaculate Conception in the Eastern Churches," in *Marian Studies* V (1954), 146-185). In fact, it had never entered the mind of anyone before the Latin Middle Ages that her conception was "immaculate"; and to find it in the Scriptures or the writings of the Fathers is to have put it there (See J. Pelikan, *Mary Through the Centuries*, pp. 194-200).

ant with Divinity, even as the Prophet says, 'God is in the midst of her, she shall not be shaken' (Ps. 45:5)".[22] This glorification began with her humility, "Behold, the handmaid of the Lord; be it unto me according to thy word" (Luke 1:38).

That Orthodoxy has some agreement with Roman Catholicism on this matter is not entirely welcome. Its marian doctrines require a logic for which the Church has no sympathy inasmuch as they involve a subtle manipulation of the facts with which the Church's wisdom has never been associated and which even the first Protestants recognized as more logomachy than Gospel. Throwing out the baby with the bathwater, however, the Reformers dismissed all devotions to the Mother of God and the doctrinal "problems" which come with it. It seems not to have occurred to them, then and now, that the devaluation of the Theotokos is itself the product of a human "tradition"; or, even more, that their entire theology itself is the product of the West's developing culture, concepts and principles. Protestantism has never understood "the mystery of the Mother of God," because it has never understood "the mystery of the Church."[23]

H   The apex (or nadir) of Roman Catholic mariological development was reached with Vatican II—"The Role of the Blessed Virgin Mary, Mother of God, in the Mystery of Christ and the Church"—a statement which urged the Faithful to "painstakingly guard against any word or deed" which might "shock" Protestants and non-Christians (*Dogm. Const. of Ch.*, ch. 8). It is no accident that the emasculation of Papal ecclesiology has led also to the diminution of the Virgin and, to be sure, of Christ Himself. It is to this misfortune that Roman Catholicism has come on account of its fascination with the "development of doctrine."

3   SACRAMENTA FUTURI

The word "mystery" has several meanings in Christian parlance, but none more fundamental than the *mysterion* which is the revelation of the divine Economy in Jesus Christ; or, what is almost the same, the Church. "The mystery passes into the life of Church," wrote St Leo the Great (*Serm* LXXIV, 2 PL 54 398A); and, consequently, into her sacraments. As St Ambrose put it, "I find Thee in the mysteries of the Church" (*Apol. proph. David*, XII, 58 PL 14 916B); hence, another meaning of the word "mystery," alluding to the

---

    22 Lossky, "Panagia," p. 209.

    23 St Gregory Palamas, *A Homily on the Dormition of Our Supremely Pure Lady Theotokos and Ever-Virgin Mary*. Trans. by Holy Transfiguration Monastery, in *Orthodox Life* XXXII, 4 (1982), pp. 4, 8.

description that the Apostles and their successors are "stewards of the mysteries of God"—οἰκονόμους μυστηρίων Θεοῦ (I Cor. 4:1), especially the Eucharist (I Cor. 12:23-34). St Dionysius the Areopagite called it, "the Mystery of Mysteries" (*de eccl. Hier.* III, 1 PG 3 424C), that is, the rite by which Christ, His Body and Blood, is communicated to the Faithful.

To this Mystery, then, all the Mysteries or Sacraments of the Church are ordained as to their end. Baptism "of water and of the Spirit" (John 3:5) is the Mystery of incorporation, the Mystery of initiation into the Eucharist, into Christ. It is a mystagogy illustrated by the act of threefold immersion, the reception of the Holy Spirit (generally called, "chrismation" or "the anointing" with sacred oil), crowned by participation in the Holy Communion. All the other sacramental rites of the Church (Ordination, Marriage, Pen-ance, Prayer Oil or Unction, etc.) have this purpose; therefore, it is impossible to treat any of the Mysteries as autonomous subjects, since all of them are aspects of "the *mysterion* hid from before the ages," the Incarnate Lord, in Whose divine-human Life the Faithful share with God and with one another through the Eucharist.

So, then, the Mystery or Sacrament of Penance or Confession is understood as the means of reconciliation to Christ and the Eucharistic community from which the obstinate have been "ex-communicated" by sin or heresy. The rite of the Priesthood (bishop, presbyter, deacon) provides the earthly Church with her sacerdotal ministries, the bishop, presbyter and deacon acting in and through the priesthood of Christ, the prototypical High Priest, for the edification of the Church.[24] Holy Matrimony, the icon of Christ's union with the Church, hallows the union of man and woman and welcomes the family into the Eucharistic unity of the Church. Unction bestows the healing of Christ to flesh marred by sinful behavior, and thereby returns the believer to the active life of the Church. The coronation of the Orthodox king, God's Anointed, an earthly Sovereign of His People, an image of Christ, also occurs during the Liturgy; and the ceremony of the monk's tonsure, "the model Christian," as St Basil the Great calls him, "*mimesis* of the Virgin Christ," as St Methodius of Olympus describes him, is likewise completed in connection with Eucharistic Liturgy.[25]

---

[24] All Mysteries should be celebrated in connection with the divine Liturgy, including "ordination." The presbyter is bound to the local church in which he was ordained (See. J. Zizioulas, "Ordination—A Sacrament?" *The Plurality of Ministries.* Ed. by H. Kueng & W. Kasper. New York, 1972, pp. 33-39).

[25] The Orthodox Church does not limit the number of Mysteries to seven. All ecclesial acts of the Church are "sacramental" (See Hieromonk Taras Kurganzky, *Sacraments or Holy Mysteries? The Orthodox Christian Doctrine of Holy Mysteries and Divine Grace.* Dewdney (Canada), n.d.

In truth, all the Church's actions which sanctify the Faithful are "sacramental" or "mystagogical." Each of them are a means of deification. But they are also the major source of teaching. We recall that St Basil explained that Tradition, παράδοσις, is inseparable from the Mysteries—ἐν μυστηρίῳ—to the end that "your faith should not stand in the wisdom of men, but in the power of God" (I Cor. 2:5). The Grace of the Mysteries are the source of wisdom and power, and transformation, the creation of the "new man."

A   St John of Damascus offers a summation of patristic thought on the holy Eucharist. There is no doubt, he asserts, that Christ spoke in literal terms to the Jews, saying, "Except you eat the Flesh of the Son of man, and drink His Blood, you have no life in you. Whosoever eats my Flesh, and drinks my Blood, has eternal life; and I will raise Him up at the last day (ἐσχάτη ἡμέρα)" John 6:54-55). "The body which is born of the holy Virgin is in truth joined to His Divinity, not that the body which ascended into the heavens descends, but that the bread itself and the wine are changed into God's Body and Blood. Inquiring how this happens, it is sufficient to hear that the change was accomplished by the Holy Spirit, just as the Lord assumed flesh from the holy Mother of God though the Holy Spirit." St John rests the Mystery of the Eucharist on the Incarnation.

In a word, even as the Holy Spirit causes the Theotokos to beget Christ, He is likewise the Agent in the "conversion"[26] of bread and wine into His Body and Blood. "So the bread on the table with the wine and water are supernaturally transformed into the Body and Blood of Christ by the invocation[27] and presence of the Holy Spirit." Consequently, "the bread and wine are more than images of the Body and Blood of Christ (God forbid!), but the deified Body of the Lord Himself...." The Eucharist is the Body and Blood of the risen and deified Christ, "the first-born of many brethren," or, as St

---

[26] The Fathers used μεταβολή, μεταποίησις, μεταστοιχείωσις, transformatio, etc. to indicate the "conversion" of the sacramental bread and the wine to the Body and Blood of Christ. These words do not anticipate "transubstantiation" (S. T. IIIa, q. 75 a. 8) which not only presumes to decipher the inexplicable, but assumes an Aristotelian metaphysics of "substance" and "accidents." From a philosophical point of view, it is arguable that bread and wine might displace Christ's physical attributes; and it is equally true that the "accidents" and "substance" in Christ should not be inseparable from Him, especially since they are deified. Finally, if we accept the Thomistic scheme, we may validly insist that the humanity of Christ is an "accident" to the "substance" of His divine Person.

[27] The "invocation" (ἐπίκλησις) of the Holy Spirit for the "conversion" or "transformation" of the physical elements of the Mystery into the Body and Blood of Christ—or, for that matter, the efficacy of all the Mysteries—is commonplace in Eastern Liturgies. The usual explanation for the absence of the epiklesis from Western liturgies is a different theology. "In view of the lack of development of the Spirit in the pre-Nicene Church," bemoans J.G. Davies, "one could not expect otherwise" (The Spirit, the Church and the

John restates it, "the first-fruits" or "earnest" of things to come. Christ is "He Who is of the future age, Him of Whom we partake for the preservation of our essence...." As Christ is, so is His Church and her Mysteries, the *sacramenta futuri*, μυστήρια τοῦ μέλλοντος αἰῶνος.

B   Salvation or deification is obtained by union with Christ. To be "recapitulated" by Him is to be joined to His humanity which has been forever penetrated by His Divinity and united to It. The Eucharist is in the image of Christ's Incarnation, meaning that the visible and invisible dimensions of this Mystery or Sacrament are linked in the same way as His becoming flesh, as His Incarnation. Thus, "whoever eats (ὁ τρώγων)[28] my flesh and drinks (πίνων) my blood," declares the Savior, "has eternal life: and I will raise him up on the last day" (John 6:54). We have eternal life, said St John Chrysostom, because in the Eucharist we have "communion" with Him. "And what do they who partake become? The body of Christ, not many bodies, but one body" (*In I Cor.* XXIV 2 PG 61 200).

The Body of Christ encompasses both the heavenly and earthly aspects of the Church, even as the Savior was Divine and human, united without disorder or division. He who "communes" with Christ is united to his brethren in eternity as well as time, because the humanity and Divinity are united, as the divine Liturgy demonstrates: Christ, the Mother of God, the

Sacraments. London, 1954, pp. 136-140). But the eighth book of the *Apostolic Constitutions* shows that it was known to the West, at least by the fourth century.

One need not look to "the lack of development" for its absence in Western worship, but to the lack of apologetical need. In the Church, nevertheless, the Holy Spirit is responsible for the operation of all the Mysteries. The danger of the Pneumomachian heresy encouraged the churches in the East to highlight the *epiklesis* in the divine Liturgy. The heresy may not have impacted the West in the same way; hence, the missing invocation. Yet, the belief that the Holy Spirit causes the change in the Eucharist is found everywhere in the early Church, for as the Latin Father, St Neketas of Remesiana said, "nothing is created without the Spirit"—*non sine Spiritus esse creata* (*De Sp. Sanct. Pot.*, 7 PL 52 857A).

If, as St Ambrose teaches, the Holy Spirit "descends and consecrates" the waters of Baptism (*De Sacr.* I, v, 15 PL 16 440A), then, with *Descendit Christus, descendit Spritus sanctus. Quare prior Christus descendit, postea Spiritus sanctus* (*ib.*, 18 441A), we have every reason to believe that the Spirit descends to transform the Gifts on the Altar. In the words of St Faustus of Riez, "...so when the species represented on the altar are blessed by the heavenly words, before they are consecrated by the invocation of His Name, the substance which is bread and wine, after the words, have become the body and blood of Christ" (*Hom. Corp. et Sang.* [among the works of St Jerome, PL 30 284]). Cf. *Miss. Gall* (St Germanus of Paris) PL 138 873B; *Miss Goth* 2 PL 77 316.

[28] The Greek verb τρώγω means "gnaw, nibble, munch." Jesus is purposively graphic here. St John recorded the word to offset any docetic explanation of his words (W.F. Arndt & W. Gingrich, *Greek-English Lexicon of the New Testament and Other Early Christian Literature*. Chicago, 1957, pp. 836-837). All the Fathers took Him literally.

Angels, the Saints and all the elect, living and dead, are present to enjoy the celebration of the Kingdom. The Eucharist is "the Sacrament of unity." The fullness of the *mysterion* is adumbrated at every Liturgy. Past and future are realized "now," and together the *communio sanctorum* stands already in God's everlasting "today," taking part in the divine Life.

This theanthropic experience, however, is impossible if, as Roman Catholicism teaches, the Divine and the human Christ are not interwoven; for the human Nature of Christ is then only an assurance of the divine Immanence, the Divine is simply "superadded" to the created as Grace "crowns" nature; or, in mystagogical terms, the physical aspects of the Sacraments merely signify the divine Presence, not their conjunction. He who merely "eats" and "drinks" the "signs" of the Eucharist whose "virtue" is somehow communicated to him, has consumed only what he sees. He who denies the physical reality of the Church has nothing of Christ. "They abstain from the Eucharist and from [liturgical] prayer," St Ignatius of Antioch might have said concerning them, "because they do not admit the Eucharist is the flesh of our Savior, the very flesh which suffered for our sins and which the Father, in His graciousness, raised from the dead" (*Ep. ad Smyr.*, 6 FC). If, then, the Eucharist is the flesh and blood of the Risen Lord, then, it is also the flesh and blood of the Church, which is His Body. But holding the ecclesiology of an invisible Church and the Real Presence in the Mystery of the Eucharist, as some Protestants do, is to deny the Incarnation.[29]

·

C   What is the origin of these mystagogical heresies? They are an Augustinian legacy. Judging from his writings prior to the year 400, Augustine acknowledged the Mysteries or Sacraments to be types of the Age to Come, *sacramenta octavi (cf. Epp.* IX, XIII, XV, LV). He did not think of them apart from the Church's Liturgy; neither did he seem interested in a "scientific analysis" of them. Gradually, his understanding of them began to change with the growing influence of Neo-Platonism upon him. The Sacraments became less and less interesting to him as *secretum*, mysterious acts of the Church by which the Faithful are deified. His dualism forced him to conceive them as *signa. Sacramentum-secretum* became *sacramentum-signum*, that is, a ritual of visible signs which magically demand the Presence of an invisible (and created) Grace.[30]

---

[29] Some Lutherans understand the Eucharist to be the Body and Blood of Christ. They accept the Roman Catholic construction, albeit substituting "consubstantiation" for "transubstantiation" (see the glossary).

[30] See J. Fitzer, "The Augustinian Roots of Calvin's Eucharistic Thought," *Augustinian Studies* VII (1976), 73f. "His definition of *sacramentum* in terms of *signum* has become classical," comments R.A. Markus, who seems convinced, too, that Origen is the

According to Augustine, the Eucharistic sacrifice, like all Sacraments, is a *sacrum signum*, "visible signs of an invisible sacrifice" (*De Civ. Dei* X, 11, 5 PL 41 282). He believed that every *sacramentum* has three components: matter (water, wine, oil, etc.), the "word of truth," and the Holy Spirit. The right "matter" and "word" (formula) insure the Presence of the Holy Spirit. The Sacrament is the visible sign of God's (created) Grace (*signum gratiae Dei*) or the efficacious sign of sanctifying Grace (*signum efficax gratiae sanctificantis*). He nowhere states that the physical and spiritual dimensions of the Sacrament are mysteriously and inextricably joined. He seems not to be thinking in christological terms.

In the same way, Augustine distinguished between "the sacrament" and "the virtue of the sacrament"—*aliud est sacramentum, aliud virtus sacramenti* (*Tract. in Ionn.* XXVI, 11 PL 35 1611). The word *sacramentum* applies (as it will during the entire Latin Middle Ages) to the empirical aspect of the rite while *virtus* is its unseen reality. *Sacramentum*, then, is the *signum* of its *virtus*. In other words, the Bishop of Hippo cannot bring himself to bind things visible with things invisible as two aspects of the Eucharist (or the Sacraments in general), as even Calvin testifies (*Institutes* IV, xiv, 15 B). Augustine's mystagogy mirrors his doctrine of the Church which mirrors his doctrine of Christ.

"We live by Him," Augustine wrote in his commentary on the Gospel of St John, "by eating Him; that is, by receiving Him as eternal life, which we do not have from ourselves" (*ibid.* XXVI, 19 1615). He wants us to believe that eating and drinking the *sacramentum* or *signum* the believer somehow consumes the *virtus*. Thus, he often spoke of "figurative eating," that is, ingesting the Eucharist with true (subjective) faith. Moreover, since the sacrament is one thing and the power of the sacrament another, the grace of the sacrament is not received by all members of the Church, but restricted to "the elect (i.e., predestined) in whom alone does the sacrament effects what it represents" (*Comm. Joh.* XXVI, 11 PL 35 1611).

---

source of this definition of the Sacrament, that is, as a kind of "visible word." The same is to be found in the tenth chapter of Augustine's *The City of God* ("St Augustine on Signs," in *Augustine: A Collection of Critical Essays.* ed. by R.A. Markus. Garden City [NY], 1972, p. 61; and J. Engles, "La *doctrine du signe chez Saint Augustine*,' in *Studia Patristica* [vol. IV, 4]. Ed. by F.L. Cross. Berlin, 1962, 366-373; and Augustine's Sermon 227).

Commenting on this matter, Calvin alerted his readers to the "error" concerning the Eucharist. It was "written a little too extravagantly by the ancients to enhance the dignity of the sacraments. That is, to think that a hidden power is joined and fastened to the sacraments by which they [i.e., priests] of themselves confer the graces of the Holy Spirit upon us, as wine is given in a cup; while the only function divinely imparted to them is to attest and ratify for us God's good will towards us.... The sacraments...do not bestow any grace of themselves, but announce and tell us, and (as they are guarantees and tokens) ratify among us those things given by divine bounty" (*Institutes* IV, xiv, 17 B).

In view of this theory, none should be astonished that he argued for the existence of the Mysteries beyond the visible borders of the Orthodox Church. He refused to identify the historical Church completely with the true Church. Among other things, the effect of Augustine's mystagogical position was to deny that the objective reality of the Eucharist was dependent upon true Faith. His mystagogy implied that without this Faith, there can be Mysteries, the Grace of the Holy Spirit, a Christian unity. He could insist, as he did, that outside of the Church—outside of Christ—the Sacraments of the Church are "valid" and "efficacious"; and, therefore, that there can be spiritual life and salvation outside the Church.

If he could distinguish between *signum* and *res*, *sacramentum* and *virtus*, it was not difficult for him to distinguish between "to have the Sacraments" and "to have them with profit," he could maintain, for example, that "heretics have lawful Baptism" (etc.) unlawfully"—*Baptismum ergo legitimum habent, sed non legitime habent* (*De Bapt. c. Donat.* V, vi, 7 PL 43 181). Apparently, the Holy Spirit seems to be indifferent to heresy, bestowing the Grace of the Mysteries sometimes to the Church, sometimes to anti-Church. One must acknowledge, writes the hieromartyr, St Hilarion Troitsky, that Augustine must "make the strange assumption that. . .the Holy Spirit operates outside the Church," that is, the Holy Spirit gives "validity" to "heretical sacraments" on account of the right "signs," without the true Faith, leaving us with the singular impression that "the essence of Christianity" is "a collection of incantations by means of which man can extract from the Divinity the supernatural help he needs."[31]

Augustine did not conform his understanding to the Tradition of the Church. He recognized the Action of the Holy Spirit Who is the Spirit of unity, a unity found only in the regenerative life of the Church, a unity from which heretics have departed or been expelled, that is, the Catholic Church. It is a unity, moreover, which they reject (or arrogate to themselves) and to which they have no desire to unite themselves or others. But if Augustine is right, then, the Holy Spirit hearkens to the plea of heretics and gives their rites efficacy in opposition to the Church and, therefore, to Himself. One can only wonder whether Augustine had heard St Irenaeus' phrase—"where the Church is, there is the Holy Spirit (*ubi Ecclesia, ibi est Spiritus sanctus*)?

---

[31] *The Unity of the Church and the World Conference of Christian Communities.* Trans. by M. Jerinec. Montreal, 1975, p. 31. Compare the teachings of St Cyprian, "For when we say, 'Do you believe in eternal life and the remission of sins not granted except through the holy Church?' we mean that among heretics where there is no Church, sins are not put away. Therefore, they who assert that heretics baptize must either change the interrogation or maintain the truth—unless, of course, they believe heretics have a Church and, therefore, have baptism" (*Ep.* LXIX., 2 ANF).

Believing that the Holy Spirit acts sacramentally outside the visible unity of the Church, Augustine alters traditional ecclesiology, something we no longer need to debate. He seems unable to convince himself that the Orthodox Church in which he was a bishop is the sole "steward of the Mysteries."[32] It is an attitude with luckless consequences. Augustine finds himself "in a kind of dead end," observes St Hilarion, "because for him the only path of salvation is *via* the Catholic Church. To recognize as valid mysteries administered outside the Church means that he recognizes the operation of Grace outside the Church in hostility towards her; in a word, this means to recognize [the stewardship of] the Church is not obligatory; and, in effect, to cast away the Faith in the One, Holy, Catholic and Apostolic Church."[33]

There is no greater evidence for St Hilarion's critique than Augustine's remarkable statements: "If anyone compelled by urgent necessity, being unable to find a Catholic from whom to receive Baptism, and so, while preserving Catholic peace in his heart, should receive from one outside the pale of Catholic unity, the sacrament which he was intending to receive within the Church, should this person be suddenly dispatched from his life, he would nevertheless be deemed a Catholic" (*De Bapt. c. Donat.* I, ii, 3 PL 43 110). And the one like it, "Therefore, it is possible that some who have been baptized outside the Church may be considered to have been really baptized within, while some who seemed to have been baptized within may be understood, though the same foreknowledge of God, more truly to have been baptized outside of her" (*ib.*, V, xxviii, 39 196).

There are no more patently Nestorian statements than these in the entire corpus of Augustinian literature. It should be apparent that he had ceased to think christologically. For him the visible Church is a fellowship of believers, but she is not herself the means of salvation. Hidden within her general membership are the saved, the predestined. Curiously, all members of the visible Church may partake of the Eucharist, but not with spiritual benefit to all, excepting the predestined on whom God has imposed the Grace of salvation.[34] One is compelled to ask to what end the reprobate offer

---

32 F. Van der Meer states that the Sacraments "appear in Augustine's writings as a number of particularly holy and effective allegories in the process of salvation; but they do so in the company of a thousand others that are not sacraments at all, rather mere signs and indications. All boundaries become blurred and the whole creation is transformed into a mystical ladder to heaven which is erected within the narrow limits of man's own soul" (*Augustine the Bishop: the Life and Work of a Father.* Trans. by B. Waltershaw. London, 1961, p. 304).

33 *The Unity of the Church...*, p. 29.

34 Harnack observed that Augustine identified as the true Church only those members who had received the gift of perseverance, that is, the special Grace *(continued)* where-

"the sacrifice of the Liturgy" and receive the Holy Communion? Not being
elect, however pious, it must be true that these "other Christians" always partake of it unworthily and, therefore, unto condemnation.

D   Also, if he is not predestined, to what end is the catechumen baptized?
The threefold immersion into water sanctified by the Holy Spirit is not a
juridical formality, not pious allegory, nor religious theatre. "For in the rite
of Baptism," St Leo says, "death comes from the slaying of sin, and the triple
immersion imitates the three days of His burial, and the rising from the
water, like His rising from the grave (*Ep.* XVI, 3 PL 54 968C-969A). "Thus,
the body receives the water as its grave while the Spirit pours out the quickening power of our new life through the renewal of our souls from the darkness of sin," confirms St Basil. "In three immersions, then, and with three
invocations, the great Mystery of Baptism is performed to the end that
Christ's death may be realized in us and that, according to tradition, the
knowledge of God may enlighten the souls of the baptized. . ." (*De Sp. Sanc.*
XV, 35 PG 32 132A).

Baptism is the introduction to new life, the theanthropic life of the
Church, a life of sanctification by the Spirit. The rite of Baptism is often
viewed as a separate Mystery from Chrismation ("the seal [σφραγίς, *consig-
natio*] of the gift of the Holy Spirit); in fact, they are two phases in the regeneration of human nature, as Sts Leo and Basil intimate. Threefold Immersion
in sanctified water in the Name of the Trinity[35] engrafts a person into the life-
giving organism of the Church, completed by Chrism (the reception of the
Spirit) and Communion (union with God and His People). The Mysteries of
Initiation are efficacious for all, adult and infant, who are incorporated into
Christ, and not to any secret elect who apparently have entered into and are
justified by a personal "relationship" with Jesus Christ.[36]

---

by the falling away of the elect or predestined becomes impossible. "Thus the
thought of predestination shatters every notion of the church...and renders valueless all
the divine ordinances, the institution and all [visible] means of salvation" (*History of
Dogma* [vol. 5], p. 166).

[35] In his first Canon, St Basil stated that "those persons who have not been baptized according to the Names [of the Trinity] which have been handed down according
to traditional teachings" remain unregenerate. In short, the heterodox have no Baptism.
St Cyprian of Carthage stated that "those who come from heresy are not re-baptized
among us, but simply baptized" (*Ep.* LXX, 1 ANF). St Cyril of Jerusalem wrote the same.
"Heretics are not rebaptized, but baptized, since they were previously unbaptized"
(*Procat.*, 7 LCS).

[36] Some of the Reformers demanded that all who were baptized as infants, having
no faith and, therefore, no "personal relationship" with Jesus Christ, must be rebaptized
as adults (Anabaptists). Others, permitted the baptism of children because the infant is

E   As already observed, the word "justification" (δικαιοσύνη) is better translated "to become righteous," that is, a status received by the baptized when they enter the Church, and which allows them to grow in Christ and through the Spirit. The Christian is "justified" at the moment of his union with "the Holy and Righteous One" (Acts 3:14), that is, he is "reborn of water and of the Spirit" (John 3:5) into Christ's Body, the Church, the "chosen generation, a royal priesthood,[37] an holy nation, God's Own people. . ." (I Pet. 2:9). In the Church, he receives freedom from satan's domination, the power of death, the passions which are the matrix of every sin—from the "old man"[38]; in a word, he shares in "the liberty of Christ" (Gal. 2:4), that is, of the Spirit, for "where the Spirit of the Lord is, there is liberty" (Gal. 3:17). As St Valerian of Cimiez said, "Our Christ has granted liberty to the Faithful through the regeneration of the life-giving bath" (*Hom.* III, 3 FC).

Regeneration recreates the catechumen into "a reasoned-endowed [Logos-endowed] sheep in the holy flock of Thy Christ, an honorable member of Thy Church, a child of the light, an heir of Thy Kingdom." A "child of the light," he becomes like Christ Who is the Light (Φῶς). He is "illuminated" (φωτισμένος) with the *gnosis* by which the initiate is able to comprehend the revealed Faith which also nourishes his spirit. "For therein is the Righteousness of God," the Apostle declares, "revealed from faith to faith; as it is written, 'the righteous (δίκαιος) shall live by [the] Faith" (Rom. 1:17; Gal. 3:24; Heb. 10:38). The Faith by which "the newly-illumined" shall live is the Faith of the Church. "Brethren, Faith is to Baptism what the soul is to the body," instructs the Archbishop of Ravenna, St Peter Chrysologus. "Hence, he who is generated from the font lives by faith. 'He who is just [righteous] lives by

---

sustained by the faith of its sponsors, and the prayers of the church. The infant is renewed by an infused faith (Luther). Still others taught that the baptismal ceremony brings infants under the covenant relationship that Christ has with his believing parents (Calvin). Baptism sometimes involved immersion, otherwise effusion (See R.H. Bainton, *The Age of the Reformation*. Toronto, 1956).

37   In his *Babylonian Captivity* (1520), Martin Luther exclaimed, "We are all priests and those we call priests are ministers chosen by us to act in our name. The priesthood is nothing but a ministry and the 'sacrament' of ordination is nothing other than a rite of choosing a preacher for the church.... No one, however, is to assume this office without the consent of the community or the call of a superior" (*Luther's Works* [vol. 36], p. 116 Pel.). Since everyone baptized into Christ has "put on Christ" (Gal. 3:27), all do indeed share in His Priesthood; hence, "the priesthood of believers." But there is also a "sacerdotal priesthood" (bishop, presbyter, deacon) who govern the Church and lead in her worship. This stratification of the Church has existed from the beginning, as St Ignatius of Antioch, St Polycarp of Smyrna, St Irenaeus of Lyons, St Hippolytus of Rome, etc. testify.

38   See the Prayer at the Reception of the Catechumen (*Service Book of the Holy Eastern Orthodox Catholic and Apostolic Church*. Brooklyn [NY], 1960, p. 151).

faith' (Rom. 1:17). Therefore, everyone who lacks faith dies" (*Sermo* LXXXVII FC). The "bath," then, is the introduction into the "abundant life," the life of the Spirit, the life of the "new creature" whose destiny is the Kingdom of God.[39]

4   EPISCOPATUS UNUS EST

The argument that the *Church* (ἐκκλησία) requires no visible head is "theological nonsense."[40] She is the Body of Christ, a visible Body; she must also have a visible head. To be sure, the risen and ascended Christ is the Head of the universal Church, visible and invisible, both in heaven and on earth. He visibly reigns even now, seated at the Right Hand of God the Father. But the tangible dimension of the Church, the temporal Church, also has a visible head, the bishop (I Tim. 3;1; 3:2; Tit. 1, 7; I Pet. 2:25; and Heb. 3:1; 4:14; 5:1), without whom there can be no Church, because a body cannot exist without a head. He is "the living image of Christ," and, therefore, the "high priest" and "president" of the Eucharist, and teacher of the Faithful.

A   St Paul opens his letters with the greeting, "...unto the church of God (τῇ ἐκκλησίᾳ τοῦ Θεοῦ) which is at Corinth. . ."; or "unto the churches (ταῖς ἐκκλησίαις τῆς Γαλατίας) of Galatia...; or "unto the church (τῇ ἐκκλησίᾳ) of the Thessalonians..."[41] Each local community is the equal of the other and icon of the heavenly Church. Each one is immediate to God, for wherever "two or three are gathered together in my Name," the Lord said, "there I am in the midst of them" (Math. 18:20). His "Name" indicates His Presence in each community—in His life-giving Word, in His high priest, the bishop, and in the Eucharist surrounded by the His People.

Furthermore, as God is one, the Church is one; as God is Trinity, so the churches are many and equal. The many are one universal Church. The local Orthodox ἐκκλησίαι each represent the whole in a particular place. All the ontologically equal churches have an "immediacy to God," the Lordship of Christ, the indwelling of the Holy Spirit Who accounts for their common

---

[39] *Ibid.*, The Ablution, pp. 160-161. Cf. I Cor. 6:11, "But you are washed, you are sanctified, you are justified in the Name of the Lord Jesus Christ, and by the Holy Spirit"; and Titus 3:5-7, Christ, "according to His mercy saved us, by the washing of regeneration and renewing of the Holy Spirit. . .that being justified by His grace, we might be made heirs of hope unto eternal life."

[40] A. Schmemann, "The Idea of Primacy in Orthodox Ecclesiology," *St Vladimir's Seminary Quarterly* IV, 2-3 (1960), 53.

[41] St Paul sometimes addresses the churches as "the saints which are at Ephesus ...the Faithful in Jesus Christ"; or "to the saints and faithful brethren in Christ which are at Colosse," but "saints" or "faithful" or "brethren" or "in Christ" refer always to the church in a particular place; not to a "part" of her.

Faith, common Mysteries, common Law, and a canonical succession of bishops (ἐπίσκοποι)[42] whose origin and succession were instituted by Christ through the Apostles. Necessarily, then, the bishop of each local church is the equal of every other, despite the organizational ranks (Bishop, Archbishop, Metropolitan, Patriarch).

The first bishops, all bearing the same *charisma*, were appointed by the Apostles who "received the Gospel for us from the Lord Jesus Christ," St Clement of Rome reports. "Jesus Christ was sent from God. Christ, therefore, is from God and the Apostles from Christ" (*I Ep. ad. Cor.*, xlii, 1-4 FC). These bishops of the Orthodox Church were appointed by the Apostles as their successors, enjoined to continue their work: the propagation of the Faith, to preach and teach the Word or saving Truth, and to preside over the Eucharist, which brings together the Faithful in heaven and on earth, uniting all to God. The Eucharist, the ritualization of "the *mysterion* hid from before the ages," is the "earnest" of our salvation.

B   Along with the writings of St Pope Clement of Rome, the seven letters of his Eastern contemporary, St Ignatius, Bishop of Antioch (d. 110), are among the earliest testimony outside the Scriptures to the Christian episcopacy. "Apart from the bishop," he charged the church at Smyrna, "let no one perform any function pertaining to the church. Only that Eucharist is authentic which is offered by the bishop or by one whom the bishop has appointed for the purpose. Wherever the bishop appears, let the people gather, as wherever Jesus Christ is, there is the Catholic Church" (*Ep. ad Smy.*, 8 PG 5 713B).

In another letter, the Saint wrote, "Come together in common, one and

---

42   The bishop was "president of Eucharist," "ruler of the church," "the ruler of the brethren," ὁ προεστώς, the equivalent of the LXX ὁ ἄρχων (T. J., Jalland, "Justin Martyr and the President of the Eucharist," *Studia Patristica* V. Berlin, 1962, pp. 83-85). Eusebius equates προεστώς and *episcopus* with reference to Publius of Athens (*Hist. Eccl.* IV, 23), while in his letter to Victor, "the bishop of Rome," Eusebius invokes "the presbyters before you," including Pope Anicetus who, in his dispute with St Polycarp, could not be persuaded. He was obliged to follow "the practice of the presbyters before him" (V, 24).

St Clement of Rome used the words "bishop" and "presbyter" or "elder" interchangeably. Hegesippus called Symeon of Jerusalem "bishop," as Polycrates applied the title to Polycarp. St Ignatius addresses a letter to "Polycarp and the Presbyters and to the Church of God abiding at Philippi." St Dionysius of Corinth wrote to "your blessed bishop Soter" (*ib.*, IV, 23). St Irenaeus refers to St Polycarp as "bishop" (*Adv. Haer.* III, iii, 4 ANF). In his letter to Severianus (c. 134), the Emperor Hadrian shows knowledge of Christian "bishops" and "presbyters" (Vopiscus, *Vita Saturni*, 8).

The evidence in favor of a monarchical episcopate in the primitive Church is overwhelming—with this reservation that, as Fr Schmemann observed (*ib.*, 61), we must not expect to find there the legalism so commonplace today. "Apostolic succession" involves both "canonical" and "charismatic" aspects. Without the true Faith, there is no "succession"; ultimately, episcopacy depends on ecclesiology.

all, without exception in the same love and faith, and in one Jesus Christ
Who belongs to the race of David according to the flesh, the son of man and
Son of God, so that with undivided mind you may obey the bishop and the
presbyters, and break one bread (Acts 2:46; 20:7) which is the medicine of
immortality and the antidote to death, enabling us to live forever in Jesus
Christ" (*Ep. ad Eph.*, 20 FC). The comparison between Christ, the bishop and
"the Mystical Supper" (as St John Chrysostom will call it) or Eucharist is palpable. St Ignatius becomes even clearer when he declares that "the whole
community is received in the person of...your bishop" (*ib.*, 1), even as the universal Church is received in the Godmanhood of Christ.

St Cyprian of Carthage characterized the episcopacy as *sacramentum
unitatis*. "They are the Church who are a people united to the [high] priest,"
he wrote to Florentius, "and the flock which adheres to its pastor. You ought
to know, then, that the bishop is in the Church, and the Church in the bishop *(episcopum in Ecclesia esse et Ecclesiam in episcopo)*; and if anyone is not with
the bishop, he is not in the Church. They flatter themselves who, not having
the peace with God's priests, secretly communicate with others; while the
Church, which is Catholic and one, as neither severed nor divided, is indeed
connected and bound together by the cement of priests who cohere with one
another" (*Ep.* LXVIII, 8 PL 4 418C-419A).

The "cement of priests" (i.e., bishops) is "the cement of concord" of the
Church (*de un. Eccl.*, 23 PL 4 534A).[43] Unity with them is necessary for the
life of the Church, including the reception of the Mysteries. We need not
worry, for instance, that St Cyprian stressed *ecclesia in episcopo* seemingly at
the expense of the Eucharist and of the Faith. They are certainly presupposed
in his understanding of the Church and heresy. He gave special attention to
ecclesiology as other Fathers emphasized her other needs, such as the exposition of Christian cosmology or discussions over contemplation of God. But
they did forget the Eucharist or the other aspects of the Faith on account of
their preoccupation. In the case of St Cyprian, he pushed the role of the episcopacy into the foreground because there was an attack upon the traditional
concept of unity. The occasion seems to have been a controversy over hereti-

---

43 Cyprian held that the unity of the Church, local and universal, was founded on
the unity of the episcopate—"the mystery of unity" (*de unit. Eccl.*, 7 PL 4 520A). Cardinal
Newman agreed, but insisted that Cyprian recognized the Church of Rome as the See of
Peter as the visible manifestation of episcopal unity; and, therefore, the source of ecclesial unity, a unity comprehended by an even greater unity: the Roman church whose pre-
eminence "developed" naturally and necessarily into the nineteenth century theory of
Papal primacy (i.e., Vatican I) as Newman knew it (*Essay*, pp. 212-219). The Cardinal
relied on Augustine as "the principal witness of the factual development, which he
helped carry out" (P. Misner, *Papacy and Development: Newman and the Primacy of the Pope.*
Leiden, 1976, p. 78).

cal baptism, and the pretensions of the Bishop of Rome "who set himself up as a bishop of bishops" (*proemium* to the Seventh Council of Carthage).

If St Cyprian rejected the Bishop of Rome as "bishop of bishops," he did not deny to him the rank of first hierarch of Christendom (*Ep.* LIV, 7 ANF). Although the risen Lord, gave equal power to all the Apostles, "yet that He might set forth unity, He arranged by His authority that the origin of that unity should begin with one," Cyprian exclaimed. "Assuredly, the rest of the Apostles were endowed with the same power as Peter, with like partnership of honor and power; but the beginning proceeds from unity" (*de un. Eccl.*, 4 PL 4 516A). The unity of the Catholic Church proceeds from St Peter and, therefore, to his Roman successors. This privilege was given him since the Apostle Peter was the first to confess Jesus the Christ or Messiah as "the Son of the living God" (Matt. 16: 18).[44] In the quarrel over Baptism, Cyprian showed great concern that the Pope was exceeding the limits of his office and betraying his trust.

C   In the West only the Roman church had been founded by Apostles (Peter and Paul), giving her a certain eminence, aside from the fact that she was situated in the capital of the Empire. Also, she was the only *sedes apos-*

---

[44] St Cyprian, *Ep.* LXVIII, 8 ANF. The Fathers universally teach that St Peter established the Roman church (and also the church of Antioch). He appointed her first bishop, St Pope Linus. Roman "primacy" was related to her apostolicity; she was founded by Sts Peter and Paul, first among the Apostles. In particular, Peter had been called the "rock" by the Savior, having been the first to confess His Divinity. The privileges of Rome's bishops, however, were contingent upon their preservation of Peter's Faith. As John Chrysostom said—τὸ μὲν γὰρ σῶμα Πέτρου οὐ κατέχομεν, τὴν δὲ πίστιν Πέτρου κατέχομεν ὡς Πέτρου· τὴν δὲ πίστιν Πέτρου κατέχοντες, αὐτὸν ἔχομεν Πέτρον (*In Inscrip. Act.* II, 6 PG 51 86). See V. Kesich, "The Problem of Peter's Primacy in the New Testament and Early Christian Exegesis," *St Vladimir's Seminary Quarterly* IV, 2-3 (1960), 2-25.

The words of St John Chrysostom were commonplace among the early Fathers. Nothing changed with the passage of time. "One should not contradict the Latins," stated St Symeon of Thessalonica (14th c.), "when they say that the bishop of Rome is first. This primacy is not harmful to the Church. Let them only prove his fidelity to the Faith of Peter.... Then let the Pope enjoy all the privileges of Peter. Indeed, let him be first, the head, the chief and supreme Pontiff. If the bishops of Rome were to show themselves to be the successors in the Orthodoxy of Sylvester and Agathon, of Leo [the Great], Liberius, Martin and Gregory [the Great], then we shall call him Apostolic and the first among bishops. We shall obey him, not only as Peter, but as the Savior Himself. But the one who is now called Pope is in fact no Pope, for he has not the Faith of Peter" (*Dial. contra haer.*, 23 PG 155 121C).

Parenthetically, the East never coveted a position superior to Rome as it never challenged Rome's "apostolicity and petrinity" (J. Richards, *The Popes and the Papacy in the Early Middle Ages: 476-752.* London, 1979, p. 10). Also, see J. Meyendorff, "St Peter in Byzantine Theology," in *St Vladimir's Seminary Quarterly* VI, 2-3 (1960), 26-48; and M. Winter, *Saint Peter and the Popes.* London, 1968, pp. 38-81.

tolica in the West, a fact "which made it easy for her to maintain and to strengthen her authority in the western provinces."[45] The influence which Rome enjoyed was indeed universal, that is, she was chief among the "mother churches," churches directly founded by an Apostle.[46]

Their "authority was a *fact* based on the real influence which they exercised," says Fr John Meyendorff. "No decision could be considered definite until they had pronounced their opinion."[47] Moreover, the churches which their missionaries established, although without the same authority, were completely equal. All the churches had a certain independence, canonically governed without the interference of another community or bishop.

Thus, there is no reason to believe that the Roman church had juridical authority over other churches or that their bishops were mere lieutenants of his supreme ecclesiastical power.[48] In the early Church the Pope held no power of supremacy, no *plenam et supremam potestatem iurisdictionem in universam ecclesiam*, for such power could not be reconciled with the ontological equality of all the communities. He was not the visible head of the Catholic Church, nor endowed with a "charism of primacy" which, of course, is found nowhere in the Tradition of the Church.[49] If nothing else, such a "charism"

---

45 Dvornik, F., *The Idea of Apostolicity in Byzantium and the Legend of the Apostle Andrew.* Cambridge (Mass.), 1958, p. 46.

46 Tertullian tells us that "by those very churches which the apostles founded in person...it (the gospel) was manifested in the same way so that all doctrine might agree with these apostolic churches—mothers and original sources of the Faith (*matricibus et originalibus fidei*)— and be accounted as holding the truth and undoubtedly containing that which the churches received from the apostles, the apostles from Christ, Christ from God" (*de presc.*, 21 PL 2 38AB); hence, the basis of Roman authority in West.

47 "Ecclesiastical Organization in the History of Orthodoxy," *St Vladimir's Seminary Quarterly* IV, 1 (1960), 3.

48 As the Roman Catholic scholar, M.J. Congar admits, "Roman theology seeks a definition of the Church in which its parts would be received within the whole, conceived really as a whole, earning thereby the status of genuine parts" (*Chrétiens Desunis.* Paris, 1937, 241).

49 The Council of Trent numbered only seven Sacraments—including, of course, Ordination—the result of further Roman Catholic rationalism (see note 25 above). "The ministry of power and government, as all other ministries within the Church, is a *charism* (χάρισμα), a gift of grace," writes Fr Schmemann. "It is bestowed through the sacrament of orders, for only sacramentally received power is possible in the Church, whose very nature is [uncreated] Grace and whose very institution is based on grace. And the Church has only three charismatic orders with no gift of power superior to that of a bishop. No sacramental order of primacy, no charism of primacy exists; therefore, in the Orthodox Church. If it [charism of primacy] existed, it would have a nature different from Grace and, consequently, its source would not be the Church" ("The Idea of Primacy....," 51).
As it is, the rank of Pope is a rank above bishop, above the Church. The existence

would have implied an "eighth Sacrament" which would indeed have placed him above the Church and over all other Christian hierarchs.

Later, some Roman bishops will claim more privileges for their See than commonly recognized. St Pope Leo I the Great (440-461) conceived his authority in terms of universal jurisdiction by virtue of his reception of "the apostolic primacy" from St Peter (*Ep.* IX, 4 PL 54 163B). The Saint, writing to the Patriarch Anatolius of Constantinople (*Ep.* LXXX, 2 914A), asserted that it was necessary to be in communion with the Roman Church in order to be a member of the Catholic Church, an inflated claim which nevertheless did not imply an identity of his local church with the universal Church. For example, he wrote to the Emperor Marcian that neither Eutyches nor Nestorius "is in good standing with this See, since the universal Church has already condemned them" *Ep.* CXXX, 3 1080B). Also, he everywhere confessed his obedience to "the authority of the Fathers" (*Ep.* X, 1 164A). The privileges of the Roman church, he said, were established by "the canons of the holy Fathers and fixed by the decrees of the venerable Council of Nicea."[50]

Contrary to medieval and modern Roman Catholic ecclesiology, St Leo did not view his "primacy" as placing him over the Church and himself as the sole interpreter of Tradition. Two centuries later, Pope St Gregory I the Great (590-604) made supremely clear the position of the Roman Orthodox Church. In a letter to St John the Faster, Patriarch of Constantinople, Gregory advised him not to assume the title "universal bishop." Although it had been given to his predecessors by the Council of Chalcedon,[51] neither he nor any

---

of such a position demands an *eighth sacrament* (outlawed by Trent). Tradition affords no example of a Sacrament of "primacy," certainly no infallible "primacy." It would contradict Christian ecclesiology. Fr Sergius Bulgakov decried the addition of "infallibility"—"that fatal formula"—which extinguished Roman Catholicism (*The Vatican Dogma.* South Canaan [Pa.], 1959, p. 59)

50   T. G. Jalland draws several conclusions from his study of St Leo, not the least of which is that the Saint "claimed not only supreme jurisdiction over the whole Church, [but] holds himself to be the final and sovereign interpreter of the laws of ecclesistical discipline." Leo's rejection of Chalcedon's Canon 28 is illustrative (*The Life and Times of St Leo the Great.* New York, 1941, p. 477). Jalland will not concede that his denunciation of the Canon was as much a defense of Nicea as it was to uphold Rome's special place in the Church. The author is too eager to find in Leo's protest some dramatic gesture of his superiority over the ecumenical Council; but the Saint everywhere swore allegiance to the authority of the Fathers (*Ep.* CIV, 3 PL 54 995A; cf. *Ep.* X, 2 629C; *Ep.* XII, 5 652B; 9, 654A; 10, 654B) who were not "papists."

51   St Gregory was mistaken. The fourth Ecumenical Council of Chalcedon (451) offered to his predecessors not the dignity of *universalis episcopus*, but the honorary title of οἰκουμενικὸς ἀρχιεπίσκοπος (J.D. Mansi. Ed., *Sacr. Concil.* [vol. VI]. Paris, 1901, 1006B, 1009B, 1012B, 1048A). The title "universal bishop" was later *(continued on next page)*

Pope before him "seized upon the ill-advised title," lest "by virtue of the pontifical rank, he took to himself the glory of singularity which denies the office of bishop to all their brethren"—*Sed tamen nullus unquam tali vocabule appellarii voluit, nullus sibi hoc temerarium nomen arripuit, nesi sibi in pontificatus gradu gloriam singularitatis arriperet hanc omnibus fratribus denegasse videretur* (*Ep.* XVIII, bk V PL 77 740C).

St Gregory wrote the same to Patriarchs Eulogius of Alexandria and Anastasius of Antioch. "Not one of my predecessors ever consented to the use of this profane title, for, to be sure, if one Patriarch is called 'universal,' the name of Patriarch is denied to the others"—*Sed nullus unquam decessorum meorum hoc tam profano vocabulo uti consensit, quia videlicet si unus patriarcha universalis dicitur, patriarcharum nome caeteris derogatur* (*Ep.* XLIII *Lib.* V 771C). No one, no council, may act "contrary to the statutes and canons of the Fathers committed to us" (*Ep.* VII, *Lib.* IV 674A). Undoubtedly, to St Peter was given "the keys of the kingdom to bind and loose" and to him and his successors the first place (*principatus committitur*) in the Catholic Church,[52] but such an honor was also the responsibility of care (*cura*) of all without also giving them rights over the Church. Gregory perceived the claim of the Patriarchs to have been pretentious. He considered the appellation to be a "blasphemy" (*Ep.* XX *ad Emp. Maur.*, bk. 5 746AC).[53]

D   What, then, led the later Popes to seek that "special position"? There were a number of events which prompted them to aspire to it, perhaps beginning with Papacy's struggle against the Byzantine Emperor in the eighth and ninth centuries. The Popes resented the control he exercised over the Western churches in Sicily and southern Italy, his shifting of Italy's capital from Rome to Milan then to Ravenna or appropriating church properties (the Popes had became the single biggest landowner in Western Europe).

(*contd.*) surreptitiously introduced into the Latin translation of its canons by the Franks. Also Chalcedon addressed St Leo as "the most holy and most blessed archbishop of great and ancient Rome" (Mansi [vol. VI], 1048) which in the Latin edition of its Acts mysteriously became, *Sanctus ac beatissimus Papa, caput universalis Ecclesiae, Leo* (*Ep.* CIII PL 52 992A). Some Latin editions of St Leo's *Ep. CIII* begin, *Romae et universalis catholicaeque Ecclesiae Episcopus Leoni semper Augusto salutem* (Wanting in Migne. See the remarks of Philip Schaff in NPNF [vol. 12]. New York, 1895 p. 167 [sec. 2]). The ecclesial language clearly belongs to another time.

[52] To Queen Theodolina, St Gregory wrote that every respect should be paid to the Church of Rome, "the Church of the blessed Peter, Prince of the Apostles." She is best honored by our persistence in the true faith, "making firm your life on the rock of the Church, that is, the confession of the blessed Peter, Prince of the Apostles"—*hoc est in confessione beati Petri apostolorum principis apostolorum* (*Ep.* XXXVIII, bk IV 712C-713C).

[53] St Gregory concluded that a "universal bishop" would be the "sole bishop"—*solus episcopus* (*Ep.* XXII, bk. 5 749B).

Finally, when the Emperor failed to protect Italy from foreign invasion, the Pope turned to the Franks for protection against the Lombards. Without precedence and on his own initiative, Pope Leo III crowned the Frankish King, Charlemagne, as "Emperor of the Romans" on Christmas Day, in the year 800 in Rome.

Leo justified his usurpation with a forgery, the so-called *Donation of Constantine*, probably written in the Frankish Cloister of St Denis during the pontificate of Stephen II (752-757), perhaps before. It gave to the Pope authority over the Western provinces of the Roman Empire.[54] Elevated to imperial rank by this document, the Pope presumed to raise Charlemagne to the position of his protector. To have created a rival to the lawful ruler in Constantinople signaled the existence of a new empire—albeit Leo III and Charlemagne pretended their motive to be the restoration of the Christian Rome in the West. The major consequence of their conspiracy was the eventual creation of a new Christianity, a new Papacy, and a new vision: "St Peter as Landlord, the Pope as deputy of a worldly dominion—that is an utterly new phenomenon."[55]

The "phenomenon" continued to proliferate so rapidly that it become necessary to compound the first imposture with another. In the same century, the *Pseudo-Isidorian Decretals* reinforced, even amplified, the claims of the *Donations*. Noteworthy is the characteristically legal character of the documents. The *Decretals* discussed the corporational nature of the Church together with the elements necessary for "a strict monarchical rulership" of this one body, placing in the Pope a plenitude of power according to the

---

54 According to the *Donatio Constantini*, the Emperor Constantine, thinking that St Pope Sylvester was responsible for his recovery from leprosy, bequeathed to him and his successors forever not only the spiritual supremacy over the other great patriarchates, but also temporal dominion over Rome, Italy and "the provinces, places and cities of the West." The *Donations* were subsequently included in the ninth century collection known as the *Isidorian Decretals,* also forgeries, upon which later Popes will build their power. These documents were unknown to the puzzled Byzantines who always explained Papal claims to universal jurisdiction over the Church to be "inflated, misguided and without historical foundation" (D.M. Nichol, "The Byzantine View of Papal Sovereignty", in *The Church and Sovereignty, c. 590-1918: Essays in Honour of Michael Wilks*. Ed. by D. Wood. London, 1991, p. 179).

Finally, in the fifteenth century, Lorenzo Valla in his *De Falso Credita et Ementia Constantini Donatione Declamatio* (1440) showed these documents to be fabrications. The controversy was renewed in the nineteenth century. Roman Catholic scholarship has been dedicated to proving that the forgeries were not composed in Rome. The energy seems misspent, since the Popes employed them not only in defense of their patrimony but against the "heresy" of "the Greeks" (See "Donations of Constantine," in *Encyc. Brit.* [vols. 7-8]. New York, 1911, pp. 408-409).

55 *Sankt Peter Landesherr, der Papst als sein Vertreter eine weltliche Herrscher—dass ist eine voellig neue Erscheinung* (J. Haller, *Das Papsttum* [bd. 1]. Basel, 1951, s. 462).

model suggested by the *Donations*, that is, the fusion of sacredotal and royal functions.[56] The forgeries formed the basis of Rome's posture toward Constantinople, as is evident in the Papal missionary activity.

Nowhere were the falsehoods of the *Decretals* more profoundly exhibited than in the dispute of Pope Nicholas I (858-867) with St Photius, Patriarch of Constantinople, over the jurisdiction of Bulgaria. In early 867, a local synod held at Constantinople condemned the Latin missionaries in the Balkans, particularly for spreading the heretical dogma of the double procession of the Holy Spirit. Photius convened yet another synod in the Eastern capital, attended by delegates from the other Orthodox Patriarchs. Together they censured the Pope. The outraged Nicholas fulminated against St Photius and "the Greeks" for their audacity. "The See of Peter," he pontificated, "has received the total power of government over all the sheep of Christ"—*eam totius iura potestatis pleniter meriusse et cunctarum Christi ovium regimen accipisse*.[57]

Inasmuch the "the sheep of Christ" necessarily includes all Christians, most of whom were subjects of the Roman Empire, Nicholas conceived the Empire and the Church as virtually identical: the *societas christiana or societas omnium fidelium* to which even the Christian Emperor was a member caused him to be subject to the Pope. In the tenth century, Walafridus of Strabo, the Abbot of Reichenau defined the Papacy, "As the race of Romans is said to have held the monarchy of the whole world, so the Supreme Pontiff, holding the place of Saint Peter in the Roman See, is raised to the highest position in the Church. . .the Roman Pope, therefore, is compared with the Augusti and the Caesars in the Empire" (*De Rebus Eccl.*, 31 PL 114 963D-964A).

The Popes after Nicholas made the same boast, but not until the pontificate of Gregory VII (1073-1085) does the new ecclesial ideology evoke a revolutionary "political" vision. His problem was first to establish forever the proper order within Christian society, an impossible task if the "church" (= clergy) were not free from imperial encroachments, as exemplified by the so-called "investiture contest."[58] His ultimate goal was to create a *civitas Dei*

---

56 W. Ullmann, *Principles of Government and Politics in the Middle Ages*. New York, 1961, p. 184. See the discussion in W. Ohnsage, "Die Patricius-Titel Karls des Grossen," in *Konstantinopel und der Okzident*. Darmstadt, 1966, ss. 1-28.

57 Quoted, Abbé Guette, *The Papacy*. Trans. by A.C. Coxe. New York, n.d., p. 300.

58 "Lay investiture" was the practice, begun probably after the ninth century, in which the newly-consecrated bishop accepted his diocese from the king through bestowal of the pastoral staff. German and Italian bishops considered themselves to be officials of the king or emperor (See G. Tellenbach, *Church, State and Society at the Time of the Investiture Contest*. Trans. by R.F. Bennett. Oxford, 1959; and also, I.S. Robinson, *Authority and Resistance in the Investiture Contest: the Polemical Literature of the Late Eleventh Century*. New York, 1978).

which Gregory detailed in *Dictatus Papae* as well as in his canonical *Collection in Seventy-Four Titles.* In them, he demands the right to depose Caesar and to bear the Caesaric insignia itself—not at all a new idea, Gregory said, but an old right which traces its history from Augustine to the *Decretals* to Pope Nicholas.[59] Only with this agenda could a society be erected that was pleasing to God.

"Kings and princes of the earth, seduced by empty glory, prefer their interests to the things of the spirit," Pope Gregory exclaimed, "whereas pious pontiffs, despising vainglory, set the things of God above the things of the flesh."[60] The boundaries between the spiritual and secular, never clear in the post-Orthodox West, become more distinct under the auspices the eleventh century "Gregorian reform," essential to which was the separation between clergy and laity, as Gratian tells us in his *Duo sunt genera Christianorum* ("There are Two Kinds of Christians"); but even more, the "reform" represented "a fundamental break in the historical continuity of the Church"[61] which too many medieval thinkers failed to understand was indeed a "break" with the traditional christology.

M. Bloch finds something more. He theorizes that this "break" was "the definite formation of Latin Christianity; and it was no mere coincidence that this happened at the very moment of the final separation between the Eastern and Western Churches."[62] There is some truth in Bloch's statement, for what will henceforth characterize "Latin Christianity" is a cultural revolution at the center of which was the revival of jurisprudence. Yves Congar points out that "the search for legal texts to support Gregory's position marks the beginning of the science of canon law," understood as "a translation of absolute justice, or divine law, into a new system of church law, at the heart of which was the legal authority of the Pope."[63] The "reform" will not stop with Pope Gregory.

---

[59] *Das kirchenpolitische System, das er entwicklete,* contends K. Hampe, *war in seinen einselnen Gedanken durchaus nicht neu, lebte er doch selbst in der Vorstellung, nur das alte Rechte zu erneuren; aber indem er an Augustin, an Pseudoisidor und Papst Nikolaus I ankne-upfte, Formulierung und de geschlossenen Bau des Ganzen* (Deutsche Kaisergeschichte in der Zeit Salier und Staufer. Leipzig, 1912, s. 46). Nevertheless, *Die Idee der paepstlichen Weltherrschaft ist die personlichste Schoepfung Gregors VII* (Haller, *Das Papsttum* [bd. 2], s. 429). See also Z.M. Brooke, "Gregory VII and the First Contest Between Emperor and the Papacy," *Cambridge Medieval History* (vol. 5). Cambridge, 1948, 51-111.

[60] Quoted, in Berman, *Law and Revolution,* p. 110.

[61] *Ibid.,* p. 374.

[62] *Feudal Society.* Trans. by L.A. Manyon. London, 1961, p. 107.

[63] "The Historical Development of Authority in the Church: Points for Christian Reflection," in *Problems of Authority: Anglo-French Symposium.* Ed. by J.M. Todd. London, 1962, p. 139f.

Pope Gregory's partisans searched the Lateran archives for Papal *(continued on next page)*

E   The idea of papal infallibility, which surely tantalized Pope Gregory VII,[64] had little or no advocacy in the Latin Middle Ages before the thirteenth century and no currency until after the Council of Florence.[65] Chiefly responsible for the development of the idea of papal infallibility, albeit inadvertently, were the medieval canonists, especially Gratian (c. 1140) whose *Decretum* "displaced all the older collections of canon law and became not only the manual but the repertory for the Scholastic theologians."[66] Doellinger believed the idea of Papal infallibility was firmly established in the canonical literature of the Latin Church by the middle of the twelfth century.

(cont'd.) documents—"arguments" (*rationes*) and "precedents" (*exempla*)—which would support the Reform against its opponents, in particular King Henry IV of Germany. They were already in possession of the *Pseudo-Isidorian Decretals* which Gregory quoted in his letter of October 1090 and subsequently appeared in chapters 67 and 68 of the *Collection in seventy-four Titles*, a canonical manual, largely the work of Anselm of Lucca and Cardinal Deusdedit. Its intention was to show the people the meaning of papal "authority" (*auctoritas*), or to quote the Collection's preamble, "how great is the privilege of the Roman Church in ecclesiastical cases" (I.S. , *Authority and Resistence*, p. 40). Note also that all the Popes between 1159 and 1303 were lawyers (R.W. Southern, *Western Society and the Church in the Middle Ages*. Harmondsworth [Eng.], 1975, pp. 131-133).

[64] *Bis zur Erscheinung der Isidorian Decretalen war also noch nirgends ein ernstlichere Schritt zur Einfuehrung der neu-Roemisch Unfehlbarkeitstheorie geschehen,* asserted Professor Doellinger. *Die Paepste dachten noch nicht daran ein solches Vorrecht sich beizulege. Erst musste die Stellung der romischen Bischoefe zur Kirche von Grund ausumgestalt es musste die Idee des Primats alterirt werden, ehe Raum und empfangler Boden fuer die untruglichkeitslehre gewonnen war, dann aber entwickelte sie sich mit einer gewissen natur nothwendigen consequenz.... Ein Mann, wie Gregory VII, musste, wie wenig er sich auch theologischen Dingen zu beschaftigen pflegte doch das privilegium der Unfehlbarket also das kostbarste Juwel seiner Krone doch halten* (Doellinger, *Papst und das Concil.* Leipzig, 1869, ss. 81-82, 119).

[65] Joseph DeMaistre believed that infallibility was "first broached at the Council of Florence." It was promoted vigorously by the Dominican, Cardinal Tommaso Cajetan (1470-1534), during the pontificate of Julius II (1503-1513). He described the Pope as "the mirror of God on earth" (*The Pope*. Trans. by A.McD. Dawson. New York, 1975, p. 7). Not all scholars agree with DeMaistre's history. See B. Tierney, *Origins of Papal Infallibility, 1150-1350: A Study of the Concepts of Infallibility, Sovereignty and Tradition in the Middle Ages.* Leiden, 1972; *Foundations of the Conciliar Theory: the Contribution of the Medieval Canonists from Gratian to the Great Schism.* Cambridge (Eng.), 1953; M. Wilks, *The Problem of Sovereignty in the Later Middle Ages.* Cambridge (Eng.), 1963; P. Granfield, *The Papacy in Transition.* Garden City (NY), 1980.

[66] Doellinger, s., 116. If we may believe Tierney, all the medieval canonists—found in the *Glossa Ordinaria* of the Decretists (followers of Gratian), and the Decretalists (commentators on papal decretals)—taught that the Pope's power was so enormous that he could modify the precepts of the Apostle Paul, albeit not in matters extending to the articles of Faith (*Papa contra Apostolum dispensat: non tamen in his quae pertinent ad articulos fidei*). Although Sts Peter and Paul were equal as Apostles, Peter was nonetheless superior to Paul by virtue of his special commission from the Lord; also, according to the principles of Roman law, "he was not bound by an equal"—*par in partem non habet imperium*—Peter was a higher authority than Paul.

Yet, the canonists could not find proof of papal infallibility (nor in Gratian's great

Whatever the truth, down to the thirteenth century "dogmatic theology remained unaffected by the canonist theory, for the theologians rarely wrote on the question of papal authority in their technical treatises. It was Thomas Aquinas who made the doctrine of the Pope a formal part of dogmatic theology."[67] Thereafter, canonists and theologians, began to reconceive the Church and the headship of the Pope. They were responsible not only for defining the idea of Papal sovereignty, but for launching the new doctrines which depicted the tradition of the Papacy as the fount of divine revelation apart from the Scriptures, a logical step which allowed for the decrees of the Pope—the supreme diagnostician of all ecclesiastical traditions—to possess an authority equal, if not higher, than the Scripture in matters of the Faith.[68]

The "keys of the Kingdom" given to St Peter and inherited by his successors were acknowledged as the source of the Pope's authority—at least, such was the contention of the Gregorian Reformers upon which the later canonists built. The "keys" signified both "the key of jurisdiction" or "power" and "the key of knowledge." Some twelfth century canonists argued that the keys were given to all the Apostles, ostensibly taking their cue from the Latin Fathers, such as St Maximus of Turin, who stated that St Peter received from the Lord the "key of power" and St Paul (the other founder of the Roman Church), "the key of knowledge" (*Hom.* LXXII PL 57 403-404). Nevertheless, the keys were not at first taken as symbols of papal infallibility.

If eventually they came to have that meaning, it was not that the emergence of the doctrine of papal infallibility was somehow inevitable, that it had always been a tacit principle of the Christian dispensation, a "dormant power" which burst upon the stage of history by the Will of divine Provi-

---

compedium whose texts were drawn from every age of the Church's past). In fact, they discovered several accounts of pontiffs who erred in doctrinal matters, e.g., Anastasius II (469-498). Although a part of the Church or even the Pope himself might err, divine Providence would always protect the whole Roman Church against apostasy (*Origins of Papal Infallibility...*, pp. 29-32).

67 Doellinger, *ibid.*, s. 215. According to J. Langen, in his quest for arguments against "the Greeks," Thomas turned for help to the forgeries listed in Gratian's *Decretum*, the effect of which was to introduce "the idea of papal infallibility into the dogmatic system of the scholia" (*Das Vatikanische Dogma von dem Universal-Episcopal und der Unfehlbarkeit des Papstes* [bd. 3]. Bonn, 1873).

68 Innocent III (1198-1216) insisted on the right to revoke the decrees of his predecessor—in accordance with the Roman legal theory of sovereignty—a right he possessed by virtue of his standing "Higher than man, less than God." No wonder he felt himself to be "the emperor of Christendom" whose authority (*plentitudo potestatis*) was given to him directly from God (*Serm.* II, PL 217 656C). This new development of the the the Papacy directly led to Boniface's famous utterence not a century later, *Ego sum Caesar, ego imperator*; and, of course, his notorious bull, *Unam Sanctam* (1302), "Furthermore we declare, state, define and pronounce that it is altogether necessary to salvation for every human creature to be subject to the Roman Pontiff" (See E. Kantorwicz, *Frederick the Second, 1194-1250*. Trans. by E.O. Lorimer. New York, 1957, p. 40f.).

dence at the right moment. Rather it arose because the doctrine was the product of the canonists' art, and the canonists' collaboration with the theologians, medieval state-craft and political theology and, to be sure, because the idea of "papal infallibility" was useful to a particular group of controversialists.

Given these historical circumstances, such an idea was the unavoidable extension of the Gregorian Reform which had, as a part of its program, the desacralization of the King and his power. To that end, the Pope misappropriated the title *vicarius Christi* which had formerly been the property of the Emperor or King. Never before had the civil ruler been regarded as a mere laymen, never before his kingdom demoted to a secular state. "In the king truly," wrote Peter Damian, "is Christ recognized to reign"—*in rege suo vere Christus regnare cognoscitur* (*Ep.* VII, 2 PL 144 436). The king was *salvator mundi*, "Christ by grace," as the Norman Anonymous of York declared him to be.[69]

Assumption of the king's title by the Pope was also designed to diminish the traditional authority of the bishops and, consequently, the councils of the Church. They were individually no longer "living images of Christ." And, since Christ and the Church formed "one Man"—*una persona Ecclesiae*, as Augustine said—she was conceived as a universal organism of which the the Pope became the Head, the vicar and visible representation of Christ on earth—*ubi repraesentatus est Christus, ibi repraesenatus est qui est vicarius Christi.*[70]

If where the Pope is there is Christ, and where Christ is there is the Pope, he is not a substitute for the Lord, He alone represents or "presents again" the Person of Christ—*quia papa non dicitur caput nisi in quantum gerit vicem Christi et eiius personam repreasentat.*[71] As *vicarius Christi*, the powers of the Pope extended not only to the whole world, but reached to heaven and to purgatory; or, as Thomas Aquinas said, *Habet [papa] autem tres partes: una est in terra, alia est in coelo, tertia est in purgatorio* (*In Symb. Apost.*, ch. 9). Curiously, none of this theorizing compelled even the "extreme papalists" of the Middle Ages—Giles of Rome, James of Viterbo, Henry of Cremona, Augustinus Triumphus—to publically subscribe to a doctrine of Papal infallibility.

---

[69]   E. H. Kantorwicz, *The King's Two Bodies: A Study in Medieval Political Theology*. Princeton, 1957m ch. 3. Byzantium was a dyarchy. No part of the Commonwealth was ever secularized. The Basileus represented the humanity of Christ, the Patriarch His Divinity, a societal unity "without confusion or separation."

[70]   Augustinus Triumphus, *Summa de potestale ecclesiastica*. Rome. 1854, VIII. ad. 1, p. 67.

[71]   James of Viterbo, *De regimine christiano*. Ed. by H.-X Arguilliere. Paris, 1926, II, 9, p. 308.

Not without a certain irony, the design of Papal apologists was to disassociate the authority of St Peter from the "keys" with which the Lord had endowed him. From the beginning of the Gregorian Reform, there was an unspoken attempt to convert the office of Peter to the Office of Christ; hence, to the office of Pope. "With the development of papal sovereignty," Michael Wilks notes, "the papal identification with Christ had to be emphasized at the expense of the succession from Peter, and this could not be done whilst papal power was dependent upon the Roman Church."[72] The Franciscan theologian, Bonaventura, suggested that all bishops were mere delegates or "vicars" of the Pope and, therefore, his power is unrestricted by the decisions of episcopal Councils, even in matters of Faith. He summed up his position with the exclamation, "The Pope stands in the place of Peter; nay rather of Jesus Christ"—*est loco Petri, imo loco Iesu Christi.*[73]

How did the Papacy reach such heights? The discussion in the first chapter on the Eucharist debate provided the christological first principles. The "history of dogma" shows us their ecclesiological implications. Anyone familiar with the New Testament knows that St Paul called the Church "the Body of Christ." The term "mystical body" to describe her is not heard until the Carolingian period, during that controversy over the Eucharist. On one occasion, Ratramnus of Corbie distinguished between Christ's "true and proper body" and His "mystical body,"the Eucharist. But, since the Church is formed through the Eucharist, it was not difficult, in the course of time, to identify the Church with the "mystical body." In the heat of a twelfth century debate over transubstantiation, the idea of "proper and true body of Christ," and His "mystical body" were switched. Because several dogmaticians spiritualized the Sacrament of the Altar, others devised arguments which demonstrated he "real Presence" of the human-Divinity of Christ in the Eucharist.

---

[72] *The Problem of Sovereignty....* , p. 406.

[73] *Comm. in Ev. S. Luc.*, cap. 9 (*Opera om.*, IV). Quaracchi, 1882-1902, p. 212. "Bonaventure evidently was certain that the Popes were not in error in their teaching on the immediate point at issue...," Tierney writes, "but he nowhere explicitly asserted that all doctrinal decrees of the Roman church—still less of individual Pontiffs were necessarily infallible" (*The Origin of...*, p. 89). To the argument that the decrees of the Pope are infallible only when he speaks *ex cathedra* (See e.g., H.E. Manning [Cardinal], *The Oecumenical Council and the Infallibility of the Roman Pontiff.* London, 1869, p. 174). Tierney responds that such a concept presupposes a distinction between the Pope's fallible and infallible pronouncements, of which the medieval canonists knew nothing. Canonists and theologians generally attributed infallibility to the Roman Church not to the Pope (See T.P. McLaughlin, ed., *Summa Parisiensis on the Decretum Gratiani.* Toronto, 1952, p. 20).

In short, the expression "mystical body" now applied to the Church acquired a sociological connotation; thus, Pope Boniface VIII defined the Church as "one mystical Body the Head of which is Christ" (*Unam Sanctam*, VIII, pp. 161-163 in *Documents of the Christian Church*. Edited by Henry Bettenson. New York, 1947). Moreover, the *corpus mysticum* as a designation of the Church became the soil for further ecclesiological speculation. After the Investiture Struggle, the church gradually developed into a "mystical corporation," that is, a divinely established organism justified by natural and positive law. Indeed, the omnivorous growth of law in the Middle Ages generated the conception of *corpus Christi mysticum*. Many theologians, such as Thomas Aquinas, began to speak of "the mystical Body of Christ," because they viewed her precisely as a legal entity. Not without interest is the fact that theologians and jurists could discourse on the "proper and true" as well as the "mystical body" without any reference to the Eucharist.

The ecclesiological development went even further. Aquinas frequently used the expression "the mystical Body of the Church" along with "the mystical Body of Christ," meaning that the Church was now a "mystical body" in its own right: the Church is a "legal person"—*Dicenum quod caput et membra sum quasi una persona mystica (S.T.II. Q. 48 a. 2)*. The Church had become a juridical abstraction, a "mystical person," a creature of juristic theorizing.

The new ecclesiology was used by the partisans of the Pope to position him as "the chief Prince moving and regulating the whole Christian polity," as the anonymous fourteenth century writer called him in *De Potestate ecclesiae*. The Pope was sometimes envisioned as the head of the Church in opposition to the emperor as the head of the Roman Empire; hence, the papal adaptation of the classical phrase, "Rome is where the emperor (Pope) is." This is in strange contrast to the words of St Ambrose—*Ubique enim nunc Christus ibi quoque Jordanis est (Serm. XXXVII, 2 PL 17 702B)*—that is, every baptismal font is the Jordan where Christ acted as the type of every Christian baptized. Again, some Scholastics amplified the new theory, saying not where the Eucharist is the Church is, but where the Pope is, there is the Eucharist. And even more, inasmuch as the Pope is identified with Christ, the Church is the "mystical Body of God"—*corpus mysticum Dei*.

By the fourteenth century, the christological interpretation of the Church and the king had disappeared completely. It was replaced by the idea of the Church as a corporation—and, therefore, Christian society—and the Pope as its lawful head. The medieval Papacy became a "body politic" despite the old and conventional rhetoric. There is, to be sure, a certain irony here: having secularized the Church, the state which always boasted of a transcendental dimension, also claimed to be a "body politic" and a "mystical body," a "legal person." Some political theoreticians, anticipating the utopianism of the Renaissance, visualized the rise of a perfect kingdom directed by a "sacred" king. Finally, during the "autumn of the Middle Ages," there appeared a new concept—a reaction to imperial and papal hauteur—the *populus* as a "mystical body"; it was the dawn of democracy.

F   No man sat upon the papal throne with greater aspirations to world-dominion than Boniface VII (1294-1303). His *Unam sanctam*, "the high-water mark of papal claim to supremacy over civil powers,"[74] resulted in his imprisonment by the French King, Philip "the Fair" (1285-1314), who also transferred the Papacy to the French city of Avignon (1309). By 1367 the Pope returned to Rome, but then again to Avignon. Although the College of Cardinals appointed Urban VI (1378-1389) as Pope for Rome, Boniface's successor, Clement VII (1378-1394), governed from Avignon ("the Great Schism"). Previously, there had been rival Popes, but never before duly elected by the same body of Cardinals.

Meanwhile, a number of theologians and philosophers were giving serious attention to the resolution of "the Great Schism." There had been a history of speculation on church government, reaching beyond even Pope Gregory VII, so the idea of its resolution—especially now that the Roman church was constricted by this ecclesial anomaly—by means other than papal action was not revolutionary. Termination of the Schism, as they saw it, must involved the calling of an ecumenical Council; hence, "the conciliar movement." According to Brian Tierney's *Foundations of the Conciliar Theory* (Cambridge, 1953), the principal conciliar ideologues were the Paris Masters, John of Paris (d. 1306), Marsilius of Padua (see chap. 6) and William of Ockham, all of whom were Nominalists and Aristotelians. Their motto was, "A Pope with a Council is greater than a Pope alone"—*papa cum concilio major est papa solo*.

Neither the conciliarists before or after the Schism denied that Papal headship was a necessary condition for the unity of the Church. Although they believed that in matters of doctrine the Pope had the right of jurisdiction, the Pope could not, for example, define, alter or augment articles of Faith capriciously. The Faith of the Church was not within the province of the Pope alone to determine, but should always involve a general council of the whole Church. As John of Paris argued in his *De Potestate Regia et Papali*, authority in the Church inhered not only in the pope and magisterium, but was diffused among her other members. In addition, a Pope might be deposed not only for heresy, but for a crime, even incompetence. This was

---

[74] Walker, W., *A History of the Christian Church.* New York, 1952, p. 291.

true not only because the Pope received his authority in the Church *propter ecclesiam* (as John was found of saying), but because his power could not have been endowed nor retained without the will of the Church. He acts in behalf of the whole Church and if the Pope fails to serve her, he can be deposed by the Faithful through the instrumentality of an ecumenical council—*collegium cardinalium quia ex quo consensus eorum facit papam loco ecclesiae, videtur similiter quod possit eum deponere.*

The *Epistola Concordiae* (1379) of Conrad of Gelnhausen called upon King Charles V of France (1364-1380) to convoke a council which would end the scandal, if necessary without the consent of the Popes. In this first major work of the Conciliar Movement, Conrad maintained that the Catholic Church (*congregatio fidelium*) and the Roman Church are not identical, if only because so many of the Popes had erred in matters of faith. Christ promised that "the gates of hades would not prevail" against the universal Church, protecting her by the Holy Spirit, "the Spirit of Truth," Who would insure the integrity of the faith.[75] No such promise was made to the Popes or the Roman church.

Conrad would not be the last to express such opinions. Pierre d'Ailly (1350-1420), Jean Gerson (1363-1429), etc., great lights of the conciliar era, extended and modified Gelnhausen's views, views which, with their own, reflected the ideas of the "pre-Protestant reforms," such as those undertaken by Wycliffe and Huss. If we may believe the familiar explanation, the whole purpose of the conciliarists was not only to unify Roman Catholicism under a single head, to end the Schism, but also to so redesign the Church as to making her a living organism which would function effectively in the time of crisis, including the death, incapacity or deposition of the Pope. For them, this was precisely one of those times.

G   The thought of a general council as the only means for healing the Schism found immediate support among many religious, scholars, and clergy. An assembly was held in Pisa in March of 1409. Neither of the Popes attended and both were deposed, a practical example of the Council's supe-

---

[75] The canonists, Joahnnes Teutonicus concurred—*sed certum est quod papa errare potest…ipsa congregatio fidelium hic dicitur ecclesia* (the universal Church)*…et talis ecclesia non potest non esse…quod verum est ubi de fide agitur et tunc synodus major est papa* (*Glossa Ordinaria.* Ed. by B. Brixiensis. Paris, 1601, ad c. 24 q. 1 c. 9). Later canonists were determined to unite the Church under a single head, without which, they argued, the Church could not function effectively as a unitary organism. Running through their glosses, however, one finds two separate concepts of "unity" which have existed in "troubled association to the present day": "the mystical body" and the "dogmatico-legal Church" (B. Tierney, *Foundation of the Conciliar Theory….*, pp. 50f., 135, 240).

riority to the Pope. The Cardinals now elected the Archbishop of Milan as Alexander V (1409-1410). The result was not unity but a greater division. There were now three Popes—the excommunicated Gregory XII (1406-1415) and Benedict XIII (1394-1417), as well as Alexander. Hence, the counciliarists pressed with even greater vigor for a resolution to the ecclesiastical turmoil.

A Council was called for the city of Constance by the Holy Roman Emperor-elect, Sigismund (1410-1437). He supported John XXIII (1410-1415), successor to Alexander. As an instrument of reform Constance was a bitter disappointment. It chose Pope Martin V (1417-1431)[76] who summoned a Council to meet in Basel. Two months later he was dead and was succeeded by Eugenius IV (1431-1447). This Pope ordered Basel adjourned (1431) and convoked another council for Bologna (1433). The conferees refused, appealing to Constance which declared a council of bishops superior to the Pope. Proceeding with its agenda, Basel issued all resolutions as bulls in its own name, and the recalcitrant Pope Eugenius, finding little help from clergy or laity, formally recognized the Council of Basel (1434). He was, to say the least, not committed to its aims. Also, he seemed preoccupied with idea of reconciliation with "the Greeks" which the Pope hoped would be achieved at the Council of Ferrara-Florence (1439).

Because he refused to enforce its decisions, Basel deposed Eugenius in the same year, and replaced him with Duke Amadeus of Savoy, who took the name Felix V. Eugenius never accepted his deposition nor the counciliarization of the Roman church. Backed by the German King, Frederick IV, the Pope denounced Basel in his bull, *Moyses vir* (Sept. 1439). In December of the same year, he promulgated another, *Dudum Sacrum*, in which he retracted his dissolution of Basel. He was eventually succeeded by Nicholas V (1447-1455). Felix laid down his office in 1449. With unity restored, the Council

---

[76] Pope Martin V was elected by a general Council which claimed that its power came *a Christo immediate* and was, therefore, superior to the Pope. He replaced Pope John XXIII whom the Council of Pisa was about to try for a number of offenses. None contested the election of Martin, for if they had, if Pope John were in fact not deposed, then Martin was not Pope and neither was his successor, Eugenius IV, nor his successors, Nicholas V, Pius II, Paul II, Sixtus IV, etc. "But according to the principle *prima sedes a nemine iudicator*, and, *a fortiori*, according to the Vatican I dogma," Fr Bulgakov reminds us, "the act of trying and deposing a pope, and electing a new one in his place, is unlawful and revolutionary."

"If, however, the council had a right to act as it did, it obviously had dogmatic and canonical reasons for it, as expressed in the resolution passed at the 4th and 5th sessions [of Constance]. The deposition of one pope and election of another is a dogmatic, or as lawyers always say, a conclusive fact, either disproving the absolute primacy of popes or interrupting their canonical succession: if Martin V is not a lawful pope, his successors are not lawful either; papal succession is discontinued" (*The Vatican Dogma*, p. 27f.).

closed its troubled career. Though the conciliar idea lived to become a powerful force during the Reformation age, the hope of return to an Orthodox
ecclesiology evaporated with the Catholic Counter-Reformation.

Nevertheless, this episode in Latin church history led to something
unexpected. It centered the dogmaticians attention on the problem which
arises from the death, heresy or incapacity of the Pope—especially his claim
to the headship of the Catholic Church, in which he possesses "the plenitude
of power" and the "infallibility" which the Lord promised not to the universal Church, as the Roman Catholics insist, but to Peter and his successors.
How, as it was in the case of Constance and Basel, may Councils of Bishops
judge, depose and appoint their superior? How can the lesser rank elevate
a bishop to a place above the episcopacy? The higher must raise the lower.
But there is a far more perplexing question resulting from the dogmatic decisions of Constance and Basel: Roman Catholicism must accept, as did these
Councils, the superiority of the bishop's assembly over the Pope, lest Roman
Catholicism be forced to concede that the succession of Popes ended in fifteenth century. Was it not these Councils which gave to the medieval Latin
church a number of Popes? Its ecclesiology had been faced with a terrible
conundrum, only exacerbated by Vatican I.

H   Papal infallibility, which for centuries had been the *de facto* ecclesiology
of Roman Catholicism, became a dogma with the first Vatican Council.[77]
This dogma consists of two parts—*Constitutio dogmatica de fidei Catholica* and
Constitutio. The new ecclesial definition was divided into four canons, complete with anathemata against opponents of papal infallibility, including the
so-called *fratres separati* (i.e., the Protestants, the Orientals and the Orthodox).

The first Canon makes the familiar assertion that St Peter was appointed by the Lord "as head of all the apostles and the head of the whole church
militant...the primacy not only of honor but of true and actual jurisdiction."
The second Canon anathematizes anyone who confesses that "the Roman
pontifex is not the successor of the blessed Peter in such primacy." The third
Canon affirms that the Pope has "not only the power of supervision and
direction, but the full and supreme power of jurisdiction of the whole
Church, both in matters of faith and morals." His authority extends "ordinarily and directly to all and every local church and to all and every pastor
and believer." Therefore, Canon four concludes, "The Roman pontifex, when
he speaks *ex cathedra*, i.e., when fulfilling his office of pastor and teacher of

---

[77]   Only after Vatican I (1870) "papalism ceased to be merely a fact and became a
dogma: the question was closed," remarks Fr Bulgakov. *"Roma locuta est*—in the face of
the whole world, in the full light of publicity" (*Ib.*, p. 8.).

all Christians, in virtue of his supreme apostolic authority, whenever he defines a doctrine concerning faith and morals is binding upon the whole Church, for he enjoys, with God's help promised to him in the person of the blessed Peter, the infallibility which the Divine Redeemer promised to His church. . .in this wise, the definitions laid down by the Roman pontifex are as such, apart from the assent of the church, not subject to correction"— *Romani Pontificis definitiones ex sese, non autem exconsensu Ecclesiae, irreformabilis esse.*[78]

The Vatican dogma was not the inevitable realization of a divine Truth, as the Council boasted; it was a critical moment in the development of the Papacy, of its form and its substance. In contradistinction to other Latin Councils, for example, the resolutions of Vatican I were put in the form of a bull published as the Pope's personal decree. Indeed, there was no need for the Council at all, except as an advisory body, since the Pope may act *ex sese, non autem exconsensu Ecclesiae irreformabilis esse.* The Vatican dogma, and especially this phrase, places the Bishop of Rome above the episcopacy, above the Church universal; it is as if a new and fourth degree of holy Orders was created for him, *episcopus episcoporum,* a position discoverable absolutely nowhere in the Scriptures, the Fathers, nor the ancient Councils. Only a tendentious manipulation of the Christian Tradition explains it.

Thus, unlike his bishops, the Pope has a "universal ordinary," to use the words of Pope Gregory VII. His privileges, such as infallibility, are intrinsic to his office. He has more than "the power of supervision and direction" (*officium inspectionis vel directionis*), but has "the full and supreme power of jurisdiction in the whole Church" (*plenam et supremam potestatem iurisdictionis in universam Ecclesiam*). Because the Pope is infallible *de fide vel moribus,*[79] a Council of bishops becomes virtually superfluous, having no authority to make final decisions in theological matters. But more, since the power of the Pope extends "ordinarily and directly to all and every church and to all and every believer," the local church is monsterized by two heads—its bishop and the Pope—while the local bishop becomes to the Pope what the presbyter is to his bishop.[80]

---

[78] The four Canons are recorded by Bulgakov's *The Vatican Dogma* in both English (pp. 49-50) and Latin (pp. 83-84).

[79] The infallibility of the Pope in "faith and morals" is actually indefinite and unlimited, for there is no human activity which is not related to them. Nothing in the life of the Church escapes the Pope's competence. *Undoubtedly, not all that he does or says require an infallible pronouncement, but since no aspect of thought and action is without its religious implications, any idea or occurrence might very well invite one.*

[80] The *De Ecclesia* of Pope Paul VI (21 Nov 64) attempted to correct the ecclesial problems of Vatican I with its formulae about "the collegiality of bishops." *(continued)*

Ironically, the Vatican Council could in fact not proclaim Papal sovereignty without simultaneously annulling its right to legislate, which is precisely what it did. Also, "How could a Council be expected to pass the resolution if it has no power to decide anything on which the Pope alone has the right of final judgment?" asks Fr Bulgakov. "How could the Council have consented even to debate such an absurdity? It can, of course, be argued that the Vatican Council had to carry out the Pope's behest from obedience, regardless of content; but even as infallible, the Pope cannot do meaningless and self-contradictory things, such as submitting to a Council's decision a motion when the power to decide belongs not to it, but to him."[81] An assembly of the Latin bishops, therefore, is only a "rubber-stamp" of the Pope's *res iudicata*. In truth, the assent and cooperation of the Council is pointless, because to confess Papal infallibility is to believe it because the Pope has spoken *ex cathedra*, and not because 533 ecclesiastical dignitaries voted for it.

Unlike Vatican I, none of the eight Ecumenical Councils of the Church (325-787)—called by the Christian Emperor, not the Pope—met to simply reaffirm the Pope's decree; nor did the formulation and publication of the Creed require his infallible seal of approval. He could not have spoken *ex cathedra*, an idea with no meaning until the Latin Middle Ages. Everything taught in the Creed was transmitted to the Church from Christ through the Apostles. If the Orthodox Bishop of Rome had failed to ratify the Creed, he would himself have been anathematized, because a Council of the universal Church is a Voice of the Holy Spirit *de fide vel moribus*.

Finally, if we remember that every bishop is "the living image of Christ" and "teacher of the Faith" as well as the "president" and "high priest" of the Eucharist, we understand why he and his flock constitute a Eucharistic com-

---

(cont'd.) The "sacred Council" teaches that the episcopacy is a divine institution succeeding to the place of the apostles, as Shepherds of the Church, "and he who hears them, hears Christ, and he who rejects them, rejects Christ and Him Who sent Christ." At the same time, "the college of bishops has no authority unless it is understood together with the Roman Pontiff" (III, 22). Although individual bishops "are the visible principles and foundation of the unity in their particular churches" (III, 23), the definitions of the Pope are not subject to the review of the episcopacy or the faithful, for "of themselves, not from the consent of the Church, are justly styled irreformable, since they are pronounced with the assistance of the Holy Spirit, and therefore they need no approval of others, nor do they allow an appeal to any other judgment" (III, 25). Pope Paul adds (III, 25) that "the charism of infallibility of the church" is individually present in the Pope (trans. by National Catholic Welfare Conference. Washington, D.C, 1964). See also Vatican II, *Lumen Gentium*, 21 Nov 64).

81   *The Vatican Dogma*, p. 62.

munity.   If, then, the Pope is the head of the Catholic Church, the local churches are not the Catholic Church "in a particular place." They are merely cells or "parts" of the "whole" (as Roman Catholic ecclesiology requires). Then, surely his Eucharist is the only Eucharist of the Catholic Church. The Eucharists of the individual bishops (and their presbyters) are "valid" only as part of the Pope's Eucharist, for the Bishop of Rome is "the Bishop of Bishops, the Bishop of the Catholic Church," "the ordinary and immediate head" of all the Faithful.

CHAPTER 6

THE EIGHTH DAY

The West has had to endure two world wars before it came to the realization that "Western civilization in its secular form is coming to the end of an era and needs radical transformation."[1] In a sense, both Bury's humanist ideal of civilization's inevitable progress and Spengler's prognostications of its unavoidable decline, are right—technological progress, moral and cultural decline. This paradox (if such is the right word) has reawakened interest in what, since Voltaire, has been called "the philosophy of history,"—"historiosophy" as some refer to it—or, in other circles, "theology of history." Whatever the position, asking the same questions leaves the same futility. Likewise, to resolve them by rewriting the first principles of history, and to determine, if any, what bearing the "supra-empirical" has on the creation (especially man), has no promise but bitter frustration.

For the last two hundred years the search for a "meaning in history" has been motivated by the question which the previous ages of human history have failed to produce concerning the foundation of a new world in which all the ancient enemies of man have been shed—poverty, war, sickness, hatred, etc. Sadly, this pursuit of a "bright and happy future of beauty and justice" has become increasingly secular, that is, premising man's purpose on his material and emotional well-being. The quest for "the holy grail" has been abandoned in favor of a quest for material happiness and enlightenment in this world. But "those who do not learn the lessons of history are

---

[1] C.T. McIntire's Introduction to the anthology, *God, History and Historians: Modern Christian Views of History.* New York, 1977, p. 7. "...the philosophical and religious presuppositions by which we live," observes the famous Protestant theologian, Reinhold Niebhur, "are as seriously challenged by world events as are the political institutions by which we have ordered our lives" (*The Nature and Destiny of Man.* New York, 1943, I, vii). His solution was a return to "the Biblical sources of the Christian Faith," as if the way in which these "sources" have been understood and interpreted in the West have had nothing to do with "the philosophical and religious presuppositions" by which the post-Orthodox West has "ordered" its life for nearly a millennium.

condemned to repeat them," if I may quote Santayana. Without the God of Revelation, nothing will be found but the sure path to spiritual oblivion.

Refusing to accept this ominous forecast, modernity has begun to search for man's beatitude where he seems always to begin, with himself or, more precisely, with a radical critique of all cultures, beginning with man himself. An inauspicious beginning, since "at no other time in his history has man become so much a problem to himself as the present," wrote the German philosopher, Max Scheler (1874-1928). He cannot determine what is his true nature and destiny, because, where he simply ignores or denies God, he has created an idol of himself, unaware that he cannot escape his dead dreams without genuine repentance and the revealed Faith. He refuses even to invent God, as Voltaire suggested he do. Adding to his woes are the obstacle of Western secular culture and ideology, the rationalism which generated, with the assistance of false religion and occultism, the philosophical and theological heritage of the post-Orthodox West.

The "problem of man," therefore, is also the "problem of God." The twentieth century gives sufficient proof of that contention. It seems to have lost all confidence in the Christian religion; it is a sick whale beached on the wet sands of a sullen shore. If the West has generally ignored the Moslem "God," it is because He cannot walk among us; and if the West has generally hesitated to adopt the "ultimate reality" of Eastern religions, the idea of losing personal identity in an infinite ocean of loveless being is intolerable to us. None of these "foreign"religions have invested much hope in history.

If Orthodox Christianity is not recognized in the West as the alternative to all these choices, we may believe that most people think she is just an Eastern version of what they already know. In point of fact, she is unique, a religion which teaches that the true God has entered the world as a man not only to eradicate evil, but by Grace to make divine all that He created and governs. In truth, God's Plan is already unfolding: the transfiguration of the cosmos is coming. The fulfillment of His Plan is being realized even now throughout history, especially through those great events of time and place, turning-points of religious, political and cultural history, driven not only by "heroes" and "grand ideas," but by forces vast and imponderable.

In the midst of all these epochal events, persons and ideas, which have shaped and reshaped the face of time, if we believe the holy Fathers, there is a milieu of centrifugal importance: the Roman Empire—the last of the great Kingdoms foretold by the Prophet Daniel—which with Constantine the Great became the *romanum imperium christiana*, surviving until its violent overthrow in the second decade of twentieth century. With the martyrdom of God's Anointed, St Nicholas II, Tsar of all the Russias, Lord of the "Third Rome," the world has entered the *apocalypsis* of history.

Along with the murder of the last Orthodox emperor, the socialist revolution is the central fact of the twentieth century. Camus' description of regicide as "the crux of our contemporary history, its secularization and the disincarnation of the Christian God" has been trivialized into political insignificance. Lost is the truth that "God played a part in history through the medium of kings" (say rather, the Orthodox emperors). His "human representative in history has been killed. . .there is no longer a king."[2] The "Constantinian era" is over, "that which restrains," κατέχον (II Thess. 2:6), has passed away with little report. In its place, has come the materialistic worldview of socialism—a mechanistic historiosophy, a new concept of man as the soulless deity whose collective task is the construction of a new reality, a Graceless thing, with spirit, at best, an epiphenomenon, which both modern politics and religion—socialism and ecumenism—endeavor to exploit to their peculiar ends. The way for "the Antichrist" has been opened.

Knowing these things, it is yet impossible with any gratifying certainty to trace the course of history that has brought the West and the human race to this κρίσις (crisis), or what occurrences will lead it to the *eschaton*; for the truth of things is not always visible, and not every phenomenon is amenable to theological explanation, let alone philosophical diagnosis.[3] By revelation the Church knows the meaning of history. Only "through a glass darkly" does she see the things which have been, things that are, things to come, a meagre vision divinely bequeathed to the holy.

1   MEANING IN HISTORY

The Orthodox Church espouses no "philosophy of history,"[4] as commonly understood—no scheme *a la* Hegel or Herder, no rational search for causes, not even Scriptural exegesis which give mortal eyes a glimpse of future political events, which today is in vogue among so many Protestant groups.

---

[2] *The Rebel*. Trans. by A. Bower. New York, 1956, p. 120. We supplement the words of Camus with the words of St Cyril of Jerusalem. The death of the Tsar signals the end of the Christian Roman Empire, fortelling "the Antichrist which is to come when the times of the Roman empire shall be expired, and the end of the world draws near" (*Catech*. XV, 12 NPNF).

[3] "Christian speculation about the meaning of history," surmises Bernard McGinn, "grew out of intertestamental Jewish apocalyptic eschatology" (*The Calabrian Abbot: Joachim of Fiore in the History of Western Thought*. New York, 1985, p. 51). Western scholarship will abide by such conclusions so long at it fails to recognize Christianity as the final revelation of God.

[4] They are very much mistaken who believe that "the Greek Orthodox view" is represented by the Russian Boehmist, Nicholas Berdiaev (F. E. Manuel, *Shapes of Philosophical History*. Stanford [Ca.], 1965, p. 144). Among other (continued on next page)

Nevertheless, there is meaning or purpose in history which, to be sure, implicates things political and cultural, economic and military. The Church is also cognizant that the grand dynamics of history is ultimately controlled by God, while, strangely, men also, with their passions and their schemes, and the evil one with all his machinations, have a free hand. Whatever happens in time and space, the divine Plan unfolds freely, mysteriously, under the seven heavens and through the seven Ages of history, the direction of things always moving towards their preordained *telos*.

History is *"salvation history" (heilsgeschichte)* set in the form of a cosmic drama. It is cosmic, because the history of the world is the history of the great and unseen battle between the triune Good and the evil one. It is cosmic because God became man in order to recover the universe lost to the devil by our disobedient first-parents. It is cosmic because the Crucified Lord has overwhelmed the omniverous death which was their penalty. It is cosmic, because, despite what stands stridently before our eyes, the profane is in full retreat before the sacred. Thus, the Church is contemptuous of any theory which declares the *arche* and *telos* of the creature to be determined either by impersonal fate or human ingenuity. God's Providence and Grace silently guides man and the universe to their destiny: the participation in the divine Nature which He had originally intended for all physical and noetical creation.

A   Several things are clear to Orthodoxy about the temper of temporal and historical existence. The eternal God is the omnipotent Creator of the heavens and the earth. From this fact, a simple ontological distinction is drawn: the disparity between the eternal and uncreated God, and contingent and created being. The difference between them is so enormous as to be incomprehensible. What the creation commonly experiences of Him are His communicable Uncreated Energies. The first creature was time (αἰών); hence, the further division between the spiritual or noetical and the physical. They are distinct orders of being, but not autonomous.

The two created realms, the spiritual and the physical, compose all created reality. Although the spiritual is not encompassed by the physical, spirit permeates the physical or material world. History, therefore, is not independent of that unseen realm and may not be written as if it were. They are

---

(cont'd.) things, he taught erroneously that the Russian monarchy was Caesaropapist, a "sin" which doomed Russian culture and led the nation to the Communist Revolution (*The Origin of Russian Communism*. Trans. by R.M. French. London, 1948, pp. 131-132). His *The Meaning of History* (trans. by G. Reavy. London, 1949) offers a metaphysics foreign to the thinking of the Church, most especially Berdiaev's Platonic doctrine of redemption as deliverance from history.

united without "separation or confusion": Christ is the pattern. His Coming introduces another dimension, the Kingdom of God. Whereas God (and, therefore, eternity) has always been present in time through His Uncreated Energies, now with the Incarnation the Divine has appeared personally and visibly created to return His creation to fellowship with the Creator.

History, then, has a meaning which is perceptible to the eyes of faith, a meaning which concedes to time no neutral ground, neither in its beginning nor its end; hence, persons, places and things do not occur by chance or pre-determination. Nevertheless, there is a temporal order, not at all hostile to human freedom, moving human history towards a terminus by spans or intervals of time called "ages." Time (and history), reflecting the Genesis week, is allotted to seven Ages,[5] with the eighth and everlasting Age or "Day" to follow, that is, the Kingdom of God. St Basil the Great writes,

> God fashioned the nature of time and set the intervals of days as its measure and sign. Calculating the week as seven-day periods, He commanded that the week continually revolve upon itself, so as to number the movements of time. Again, He ordered that one day, revolving seven times upon itself, completes a week. This has the form of a circle, since it begins and ends with itself.
>
> Such is the character of an 'age,' that is, to revolve upon itself without limitation. If, then, the beginning of time is called 'one day' rather than the 'first day,' it is because Scripture seeks to associate that day with the age. Surely, it was fitting to describe by the name 'one' the day whose character is unique and shared with no other.
>
> If the Scripture speaks of many ages, saying everywhere 'age of ages' or 'ages of ages,' they are nowhere enumerated as first, second, third. In this way, we are shown not so much limits, ends and succession of ages as the distinction between various stages and objects. It is written, 'the day of the Lord is great and very bright' (Joel 2:11); and

---

5   Generally, the Fathers do not define the content and duration of the world's ages. Augustine was at one time not so reluctant. The first, he said, extended from Adam to Noah, the second from Noah to Abraham, the third, from Abraham to David, the fifth from David to the Captivity in Babylon, the sixth from the Captivity to the Advent of Christ—through which we are now passing—and, finally, the seventh day, the day of "the Sabbath rest" when Christ will return to reign [a thousand years] on earth with the saints. "The eighth day signifies the new life at the end of the historical ages" (*Serm.* CCLIX PL 38 1197f.).

Elsewhere Augustine added that "the seventh day will be brought to a close not by an evening, but by the Lord's Day, as an eighth and eternal day, already consecrated by the resurrection of Christ, and prefiguring the eternal repose not only of the spirit, but also of the body. There we shall rest and see, and love, love and praise. This is the state which will be without end" (*De Civ. Dei*, XXII, 30 PL 41 667f.). Although he seems to have rejected millennarianism, his attitude towards it remained ambivalent to the end. See Danielou, *The Bible and the Liturgy*. Notre Dame (Ind.), 1956, pp. 276-286.

elsewhere, 'Why should you seek the day of the Lord? This day is darkness and not light' (Amos 5:16). 'Darkness,' that is, for those worthy of it.

This day without evening, without succession and without end is not unknown to Scripture, and is the day which the Psalmist calls 'the eighth,' because it is outside the time of weeks.

Thus, whether one says 'day' or 'age,' he expresses the same idea. Give this state the name of 'day'; it is one, not many. Or if you call it 'age,' it is still single and not multiple. Thus, that you may project your thoughts towards the age to come which the Scripture marks by the word 'one,' the day of which Sunday, 'the first-fruits of days,' is the icon, the contemporary of Light, the holy Day of the Lord, honored by His Resurrection.[6]

The "one day" is the "beginning" of time, "the instantaneous and imperceptible moment of creation." St Basil adds,

But just as the beginning of the road is not yet the road and the beginning of the house is not the house, so the beginning of time could not be time, nor even the least portion of it.... It is absurd to imagine the beginning of beginning.... Thus, when it is written, 'In the beginning God created,' it is to teach us that the Will of God made the cosmos to arise in less than an instant" (*Hexa.*, I, 6 PG 32 145D).

As time has an absolute beginning, it shall have an end, and he who denies one or the other blasphemes against the Only-Begotten Son of God (*De Sp. Sanct.* 43 PG 32 145D).

B   For St Basil, the Word or Logos of God is both Creator and Savior. Before His Incarnation, He was not only the Maker of the heavens and the earth, but also served as their Providence. Relative to his human sojourn, the pivotal event in history is the Lord's bodily Resurrection which inaugurates the restoration of the creation and its return to Him Who fashioned it. That moment is the promise of a cessation to the relentless roll of hours, days, weeks and years, and an end to the mutability of man's life; indeed, His bodily Resurrection typifies things to come.

---

6   *Hexa.* II, 8 PG 29 49D-52A. The late Cardinal Danielou has demonstrated that the doctrine of the Eighth Day was universally held by the Fathers, as well as by Augustine and Origen. According to Danielou, this doctrine has "completely emptied history of all significance. We are here in the midst of Hellenistic thought" (*The Bible and the Liturgy*, pp. 265). He is mistaken in several ways: 1) the Greek idea of "time as the image of eternity," presupposing fated, interminable and necessary recurrence of ages is not found in patristic literature; 2) time is conceived differently in the Fathers and Hellenism: the first is linear, the second cyclical; 3) the creation, recovered from the devil, is returned to God in Christ. There is no "Great Year." The Eighth Day, the Age to Come, is endless, without repitition, because God is eternal and immutable (Ps. 89:2; 101:26-27 LXX; James 1:17).

By contrast, the Greek idea of time has no beginning and no end and, as Plotinus dreamt, man's resurrection *is from* the flesh, not in the flesh. Aristotle describes the common Greek view of time.

> We cannot truly say, e.g., that 'it is absolutely necessary for a house to come-to-be when foundations have been laid'; for (unless it is always necessary for a house to be coming-to-be), we should be faced with a consequence that, when foundations have been laid, a thing which need not *always* be, must always be. No; if its coming-to-be is 'necessary', it must be 'always', it must be 'always' in its coming-to-be. For what is 'of necessity' coincides with what is 'always', since that which 'must be' cannot possibly 'not-be.' Hence a thing is eternal if its 'being' is necessary. And if, therefore, the 'coming-to-be' of a thing is necessary, its 'coming-to-be' is eternal; and if eternal, necessary. It follows that the coming-to-be of anything, if it is absolutely necessary, must be cyclical, i.e., must return upon itself...(*De Gen. et Cor.*, II, XI, 11 337b-338a).

Time has *diastole* and *systole*, a coming into existence and a going out of it, by which the Greeks detailed both cosmic and human existence as a cycle of ages—birth, thriving, acme, decline—without end. They applied this scheme to nations, none doing it better than the ancient *Histories* of Polybius (2nd c. BC) who foretold the demise of Rome, which caused the Greek-educated Scipio Africanus, the conqueror of Hannibal, to weep bitterly. Hellenism recognized no Providence, only the unyielding laws of time, or fate, to which the gods (if any) were themselves subject.

C The fact that the Fathers explained the Christian Faith in the language of current thought is no reason to characterize Christianity as a synthesis of religion and Greek philosophy which was "dominated by the ideas of permanence and recurrence." The new vision of human destiny, in the light of Christ, could not be accurately and adequately expressed in the terms of Greek philosophy; and, in fact, old words had to be given new meanings in order to provide the Christian message with a voice to the culture. As St Basil's exegesis of Genesis shows the "problem" of the Fathers was not "adjustment" and "relevance," but "a radical change in the basic habits of mind."[7]

Only with the spread of the Christian Faith did things physical and temporal come to have spiritual value. The Fathers undertook the "refutation of the cyclical conception of time" but "only in the context of a coherent doctrine of creation."[8] The Christian cosmogony presupposed a theology unknown

---

[7] Florovsky, G., "Eschatology in the Patristic Age: An Introduction," *The Greek Orthodox Theological Review* II, 1 (1956), 31.

[8] *Ibid.*, 33.

to the classical world; and, therefore, a perspective on man and history unimagined by the pagan by whose admission freedom was illusory, and death was the only escape from the cosmic *perpetuum*, a flight which promised not redemption of but the liberation from fleshly suffering. Thus, St John Chry-sostom asks with no little mockery, "Where are they who disbelieve the Resurrection? Who are they, I pray. For I am an ignorant man—nay, certainly I know. Are they Gentiles or Christians who deny the work of creation. The two denials go together: the denial that God created *ex nihilo*, and the denial that He raises the dead" (*Acta. Apost.* II, 4 PG 60 31). It is not an impersonal fate which governs the universe, he rejoiced, but the Almighty God Who rules and informs the course history by His Providence; hence, "meaning" is something bestowed by God, and revealed according to the Creator's good pleasure.

D   Early Christianity produced historians in the familiar sense—Eusebius of Caesarea, Theodoret, Socrates, Cassiodorus, Orosius, Sulpicius Severus, St Gregory of Tours, St Bede the Venerable, etc.—but their facts assumed a peculiar "theology of history" (as all histories do) and their writings were not lacking apologetical intent—an intolerable "bias" which, if we believe modern historians, spoils their credibility. These writings were "ecclesiastical histories," albeit unlike Augustine's *The City of God*, which was the first attempt to compose a "universal history," a "Christian interpretation of history," as some call it. A record of much more than past events, *The City of God* pretended to be offer a demonstration of history as the working out of the divine Plan which embraces all peoples and ages. Augustine explicates the application of timeless principles which predetermine the whole story of human spiritual development.[9]

Since the Fall of Adam, explained Augustine, the human race has been divided between those of his posterity "who live according to man, the other according to God. And these we also mystically call the two communities of men, of which the one is predestined to reign eternally with God and the others who will suffer eternal punishment with the devil." One of Adam's two sons, Cain, founded the city of man (Gen. 4:17) and Abel belonged to the City of God (*civitas Dei*)...whence it comes to pass that each man, being derived from a condemned stock, is born of Adam both evil and carnal, becoming

---

[9]   Christopher Dawson maintains that Augustine's "theory of history is strictly deduced from his theology of creation and Grace. It is not a rational theory in so far as it begins and ends in revealed dogma; but it is rational in the strict logic of its procedure and it involves a definitely rational and philosophical theory of the nature of society and law and of the relation of social life to ethics" ("St Augustine and His Age: The City of God," in *Saint Augustine: His Age, Life and Thought.* Ed. by M.C. D'Arcy. New York, 1957,

good and spiritual only when grafted into Christ by regeneration; so it is with the human race as a whole." Furthermore, "when these two cities began to run their course by a series of deaths and birth," Augustine continued, "the citizen of the world was the first-born [i.e., by natural propagation], and after him the stranger in this world, the citizen of the City of God, predestined by Grace, elected by Grace, by Grace a stranger below, and by Grace a citizen above" (*Civ. Dei* XV, 1 MD). These two cities, *civitas Dei*—to which those before Christ were His "faith" (Heb. XI, 1-40; Augustine, *Ep*. CII, 2, xii 2 PL 33 374); and *civitas terrena*, a city of men who have rejected Him—have defined history from its tragic inception.

The City of God, which antedates the creation of the physical world, is "a great City, new Jerusalem, coming down from God out of the heavens" (Rev. 21:2). She is the true and invisible Church (*Civ. Dei*, XX, 17) and, therefore, neither the hierarchical Church[10] nor the state, not even the Christian Empire of Constantine, may be equated with the eternal City.[11] Although a shadow of that celestial realm, a symbol of the heavenly City,[12] the Catholic

---

[10] "It is impossible to identify the City of God with the Church, as some writers have done, since in the heavenly City, there is no room for evil or imperfection, no admixture of sinners with the saints," writes Christopher Dawson. "But, on the other hand, it is an even more serious error to separate the two concepts completely and to conclude that St Augustine assigned no absolute and transcendent value to the hierarchical Church. Certainly the Church is not the eternal City of God, but it is its organ and representative in the world. It is the point at which the transcendent spiritual order inserts itself into the sensible world, the one bridge by which the creature can pass from time to eternity" ("St Augustine and His Age...," 72).

If Dawson is correct about Augustine, and he seems to be (*Ep*. CXXXVIII, 5 NPNF), the Bishop's ecclesiology is uncommon. The Fathers, East and West, identify the Church on earth with the City and Kingdom of God. For example, St Basil the Great asserts that membership in the visible Church is confirmation of our heavenly citizenship, for God is in "the midst of the city...the name 'city' applying to Jerusalem above as well as below" (*Hom. on Ps*. XVIII, 5 PG 29 424B); and Jerome says that the Church is "our heavenly Jerusalem," *municipatus in Deo* (*In Zachariam* PL 25 1529D). The "hierarchical Church" is becoming what she is (see footnote 12).

[11] Augustine called Rome a "second Babylon" (*De Civ. Dei*, XVIII, 2 MD), while insisting that the Christian emperor live modestly, governing with mercy and benevolence, without vainglory, acting with "love of eternal felicity, not neglecting to offer to the true God, who is their God, sacrifices of humility, prayer and contrition for their sins, such Christian emperors, we say, are happy in the present time by hope, and are destined to be so in the enjoyment of that reality which we all await" (*ib.*, V, 24).

[12] The Fathers refer to the Church as an "icon" of the Age to Come, meaning that although the Orthodox Church is the City and the Kingdom, she is imperfect. Augustine's nestorian ecclesiology separates heaven and earth, what is and what is to come (See K. Loweth, *Meaning of History*. Chicago, 1949, p. 165f.). With a hidden pride, it would seem, Dawson compares Augustine's City of God with "the Neo-Platonic concept of the Intelligible World—κόσμος νοητός; indeed, the Christian Platonists of later times who were equally devoted to Augustine and Plotinus, deliberately *(continued on next page)*

Church is a mixture of "the elect," "the predestined," that is, "the hidden People of God" and the reprobate, indicating thereby that the historical Church is not a vessel of salvation;[13] while the state, according to the Bishop of Hippo, was wholly conceived, born and nurtured in sin.

Augustine recognized no secular progress, no perfection of man by education, no utopian state or cosmopolis; nevertheless, he admitted some spiritual progress in all individuals—a curious notion considering his views on irresistible Grace. His theology was almost unknown in the East, but of those Latin Fathers who were familiar with his writings (Sts John Cassian, Vincent of Lerins, Faustus of Riez, etc.), they had little sympathy for too much of it, especially his novel bifurcation of the temporal Church and the true Church, the City of God. They did not hold with his opinion that one could belong to Christ without first belonging to the Eucharistic, hierarchical community of believers.

E   History is composed of two races—the race of Christ and the race of Adam, that is, the Church and the world: those reborn of "water and the Spirit" (John 3:5) and "those who shall perish in their own corruption" (II Pet. 2:12). Although Christians "are not different from other men in nationality, speech or custom" (*Ep. ad Diogn.*, 5 FC), they are obligated "not to be unequally yoked together with unbelievers: for what fellowship has righteousness with unrighteousness? And what communion has light with darkness? What concord has Christ with Belial?" (II Cor. 6:14-15). This division of humanity into two races began when Yahweh (God the Son) selected Old Israel as His People, as His Bride. Liberating her from Pharoah and Egypt,[14]

(*cont'd.*)   made a conflation of the two ideas" ("St Augustine and His Age...., 67). The notion that members of "the hierarchical Church"—and for that matter her hidden members—have spiritual prototypes in the *kosmos noetos* (Ideas in the divine Mind), dovetails perfectly with Augustine's predestinarian soteriology.

[13] H. Chadwick, *Augustine*. Oxford, 1986, p. 55. Harnack opined that Augustine's ecclesiology does not identify the "true Church" with the earthly Church. The former he calls "the communion of the saints" or the "elect," members of the earthly Church who have received the gift of perserverance. "Thus, the thought of predestination shatters every notion of the church," he adds, "...and renders valueless all the divine ordinances, the insitution and [visible] means of salvation (*The History of Dogma* [vol. 5], p. 166).

[14] Vladimir Soloviev asserted that the Jews knew "Egypt" (Αἴγυπτος in Greek) under its more ancient name of *Chemia* ("the dark land"). The goddess Isis, the sensible image of the spiritual world, gave her children the power to become "gods." Escape from Egypt signified for Israel, among other things, freedom from idolatry (*Deutsche Gesamtausgabe: der Werke von Wladimir Solowjew* [bd. 6]. hrgs. W. Szyklarski, L. Mueller. Frieburg im Brerslau., 1965, 108-112). According to patristic typology, the Exodus prefigures the liberation of the new Israel from from the devil ("Pharoah") and the "darkness" of the world ("Egypt"). See the discussion in J. Danielou, *From Shadows to Reality: Studies in the Biblical Typology of the Fathers*. Trans. by W. Hibberd. London, 1960, bk. 4).

Israel was led to the land of Canaan, to Zion and Jerusalem—prefiguring thereby the Church's trek to the heavenly Kingdom. God promised to be Israel's God so long as she kept herself free from idolatry and obeyed His Law. "Beware lest thou forget the Lord, Who brought thee out of the land of Egypt, out of the house of bondage. Thou shalt fear the Lord thy God and Him only shalt thou serve; and thou shalt cleave to Him and by His Name thou shalt swear. Go ye not after after other gods, the gods of the nations which are round about you" (Deut. 6: 12-14 LXX).

With the conquest of the land, the establishment of her Kingdom, with Jerusalem as its capital, the City of David "where the Name of God is praised" (Ps. 103:21), Old Israel became manifestly "the shadow of good things to come" (Heb. 10:1), not the least of which was the prophecy concerning the

> Son of man coming in the clouds of heaven, and came to the Ancient of days, and they brought Him near before Him. And there was given Him dominion and glory, and a kingdom, that all peoples and nations, and languages, should serve Him: His dominion is an everlasting dominion which shall not pass away... (Dan. 7:13-14 LXX).

According to the divine Plan, with the fulfillment of the Old Testament prophecy, the Messiah (Dan. 9:25-26) will appear and build the new Israel, which shall include both Jews and Gentiles, His Church, a universal and historical religion, erected on historical facts—the Virgin Birth, the Cross, the Resurrection, the Descent of the Holy Spirit at Pentecost, etc.

The Church, the race of Christians, is His final revelation before the consummation of the divine Plan. She is the new beginning which is now what she will become—the Kingdom of God. Until that time, even though the devil has been defeated, he continues to battle God for the souls of men. The devil repeats in history his triumph in Eden ("ye shall be as gods"), luring the Faithful to apostasy with the same promises he made to Adam, promises with which he tempted the Savior as He fasted in the wilderness—"the lust of flesh, the lust of eyes and the pride of life" (I John 2:16).

Such must be the condition of the humanity outside of the Church, that is, the humanity which denies Christ's Lordship. Whatever Adam's children may do to improve the social and economic, even the moral lot of men, the result will always prove disappointing. Without the divine Truth and Grace, no shade of excellence or valor, however noble the cause pursued, whatever the scientific and technological advance, nothing can alter fundamentally the spiritual nature and status of the unregenerate. Outside of Christ, men remain under the power of the devil, sin and death. Without his freedom from these forces, man lives by his illusions.

2   Man and the State

If nothing else, the history of Western political thought demonstrates that the origin and nature of the "city" or "state" or "commonwealth" presupposes an understanding of man and the God or gods in whom its citizens believe. Whatever the variations of this idea, our statement is true everywhere, for everyone, always. In antiquity, the Greeks and Romans created the state for the purpose of constraining man's passions and reforming him into a being who lived in a community governed by reason. In the Middle Ages, the principal goal of the city was *iustitia*—ordained by "the Supreme Being"— with its classical and Augustinian antecedents, resting on the *lex natura (an image of the lex aeterna)*, discovered by the conceptual exercise of the intellect. The law signified that the Christian state was primarily a moral being, especially as its existence was crowned by faith.

The Renaissance, whose "rebirth" was spurred, in large part, by Byzantine exiles, was as much an heir to medieval political thought as it was to Hellenism. Renaissance humanists, in particular, were prone to elaborate mythical, ethical utopias. They discussed, contrary to both Scholastic and Reform theology, the idea of a "new man" and a "new society"—without taking into account the intrusion of sin. The Reformation was no less intrigued than Renaissance writers by the theory of "the two kingdoms," a part of the Augustinian (Platonic) heritage. The Reformers agreed with Wyclife, Marsilius of Padua and Occam that the authority of the state is not derived directly from God, but from the people, *vox populi, vox dei*. This idea, as it developed, eventually led, after the banishment of God, to Niccolo Machiavelli (1496-1527), and the secular science of politics. He is often credited with coining the word "state," conceived as an amoral being, the product of statecraft, whose existence and actions result from enlightened self-interest (*raison d'état*).

It would be interesting to learn what, if anything, Machiavelli, the Renaissance and the Reformation knew of the political theology ("political christology") of "the Eastern Empire and Church." Perhaps, they assumed that "the Greeks" and their dead empire with its Church in captivity had nothing to offer. Nothing, perhaps, save some old classical political ideas hardly deserving their attention, particularly if they assumed that its "idea of the city" was really no different from the medieval theories of the state which were even now only fodder for the new political world emerging before their eyes. It was a lamentable ignorance or indifference, because a genuine understanding of the Byzantium's "chalcedonian" political doctrine informing the West's political revolution would have radically altered its direction, providing it with an authentically Christian vision of God and history.

Instead the development of Western culture followed a predictable course, wounded by the familiar bifurcation of time (nature) and eternity (Grace) which, with the passage of time, only widened with the introduction of ideas which ordained the absolute separation of the secular and the sacred. How fascinating that by the nineteenth century all Western speculation about the city and history, God and man, should climax in what Nietzsche described as "the malignant historical fever," driven, on the one hand, by the spiritual pantheism of Hegel, and, on the other, with the materialistic monism of Marx. Since then the West has entered the positivist, postmodern era with the greatest dualism of all, the subjectivism of the irrational self and the objective world of science and technology. These have stung the Western religions to death, particularly Roman Catholicism, which, despite Pius IX's *Syllabus of Errors* (1864), has finally surrendered to most of what the Papal document condemned, including "tolerance" (ecumenism), "laicism," "liberalism," etc.

A   Most contemporary political thinkers, religious and secular, view the modern state as historically the antithesis of both the classical and Christian "theory" of government; and, therefore, have composed a new idea of man; or, perhaps, the reverse is more true. If there is any recognition of deity in the West, he is still *mutatis mutandis* the idol devised by Augustine and Thomas. Yet, however disdainful modernity may be of its religious past, of its "dark ages," nothing is more repugnant to it than the patristic conception of the state best expressed by St Irenaeus.

> God imposed upon mankind the fear of man as some do not fear God. It was necessary that they be subject to the authority of men, and kept under restraint by their laws whereby they might attain to some degree of justice and exercise mutual forebearance through dread of the sword...as the Apostle says (Rom. 13:4), 'For the higher power [the state, *exousia*] does not bear the sword in vain but is a minister of God, a revenger to execute wrath upon them that do evil' (*Adv. Haer.* V, xxiv, ii ANF).

Such was the position of the Church before and during her nearly seventeen hundred year alliance with the Roman Empire; and likewise in the West the words of Irenaeus prevailed until the rivalry between pope and king forced medieval philosophers, theologians and jurists, to find some resolution to the conflict, at the expense of Tradition. The result was a diversity of political theories which, on the face of them, called for further developments, for the "reform movements" that came.

B   From the moment that the Savior uttered His command, "Render therefore unto Caesar..." (Luke 20:25), and St Paul declared, "Let every soul be
subject unto the higher powers. For there is no power but of God..." (Rom.
13:1), the Orthodox Church has understood these and like statements to
mean that the state, whether pagan or Christian (John 19:11), exists by the
divine Will. The state, therefore, is the product of God's Providence and the
authority of the ruler originates with Him. Government exists everywhere
by virtue of the divine Providence or, if we may use the language of St
Justinian's *Digest* and *Institutes,* "natural law" (*ius naturale*)—i.e. the face of
the divine Energies—while the state is the "law of the nations" (*ius gentium*).[15]

By virtue of such legal concepts (and Aristotle), the Latin Middle Ages
produced a political theory in which "law" became the basis of the state
(regime). For Aquinas, law fell into several classifications, an ordered hierarchy of the natural law derived from "participation" in the eternal law
which is God's *ratio* or *logos*—*lex est aliquid pertinens ad rationem* (*S.T.* IIb, 1 q.
90 a. 1); while human law is obtained from natural law by deduction and
determination. If we look at the Fathers, the *ratio* or *logos* is God the Son—
the pre-incarnate Word, the Creator Who "enlightens every man that comes
into the world" (John 1:9). He is the Author of the moral and cosmic law. It
is in Him, exclaims St Gregory the Theologian, that "we live, and move, and
have our being" (*Theol. Ora.* IV, 20; Acts 17:28).

The divine Logos is the Source of government; and it is He Who
ordains, as the result of sin, that "there should be rulers, rule and ruled,"
affirms St John Chrysostom, an order established by Him "to prevent confusion, the people swaying in every direction, like waves of the sea" (*Ep. ad
Rom.,* 23 PG 49 93). If the human or positive law *(lex civile)* is faithful to His
Will—the eternal *Nomos*—it achieves its purpose. There is no disagreement
among the Fathers on this matter, and none on the details of the formula of

---

[15] Roman jurisprudence recognized three kinds of law: "natural law," "the law of
the nations" and "positive" or "civil law" (*ius civile*). The great task of Byzantine legisla-
tion was to christianize it, to bring legal concepts into harmony with the piety of the
Church. The Fathers were largely responsible for the transformation of the presuppos-
tions of *lex natura, lex gentium, lex civile.* First, informing them with the knowledge of
God's relation to all the nations (Rom. 2:12-14; Acts 27:28). The "laws of nature" are in
fact God's Providence, the action of His Uncreated Energies, everywhere in time and
space. Second, it is a mistake to think that nature exists in a normal condition. Third, the
fact that Christianity shares with Stoicism, to some degree, the belief that man is a social
creature and government is an institution necessary to the development of human life, is
no reason to look to Greek philosophy as the source of Christian political teaching (R.W.
Carlyle & A.J. Carlyle, *A History of Medieval Political Theory in the West* (vol. 1). Edinburg,
1930, p. 98). As we shall see, the Christian city, whatever its debt to paganism, is fundamentally different in purpose. The pagan city, metaphysically, is pretentious, a vainglo-
rious ambition, unaware of itself as a mythic, that is, only a racial, memory of Paradise.

"rulers, rule and ruled" which presuppose the "invisible Hand" of the Logos Who is also the Creator. In connection with this, they recognized also the Old Testament declaration, "By Me kings reign and princes decree justice" (Prov. 8:14), meaning that political authority comes form God, not the devil, as some heretics wrongly believed. Finally, by referring to God as the source of this authority, the Fathers confirmed the Old Testament conception of kingship, and differed with the theory of some pagan Roman jurists (e.g., Ulpianus, Gaius, Marcianus) that political authority was conferred on rulers by the people.[16]

St Gregory the Great ("Dialogist") is a representative voice of the Fathers on the relation between ruler and ruled. He writes that by nature all humans are equal—*omnes namque natura aequales sumus*—and that, although men were set over the animals, one man should not rule another—*homo quippe animalibus irrationalibus, non autem caeteris hominus natura est praelatus*—and only by His "secret dispensation," necessitated by sin, do some men rule over their fellows—*alios aliis dispensatio occulta postponit* (*Expo. Moral. in Beat. Job* XXI, 15, 22-23 PL 76 203). He who rules, then, even if an evil ruler, must be reverenced as one who derives his authority from God. St Gregory recalls for us the conduct of David towards Saul, observing that the former would not lay his hand on the Lord's anointed, and repented that he had cut the hem of Saul's garment. To resist the lawful ruler of a sacred society is to offend against Him who has set him over men (*Pastoral Care* III, 4 ACW).

St Gregory was certainly aware, having lived in Constantinople for seven years as the *apocrisarius* (*nuncio*) of Pope Pelagius II (579-590), that the supernatural authority of the emperor had limitations. He must have been known about the Nika revolt which occurred at the time of Justinian's accession to the throne (527). But more, he knew that Roman citizens had been granted various legal rights long before the christianization of the empire; and also that by the fifth century, the emperor was formally obliged to make a solemn declaration to the senate, the army and the people, who had cooperated in raising him to office, to preserve inviolate the Orthodox Faith, the canons and decrees of the Church's councils as well as her rights and privileges.

---

16 *Quod principi placuit, legis habet vigorem,* stated Ulpianus, *utpote cum lege regia, quae de imperio ejus lata est, populus ei et in cum omne suum imperium et potestatem conferat* (quoted in Carlyle, *History...* p. 64). There is a certain ambivalence on this question in the political history of the Christian Roman Empire. On being raised to the imperial rank by the army, Emperor Leo I (457-474) declared, "...the Almighty Lord and your choice has apppointed me emperor"; and Justinian affirmed in one of his famous novels the words, "...since God has placed us at the head of the Roman Empire..." Carlyle maintains that ultimately the Byzantines believed that imperial sovereignity was derived from God (*ib.,* p. 272).

By virtue of his *philanthropia* or *clementia*, the new emperor promised to be a "just and mild sovereign" who would refrain, as far as possible, from inflicting death and mutilation upon his people. Finally, he was made liturgically cognizant of the restrictions on his powers by the rite of royal unction, a Mystery which linked his authority to membership in the Church, by virtue of his reception of that unction at the hands of the patriarch. These were not mere formalities, but the binding obligations of a long tradition, which the Fathers would not permit him to forget.[17] Nevertheless, from time to time, the emperor presumed to play the ancient *pontifex maximus* or *sacerdos-rex* (pagan priest-king), intimidating the clergy and packing their councils with his sycophants. Already in the fourth century, the emperor was admonished,

> Intrude yourself not into ecclesiastical matters, wrote St Hosius of Cordova to the Emperor Constantius, neither give any command to us concerning them; but learn from us. God has put into your hands the empire, but to us He has entrusted the Church. If anyone should steal the empire from you, he would be resisting the ordinance of God; similarly, be fearful to usurp to yourself the things which pertain to the Church and avoid that which would make you guilty of great offense. It is written, Render unto Caesar the things of Caesar, but unto God the things of God (Matt. 22:21). Therefore, as we have no right to exercise earthly rule, so you, O emperor, have no authority to burn incense.[18]

In a word, the emperor shared his rule of Christian society with the bishops of the Church. Justinian put into law the ideal of two governing ministries ("dyarchy") of the Christian Roman Empire. "The priesthood and the imperium are the greatest gifts of God to man, a bestowal of His supernal care for mankind," he declared in his sixth Novel. "The former governs divine matters, the latter presides over and exhibits the diligent concern of men. Both, however, proceed from the same Source to adorn life." He described the relationship of the priesthood or *sacerdotium* to the government or *imperium* as a *symphonia*;[19] thus, the great symbol or emblem of the Byzantine christocracy,

---

[17] See W. Ensslin, "The Emperor and the Imperial Administration," in *Byzantium: An Introduction to East Roman Civilization*. Ed. by N.H. Baynes & H. St. L.B. Moss. Oxford, 1962, pp. 271-280.

[18] In *Hist. Arian.*, 44 PG 25 745D-748A. Also, St Athanasius, *Hist. Arian.*, 52 PG 25 756C; St John Chrysostom, *Ad pop. Antioch.* III, 2 PG 49 50; Ambrose, *Ep. 3 ad Emp. Theod.* FC; St John of Damascus, *De imag.* II, 12 PG 94 1296C, etc.

[19] Two fundamental categories of Byzantine political thought, were the hostility between the "light of Christ" and "the darkness of the world"; and relative to the Christian Empire itself, there is no distinction between secular and sacred spheres, only the distinction between the sanctified human (*imperium*) and the incarnated Divine (*ecclesia*) united "without separation of confusion." In the juridical language of the Emperor Justin-

the double-headed eagle, each pointing in opposite directions, holding the cross in one talon, the world in the other, the realization of the Chalcedonian principle of unity without "separation or confusion." The post-Orthodox Popes and kings of the West jousted for leadership of the medieval theocracy, a strange dualism which permitted only one head of the one body politic.

Ⅽ   Other than its Christian component, what was the difference between the Christian and classical city? Was not the Church heir to the Greek *polis* and the Roman *civitas*? The pagan kingdoms were caesaropapist, their rulers both "head of state" and head of the religion. Christian Rome had no such ideology, whatever the occasional pretentions of the emperor. He was the successor to Saul, David and Solomon, as well as to the Roman Augusti.[20] But there was something more fundamental, something even the medieval city could not manage with its adoption of the classical political theories. Glanville Downey's research[21] brought him to the conclusion that the pagan

---

ian: *Maxima quidem in hominbus sunt dona dei a superna collata clementia sacerdotium et imperiuim, illud quidem divinis ministrans, hoc autem humanis praesidens ac diligentiam exhibens; ex uno eodemque principio utraque procedentia humanam exornant vitam...erit consonantia (symphonia) quaedam bona, omne quidquid utile est humano conferens generi* (*Corpus juris civilis: Novellae* 4. col. 1, tit. 6 (ed. R. Schoell. Berlin, 1959).

This christological "distinction" is clearly embodied in the duties of the government or *imperium were the conduct of war, diplomacy, social philanthropy, defense of the Orthodox Faith; while the competence of the priesthood or sacerdotium was doctrine, canons, sacraments, evangelism. The line between the ministries was not always clear; for example, both had a profound interest in education, the government subsidized missionary activity, the clergy admonished the emperor and the bureacracy in their ethical behavior, etc. The people had the right to demand responsibile leadership from both.*

[20] Whatever the pagan elements in Byzantine monarchy, its prototype is the Hebrew monarchy. Note the suggested parallel between Jerusalem and Constantinople in the words of Justinian at the completion of Hagia Sophia: "Glory be to God, who has deemed us worthy of this deed. Solomon, I have conquered thee!" In the eighth century, with the recovery of the true Cross from the Persians, a troparion was composed to celebrate the event, "O Lord, save Thy People and bless Thine inheritance, granting to our believing emperors victory over the barbarians and by the Cross preserve Thy *politeuma* (πολίτευμα)" (First Tone, Feast of the Elevation of the Cross). The language is taken from Psalm 27:9. On some of the artistic evidence which relates the kings of Old and New Israel, see D.J. Geanakoplos, *Byzantine East and Latin West*. New York, 1966, p. 63f. Also, the Council of Chalcedon greeted the Emperor Marcian with the words, "May your empire be eternal!" (Mansi VII, 169), an allusion to the Hebrew, not the Roman or Greek, monarchy, inasmuch as God promised David—the Council called Marcian "the new David"—an everlasting house (II Kgs. 16) and dynasty that would exist forever (II Kgs. 1:31; III Kgs. 2: 45; Ps. 21:6 LXX).

[21] "From The Pagan City to the Christian City," *The Greek Orthodox Theological Review* X, 2 (1964), 121. Constantinople, New Rome, was in fact "the City," the model of all Christian cities. It was not only the abode of Hagia Sophia and the University, but also of countless monasteries.

city, although, in some ways, the model for the Christian city, had neither the
same presuppositions nor the same purpose. Like Athens, the city of Constantinople was "an educational institution and a creative organism."[22]

Athens and Constantinople differed not only in their theology, but also
on the questions of man's nature, something seen very clearly in Plato's
Republic. In describing "justice" as the chief attribute of "the good *polis*," he
turns to the idea of the "good" or "just man" to determine what justice is; that
is to say, answering the question, "What is the good or just *polis*?" with "What
is a good man?" The patristic creators of Christian culture did not oppose
how Plato framed the question of the Greek concept of man, since it was an
optimistic view which held out the promise that the sinner could, by the use
of reason, achieve perfection or "excellence" (ἀρετή). The Christian view of
the "good *polis*" and, therefore, the "good man" involved more than extending the range of man's knowledge. Werner Jaeger never tired of pointing out
that the Greeks believed the city to be capable of rationally forming "the
good life" and "the good man." For Christians such an objective was impossible without Christ and the Church.

But the hand of the Fathers was strengthened also by the disillusion-
ment of Plato who watched the traditional Hellenic ideal fail before his eyes.
He wanted to replace it with a new theory of the *polis*. At first, he urged the
wise man to find a place in human affairs, but after the martyrdom of
Socrates, he came to regret his advice. He now urged the wise man to make
a journey to "the *polis* above" through the perfection of "the *polis* within," a
conception based on the premise of the body/soul dualism, an immortal
soul seeking to free itself from its corporeal prison.[23] According to Plato,
God gave "the sovereign part of the immortal soul (reason) to be the divinity of each man" (*Rep.* VI, 508bc). Reason, rightly educated, learns that the
"earthly region," the "cave" is haunted by "evil" (negation of good). "That is
why we should make all speed to take flight from this world to that other
and that means becoming like the divine as far as we can, and that is to
become righteous with the help of wisdom" (*Theat.* 176b).

---

[22] *Ibid.*, 124.

[23] Orthodox anthropology is not dualistic. The body is physical, and the soul (and
angels) was created by God with a certain materiality. Following Plato, Augustine taught
that the soul is utterly spiritual. In his *De quantitate anima,* he denies that the soul has any
"quantity." The questions about its union with the body, the consequence of that union,
and the state of the soul when seprated from the body "are practically brushed aside"
(*The Greatness of the Soul.* Trans. by J.M. Colleran. Westminster [Md.], 1950, p. 5). The
Church, in fact, permits no comparison between the totally immaterial Creator and the
creation. Orthodox spirituality demonstrates her opposition to Platonic-Augustinian
dualism and her position on the body-soul connection.

Platonic mysticism remained along side the "traditional" view of the *polis* and its *paideia*, two currents of "political" thought which intrigued the Greek consciousness to the end, thanks in large part to Aristotle. As champion of the earthly *polis*, the student of Plato, unlike his teacher, had no celestial aspirations. He wanted Greeks to be "trained and habituated" to the pursuit of worthy occupations" (*Nich. Eth.* I, 4 1095a30). He could not imagine any other kind of life save the life of reason which is the happiest. "If reason is divine, then, in comparison with man, the life according to it, is divine in comparison with human life," he wrote in the tenth book of the *Nichomachean Ethics* (7 1177b30). "But we must not follow those who advise us, being men, to think of human things, and, being mortal, of mortal things, but must, so far as we can, make ourselves immortal, and strain every nerve to live in accordance with the best thing in us..." Man is a "political animal" who can find neither happiness nor perfection without the city. "He who is unable to live in society, or who has no need because he is sufficient for himself, must be either a beast or a god; he is no part of a *polis*" (*Pol.* I, 2 1253a25). The God of Aristotle is the "unmoved Mover," he would seem to have no direct role to play in the life of the *polis* or its citizens.

D   The Christian city, whose emergence was possible only after the Church's union with the Roman Empire, along with the development of a Christian culture, was the work of the Church Fathers and other ecclesiastical writers. They, too, called for the acquisition of "virtue" or "excellence," but of a spiritual kind. It was a perfection of the total man, body and soul, accomplished by the Faith and eternal Grace which, incidentally, did not exclude the profitable use of reason. Unlike ordinary Greek education which prepared the citizenry for a happy and useful life in this world, the education of the Christian city prepared the Faithful for the Age to Come; and unlike the "journey" of pagan philosophers and mystics to the "*polis* above," the Orthodox Christian's "journey" to the Kingdom of God began with the historical Church "below."

As Homer was at the center of pagan education, "the Bible as a new instrument of teaching became the center of the educational program of the Christian community."[24] The Bible contained not only defined "virtue" or "dispassion," but was a primer for its acquisition. The holy Mysteries or Sacraments were also a source of instruction, e.g., catechumens were "trained" in the Faith before and after Baptism. In addition, they put the believer in contact with realities found nowhere else on earth. The soul was

---

[24] Downey, p. 126-127.

cleansed from sin by the Mysteries, which convey the presence of things unseen. Another source of wisdom and Grace were the Canons. Presupposing the doctrine and spirituality of the Church, they taught humility along with discipline in ecclesial administration and organization. Unlike the civil law which hoped to insure justice and bring some order into human relations, the Canons[25] sought to engender the spirit of voluntary obedience in both clergy and laity, "the whole body of the Faithful" —for it was by the sin of disobedience that the human race had fallen.[26] Voluntary obedience was, therefore, the "virtue" which lay at the heart of Orthodox piety.

E   Unlike the modern state (see below) with its own secular agenda, justified by its own selfish interests, the *raison d'être* of the Christian Roman Empire was spreading the Gospel. It resembled, in some ways, the ancient kingdoms of Egypt, Persia, Babylon, and perhaps, even Homeric Greece whose cities were founded as "sanctuaries" for common worship,[27] whose

---

[25]   All the canons, ethical or adminstrative, presuppose dogmatic truths. They must not be compared to civil laws which exist for the promotion of equity and justice between individuals. The canons were designed to produce righteousness. Therefore, the principle of "economy"—the mitigation of canonical severity—is not the side-stepping of the canonical injunction and has nothing in common with the Latin legal aphorism, "Necessity creates what is not permitted by law" (*quod non est licitum lege necessitas facit licitum*). The canons are not laws, but unchangeable mandates of the Spirit (See my "Oikonomia and the Orthodox Church," in *The Patristic & Byzantine Review* VI, 1 [1987], 65-79). For a systematic treatment of the Canons, consult A. Bogolepov, *Canon Law of the Early Church*. New York, 1957.

[26]   There are two errors concerning the Fall of Adam that need correction. First, Westerm catechisms teach that the first man and woman were driven from Eden as punishment for the "original sin"; but the Fathers tell us something else. "Partaking of the tree, the man (and woman) became liable to death and subject to the future needs of the body," states St John Chrysostom. ". . .Adam was no longer permitted to remain in the garden, and was bidden to leave, a move by which God showed His love for him. . .he had become mortal, and lest he presume to eat further from the tree which promised endless life of continuous sinning, he was was expelled from the garden as a mark of divine Solicitude, not of necessity" (*Hom. in Gen.* XVIII, 3 PG 53 151).
       Secondly, Adam and Eve ate from fruit of the Tree forbidden to them. They sinned and "the wages of sin is death" (Rom. 6:23). "He (Adam) had heard, *Earth thou art and to the earth shalt thou return*, and from being incorruptible he became corruptible, and was made subject to the bonds of death," writes St Cyril of Alexandria. "But since he produced children after falling into this state we, his descendents, are corruptible coming from a corruptible source.   Thus it is that we are, heirs of Adam's curse" (Doctrinal Questions and Answers IX, 6 in Cyril of Alexandria, Selected Letters. Ed. R. Wickham. Oxford, 1983). Although the race of Adam is not guilty of his sin (contrary to Augustine *and his tradition*), mankind nonetheless shares the mortal substance of our first-parents, inheriting with it the ability to sin; for "the sting of death is sin" (I Cor. 15:56).

[27]   See the interesting study by Fustel de Coulanges, *The Ancient City: A Study of the Religion, Laws and Institutions of Greece and Rome*. New York, n.d., pp. 134-141.

conquests were inspired by the desire to extend the light of their religions to the darkness of unbelief. One need have no illusion that the ambition for empire ("the rule of many peoples") was always driven by missionary zeal; nevertheless, the fact that the king was, if not a god, the representative of his god, and the high priest of his religion, propagation of the Faith was always fundamental to the understanding of sacral monarchy. In Byzantium, the *basileus*, not unlike the early medieval Latin kings (sometimes called, *summus typus Christi*), was an analogue of the God-Man, his coronation and marriage compared to Christ in triumph, Christ united to His Bride, all of which is symbolic of the transcendent source and purpose of the king and his kingdom.

None should be surprised that monarchy was the government of the Christian Roman Empire; nor that the peoples of the Latin Middle Ages were ruled by kings, and even that kingship, albeit in its constitutional form, should reach the twentieth century. In the West, at least, the great longevity of the monarchical government is not difficult to explain. We should remember that it was "Christendom" before it was "Europa"; and that earthly king and kingdom mirrored heavenly Prototypes. If, as the Gospel of St Matthew (28:19) relates, the Lord instructed the Apostles to teach all nations "the Faith once delivered to the saints," we must conclude that a Christian nation would possess a Christian government; and, inasmuch as the Lord proclaimed in His Prayer, "Thy Kingdom Come (not "Thy democracy come"), Thy Will be done, on earth as it is in heaven," that the head of a Christian government of a Christian nation should be a Christian king.

Neither is it accidental that the importance of religion in Western culture (or anywhere) should shrink with the diminution of sacred monarchy (or perhaps the reverse is true); and that the growth of the democracies should accompany the ascendency of atheism. Significant, too, is the new political dogma that democracy is sacrosanct; and that the rise of the new secular "evangelism," or the universal propagation of this form of government, should be undertaken by a secular state, as the "manifest doctrine" of the United States urges. Having no divine commission, there is a curious arrogance in demanding that all nations adopt democracy, especially when egalitarian societies have never existed in fact, not even in Periclean Athens which boasted of its democracy. Historically speaking, also, they have never been admired. Plato and Aristotle had little good to say about them, finding in democracy the strong tendency not only toward anarchy, but conformity and mediocrity.

In the ideology of the Fathers, democracy is not the icon of God's Kingdom. St Gregory the Theologian (*Theol. Ora.* III, 2 FC) argued that monarchy in general is the best form of government, because it is the rule of one and naturally associated with monotheism, even as the rule of the "best" or the "few," aristocracy, is linked to polytheism, while the rule of the "many," "democracy," is related to atheism.[28]   Perhaps, the truth of this political analysis explains St Hippolytus' exegesis of Daniel in which the democracies are seen in prophecy as the harbingers of the Antichrist (*Treatise on Christ and Antichrist* II, 27 ANF).   Interestingly, if democracy is the prelude to the advent of the Antichrist, it is also connected with the extinction of the Christian Roman Empire—that which withstands Antichrist—along with the great "falling away" or ἀποστασία which reveals "the mystery of iniquity" (II Thess. 2: 1-7). The global dominance of democracy therefore has an immense eschatological significance.

Yet, none of these conditions for the coming of the Antichrist and the *eschaton* were present at the fall of Constantinople, suggesting that the demise of the Byzantine Empire was not the end of the Christian Roman Empire. The "first Rome" had been overthrown by the "barbarians," the second by the "Hagarenes" (the sons of Hagar, the Turks); but there was another, a "third Rome," a final stage of the Christian Roman Empire. This famous image of the Orthodox Russian monarchy originated with Philotheos of the Eleazar Monastery in Pskov, who wrote to Tsar Vasily III in 1531,

> "The Church of ancient Rome fell because of the Apollinarian heresy, and the second Rome—the Church of Constantinople—has been hewn by the Hagarenes. But the third, new Rome, the Universal Apostolic Church has come under thy mighty rule which radiates forth the Orthodox Christian Faith to the ends of the earth more brightly than the sun... .In all the universe thou art the only Tsar of Christians.... Hear me, pious Tsar, all Christian kingdoms have converged in thine alone. Two Romes have fallen, a third stands, there shall not be a fourth...." (in N. Zernov, *The Russians and Their Church*. London, 1945, p. 71).

---

[28] Erik Peterson states that the Fathers of the fourth century were familiar with Homer's axiom "the rule of many is not good, let there be one dominion" and Alexander of Aphrodisas, "one rule, one source, one god" was the basic assummption of Hellenistic kingship. This idea was delineated in the anonymous but highly influential treatise, *De mundo*, which appeared in Alexandria around 40 B.C. It is noteworthy that the Alexandrian Fathers (e.g., Sts Timothy, Athanasius, Cyril, etc.) have very little to say about kingship. Peterson mentions Cyril's *Contra Iulianum* (on Emperor Julian the Apostate's helleninstic revival), conceding that this Father discusses kingship *doch ohne monotheismus zu sprechen* (*Die Monotheismus als politisches Problem: Beitrag zur Geschichte der politischen Theologie im Imperium*. 1935, s. 147). In the festal menaion, the Orthodox Church ritualizes her political theology: the empror is likened to the humanity of Christ, not to God the Father, and the priesthood to His Divinity; also, in his coronation and marriage (see E. Kantorwicz, "Oriens-Augusti/Lever du Roi," *Dumbarton Oaks Papers* XVII. Cambridge, 1963, 117-162; G.H. Williams, "Christology and Church State Relations in the Fourth Century," *Church History* 20 (1951), 9f.; and my "Sacerdotium et Imperium: the Constantinian *Renovatio* According to the Greek Fathers," *Theological Studies* XXXII, 3 (1971), 448-455).

Behind the Philotheos political theology, a Byzantine inheritance, lay the same "theology of history" whose literary sources are the prophecies of Daniel and St Paul.[29] Before the Birth of Christ four Kingdoms shall rise, said the Prophet, the last was also the greatest of them—Rome "a fourth beast, dreadful and terrible, and strong exceedingly" (Dan. 7:7). Of course, if the entire Roman Empire fell in 476 with the Western part (*pars occidens*), then, to be sure, the ideology of the three Romes is nonsense.[30] But if it is true, if the life of the "fourth beast" was extended far beyond the conventional Western dating of its rise and fall; and if it survived by virtue of the Christian Faith among the Slavs, the Rus, Christian Rome did not vanish with the fall of Constantinople (1453). Thus it is hardly ridiculous to accept that the Orthodox monarchy of Russia was indeed the third phase of the Roman Empire;[31] and, then, it is also true that its collapse, as forseen by many Saints, is essential to the understanding of Christian eschatology.[32]

---

[29] Quoted in J.H. Billington, *The Icon and The Axe: An Interpretive History of Russian Culture*. New York, 1966, p. 58.

[30] If the Roman Empire is the last of great world-governments, how do we describe the kingdom of the Arabs, Carolingians, Saxon Germany, the Chinese and the Mongols, of the Turks, the Spanish and British in modern times? Daniel's purpose was prophecy: four kingdoms would appear before the Birth of Christ, a series of political systems that would prepare the world-stage for His Coming. Hence, the words of the Nativity troparion (Second Tone) of the Orthodox Liturgy, "When Augustus became supreme ruler of the earth, the multiplicity of governments among men ceased. And when Thou became human from the spotless Virgin, the worship of heathen gods also ceased. The cities came under one worldly rule, and the nations believed in one divine Supremacy; but we believers were enrolled in the Name of Thy Divinity, O Incarnate God..."
All non-Christian kingdoms *annos Domini* are antitypes of the Kingdom of God; hence, the words of Philotheos, "In all the universe thou art the only tsar (emperor) of Christians..." Such a claim was possible, because Russia was claimant to the true Faith which the Byzantines squandered with their ill-fated union at the Council of Florence (1439). The Greeks were punished with the loss of their empire. The apocalyptic "woman dressed in the sun" (Rev. 12:1) has fled to the "desert" (*pustynja*) of the North, to Russia, where alone the great Orthodox tsar saved her from destruction (See the discussion in Dimitri Stremooukhoff, "Moscow the Third Rome: Sources of the Doctrine," in *The Structure of Russian History*. Ed. M. Chernievsky, New York, 1970, p. 114-118).
Whether the Renaissance was aware of the "Third Rome" doctrine, I cannot say; but there is no doubt that its historiosophers had a keen interest in "exploding" the traditional four-empire prophecy of Daniel (see E. Cassirer, etc., ed., *The Renasissance Philosophy of Man*. Chicago, 1961; and R.G. Collingwood, *The Idea of History*. New York, 1956, p. 57f). Whether under the spell of Joachim of Fiore, or devoted to Augustine, in either case, they were seeking a new vision of the city to fit their new understanding of man. They were drawn to Joachim's idea of a *novum ordo*; and to the millenialism which, as we mentioned, Augustine never fully abandoned (*De Civ. Dei.*, XX, 7 PL 41 666-667; *Serm.* CCLIX PL 38 1197-1198).

[31] See the valuable article, I. Sevcenko, "A Neglected Byzantine Source of Muscovite Political Ideology," *The Structure of Russian History*, pp. 80-125.

[32] The nineteenth century Russian Slavophile and Old Believers complained that Peter the Great was responsible for the "decline of the Russian   (continued on next page)

F   For any number of profound and complex reasons, the post-Orthodox
West has given this "theology of history" very little consideration and even
less credence. One thing is certain, it was no longer prepared to endorse a
view of state and man (i.e., history) which was so clearly opposed to its own
religious and cultural development, a development which, in the most general terms, our study has hitherto sought to trace. To be sure, the West is
indebted to ancient Greece for much of its political theory; but we cannot
blame antiquity for the way in which european empires and nations exploited that legacy. We cannot forget the powerful Roman, German and Christian
components of its history in explaining the problems peculiar to its post-
Orthodox milieu, especially the origin and nature of political power.

Two currents of political thought may be found in the middle ages.
There seemed to be little doubt that all political authority descended from
God. Some believed, however, that the Almighty bestowed such political
power upon the king, and religious authority or power directly on the Pope.
Others held that such authority came to the people who leased it to their
leaders. Typical of the first is Thomas Aquinas (1225-1274), "the greatest representative of Scholastic philosophy" and "the most constructive and sys-
temtic thinker of the Middle Ages,"[33] and, of the second, Marsilius of Padua
(c. 1275-1342), "the great prophet of modern times and precursor of nearly
every modern doctrine, and development."[34]   Thomas and Marsilius, al-

(cont'd.)   Orthodox Empire." Russian historians have argued that "the St Petersburg revolution" led directly to the Bolshevek Revolution of 1917. Aside from the class division
caused by his introduction of Western mores and customs, the suppression of the
Patriarchate, the introduction of Protestant Scholastsicism into Orthodox seminaries, etc.,
Peter's endeavors involved something more fundamental: the reinterpretation of the
political theology that the tsars inherited from Byzantium. He replaced the traditional
Orthodox christocracy with the Reformation theocracy.

The ideological revision was undertaken by the Protestantizing Theophan
Prokopovich (1681-1736) who taught that the emperor was the image of the genderless
God the Father rather than, as formerly, the male humanity of God the Son. In this con-
ception of kingship, there is an implicit dualism between nature and supernature. The
Prokopovichian "reform" was in fact the revival of a theory first adapted from Hellenism
by Eusebius of Caesaria for St Constantine, a theory also found in the erastianism of the
medieval Ambrosiaster, Cathulfus, and Marsilus of Padua, and practiced in various
European countries (See G. Florovsky, *Ways of Russian Theology* [vol. 5, pt. 1]. Trans. R.L.
Nichols. Belmonst, 1979; and M. Chernievsky, "The Old Believers and the New
Religion," in *The Structure of Russian History...* , pp. 177-178). The Petrine theocracy also
permitted women to lawfully rule in their own name, a novelty which, in the dualistic
atmosphere of post-Reformation Europe, became a trend.

33 D'Entreves, A.P., *The Medieval Contribution to Political Thought: Thomas Aquinas,
Marsi-lius of Padua, Richard Hooker*. New York, 1959.

34 A. Gewirth's Introduction to *Marsiius of Padua: The Defender of Peace* (vol. 1). New
York, 1956 p. 4. The Latin text is found in *The Defensor Pacis of Marsilius of Padua*. Ed. by
C.W. Previte-Orton. Cambridge, 1928.

though expounding entirely different answers to the same problems of medieval political speculation, shared a common affection for Aristotle and, employing his genius to their own advantage, attempted to devise a theory of the state with no reference to revelation and none to sin,[35] unlike Augustine and the Fathers. In other words, recognizing a separation between faith and reason, as they saw it politics need not make obeisance to faith, but could in fact elucidate theories of state on purely philosophical and legal grounds.

G   There is no more basic Thomistic principle than "Grace does not destroy nature, but perfects it"—*gratia non tollit naturam, sed perficit*—implying that Aquinas recognized the independent existence and integrity of the natural order; or, in political terms, one may find and develop human standards of justice and truth without the assistance of Grace, without revelation. Man is able to achieve certain of his goals, because the created order in which he lives is governed by the natural law (*lex natura*) which is itself a reflection of the eternal law (*lex aeterna*). Nevertheless, without Grace man cannot find perfection and may surely lose his way.

His metaphysics did not require Thomas to think of the state as an institution divinely appointed to restrain human evil. Instead he "followed Aristotle in deriving the idea of the state from the very nature of man," that is, man is by nature a social and political animal—*homo naturaliter est animal sociale et politicum*.[36] He has the desire to live in a group, because the solitary man is neither capable of protecting himself against his enemies nor procuring the moral as well as the material needs of life.[37] In addition, man is essentially good, despite Adam's folly: "the original sin" was only the loss of the "superadded gifts" (e.g., immortality) later restored in Christ; and, therefore, man is able to live according to the *lex natura* without Grace or the divine Wisdom as the precondition for political association. The success and longevity of a Christian state, however, depends on its leadership. In imitation of the monarchy of heaven and the ways of nature, God has appointed the king as His "minister," His "avenger to execute wrath upon those who do evil" (Rom. 13: 1, 4). Obedience to the king is demanded by the Scriptures as central to the natural *ordo iustitiae*.

The duel between king, whether tyrant or true, and the Pope, raised for Thomas that grand political question of medieval life and thought: "Who is

---

[35] In the thinking of both Aquinas and Marsilius, "the idea of sin has no part in the rational justification of the state," writes D'Entreves, "and the way was thus cleared for the reception of a large part of Aristotelian teaching" (Ib., p. 31).

[36] *Ibid.*, p. 23.

[37] *On Kingship: to the King of Cyprus*. Trans. by G.B. Phelan. Toronto, 1949, I, 4-7, 14.

the visible head of Christendom?" The king is God's anointed (*On Kingship* VII, 61) and the Pope God's vicar. The Church of Christ is the foundation of a single hierarchical *societas christiana*—the number of rulers and nations notwithstanding. Medievalists generally agreed that one body cannot have two heads; hence, the quarrel between the "papalists" and the "royalists." Thomas numbered himself among the Pope's champions, defending his spiritual and legal sovereignty. He is *summus sacerdos*, the successor to Peter, heir to the *Donatio Constantini*, and, therefore, the one to whom all Christians, including the king, must submit. God's power comes to the Pope as head of all Christian peoples.

G   Marsilius of Padua was a medieval nominalist under the influence of Aristotle and Averroes.[38] Unlike Aristotle and Aquinas, he refused to describe man as a "political animal." The state was initially formed to satisfy man's biological and economic needs, rather than for rational and theological reasons. Thus, he differed with Machiavelli as much as he did with his medieval predecessors. Against the former Marsilius argued that the state is not the design of a cunning and ambitious prince, but the confluence of human and individual values; and against the latter he placed a "republicanism" (as Gewirth calls it) which denied to the autocrat the support of "natural law" and "religious principles" which placed the monarch above the people and invariably led to self-aggrandizement.

Marsilius proposed a revolutionary solution to the political variance between temporal and spiritual powers. He not only incorporated the *sacerdotium* within the *regnum,* but also set earthly and eternal happiness side by side as two kinds of "sufficient life" or "ends deserved by man" (*Def. Pac.* I, iv, 3); in a word, he placed secular and religious values "in stark opposition," not by holding that only the latter was true, as Augustine did, but rather affirming the validity of both despite their contrariety.[39] In this way, he rejected the position of the "royalists" who declared that the power of the king descends from God; and the "papalists" who insisted that the Pope possesses "the plenitude of power" from the Creator; but also the so-called "moderates" who hoped to strike a balance between the extremes. In the simplest terms, he

---

[38] The philosophical movement known as "Latin Averroism" was based upon a complete acceptance of Aristotle even where he was in opposition to Roman Catholicism. Marsilius' *Defensor pacis* was viewed as the leading, perhaps the first, exponent of "political Avereroism," i.e., to oppose faith and reason in such a way that one could believe by reason what was forbidden by faith. Thus, professing Christianity "by faith," he held political values antithetical to Scriptures, the *doctores ecclesiae*, and even the pope (Gewirth [vol. 1], pp. 39-44).

[39] *Ibid.*, p. 79.

defined political power as wholly the power of the state, an earthly *regnum* not without similarity to Augustine's *civitas terrena*,[40] a secular state founded on "civil happiness" and "socio-economic stability." The ruler (*pars principans*), who reigns by the choice of the people—an authority which once given he exercises indisputably—is under no obligation to rule in obedience to God or in the name of justice for all.

The state is regulated by human laws which are composed at the behest of the people ("legislator"). The conventional medieval idea that without law there is no justice, had no meaning for Marsilius. Laws are human conventions, "coercive commands," acts of the will, not of reason. "Law, then, is a 'discourse' or statement emerging from prudence and political 'understanding,' that is, it is an ordinance made by political prudence concerning matters of justice and benefit and their opposites; and having 'coercive force,' that is, concerning whose observance there is given a command which one is compelled to observe, or which is made by way of such command" (*ib.*, I, x, 4). According to Marsilus, the purpose of law is not to prepare men for eternal life, nor even to make them "good," but merely to regulate their "external acts" which may infringe upon the legitimate rights of other citizens.

Such a doctrine not only reversed the claims of the "papalists" based upon divine law, "but marks the attainment of a kind of sovereignty without parallel in the tradition of medieval political philosophy, the complete independence of the secular state."[41] The people or "the whole body of citizens" are "sovereign" with the power to choose their rulers and to invest them, conditionally and temporarily, with the power which belongs innately to the electorate. Also, "the whole body of citizens" are, in a Christian state, the counterpart of "the whole body of the faithful," members of the Church together forming one *respublica christiana*. By the word "church," Marsilius meant *de universitate fidelium et invocantium nomen Christi*, the people as *viri ecclesiastici* formerly equated with priests now applied to both laity and clergy—*dici debent omnes Christ fideles, tam sacerdotes quam non-sacerdos* (*Def. Pac.* II, ii, 31). The clergy (*pars sacerdos*) are also part of the state. This "part" is largely responsible for producing unity in the commonwealth, unity by voluntary faith.

---

[40] According to Gewirth, Augustine's theory of the "city of man" and the "city of God" permeates Marsilius' political philosophy. The basis of this dualism are the objects of love, God and man. As the Bishop of Hippo wrote: *Fecerunt itaque civitates duas amores: terrenam scillicet amor sui usque ad contemptus Dei, coelestem vero amor Dei usque ad contemptum sui* (*De Civ. Dei* XIV, 28 PL 41 436). "The importance of Augustinianism for Marsilius' political thought has received almost no recognition, despite the fact that Augustine is the chief interpreter of the profusion of Biblical citations in Discourse II of the *Defensor*" (*ib.*, p. 37).

[41] *Ibid.*, p. 174.

It would not be unfair to say, therefore, that Marsilian erastianism wholly subverts traditional Papist ecclesiology, a hierarchical structure which placed the Pope, his bishops, and priests over people. The sage of Padua denied to the clergy the right to govern by a law which is normally coercive; for, in fact, "the whole body of canon law" was simply a human invention designed to secure Papal power. In truth, the Pope and the magisterium exist for the sake of organizational church order. Their judgments are subject to review by the Faithful whom they serve (*ib.*, II, ii, 3; xxvi,7). The councils of the Church, which represent the people, are infallible in their decisions when they agree with the Scriptures (the supreme authority in matters of religion),[42] and confirmed by the Faithful.

The immediate impact of Marsilius's political philosophy (and theology) was slight, although he seems to have influenced the fifteenth century conciliarists. His accomplishments will need to wait to be appreciated. "The questions with which Marsilius dealt," observes Professor Gewirth, "and the answers he gave, are of profound importance for the understanding of the modern world. They involve the basis, content, and veracity of a secular morality and politics, and the nature and justification of popular sovereignty; issues whose contemporaneity is continuous, as indeed the shifting interpretations and reevaluations of Marsliius have made clear."[43] For our purposes, however, we see him, along with Aquinas, as another instance of that philosophical and theological dualism which characterizes the Latin Middle Ages, the Protestant and Machiavellian worlds.

H   The enormous disfavor done to posterity by the medieval Aristotelians was to declare that the sphere of human values could win complete expression in the concept of natural law; thus, the legitimacy of the state could be demonstrated without any reference to God and Christianity. Thomas Aquinas' *cum sui* prepared the way for future generations to theorize about the state, its origin and purpose, without appeal to the Scriptures or the Church Fathers. Nevertheless, medieval thought reaffirmed the truism that any attempt to construct or to explain the existence of the state always begins with our understanding of man and his deities. Nowhere is this clearer than

---

[42] Marsilius held that the truth of any theological opinion depended upon its agreement with the Scriptures, including the holy Fathers who sometimes contradicted each other —*Quoniam et ipsi quandooque circa Scripturam et praeter Scripturam sententiis ad invicem dissident, ut Hieronymus et Augustinus...et rursum Ambrosius cum Hieronymo...(Def. Pac.* II, xxviii, 1).

[43] Gewirth (vol. 1), p. 304. Regarding his doctrine of the Church, L. Strauss says that it was "of the greatest political importance, especially during the Reformation, for that doctrine belongs to politial theology rather than political philosophy" ("Marsilius of Padua," in *The History of Political Philosophy*, p. 276).

in atheistic modernity, from Machiavelli to Marx, where philosophers, perhaps inadvertently at times, have demonstrated this political axiom.

Machiavelli was the first to completely emancipate the state from its historic association with the Church and, consequently, to leave the subject of morality out of political discussion. No longer is a good society conceived as a society in which good men rule, but rather Machiavelli equated the interests of the state with the interests of the ruler whose ends are justified by whatever means he uses to maintain power and win "glory." In his *The Prince* (1513)[44], he based his theories on several postulates: that man is everywhere and always the same; that human nature, whether good or bad, must be treated as bad inasmuch as most people are "civilized" and civilization accounts for their corruption. Religion, he said, was sometimes helpful as a cohesive social force, but not as the basis for political policy and direction. In any case, God's intervention in the affairs of men is not required. *Fortuna* brings to them enough excitement and uncertainty. Machiavelli had laid the ground for modern political science.

Henceforth, nothing will stand in the way of individual speculation on God, man and the city, beginning with the English deists, Thomas Hobbes (1588–1679), a materialist and monarchist, and later, John Locke (1632–1704), "the father of the American revolution," who stated the case for parliamentarianism and the "liberal state"; and, in Holland, Benedict de Spinoza (1632-1677), the Jewish pantheist, who, following the Stoic tradition, disagreed with Hobbes and Locke, insisting that the state exists as the condition under which men search for the ideal order of things which are found only in that eternity which exists prior to anything human. Meanwhile, in the name of tradition, Martin Luther (1483-1546) and John Calvin (1509–1564), translated Augustine's "two cities" or kingdoms into "Biblical" terms, but do nothing to alter the West's ontological schizophrenia: time opposed to eternity, the visible to the invisible: European man cannot find an integrated existence. The Reformers defined the state as a work of reason, and the business of the Christian religion the salvation of soul. At first, nevertheless, Protestantism gave to the state the function of protecting the church, that is, the freedom of her members; and to religion the right to morally admonish political leaders.

They agreed with the monarchist, Richard Hooker (1553–1600), that the organization of the state and the organization of the churches must be sepa-

---

44 The term "machiavellianism" describes the philosophy of *The Prince*, although the author wrote numerous other books, most on war and glory. Machiavelli represented "the culture that is born of humanism becoming aware of political problems because they are at a crisis," wrote J.H. Witfield. "It is because of this that he seeks to solve them from the elements with which humanism has endowed the western mind" (*Machiavelli*. Oxford, 1947, p. 18).

rate, with both having a role in restraining the sinner, the one by law the other by preaching. In the Genevan theocracy, Calvin did both. Like Hooker and the Reformers, Hugo Grotius (1583-1645), followed Aristotle and Aquinas in teaching that man is a social animal whose passions could be restrained only if sublimated by organized contact with other men, as Descartes (1596-1650) suggested. Grotius was the first to hold that natural law was valid even without God. In his *Spirit of the Laws*, Montesquieu (1689-1755), concurred with him, adding that natural law acted by "blind necessity" rather "than governance rationally aimed at the good,"[45] which, of course, left no room for the miraculous. The eighteenth century philosopher, David Hume (1711-1776) was not insensitive to the implications of deism. To the idea of natural law, he delivered a fatal blow. A severe critic of idealism, he stubbornly refused any rights to human reason beyond the senses. His scepticism led him to reject the "social contact," because, he said, the government will surely become oppressive and the governed will break their promise. Hume wanted government, monarchist or republican, to do nothing more than secure man's freedom.

Jean-Jacques Rousseau (1712-1778), set aside Hume's critique of what the Frenchman called the "social contract." Born free, man is not a social animal, but voluntarily joins in an association with other men to protect his rights and his property; to this end, he submits to the "general will." The corrupting influence of civil society is overcome by education. In these ideas, according to Alan Bloom, Rousseau had discovered the fundamental truth that man's freedom is independent of, and opposed to, moral rule, a truth which "completes the break with the political teaching of classical antiquity begun by Machiavelli and Hobbes."[46] An admirer of Rousseau, the German, Immanuel Kant (1724-1804), viewed the state as part of nature whose laws allowed man no autonomy. His freedom and his morality are found by faith and experience in the invisible world of the νοούμενον, of the soul, where the knowledge of God and his own immortality are hidden.

Kant's vision was dualistic. Until the time of Georg Hegel (1770-1830), the political landscape remained divided, ravaged by the debate in which Edmund Burke describes man as a "religious animal" while John Stuart Mill saw government's task as opening the way for the individual to achieve maximum pleasure with minimum pain. Hegel attempted to effect a synthesis between "the Christian-Kantian" ideology and the politics of Machiavelli, Hobbes, Bacon and Locke. Reality is Spirit, God, and Hegel is its prophet proclaiming that through the state history would realize all human

---

[45] D. Lowenthall, "Montesquieu," in *The History of Political Philosophy,* p. 514.

[46] "Jean-Jacques Rousseau," in *The History of Political Philosophy,* p. 569.

aspirations, resolving what all human theorizing had hitherto failed to attain. History explains the origin, meaning and end of all human endeavor, whether religion, art, science, economics, politics or philosophy. We are told that Karl Marx (1818-1883) "turned Hegel on his head," that is, he has used the same dialectical method to demonstrate that matter not spirit constituted the essence of history. Marx was an atheist who saw the end of history as "beauty and freedom," achieved economically through the class struggle. Once the state was the servant of man's heavenly beatitude, now it becomes the tutor of his earthly happiness; and, finally, according to Marx, the state will vanish, as God and the supernatural did before it.

The only response to Marxian socialism has been the liberal democracies; but they are no less secular. The religions of Islam and of the Far East are slowly retreating before the onslaught of "the new world order." As citizens turn ever more to the state for solutions, the state becomes increasingly the problem. The conflict between human law and human freedom has never been so sharp, the passions never so uncontrollable. God has no place in public discourse. Reason is overcome by power and fanaticism. The "human predicament" has become more perplexing, insoluble. Where people do not retreat into religion, the sober man discovers himself isolated in a vast desolate universe which may explain his search for extra-terrestrial life. He is paying the price for what Bonhoffer called "coming of age." Without the true God and His revelation, he has nothing in which to believe, to love, to worship but himself. Perhaps, a desperate humanity will begin to look for "salvation" where very few have looked before.

3   MONASTICISM

The life of Orthodox Christians is essentially ascetical. Asceticism prepares us for eternal life. The preparation begins with Baptism, because the Age to Come is already among us. We follow the way of the Cross, because it is the way of deification. But the way of the Cross is arduous; it is the "narrow way," the way of repentance, the way of self-denial, the way of humility which the Gospel defines as voluntary obedience, an obedience which took the Lord "even to the death of the Cross." To that end, He possessed nothing, He had nowhere "to lay His Head," He made Himself a "eunuch. . .for the Kingdom of the heaven's sake" (Matt. 19:12). Christians are called to follow Him. To follow Him is the only way to understand human nature, to achieve not only moral and intellectual rebirth, but the transformation of our fallen nature. The way of the Cross is the answer to the sins of our first-parents, "the lust of the flesh, the lust of the eyes and the pride of life," by which their offspring was deprived of immortality. "But he who does the Will of God abides forever" (I John 2:16-17).

A   Monasticism is maximal Christianity, piety *par excellence*. Whatever its form and method (rule)—"coenobetic" (communal), "anchoretic" (solitary), "semi-anchoretic" (Elder with several monks)—monastics have the same spiritual aim as all members of the Church: to liberate themselves from sin and death. Male and female monks, to quote St Gregory the Theologian, "hasten forth from earth to become a god"—γαίηθεν ἐπιγόμενος θεὸς εἶναι (*De Virg.*, 210 PG 37 538A). By this uncompromising zeal, monks do not thereby constitute an elite above the Church; neither should we depict the "development" of this vocation as "the protest of the lay spirit against sacerdotalism," a temperament which in fact places monks "against and outside the Church"; nor, as so many have suggested, are monks "mystics" in the Greek sense of implying hatred of the flesh.[47]

Because the monk deprives himself of the things upon which ordinary men and women rely—particularly marriage and the "lawful intercourse" natural to it—one may not conclude monasticism signifies a contempt for marriage. From the beginning, virginity has been honored by the Church.[48] Indeed, "marriage is good" (Heb. 13:4), wrote St John of Damascus, "but virginity is better." "Celibacy is an imitation of the angels" (*De Fid. Orth.*, IV, 24; Matt. 22:30). "Stood virginity at the Right Hand of God," exclaimed St Gregory the Theologian, "and wedlock at His Left, also of great honor" (*De Virg.*, 750 PG 37 578A). The difference between them and where virginity finds its clear justification is the effort to realize immediately and totally within oneself the chaste and nuptial union of Christ and the Church which shall come to all who are "in Christ" at the consummation of the world.

Aside from their evangelically heroic effort to achieve perfection through the Grace of prayer and self-denial, monks have served the Church as clergy, apologists, polemicists, hymnographers, iconographers, poets, counselors and healers. Also, it is the presence of the monk which constantly alerts the rest of the Church to her transcendent origin, nature and destiny. Historically speaking, it was monasticism which saved the Church from the terrors of Iconoclasm, Islam, the Latin Crusades, Protestant proselytizing, the Turkish domination (*Turkokratia*), and Socialism. Surely, since the eighteenth century, monasticism has protected her against "secularism," that peculiarly Western scourge which excoriates all asceticism as fanatical, world-hating paranoia. It was St Nicodemus and the Athonite monks who saved Greek Orthodoxy from that philosophy which came to Hellas as the European

---

[47] Workman, H.B., *The Evolution of the Monastic Ideal*. Boston, 1930, p. 13.

[48] See L. Bouyer, *The Spirituality of the New Testament and the Fathers* (vol. 1). Trans. by M.P. Ryan. New York, 1963, pp. 303-305; and H. Koch, *Quellen zur Geschichte deer Askese und des Monenchtums in der alten Kirche*. Tuebinger, 1931, ss. 23-76.

Enlightenment. St Paisius Velichovsky, the Optina and Kievan monastics, preserved the Russian Church from the westernizing designs of Peter the Great.[49]

Not without good reason, then, did St Basil the Great long ago call the monk "the true and authentic Christian," the "role-model" for all Christians, while St John of Climacus called them "the light to all men" (*The Ladder of Divine Ascent* XXVI, 31 LM). The monastic life reflects the mystery of the Age to Come wherein, it is said, men transformed by Grace shall be like angels, neither giving nor taking in marriage (Matt. 23:30). The monastery is a breach in the concatenation of temporal events; it is the city on the edge of tomorrow. The life of the monk is the life of another world, so that, in the words of St Symeon the New Theologian, monasticism is truly the "self-alienation from material things, from the modes, attitudes and forms of this present life, as well as the denial of one's own body and will" (*Practical and Theological Texts*, 5 Ph). It is a free and total surrender to God.

To varying degrees, the same piety belongs to those who live in the world, those who have married or have remained single. It is sorry bigotry which opposes monasticism to the married state when countless times the Church has clarified her world-view. The ideals of the monastic life do not negate the purpose and ideals of marriage. They have the same goal. Monasticism is indeed a superior way of life, the deliberate sacrifice of legitimate earthly joys for the joys of eternity; it is the exchange of something good for something better, that is, voluntarily forfeiting what is pleasing and blessed, in order to embrace now the Age to Come. Yet, marriage is a sacred Mystery (Eph. 5:21-33), an icon of the divine matrimony of Christ and the Church, whose purpose is no less the quest for the Kingdom.

Thus, the holy estate of matrimony exists not simply for companionship, to escape fornication, to find happiness, not even for the propagation of the race. To repeat, Christian marriage is ultimately a relationship, imitating the union between Christ and the Church, in which the interaction between male and female, through the service of the first and the obedience of the second, brings salvation to both and their family. Khomiakov wrote that marriage "is not a contract, not an obligation, and not legal slavery, but the reproduction of the image of Christ and the Church established by divine law..." It is no exaggeration to say that husband and wife, by their struggle with their individual passions (anger, hatred, sloth, envy, etc.), their life of giving and receiving, of common worship and the practice of their Faith, bring not only sanctification to the themselves but sanity to friends and neighbors, and even their community.

---

[49] A. Schmemann, "Orthodoxy," in *The Study of Spirituality.* Ed. by C. Jones, G. Wainwright, E. Yarnold. Oxford, 1986, pp. 519-524.

B   The scholarly consensus seems to be that monasticism originated in the
fourth century.[50] We are told that no data has been uncovered which justifies dating it before that time. On the other hand, some are unconcerned
only with "evidence" that confirms their prejudices. The Protestant liberalism
of H.B. Workman is a case in point. He argues that the rise of monasticism
coincided "roughly speaking" in the third century, with the loss of Church's
"chiliastic expectations" (i.e., the imminent return of Christ). Confronted by
the "world" with which she hitherto had never come to terms, she welcomed
to that end the assistance of Greek culture. The result was her "acute hell-
enization." From this tragic merger came the Christian adaptation of Platonic mysticism commonly called monasticism.[51]

    For Workman, "hellenization" means essentially Platonism. On account
of it, monasticism developed all those aspects of the solitary life which have
become so familiar, not the least which was "the mystical flight of the alone
to the Alone," an idea drawn from Plotinus. The monk despises his own
body and its natural desires. Unwed, unattached, intoxicated with the
Divine, monks struggled then, as they do now, to escape the flesh by contemplation, prayer, and self-flagellation. Domination by transcendental consciousness, monks think themselves entitled to a higher level of knowledge
and experience than ordinary people. The "vision" (θεωρία) and "union"
(ἕνωσις) with God is the whole purpose of his monastic experience, as it was
for the Greeks.

    Workman is part of that broad circle of church historians who believe
that monasticism is pagan Greek not a Christian phenomenon. They are not
unaware that most of the Fathers were monastics. Patristic theologies (e.g.,
the Cappadocian Fathers), we are incessantly reminded, are based on theo-

---

[50]   Owen Chadwick (*John Cassian*. Cambridge [Eng.], 1968, p. 25f.) is uncertain for
how long before 360 A.D. monasticism existed in the Church. Certainly no organized
monasticism existed prior to that time. An earlier date is not mentioned in histories of
Eusebius of Caesaria, Socrates, Theodoret, Palladius; nor the *Adhorentes Patrum, Verba
Seniorum, Apophthegmata*, etc. Chadwick is certain that an inchoate Christian monasticism began in Egypt, but not before the time of Origen of Alexandria He holds the common opinion that "the Alexandrian theology" of Origen (as expounded by Evagrius of
Pontus) provided the principles of later monastic spirituality. Chadwick is not the only
historian to explain the piety of monks by "Alexandrian theology" (e.g., A.J. Festugiere,
The Child of Agrigente. Paris, 1941, p. 13).
    By this, we are ever reminded that many of Origen's writings were memorized by
the monks of the Egyptian Thebaid, and were even included in the *Philokalia*. Chadwick,
etc., do not take into account that Origen consulted the Apostolic Tradition (to which he
claimed fidelity) and, also, that Origenist literature, if not always sound doctrinally, is
nonetheless open to Orthodox intepretation. The Church was not ungrateful for the arsenal of concepts and language which Origen, Clement, Evagrius, and Didymus the Blind
provided in her struggle with Hellenism and heresy.
[51]   *The Evolution. . .* , p. 11f.

ries of the Platonic tradition. Workman is not the only historian to share with Père A.J. Festugiere the debatable conclusion, "When the Fathers 'think' their mysticism", he declares, "they Platonize. . . . There is nothing original in the edifice."[52] We may agree that Christianity is a "mystical" religion, but not "mysticism" as Festugiere *cum sui* know it.[53] Their judgment of Fathers, Saints and monks, is clouded by a version of Christianity which hardly matches anything found in the history of Orthodoxy.

The Christian "mystic" (μυστικός) earns his name from his identification with Christ, his membership in the Church, the Body of the God-Man, wherein every baptized person, a "temple of the Holy Spirit," is a "mystic," to some degree, as St Dionysius the Areopagite suggests (*Eccl. Hier.* I, 1 PG 3 372B). He is a "mystic" by virtue of his "royal priesthood," his offering of himself in the "mystic gifts," sharing in Christ's "sacrifice of praise" to the Father, his reception in return of "the Body and Blood of God," "the mystical supper," as St John Chrysostom refers to it. Finally, as his piety increases, he ascends the "ladder" of perfection, until there may be moment in which his union with God allows him to glimpse eternity, the state which is the final end of all the deified.

Therefore, it is an error to picture the monk as "a curious and definite type of personality,"[54] totally indifferent to the misery of the human race by virtue of his obsession with his own peculiar quest. And it is equally wrong to conceive, as part of the "monastic syndrome," the "philosophical spirituality" of Origen which demands repentance for the soul's pre-cosmic sin.[55] As some writers would have it, the monk's determination to assuage his guilt led to his or her flight into the desert where sometimes, of course, they dwelt in isolation in religious communities with like-minded neurotics, forming a para-ecclesial corp of *viri spirituali*. They are often indifferent to the creed and discipline of the "official" Church, unable or unwilling to share their superior visions and experiences with simple Christians. In other words, monastic piety, as most of Christian theology, is inherently contrary to the Gospel.

---

52 *Contemplation et Vie Contemplative selon Platon.* Paris, 1967, p. 5.

53 *L'Enfant d'Agrigente*, 141-142.

54 Underhill, E., *Mysticism.* New York, 1955, p. 3

55 An excellent example of Origenist (Platonic) thinking are the ruminations of Nicholas Berdiaev. "...from the very beginning I was aware of having fallen into an alien realm. I felt this as much on the first day of my conscious life as I do at the present time. ...The consciousness of being rooted in the earth is alien to me, and I was strongly attracted by the Orphic myth (to whom Plato was indebted) concerning the origin of the human soul, which speaks of a falling away of man's spirit from a higher world into a lower..." (*Dream and Reality: An Essay in Autobiography.* Trans. by K. Lampert. New York, 1950, p. 15).

But this thesis only makes sense if we assume that Christianity is not a revealed religion, and the Faith of the Church is without divine origin or direction. Nevertheless, the Orthodox Church has never denied her indebtedness to Hellenism which is "a standing category" (to borrow Fr Florovsky's celebrated phrase) of Christian thought, that is, as a means for access to the arena of rational discourse and public communication.[56] Yet, whatever its form, Christian spirituality, *a fortiori* monasticism, in its hidden depths exceeds the power of unbelief to understand and, therefore, to judge. Failing to recognize this truth, the scholar, at every level, will continue to distort the truths of the Faith of Orthodoxy. We need only mention "Byzantine theology" and the fourteenth century Hesychast controversy.[57] The historical analysis of this and most religious issues, especially on the part of university academicians, generally involves favoring a solution to the controversy which is contrary to the position taken by the Church. Problems are discovered where none exist, questions are asked where none should have been raised, answers are given to numerous phantom inquiries. Everything seems to be done to reconfirm the historians religious and philosophical prejudices.

---

[56] See Vladimir Lossky's discussion on St Dionysius the Areopagite ("Pseudo-Dionysius"), *The Vision of God*, pp. 99-100.

[57] The Christian idea of hesychasm ("inner silence" or "stillness"), whatever its application by the monks, has no other aim than creating tranquility of mind and body without which "pure prayer" and "contemplation" are extremely difficult. The monks of Mt Athos were not its originators; and St Gregory Palamas not its only defender. *Apatheia* and *hesychia* are inseperable. It has been a spiritual ideal of the Church everywhere from the beginning, not merely Egypt and Syria. Cf. II Thess. 3:12; St Ignatius of Antioch (*Ep. ad Eph.* VIII, 2 FC).

Along with obedience and humility, silence was part of St Benedict's trilogy of monastic virtues (*Rule of St Benedict*. Ed. by T. Fry. Collegeville, 1981, ch. 5-7); it has a history among the Greek Fathers (e.g., St Gregory of Nyssa, *Cant.* XV PG 44 1108A). The *Philokalia* is a diary of it. St John Cassian brought to the West a record of his experience with the monastic practices (including hesychasm) of the Egyptian desert. Judging from the eager reception by the Italian, French and Irish monastaries, those practices were consistent with their own spirituality. St Columban of Luxeuil wrote a brief address, *De Octo vitiis*, following Cassian's order of passions and the the mortification of these "perverse effections" (See E.S. Duckett, *The Gateway to the Middle Ages: Monasticism*. Ann Arbor, 1961, pp. 95-98); Chadwick, *John Cassian*, pp. 148-162; and A. Wathen, *Silence: The Meaning of Silence in the Rule of St Benedict*. Washington, DC, 1973).

For Augustine, on the other hand, "silence" or "quiet" (*quietus*) was merely the cessation of intellectual activity, a "calm" necessary for contemplation. He seemed to admit no connection between "silence" and "mortification" (dispassion). See his *True Religion* XXXV, 65 (PL 34 151); and G. Lawless, *Augustine of Hippo and His Monastic Rule*. Oxford, 1987, p. 51f.).

C   There are very few church historians without some knowledge of St
John Cassian's history of monasticism delineated in his *Conference XVIII* with
Abbot Piamum, but only a few take it seriously. John writes that Coeno-
bitism is the primitive form of monasticism, practiced already in the days of
Apostles; it was the state of the Christian religion in Jerusalem (Acts 2:45; 4:
32-35). Until the death of the Apostles, "the whole Church, I say, was then
such as now are those who can be found in coenobia..." These Christians
took up the life of virginity, self-denial and prayer, receiving the name of
"monk" on account of their strict and solitary lives. Only later, with the peace
between the Church and the empire, did monasticism become a flight into
the desert, a reaction of the Christian spirit to the ostensible reconciliation of
the Church with the "world." Monks were suspicious of all intercourse
between the Faithful and the philistines; and in the fourth century the reason
for their caution was dramatically illustrated. Monks became a kind of permanent "resistance movement."[58]

For example, St Paul the Simple and St Anthony withdrew into the
desert "not as from faintheartedness and the evil of impatience," wrote Cassian, "but from a desire for loftier heights of perfection and divine contemplation" (XVIII, 6). They lived alone, eager to fight the demons,[59] imitating
the Prophets Elias and Elisseus, St John the Baptizer, "who became like a pel-
ican in the wilderness" (Heb. 11:37-38; Job 39: 5-8; Ps. 102:7-8; 107:2, 4-6; Lam.
3: 27-28). The Lord Himself was an ascetic. His forty days in the desert, His
fasting, His temptation by the devil, was an admonition to Christians that
they "wrestled not against flesh and blood, but against principalities, against
powers, against the rulers of the darkness of this world, against spiritual
wickedness in high places" (Eph. 6:12).

D   Early monasticism, of course, was not organized, as St John Cassian
indicates, and we should not expect to find rules, methods and vows, either
in the East or the West. Organized monasticism began with St Pachomius
(c. 307) in the East, and with Cassian in the West. The reasons for the spread

---

58   Florovosky, "Empire and Desert: Antinomies of Christian History," *The Greek
Orthodox Theo-logical Review* 3 (1957), 146-150.

59   Bouyer (*The Spirituality of the New Testament and the Fathers* [vol. 1], p. 312). He
observes that the monastic irruption into the desert was not motivated simply by a desire
for tranquility and contemplation. On this point the *Vita Antoni* is clear. He entered the
desert to combat demons, an idea with a Gospel origin. There is where the Lord met the
devil and faced His three temptations (Matt. 4:1-15; Mark 1:12-13; Luke 4:1-10). The
Lord's Prayer ends, "Deliver us from the evil one" (See K. Heussi, *Der Ursprung des
Moenchtums*. Tuebingen, 1936, s. 111f.).

of Western monasticism were no less cogent than it was in the East. Saint John Cassian's experiences in the Egyptian Thebaid fertilized his mind, and, to repeat, with very little inspiration from Hellenism.[60] On returning home, his efforts were not without success, as we learn from the construction of male and female monasteries by St Honorius of Lerins, Caesarius and Aurelian of Arles, etc.; and even from the zeal of the sixth century Merovingian kings who would erect them everywhere in their realm, while the last of their line even found sanctuary in a monastic cell.

Finally, St Benedict of Nursia (480-547), whose hagiography is written in the *Dialogues* of St Gregory the Great, initiated a monastic order which thrived in the West until the time of the Crusades. For his Rule, Benedict was, in large part, indebted to "our Father" St Basil, and to St John Cassian from whose writings Benedict's monks were instructed to read every day.[61] For Benedictines, prayer, worship and contemplation were the first order of business. The Saint also laid great emphasis on physical work. "Idleness is the enemy of the soul," he wrote. His monasteries, as others, also had libraries, instrumental in the preservation of Christian literature. In general, Benedict's Rule outlined a strict life, but not one that was impossible for the devoted Christian to practice. First, he demanded obedience to the Abbot "without delay." Typically patristic, he urged his monks to follow the path of obedience as the sure path of salvation, for obedience produced humility, and humility the mortification of the flesh, that is, of "vices" (passions).

By the twelfth century Benedictine monasticism finally lost its popularity and, perhaps, its vigor, and the number of candidates declined. The most obvious reason for its transformation, however, was the post-patristic worldview of the heretical West, one in which traditional Benedictines could not

---

[60] A. Louth refers to Cassian as a "convinced Origenist," a dubious conclusion even from the available facts. Cassian never mentions Origen (or Evagrius, a "convinced Origenist"); and, if we have not totally misunderstood the eighteenth *Conference*, Christian perfection was not limited to monks, as Louth thinks (*Discerning the Mystery: An Essay on the Nature of Theology*. Oxford, 1983, p. 218). Also, one might assume that St John had sufficient comprehension of Origen's eschatology, to understand that "the restoration of all things" (ἀποκατάστασις τῶν πάντων) would render not only monasticism but the entire Christian Economy superfluous. It is a serious mistake, therefore, to speak with any enthusiasm about Origen's influence on Cassian.

[61] Bouyer calls St Benedict "a prudent legislator" who does not exclude (as St Basil seems to have done) the anchoretic form of monasticism, but who nevertheless "holds for his part to a well-regulated cenobitism, a mind wholly impregnated with moderation and discretion. On the other hand, we find no trace in him of the pastoral concerns which led *à la* Augustine "to a mutation of the very idea of what a monk should be" (*The Spirituality of the New Testament...* , p. 512). To cite an instance, St Benedict declared that "freedom" is born of obedience and inward purification, while for Augustine "perfect service becomes perfect freedom" (G. Lawless, *Augustine of Hippo...* , p. 23).

survive. Père M.D. Chenu attributes the change in Western attitudes towards monasticism in general and Benedictinism in particular to a new culture, a new learning which developed under the influence of the Moslem renaissance in Spain. From that moment "controversies no longer had to do with dogmatic formulations of this or that mystery as they had in the fourth century, but with intellectual or institutional behavior."[62] He adds to this explanation another which had gradually become common in the Latin Middle Ages: church history. Anselm of Havelberg believed, as did so many of his contemporaries, in the periodical renewal of the Church as she grows in the Truth from one age to the next. "The holy Church," he wrote, "passing through diverse stages which in turn gradually successed themselves to the present day, rejuvenates herself as the eagle, as she always renews herself"—*Sancta Ecclesia pertransiens per diversos sibi invicem paulatim succedentes, usque in hodiernum diem, sicut juventums aquilae renovator et semper renovabitur* (*Dial.* I, 6 PL 188 1149).

Chenu seems satisfied with these answers. They are, however, *petitio principi*, begging the question; and he seems aware of it. He takes a little more time to delineate the reason for the West's "new culture." He wants his readers to think it was "a sensational apostolic awakening"; but these so-called renovations had been occurring since the time of Pope Nicholas I in the ninth century. Chenu argues, therefore, that the "apostolic awakening" and the "new culture" are the result of historical circumstances of the twelfth century and the natural evolution of the Church, as her apologists have always contended. But which came first, the "new culture" or the "apostolic awakening"? He does not handle well the coincidence between "advances in culture and religion" and the question of doctrinal innovation. One cannot be certain that he ascribes the changes in Roman Catholic theology to the changes in Western culture, as we do.

E   This 'new culture' was not without impact upon the development and proliferation of monastic orders; or, perhaps, it was the reverse. Nothing was more important to their propagation in this period than the great Cistercian monk, Bernard of Clairvaux, and specifically his *Commentary on the Song of Songs*. He was indebted to Origen whose allegorical commentary on this same book has been called "the first great work of Christian mysticism"—not an untypically provincial Western judgment. Following Origen, Bernard taught that the human soul not the Church is "the bride of Christ," an idea which spurred the growth of female monasticism with an eroticism (and individualism) which reconceived the Eucharist as union with "the

---

62   *Nature, Man, and Society in the Twelfth Century*, xvii.

beloved Groom"—"bridal mysticism," as some medievalists refer to it. Although under a new form, this understanding of monasticism was simply a renewal of the unique Augustinian juxtaposition of God and the soul. On this point, there was no conflict between Origen and Augustine, both of whom were Platonists. The discovery of Augustine's "lost letters" on monastic life[63] likewise promoted the development of the new forms of monasticism.

Pope Urban II, who apparently was an advocate of the "new culture" favoring the Augustinians, was not unaware of the venerable Benedictine tradition and propounded a theory to explain his preference. The primitive Church, he said, had two forms of religious life: "monastic" and "canonical." In the former, men and women abandoned temporal pursuits in order to devote themselves to contemplation. The latter, however, were monks who made use of earthly things "to redeem the time with tears and almsgiving." In the Pope's view, the Augustinians and the orders it spawned revived a neglected primitive tradition of the Church and thereby restored the balance which Benedictine monasticism and orders like it were later to obscure.[64]

The Cistercians had sought to revitalize the Benedictine Rule, but the Augustinian Canons complained against their severity, against what they felt was the Cistercian trust in outmoded monastic practices. Against them, the Augustinians stressed "the apostolic life" or "primitive simplicity" in reaction to those eccentric rules which had dominated monasticism for so long. In a time of cultural and political turmoil, the dawning a new spiritual climate, the Canons wanted to keep pace with the contemporary needs of the Faithful. Perhaps, too, it was the call for moral reformation in preparation for a new age. The Sicilian monk, Joachim of Fiore, caused a stir in Europe, announcing the formation of the "angelic order" whose monks, walking among the people, would stir them to purge the Church of all its corruptions while also looking for the end of the world as they knew it.[65]

---

[63] Before the year 1000 the Rule of Augustine was little known in the West. However, late in the eleventh century the Augustinian order began to form as a definite group of religious, part of the general ecclesiastical reform (R. Canning, trans., *The Rule of Saint Augustine: Masculine and Feminine Versions*. Introduction and Commentary by T.J. Van Bavel. Kalamzoo, 1961, p. 7). Like the Bishop of Hippo, medieval Augustinians placed no stress on obedience, wore no special habit, commanded no fasting. He taught that true religion grows "out of a group of friends" who love and respect one another. The traditional authoritorian director was replaced by a *praepositus* ("one who is put forward"), that is, the "prior" or "prioress" (*ib.*, pp. 103-104).

[64] See R.W. Southern, *Western Society and the Church in the Middle Ages*. Harmondsworth (Eng.), 1975, p. 244.

[65] *Ibid.*, p. 270.

The spirit of reform was everywhere driven forward largely by the socially conscious, active monastic orders; yet, it was a reform which only illustrated once more the Latin medieval mentality which only perpetuated and reinforced its crypto-nestorian duality. Two symptoms of this mentality were the appearance of the Dominican and Franciscan monastic orders. The first followed the Augustinians, the second, in some ways, emulated the Cisterians. At the same time, some Franciscan chapters, adopting Joachim's apocalyptic vision of history, placed great stress on poverty and service, carrying the eschatological hopes of this monasticism outside the monastery. The Dominicans were from the beginning an order of preachers and mendicants, a task for which they readied themselves by theological studies. Some of the greatest theologians of medieval theology from 1250–1350 are found among them: Albertus Magnus, Thomas Aquinas, and Meister Eckhart were Dominicans; Bonaventura, Duns Scotus, and William of Ockham are numbered among the Franciscans.

Later to become a source of so much mischief in the Middle East, these orders were founded by two men of extraordinary energy and enthusiasm, the Augustinian Canon, Dominic of Spanish Calaroga (1170-1221), and Francis of Assisi (1181-1226). Dominic was sent by Pope Innocent III (1206) to preach among the Albigensians (Neo-manicheans). He and those who joined him in southern France formed the new order. Preaching to the masses enflamed his desire to spread his mission beyond the Western nations. He wanted to reach wider circles of people, even the whole world. At the end of his life, he hoped to bring "holy preaching" to the Tatars on the Dnieper and Volga. His significance, not unlike that of Francis, was "to open up a place in the church for popular movements."[66]

There is something far more portentous about these men, especially Francis. Nothing states his cultural significance better than the "official" or festal icon of Francis, painted in Pisa; and later the allegorical paintings of him by Giotto di Bondone (1267-1337). How fascinating, too, that these icons were executed during a Byzantine revival in thirteenth and fourteenth century Western Europe. The official or Pisan icon depicts a bearded Francis with a striking resemblance to Christ, including the stigmata. He is the image of suffering. In other icons, the wounded Francis is shown carrying the Christ child with a dove hovering over their heads. In some icons, he holds the Gospel in one hand while making a gesture of benediction with the other. Medievalists were not diffident about their interpretations of this Franciscan iconography. They seemed to agree that his stigmatized visage presents the monk as the living image of Christ. The mission of the monk, in

---

[66] G. Barraclough, *The Medieval Papacy*. New York, 1968, p. 129f.

imitation of Christ, is service to the poor; hence, his own poverty and suffering. Most interesting of all is Francis holding the Christ child, an iconic privilege generally reserved for the Mother of God. Likewise, his possession of the Gospel—the iconographical symbol of episcopal authority—and, finally, the blessing with the hand commonly associated with the priesthood. Francis was not a priest. We have here, then, not only a new conception of monasticism, but of the Church.[67]

Francis himself seemed to manifest the new and unspoken European assumption regarding the inner man and the ultimate Reality—the Augustinian polarity of being—God and the self. The priesthood and the Sacraments no longer held any monoply on Grace. Whatever Francis' devotion to the Papacy may have been, the traditional understanding of the institutional Church was being revised by his followers and apparently to his iconographers. His icons suggest, moreover, that the Church as the world had known her was not everywhere perceived as the necessary mediator between God and man. God now comes directly to the believer—hence, the depiction of Francis standing alone with Christ and the Holy Spirit. Here are the first winds of Protestantism, a new sense of things in which the institutional Church has become an obtrusion into the immediate relationship between Christ and the soul.

F   That "new sense of things" surely inspired the quest for mystical revelations, judging by religious revolutionaries like Meister Eckhart (1260-1328), a student of Plato's *Timaeus* and of the writings of Augustine and Aquinas. He was one who pursued the life of solitude and learning whereby he could elude worldly affairs and the excesses they wrought. He retreated into the

---

[67] Friedrich Heer offers an interpretation of these icons. He finds the stigmata highly significant. They identify Francis with Christ, particularly as he stands with the infant Jesus in his arms. "It was the birth of the new imitation of Christ. To be a Christian now meant to do as Christ did, to suffer as He suffered, to love Him and live in Him, in obedience to the new father and in the service of the brethren. This alliance between the Roman Pope Innocent III and Francis, the son of the Italian people, had deep foundations on both sides. In the Franciscan crib, the *filioque* was safe for the first time. It showed how the Spirit of God was born in God the Son [*filioque*], and thus it was also the basis of the emancipation of Italian art from Byzantium. Every representation of the crib from then on was a *trionfo* over the East. Stigmatics arose again and again after Francis's day, but never in the East. By these marks Francis outshone all the most ancient and most venerable tombs of saints and sees of patriarchs in all the East. His stigmata proved that the true *auctoritas*, the power of the new holy Father, resided in Rome" (*The Intellectual History of Europe*, p. 128f.; and his *The Medieval World*. trans. by J. Sondheimer. New York, 1961, pp. 222-224; and E. Benz, *Ecclesia Spiritualis: Kirchenidee und Geschichtestheologie deer Franciskanischen Reformation*. Stuttgart, 1946, ss. 97-104; and Hans Belting, *Likeness and Presence: A History of the Image before the Era of Art*. Trans. by E. Jephcott. Chicago, 1994, pp. 381-387).

"hidden sanctuary of the soul" where, he said, the birth of Christ takes place no differently than it does in eternity, an experience which Eckhart claimed required detachment from all external things.[68] Eckhart explained this encounter with timelessness in a Sermon entitled, "This is the Meister Eckhart from whom God hid Nothing." Not to be taken literally, his allusion was to a contact with God in the soul, superceding the knowledge of the senses and the intellect. Unlike the subjectivism of the post-Cartesian world, he was certain that what he sought, the transcendental, was experienced outside of the human intellect. Eckhart was no Bishop Berkeley for whom "to exist is to be perceived." The mental idea, the Meister said, always pointed to something higher, "of which it is the symbol."[69]

The theosophy of Eckhart is revealing. It is another instance of a new direction that medieval monasticism had taken: an inwardness which signaled a further devolution of the "objectivism" of the great monastic tradition represented by Sts John Cassian, Benedict of Nursia and Pope Gregory the Great. The German's monasticism, if we may call it that, is the self-conscious spirituality of a milieu ever more consumed with man and his uncomfortable place in time. One could indeed criticize this transformation in medieval monasticism for its manicheism, scholasticism, eroticism, social activism, even its "mysticism," but far more important are the consequences of this transformation from a culture of transcendentalism to a homocentric worldview. Monasticism, intended *ab initio* to be the icon and foretaste of eternity, an instrument of sanctification, a "culture of self-denial," had become the laboratory of social and intellectual change.

To be sure, there were then, as there are now, Roman Catholic monks who resisted the "revolution in faith," but their efforts did not then, as they do not now, herald a return to the Fathers. Nothing is more crucial in this regard than the paucity of medieval literature on the subject of deification,[70] a subject about which monasticism had less and less to say as Scholasticism increasingly informed the monastic studies, preaching and values. The ascetic spirituality of the medieval monk, if not emasculated by the philosophical debates and vigorous social ministries, was otherwise impover-

---

[68] For example, Sermon IV ("On Eternal Birth"), in R.B. Blakney (Trans.), *Meister Eckhart*. New York, 1941, pp. 118-124; Southern, *Western Society. . .* , pp. 301-304.

[69] Sermon I, p. 98.

[70] Deification seems not to have been the aim of medieval Latin monasticism. The idea was ordinarily associated with pantheism. An exegesis of II Pet. 1:4 (". . .partake of the divine Nature") can, for example, be found in Spanish monasticism; thus, John of the Cross believed the verse to mean that ". . .He descends upon the soul in mercy, impressing and infusing His love and grace in her, making her beautiful and lifting her so high as to make her a partaker of the very divinity (2 Pet. 1:4)" (*The Spiritual Canticle, in The Collected Works of St John of the Cross*. Trans. by K. Kavanaugh &   *(continued on next page)*

ished by the personal quest for the the mystical state which, many came to believe, was the only way to satisfy the craving for absolute truth, as the world around them spiritually devolved.

Monasticism mirrored the spiritual schism in the medieval soul, a tension which was its most dubious legacy to the modern world. Never did medieval man reconcile contemplation and action, as it failed also to unite faith and reason, the detemporalized and the secular. Taking into consideration what the world has become and the hope of the modern Papacy to accommodate the new philosophies and theologies, we should not be surprised that the scales have tipped heavily in favor of social activism. There is no longer much trust in "poverty," "obedience" and "virginity." Monks have become scholars, lawyers, politicians, teachers, social workers. The Western monk no longer goes in quest of the holy grail—deification—which is known by few, sought by less.

4   THE ICON

The icon has existed in the Christian Church from the time of the Apostles; it also has antecedents in Judaism, as St John of Damascus shows in *Orationes tres adversus eos qui sacras imagines abiciunt*. Thus, to say that the early Church inherited a hostility towards religious art from the Synagogue out of which Christianity ostensibly emerged, is untrue. No support for this position will be uncovered in the Christian Apologists of the second and third centuries who, not unlike the great Hebrew prophets, condemned idolatry, such as the cult statues of paganism. There is too much Christian art in antiquity for anyone to confuse iconography with idol-worship.

Neither is there is any reason to believe, as does Professor Paul Alexander, that the Church, initially hostile to art, later modified her sub-apostolic attitude towards it "largely" under the influence of converts from paganism.[71] It may be true that the primitive Christian left no cache of icons, but the persecution of the Church, not a repugnance for art, explains the reluctance of believers to artistically portray Christ, the Virgin and the Saints.

(cont'd.) O. Rodriguez. Washington, DC, 1979, XXXII, 4). In her *Soliloquies*, alluding to the same verse, Teresa of Avila denotes deification as the "changeable will; now, there shall be no more change. For God's [*created*] grace will have done so much that by it you will be a perfect sharer in the divine nature so that you shall no longer be able, or want to be able, to forget the supreme Good or fail to enjoy Him together with His love" (*The Collected Works of St Teresa of Avila* [vol. 1]. Trans. by K. Kavanaugh & O. Rodriguez. Washington, DC, 1976, XVII, 5). Augustine was the "church father" they most admired (See B. McGinn, *The Foundations of Mysticism* [vol.1], p. 251).

[71] P.J. Alexander, *The Patriarch Nicephorus of Constantinople: Ecclesiastical Policy and Image Worship in the Byzantine Empire*. Oxford, 1958, p. 214f.

In addition, there was a certain reluctance among Christians to "theologize in color," or to make public, in any medium, what belonged to the mysteries of Faith, to what the Church sought to keep hidden from the uninitiated. At the same time, more and more icons began to appear with the attack of pagans and Jews on the Christian Faith.

The first iconographer of the Church was the Savior Himself. I refer to "the Holy Face," the *acheiropoietos* ("made without hands") or the *mandylion* ("handkerchief").[72] Orthodox Tradition ascribes the first "made with hands" icon of the Theotokos to St Luke. Theodore, a Reader (c. 530) in the Temple of Hagia Sophia, is the oldest historical witness we have concerning it.[73] This iconic prototype, like so many others of Christ and the Virgin, have not survived to our time. Of first century iconography the frescos and sarcophagi reliefs of the Roman catacombs alone remain. Nevertheless, there is a long history of conciliar and patristic statements about icons and their prototypes in general, of iconographic schools, diversity of styles, icons of great antiquity and miraculous powers,[74] to say nothing of iconology itself.

But our discussion here goes beyond such things to the icon as a manifestation of the Christian conception of time—therefore, of a "chalcedonian" history—the embodiment of its christological principles which have always been part of the Church's Faith. The articulation of those principles is nowhere better shown than in the deliberate effort of the Orthodox iconog-

---

[72] The Lord gave to the emissary from King Abgar of Edessa a portrait of Himself. After washing His face, Christ wiped it with a piece of linen, and His features remained on it. For a history of "the icon not made with hands," see L. Ouspensky, *Theology of the Icon.* Crestwood (NY), 1978, pp. 59-66. Most historians, of course, consign this episode to legend; likewise the icons of St Luke the Evangelist.

[73] Theodore mentions the Lucan icon of the Virgin sent from Jerusalem by the Empress Eudoxia to her sister-in-law, St Pulcheria, in Constantinople, around the year 450. Later, St Germanos, the Patriarch (715-733), spoke of an icon painted by St Luke found in the city of Rome. It may have been the very icon (*quam dicunt a sancto Luca factam*) which Deacon (Pope) St Gregory the Great (590-604) carried in solemn procession to the basilica of St Peter (Ouspensky, *Ib.*, pp. 71-79).

[74] Aside from the Ouspensky book, consult his collaboration with V. Lossky, *The Meaning of the Icon.* Olten, 1969; C. Cavarnos, *Byzantine Thought and Art.* Belmont (Mass.), 1968; C. Mango, ed., *The Art of the Byzantine Empire, 312-1453: Sources and Documents.* Englewood Cliffs (NJ), 1972; A. Giakalis, *Images of the Divine: The Theology of Icons at the Seventh Ecumenical Council.* New York, 1994; C. Galavaris, *The Icon in the Life of the Church.* Leiden, 1981; A. Grabar, *Christian Iconography: A Study of Its Origins.* Princeton, 1968; P. Kontoglou, "The Hopelessness of Death in the Religious Art of the West and the Peace and Hope of Orthodox Iconography" (trans. by Bishop Ephraim), *The True Vine* VI, 1 (1994, 6-35; C.D. Kalokyris, "The Essence of Orthodox Iconography," *The Greek Orthodox Theological Review* XIII, 1 (1968), 65-102; XIV, 1 (1969), 42-64; Archmandrite Cyprian, "Our Task in Iconography", in *Orthodox Life* XXX, 1 (1983), 33-38; G. Florovsky, "Origen, Eusebius and the Iconoclastic Controversy," *Church History* XIX (1950)., 77-96.

rapher to depict the figures (including angels) on their work as historical, that is, in their geographic setting and to represent genuine portraits of the Savior, the Virgin, the Saints. The Christian artist was not permitted creative license. He or she was required to use a model which often was a copy of a copy, etc. In addition, the physical attributes of the icon had to express the spiritual or noetical reality to which the physical image was connected "without confusion or separation." Therefore, the visible icon invited the viewer to pass from it to the invisible prototype, as Nicea II (787) defined it.

A   Although modern philosophers confess that time is the most difficult metaphysical problem of all, they are generally inclined to deny the existence of anything beyond it, beyond this *cosmos*. Whatever their final verdict on the subject, our contemporaries would generally agree with Kant, "Time is the formal condition *a priori* of all appearances in general"—*Die zeit ist die formale Bindung a priori aller Erscheinungen uberhaupt* (*Krit. der rein. Vern.*, Trans. Aesth., zweit. absch. VIc [sec. ed]). Time, history, is conceived as linear— with no beginning, and no end—but infinite in either direction, that is, with no discernable beginning or end.

With the exception of Nietzsche and the Idealists, the Greek idea of cyclical time has no place in modern philosophical and scientific discourse. "Positivism is the accepted world-view among educators," observes P.E. Meland, that is, the modern world has rejected cyclicism.[75] Time may be dynamic or static, but it does not repeat itself, neither will it predictably end in some future "great year," with some cosmic crisis, swallowing all the elements of the past, disgorging a new age which finally vanishes into another age, only to begin again and again *ad infinitum*. In this connection, some Greeks, like Plato, conceived reality as dual—time and eternity—others, like Plotinus, were monists, even pantheists, who saw reality hierarchically fused from the highest to the lowest existence. Time is the human measure of a dynamic reality.

When compared to the ancient cosmology, the modern Western concept of time appears as a secular parody of that vision generally associated with Judaism and Christianity or, to be precise, with the storied cosmology received from Augustine. He proposed an usual theory: from creation to resurrection, history runs in a straight line from *arche* to *telos*, with eternity as its unavoidable companion. But he adds that nothing stands between Truth (God) and the mind—*inter mentem nostram et veritate nulla interposita creatura est* (*De vera Rel.*, LV, 113 PL 34 172)—a remark, seminal and revolutionary, with immense religio-philosophical consequences far beyond anything Augus-

---

[75] *The Secularization of Modern Culture*. New York, 1960, p. 117.

tine might have anticipated. Put another way, here is a rationalism which imagines itself to have emancipated the soul from servitude to time; however, as human experience shows, man's reason, detached from the discipline of religions, will always seek what is too wonderful for it; so it was with the Bishop of Hippo.

Augustine's epistemology—however modified later by medieval nominalists and realists—was yet the tacit assumption of medieval philosophical and theological speculation. Thomas Aquinas, as already noted, conceived nature as crowned by Grace, as if eternity had condescended to set gently atop the created order. He would not turn against his master, although Aristotle compelled him to make adjustments in the "traditional" cosmology. The Protestant Reformers, trusting in the *Scriptura sola* (and revisiting Augus-tine), likewise recognized eternity as parallel to time, to history, with the Sovereign God, from time to time, violating (miracles, visitations, the Incar-nation) the laws of nature which He Himself had erected and, therefore, has the right to suspend.

B   The Orthodox Church has another vision of time which is illustrated by her iconology—even as sacred art (or lack of it) in the post-patristic West rests on its understanding of time. We have already touched on this matter with a previous discussion of the Eighth Day and its relation to Sunday and the divine Liturgy, and in connection with these, the theme of "today." If we remember that the icon, in the words of Photius Kontoglou, has "a liturgical and dogmatic character,"[76] the Christian idea of time comes slowly into focus. The icon is "liturgical," because it is essential to Orthodox worship, "dogmatic" because it reflects the Chalcedonian christology. The "liturgical" presupposes the "dogmatic" and the "dogmatic" also reveals the divine cosmology.

Christ is the Archetype for time's relationship to the spiritual, including eternity: as with His two natures, so they are united "without confusion or separation." As He was "first-born from the dead," the future, the Age to Come reaches back into the course of history. Time and eternity are not parallel or complementary; time is not "the moving image of eternity" (Plato), but eternity, immanent to creation, gradually deifying it with the Uncreated Energies, sinks into time as water into a sponge. There are, to be sure, moments when past and future paradoxically merge in the present, most especially in the divine Liturgy of the Church when time ceases to exist as periodic or sequential.

---

76 *The Expression of Orthodox Iconography* (vol. 1). Athens, 1979, p. 75 (in Greek).

In the words of Constantine Kalokyris, these three modalities of time become "a mystical life-experience in which, while eternity is lived in the present, the things of the past and of the future and even the eschatological things, that is, prehistory and the main stations of the redemptive work of Christ, and all the salutary gifts extending to the last days which flowed from Him, are condensed and lived mystically as alive and present before us".[77] Time (and space) are not "adamant categories." There is no better manifestation of "iconographic time" than the Orthodox worship which abolishes time in its scientific sense.[78] In the divine Liturgy, where the believer shares in "the Mystery," the icon is visible testimony to the unity of the Church, by the presence of sacred persons and events through it; that is, time and space are "contemporized" (συγχρονιζόμενα) with the transcendent and the "communion of the saints" is realized in those liturgical moments when the Age to Come permeates the Now, when the heavenly and earthly Church join in "the sacrifice of praise."

The Eucharist identifies the *mysterion*, that "mystical" moment when all the Faithful participate in the Life of God. The fact of this participation, shared by "the terrestrials and the celestials," is exquisitely displayed in the icon whose timeless personalities, vivid colors and shapes, all announce the grand purpose of the divine Economy, of Christ the Archetype.[79] The music and the liturgical rites, the iconic architecture are more than the setting for the consummate unity of the Church in the *koinonia* of the Eucharist. Like the incense whose odor betrays the Presence of the Holy Spirit, everything which decorates the temple informs the initiates of their collective participation in the Divine. In a real sense, the whole temple, "the House of God," is iconic, because everything which takes place there suggests the unity of time and eternity. Because the Eucharist brings to us the incarnate Christ as food and drink, it is also an icon, the revelation of the Divine in the human: access to the Uncreated by the created.

C   The iconographer portrays the sanctification of the Saint by painting large eyes to behold the Lord (θεωρία), large ears to hear His Voice, large

---

[77]   "The Essence of Orthodox Iconography," 1, 45.

[78]   *Ibid.*, 46.

[79]   The Fathers sometimes used the word prototype (πρωτότυπος), sometimes *archetype* (ἀρχέτυπος) for persons or events which the icons imitates. Scholars commonly trace their language and concepts to Greek philosophy. "...an Orthodox cannot accept the idea that the iconographic doctrine of the Church was formed under the influence of ancient philosophy, in particular of Neo-Platonism," writes L. Ouspensky. "In fact, the doctrine of the image has always been rooted in the heart of the Christian vision of the world. From its very origin, it existed with an implicit fullness" (*Theology of the Icon*, p. 113).

nose to inhale the fragrance of the Holy Spirit, a small mouth as the sign of abstinence, wearing garments which, by their folds and color, project the spiritual bodies of the Saints, with their heads surrounded by a crown of light—Christ alone displaying a cruciform halo, *nimbus crucifixus*, with the Greek word ὁ Ὤν *("the Existent One," the "He Who is" of Exodus 3:14)*—to represent splendor and glory of the Age to Come in which the *cosmos* is transfigured. Furthermore, the use of symbolic colors and shapes implies the theological truth that what has not nor cannot be seen is not able to be depicted. Hence, God the Father Who has never been seen (or ever shall be) cannot be painted.[80] He has no form, neither did He ever manifest Himself. He has no icon, but is worshiped. The Holy Spirit is ordinarily depicted as a dove, but is not worshiped in that form. Christ was incarnate, the angels are not without a certain materiality, which allows them to appear to man as shown on icons. The Saints, of course, were body and soul, and shall be again, and it is in this form that they are "written." God alone is worshiped, the icons of Christ, the Virgin, the Angels and the Saints venerated or, as St Basil said, "the honor given to the icon passes over to the prototype" (*de Sp. Sanct.*, 18 PG 32 149A).

In other words, icons present "the mystical world of faith"—τὸν μυστικὸν κόσμον τῆς πίστεως, to borrow Kontoglou's phrase. They are a "transcription of the holy word," he adds. Yet, although the icon makes things holy and spiritual visible to the eyes of faith, they are not the subject of demonstration and persuasion.[81] Iconography is an ascetical and prayerful art, arousing compunction, translating the believer beyond the vicissitudes of time and the senses. It is not naturalistic; it sets no mirror before nature; it conjures no abstraction; it is not theatre, but is the art which aids man in his experience of the mysteries of the Christian religion, mysteries which the saved will continue to search out endlessly in the Age to Come. Thus, the iconographer, a person of "humility and contrition," does not go where his genius would otherwise take him—neither is the icon a medium for it—but he is guided by Tradition. Orthodox iconography is a spiritual art.

---

80 According to Kalokyris, "icons" of the Holy Trinity and God the Father began to appear in eleventh century Byzantium, the prohibition against idolatry notwithstanding. In twelfth century southern Italy (Brindisi), perhaps for the first time, the Father is portrayed as Daniel's "Ancient of Days" on a wall-painting in the church of San Biagio. Kalokyris mentions also a depiction of the Trinity on the fourteenth century Psalter of Munich. He alludes, finally, to Rublev's Hospitality of Abraham with the three Angels as the Three Persons of the Trinity ("The Essence of Orthodox Iconography," XIII, 1, 70). To be accurate, the three Angels are a symbol not an icon of the invisible Trinity which cannot be depicted.

81 *Expression. . .* (vol. 1), 415.

D   Whether through its paintings or statues, the sacred art of Roman Catholicism depicts its doctrines of man and the Fall, and by implication its ontology and, therefore, its christology. In the steps of Aquinas, it describes the
loss of primordial innocence—the original sin—as the forfeiture of the supernatural gifts of Grace, that is, natural justice, control over nature, and immortality. The purpose of the Incarnation is the reacquisition of the those very
"superadded gifts" which Adam possessed in Paradise. Man's nature was
not fundamentally changed either by the Fall; nor, indeed, by the Crucifixion
and Resurrection. Their Grace, the Grace of Christ punished and risen, being
a created power, is the promise of man's restoration to his original Edenic
condition. The "state of Grace" in which the saved must live and die is by no
means anticipation of man's deification. At best, he or she will be a God-
bearing vessel, very much like the Nestorian Jesus. Roman Catholic art
shows nothing else.

Thus, two different conceptions of God have produced two different
dogmatic conceptions of holiness,[82] and, consequently, two different conceptions of sacred art. "The representation of man in Western art corresponds
to the theoretical impossibility of deifying human nature, of transfiguring it
radically, its corporeal reality included," remarks Leonid Ouspensky.[83]
Man's contact with created Grace does not allow for a partaking of the
divine Nature; nor does the presence of the Holy Spirit in the soul radically
alter his being. Holiness is depicted in such art by the "beautiful" man or
woman with a halo hovering above the head, rather than around it. For reasons of perspective, the halo is elliptical, implying that Grace is external,
something "superadded" to human nature, rather than a radiance exuding
from the being of the Saint. Also, the flatness of the icon seeks to represent
the state of the noetic world where the "holy ones" of dwell, a state impene-
trable to reason or the senses. A religious statue must imply only a certain
coincidence or analogy between the visible and invisible creation.

E   To explain these differences in the sacred art of the Church and the post-
Orthodox West, one must, as already suggested, turn to the differences in the
Faith, a European Faith, continuing to change,which altered the art that was

---

[82] "The two traditions have separated on a mysterious doctrinal point, relating to
the Holy Spirit, who is the source of holiness," observes Lossky. "Two different dogmatic conceptions correspond to two different experiences, to two ways of sanctification,
which scarely resemble one another. Since the separation, the ways which lead to sanctity are not in the same in the West as in the East. The one proves its fidelity to Christ in
the solitude and abandonment of the night of Gethsemane, the other gains certainty of
union with God in the light of the Transfiguration" (*The Mystical Theology..*, pp. 226-227).

[83] *Theology of the Icon*, p. 216.

part of it. Unlike Orthodox iconography which shows little change, the Western iconography is a map of the culture which produced it, a history which divulges the effect of the culture on that art and surely *vice versa*. To the eleventh century, icons, East and West, were understood very much in the same way—as liturgical and dogmatic. But various intellectual developments (too vast and complex to discuss here) reshaped the piety of the West, perhaps beginning with art, such as the tenth century iconography of Ottonian Germany where, for the first time, someone dared to artistically depict, perhaps innocently, the initial movements of the resuscitated Christ. Traditionally, iconographers were intent on not exceeding the testimony of the Evangelists, relying upon the eye-witness of the apostles and three Marys.[84]

Iconographic innovations, mayhaps the catalysts to the new art of the West, were, in part, the result of the new spirituality, especially the distinction between "the external" or "active life" and "the inner" or "contemplative," "the mystical life." The "spiritual exercises" of the contemplatives held the promise of union with God through the gradual exclusion of anything visual or sensible. "Meditation" was the limit of clergy and monastics who remained in "active life," while the ordinary believers had to be satisfied with even less: the Sacraments, fasting, prayer, hearing the lives of the saints, veneration of images, statues, and reliquaries, etc. Gradually, the latter increasingly lost their importance in public worship, a demotion which eventually extinguished the liturgical character of religious art. The religious value of it became largely an educational tool, if not merely decorative accessories to lend an aesthetic atmosphere to the place of worship. Thus, too, where they were not used for private devotions and personal needs, images became part of the *stadtkultur*, serving as patrons of the city or emblems of social groups. "As a result the images passed from hand to hand," Belting says, "changing as they did so."[85]

F   Although not until our ecumenical era are statues or images being removed from the Roman Catholic temples, they have for a long time been nothing more than an aid in prayer. Devotion to images, as the Faith itself, has became increasingly privatized. They began to lose their "chalcedonian" character already in the thirteenth century; and even the nineteenth century liturgical revival failed to integrate the image into liturgical worship. Thus, the vision of the painter took on increasing importance, so by that period

---

84 Grabar, *Christian Iconography*, p. 123.
85 *Likeness and Presence*, p. 410.

which John Huizinga called "the autumn of the Middle Ages,"[86] Latin iconography had lost all contact with the ancient tradition. Medieval art, like its life and thought, slipped with little difficulty into modernity, a transition prepared by its Aristotelians and Platonists, the new monasticism and mysticism, the growth of individualism, humanism and secularism, etc. There was no alarm when the Renaissance turned the holy subjects of religious art into the *quasi-sacral* subjects of its naturalism, when things Divine became things human; hence, the blasphemy which dared to depict God the Father Himself in human form, artistic creations which in fact were no more than the creatures of the artists' imagination, as we see in the works of Michaelangelo, DaVinci, Raphael, El Greco, etc.[87]

The Platonism of the Renaissance completely severed heaven from earth and thereby redefined the personalities and events of religious history as splendid allegories of their transcendent prototypes. The elevation of the Crucifix (usually behind the altar), the statues of the Virgin and the Saints to pedestals, placed them beyond immediate contact with the celebrant and the worshippers. The statuary did not signify the presence of the holy ones, but lent to the Mass an aesthetic and emotional ambience, hoping to lift the mind of believer to heavenly things.

Likewise the architecture of the temple which formerly was constructed as something profoundly more than the environment for worship came to mean little more. In the past, churches were constructed as "icons" of the new creation: sometimes cruciform, sometimes rotund (circle = eternity), sometimes both, to prefigure the transfigured universe, the realization of God's Kingdom, the perfect communion of the Saints; but, also, the temple was the symbol of the new man, outwardly simple, dignified, resolute, while inwardly beautiful and spiritually glorious, bathed in the Uncreated Light. Furthermore, by its lines, use of color and space, the temple provided a sense of brotherly intimacy and warmth, *a fortiori* as the temple, crowned by the dome, spoke of "God with us." Finally, the temple was architecturally represented as the vessel of salvation, an image of Noah's Ark.

Medieval architecture (plastic art), like its icons, became, with the change in Roman Catholic theology, a reflection of that change. Thus, lost was "the theology of the senses," of light and color, and sound and taste—of "wheat, wine and oil" (Psa. 4:7)—which demonstrates the resurrection of the

---

[86]　Art, increasingly sensuous and photographic, was an integral part of the age. Its task, now not exclusively religious "was embellishing the forms in which life was lived with beauty" (*The Autumn of the Middle Ages*. Trans. by R.J. Payton and U. Mammitzsch. Chicago, 1996, pp. 294-328).

[87]　See J. Hale, *The Civilization of Europe in the Renaissance*. New York, 1944, chaps. 9-10.

flesh. Henry Adams offers us, in his *Mont-Saint Michel and Chartres* (New York, 1959, p. 324f.), an example of the medieval "philosophy" of the Christian temple. Its builders, he states, believed that with Aristotle's help, the pointed arch and the magic of mathematics (which revealed the cosmic secret of numbers), they could solve, architecturally, the grand intellectual problems that philosophers had failed to resolve, such as spanning the "chasm between unity and multiplicity." They used the Trinity as a model; thus, as they saw God as Geometer of the universe, so the architects conceived the church building as a triangle: the first line, infinite in extension, must be assumed, while a second became a reflection of the first; but where is the third? The Father and Son are extension and reflection—how is the Holy Spirit to be represented on the structure? He is the diversity which emanates from the unity of the other Persons. From the outside, the towering spire of the cathedral projected a sense of divine transcendence, and within the dark corners sequestered among the lofty arches emitted a sense of mystery, and the tall and stately columns symbolized the majesty of God.

The temple, with its stained glass windows, welcomed beams of light from the *outside*, suggesting the Light of God came from without rather than from within the soul purified by Grace. The sun's light suggested the *lumen gloria* by which man will see God. Such architecture was the background to liturgy and sacred art. The Mass was celebrated in Latin (instead of the language of the people), a practice which led gradually to a difference in the piety of the Faithful and the clergy, a difference only exacerbated by the subsequent introduction of pews, kneeling on Sunday, new music, the rosary, etc. The Western Mass came to resemble more and more a court ceremonial.

ᘓ   The empty walls of the Reformed temples (under no obligation to face the East) were, historically, a statement of the Protestant rejection of "papal idolatry." Christianity, as the Reformers conceived it, was a purified, desensualized "religion of the Word." "The Reformation taught the dominion of 'the word' which surpassed every other religious sign," states Belting. "Christianity had always been a revelation through the word, but now the word took on an unprecedented monoply and aura."[88] The Reformation had profited from the new humanism which also proclaimed the reign of the Spirit through "the mirror of the word." As if visited by the eighth century iconoclasts (and drawing arguments from Thomas Aquinas), Protestants argued that the painter can represent only the body; hence, the word ranked above any painted or sculpted image. Not unexpectedly, then, the Reformers' temples and liturgies were plain, without iconography, without

---

[88]   *Likeness and Presence*, p. 465.

corporeal language or symbolism, whether medieval or Renaissance, which had until then characterized religious structures.

Although Martin Luther did not object to sacred images if they remained in the picture-cabinets of private homes as aides in the believer's devotions, he seems to have held with the other Reformers, that they had forever lost their place in the house of worship. Opposing Carlstadt in *Against the Heavenly Prophets with Regard to Images and the Sacraments* (1525), he described images as "a remembrance and a sign," that is, assistance in prayer and a source of education (*WA* XVIII, 82-85). He, therefore, did not discourage religious art, so long as the work was infused with the "authentic message of the gospel." He urged religious painters to depict the humanity of Jesus which alone mirrored the eternal. Albrecht Duerer (1471-1528) adopted Luther's ideas and reflected them in his art. John Calvin, on the other hand, condemned as "hair-splitting" the distinction between "worship" (λατρεία) and "veneration" (προσκύνησις or δουλεία). He insisted that an image or icon can never be anything but a sacrilege, an anthropomorphic idol, constituting an insult to God Who gave an express Commandment against their creation and use. God manifests Himself in "the Word" (*Institutes* IV, ii, 4; viii, 11 B). More than Luther, Calvin demanded that God should be honored "only in the living temple and in the hearts of men"[89]

Yet, the Protestant attitude towards sacred image or icon was not revolutionary. They learned from the Scholastics that such art gave no access to the spiritual world, was no instrument of Grace; and, therefore, adopting the ecclesiology of the invisible Church, it was only logical that they marginalized if not eliminated images of the holy as a liturgical art altogether. They found no Biblical foundation for it; and, on account of this revulsion for "the mysticism of the icon," the Reformers rejected the compromise of the Council of Trent whose decree[90] might have been the basis for dialogue between them. If later some Protestants will paint or draw Biblical events and persons, their purpose was not "mystical," but educational, perhaps "inspirational."

---

[89] On readings from the Reformers' works on the images, see R.H. Bainton, *The Age of the Reformation*. Princeton, 1956, pp. 36,40, 114-119, 172; also, Belting, pp. 458-460.

[90] Trent declared that images are owed *honorem et venerationem*, not because "some divinity or power (*divinitas vel virtus*) is believed to lie in them as a reason for cultus or because anything is expected from them, nor that confidence should be placed in images as was done by pagans of old; but because the honor showed them is referred to the original which they represent." Trent also cautions that images not be painted with "seductive charm" and "sensual appeal"—which had become too common since the Renaissance (*The Ecumenical Councils* [vol. 2]: *The Council of Trent*. Ed. by N.P. Tanner. London, 1990, pp. 774-776). Except for the relics sometimes put into the images, they were no longer "honored and venerated," surely not as "the windows to eternity." Also, Trent might have better called Latin "images" imaginative analogies rather than representations.

H   If there has been little taste for sacred art in Protestantism, it is because the Lutherans, Calvinists, Baptists, Methodist, Congregationalists, etc. are the proponents of false ecclesiologies, false doctrines of the Church which evoke heretical christologies. To repeat, in understanding Christianity as a "religion of the Word," of inwardness, a religion of the soul, with no obvious ties to anything material, there is no reason for the body and the senses to share in the worship of God; hence, there is no need for art, at least, not at the level of faith. Roman Catholicism, on the other hand, has lost its memory of the icon which was eventually replaced by the three-dimensional sculpture.[91] Why the change? Why the porcelain, sensuous, life-like figures ("realism") decorating its temples instead of the "mystical" icon which covers the interior of Orthodox churches? A new world-view in which the natural man is "perfected" by created Grace rather than deified by Uncreated Grace.

The present state of Western art, sacred or secular, is the unavoidable consequence of the West's nestorian dualism, its competing theologies, and its philosophical consciousness. This mind-set picks up new modalities with the Reformation, after which came the periods of the so-called Enlightenment, of Romanticism, Pragmatism, and Positivism. Each contributed to the development of Western art until it has become homocentric, despite pockets of ecclesiastical resistance. As with Western man himself, art and culture, has generally ceased to be the product of religion. Religious art is almost unseen, except in museums and some churches. Thus, painting, sculpture, architecture, etc. come to express the personal vision of the profane and pelagian man. His art, like his theology, is written in the idiom of abstraction and psychology. There is no perception of eternity, of revelation or the divine Good and preternatural evil.

Without this objective spiritual dimension to created reality, without the presence of God and His divine economy, what is left? Merely the compulsive and futile quest for answers to the human predicament, a compulsion and futility which is nowhere more conspicuous than in contemporary art, especially with the emergence from the very bosom of modernity of a new cultural movement—"post-modernism" (a term coined in the 1930's). It seeks liberation from the idea of a hidden and permanent truth behind the world of visible multiplicity, a dualistic view of reality which has characterized the West since the Middle Ages. In a word, post-modernism wants mankind to celebrate diversity; hence, it follows that in art, as in every other

---

[91] The history of the early medieval papacy and kingship has been memorialized in sacred art, almost always flat, from the seventh century Psalter of Echternach to the twelfth century "Donations of Constantine." After a brief Byzantine revival, statuary begin to appear with regularity in the fourteenth century, such as the famous sculpture of Boniface VIII (See the illustrations in G. Barraclough, *The Medieval Papacy*).

human endeavor (including science), the individual must look not for the knowledge of a united and intelligible reality to which he may relate, but is permitted to provide society only with an interpretation of what he sees around him (relativism). So it is that much of contemporary art reflects (if it does not share in the guilt of creating it) the predicament to which the West (and much of the world) has been brought by the ancient dualism: first the loss of God, now the loss of self.

The privatized deities of a thousand beliefs plays "no role whatever in the public life of the secular metropolis."[92] The supernatural has little appeal for modernity—unless we define pantheism in those terms. As Van Gogh said, life is "the power to create." To "create," not to "interpret" as was the inclination of ancient and medieval artists and philosophers. "The artist constructs the world to his plan," writes Camus.[93] Hence, "the terrifying castles of the surrealist," the desperate abstractions of the cubist, the impressionists' passion for coherence. Late in our century, the modern "iconographer" has gained ecological consciousness on account of which he paints man as another aspect of nature, another animal species on earth. Without God, art is dehumanized. Exalting himself, man is abased.

---

92 H. Cox, *The Secular City*, p. 2.
93 *The Rebel*, p. 255.

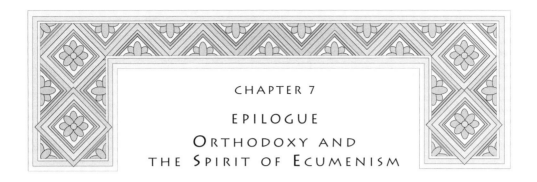

CHAPTER 7

EPILOGUE

ORTHODOXY AND
THE SPIRIT OF ECUMENISM

Ecumenism[1] is a religious phenomenon of Western culture, a culture whose evolution, since the French Revolution, has rushed toward political and spiritual homogeneity. It is an idea of world-unity spurred by socialism and the Hegelian milieu of the nineteenth century, complemented in the twentieth century with the influx of far Eastern religions. No doubt two world wars have fueled the persistent but futile aspiration for "perpetual peace," the ancient dream of cosmopolis, or to invoke the popular platitude, a "brave new world." Not a few ecumenists rightly believe that ultimately all problems are religious problems, all solutions are religious solutions; but what kind of religion?

1   THE TWENTIETH CENTURY

Ecumenists (and politicians) have a grand scheme: the unity of humanity through the unity of the Church: universal Church, universal religion, all part of, if not coordinated with, the political solution: a "new world-order," if not a world-state. After World War I, this religio-political scheme was adopted as central to the ecclesial agenda of the Patriarchal Synod of Constantinople in its Encyclical of 1920, an Encyclical which envisioned a League of Churches to complement the League of Nations. Both ideas failed, but did not expire. They were reincarnated in 1948 as the United Nations (UN) and the World Council of Churches (WCC). The evidence does not permit us to speak of planned global conspiracy, only an unconscious collusion of minds.

---

[1] Originally, the word "ecumenism" referred to "a movement of thought and action" whose end was "the reunion of Christians" (G.H. Tavard, *Two Centuries of Ecumenism: The Search for Unity. Notre Dame* (Ind.), 1962, xi-xii). Its current reach far exceeds its intitial grasp. The World Council of Churches which it spawned, now strives to become a world religion.

A   The inclusiveness of the United Nations should hold no surprises; neither the exclusiveness of a Christian organization. Under these circumstances, however, there could be no alliance between them, since "politics"
and "religion" and the grand vision of humanity united as cosmopolis with
a pantheon had no chance of realization. How fortunate it is, then, that in
Pacem in terris (1963), Pope John XXIII[2] approved the United Nations
"Universal Declaration of the Rights of Man," and a year later convoked the
second Vatican Council which "received from the Holy Ghost the charism of
transforming the Church" (*L' Osservatore Romano*, 7 August 1989, p. 9). One
might find further coincidence in the speech of Pope Paul VI (4 Oct. 1965)
before the United Nations, saying, "We are tempted to declare that your spirit reflects in some way, in the temporal order, what our Catholic Church
wishes to be in the spiritual order, unique and universal."

The plan of religio-political monism, reflected in the Pope's speech to
the United Nations, was bolstered two months later with the so-called "lifting of the Anathemas." The condemnation of papal heresies by the four
Patriarchs of the East in 1054 (and later reaffirmed by the Russian Orthodox
Church) had persisted until then as a monument to Orthodoxy's witness to
an imperishable Faith. In December of 1965, the plenipotentiary of Patriarch
Athenagoras I, Metropolitan Meliton, stood at the altar of St Peter's Basilica
in Vatican City where he publically proclaimed that "the baseless reproach-
es" and "blameworthy symbolic acts...on both sides" were negated and for-
given. Although the fatuous gesture was meaningless—Patriarch Athenagoras, having no authority to act unilaterally—he announced before the
world that what was enacted, accepted and ratified by all, for all, everywhere was now superceded by the will of a single man for the sake of an idea
inimical to the Faith that he was obliged by a sacred oath to defend.

The Masonic Athenagoras expunged a millennium of Orthodox fidelity
to the Apostolic Truth. His motive became apparent in his terse expression,
"the task of refounding the Church." Some Orthodox denounced him as a
"heretic," "uniate," as "neo-Papist," but these criticisms, albeit true, largely
missed the mark. The Roman-Constantinoplean liaison was the first giant
step in the history of contemporary religion toward spiritual universalism.

---

2   A small but intriguing detail in the life of Angelo Roncalli (Pope John XXIII) was
his friendship with the Belgian monk, Dom Lambert Beauduin (1874-1960). To him the
Pope owed no little debt for ideas concerning Christian unity and the calling of an "ecumenical Council." Beauduin had close ties to the Russian *émigrés*, including the Parisian
disciples (Bulgakov, Berdiaev, etc.) of Vladimir Soloviev, the nineteenth Russian
theosophist and philosopher, whose book, *Russia and the Universal Church*, was to them
an ecumenical manual (See Nicholas Zernov, "The Significance of the Russian Orthodox
diaspora and its Effect on the Christian West," in *The Orthodox Churches and the West*. Ed.
by D. Baker. Oxford, 1976, pp. 315-327).

The Ecumenical Patriarch had formally rejected the "classical consciousness" of the Church (chap. II) with his "lifting of the anathemas," a tragedy which was antedated four decades earlier by the adoption of the New or Gregorian Calendar.

B   Athenagoras' presumption had implications for a new direction in ecclesiastical affairs, something which had been visibly initiated at the New Delhi Assembly (1961) with the admission of the Communist-dominated Moscow Patriarchate. The injection of Marxian Socialism was a boost to the growing inclination of ecumenism towards one-world religion, an inclination augmented in Nairobi, Kenya (1975), where the Fifth Assembly decided "to advance towards unity in order that the world may believe... to express the common concern of the churches in the service of human need, the breaking down of barriers between peoples, and the promotion of one human family in justice and peace."[3]

The theme for the next meeting of the WCC, gathering in Vancouver, Canada (1983), was "Jesus Christ—the Life of the World." However, this was a "New Age" Christ who instilled a novel advocacy—"the fruitfulness and importance" for dialogue with non-Christians who by invitation had sent delegations to the Vancouver Assembly. Common worship included, among other things, an exhibition of American Indian religious rites. "To profess a faith in Jesus Christ as the Savior was apparently no longer to be characteristic of the World Council," observes Fr Degyansky. "To the ecumenists, Vancouver became an ideal opportunity for the World Council of Churches Assembly to look seriously at issues of religious and cultural pluralism, recognizing that, indeed, 'our future is one'."[4]

C   If such an ecumenical ideology were the basis of Vancouver convocation, it took on a more ominous meaning—albeit Rome is not officially a member of the WCC—at the Assisi Conference (1986), "the pantheon of Assisi," as Abbé LeRoux describes it.[5] Leaders from every religious community in the world—including the Orthodox—were represented. Pope John-

---

3   C. Patelos, ed., *The Orthodox Church and the Ecumenical Movement*. Geneva, 1978, p. 19.

4   *Orthodox Christianity and the Spirit of Contemporary Ecumenism*. Etna (Cal.), 1992, p. 58. With regard to the theoretical justification for "Christian" relations with non-Christians, see, e.g., S. Fritsch-Oppermann, "Trikaya and Trinity: Reflecting on Some Aspects of Christian-Buddhist Dialogue," in *Journal of Ecumenical Studies* XXX, 2 (1992), 47-54; and B.J. Redman, "One God: Toward a Rapprochement of Orthodox Judaism and Christianity," *Journal of Ecumenical Studies* XXXI, 3-4 (1994), 307-331.

5   D. LeRoux, *Peter, Lovest Thou Me? John Paul II: Pope of Tradition or Pope of Revolution*. Gladysdale, Victoria (Aust.), 1990, p. 160.

Paul II greeted his guests not with a declaration of his faith in the God-Man, but rather with an exhortation to cooperation and good will. "The fact that we profess different creeds does not take away from the significance of this day," the Pope declared. "On the contrary, the churches, the ecclesial communities and the religions of the world show that they profoundly desire the good of humanity."[6]

That the Pope brought together Christian, Jew, Muslim, the American Indian and oriental pagans into a single company of prayer, of discourse and of purpose stands as an obscene indifference to the Lordship of Christ. Assisi was an event the likes of which had never occurred before in the history of Christendom, a blasphemy so deliberately perverse that it is difficult to imagine that even the most notorious heretics of the past would have participated. The *pièce de résistance* of the Assisi Conference was the placing of a statue of Buddha on the altar of a Christian temple. The Italian newspapers made special note of the incident, incredulous and chagrined. It was, therefore, consistent of the Pope to close the assembly with the same humanistic tolerance that opened it. "With the religions of the world, we share a profound respect for conscience and obedience which, with all, we try to find truth, to love and serve every person and every people.... Yes, we consider both conscience and obedience to conscience an essential element along the road to a better world and to peace."[7]

Even the most vocal critics of Roman Catholicism must have been overwhelmed by the syncretism of Assisi. They surely noticed that the Only-begotten Son of God had been dethroned by one who calls himself, *vicarius Christi*, reducing by implication the eternal God to one of many saviors—Buddha, the Great Spirit, Lord Shanti, etc.—while the Orthodox by remaining silent , stood consenting to the injustice. How grievous to see the whole meaning of the Christian Faith vitiated in a few days of bewitching sacrilege.

D   More concessions were expected of the Orthodox Church. The Geneva center of the World Council of Churches released the text of a draft, "Towards a Common Understanding and Vision."[8] The preliminary document anticipated the agenda of the Eighth Ecumenical Assembly of the WCC in 3-14 December of 1998 that was to be held in Harare, Zimbabwe. The draft called on members to "recognize in other churches elements of the true

---

6   Quoted, *ibid.*, p. 163.

7   Quoted, *ibid.*, p. 166.

8   For the full text of this document: E-Mail-mal@wccoe.org.

Church"; and to enter into a "spiritual relationship through which they seek to learn from each other and give help to each other in order that the body of Christ may be built up and the life of the Church may be renewed" (para. 1.13).

According to the WCC, the present goal of the ecumenical movement is the reconciliation of both the Church and humanity to God's revealed purpose (para. 2.4). Once more comes the call to "mutual commitment which the churches have established with one another," "rooted" in the indivisible Christ Who "has made us His own" (para. 3.4).

Hieromonk Ambrose (Russian Synod) observed that in these few sentences the Central Committee has mandated cooperation with "any religion in the world . . . if the goal is unity," while implicitly repudiating "the Orthodox dogma of the one Church, from which heretics and schismatics fell away."[9] In a word, "mutual recognition of other churches" is mandatory upon those who seek or hope to retain membership in the WCC (para. 3.4, 7), all premised on the notion that "our knowledge of the unchangeable evolves; each Christian community must render its contribution to the full understanding of the (Gospel) message."[10]

With the resistance of many Orthodox to such an ecclesiology—including the withdrawal of the Orthodox Churches of Georgia and Bulgaria from the World Council of Churches—the Harare Assembly moderated the demands of the Geneva draft and all other declarations that might express like sentiments. The General Secretary's Report and the Policy Statement were less strident, but hardly compatible with the traditional Orthodox doctrine of the Church. The Assembly kept the slogan, "Common Understanding and Vision," couching the new proposals in the safe rhetoric of goals and ideals. A common language must be found, it stated, a "language inspiring to all the baptized, not simply to specialists." The "language" must no longer reflect that "institutional preoccupation" which obscures "the wider ecumenical movement's evangelical commitment to the mission of God." The Policy Statement stressed the importance of "self-critical evaluation" as part of "our membership and participation." Helpful in realizing on earth "the unity of God's People already given in Christ," is the development of "an ecumenical spirituality," perhaps beginning with a common celebration of Easter on 15 April 2001 (see WCC Website).

---

[9] "On Membership in the World Council of Churches," in *Orthodox Life*. XLII, 1 (1997), 25.
[10] Timiadis, E. (Metropolitan), "Neglected Factors Influencing Unity," *The Greek Orthodox Theological Review* XIV, 2 (1969), 137.

2　The Oberlin Statement

Some Orthodox may wonder how so many of their leaders have lost the "classical consciousness" of the Fathers. What reasons could they have for adopting a religious philosophy whose very existence is antithetical to the divine privileges of the Church? Although a plausible case was originally made for an Orthodox presence in the WCC—"witness" to the apostolic Faith of which she alone is the guardian—the current aims of the WCC are not something reconcilable with Orthodox ecclesiology, especially now that ecumenism has abandoned its original motive—"reunion of Christendom"—for the illusion of one world religion.

A　Some may remember the proud stand the Orthodox took at Amsterdam and Evanston, listening with satisfaction to the Statement of Faith delivered to the North American Faith and Order Study Conference, in Oberlin, Ohio (1957).[11] There is an interesting, although incidental, detail about the Orthodox delegation led by Athenagoras Kokkinakis, the Greek Orthodox Bishop of Boston, and later Archbishop of Thyateira in London. To a man they were New Calendarists (see below), who subsequently either became rabid ecumenists (save for the redoubtable and mystifying Georges Florovsky) or died in the jurisdiction of the Constantinopolitan Patriarchate. There is the isolated case of Father Eusebius Papastephanou, a Greek Orthodox priest, who has since become a charismatic (the new Montanism), a spiritualistic variety of ecumenism.

At Oberlin, however, they declared with conviction that "the unity we seek" is "a given unity which has never been lost, and as a divine gift and an essential mark of Christian existence could not have been lost. This unity in the Church of Christ is for us a unity of the historical Church, in the fullness of faith, in the fullness of continuous sacramental life. For us, this unity is embodied in the Orthodox Church. ..." The Orthodox conceded that "the unity of Christendom has been disrupted," that is, Protestantism and Roman Catholicism who make the confession that Christ is God and Savior, are nevertheless estranged from the unity of the Church on account of a faith which lacks fullness. But the true faith, the faith without which there can be no unity, exists, the Orthodox Church; and, therefore, the unity of the Church "has never been broken or lost, so as to be now a problem of search and discovery."

---

[11] Final Report II, 2, in *A Documentary History of the Faith & Order Movement: 1927-1963*. Ed. by L. Vischer. St Louis, 1963, p. 29. To quote Justin Popovich, "Intercommunion, that is, participating with heretics in Holy Sacraments, and especially the Holy Eucharist, is the most shameless betrayal of our Lord Jesus Christ... The idea of intercommunion is contradictory and totally inconceivable for the Orthodox Catholic conscience" ("Humanistic Ecumenism," in *Orthodox Faith and Life in Christ*. Trans. by A. Gerostergios. Belmont [Mass.], 1994, p. 173).

"The Orthodox Church...is the Body of Christ and, as such, can never be divided. It is Christ as her head and the indwelling of the Holy Spirit that have secured the unity of the Church throughout the ages." "The Orthodox Church teaches that she has no need to search for a 'lost unity,' because her historic consciousness dictates that she is the *Una Sancta* and that all Christian groups outside the Orthodox Church can recover their unity only by entering the bosom of that Church which [alone] has preserved her identity with early Christianity. These are claims that have arisen not from presumption, but from an inner historical awareness of the Orthodox Church. Indeed, this is the special message of Eastern Orthodoxy to a divided Western Christendom."

Uniquely, she has maintained "an unbroken continuity with the Church of Pentecost by preserving the Apostolic Faith and polity unadulterated. She has kept 'the faith once delivered to the saints' free from the distortions of human innovations. Man-made doctrines have never found their way into the Orthodox Church, since she has no necessary association in history with the name of one single father or theologian. She owes the fullness and the guarantee of unity and infallibility to the operation of the Holy Spirit and not to the service of one individual. It is for this reason that she has never felt the need for what is know as 'the return to the purity of the Apostolic Faith'"; indeed, Orthodoxy is the Apostolic Church.

"We are bound in conscience to state explicitly what is logically inferred: that all other bodies have been directly or indirectly separated from the Orthodox Church. Unity, from the Orthodox standpoint, means a return of the separated bodies to the historical Orthodox Catholic and Apostolic Church." Her unity, the document continues, "rests on identity of faith, order and worship." All three aspects of the life of the Church are outwardly safeguarded by the reality of "the unbroken succession of Bishops which is the assurance of the Church's uninterrupted continuity with Apostolic origins." "Adhering tenaciously to her Apostolic heritage, the Orthodox Church holds that no true unity is possible when episcopacy and sacrament are absent." But also, there can be no agreement in Faith where there is no conformity with the decisions of the Seven Ecumenical Councils which implies that the Church is a visible organism. "It is a unity in the Spirit that is expressed in a unified visible organization."

B   The ecclesiology of the one true Church, the Orthodox Church, also "dictates" that no "intercommunion," no common acts of worship and prayer, no attendance at inter-denominational Communion services are permissible. "A common Faith and a common worship are inseparable in the historical continuity of the Orthodox Church." In other words, "An 'inter-communion' presupposes the existence of several separate and separated denominations which join occasionally in certain common acts or actions. In the true unity of Christ's Church there is no room for several 'denominations.' There is, therefore, no room for 'intercommunion'," no sharing of the Common Cup. "Communion is worship only possible within the unity of faith." Communion in the Eucharist is possible only within the Orthodox Church, for she is the Church.

3   GEORGES FLOROVSKY (1893-1979)

The question recurs, as when it was first asked: how is it possible for the Orthodox participants in the WCC, conscious of their Church as the one, holy, catholic and apostolic Church, to have surrendered this divine honor? When did the ecclesiology of the Oberlin Statement become obsolete? When did the canons become "toilet paper," as one Greek hierarch so eloquently put it. What caused these bishops, priests and theologians to come gradually to the position that the Orthodox Church could not be identified as the *Una Sancta*? Were they persuaded by argument? We have heard none. What compelled them to embrace a new religious consciousness?

A   There is a clue in the career of Fr Georges Florovsky, the symbol of his generation, of an Orthodoxy conscious of itself as the true Church but unable to endure the *embarras de richesses*. Here is a troubled Orthodoxy, dogged by a predatory West and demeaned by a repressive East, an institution which in the nineteenth century seems to have lost her nerve, so that in the twentieth century she is ready to cede her patrimony. Florovsky was the embodiment of the crisis, struggling to remain faithful to the patristic heritage of Orthodoxy while enamoured of occidental ways. His writings, profound as they sometimes were, show a desperate effort to reaffirm "the Faith of the Fathers" while welcoming heretics as "separated brethren" and their religious and intellectual values as saving Truth.

A student of Florovsky's at Princeton, His Grace, Bishop Chrysostomos of Etna (Cal.), offers some useful insight into his mentor's life and thought. Florovsky, he asserts, "was above all a scholar," a profession which seemed to dwarf his priesthood. Calling for "patristic revival," he, nevertheless, described the theology of the Fathers as "incomplete." Unwavering "in his dedication to the immutable truths of the Church," Fr Georges advocated a Christian Faith "which does not compel a man to draw on the Fathers as a source of action." His Orthodoxy, the Bishop concludes, was "cerebral...sterile and academic".[12]

---

[12] "A Tragedy of Orthodox Theology," *The Orthodox Word* XVI, 5 (1980), 237-242. For a more sympathetic picture of Fr Florovsky, see A. Blaine, "A Sketch of the Life of

B   Bishop Chrysostom passes over Florovsky's ecumenism with little comment, save that he "marvelled" at his loyalty to the Patriarch of Constantinople, who was zealous in his devotion to the movement. Ecumenism had
gripped the Patriarchate well before Fr Georges entered its jurisdiction, subsequent to his migration to Paris in 1926 (ordained to the priesthood, 1932)
where he joined the faculty of the St Sergius Theological Institute, a pesthole
of theological liberalism. At the time, he accepted the patronage and authority of Archbishop Eulogi (Georgievsky), a hierarch of the the Russian Orthodox Church Outside of Russia (Sremski Karlovci, Yugoslavia),[13] whose president was Metropolitan Anthony (Khrapovitsky), formerly of Kiev. In 1931,
Eulogi and much of the Orthodox emigration—including the Institute—bolt-
ed the Russian Synod, in order to avoid its censure and the excommunication of the Moscow Patriarchate, putting themselves uncanonically under
the *omophor* of Patriarch Photius III of Constantinople.

    The reason for the Archbishop's action, aside from the faculty's unre-
strained ecumenical activities, was the controversy over the heterodox theological and philosophical opinions of several professors at St Sergius. Of par-
titular offense was the sophiological heresy of the Institute's Dean, Fr Sergius
Bulgakov. Although disapproving of his doctrine, Florovsky would not con-
demn him "out of respect for the charisma and the personality of his revered
friend."[14] A leading member of a group of Russian intellectuals, the self-
styled "Neo-Christians" who demanded the right to create new doctrine for
the Church, Fr Sergius "modernized through the prism of German Idealism,"[15] arguing for the introduction of Vladimir Soloviev's pantheistic metaphysics—particularly, the Gnostic idea of Sophia—into the Christian Faith.

Georges Florovsky," in *Georges Florovsky: Russian Intellectual and Orthodox Churchman*. Ed.
by A. Blane. Crestwood (NY), 1993, 13-217. One can hardly miss the wording of the
book's title. That Fr Georges was first "a man of high intellectuality" (Blane's expression)
is precisely the impression he left on me during my student days at Holy Cross Greek
Orthodox Seminary (1954-1956). Perhaps, he had the same feeling about himself, which
may explain why, when he celebrated the Liturgy and preached, he seemed almost shy,
perhaps uncomfortable.

    [13] The Karlovic Synod was established by Patriarch Tikhon. All bishops of the
Russian diaspora originally belonged to it, both in Europe and the Americas (consult M.
D'Herbigny & A. Deubner, "Évêques Russes En Exil: Douze ans D'Épreuves [1918-1930],"
in *Orientalia Christiana* XXI, 67 [1931]).

    [14] Williams, G.H., "Georges Vasilievich Florovsky: His American Career (1948-
1965)," *The Greek Orthodox Theological Review* XI, 1 (1965), 29. Bulgakov was nevertheless
formally condemned (7/20 Sept. 1935) by Metropolitan Sergius, Acting Patriarch of
Moscow, and by the Karlovci Synod under Metropolitan Anthony Khrapovitsky.

    [15] *Ibid.*, 28. Florovsky saw in Bulgakov's philosophical theology the crypto-pan-
theism which reduced the individual to a cell within the cosmic body, and which
deprived him of freedom. Bulgakov described his philosophy as   *(continued on next page)*

Sophia, he said, is the *Ousia* or Essence of God, the feminine element in the Deity. By means of her (*qua* Plato's Ideas), God created the world, and with her collaboration Christ saved it.[16] Bulgakov was justly accused of injecting a fourth Person into the Trinity.

On account of his remonstrances to the Dean and his colleagues, Florovsky was particularly unpopular with them. The majority of the Institute's faculty was revising the major themes of Orthodox theology while Florovsky was promoting a "return to the Fathers." He believed that a patristic revival— a "neo-patristic synthesis"—was necessary for the reaffirmation of the Orthodox Tradition if the world were to behold the true face of his Church. Thus, when his *Ways of Russian Theology* appeared in 1937 with its insistence that the failures of Russian theology (and philosophy) were precisely their deviation from the spirit of the Fathers, the Institute faculty conspired to shield the students from his influence.[17]

Had Berdiaev *et alii* not been self-defensive, they might have asked Florovsky some pertinent questions. What is a "neo-patristic synthesis"? His reply might have been that the great wisdom of patristic literature "primarily" from the fourth to the eighth centuries should be updated. A return to the Fathers does not require "slavish imitation" of their teachings, but rather the advocacy of their spirit. But what is their "spirit"? Adapting those great themes of patristic thought to modern theological problems, Florovsky could have said. Such a program would, of course, involve the introduction of foreign elements into Orthodox theology.

Florovsky's "neo-synthesis" gave him the opportunity to validate his

---

(cont'd.) "panentheism" (everything in God), not pantheism (everything is God). A sophistry at best, since he said more than once that God would not exist if the universe did not exist, and vice versa (e.g., *The Unfading Light*. Moscow, 1917, pp. 102-103 [in Russian]). Thus, in order to counteract such thinking, writes Professor Williams, Florovsky "stressed individual personality (harking back to the philosophy of freedom and the personalism of Charles Renouvier [1815-1903]); and he rejected theological abstractions [found also in Bulgakov] in what he always disparaged as the theosophical or anthroposophical algebra of such systematic theology, both Roman Catholic and Protestant" ("The Neo-Patristic Synthesis of Georges Florovsky," in *George Florovsky: Russian...*, 292.

16 See Bulgakov's *The Wisdom of God: A Brief Summary of Sophiology*. Trans. by P. Thompson, C. F. Clarke & Xenia Braikevitch. With a preface by F. Gavin. London, 1937; also, W.F. Crum, *The Doctrine of Sophia according to Sergius N. Bulgakov*. Cambridge (Mass.), 1965.

17 Nicholas Berdiaev, editor of *The Way* (*Put'*), flayed Fr Georges in a long and scurrilous review of his book, accusing him of arrogance, of playing the avenging angel, of damning all those who disagreed with him. Berdiaev and his friends were aware that *Ways of Russian Theology* was an implicit reproach of their speculations (See the translator's Note to the English edition, volume five, *The Collected Works of Georges Florovsky*. Belmont [Mass.], 1979, xi-xv).

own extra-Orthodox philosophical and theological resources. Yet he could not legitimately argue that his incorporation of Augustine (whom he ranked among them), Soloviev, or Charles Renouvier, and the Marburg Neo-Kantians (which exercised so much influence on Florovsky's conception of knowledge, creation, time, freedom, and eschatology) into Orthodox theology was comparable to the "hellenism" of the Fathers. They saw Greek philosophy and the religion of Judaism as historical "preparation for the Gospel." Modern philosophy is not. Florovsky's brood of thinkers had no such credentials, and were not so easily adaptable to the purposes of Orthodoxy as were Plato and Aristotle. In addition, the "spirit" of his theological and historical writings are evidence that the Florovsky synthesis fell far short of the patristic achievements. He had little trouble in criticizing the Fathers, as we have seen in his treatment of St Vincent of Lerins.

In any case, it was a useful perspective which he took to the First Congress of Orthodox Theologians in Athens (29 Nov-6 Dec, 1936). In his initial paper to the Congress, "Westliche Einfluesse in der Russischen Theologie," he traced the influence of both Roman Catholic and Protestant influence on Orthodox Theology ("pseudomorphosis"); and, in his second paper, "Patristics and Modern Theology" (*Procès-Verbaux du premier Congres de théologie Orthodoxe* [29 Nov-6 Dec, 1936]. Ed. by H. Alivizatos. Athens, 1939, 238-242), Florovsky made his famous declaration concerning "Christian Hellenism" as a "standing category" of Orthodox theology. The proposals of this paper seemed to call for much more than secular Western thought as "handmaiden" to Christianity. His books and articles on the Fathers paid considerable deference to modern patristic research, heterodox and secular.

Florovsky told the Congress of his disappointment with the present course of Orthodox theology, that is, the perpetuation of the "pseudomorphosis" which had obscured Truth for more than a three centuries. He reserved not a few words of criticism for the Russian Church. Her theologians were not alone, however, in writing theology by interpolating quotations of the Fathers into theological systems borrowed from the West, a practice which misleads and distorts rather than illuminates the traditions of Orthodoxy. Florovsky had special praise for Metropolitan Anthony Khrapovitsky, president of the Karlovci Synod, for his efforts to bring Orthodox theology back to the Fathers, albeit he found Vladika's assessment of them "in many points more than inadequate." Surely, in the light of Florovsky's own theological "inadequacies,"[18] this is a curious remark considering the traditionalism and sanctity of the Metropolitan.

---

18   Fr Alexander Schmemann makes the pertinent observation that Fr Florovsky failed "to clarifiy and explain what he meant by the 'Neo-Patristic synthesis'" ("In Memoriam", *St Vladimir's Seminary Quarterly* XXIII, 3-4 [1979], 139).

Not unlike most of his colleagues at the Congress, the thinking of
Florovsky reflected a certain ambivalence towards the Orthodox Faith.
Before this illustrious assembly, he referred to the Orthodox Church as *Una
Sancta;* but he also added that, if she was to win the ear of modernity, she
would need to reshape the great ideas of patristic literature, i.e., he wanted
to undertake a critique of the entire Orthodox ethos in order to find a place
for her in the twentieth century. Lastly, Fr Georges was not opposed, with
some qualifications, to the application of modern scientific research to patristic Biblical exegesis.[19] It is noteworthy that nearly every theologian attending the Congress in Athens had studied in Europe, especially Germany; and,
also, that most of them took part in ecumenical meetings before and after the
Congress.

C   An important, but generally ignored fact, is Fr Georges' attachment to
Augustine of Hippo. With his idea of "the neo-patristic synthesis," the erroneous opinions (e.g., on the validity of heretical baptism) of the Latin Bishop
were easily ingested by Florovsky. He might better have adopted the ecclesiological "radicalism" of Metropolitan Anthony Khrapovitsky, excising the
influence of Augustine, "the father of the Schoolmen" (Khomiakov) from his
own theology. His attraction to the Bishop of Hippo was a fundamental element in Florovsky's theological ambivalence, an attraction which might be
traced to the impact of the "liberal" nineteenth century Metropolitan Philaret
(Drozdov) of Moscow (see below) on his thinking. Philaret also respected
Augustine and his notion that one could belong invisibly to the Church.
Thus, he refused to deny the name "Christian" to any religious body which
confessed Christ as Lord; and, for that reason, His Eminence was willing to
publically acknowledge that the Sacraments of Roman Catholics and Protestants were not without some real "charismatic" significance, despite the separation of these bodies from the Orthodox Church.

D   Professor Williams highlights the words "charismatic" and "canonical"
in a literary tribute to Florovsky, words which had become in Florovsky's
theology "nearly technical terms for designating the still undetermined
boundary between the empirical (historical) and true Church." In other
terms, Fr Georges conceived the Church visibly as "canonical" and invisibly
as "charismatic." He never clarified for his readers the nature of their relationship, that is, the Church as an historical institution and the Church as a
living organism, the Church in heaven, the Church on earth. For him it was
an *a priori* truth that the Church cannot be divided, but he anguished over
"the challenge of disunity." He formally rejected such facile solutions as the

---

19 Blaine, "Geo. Vasil. Florovsky," *ibid.,* 83.

Anglican "branch theory." Orthodoxy is the true Church, Florovsky confessed, but, like Philaret, he would not "unchurch" anyone.

Florovsky's "ecumenical" statements manifest no repugnance for heresy. For him the word seemed to have no specific target, at least, not in the modern world. He made no public declaration that heresy, hateful to God, was the promise of damnation (Gal. 1:8). We may credit him with repeating the words of Khomiakov, "heresy has no place among us"; but he invariably avoided the conclusion that the false doctrine espoused by "other Christians" excludes them from the Catholic Church. His writings do not show that he came to grips with this truth everywhere taught by the holy Fathers. His experience and logic insisted the faith of the Orientals, Protestantism and Roman Catholicism, must not be discounted. His mind took refuge in historical analysis and analogy.

E   There are two ecclesiological statements which exhibit this tortured contradiction. "I have no confessional loyalty," he said; "my loyalty belongs solely to the *Una Sancta*....Therefore, for me, Christian reunion is just a universal conversion to Orthodoxy...."[20] Another time, he wrote, "All local churches indeed have their particular contributions." The contribution of "the Eastern Church" is unique. "The witness of the Eastern Church is precisely a witness to the common background of ecumenical Christianity, because she stands not so much for a local tradition of her own, but the common heritage of the Church Universal. Her voice is not merely a voice of the Christian East, but a voice of Christian antiquity."[21]

The ambiguity of these remarks displays Florovsky's unwillingness to affirm that, on account of her pure doctrine, the Orthodox Church is precisely the *only Church*. Intimidated by his own scholarly "objectivity," he refused to define the "borders" of the "charismatic" Church as the "borders" of the "canonical" Church.[22] His error was, of course, to approach ecclesiology from these two categories, rather than taking the patristic or christological

---

20   "Confessional Loyalty in the Ecumenical Movement," in *The Student World* XLIII, 1 (1950), 204.

21   "The Eastern Orthodox Church and the Ecumenical Movement," *Theology Today* VII, 1 (1950), 68-79.

22   The word "canonical" here has a juridical ring. Although the Canons of the Orthodox Church take the form of Roman laws, they have a different purpose. Thus, whenever the canons are invoked to define the visible "borders" of the Church, the implicit purpose is to draw a sharp line between the Church and the world. Furthermore, Canons, as we said before, manifest Christian doctrine; but also they exist "to protect the Orthodox from infection by an heretical spirit" as well as from "indifference to the Faith" (Bishop John of Smolensk). There is every reason to be alarmed over the selective use of them by the hierarchy of so-called "world Orthodoxy" (i.e., ecumenists) and even some Old Calendar bishops.

position which combined them. It would then have been evident to him that the Christian Revelation requires the borders of the Church to be palpable. Instead he chose the flawed Augustinian (nestorian) ecclesiology. In other words, as there is one Christ, there is one Church; and if Christ's Divinity and humanity are united "without confusion or separation," so likewise are the visible and invisible dimensions of His Body, the Church, that is to say, as the Divinity and humanity are one, so likewise the invisible or "charismatic" and visible or "canonical" dimensions of the Church. The one is perfectly coterminous with the other.

It follows that the "borders" of the Church established by the Lord must be identifiable by everyone who encounters her, as the "borders" of the Body of Christ. None may say they could not find her. Again, if, as Florovsky insisted, the Church is indivisible; and, if, according to the Oberlin Statement, the unity of the Church has not been broken or, what is the same thing, that the Orthodox Church is the Body of Christ and the "problem of unity" is resolved by universal conversion to Orthodoxy, then, she is not "the Eastern Church," but the Church, the only Church of the living God. But Florovsky refused, as he said, to "unchurch anyone"; he need not have troubled himself. In truth, Orientals, Latins and Protestants cannot be "unchurched," because they were never "churched." They have no Sacraments, no priesthood, no saving Grace. For these belong to the Church alone, the cause and expression of her unity, testimony to the indwelling of the Holy Spirit. Where heresy is God will not abide, for He is the God of Truth, not of confusion.

It is impossible, therefore, that heretics share in her Grace, lest we believe they are part of the Church, and the Church is "with heresy"; or that the Grace of the Holy Spirit operates outside the Church, and the Spirit acts against Himself. Such apologetics are not to be found in the writings of Georges Florovsky. I am not persuaded he knew or could have appreciated them. He did not hesitate to caution me in our correspondence about taking too seriously the patristic denunciations of heresy. There is some irony in his refusal to recognize in himself "pseudomorphic" judgments on the Fathers and the Church which venerates them.

4   MEGALE IDEA

Double-mindedness seems to be characteristic of not a few Orthodox today. We should not be astonished that, since the days when Florovsky's views of Orthodoxy prevailed amongst ecumenists, the world has changed and ecumenism has changed with it. There is a greater number of twentieth century Orthodox, clergy and laity, who, if not ignorant, are simply indifferent to the great problems with which Florovsky wrestled. It is a new generation which suffers far less conflict from anything that plagued Fr Georges. How do we explain the existence of this new breed? Was he a forerunner to them? Are they the inevitable next stage?

Let me suggest that, historically speaking, the antecedents of the twentieth century ecumania of "world Orthodoxy" may be traced not unreasonably to the intellectual and social ferment of the nineteenth century. In reviewing the history of the Church of Greece and of Russia in the last century, we uncover two basic causes for the development of the contemporary ecumen-ical mentality. First, the Church's leaders were educated abroad, mostly in Germany. They returned home to teach in the local seminaries from which many candidates were plucked to become her bishops. Traditionally, the Orthodox episcopate has been chosen from the monasteries of Greece and Russia, for the reason that although learning is valuable, holiness is the mark of the true hierarch; and holiness is the result of ascetical struggle. The omnipresent "academic" and "bureaucratic bishop" is the heavy burden of the European legacy, the result of its "humanism," as Fr Justin Popovich observed.[23]

Second, Greece and Russia were stricken with the demonic fever of nationalism, the offspring of a secular Western culture, clearly observable in the Greek *Megale Idea*, the pathology of Greek imperialism (including the recovery of Constantinople). Among the Russians, the tension between the Slavophiles and the Westernizers was the manifestation of that same Western incursion, the same socio-political ideology. In reaction the Slavophiles raised the banner of "nationality," "Orthodoxy," and "monarchy"[24] even as the Westernizers aspired to transform Russia into a Western nation. The forms which nationalism generally took in nineteenth century Greece and Russia affected both Orthodox spiritual life and the attitude towards doctrine.

---

[23] Fr Justin rebuked European humanism as "the longing for power, pleasure and knowledge." This is what the foreign-educated hierarchs brought into Orthodoxy, he complained, rather than the humility of the monk, trained in the *knowledge* and piety of the Fathers ("Humanistic Ecumenism," p. 182). Fr Justin said that Napoleon, Pope Pius IX, and Friedrich Nietzsche epitomized the nineteenth century. They are "the three fatal names of the three sickest people of the hereditary sickness—Caesar, Pope and the Philosopher." Bonaparte laughed in front of the holy churches of the Kremlin, Pius proclaimed himself infallible, Friedrich Nietzsche publically declared the worship of the Antichrist (*ib.*, pp. 184-186).

[24] The slogan of the French Revolution (1789) was "fraternity," "equality" and "liberty," ideas which grew out of the Enlightenment, an intellectual movement which strongly influenced Greece in the first half of the nineteenth century, even providing political ideology for the revolution. Aware of this fact, neither Tsar Alexander I nor Tsar Nicholas I intervened on the side of the Greeks against Turkey, which was, of course, also a monarchy. The Russian Slavophiles proclaimed "Orthodoxy, Monarchy, Nationality," in reaffirmation of "the Third Rome" (See A. Gratieux, *A.S. Khomiakov et le Mouvement Slavophile* [vol. 1]. Paris, 1939, 1-40).

A   On 25 March 1821 o.s. (the Feast of the Annunciation), Alexander Ypsilantis, a Freemason and president of the revolutionary *Philike Hetaerea*
(Society of Friends), and former *aide-de-camp* to Tsar Alexander I, entered
Moldavia from Russian territory at the head of a small force of Greek sol-
diers. In the same month, Arcbishop Germanos of Patras unfurled the standard of revolt at Kalavryta in the Morea. The Greek revolution had begun,
and something more. The Greeks, who had hitherto been drawn together by
a common religion, were now animated by the sentiment of nationality, and
too many of them viewed the Church as simply the bearer of national ideals.

The "national reawakening" had been preceded by a literary revival.[25]
The spirit of the French Revolution, which pervaded Western Europe, was
seeping into the Aegean world through the political writings of Adamantios
Koraes (1748-1833) and Theophilos Karis (1781-1853), etc., an influence
which virtually assured the establishment of a Greek Republic. Politicians
and theologians swiftly employed their skills to engineer a new Church-State
relationship, and to suppress every sign of nostalgia for the old Byzantine
symphonia which, they believed, if reinstated, would deny Greece a place in
the modern world. Their traditionalist opponents, such as Benjamin of
Lesvos (1762-1824) and Konstantinos Oikonomos (1780-1857), etc., were far
less concerned with the aims of the Westernizers than with the perpetuation
of sacral society in Greece, which included a close association with the
Patriarch of Constantinople.

Therefore, Oikonomos, *et alii* were greatly disappointed when in July of
1833 the new Greek Parliament, meeting at Nauplion, declared the autonomy of the Greek Church and, in imitation of the Russian (Lutheran) model,
established a Holy Synod with an Archbishop of Athens to preside over it.
The traditionalists decried the separation from Constantinople as destructive
to the true Faith inherited from the Fathers and a perversion of the Orthodox
synodal system which seemed to motivate the separation. The whole
scheme of the republicans, as many saw it, was no more than to Westernize
Hellas and the Church by "protestantizing" them.

---

[25] Less than fifty years before the Greek revolution, St Nikodemos of the Holy
Mountain (1749-1809), edited many of the ancient classics of Orthodox theology. He col-
laborated with St Makarios of Corinth to publish in 1783 the famous *Evergetinos*, the
eleventh century collection of sayings by the early desert Fathers. Together they produced editions of St Symeon the New Theologian. Also with Makarios, he published the
Philokalia, the ascetical writings of not only the desert Fathers, but also those of Mt Athos,
principally the hesychasts. With Agapios Leonardos, he collected all the principal canons
of the Orthodox Church with commentaries and notes (*Pedalion*), published in 1800. In
other words, the Greek-speaking world could not plead ignorance of the Fathers. Not
only the industry of Sts Nikodemos and Makarios, etc., but the patriarchical and monastic libraries, were filled with patristic literature. Too many of its leaders chose to ignore
them and feed at the literary trough of Freemasonry, atheism, and romantic nationalism.

Oikonomos wrote an epistolary *Treatise on the Three Hierarchical Orders of the Church* (1835) in protest. He complained to the Patriarch of Constantinople that "presbyterianism" was not a frivolous worry, but was in fact even now insidiously creeping into the thinking of too many Orthodox. Gregorios VI issued an encyclical against "the spreading of presbyterianism in Greece," which the historical record shows was indeed part of the deliberate mischief of the English Bible Society.[26] Its plan was to dispense Bibles to the Greek masses. It employed, after several abortive attempts, the services of Neophytus Vamvas to translate the Bible into the vernacular (1828). He was a Paris-educated intellectual who, while in France completing studies in philosophy, came under the influence of Koraes. Perhaps, it was he that recommended Vamvas to the Society.[27] The Holy Synod and Constantinople initially proscribed the new Bible and forbade any further distribution of it.[28] It found objectionable Vamvas' defense of Protestant agents for whom he was working, but also the Synod was cognizant of the motive for its translation: to

---

26   The motivation of the British Bible Society was proselytism or, in the words of Mark Siotes, "to ensnare Orthodox thought and destroy it in the nets of Western scepticism and Protestant rationalism." Years before her liberation, the Society came to Greece for the express purpose of replacing holy Orthodoxy with Protestantism. Its agents busied themselves not only with distributing Bibles, but with erecting foreign schools, writing tracts, holding rallies, etc. Such activities were protected by the new Greek governments decree of toleration ("Constantine Oikonomos of the House of Oikonomos and the Operations of the British Bible Society in Greece [1780-1857]," in *The Greek Orthodox Theological Review* VI, 1 [1960], 7-55).

27   The Bible Society's archives indicate a correspondance between itself and the notorious Adamantios Korais (Koraes). Of his letters, only the one written in 1808 is extant. The Society took his counsel not only on the translation of the Scriptures into modern Greek, but also about the temperament and customs of his people. "The high respect which the Society in fact held for Korais' is apparent in the passages from the Society's deliberations...," says Richard Klogg. "The relationship of Korais and the Bible Society was hardly a major event in Korais' career; nevertheless, it has some significance in the history of the religious and cultural development of modern Greece." ("The Correspondance of Adhamantios Korais with the British and Foreign Bible Society (1808)," in *The Greek Orthodox Theological Review* XIV, 1 (1969), 84.

28   The Vamvas translation was later approved with some correction of his modern Greek, and accompanied by the Old and New Testament text in their original Greek (Septuagint, *koine*). His Bible was released serially, beginning with the Pentateuch in 1833. Five years later the four Gospels and the Acts appeared for the first time. In 1840 the entire Old Testament with the *deuterocanonica* (Esdras, Tobit, Judith, Baruch, etc.) was published; and in 1844 all the books of the New Testament were issued. 1851 saw the books of the Old and New Testament distributed together. In this form they were reprinted in 1862; and from 1866, they were again reprinted with the name, *Ta Hiera Grammata* or *The Sacred Writings* (Siotes, "Constantine Oikonomos...," 33-35). On Oikonomos' philological and spiritual objections to the "new Bible," see his *Animadversion against 'On the New Greek Church': a Brief Reply to the Most Erudite Master, Mr Neophytos Vamvas*. Athens, 1838 (in Greek).

encourage private interpretation, a practice which would not only lead to a denial of the Orthodox Tradition but to the moral disease of subjectivism.[29]

B   The University of Athens would probably have opened its doors in 1837, whatever the intellectual climate of post-revolutionary Greece. The first professors were Michael Apostolides, Theoklitos Pharmakidis (arch-enemy of Oikonomos), and the renowned Konstantinos Kontogones who, according to Fr Stylianopoulos, "carried most of the academic burden at the University for more than a quarter of a century."[30] In 1846, he published his lectures as a book, *Philological and Critical History of the Holy Fathers of the First Three Centuries*. As he wrote in the preface, his work was the first of its kind, introducing scientific theological scholarship to modern Greece.[31] He knew before he wrote the book that any critical treatment of "the God-bearing Church Fathers" in the *History* must necessarily involve an unwelcome reex-amination of "the mysteries of our blameless Faith."

Thus, Kontogones was faced with a double problem. He admitted that the Fathers are the "key" to the understanding of Scriptures. But the Western scholarship in which he was trained directed Kontogones to undertake a his-torical criticism of them, with the method that would not permit anything or anyone to stand between the student and the Biblical text. "Internal evi-dence" alone was the criterion for the examination of the documents; hence, the Fathers cannot be taken as authorities on the authenticity of any part of Scripture, especially not when their own writings require literary reevalua-tion. Kontogones seems not to have experienced any mental conflict between the demands of his Orthodox Faith and the discipline of the science which urged him to question it.

The attitude of Kontogones is, at the very least, perplexing in the light of the new Greek Constitution of 1843. The second article declared the Orthodox Church of Greece is "...organically and canonically united by an indissoluble bond with the Great Church of Constantinople, and with all other Orthodox Churches. . .administered according to the Apostolic and

---

[29] On the intellectual turbulence of the decade following the Greek revolution, see first chapters of C.A. Frazee, *The Orthodox Church and Independent Greece, 1821-1852*. Cambridge (Eng.), 1969; and G.A. Maloney, *A History of Orthodoxy Theology Since 1453*. Belmont (Mass.), 1976, pp. 179-186.

[30] "Historical Studies...," 400-401.

[31] "Here is a scholar who studied at the universties of the West for more than five years," Stylianopoulos informs us, "returned to a university chair in Greece and printed his first fruits in the form of a 'philological' and 'critical' history—the play-words of Western scholarship" (*ib.*, 401). More important are the remarks of Fr Theodore that such a book "cannot co-exist peacefully with the heart" (*loc. cit.*). Kontogones was unfortu-nately the prototype of "the modern Greek Orthodox theologian."

Conciliar Canons and the holy traditions...."[32] The Constitution makes an important allusion to Canon XIX of the fifth Ecumenical Council (Trullo):

> We declare that the deans of churches, on every day, but more especially on Sundays, must teach all the clergy and the laity words of truth out of the holy Bible, analyzing the meanings and judgments of the truth, and not deviating from the definitions already laid down, or the teaching derived from the God-bearing Fathers; but also, if the discourse be one concerning a passage of Scripture, not to interpret it otherwise than as the luminaries and teachers of the Church in their own written works have presented it; and let them rather content themselves with these discourses than attempt to produce discourses of their own, lest, at times, being resourceless, they overstep the bounds of propriety. For by the means of the teachings afforded by the aforesaid Fathers, the laity, being apprised of the important and preferred things, and of the disadvantageous and rejectable, are enabled to adjust their lives for the better, and do not become prey to the ailment of ignorance, but, by paying due attention to what is taught, they sharpen their wits so as to avoid suffering wrongly, and for fear of impending punishments they work out their salvation.[33]

Kontogones was probably not alone in his apparent indifference to the decree of the National Assembly or the Canons. If his desire was to establish "a solid academic tradition," to borrow Fr Theodore's phrase, it should not have been at the expense of the holy Fathers and in defiance of the Canons. Kontogones did not endorse the opinion that if historical criticism would not be a servant of Church, it must be dismissed as any other innovation.

C   If nothing else, the Patriarchal Encyclical of 1848, should have made it clear to Kontogones and those like him that the Greek Orthodox Church would not abandon her traditions. The Encyclical was a response to Pope Pius IX 's *In Suprema Petri Apostoli Sede* in January of the same year. The Pontiff called the Orthodox "lost sheep" and invited them "to return at last to the flock of Christ." He assured them that they had no reason to fear that "any burden shall be imposed on them which is not necessary." The papal Encyclical exasperated the Orthodox both in Greece and in the Ottoman Empire.

The Ecumenical Patriarch, Anthimos VI, along with Hierotheos II of Alexandria, Methodios of Antioch, and Cyril II of Jerusalem, in addition to 29 metropolitans, responded with a passionate rejection. They fulminated against the Papal document as "a fraud and plague," stating that "of those heresies which the Lord knows, have now spread over a great part of the

---

[32]   Quoted in Frazee, *The Orthodox Church...*, p. 161.

[33]   *Pedalion*. Trans. by D. Cummings. Chicago, 1957, p. 313.

world, at one time it was Arianism, today it is Roman Catholicism. But this, too (as the first), although successful for the moment, will not last to the end, but will disappear and be cast down, and a great voice shall cry out, It is destroyed!"[34] All the Orthodox, whatever their political or theological persuasion, united in their opposition to papal audacity.

Almost fifty years later, the Patriarch Anthimos VII of Constantinople and his Synod replied to the reunion Encyclical of Leo XIII, *Pareclara gratulationis* (1895). What might seem curious to some is that the Patriarch addressed the Pope as "most blessed" (μακαριώτατε πάπα)—the courtesy of protocol—but not "all holy" (παναγιώτατε) which he reserved for his office. There is deference here, whatever the subtlities of diplomacy, that seems out of place in a Patriarchal encyclical which refers to the Orthodox Church as "the one, holy, catholic and apostolic Church of the seven Oecumenical Councils." Following the example of the 1848 Encyclical, the Patriarch repeated the heresies of Rome, to which were added the novelties of the Immaculate Conception and, more recently, the dogma of Papal Infallibility. The Patriarchal Encyclical concluded with affirmation, "Let us, who by the Grace and Goodwill of the most gracious God, are precious members of the Body of Christ, that is to say, of His one holy, catholic and apostolic Church, hold fast to the piety of our fathers, handed down to us from the apostles."

Yet, there is something deeply troubling in the Encyclical of 1895, which refers to the Old Catholics as "the Christian conscience which rose up in one body in the year 1870, in the persons of the celebrated clerics and theologians of Germany, on account of the novel dogma of the infallibility of the Popes, issued by the Vatican Council, a consequence of which rising is seen in the formation of the separate religious communities of the old Catholics, who, having disowned the papacy, and are quite independent of it" (sec. XIX).[35] The Patriarch's reference to the Old Catholics is provocative from several points of view, especially as he praises their opposition to the new dogma without immediately calling upon them to join the Orthodox Church. Anthimus also describes them as "separate religious communities" rather than another form of heresy.

What, too, is the nature of the Patriarch's ecclesiology which allows him to confer the title of "Christian" upon the Old Catholic sect while they remain outside the fold of the one, holy, catholic, apostolic Church, as he defined the Orthodox Church? The generosity of the Encyclical is explained by the bud-

---

[34] Quoted in Frazee, *ib.*, p. 169.

[35] *The Reply of the Orthodox Chuch to Roman Catholic Overtures on Reunion: Being the Answer of the Great Church of Constantinople to a Papal Enyclical on Reunion.* New York, 1958.

ding relationship between the Church of Greece and the Old Catholics. The Old Catholics held four Conferences—Bonn (1871), Koeln (1872), Konstanz (1873), Freiburg (1874)—at which the Orthodox, both Russian and Greek, participated, as well as the Anglicans. The Orthodox took part in meetings with sectarians whom the they called "a faithful remnant" in the West, Old Catho-lics who presented an agenda in which the *confrères* addressed the "problems" of the Trinity, the perpetual Virginity of the Theotokos, the inter-cession of the Saints, etc., subjects long ago settled by the ancient Councils and Fathers.

Furthermore, although the Old Catholics defected from Rome, none of its leaders for one moment denied to either themselves or Roman Catholi-cism membership in the universal Church. Their guiding spirit, Johann Ignatius von Doellinger, turned to the Orthodox for "reunion" because, as he asserted, rejoining "the despotically constituted" Roman Catholicism would have been a situation intolerable to them. Doellinger was confident, never-theless, that the "racial hatred" which caused the breach between East and West could eventually be overcome. Two things greatly disturbed him: the *filioque*, "an offense to the orientals, who say that the Latin Church had no right to insert it"; and, the persistent rumor that "the Greek Church consid-ered herself the universal Church apart from the Roman."[36] Herr Doellinger's worries may not have been shared by the Ecumenical Patriarch, but they would have consequences.

Ϲ   It is strange, too, that the Patriarchical Encyclical of 1895 made no men-tion of the Anglicans who likewise rejected the "tyranny" of Rome, and who established contact long before the Old Catholics with Constantinople, the Orthodox Church of Greece, as well as the Church of Russia. Relations were not always friendly–largely the fault of the British Bible Society–but the ani-mosity was eliminated when its proselyting of the Orthodox in Greece and Asia Minor ceased. Serious *rapprochement* was attempted by the members of the Oxford Movement (1833-1845), an overture which inclined many Anglicans to reevaluate their conventional attitude towards the other "branches" of the Church. Self-conscious about the catholicity of Anglican-ism, assured that they themselves could have no intimacy with Rome, the Oxfordians decided to inquire of "the Orthodox Greek Church" about the possibilities of communion. Members of the group urged the Archbishop of Canterbury, A. Campbell Tait, to correspond with the Patriarch Gregory VI (1835-1840, 1867-1871) of Constantinople.

---

[36] See his *Lectures on the Reunion of the Churches*. Trans. by H.N. Oxenham. New York, 1972, pp. 43-54, 136-155.

The result was an era of friendship between "the Orthodox Greek Church" and "the Anglican communion," with the establishment of contacts with the Episcopal Church in the United States through the so-called Russo-Greek Committee (1862) and the Eastern Churches Association (1863) in England. The third Lambeth Conference (1888) raised the hope "that the barriers to fuller communion may be, in the course of time, removed by further intercourse and extended enlightenment." In 1898, Bish-op John Wordsworth of Salisbury visited Constantinople and the East. The year after the Archbishop of Canterbury, Frederick Temple, began a correspondence with the Ecumenical Patriarch, a special committee was subsequently organized to study various aspects of Anglican teachings, a concession which further reflected the new direction in Orthodox ecclesiology.

The question of Anglican Orders, after Rome's judgment of them as invalid (1896), stirred the interest of the Patriarchate, especially when Constantinople heard that some Russian Orthodox theologians had already given a favorable answer to the Anglicans on this matter. At the turn of the century, Patriarch Joachim III, called upon Chrestos Androutsos (1869-1937), then Professor of Dogmatics at the Halki School of Theology (opened in 1844), to examine the question of Anglican Orders. The results of his study, *The Validity of Anglican Orders from an Orthodox Point of View* (1903), concluded that the evidence does not warrant any decision on its status. Moreover, even if they are "valid," any intercommunion must presuppose "dogmatic union." Lastly, Anglicans entering the Orthodox Church may be accepted on the principle of *economia* or condescension. This was the first insinuation of this principle into ecumenical relations.[37]

Although influential, Androutsos' monograph was subject to criticism by other Greek Orthodox theologians. For instance, Konstantinos Dyobouniotes argued that the "validity" of Anglican Orders depended on "proof" that the consecration of the first Anglican prelate after the Reformation, Archbishop Parker, was canonical. Dyobounites was not convinced, as was Androutsos, that it had been provided. Furthermore, he had very serious reservations about the correctness of the Anglican doctrine of the priesthood in particular, and its Sacraments in general. Of these two "problems," the first may be solved by historical research, he said; and the second, when Anglicans shall define "officially and authoritatively" their teachings on the Sacraments (including holy Orders), which at present has an "inconsistency and indefiniteness which does not now allow the formation of certain conclusions based on sure and unquestioned teachings."[38]

[37] G. Florovsky, "Orthodox Ecumenism in the 19th Century," in *St Vladimir's Seminary Quarterly* IV, 3-4 (1956), 45.

[38] *The Mysteries of the Eastern Orthodox Church from a Dogmatic Point of View*. Athens, 1912, p. 336 (in Greek).

Whatever the disagreement of Greek theologians on the "validity" of Anglican Orders, they uniformly approached the matter from the wrong "point of view"—as the unfortunate word "validity" testifies—which reflected their westernized mentality. The first smacks of legalism, the second of relativism. "Anglican Orders" should have been examined from the christological "point of view." More disturbing here is the suggestion that the so-called "Church of England" is a Church at all or, what is the same thing, that the customary rites of the *Book of Common Prayer* have any efficacy whatsoever. In some ways, the reaction of these Greek theologians was a *volte-face*, if not simply a contradiction, especially when, throughout the last half of the nineteenth century, the great lights of "Greek theology" made unmistakable pronouncements about the exclusivity of the Orthodox Church, even quoting, as Androutsos did, the *Catechism* of Platon, Metropolitan of Moscow, "The Orthodox Church is not merely the true Church, but the only Church."[39]

If this is true, then, why did these academicians employ language, ideas and methodologies which in themselves have no application to Orthodox theology? Why the swarm of subtle and scholastic theories about the Mysteries? Why was implicit credence given to the claims of apostolic succession by Anglicans and Roman Catholics? Why the legalistic manipulation of the honored principle of "economy"? To repeat, the answer is the influence of foreign educations on the Orthodox proponents of ecumenism; and, the national pride in Orthodoxy as the major attribute of the Greek character, and therefore, the fear that any form of ecclesial exclusivism would find Greece shunned, unwelcome among the family of nations.

D   But these ecclesiological "problems"—aside from double-mindedness—became inevitable when the reborn Greek nation, fearful of standing alone, succumbed to Western political and religious blandishments. Attending the Old Catholic and Anglican conferences was *une grande méprise*. First, encounters of this sort require tolerance of heretical opinions, which, if the meetings are to continue, demand accommodation, and which finally, if explorations into "Christian unity" are to have any meaning, they must entail compromise with false doctrine. The last has come gradually, a concession that could not have appeared in the nineteenth century, but for which, nonetheless, the Greek theologians born and raised in that confusing and fascinating era are, in part, accountable; that is, for the conversion of Orthodox ecclesiological categories into an idiom amenable to their ecumenical purposes, a labor which has left the "borders" of the Orthodox Church both tenuous and unin-

---

39   *The Basis of the Union of the Churches according to the Recent Pronouncements of the Orthodox Churches.* Constantinople, 1905, p. 21. Cf. F. Gavin, *Some Aspects of Contemporary Greek Orthodox Thought.* London, 1936, p. 249-263.

telligible. Thus, the genuine Biblical and/or patristic doctrine of the Church was slowly eroded out of fear and pride.

E   After Patriarch Joachim III invited all the autocephalous Orthodox Churches to express their attitudes towards relations with "other Christian bodies" (from whom he received favorable responses), relations warmed even more, especially with the Anglicans, including the Episcopal Church in the United States. In 1907 the first Anglican student entered Halki, an exchange program which anticipated the proposal of the 1920 Patriarchal Encyclical. In response, the fifth Lambeth Conference (1908) resolved to admit Orthodox individuals to the Sacraments; and requested the Archbishop of Canterbury to appoint a permanent Committee on Orthodox affairs.[40]

With the coming of World War I, the Anglicans displayed a "brotherly philanthropy" toward the Orthodox, and in the spirit of "brotherly love" gave every assistance to the needy Orthodox Churches of the East. They helped in the education of candidates for the priesthood of the Orthodox Church both in England and the United States. Conferences held between the Orthodox and the Anglicans in the United States and England discussed a whole range of theological and pastoral questions important to both. Such meetings continued through the war years. Closer ties with the Anglicans made it more difficult for the Orthodox to think of them as unbaptized and unchurched.

Two events occurred in order to permanently cement the "friendly relations" between the Orthodox, the Anglicans, and, indeed, "all the Churches of Christ wheresoever They may be." Prior to the World Conference on Faith and Order, the *locum tenens* of the Ecumenical Patriarchate, Metropolitan Dorotheos of Brussa[41] and eleven supporting hierarchs, sent an open letter to all the autocephalous Orthodox Churches. Considering Orthodox ecumenism over the past seventy-five years, there was nothing startling in its provisions. The letter called for "a closer relationship" between the Orthodox and "other churches" despite the doctrinal differences. The elimination of "old prejudices, traditions, and even pretenses" would prove an auspicious beginning.

----

[40] According to Vasil T. Istavridis, the only example of an American Orthodox hierarch urging his flock to partake of Anglican Sacraments was the Antiochian Bishop, Raphael Hawaweeny, of Brooklyn, New York (1910). He was later forced to rescind this decision ("Orthodoxy and Anglicanism in the Twentieth Century," in *The Greek Orthodox Theological Review* V, 1 (1959), 15).

[41] Metropolitan Dorotheos would later pay a visit to England to meet the Archbishop of Canterbury, Randall Davidson (1921). He gave the *enkolpion* (icon-medallion) made for Joachim *III* to the Briton. Dorotheos died suddenly during his stay. He was the highest ranking member of the Patriarchal See of Constantinople to visit the West since the Council of Florence (1439).

We, therefore, on the occasion of the establishment of the League of Nations, which has now been effected with good omen, view the matter to be both feasible and more timely than ever; we proceed, full of hope, to herein state in summary our thoughts and opinions as to how we may conceive this relationship and understanding, and how we may consider it possible, earnestly seeking and inviting the judgment and opinion thereon, both of the other brothers of the East and the venerable Christian Churches of the West wheresoever they may be.

The letter recommended an end to proselytism, a renewal of exchange seminary students and teachers, pan-Christian conferences, mutual respect of local customs, settlement of the question of mixed marriage, etc., but of all the proposals none will be so volatile and far-reaching in its consequences as the call for a "uniform calendar," the new or Gregorian calendar.[42]

The victory of Eleftherios Venizelos sent King Constantine of Greece into exile. The new Metropolitan of Athens, Meletios Metaxakis (1918-1920), an ardent Venizelist and enthusiast for Church reform, believed that his cause would bring him assistance from the West. In the year of his election he visited Britain, took part in a conference at Oxford, dined at Lambeth Palace with the Archbishop of Canterbury, and addressed a public meeting at West-minster central hall. Meletios also hoped that his ecumenical goodwill tour would gain the support of the British government in the forthcoming Paris peace conference, with the particular object of securing the return of Hagia Sophia to Greek hands.[43]

Metaxakis became Patriarch of Constantinople in 1921, a post he kept for less than two years. With the intervention of the British, he will later

---

[42] The Encyclical of 1920 has been translated into English (*The Greek Orthodox Theological Review* I, 1 [1954], 7-9). Degyansky finds no little coincidence between this "infamous encyclical" and the consolidation of political power under a secular Turkish government led by Attaturk. Fr Daniel contends that the new government had no liking for the Patriarchate which it considered a political threat. The Patriarch was not innocent of connivance with the Western nations. No wonder the Turks expelled thousands of Orthodox Greeks from Asia Minor. Thus, the Encyclical was as much an appeal for help from the West as it was a call for Christian unity (*Orthodox Christianity and the Spirit of Contemporary Ecumenism*, pp. 36-38).

[43] The reasons for the hostility of the Turkish government towards both the Patriarchate and its Greek population from its new Republic are numerous. It had no confidence that the Greeks would abandon the *Megale Idea*. The activity of Meletios was proof of it. When this same Meletios became the Ecumenical Patriarch, the Turks saw the confirmation of their fears. As the Greeks were instrumental in the demise of the Ottoman Empire, the Turks suspected that they might also have designs on the new Republic. The Ankara regime calculated also that the expulsion of the Patriarchate (along with the Ottoman royal family) was a way to sever all ties with Turkey's own theocratic past (See. H.J. Psomiades, The Ecumenical Patriarchate Under the Turkish Republic: the First Ten Years," in *The Greek Orthodox Theological Review* VI, 1 [1960], 56-80).

become Patriarch of Alexandria.[44] In the summer of 1923, he undertook to implement his reforms, beginning with the recognition of Anglican Ordination and the adoption of the New Calendar ("the Papal Calendar"). Almost at once (1924), the Archbishop of Athens, Chrysostomos Papadopoulos, on behalf of the Church of Greece, exchanged the traditional Julian for the Gregorian Calendar, knowing too well, as Meletios must have known, that the latter was more than once condemned by the Orthodox Church—by Jeremy II, together with Sylvester of Alexandria in 1583, Sophronios of Jerusalem in 1587, the Local Council of Constantinople in 1593, and Dositheos, the Patriarch of Jerusalem in 1694. Until 1924, the Orthodox Patriarchates resisted any change in the Calendar.[45] But the spirit of the times prevailed, and gradually other Orthodox Churches acquiesced in the innovation.

Neither Metaxakis nor Archbishop Chrysostomos, nor those Churches that eventually followed them, were able to justify the change to the New Calendar. One cannot ignore the fact that the introduction of the Gregorian Calendar into the Orthodox world was uncanonical, the negation of an ancient and sacred custom. It represented an arrogant disregard for her synodal machinery, and a total indifference to the rationale of the first Nicean Council which formally adopted the Julian Calendar. At the same time, it required the Church to accept the new ecclesiology, indeed, the alien "mind," that the modern innovation presupposed. "The Julian Calendar and its Paschalion were accepted by the First Ecumenical Council and have been sanctified by more than a millennium of Church use," writes Bishop Gregory (Grabbe). "For this reason, to abandon or pervert it, is a violation of dogma concerning the Church."[46] The Fathers of Nicea, Vladika reminds us, were not so much concerned with astronomical precision "as with unity in prayer life of all the local Churches," especially the holy Pascha "in whatsoever land they [Orthodox] may dwell."[47]

---

[44] See Stuart Mews, "Anglican Intervention in the Election of an Orthodox Patriarch, 1925-1926," in *The Orthodox Churches and the West: Papers Read at the Fourteenth Summer Meeting and The Fiteenth Winter Meeting of the Ecclesiastical History Society.* Ed. by D. Baker. Oxford, 1976, pp. 293-306.

[45] See Fr Basil Sakkas, "The Calendar Question: The Festal Calendar as a Tradition of the Church," in *Orthodox Life* XXII, 5 (1972), 18-34; Bishop Gregory, "The Betrayal of Orthodoxy Through the Calendar," in *Orthodox Life* XXXIII, 6 (1983), 34-46; Bishop Photius of Triaditsa, "The 70th Anniverary of the Pan-Orthohdox Congress in Constantinople"; and L. Perepiolkina, "The Julian Calendar," in *The Orthodox Church in Defense of the Julian Calendar.* Jordanville (NY), 1996. Their reference is to the revision of the solar Julian Calendar accomplished by Pope Gregory XIII (1582).

[46] "The Betrayal of Orthodoxy…, 41.

[47] *Loc. cit.* According to Bishop Gregory (quoting A.N. Zelinsky), the Council of Nicea undertook a reform of the solar Julian Calendar, introducing a "lunar course," i.e., the passage of the moon through its phases. This was necessary in order to fix precisely

5   SCHISM IN THE SOUL

In many respects, the experience of the Orthodox Church in nineteenth century Russia was considerably different from the ordeal of the Orthodox Church in Greece. Russia was ruled by Christian Tsars, Greece by limited monarchy after the failure of a post-revolutionary dalliance with Republicanism. The intellectual invasion from the West in Greece was primarily the Enlightenment, in Russia it was romanticism, pietism and theosophy.[48] In fact, Tsar Alexander I (1801-1825), victor over Napoleon, was reared in his youth by teachers enamoured of the "sentimental humanism" of Freemasonry (his father, Pavel I, was Grand Master of his Lodge). Alexander acquired a taste for Francis de Sales, Teresa of Avila, *The Imitation of Christ* and Tauler; and later, for the theosophy of Baroness Kruedener, Jung-Stilling, Josef DeMaistre and Franz von Baader.

A   Perhaps, the man with the most immediate access to the Tsar was the Procurator of the Holy Synod and later Supervisor of Foreign Confessions and the Bible Society, Prince Aleksander Golitsyn (1773-1844), a zealot of "the inner church" ideal. He persuaded the Tsar to read the Scriptures and, given the occultism which already preoccupied him, Alexander came to envision "a new world opening before me." He was certain that an interconfessional Christianity was possible if the churches would adopt the teachings of the Bible, that is, as the divine well of morality and lore, and not primarily as a liturgical book, as Orthodoxy taught. The divinations of Baroness von Kruedener persuaded him that he was ordained to save Christendom. In the Spring of 1814, the Tsar received a memorandum from Franz von Baader (1765-1841), the German Romantic, (which he also sent to the monarchs of Austria and Prussia), *On the Need Created by the French Revolution for a New and Closer Union of Religion and Politics*. He came to Russia with plans for "the reunification of the Church," hoping to enlist the Tsar in his cause.[49] He

---

the feast of Pascha inasmuch as its date was determined by the time of the Jewish Passover which, from the time of Moses, had been celebrated by the Jews only at the time of the full moon. The synodal adjustment was able to unite the rhythm of the moon with the rhythm of the sun ("Betryal..., 35). The modern Church Fathers (St Nectarios of Aegina, Metropolitan Anthony Khrapovitsky, and Justin Popvich) were Old Calendarists.

[48] "The Russian soul passed through the ordeal or seduction of pietism at the outset of the nineteenth century," remarks Fr Florovsky, "the *apogée* of Russia's Westernism" (*Ways of Russian Theology* [vol. 5, pt. 10, in *The Collected Works of Georges Florovsky*. Trans. by R.L. Nichols. Belmont [Mass.], 1979, p. 162). One would have thought that the Communism was "the apogee of Russia's Westernism." Marxian Socialism is the spawn of Western secularism.

[49] Baader admired Russia's *symphonia* of Church and State, but above all he loved Orthodoxy because it was "the mystical part of the Church, the   (continued on next page)

believed that the first imperative of "ecumenism" was love, since "the division of the churches" was caused by hatred. Love, von Baader said, is the very principle of cosmic unity, and the absence of it among men is the source of their disunity. God is Love, He Who draws all things to Himself. The abolition of hatred must begin with monarchs. If they rule their countries in the spirit of love, he announced, they will lead the Churches to reunion, that is, inasmuch as the Christian religion is the God-ordained force for human unity in history, its reunification must lead naturally to the reconciliation of all religions and thereby all nations.

The sanguine dream of von Baader triggered a new sense of urgency in Alexander, almost a frenzy to realize his calling. Not by accident, the Tsar chose 14/27 September, 1815, the Feast of the Elevation of the Cross, to announce his famous "Holy Alliance" which was both "the Christian answer" to the French Revolution and a petition to all the rulers of Europe to pledge themselves to the "sublime truths which the holy religion of our Savior teaches."   They were exhorted to conduct their relations with other nations according to "the precepts of justice, Christianity, charity and peace." All the European monarchs signed with the exception of England, the Papal State, and Turkey.[50]

B   Prince Golitsyn supported the Holy Alliance in all its dimensions. Florovsky describes him as "perhaps the most characteristic man of that age."[51] He converted to "universal Christianity" long before the Tsar enacted his utopian scheme. Golitsyn's "religion of the heart" was one of the reasons that

(cont'd.) tertia pars" (Briefe 1840 zu V. Stranskii, in *Saemtliche Werke* [bd. 15]. hrgs. v.F. Hoffmann & J. Ham-berger. Aalen, 1963). See also L. Hein, "Franz von Baader und sine Liebe zur Russichen Orthodoxen Kirche," *Kyrios* XII, 1-2 (1972), 31-59. Baader was only the first injection of German Idealism into the veins of the Russian body politic.

Schelling (1775-1854) and Hegel (1770-1830) were very popular among the Russian intelligentsia, figures intrinsic to the national debate between the Slavophiles (*slavophili*) and Westernizers (*zapodniki*) which raged until the end of the nineteenth century (A. Hare, *Pioneers of Russian Social Thought*. London, 1956; D. Cizevsky, *Aus Zwei Welten:; Beitrage zur Geschichte der Slavisch-Westlichen Literatischen Beziehungen*. hrsg. C.H. van Schoonveld. The Hague, 1956). Baader, *et. al.* were *sine qua non* to Vladimir Soloviev and his followers (L. Sabaneff, "Religious and Mystical Trends in Russia at the Turn of the Century," *Russian Review* XXIV, 4 [1956], 2354-368; B. Schultze, "Philosophie, Theologie und Mystik der Ostkirche," *Stimmen der Zeit* CXXXVI, 3 [1936], 139-150; L. Walton, "The Sophianic Lure: A Study in the Sources of Soloviev's Philosophy," *The Dublin Review* CCXXXV, 2 [1951], 27-51).

50   Although the Holy Alliance exerted some influence on European affairs, it was "generally regarded as too vague and mystical to be practical" (Ivar Spector, *An Introduction to Russian History and Culture*. New York, 1951, p. 110).

51   *Ways of Russian Theology*, p. 166.

he promoted the Russian Bible Society, a largely autonomous branch of the British and Foreign Bible Society. It included people from all religions, including Uniates. At first the Society limited its work to the distribution of Bibles among foreigners and the non-Orthodox. In 1814, it decided to make Bibles in the Slavic language available. Two years later it printed and disseminated a Russian Bible. A prominent Freemason, A.F. Labzin (1766-1825), who was doing much the same thing, coordinated his activities with the efforts of the Bible Society.

Like Labzin, important members of the Society began to publish "mystical literature," particularly the works of the German theosophists, Jung-Stilling and Eckhartshausen, who were critical of "formal church life and doctrine" and quick to denounce "the absurd and superstitious blindness of those who profess the traditional Faith of the Eastern Greek-Catholic Church, which must be driven out with the divine Book" (the Bible).[52] The industry and propaganda of the Society and the Freemasons were a subtle and invidious complement to a new scholasticism invading Russian seminaries and schools. At first, the government was slow to act, but when finally the wave of alien ideas was seen as a threat to the Christian monarchy itself—particularly after the Decembrist Revolution (1825)—the government struck with a vengeance.[53] It was futile because it was too late.

There was an "uprising" against the Bible Society and the whole "new order." But the result was not a return to the Fathers, it was a reversion to seventeenth century "Protestant scholasticism," to the rationalism of Archbishop Theophan Prokopovich (1681-1736), Peter the Great's Procurator and political theologian.[54] Like him, Philaret (1782-1867), fifty years Metropoli-

---

52   *Quoted, ibid*, p. 184.

53   Freemasonry has taken different political stances throughout its long history in Russia, sometime pro-, often anti-monarchist. In the nineteenth century, it was allied with the Enlightenment. Yet, the Lodge was not without its "mystics" who had studied Romantic historiosophies (see A. Koyre, *La Philosophie et la Problème National en Russie au début du XIX siècle*. Paris, 1929). Here may be the explanation for this secret fraternity's ability to cooperate with the Bible Society. Most of the Russian Decembrists were "students of the French Encyclopaedists." They symphathized with the Greek revolution of 1821. Anatole Mazour holds that "the affliation of the Decembrists with the Masons, though temporary, left an indelible imprint upon the later secret political organizations . . .in Russa" (*The First Russian Revolution, 1825: The Decembrist Movement, Its Origins, Deelopment and Significance*. Berkeley [Cal.], 1937, p. 52.

54   An interesting, and not entirely incidental, fact, is the anti-Latin Prokopovich's addiction to Protestant thought. Thanks to his efforts, while Professor of Dogmatic Theology at the Seminary at Kiev (1711-1717), the works of Augustine were gradually translated into Russian. Knowing Latin, he had several leather-bound editions of Augustine in his personal library (See M. Jugie, "Saint Augustine dans la litérature théologique de l'Église russe," in *Échos d'Orient* XXXIII, 160 [1930], 390).

tan of Moscow, was educated in the spirit of the West from Protestant texts, texts which supposedly encouraged his belief that Orthodoxy and Protestantism had very much in common (Trinity, Christ, the Cross, heaven and hell, etc.). Unlike Theophan, Philaret vowed a special love for the writings of St John Chrysostom and St Gregory the Theologian, whom he regularly quoted in his sermons; but not even his affection for "the other eastern Fathers" lifted from his mind the load of foreign religion, as his doctrine of the Church demonstrates.

Philaret wanted to write new commentaries on the epistles of St Paul, despite the fact that there was an abundance of patristic literature on the subject—not the least was the work of his beloved St John Chrysostom—which could provide him, along with the Scriptures, all the knowledge an Orthodox hierarch would need. Philaret's favorite aphorism, "theology reasons," was apparently his way of saying that the human personality was also shaped and perfected by the achievements of human reason. Thus, the understanding of Scripture was not limited to the few, but to everyone who sought divine Truth. Not without merit was his desire to make "theology" accessible to all, but the idea was flawed by a misconception of it. Whether the word "theology" was used in a broad sense (anything pertaining to religion) or in the traditional sense (God in Himself), Philaret should have recalled from his reading of the Fathers that the knowledge of God (theology) is the reward of sanctity.

Fr Florovsky wants us to believe that Philaret was "the first person in the history of modern Russian theology for whom theology once more became the aim of life, the essential step toward spiritual progress and construction."[55] It is more than confusing to hear Florovsky praise the Metropolitan for "firmly and judiciously teaching the lessons of faith," warmly praising him as a "Biblicist," when we read about Philaret's effort, for the sake of the Bible, to "minimize the importance of Tradition in the Church." One should not be surprised to hear that the Metropolitan "held firmly" to the Protestant notion of "the self-sufficiency" of holy Scripture.[56] "Philaret was

---

[55] *Ways...*, p. 212. Serge Balshakoff reserves that honor to Metropolitan Antony Khrapovitsky, refering to him as "the greatest Orthodox theologian of recent times" (*The Doctrine of the Unity of the Church in the Works of Khomyakov and Moehler*. London, 1946, p. 149).

[56] It is a strange devotion Florovsky had for Philaret. "When he (Philaret) spoke of Scripture as the 'sole and sufficient' source of teaching about faith, he did not have in mind a book with leather covers, but the Word of God which lives in the Church and awakens in each living soul that which the Church acknowledges and teaches, Scripture in Tradition. Furthermore, true and holy Tradition is not simply the visible and verbal tradition of the teachings, canons, ceremonies, and rituals, for it is also the invisible and actual instruction by grace and sanctification. And for Philaret the main thing was not

probably the greatest theologian of the Russian church in modern times,"
asserts Fr Georges, "and his influence on the life and theological thinking in
Russia was enormous."[57] If Philaret was indeed "the greatest theologian of
the Russian Church in modern times," he must also have been the most
patristic. He was not. His "influence" may have been "enormous," but an
Orthodox can take no delight in his "Westernism."[58] Judging from the available literature, including his *Longer Catechism*,[59] it would not be rash to conclude that Philaret was a major contributor to the formation of twentieth century "Orthodox ecumenism."

C   However vigorous, the "liberal" Orthodoxy of Philaret was not the only
current in the Russian theology of the last century. There is another stream
of traditional Orthodox thought which runs from St Paisi Velichovsky (1722-
1794) a century before, through St Seraphim of Sarov (1759-1833), Khomiakov and other Slavophiles, to Anthony of Kiev (Khrapovitsky), to his disciple, Hieromartyr Hilarion Troitsky (d. 1929), Archbishop of Kruitisky. They
represent a monastic (and patristic) renewal of Orthodoxy in Russia,
nowhere better practiced and preserved than the Optina Pustyn (1828-
1929).[60] Its tradition of *startsy* ("old men," "elders") reaches to the time of St

---

historical memory, but the uninterrupted flow of Grace. Therefore, only in the Church is
authentic tradition possible. Only in the Church does the Grace of the Holy Spirit pour
forth revealed truth in an unbroken stream and admonish with it" (*ib.*, pp. 213-214).

Florovsky is writing about himself. For that reason, he deliberately avoided doing
what the scholar in him was trained to do: define terms, draw distinctions, give an objective analysis and exposition. Above all, he should have subjected the "theology" of
Philaret to the judgment of the holy Fathers. Nothing he wrote in the Metropolitan's
defense has met these criteria. Neither Florovsky nor Philaret (Filaret) took heresy seriously, and both gave personal inflections to the New Testament and the Fathers. To call
Roman Catholicism and Protestantism heresies did not come easily to them (*ib.*, p. 218f.).

57   "Orthodox Ecumenism...," 6.

58   For example, Makary Glukharev (1792-1847), was "one of the most remarkable
men of that era." At the St Petersburg Academy, he was "completely under Filaret's influence." Graduating, he taught for a period and later became a monk. He translated
Augustine's *Confessions* and the *Ladder* of St John Climacus, the writings of St Theodore
the Studite and of Teresa of Avila, several works of Gregory the Great and intended to
render Blaise Pascal into Russian (*Ways...*, pp. 223-227).

59   The *Longer Catechism* of Metropolitan Philaret was approved by the Russian
Holy Synod in 1839, and subsequently by all the Orthodox Patriarchates.   R.W.
Blackmore translated the *Catechism* into English in his *Doctrine of the Russian Church*.
Aberdeen, 1845. The English edition was later republished by Archmandrite Anthony
Bashir as *Studies in the Greek Church* (New York, 1936).

60   The Optina monastery (near Moscow), under the leadership of Elder (*staretz*)
Makary, had a prolific publishing house, producing the works of the ancient Fathers as
well as twenty-five volumes of ascetic literature, such as Sts Mark   (continued on next page)

Anthony the Great. The monastery was visited by many of Russia's most famous intellectuals—Ivan Kireevsky, Fydor Dostoyevsky, Khomiakov, even Tolstoy and Soloviev, etc.

As valuable as Optina may have been as a spiritual retreat and refuge, it had greater importance as the stronghold of Orthodoxy against the rising tide of materialism, positivism and socialism in Russia. It was at this monastery, for instance, that Ivan Kireevsky, the leader of the Slavophiles, was guided from Hegel and Schelling to St Isaac the Syrian, and a new understanding of "Christian philosophy." Kireevsky had been a practioner of philosophy in the conventional and European sense, but his visit to Optina turned him to the patristic conception of philosophy, a "new philosophy" which would be a testimonial to God as well as to his beloved Russia. His *New Principles* was published in the year of his death (1856), which left his ambition for the construction of a Christian philosophy to his friend, Alexi Kho-miakov. It was the latter more than any other religious thinker in modern Russia who broke the spell of "scholasticism" through his appeal to the Fathers.[61] He believed that in the Orthodox Church there existed an order of things which is found nowhere else and, therefore, he called for the repristinization of all cultures in the spirit of Orthodoxy.

It is in this context that we are to understand Khomiakov's conception of Christian universality, that is to say, his ecclesiology. If Orthodoxy is the one Church, the one religion intended by God for all humanity, this means, among other things, that all cultures should be inseminated with Orthodoxy. On the other hand, the Western culture which has infected Russia is the expression of an heretical mind, the same mind that begat Roman Catholicism, Protestantism and socialism. He believed that the Reformation was in fact no more than an extension and development of Romanism. Both are rationalist, reaching different theological conclusions from the same erroneous premise.

In language characteristic of Khomiakov—"Romanism is an unnatural tyranny; Protestantism an unprincipled revolt. Neither of them can be accepted. But where is unity without tyranny? Where is freedom without revolt to be discovered? Both are to be found in the ancient, continuous, unadulterated tradition of the Church. There a unity is found more authoritative than the despotism of the Vatican, *for it is based on the strength of mutu-*

(contd.) the Ascetic, Symeon the New Theologian, Theodore the Studite, Abba Sabbatius, Abba Dorotethos, the letters of Isaac the Syrian, etc. The monks collected and edited the writings of St Paisi Velichkovsky. Metropolitan Philaret of Moscow displayed extraordinary interest in the literary work of Optina (Archbishop Seraphim, *Die Ostkriche.* Stuttgart, 1950, ss. 298-319).

61 S. Bolshakoff, "Patristic Foundations of Khomyakov's Theology," in *The Eastern Churches Quarterly* X, 5 (1954), 235-245.

al love. There a liberty is to be found more free than the license of Protestantism, for it is regulated by the humility of mutual love. Orthodoxy is the Rock and the Refuge."[62] Alexi Khomiakov's polemic against the Western confessions has no equal in Russia.

The heresies of the West, he continued, have a history. Examine the period from the Middle Ages to the present day and one will encounter the conflict between what Roman Catholicism accepts as the realm of faith and what it assumes to be the domain of human reason. Faith or revelation is allotted the sphere abandoned by reason—"mystery" and "authority"—which implies, of course, that reason has identified and marked off the terrain of faith (reduced to the Scriptures by the Reformation). The result is that sometimes faith has been conceived as "crowning" reason, which, as the intellectual history of Western Europe shows, only surrendered more and more of human experience to the charge of philosophy. Sometimes no restrictions were placed on reason, while at other times faith arbitrarily refused to lease any territory to it. Khomiakov agreed with Kireevsky that in Orthodoxy true faith illumines the powers of the soul, binding all its faculties into a living and moral unity. A self-critical reason, therefore, cannot oppose faith (or the Faith) because it knows the scope of its powers and that only Grace through faith can elevate it above its ordinary functions. Once it humbly recognizes its limitations, then, reason, as an aspect of the soul, participates in man's spiritual and gnostic life.

There is no better argument against the Western heterodox—which, incidentally, Khomiakov believed to be closer to Orthodoxy than the Eastern heresies—than the tragedy of their intellectual history. In fact, the West's struggle with "faith" and "reason" and the consequence of that preoccupation, is largely responsible for its narrow perception of the Christian Truth. It is her terrible pride—"the idol of pride"—which is the lesson the West has not learned about itself. "Christian knowledge is a matter, not of intellectual investigation, but of a living faith, which is the gift of Grace," Khomiakov wrote. "Scripture is an external thing, and tradition external, and works are external: that which is able to integrate and internalize them is the one Spirit of God. From tradition alone, or from Scripture or works, a man derives only a fragmented and incomplete knowledge, which may indeed in itself contain some truth, for he starts from Truth; but at the same time it must of necessity be erroneous, inasmuch as it is incomplete. A believer knows the Truth, but an unbeliever does not know it, or at least only knows it with an external and imperfect knowledge."[63]

---

62 Birkbeck, W.J., ed., *Russia and the English Church during the Last Fifty Years* (vol. 1): *A Correspondence between Mr. W. Palmer & Mr. Khomyakov*. London, 1895, p. 102.

63 *The Church Is One*. Trans. with Intro. by G. Grabbe. Seattle, 1979, pp. 23-24.

The acquisition of saving Truth comes only within the *sobornost* of the Church.[64] "No man can comprehend the eternal Truth of primitive Christianity other than in its plenitude, that is to say, in the identity of unity and freedom manifested in the law of love. Such is Orthodoxy."[65] Thus, "love" and "unity" "truth" and "freedom" are ecclesial experiences (of the corporate "we," not the separate "I"); they are not the splendid results of dialectic. They are the fruits of the spiritual life, not theorizing about ethics and spirituality, even as true doctrine is not the product of speculation. Whoever isolates himself from the *sobornost* of the Church is deprived of the Holy Spirit. The "authority" of Roman Catholicism suffocates human freedom and denies the human personality growth in the Spirit, while by denying the organic fellowship of the Church, Protestantism places the individual outside her loving and nurturing oneness, outside the unity of the Holy Spirit which alone sanctifies and transforms the soul within that fellowship.

D   It was these truths which eluded William Palmer (1811-1879), the Anglican Oxford "ecumenist" in his overtures to the Russian Church.[66] No one should have expected that a man reared in the modern culture of the post-Christian West would understand the ancient "truth in love" alive in Orthodoxy. He encountered Russian Orthodoxy with his own perspective. Palmer believed the Christian Church in its fullness was severally Anglican, Greek and Latin, so in turn each of those three was the whole Church; hence, whenever anyone of the three was present, so also the other two. Palmer failed to appreciate the essential difference between Anglicanism and Orthodoxy. He saw a similarity between them which he believed could be exploited to his advantage; and he was disappointed that, after the Procurator of the Holy Synod, Count Nikolai Protasov (1799-1855), examined his ecclesiology, he would not take up his cause. Palmer was also dismayed when Metropolitan Philaret made as a condition of his admission to Holy Communion, that he

---

64   *Sobornost'* approximates the English "cohesion," "totality," "integrality"; it applies to the Church, not to the cosmos as Soloviev and his followers believed. For Khomiakov it renders the Greek word, *katholikos*, found in the Nicene Creed. "*L'Église catholique c'est l'Église de l'unanimité libre, de l'unanimaté parfaite, l'Église ou il n'y a plus de nationalistes, plus de Grecs ne de barbares, ou il n'y a plus de différences de conditions plus de maîtres ni d'esclaves, c'est l'Églises prophetisée par l'Ancient Testament et réalisee par le Nouveau, l'Église telle enfin que saint Paul l'a definie*" (*L'Église Latine et le Protestantism*. Farnborough (Eng.), 1969, pp. 397-398).

65   Quoted in Gratieux, *A.S. Khomiakov. . .* (vol. 2), p. 47.

66   On Palmer's visit to Russia, see S. Bolshakoff, *The Doctrine of the Unity....*, pp. 77-123

"must submit absolutely and without reservation to all the doctrine, discipline and ritual of the Orthodox Church."[67]

When Palmer corresponded with Khomiakov, he should not have been distraught to hear him repeat what he had heard before. The reception of Holy Communion in the Orthodox Church, he told Palmer, compels him to accept the totality of Christian doctrine. "Union," the Russian wrote him, "cannot be understood by any Orthodox otherwise than as the consequence of a complete harmony, or *a perfect unity of doctrine*."[68] Palmer seems to have been aware of Khomiakov's "theology of culture,"[69] giving him in this alone a glimpse of his correspondent's attitude towards the West. He should not have been surprised, then, to hear him speak in theological terms of the Christian Truth, lost to the West by virtue of its many heresies, heresies which have deprived Anglicanism of genuine spiritual life. False life generates false doctrine, even as false doctrine generates false life; and one or both signify the absence of the Spirit. "Just as the pride of the separate Churches," Khomiakov wrote in seventh chapter of *The Church is One*, "which dared to change the Symbol (Nicean Creed) of the whole Church without the consent of their brethren, was inspired by a spirit not of love, and was a crime against God and the Church, so also their blind wisdom, which did not comprehend the mysteries of God, was a distortion of the Faith; for it is not preserved where love has grown cold."

Therefore, when Khomiakov contemplated "reunion," he was thinking of more than repentance or the dropping or adding of a few doctrines, even the *filioque*. Returning to the Church of Christ, does indeed impose upon Protestantism and Roman Catholicism the solemn renunciation of their doctrinal errors and submission to every teaching of Orthodoxy; but, above all, the members of "separated bodies" must acquire a new *sentiment religieux*, a *phronema*, a "renewal of the mind." For Palmer, when he had rejected Khomiakov's exhortation, it was a much simpler matter to join subsequently "the Roman communion" (1855). All he needed to do was suspend his private judgment and affirm nothing contrary to Roman dogmas.

E   Khomiakov did not stand alone in his "daring radicalism" (Florovsky's characterization), but ecumania was the fashion and the "radicals" were muffled. So many of his Russian contemporaries outstripped "the Greeks" in

    67   Palmer, W., *Notes of a Visit to the Russian Church*. Selected and Arranged by Cardinal Newman. London, 1882, p. 415.

    68   Birkbeck, p. 7.

    69   A valuable summary of Khomiakov's teachings on this subject, see Bolshakoff, *The Doctrine of the Unity....*, pp. 37-76.

their desire to meet the Old Catholics and the Anglicans in amiable dialogue and to find something "charismatic" in the rites and pseudo-Sacraments of the heterodox. In the forefront of the "ultraconservative" opposition within the Orthodox Church of Russia were Metropolitan Anthony Khrapovitsky and Archbishop Hilarion Troitsky. Neither was opposed to discussion with the heterodox—albeit Metropolitan Anthony reserved a special animus towards Latins, the consequence of his unpleasant experience with them in Volhynie.[70] For him, there is no spiritual reality, no saving Grace outside of Orthodoxy. Beyond the ecclesial perimeter was only "this world, foreign to Christ's redemption and possessed by the Devil." To hold "right beliefs" is irrelevant, so long as the individual did not seek his salvation in the Orthodox Church. What was important to the Saint, commented Fr Florovsky, was "actual membership in the Church, which is not compromised by doctrinal ignorance and frailty. 'Doctrinal agreement' by itself means little. Membership in the Body is the only thing that counts."[71]

Metropolitan Anthony's "ecumenism" had markedly nothing in common with what has become so familiar today. He preferred the traditional "monologue" to the popular "dialogue" with heretics. To delineate the genuine Orthodox position, on 18 January, 1918, Archbishop Hilarion wrote an "open letter" to Mr Robert Gardiner, *The Unity of the Church and the World Conference of Christian Communities*.[72] He responded first to Mr Gardiner's criticism of Metropolitan Anthony, initially published in *Revue internationale ecclésiastique*, in which the author thrashed the (then) Archbishop of Kiev for "a strictness of Orthodoxy" which lamentably determines "the doctrinal position of the ultraconservative elements in the Russian church, in other words, the hierarchy." He refused to conceive the Archbishop's stance as anything but "intolerant."

St Hilarion challenged Gardiner's primary assumption. "In no wise," he said, "can I acknowledge Archbishop Anthony to be a representative of 'ultraconservative' elements in our Church." The label "ultraconservative has no meaning for us." "I am of the opinion that in matters of faith there can be but one strict Orthodoxy; here we can have either truth or error, but there can

---

[70] Volhynie is near the Czech border. Metropolitan Anthony was Bishop of the Orthodox diocese there (1902-1905). Roman Catholic rivalry was intense. "...l'atmosphère de la Volhynie," says S. Bolshakoff, *"avec ses polémiques et son prosélytisme mutuel produisit en Msgr Antoine une profonde antipathie pour l'Eglise romaine et ses institutions"* ("Le Metropolite Antoine de Kiev, Président du Synode des Évêques Russes a L'Étranger," in *Irenikon* XIII, 5 (1935-1936), 567).

[71] "Orthodox Ecumenism....," 51.

[72] Translated by M. Jerinec. Montreal, 1975. Hilarion was a layman at the time he wrote the letter.

be no truth which is strict, and another which is less so." Mr Gardiner should not confuse, Hilarion continues, the Archbishop's plea for the renovation of Orthodoxy—his desire to emancipate her from the stranglehold of Western rationalism—as a mask for so-called "ultraconservatism," a pejorative appellation which better applies to those who "blindly adhere to the scholastic theology imported from the West as the only possible and exclusively true one."

The theology of the West is replete with error and for that reason those who adhere to it are outside the Church. The *filioque* heresy is only part of the reason that "there is no ecclesiastical unity in grace between us," Hilarion continued. Gardiner should not take comfort from the words of Philaret, the Metropolitan of Moscow—"No church which believes Jesus to be the Christ will I dare to call false"—a completely personal viewpoint. Also, there are a number of objections to his idea that there are many churches some of which are in possession of "the pure truth," while others have the "impure truth." "A church of impure truth seems to be evidently a false one, and there cannot be a false church; such a church ceases to be a church, and becomes an extra-ecclesiastical community. In any case, Metropolitan Philaret did not partake of the Eucharist with the Latins...."

In this connection, Hilarion stated, "If the mysteries are valid outside the one Church of Christ, if the fullness of the ecclesiastical life in grace is not limited to the boundaries of the [Orthodox] Church, then, there exist several churches. . .and the ninth article of our Creed ["I believe in one. . .Church"] should be dropped." "No, the truth of ecclesiastical unity does not acknowledge the grace of the mysteries administered within extra-ecclesiastical communities. It is impossible to reconcile church unity with the validity of extra-ecclesiasticl sacraments. Even the genius of Augustine had been unable to solve this problem satisfactorily." With him originates the unpatristic distinction between "the validity of the sacraments and their efficacy." There are no Sacraments where there is no Spirit, and the Spirit abides only in the Church.

The question is finally whether heretics and schismatics have the Grace of the Holy Spirit. The Church is the "temple of the Holy Spirit." Thus, if the Sacraments of heretics and schismatics are "valid," the Spirit is with them and they are part of the one Church of Christ—heretical doctrine and defiance to lawful authority notwithstanding. Why, then, does the Orthodox Church baptize and chrismate Protestants and Roman Catholics when they join her? Are they not already part of the Church? Is there any need to repeat their priesthood and other Sacraments? But, then, some Christian communities (Protestants) deny the necessity of both which, if true, means that one may be a Christian with or without a priesthood and the Mysteries. An essential dimension of the Church has been abrogated. Much of

Christian doctrine has been amputated. Where, then, is the unity of the Church? And if heretical doctrine is mixed with the saving Truth, where is the Church's infallibility? If she is not infallible, how do we know the Truth? Everything in the history of the Orthodox Church—from the statements of her Fathers to the implications of her Canons and liturgical practices—affirms that she is the Church, and heretics and schismatics have no part in her unity.

Nevertheless, St Hilarion did not oppose the projected Conference and the Orthodox participation in it so long as it is imposes no condition on her representatives to accept "all contemporary Christian confessions and sects" as altogether "the Church of Christ which has lost only its visible unity." Neither must Mr Gardiner anticipate that the Orthodox will confirm the existence of Anglican Orders, for, if nothing else, the way in which the question concerning the nature of its ministry is framed is "hopeless." As for himself, Hilarion had no sympathy for the debate over Anglican Orders; the "question" did not exist for him. Whether Archbishop Parker was validly consecrated or not is irrelevant. After the year 1054, it was impossible for the English Church to receive the Grace which "had already run dry in [Roman] Catholicism."

In other words, as the first Canon of St Basil implies, outside the Church there is no sacramental Grace, "and every sort of succession outside the Church is unlawful, since a layman executes the laying-on of hands upon a layman, without communicating any sort of grace to him, because there is none, nor can there by any outside the one Church, outside the unity of the Body of Christ." St Hilarion ends his remarks with the hope that his letter to Mr Gardiner will serve to advance the cause of "union," that is, all who identify themselves as Christians will embrace "the living body of the one Church of Christ." He prays, too, that God will permit him to see the day when "we will both be together in the One Church of Christ" sharing in "the Communion of the one Bread."

F　　One should expect that Archbishop Hilarion's ardor for the possibility of "union" to have cooled as he watched the extent to which so many Orthodox, especially in the diaspora, were carried away in their enthusiasm for ecumenism. We have a record of Metropolitan Anthony Khrapovitsky's reaction to it. He must already have had a premonition at the Moscow Pan-Russian Orthodox Council (1917-1918), about the nature of the involvement of some in the movement. He must have been most disconcerted by the voices, anti-monarchist and anti-patriarchal voices, which called for the abolition of the Holy Synod and the establishment of a democratic form of church government, a parliament.[73]   This "liberal" faction within the Council, when finally expelled from Russia by the Bolsheviks, gravitated toward Western Europe, particularly to France and England. They established a Theological Academy in Paris (1926), a base from which to freely launch their ecumenical sorties.

The so-called Christian intelligentsia of the Russian emigration were, from the beginning of their exile, eager participants in and advocates of every kind of ecumenical conference, symposium, and "joined very gladly in the octave of prayer for the unity of the Churches."[74] With the backing of their Archbishop, the faculty of St Sergius Academy (Bulgakov, Zander, Berdiaev, Zenkovsky, etc.) involved themselves in the World Student Christian Federation, the YMCA, the Istina Center, St Basil's House and the Fellowship of St Alban and St Sergius, *Cimadé,* the *Comité Intérorthodoxe d'action économique,* etc.

The prevailing sentiment of the intelligentsia was expressed by Fr Bulgakov, "the splits within the Church do not reach to its foundations; in its sacramental life the Church remains one, and this is especially true as regards Orthodoxy and Catholicism."[75]

Professor Lev Zander maintained that Orthodoxy possesses "the fullness of divinely ruled truth" and "is always conscious of herself as *the Church.*"[76] Nevertheless, he argued, "vestiges of truth" remain in the West, "seeds of Orthodoxy" which provide the basis and possibility of "unity" with all Christian Churches. Indeed, there is already a spiritual brotherhood between East and West. Many Western Christians, Zander exclaimed, are "unconsciously Orthodox," Orthodox without being members of the Church. Anglicanism, in particular, shelters "enclaves of Orthodoxy" which are, from "the dogmatic point of view, Orthodox." Thus, so long as they believe correctly about the Mysteries, these "Western Orthodox" possess and administer them validly and receive their Grace.[77]

---

[73]   The Patriarchate was restored. St Tikhon was proclaimed Patriarch of all Russia. Archbishop Antony was made *doyen* of the Russian hierarchy (See Bolshakoff, "Le Metropolite Antoine de Kiev...." 569).

[74]   In a letter (5 Dec 1934 n.s) of Archbishop Eulogi to Abbe Couturier (cited in G. Curtis, *Paul Couturier and Unity in Christ.* Westminster [Md.], 1946, p. 72).

[75]   Quoted, N. Zernov, *The Russian Religious Renaissance of the Twentieth Century.* New York, 1963, p. 263.

[76]   "The Ecumenical Movement and the Orthodox Church," *The Ecumenical Review* I, 3 (1949), 273.

[77]   "Die Westliche Orthodoxie," in *Theologische Existenz Heute* LXX. Munchen, 1959, p. 16.

Zander's novel opinions rose from reckless speculation about the doctrine of the Church, a sinister ideology shared in common by most of the Paris intelligentsia, an ideology concerning which few have been cautious to study. It is "democracy" or "secularism" hidden under the guise of *sobornost*, interpreted to mean the rejection of what they called "external authority."[78] The coincidence of ecumenism and the democratization of the Church was not accidental. Their adherence to ecumenism was part of that ideology, a necessary deduction from their universalist or monist philosophies; hence, also, their opposition to sacral monarchy. At Clermont (France), the fifth general Congress of the Dvigenie (1927), Professor Anton Kartashev lectured on *La Russie qui vient*, of a Russian Church without "caesaropapism" (i.e., the monarchy). In general, the Congress hailed the death of Tsar Nicholas as the end of "the Constantinian era," the beginning of another, which according to Bulgakov, signifies that *chaque membre de l'Église entre directément en relation avec le Christ, puisque la barriere de l'autorité exterieure n'existe pas*.[79] The Church about which they spoke was not the Church of the Fathers. They sought to contaminate the Russian Orthodox Church, at home and abroad, with their ecumenical phantasies.

G   If this chapter on Orthodoxy and ecumenism ends here, it is because there is nothing more to be said, unless one wishes to review the litany of mystagogical, doctrinal and canonical abuses perpetrated by Orthodox clergy for the sake of modernism; or to listen with bewilderment as Orthodox educators defend now what years ago they would have condemned.[80]

---

[78]   See the discussion in S. Bolshakoff, *The Doctrine of Unity of the Church. . . .*, pp. 263-303. This group of the Russian intelligentsia considered "external authority" to be a restriction upon their religious and philosophical freedom. Valuable insight into their thinking may found in F. Heer, "Sergej N. Bulgakow," in *Tendenzen der Theologie Im 20 Jahrhundret: Eine Geschichte In Portraets*. ed. by H.J. Schutz. Stuttgart, 1966, 114-119; L. Schapiro, "The *Vekhi* Group and the Mystique of Revolution," in *The Slavonic Review* XXXIV, 8 (1955), 56-77; N. Lossky, "The Successors of Vladimir Solovyev," in *The Slavonic Review* III, 7 (1924), 92-109; S. Bulgakov, "Vekhi (Signposts): A Collection of Articles on the Russian Intelligentsia (II): Heroism and Asceticism," in *Canadian Slavic Studies* II, 4 (1968), 447-463; M. Azkoul, "Introduction to Russian Neo-Christian Thought: Pavel Florensky," in *The Patristic and Byzantine Review* VIII, 2 (1989), 101-122; Nicholas Berdiaev, *The Russian Idea*. New York, 1947; V.V. Zenkovsky, *A History of Russian Philosophy* (vol. 2). New York, 1953;

[79]   See *Évêques Russes in Exil*, 256-269.

[80]   In his critical book review of G.D. Metallinos' *I Confess One Baptism. . .* (St Paul's Monastery, Holy Mountain, 1994), Professor John Erickson of St Vladimir's Russian Orthodox Seminary (OCA) attacks Fr George's call for the rebaptism of Roman Catholics, Protestants and the non-Chalcedonians as an "innovation" which has no doctrinal lineage before the eighteenth century, beyond the 1775 decision of Patriarch Cyril V of Constantinople who mandated the "rebaptism" of all heretics. Erickson also rejects Fr Metallinos'

Moreover, the search for the origins of "Orthodox ecumenism" might have been pursued into the eighteenth century, to the influence of the Enlightenment on the Christian East. The effect of German Romanticism (other than Baader) on Russian theology might have been further examined. How, too, did Peter the Great's Westernization of Russian foment the ecumenical mentality? What effect did the struggle between the Westernizers and the Slavophiles have on the soul of Russia? or the trauma of German kings in nineteenth century Greece? We might have also discussed the impact of Uniatism, European education, or the inundation of the Middle East with Roman Catholic monastics. Scholarly research may speculate about this or that factor and its relevance to the history of Orthodox countries, but the effort is futile, considering the biases with which such research is commonly undertaken. An autopsy does not benefit its subject.

Perhaps, more attention should be given to the kind of words spoken by the late Metropolitan Philaret of the Russian Church Abroad in his *Second Sorrowful Epistle* (1972). "It is the belief in the renewal of the whole of mankind within the new and universal Church that lends to ecumenism the nature of a chiliastic heresy, which becomes more and more evident in the ecumenistic attempts to unite everyone, disregarding truth and error, and in their tendency to create not only a new Church, but a new world," he comments. "The propagators of this heresy do not wish to believe that the earth and all that is on it shall burn, the heavens shall pass away, and the elements shall melt with fervent heat (II Pet. 3:10-12)."

---

historical data that triple immersion into sanctified water is the traditional way to baptise; and that, therefore, Latins and Protestants who generally practice baptism by "aspersion" (sprinkling) or "affusion" (pouring) must be viewed as unbaptized. According to Erickson, "immersion" cannot not be proven to be the universal custom of baptizing in the early Church (*St Vladimir's Theological Quarterly* XLI, 1 [1997], 77-81).

Erickson suggests that even the Fathers did not everywhere and always employ baptismal immersion. For example, St John Chrysostom is supposed to have said, "It is as in a tomb that we immerse our heads in the water...then when we lift our heads back the new man emerges" (*On John* XXV, 2 PG 59 151). A dubious translation from a single Gospel commentary by Chrysostom, Erickson will not even comfort us with a complete sentence—Καθάπερ γὰρ, ἐν τινι τάφῳ, τῷ ὕδατι καταδυόντων ἡμῶν τὰς κεφαλὰς, ὁ παλαιὸς ἄνθρωπος θάπτεται, καὶ, καταδὺς κάτω, κρύπτεται ὅλος καθάπαξ· εἶτα ἀνανευόντων ἡμῶν ὁ καινὸς ἄνεισι πάλιν.. Erickson might also have consulted St John's *Ad Illuminandos Catechesis*, or St Justin Martyr (*Apol.* I, 61 FC), *The Apostolic Tradition* (no. 21) of St Hippolytus, the *De Baptismo* and *De Corona* of Tertullian, or *The Teaching of the Twelve Apostles* (ch. 7 FC): "Baptize in the Name of the Father, and of the Son, and of the Holy Spirit in running water [streams, seas, etc.]. But if you have no running water, baptize in any other [pool, resevoir, etc.); and if you cannot in cold, then in warm water. But, if the one is lacking, pour the other three times on the head..."

Professor Erickson's sources (J.G. Davies, *The Architectural Setting of Bapitsm*. London, 1961; A. Stauffer, *On Baptismal Fonts. Ancient and Modern*.   (continued on next page) *(cont'd.)* Nottingham, 1994) report that many fonts in Greece and throughout the Middle East (e.g., the excavations of Dura Europos) were clearly too shallow to allow complete submersion of the human body, even one prone in the water. (Infants also?) The fonts were never more than four feet deep. He concludes that the early Church shows a diversity of baptismal practices. Erickson's conclusions are clearly disputable. "The evidence of early baptisteries and Christian art have been open to varying interpretations," according to E. Ferguson. "Some have contended that the candidate stood in a pool while water was poured over his head, a partial immersion. The literature accounts do not seem to bear this out (St Cyril of Jerusalem, *Catech.* 12.14; Basil, *De Spir. Sanct.* 15.35; Ambrose, *Sacram.* 3,1. lf; John Chrysostom, *Catech.* 2:26; *In John.* hom. 25.2.). The earliest baptismal fonts in the house church at Dura Europos were sufficient for an immersion. Dimensions and shapes of other baptismal fonts from the fourth and following centuries vary, but most appear unnecessarily large for anything other than a complete washing" ("Baptism," in *Encyclopedia of Early Christianity*. Ed. by E. Ferguson. New York, 1990, 132-133).

In another article, "Baptistery," Ferguson writes that the earliest known baptistery, Dura Europos (c. 240), had a pool with measurements five feet four inches in length by three feet one inch in depth. A ledge on the two short sides permitted a person seated to be immersed by bending over. Four hundred baptisteries from the third to the seventh century have been catalogued. "They exhibit great architectural variety .... Nonetheless, they testify to considerable unity in the Christian world and to the importance of baptism" (*ibid.*, 136f.). Then, as now, the Church recognizes baptism with "aspersion" and "affusion" as exceptions, permitted by "*economia*" (see D. Stone, *Holy Baptism*. New York, 1899, pp. 141-150).

Aside from the fact that his ecumenical sensibilities bias his critique of *I Confess One Baptism* ..., Erickson's treatment of the Fathers is unacceptable from an Orthodox point of view: He seems to regard them as resources rather than authorities, and alludes to the Canons which demand triple immersion (see Metallinos, App. I-II) only to ignore them. He is not careful to distinguish adult from infant baptism, nor Orthodox from heretical rites in antiquity. He compels Christian theology to adopt his interpretation of religious artifacts. But if the "evidence" says one thing and the teachings of the Church say another, which often happens, any Christian faithful must opt for the Orthodox Faith. Erickson, in cavalierly dismissing Fr George Metallinos' appeal to the Fathers and the Canons, shows where his loyalties lay. Palpably, he and Fr George have neither the same ecclesiology nor the same Orthodoxy.

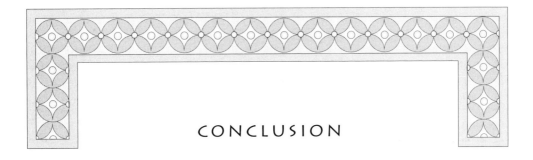

CONCLUSION

With the dramatic erosion of the medieval Christian synthesis, reformers, philosophers and scientists from the time of the Renaissance have attempted to formulate a new system of beliefs. Having never considered a return to the Fathers, the West finally surrendered any hope of reconciling traditional Christian values (as it understood them) with the new postulates of science and secular philosophy. Numerous thinkers, skeptical and religious, of the nineteenth century, had instead devoted themselves to the rebuilding of a new world with technology and science–despite the supernaturalist claims of classical Protestantism and conservative Roman Catholicism. This optimism was shattered by World War I. Indeed, the so-called "literature of decline" (Spengler, Toynbee, Jung, etc.) became popular reading. There seemed to be no answers for a world torn by ideologies which only exacerbated the contemporary mood—unreason, relativism, nihilism.

It seems to have occurred to only a few that the solution to the West's predicament was a radical transformation of its life and thought. Today some have come to that realization and turned to Far Eastern religions for consolation. Others have tried religious and philosophical syncretism. The result has been to fracture Western society with still no promise of objective truth, with no metaphysical assurances. The dichotomy of "God" and the "soul" or "self," of "faith" and "reason" continues under varying guises, the incessant working and reworking of the same elements with no meaningful change. The nineteenth century left the West divided and deracinated, with no moral compass, no metaphysical *grund*, and no confidence in the claims of Christianity—thanks, in part, to the modern christologies of Bauer, Strauss, Schweitzer, Renan, etc., and more recently, J.D. Crossan. These christologies introduced another dualism to a West in spiritual decline—the "Christ of history" (as reason determines him to be) and the "Christ of faith" (as many believe him to be). Such speculations are, of course, the outcome of a developing anti-supernatural world-view which rests on the evolving intellectual and religious tradition of the post-Orthodox West. Despite the futility of such protests as Pope Pius IX's *Syllabus of Errors* (1864), a new *pou*

305

sto has emerged: the self. This result was inevitable, on account of the mischief of Descartes, Kant, Hegel and, to be sure, scholastic rationalism and Protestant individualism ("the priesthood of believers").

From here, there was no way back to the Christian roots of Western life and thought, even if there were a consensus that such a return was desirable. To be sure, at the turn of twentieth century, Roman Catholicism attempted a patristic and liturgical revival, resulting in diversity and greater conflict within her ranks. Protestant subjectivism, invited the rationalism which generated the Romanticism and Liberalism of Schleiermacher who, along with so many of his disciples and contemporaries, viewed history as evolutionary with the "supernatural" and "the miraculous" reduced to "mythology." How ironical, too, that virtually every major philosopher (and theologian) of nineteenth century Europe should spring from a Protestant background. Fr Florovsky described this largely German phenomenon as "the direct and genetic line from the Reformation to Idealism." He saw "the crisis of Idealism as the crisis of the Reformation" ("*Die Krise des Deutschen Idealismus* [II]: *Die Krise des Idealismus als die Krise der Reformation*," *Orient und Occident*. XII, 2-12).

The final solution to the West's spiritual and intellectual dilemma seems to be ecumenism. For traditional Orthodox, it is not a compelling proposal. The quest for the "reunion of the churches" and of "the religions of the world" without the immutable truths of the Christian revelation, without the recognition of Orthodoxy as their steward, would only perpetuate those ideas and forces which have brought the world to the present state of affairs. The cultural developments of the last two hundred years have continued to provide it with the same insoluble questions about God, human nature and destiny which have taunted the post-Orthodox West since the late Middle Ages. Into this, this malignant occidental heritage, ecumenism promises to drag the Orthodox Church.

A   *Once Delivered to the Saints* has attempted to provide a preamble to any critique of Western life and thought which this study premises as a historical and intellectual continuum, from the religious rationalism of medieval scholasticism to the current pluralism and anti-intellectualism of postmodernity. Likewise, we have offered the only alternative to the dubious claims of other religions. There is only one religion for mankind as there is but one God and one disclosure of His will: the Orthodox Church. In Her alone is found the Christ of the Faith who is also the Christ of history. Any introduction to Orthodoxy must begin with the knowledge of the true God, His revelation to the human race in the person of the God-Man, Jesus Christ, and His invitation to participation (*theosis*) in the divine life through His Church. It is a message often misunderstand, especially the idea that the future, the age to come, is already present to us ("realized eschatology"). The apostate West prefers a soteriology of the beatific vision or some other nebulous version of "eternal life." The logic of the Church, however, is so evident as to be ineluctable: if "God alone has immortality" (I Tim. 6:16) as the Apostle says, He alone is eternal. Man's existence is mortal, contingent. Therefore, immortality or eternal life is possible for the creature only if he shares the eternity or immortality of God. He cannot be "partaker of the divine Nature" by entering into His very substance, as pantheists insist; nor by a created Grace, as Augustine and the West assume. Man becomes divine through the Incarnation or, to be precise, by integration into the Church, Christ's Body, through which the member has access to His Divinity, *i.e.*, God's Uncreated Energies.

If, on the other hand, the Church had adopted the "onto-theology" of the Augustinian-Thomist West, she would have fallen into the same metaphysical trap: dualism (Nestorianism) or monism (Monophysitism). Neither should we ignore the fact that the philosophical theology of the West" is the anthropological correlate of man as "value-creating" and "good-discovering being."[1] It is not difficult to find the source of this polarization (dualism) of the Divine and the human: Augustine of Hippo. Even the present opposition between the poles of reality stem from his tradition. Reducing God to a being, Augustine *et alii* could not maintain the patristic apophatic theology, or the Essence/Energy antinomy, or the "chalcedonian" relationship between the visible and the invisible. Pantheism then would be unavoidable; hence, they outlawed the very possibility of deification, while promising human reason access to realms of truth hitherto unattainable.[2]

B   Seduced by philosophy, Augustine lost contact with the "mind of the Church," with her christology, a doctrine known from the beginning, albeit not formulated by the Church until the Council of Chalcedon (451): God become man, one Person recognized in two Natures, Divine and human, "without confusion, without change, without division, without separation, the distinction of Natures in no way annulled by their union." Here is the dogma which is the *point d'appui* of the whole Christian Economy, written in the language of negation, a strategy which strikes at the very heart of rationalism, that nemesis of revelation, that pernicious and insatiable *daemon* never satisfied until all human experience has been reduced to the idiom of dialectics.

---

[1]   Bloom, *The Closing of the American Mind*, p. 160

[2]   E. Underhill, *Mysticism: A Study in the Nature and Development of Man's Spiritual Consciousness*. New York, 1955, p. 99.

Chalcedon is the guardian of the Christian *weltanschauung* in two ways: first, it provides the basis for "the theology of history," which otherwise, as modernity shows, history will be conceived as endless becoming or as something unreal before some timeless Ideal; and second, Chalcedon reaffirms the God-Man as the paradigm of creation: the unity of the physical and the spiritual in which, by virtue of their union, the things physical have access to the noetical or spiritual worlds while things spiritual inform the realm of the senses.

Historically, of course, the necessity of the Chalcedonian dogma derived from a series of challenges to traditional christology, beginning with Docetism which rejected the reality of the Lord's humanity, to Arianism which denied His Divinity; and, then, Nestorianism that could not reconcile His Divinity and Humanity, to Monophysitism which "confused" or merged them. From this point of view, all these heresies, each in its own way, negated the possibility of salvation, i.e., deification, *theosis*. Here are the fundamental falsehoods into which proud human reason falls. It fails to recognize its moral weakness, it refuses to define and observe the limitations of its nature, and to ignore "the landmarks erected by the Fathers." On account of this pride, reason is condemned necessarily to repeat its errors and worse, to suffer demonic delusion.

C   Are the various heresies radically different? What does it suggest that they stand either to the right or to the left of the Chalcedonian christology? Surely, it was not by mere chance that men fell into heresy. According to the Fathers, they reached disparate results with the principles and methods of Greek philosophy. The sectarian doctrines of Christ may appear to be opposites, but they are implicit in each other. Chalcedonian christology is not their synthesis, not the reconciliation of opposites, not another cunning turn in the dialectical process.

The history of Western Christendom leads us to the singular conclusion that all the ancient heresies are revived in both the medieval and modern ones which possess or revisit the ancient heresies. The majority of them are crypto-Nestorian if only because the West has failed to integrate "faith" and "reason," "nature" and "grace," "time" and "eternity," the "sacred" and the "secular," a translation of this dualism into "a most inexpressible calamity." Other heretical doctrines are extrapolated from these concepts, such as predestination or salvation by the divine Will alone, or by "faith alone" and "grace alone" (i.e., monotheletism). Also, the distinction between created and communicable Grace, uncreated and incommunicable Grace; or created and uncreated Glory. All these ideas demonstrate the power of secular philosophy to change the Christian Faith.

D   The first error of medieval philosophy/theology—God as being—led necessarily to the second, the failure to *methodologically envision Christ as the model of reality for them, that is, the Divine as penetrating the created physical and noetic dimensions of that reality corresponding to Christ's Godhood and Humanity of body and soul.* Not that they deliberately scorned it; not at all. The West had largely ceased to think in those terms by the "Gothic era," as we see for example, in the ideal of medieval kingship which had evolved from christo-centric to law-centered monarchy by the thirteenth century. One thing is certain about the heritage of the Latin Middle Ages; it schooled the West in the contemplation and cogitation of reality from the point of view of created things. In other words, by stressing the importance of rationally under-standing the truths in which the West also believed (*fides quaerens intellec-tum*), it approached reality from the human side almost exclusively. By contrast, Orthodox believe and think with an integrated or "Chalcedonian" vision of reality. In the language of christology, to perceive the world from a purely human point of view suggests that Christ had only a human nature; and viewing the world "under the aspect of eternity" implies that Christ had only a divine nature. The Orthodox or Chalcedonian christology gives a uni-fied perspective of reality. Therefore, it would be wholly accurate to describe Western life and thought as homocentric, that is to say, Nestorian.

If some Western theologians and savants now concede that the resolu-tion of historic, religious and cultural problems requires new methods and assumptions, and have begun, in some small quarters, to take patristic chris-tology seriously, it is in large measure the impact of Russian Orthodox *émi-grés* on European religious thought after the first World War—an opportuni-ty obfuscated by the ecumenical movement. Although they influenced the kindred *Lebensphilosophie*, phenomenology, and the revival of German Platonism, the influence of the *soi-disant* Russian "Neo-Christian" philoso-phers, Berdiaev, Frank, Nicholas Lossky, etc. was counter productive in mat-ters of religion. In fact, the result was an exacerbation of what historians of that generation called "the crisis of European humanity." Greeted by the western philosophical community as bearers of light, bringing the gifts of new insight and spirit, the Neo-Christians were wrongly identified as Orthodox philosophers. Hardly the truth, considering that they failed to bring the God and Christ of Orthodoxy that would have fundamentally altered the attitude if not the spiritual mentality of their hosts.

In general, therefore, theological discourse remains what it has been since Anselm and Aquinas and precisely because of the West's inability to rightly integrate the Divine and the human, the source of all its moral and spiritual woes. The Papal West sought to balance the extremes with the idea of law, but it invariably slipped from one side or the other, always hindered by those great intellectual struggles for which the Middle Ages has so often been praised. It did not trust itself to the Faith of Chalcedon (although some would protest), preferring to prove all that it believed, testing everything at the bar of reason, asking too many questions, searching for answers where none could be found, aspiring to knowledge which is too wonderful for man. The penalty has been the modern nihilism.

E   As always, we look to the Latin Middle Ages for the beginning of the West's devolution. Its politics is illustrative. The Scholastics tied their theories of man and the state to the theory of *lex natura*. Near the end of this epoch, the concept of natural law and all its religious, philosophical, and legal assumptions gradually lost its hold on the thinking of Western jurisprudence. Yet, the very possibility of its subversion was already present in the academic or Scholastic political theories of the period, especially the notion that the state could be rationally constructed with no reference to God or revelation; an act of human genius alone. Finally came what seemed inevitable, a secular "prince" who believed that positive law, required no natural or eternal law, and lacking such a foundation, the moral law could be broken down to accommodate "an unavoidable necessity." The transcendent or "super-empirical necessity" of an unbreachable onto-theological imperative finally collapsed before the blows of an "empirical necessity," the *staatsraison*, to borrow Friedrich Meinecke's word. European man was watching evil fighting for a place along side the good, contending that it was producing a special, even a "higher good." With Machiavelli, the forces of sin (which the Christian state struggled to suppress) had won a partial victory. The West was now beset with another dualism: a hostility between the supra-empirical and the empirical, between absolute and relative standards, which in our century, would seem to have resulted in the complete triumph of the latter.

F   The heritage of the Renaissance was the new concept of man out of which developed a new understanding of the universe. The world was no longer viewed as a "realm" of things ordered according to their ideal nature, but as events determined by mechanical causality. The period extending from 1500 to 1700 is called "the scientific revolution." Nothing aided the new science more than the new astronomy guided by Copernicus, Kepler and Galileo. They challenged the assumption, the long held assumption that the earth was the center of the universe and that man was the crown of creation. The new scientific, that is to say, secular vision was in fact only a restatement of medieval nominalism, a radical dualism now open to more than the division between time and eternity. This is the implication of Galileo's remarks in his letter to Christina, Grand Duchess of Tuscany (1615), "Nor does God less admirably discover Himself to us in Nature's action than in Scripture's divine diction." Thus, "the book of nature" becomes as authoritative as the books of the Bible. The breach between supernatural religion and scientific reason is firmly and sedulously established as the fundamental attribute of modernity.

G   The current spiritual dilemma in the secular West is unmistakable. God had been excluded from public life and discourse (the "separation of church and state," as some refer to it); hence, the dualism between the objective science and subjective religion. God is simply irrelevant, as well He might be. If the post-Orthodox Western deity was ever "the God of Abraham, Isaac and Jacob,"[3] He is no longer and has not been for centuries. As the "divine" of a philosophical theology, He is "the God of 'the proofs' which prove nothing," writes Miguel de Unamuno, "or rather, they prove nothing more than the existence of this idea of God."[4] How else may we explain that, except as a very personal faith? He is no more required by modernity as the substratum of truths and values. As a "cultural fact," this deity of the West is dead; or, if He does survive, if there be a twentieth century compromise of this theological "problem," it is that He is whatever I want Him to be.

There is no exaggeration in saying that the Orthodox and the postpatristic West do not share the same theological tradition however similar their religious glossaries and despite the ecumenical trumpeting of a "common heritage." There is no "common mind," no theological continuum between the Western heritage and the Fathers, as there is between Augustine and Aquinas, Luther and Boehme, Calvin and Tillich, Eckhart and Spinoza, Kierkegaard and Barth, etc. The God of these writers is the one "God" about whom they all theorize in one way or another, the same God in whom Westerners believe or disbelieve. That God is the filioqued deity of substance, attributes and relations, complicated by prolix theorizing about His demands (and the hypocrisy of His followers). It is, therefore, no wonder that so many of our contemporaries have rebelled against Him.[5]

---

[3]   According to Etienne Gilson, medieval theology is ordered after the pattern of a science. The existence of God is a "philosophical problem." "The position of a theologian on this point unavoidably consists in collecting philosophical evidence...a theologian cannot do much more than apply to the philosopher for philosophical information" (*The Elements of Christian Philosophy*. New York, 1960, p. 49).

[4]   *Tragic Sense of Life*. trans. by J.E.C. Flitch. New York, 1954, p. 160

[5]   There are several famous examples in Western modernity. Of course, Nietzsche's famous, "God is dead" (*Gott is tot*), but other nineteenth century writers, e.g., Proudhon, "There is no end in the battle against God" (*on nía jamais finis de se debattre contre Dieu*; and Baudelaire, "Let the race of Cain ascend to the heavens and hurl God to the earth" (*Race du Cain, au ciel montre sur la terre jette Dieu*)

H   The one, true God lives. He speaks to the race of men through the Church of His Word. His center in this world is the religious community which He Himself established, "a chosen generation, a royal priesthood, an holy nation, a peculiar people" who were formed by His Spirit to "show forth the praises of Him Who hath called you out of darkness into His marvelous Light" (I Pet. 2:9). He is "known" by none, save His own People. The blessed Trinity is the true God, the God of the Prophets and the Apostles, "the superessential and incomprehensible God," Who cannot be named. It is this God Who condescended to reveal Himself through His Uncreated Energies as Love, Mercy, Justice, and, finally, in the Person of Christ Jesus. It is this God Who is the "the God of the living," the God Who upholds today and forever "the Faith once delivered to the Saints".

The true and unchanging Faith alone proclaims the right conception of Christ, because she alone provides the world with the authentic understanding of God; or as Professor Buckley wrote unawares, "What God is, and even that God is, has its primordial evidence in the Person and in the 'event' that is Jesus Christ."[6] The writer should have gone further: to affirm that the right conception of God and Christ accounts for the right ecclesiology, iconology, ethics, gnoseology, etc.; and, indeed, that the degree of truth or veracity found in other religion hinges upon the God and, therefore, the Christ, in whom they believe or deny.[7] In other words, that religion alone is God's religion in which God is "rightly conceived," rightly glorified" and "rightly believed"—orthodoxia—because she alone is possessed by the God Who speaks to man. He alone accounts for the existence of "the faith once delivered to the saints" without any mixture of falsehood or half-truths.

To His Church, His Body—of which all pre-Christian religions and philosophies were types and antitypes; and of which all "churches" of the so-called Christian era are rivals if not caricatures—"He entrusted the mysteries and dogmas" (St Gregory the Theologian). Within her He deposited "the

---

6   M. Buckley, At the Origins..., p. 361.

7   What may be said for Western religions is also applicable to Eastern religions. Among other things, they have a false christology as reflected, above all, in their cosmologies. In addition, the "gods" of the East are fictitious, for "the gods of the nations are demons" (Ps. 95:5 LXX). They have no equivalent to the God of Christian theism, no strict equation of God with the Good. The impersonal Brahma and Tao have not condescended to visit their creatures as one of them; they cannot. They have no consciousness. Many minor deities may appear to the believer, but the ultimate Reality in Eastern thought has more in common with Plotinus' "One" (who may be indebted to Hinduism) than the God of Abraham. On the "mystical idealism" (i.e., Monophysitism) of the Hindu religion, see S. Dasgupta, Indian Idealism. Cambridge [Eng.], 1962). Historically, the oriental conception of the ego itself as neither permanent nor perishable has nothing in common with Orthodoxy or the West (A.W. Watts, The Way of Zen. New York, 1959, pp. 24f., 29f., 76.).

Faith once delivered to the saints" by Jesus Christ Himself through His Apostles to the Church for the salvation of the *cosmos*. He is "the same yesterday, and today, and forever," so that we might "not be carried about with diverse and strange doctrines" (Heb. 13:8). Therefore, only that Christianity is true whose Faith *in toto* remains unchanged from the moment it was consigned to the Apostles; and if there is no such Faith, if what is believed is the result of every historical mutation of human affairs, if it is as the individual perceives or wants it, there is no self-revealing God, no Christianity, only the relativism and spiritual chaos we have come to know.

Of course, none may deny that many of the things believed and practiced by Roman Catholicism, Protestantism, the Anglicans and the myriad "Christian sects" are correct—taken from the Scriptures and history—but they are truths which heretics have mingled with "the tradition of men" (Col. 2:8)—not the *Paradosis* the Lord instructed the Apostles to be observed everywhere in every generation by all who wished to unite with His Church (Matt. 18: 19-20). We have every reason to believe that He tolerated no human manipulation of His Gospel. The idea of a "doctrinal minimum," an evolving standard of Faith, an amalgamation of the divine Mystery with human theories has no support in the Fathers or the divine Scriptures. Salvific Faith is the Faith of the one Church. There is no Church without the Faith, no Faith without "the Church of the living God, the pillar and ground of Truth" (I Tim. 3:15). Only the Orthodox may claim to have kept the Apostolic Faith without addition or subtraction.

I   In the West only a few historians have any real comprehension (however copious the literature) of the history, doctrine and spirituality of the Orthodox Church, and even less of the cruciality of her christology to them all.[8] Judging from the mistreatment of "the Greek Church" in the past—the haughty histories of Gibbon, Harnack, Lietzmann, Schaff, Latourette, Lecky,

---

[8] Some church historians are aware of the implications of christology to the rest of Christian doctrine, but, at the same time, they refuse to draw out those implications. They interpret these doctrines as the products of an unfolding history. For example, "There is no doubt that the Monophysite christology tended to be associated with the Augustinian type of Fall-doctrine, just as Nestorianism has been logically linked with Pelagianism," exclaims N.P. Williams. Moreover, the latter "must inevitably fall under the stigma of Docetism" (*The Idea of the Fall and Original Sin*. London, 1927, pp. 353, 388). Williams might better have said that the "Augustinian type" tends to be associated with Monophysite or, more precisely, Monothelete soteriology (i.e., salvation by the divine Will alone); but, then, so is Pelagian soteriology (i.e., salvation by the human will alone). One may assume that Williams was cognizant of the Nestorian and Docetic character of Protestantism, but does not take it seriously, certainly not enough to deny the shame of innumerable Christian denominations. He also fails to consider that a false christology imperils the entire Christian Economy.

etc.; or even some of the sympathetic treatments by Runciman, Baynes, Benz, Gavin, Hussey, Pelikan, etc.—it is clear, on the one hand, that many of the writers have familiarized themselves with her only in order to test her life and thought against some personal or sectarian theology or historiosophy; and, on the other hand, to demonstrate a "fairness" by historians, which is finally no more than the pride, if not the delusion of their so-called objectivity.

The first sign of the West's historic prejudice and ignorance is the label "the Greek Church" or "the Eastern Church," although the official documents and decrees of Orthodoxy refer to her as "the One, Holy, Catholic and Apostolic Church of the Nicene Creed." But, then, we should not expect, on account of their own beliefs, that non-Orthodox would make any concessions to her claims. Next is the misleading notion that her "theological creativity" and "doctrinal originality" evaporated in the eighth century with St John of Damascus; or, perhaps, a little later, with St Gregory Palamas—as if "creativity" and "originality" were somehow the imperatives of a "living Church" which Orthodoxy has failed to meet. In any case, to acknowledge the correctness of the Orthodox view of Tradition would be an act of self-abnegation for Protestants and Latins. Finally, historians sometimes admit Orthodoxy baffles them, and if they have any concealed suspicions about the purpose of her stubborn refusal to alter her ways, historians do not always tell us what they think. In any case, it remains a basic assumption of academia that "the whole Church" is divided into rival "Christian bodies." Historians are not prepared to give serious consideration to another opinion.

J   Trusting in the conclusions of such church histories, not a few ecumenists have decided that their movement, divinely inspired, is the final stage in the growth of the Christian religion, the stage of reconciliation ("synthesis"). Looking forward confidently to the day when the unity of the universal Church will include all Faiths, all spiritualities, all the religions of the world, they are blind to the theological and philosophical history of the West which has generated its current spiritual dilemma; and to which ecumenism is seen to be the answer. As if illumined from on high, not a few Orthodox have embraced this ecclesiology, confessed the sin of exclusivism, forsaken their "xenophobia" and "rigorism" for the sake of this new and glorious religious adventure—unaware of the metaphysical and epistemological quagmire into which "the servants of the servants of God" are dragging the Church. As members of the World Council of Churches, "mainline Orthodoxy" cheerfully steps to the *danse macabre* around the ecumenical altar while its *intelligentsia* blithely fiddle the tune. Properly intimidated by their "separated brethren," too many Orthodox think themselves wiser than the Fathers. They are motivated, as far as we can see, by national and personal pride, by their education and biases, despite the apostolic exhortation, "Stand fast and hold the traditions which ye have been taught by word and our epistle" (II Thess. 2:16).

What was initially the Orthodox reason for their presence in the ecumenical movement—"witness to the Truth"—has vanished with the birth of new fantasies. As the result of Orthodox compromise and accommodation, the Fathers, the sacred Canons, the holy icons, worship of the Church, the Calendar, etc. her whole Tradition has been relativized ("an alliance of traditions"). The Orthodox offer little challenge, no virile protest to Roman Catholicism and Protestantism, no zealous refutation of heresy while, at the same time, calumniating the modern defenders ("ultra-conservative") of the ancient Faith with an animosity formerly reserved for the enemies of Christ. The Orthodox Church might have sparked a religious revolution in the twentieth century, erasing the Western rationalism and legalism,[9] and enlightening the world with the knowledge of the true Gospel; but too many of her leaders, ashamed of Orthodoxy's exclusivism, have taken their turn in emasculating the Gospel. Their enthusiasm for the heresy of ecumenism might better have been spent on a restudy of the Fathers:

> But I trust that the Church, by the light of her doctrine, will so enlighten the world's vain wisdom, that, even though it accept not the mystery of the faith, it will recognize that in our conflict with heretics that we, and not they, are the true representatives of that mystery. For great is the force of the truth; not only is it sufficient witness, but the more it is assailed the more evident it becomes; the daily shocks which she receives only increases its inherent stability. It is the peculiar property of the Church, that when she is buffeted she is triumphant, when assaulted by arguments she proves herself in the right, when she is deserted by her supporters, she holds the field...
>
> *St Hilary of Poitiers*

The unity of the Faith is the greatest obstacle to heretics. The contradiction of doctrine among heretics is the sure sign of their folly. "Amid the clash of mutually destructive errors," St Hilary of Poitiers continues,

> the Church stands revealed not only by her own teachings, but by that of her rivals. They are ranged, all of them, against her; and the very fact that she stands single and alone is her sufficient answer to

---

9 "The basic institutions, concepts and ideas of Western legal systems have their source in religious rituals, liturgies, and doctrines of the eleventh and twelfth centuries," observes H.J. Berman, "reflecting new attitudes towards death, sin, punishment, forgiveness, and salvation, as well as assumptions concerning the relationship of the divine to the human and of faith to reason." Although the theology of the Western legal systems have all but "dried up", the institutions, concepts and values have remained, as a kind of "secular theology" (*Law and Theology*, p. 165).

their godless delusions. Each heresy can defeat the others, but not one can win a victory for itself. The only victory is the triumph which the Church celebrates over them all. Each heresy wields against its adversary some weapon already shattered in another instance, by the Church's condemnation. There is no point of union between them, and the outcome of their internecine struggles is the confirmation of the Faith" (*De Trin.* VII, 4 NPNF).

The words of the sage ought to echo and reecho in the ears of the Faithful, "Do not remove the ancient landmarks erected by the Fathers" (Prov. 22:28). Defying the fashionable and defending the Truth should mean now what it has always meant to the Orthodox: adherence to the Fathers, to say only what they allow, to go only where they permit. Despite the centuries of persecution and suffering, apostasy and schism, isolation and sin, the apostolic Faith has persisted according to the promise of the Lord. No matter how cheaply she is sold on the ecumenical market by those "who will not endure sound doctrine; but after their own lusts shall heap to themselves teachers, having itching ears" (I Tim. 4: 3-4), her Faith shall never change. Her Faith cannot be diminished only deserted. What was believed by the Apostles and the first century Christians is professed today. To cite St Basil the Great, "What the Church holds now has not replaced what she believed in the beginning" (*Ep.* CCXXIII, 3 FC).

What is Orthodoxy? A divinely constituted confederation of theanthropic communities originating in Palestine by a covenant or *testamentum* between Christ, the God-Man, and the People called by His Name. She coinheres by the Faith He delivered to the Apostles, the Faith which rests on the covenant of His Body and Blood. Like ancient Israel of the old Covenant, the God of Orthodoxy is the God of Abraham, Isaac and Jacob. He is the Creator of all things, the only God; but He is Head and Spouse to His "peculiar people." The working out of His covenant or pact with the new Israel, the Church, describes also her history.[10] The significance which Orthodoxy attributes to her own history is the very dynamic of all history, the law and condition of its development and destiny. In a word, the Orthodox Church is the Chris-tian Church, the new Chosen People, the instrument of His divine Economy. Never was it her task to develop "the Faith once delivered to the saints," but to spread it, to propagate what had been established from the beginning.

---

[10] Contrary to Hans Kueng, the Orthodox Faith is not one of many evolving "paradigms," i.e., "an entire constellation of beliefs, values, techniques shared by the Christian community" (*Christianity: Essence, History and Future*. New York, 1995, intro.). Orthodoxy is the only "paradigm" revealed by God.

GLOSSARY

AGE   (Grk., αἰών; Lat. *aevum*)

Also "day" (*yom*, in Hebrew) A period of time, beginning with the first instant of creation. History is divided into seven ages. "The Eighth Day" or "Age" follows history; it is everlasting, "the Day of Lord." "Age" is not an "attribute" of God. *Aevum*, in the language of philosophy, is endless time which bridges historical time and eternity.

ALLEGORY (Grk., ἀλληγορία)

An interpretation of Scripture which uncovers spiritual rather than historical meaning of persons, places and things.

ANALOGIA ENTIS (Lat.)

"The analogy of being" is a concept of medieval philosophy. Everything has being, including God; therefore, to some degree everything may be compared to Him. For example, God and man think alike, although God is perfect and omniscient.

ATONEMENT

The Fathers do not use this term; it was conjured in the post-Orthodox West. According to Orthodox teaching of the redemption, Christ voluntarily died on the Cross as a representative of the human race. On the Cross, He offered to God the Father "a sacrifice of praise." Making Himself a "ransom" to death and the devil, He conquered them by His Death, as He cleansed the human race of sin which is the "sting of death" (I Cor. 15: 56). In otherwords, Jesus is "our Passover." The heretical West holds the novel doctrine of the "substitutionary atonement," that is, Christ endured the Cross, in the place of the human race, a punishment by which He assuaged the Wrath of God. He died to appease or satisfy the injured Majesty of God.

BEATIFIC VISION (Lat., *viso beata*).

The Roman Catholic theory that in heaven the souls of the saved will behold the divine Essence directly and intuitively. The Orthodox Church identifies salvation as "participation in the divine Nature" a part of which is "to keep festival unceasingly while delighting in the apprehension of the boundless and ineffable beauty of Thy Countenance (Christ); for Thou art the true desire and unutterable joy of those Who Love Thee, O Christ our God, and all creation hymns Thee forever" (Thanksgiving After Holy Communion).

CHRISTOLOGY (Grk., χριστολογία)

The doctrine of Christ: Incarnate God, Messiah, Second Adam, the Last Man, Redeemer; also, the relation of the Divine to the Human in Jesus. Christ is one Person recognized in two Natures: true Man and true God united without separation or confusion. He is the model for all existence.

CONSUBSTANTIATION (Lat., *consubstantia*)

The Lutheran Eucharistic teaching: in the conversion of the bread and wine to the Body and Blood of Christ, the substance of the created elements are added to the substance of Christ.

CONTEMPLATION (Grk., θεωρία, Lat., *contemplatio*)

Literally, "the vision of God." Detachment from the senses: beholding of God and spiritual things. Wrongly translated speculation.

DEIFICATION (Grk., θέωσις)

Also, divinization. The saved will become divine by Grace, that is, immortal, incorrupt and sinless. In the Age to Come, God will also deify the cosmos (II Pet. 1:4). A spiritual process which begins at Baptism.

DELUSION (πλάνη, *errore, prelest*)

Illusion; hence, led astray, beguiled by the devil.

DISCIPLINA ARCANI (Lat.)

St Basil says it covers all "dogma." Hidden doctrine of the Church taught to catechumens before and after Baptism and Chrismation. It is commonly oral instruction given by the bishop or, with his permission, the presbyter. Differentiated from the "proclamation" of those Christian truths preached to the world.

DISPASSION (Grk., ἀπάθεια)

The purging or uprooting of the passions (anger, hate, lust, envy, indolence, etc.), an inner cleansing, purity of the heart. Having the grace to successfully resist temptation. Perfect love is the sign of dispassion. Dispassion produces a change in human nature. It is a condition of *gnosis* and *theoria*.

DOCETISM

The heresy which holds that the Body of Christ was a phantom. He was not really born with a human body, nor died on the Cross nor risen from the dead in the body. The Docetists declare the Church to be invisible.

DUALISM

The teaching that reality is composed of two dimensions: time and eternity. Sometimes they are viewed as radically opposed (Plato); or interacting without interpenetration (Nestorius, Augustine, Aquinas); and, finally, the patristic mitigated dualism defined by the Council of Chalcedon: the mutual permeation of time and eternity without confusion or separation. According to the Fathers, the mono-dualism of the Church is patterned after the relationship between the Divine and the human in Christ.

E

ECONOMY (Grk., οἰκονομία; Lat., *dispensatio*)

Dispensation. The divine Plan for the salvation of the human race through Jesus Christ (Eph. 1:10). Fathers used economy as a synonym of Incarnation.

ECUMENISM

The modern heresy which seeks to fold all the religions of the earth into one. Originally desired to re-unite Christianity, ecumenism no longer requires the traditional confession of Jesus Christ as Lord, God, and Savior as a condition of membership.

ENTELECHY (Grk., ἐντελεχεία)

A word first used by Aristotle to indicate that within every living thing there a force which predetermines its development. This force or principle leads a thing to the end for which it was designed, e.g., the acorn is potentially the oak tree.

EPIKLESIS (Grk., ἐπίκλησις)

During the divine Liturgy, the priestly invocation of the Holy Spirit to convert or change the bread and wine of the Eucharist into the Body and Blood of Christ. Papists insist that it is the words of institution spoken by the celebrant which effects the change.

ESCHATOLOGY (Grk., ἐσχατολογία)

From the Greek ἔσχατος or "last things" (τὰ ἔσχατα), alluding to the end of the world and the completion of God's Plan. In the Church, the joys of the Age to Come are inexplicably foretasted in the Mysteries, implying that they have an eschatological dimension. She is the Body of the risen Christ Who is the "last Man" (ὁ ἔσχατος ἄνθρωπος).

F

FAITH (Grk., Ἡ πίστις; Lat., *fides*)

"Now faith is the substance of things hoped for, the evidence of things not seen" (Heb. 11:1). Therefore, it has two aspects: the faith by which we believe and the object of that faith: the Faith which we profess. The word "faith" used alone, sometimes refers to both; and, in Western literature, it is often the equivalent of "revelation" as opposed to "reason."

G

GNOSIS (Grk., γνῶσις)

The highest form of knowing. Spiritual knowledge as opposed to intellectual knowledge (e.g., logic); or sensual, empirical knowledge (e.g., biology). It is the gift of dispassion. There is also the "gnosis falsely so-called" of heretics (I Tim. 6:20).

GRACE (Grk., χάρις; Lat., *gratia*)

The extension of the divine Persons. It is described in the Scriptures as communion with Them, an undeserved divine Favor, the free Gift of God. In Western theology, Grace is understood as an impersonal created power or force of God. See Uncreated Energies.

H

HEART (Grk., καρδία, Lat., *cor*)

Also, spirit (πνεῦμα, Grk. or *spiritus*, Lat.), even mind (νοῦς). It does not refer to the physical organ, nor is it the seat of emotions, but the center of man's being, inner-self. Expulsion of the passions from the heart is dispassion (Matt. 15:19; Mark 7:21). God dwells in and speaks to man through the heart. God is "known" by the heart or spirit.

HIGHER CRITICISM

Rejection of the divine inspiration of the Scriptures, the scholarly attempt to scientifically discover the human authorship and authenticity of books of the Bible. Differs from Textual Criticism of the Bible which seeks only to confirm its correct chapters and verses.

K

KOINONIA (Grk. κοινωνία; Lat., *communio*)

The association, communion, fellowship (Acts 2:42) of the Faithful by virtue their "one mind," specially participation, sharing in the holy Spirit through Christ and the Church (II Cor. 13:13); and, therefore, consuming the Body and Blood of Christ. (I Cor. 10:16).

M

MERIT

In the Middle Ages, the Scholastics distinguished between two kinds of merit: *meritum de congruo*, a suitable or fit reward from God for a good deed. Merit of this sort was possible for everyone, even those outside the Church. *Meritum de condigno* is the sort of reward earned only by members of the Church in a state of Grace. The Latin Fathers employed the word to identify the good the Faithful have achieved by Grace.

MONERGISM (Grk., μονεργεία)

Literally, from the Greek "one energy" or "power," referring to the condition under which man is saved. Augustine was a monergist, insisting that the divine Will alone is responsible for man's salvation. His enemy, Pelagius, also a monergist, argued that the human will alone was the cause of a person's salvation.

MONOPHYSITISM

The heretical christology which teaches that after the union of the Divine and human, Christ had one Nature (Grk., μόνη φύσις), that is, He has a single Nature which is both human and Divine.

MONOTHELETISM

An aspect of the Monophysite heresy: one Will (Grk., θέλημα) or energy in Christ to correspond with His single Nature.

MYSTAGOGY (Grk., μυσταγωγία)

Referring to the holy Mysteries, their origin, nature and purpose; the liturgical rite.

MYSTERY (Grk., τὸ μυστήριον)

"Mystery" in the New Testament refers to the "mystery of salvation" or "the mystery of godliness" or "piety": Christ is the *mysterion*, He by Whom God's Plan for salvation would be accomplished.

NEOPLATONISM

The monistic and pantheistic system of the third century A.D philosopher, Plotinus of Lycopolis, who considered himself a disciple of Plato. Augustine of Hippo attempted to reconcile the Orthodox Faith with his philosophy.

NESTORIANISM

The christological heresy which, although recognizing two Natures in Christ (true God and true Man) separates them, so that the Divinity is said to flow through the Humanity as "water through a pipe."

NOETIC (Grk., νοητός)

Something beyond the physical or material, anything spiritual.

ORIGINAL SIN

The first sin, the sin of Adam, which introduced death and sin into the world. Augustine added the falsehood that every human being, including children, inherits the first man's guilt.

P

PERICHORESIS (Grk., περιχώρησις)

The Greek word use to explain the relationship of the Divine and human in Christ, i.e., Their interpenetration, each Nature taking some features from the other without confusion or amalgamation. *Perichoresis* is the basis of deification.

PHILOSOPHY (Grk., φιλοσοφία)

Literally, "the love of wisdom." According to the Fathers, the word philosophy applies to the "foreign philosophy" (ἔξο φιλοσοφία) or "external wisdom" (*externa sapientia*) of worldly thinkers, especially the Greeks who struggled to offer a rational explanation for the world and its causes. Christianity is the true wisdom or love of Christ, "the *Sophia* of God" (I Cor. 1:24). The supreme expression of divine Wisdom is the life of the ascetic or monk ("the highest philosophy").

PLEROMA (Grk., πλήρωμα; Lat., *plenitudo*)

Meaning "complete" or "full" with specific reference to Christ and the Church at the end of history. God has "put all things under His feet, and gave Him to be the head over all things to the Church, which is His Body, the fullness (τὸ πλήρωμα) of Him that fills (πληρουμένου) all in all" (Eph. 1:23). The realization of God's Plan.

R

ROMANTICISM

A 18th and 19th century philosophical and literary movement. It was, in part, a reaction to the Enlightenment with its reliance on reason and mathematics. Romantics held that feeling and personal experience are the best guides to living. Romantics believed that their artistic creations gave expression to beautiful forms inspired by the evolving infinite Spirit. Friedrich Schleiermacher, the founder of Protestant liberalism, was a leader of the movement.

S

SECULARISM (Lat., *saeculum*)

World. Secularism or secularization arose within the culture of the so-called Christian West. It is a body of ideas and values which turn man away from God, the supernatural and beliefs revealed by Him to His Church. To live as if the life in this world has only the meaning human beings give to it. Pluralism and tolerance are the great tentacles of secularism. It denies the holy and the absolute.

STARETS (Russian; Grk., γέροντα)

A monk who is a spiritual guide, often the head of a monastic community or cell.

SYNERGISM   (Grk., συνέργεια)

The "unity of many energies": the divine Plan of salvation involves the concurrence of the Divine and the human (Rom. 8:28) in Christ. The Incarnation exemplifies the whole process of salvation. God and man are joined in a common purpose. Man cannot save himself, God will not save him without his consent and effort.

TELEOLOGY (Grk, τελεολογία)

Any view affirming that history has a purpose or "end" (τέλος), contrary to mechanism which asserts that phenomena are explainable only by antecedent conditions, as effect follows cause, with no ultimate purpose or design.

THEANTHROPOS (Grk., θεάνθρωπος)

In the vocabulary of the Greek Fathers, "God-humanity"; its complement, θέανδρος (God-male); to describe the unity of the Divine and human in Christ. Hence, the Church as the Body of Christ is a "theanthropic community."

THEOLOGY (Grk., θεολογία)

The knowledge of God or the Trinity (θεογνωσία) revealed in Christ. It is not sharply distinguished from God's Plan of salvation in Jesus (οἰκονομία). Theology is "mystical," because the purpose of such knowledge is deification or union with God. Theology is "negative," because the Essence of God is unknowable. To reach the heights of such knowledge requires holiness, something which very few attain. In common jargon, "theology" is ordinarily attached to anything religious, such as the soul or prayer or the joys of heaven; or even the doctrine of the Church.

THEOTOKOS (Lat., *Deipare*)

Translated from the Greek as "Mother of God" or "God-bearer"; *Deipare* in Latin. The Ever-Virgin (ἀει-πάρθενος) Mary begat the human nature of Christ. Because the Nestorians viewed the two Natures of Christ as separated, they preferred the title "Mother of Christ" (Χριστοτόκος).

TRANSUBSTANTIATION (Lat., *transubstantia*)

The teaching of Thomas Aquinas that during the Mass the substance of Christ replaces the substance of the bread and wine in their conversion to His Body and Blood.

TYPOLOGY (Grk., τυπολογία)

A method of Scriptural exegesis (heremeneutics); thus, Old Testament persons and places point to persons and places in the future (e.g., Moses prefigured Christ, the Ark the Church, etc.). Also, New Testament persons and places and things foretell the Age to Come (e.g., or the Eucharist adumbrates the heavenly Banquet in the Kingdom of God).

UNCREATED ENERGY (Grk., ἐνέργεια)

Also the "operations" or "powers of God." Divinity acting outside of Itself, mysteriously communicating or extending Itself primarily as Light and Grace. God created and governs the cosmos by His Energies. The Essence of God is forever unknowable and incommunicable.

WELTANSCHAUUNG (Ger.)

A grand vision of the world, its origin, nature, purpose; the relationship between one aspect of the world to another. In modern philosophy, "world-view" is the creation of human logic and ingenuity.

ABBREVIATIONS

ACW	*Ancient Christian Writers*
Adv. Ar.	*Adversus Arius* (Marius Victorinus)
ANF	*Ante-Nicean Fathers*
B	F. L. Battles, tr., Calvin's *Institutes*
CV	Cyril Vollert, tr., *Compendium of Theology*
EH	E. Hamilton, ed. *The Collected Dialogues of Plato*
FC	*Fathers of the Church*
HTM	Holy Transfiguration Monastery
L	*Loeb Classics*
LCS	*Lectures on Christian Sacraments*
LXX	*Septuagint*
LM	Lazarus Moore, tr., *The Ladder of Divine Ascent*
MD	Marcus Dodds, tr., *City of God* (Augustine)
NG	*The Triads of Gregory Palamas.* Translated by Nicholas Gendle.
Mansi	*Sacrorum Conciliorum: nova et amplissima*
Myst.	*Mystagogy of the Holy Spirit* (St Photius)
NPNF	*Nicene Post-Nicene Fathers*
OO	*Opera Omnia* (Duns Scotus)
Pe	Pegis, A.C., *Basic Writings of Saint ThomasAquinas*
PG/PL	*Patrologia Graeca/Patrologia Latina*
Ph	*Philocalia*
Pel.	Jaroslav Pelikan, tr. *Luther's Works*
RM	Richard McKeon, ed., *The Basic Works of Aristotle*
SC	*Sources Chrétien*
S.T.	*Summa Theologiae* (Aquinas). Blackfriars edition.
Weimar	*Luther Werke* (Martin Luther)
Wickham	*The Selected Letters* of St Cyril of Alexandria

BIBLIOGRAPHY

A PRIMARY SOURCES

AIKEN, H.D., ED., *The Age of Ideology: The 19th Century Philosophers*. New York, 1960.

Ancient Christian Writers (53 vols.). Ed. by J. Burghardt & T.C. Lawler. New York, 1962.

ANSELM, *Proslogium, Monologium; An Appendix in Behalf of the Fool, Gaunilon; and Cur Deus Homo.* Trans. by S.N. Deane. LaSalle (Ill.), 1951.

Ante-Nicene Church Fathers (10 vols.). Ed. by A. Roberts & J. Donaldson. Grand Rapids, 1951- .

AQUINAS, T., *The Basic Works* (2 vols.). Trans. by A.C. Pegis. New York, 1945.

——--, *Compendium of Theology.* Trans. by C. Vollert. St Louis, 1948.

——--, *On Kingship to the King of Cyprus.* Trans. by G.B. Phelan. Toronto, 1949.

——--, The *Summa Theologiae* (vol. 6). The Blackfriars edition. London, 1965.

ARISTOTLE, *The Basic Works.* Ed. by R. McKeon. New York, 1941.

AUGUSTINE, *The City of God.* Trans. by M. Dods. New York, 1950.

——--, *The Confessions.* Trans. by E.B. Pusey. New York, 1949.

——--, *The Rule: Masculine and Feminine.* Ed. by C. Van Bavel. Trans. by R. Canning. Kalamazoo, 1961.

BAADER, F. VON, *Saemtliche Werke* (15 bds.). hrgs. vo. F. Hoffmann & J. Hamburger. Aalen, 1963.

BAINTON, P.H., ED., *The Age of the Reformation.* New York, 1956.

BETTENSON, H., ED., *Documents of the Christian Church.* New York, 1947.

BIRKBECK, W.J., ED., *Russia and the English Church during the Last Fifty Years* (vol. 1): *Correspondence Between Mr W. Palmer & Mr Khomyakov.* London, 1895.

BLAKNEY, R.B., TRANS. *Meister Eckhart.* New York, 1941.

BOEHME, J., *The Aurora.* Trans. by J. Sparrow. London, 1961.

——--, *On the Incarnation of Jesus Christ.* Trans. by J.R. Earle. London, 1934.

——--, *Six Theosophic Points and Other Writings.* Trans. by J.R. Earle. Ann Arbor, 1970.

——--, *The Signature of All Things and Other Writings.* Trans. by W. Law. New York, n.d.

BONAVENTURE, *Breviloquium.* Trans. by E.E. Nemmers. St Louis, 1946.

CALVIN, J., *Institutes of the Christian Religion* (2 vols.). Trans. by F. L. Battles. ed. by J.T. McNeil. Philadelphia, 1960.

CASSIRER, E., ETC., ED., *The Renaissance Philosophy of Man.* Chicago, 1948

DUNS SCOTUS, *Opera Omnia* (26 vols.). Ed. by L. Wadding.Paris, 1891-1895.

EUSEBIUS, *Ecclesiastical History.* Trans. S.E. Parker, Grand Rapids, 1962.

Fathers of the Church (85 vols.). Ed. by P. Halton, etc. Washington, DC, 1946.

FEUERBACH, L, *The Essence of Christianity.* Trans. by G. Eliot. New York, 1957.

HAPGOOD, I.F., TRANS., *Service Book of the Orthodox Church.* Englewood (NJ), 1975.

HEGEL, G., *Early Theological Writings.* Trans. by T.M. Knox. Chicago, 1948.

————-, *The Philosophy of Hegel.* Trans. & ed. by C. J. Friedrich. 1953.

HOBBES, T., *The Leviathan.* Ed. by M. Oakeshott. Oxford, 1955.

JAMES OF VITERBO, *De regimine Christiano.* Ed. by H.-X Arguilliere. Paris, 1926.

JOHN OF THE CROSS, *The Collected Works.* Trans. by K. Kavanaugh & O. Rodriguez. Washington, DC, 1979.

JOHN OF PARIS, *De Potestate et Papali.* Ed. By J. Leclercq. Paris, 1942.

JOHANNES TEUTONICUS, *Glossa Ordinaria.* Ed. by B. Brixiensis. Paris, 1601.

KANT, I., *Kritik der Reinen Vernunft.* Leipzig, 1920 (*zweiten auflage*).

KHOMIAKOV, A.S., *The Church Is One.* Trans. by G. Grabbe. Seattle, 1979.

LOCKE, J., *Two Treatise of Government.* Ed. by P. Laslett. Cambridge, 1967.

LUTHER, M., *Commentary on the Romans.* Trans. by J. Owen. Grand Rapids, 1948.

————-, *Werke* (64 bds.). Ed. by J.K.F. Knaake, etc., Weimar, 1883-1985.

————-, *Luther's Works* (56 vols.). Ed. by J. Pelikan. St Louis, 1958-1986.

MANGO, C., ED., *The Art of the Byzantine Empire, 312-1453: Sources and Documents.* Englewood Cliffs (NJ), 1972.

MANSI, J.D., *Sacrorum Conciliorum: nova et amplissima* (53 vols.). Paris, 1901-1927.

MARSILIUS OF PADUA, *Defensor Pacis.* Ed. by C.W. Previte-Orton. Cambridge, 1928.

————-, *The Defender of the Peace* (2 vols.). Introduction and trans. by A. Gewirth. New York, 1956.

MCLAUGHLIN, ED., *Summa Parisiensis on the Decretum Gratiane.* Toronto, 1952.

MIGNE, J.P., ED., *Patrologiae Curcus Completus: Series Graecae* (162 vols.); and *Series Latinae* (217 vols.). Paris, 1857-1890.

NASSAR, S., TRANS., *Divine Prayers and Services of the Catholic Orthodox Church of Christ: Octoechos, Menaion, Triodion, Pentecostarion.* New York, 1961.

NEWMAN, J.H., *Apologia Pro Vita Sua.* Garden City (NY), 1956.

———-, *An Essay on the Development of Christian Doctrine.* Ed. by J.M. Cameron. Hammondsworth, 1973.

———-, *Discussions and Arguments.* London, 1972.

Nicean and Post-Nicean Church Fathers (14 vols.). Ed. by P. Schaff & H. Wace. Grand Rapids, 1989-1991.

PALMER, W., *Notes of a Visit to the Russian Church.* Selected and Arranged by Cardinal Newman. London, 1882.

PATELOS, C., ED., *The Orthodox Church and the Ecumenical Movement.* Geneva, 1978.

PAUL VI (POPE), *De Ecclesia* (21 Nov 1964). Trans. by the National Catholic Welfare Conference. Washington, DC, 1964.

Pedalion: All the Sacred and Divine Canons of the Holy Catholic and Apostolic Church. Collected by Hieromonk Agapius and Monk Nicodemus. Trans. by D. Cummings. Chicago, 1957.

Philokalia (4 vols.). Trans. by G.E.H. Palmer, etc. London, 1979-1995.

PLATO, *Works.* Ed. by E. Hamilton & H. Cairns. Princeton, 1973.

POPOVICH, J., *Orthodox Faith and Life in Christ.* Trans. by A. Gerosterigos, etc. Belmont (Mass.), 1994.

———-, *Études de théologie orthodoxe.* Trad. par A. Jetvic. Athens, 1974.

ROUSSEAU, J-J., *Emile or On Education.* Trans. by A. Bloom. New York, 1979.

ANTHONY (KHRAPOVITSKY), *The Dogma of Redemption.* Trans. by Holy Transfiguration Monastery. Montreal, 1979.

———-, "The First Ecumenical Council," *Orthodox Life* XXXIV, 6 (1984), 9-14.

———-, "The Moral Aspect of the Dogma of the Church" (trans. by V. Novakshanoff), in *Synaxis: Orthodox Theology in the Twentieth Century* 2 (1976), 7-24.

ST BASIL, *Letters* (4 vols.). Greek text. Trans. by R.J. Deferrari. London, 1938 (Loeb Classics).

ST BEDE THE VENERABLE, *A History of the English Church and People.* Trans. by L. Shirley-Price. Hammondworth, 1986.

ST BENEDICT, *The Rule.* Ed by T. Fry. Collegeville (Minn.), 1981.

ST CYRIL OF ALEXANDRIA, *Selected Letters.* Greek text. Ed. and trans. L.R. Wickham. Oxford, 1983.

ST CYRIL OF JERUSALEM, *Lectures on the Christian Sacraments: the Procatechesis and the Five Mystagogical Catechesis.* Greek text. Ed. by F.L. Cross. London, 1951.

ST GREGORY PALAMAS, "A Homily of Our Supremely Pure Lady Theotokos and Ever-Virgin Mary" (trans. by Holy Transfiguration Monastery), in *Orthodox Life* XXXII, 4 (1982), 4-8.

———, *The Triads*. Trans. by N. Gendle. New York, 1983.

ST DIONYSIUS THE AREOPAGITE, *The Complete Works*. Trans. by C. Luibheid. New York, 1987.

ST HILARION (TROITSKY), *Christianity or the Church*. Trans. by L. Puhalo & V. Navok-shonoff. Jordanville (NY), 1971.

———, *The Unity of the Church and the World Conference of Christian Communities*. Trans. by M. Jerinec. Montreal, 1975.

ST HIPPOLYTUS OF ROME, *The Apostolic Tradition*. Trans. & ed. by G. Dix & H. Chadwick. London, 1992.

ST ISAAC THE SYRIAN., *The Ascetical Homilies*. Trans. by Holy Transfiguration Monastery. Boston, 1984.

ST JOHN CLIMACUS, *The Ladder of Divine Ascent*. Trans. by L. Moore. Boston, 1979.

ST MACARIUS THE GREAT, *Spiritual Homilies*. Trans. by A.J. Mason. Willits (Cal.), 1974.

ST MAXIMUS THE CONFESSOR, *Selected Writings*. Trans. by G.C. Berthold. New York, 1985.

ST PHOTIUS THE GREAT, *Homilies*. Trans. by C. Mango. Cambridge (Mass.), 1958.

———, *On the Mystagogy of the Holy Spirit*. Studion Publishers, New York, 1983, with Greek text. Trans. by Holy Transfiguration Monastery.

ST SERAPHIM OF SAROV, *A Conversation with N.A. Motovilov*. Jordanville (NY), 1962.

Septuagint, with the Apocrypha: Greek and English. Ed. and trans. by L.C.L. Brenton. Grand Rapids, 1980.

SCHAPIRO, H., ED., *Medieval Philosophy: Selected Readings from Augustine to Burdian*. New York, 1964.

SOLOVIEV, V., *Deutsche Gesamtaussgabe* (bd. 6). *hrgs. v.* Szyklarki & L. Mueller. Freiburg im Breslau, 1965.

Sources Chrétien. Ed. by J. Danielou. Paris, 1940- .

TANNER, N.P., ED., *The Ecumenical Councils* (vol. 2): *The Council of Trent*. London, 1990.

TERESA OF AVILA, *The Collected Works* (vol.1). Trans. by K. Kavanaugh & O Rodriguez. Washington, DC, 1976.

The Patriarchal Encyclical of 1920: UNTO ALL THE CHURCHES OF CHRIST WHERESO EVER THEY MAY BE. Translated in *The Greek Orthodox Theological Review* I, 1 (1954), 7-9.

The Reply of the Orthodox Church to Roman Catholic Overtures: Being the Answer of the Great Church of Constantinople to a Papal Encyclical on Reunion (1896). Published by the Orthodox Christian Movement of St John the Baptist. New York, 1958.

B   SECONDARY SOURCES:
1   BOOKS

ABELSON, J., *Immanence of God in Rabbinical Literature*. London, 1912.

ADAMS, H., *Mont-Saint-Michel and Chartres*. New York, 1959.

ALLEN, J.J., *The Inner Way: Eastern Christian Spiritual Direction*. Grand Rapids, 1994.

ANDERSON, H., ED., *Justification by Faith: Lutherans and Catholics in Dialogue VII*. Minneaplolis, 1985.

ANDROUTSOS, C., *The Great Hereafter*. Trans. by W.E.T. Roberts. Cleveland, 1956.

———-, *The Basis of the Union of the churches according to the Recent Pronouncements of the Orthodox Churches*. Constantinople, 1905.

ALEXANDER, P., *The Byzantine Apostolic Tradition*. Berkeley, 1985.

———-, *The Patriarch Nicephorus of Constantinople: Ecclesiastical Policy and Image Worship in the Byzantine Empire*. Oxford, 1958.

ARMSTRONG, A.H., ED., *The Cambridge History of Later Greek and Medieval Philosophy*. Cambridge (Eng.), 1967.

AULEN, G., *Christus Victor: An Historical Study of the Three Main Types of the Idea of the Atonement*. Trans. by A.G. Herbert. New York, 1956.

———-, *Reformation and Catholicity*. Trans. by E.H. Walstrom. Philadelphia, 1961.

AZKOUL, M., *St Gregory of Nyssa and the Tradition of the Fathers*. Lewiston, 1995.

———-, *The Influence of Augustine of Hippo on the Orthodox Church*. Lewiston, 1990.

BAKER, D., ED., *The Orthodox Churches and the West: Papers Read at the Fourteenth Summer Meeting and the Fifteenth Winter Meeting of the Ecclesiastical History Society*. Oxford, 1976.

BALSHAKOFF, S., *The Doctrine of the Unity of the Church in the Works of Khomyakov and Moehler*. London, 1946.

BARRACLOUGH, G., *The Medieval Papacy*. New York, 1968.

BARRY, F.R., *The Atonement*. New York, 1968.

BARTH, K., *Dogmatik* (bd. 1). Zurich, 1947.

———-, *Dogmatik in Grundriss*. Stuttgart, 1947.

BAUR, F.C., *On the Writing of Church History*. Ed. & trans. by P.C. Hodgson, New York, 1968.

BAYNES, N.H. & MOSS, H. ST. L.B., *Byzantium: An Introduction to East Roman Civilization*. Oxford, 1962.

BELTING, H., *Likeness and Presence: A History of the Image Before the Era of Art*. Trans. by E. Jephcott. Chicago, 1994.

BENZ, E., *Ecclesia Spiritualis: Kirchenidee und Geschichtestheologie dere Franziskanischen Reformation*. Stuttgart, 1946.

———-, *Evolution and Christian Hope: Man's Concept of the Future from the Early Fathers to Teilhard de Chardin*. Trans. by H.G. Frank. New York, 1966.

BERDYAEV, N., *Dream and Reality: An Essay in Autobiography*. Trans. by K. Lampert. New York, 1950.

———-, *The Divine and the Human*. Trans. by R.M. French. London, 1949.

———-, *The Meaning of History*. Trans. by G. Reavy. London, 1949.

———-, *The Origin of Russian Communism*. Trans. by R.M. French. London, 1948.

———-, *The Russian Idea*. New York, 1947.

BERMAN,H.J., *Law and Revolution: The Formation of the Western Legal Tradition*. Cambridge (Mass.), 1983.

BILLINGTON, J.H., *The Icon and the Axe: An Interpretive History of Russian Culture*. New York, 1966.

BLANE, A., ED., *Georges Florovsky: Russian Intellectual and Orthodox Churchman*. Crestwood (NY), 1993.

BOGOLEPOV, A., *Canon Law in the Early Church*. New York, 1957.

BORNKAMP, *Luther's World of Thought*. Trans. by H.M. Bertram. St Louis, 1958.

BOUYER, L., *A History of Christian Spirituality* (2 vols.). Trans. by M.P. Ryan. Notre Dame, 1958.

———-, *The Spirit and Forms of Protestantism*. Trans. by A.V. Littledale. Westminster (Md.), 1957.

BRINTON, H.H., *The Mystic Will: Based on a Study of the Philosophy of Jacob Boehme*. New York, 1930.

BROCK, S., *The Luminous Eye: The Spiritual World Vision of St Ephraim*. Kalamazoo, 1992.

BRONOWSKI, J. & MAZLISH, B., *The Western Intellectual Tradition: From Leonardo to Hegel*. New York, 1960.

BROSCHE, F., *Luther On Predestination: The antinomy and the Unity Between Love and Wrath in Luther's Concept of God*. Uppsala, 1978.

BRUNNER, E., *Reason and Revelation: The Christian Doctrine of Faith and Knowledge*. Trans. by O. Wyon. Philadelphia, 1946.

BULGAKOV, S., *Karl Marx as A Religious Type: His Relation to the Religious Anthropotheism of L. Feuerbach*. Trans. by L. Barna. Belmont (Mass.), 1979.

———-, *Die Tragoedie der Philosophie. ueber*. V.A. Kresling. Darmstadt, 1927.

———-, *The Vatican Dogma*. South Canaan (Pa), 1959.

BURY, J.B., *The Idea of Progress*. New York, 1932.

CAMILLE, M., *Gothic Art: Glorious Visions*. New York, 1996.

CAMUS, A., *The Rebel*. Trans. by A. Bower. New York, 1956.

CARLYLE, R.W. & CARLYLE, A.J., *A History of Medieval Political Theory in the West* (vol. 1): *The Second Century to the Ninth*. Edinburgh, 1930.

CARRAS, P., *On Eternity*. Toronto (Can.). n.d.

CASEL, O., *The Mystery of Christian Worship and other Writings*. Ed. by B. Neunheuser, London, 162.

CAVARNOS, C., *Byzantine Thought and Art*. Belmont (MA), 1968.

———, *The Hellenic-Christian Philosophical Tradition*. Belmont (MA), 1989.

CHADWICK, O., *John Cassian*. Cambridge (Eng.), 1968.

CHADWICK, H., *Augustine*. Oxford, 1986.

CHEMNITZ, M., *Examination of the Council of Trent* (pt. 1). Trans. by F. Kramer. St Louis, 1971.

CHENU, M-D, *Nature, Man and Society in the Twelfth Century*. Trans. by J. Taylor & L.K. Little. Chicago, 1968.

CHERNIAVSKY, M., ED., *The Structure of Russian History: Interpretive Essays*. New York, 1970.

CHRISTENSEN, I.O., *The History of Western Art*. New York, 1959.

CIZEVSKY, D., *Aus Zwei Welten: Beitrage zum Geschichte der Slavisch-Westlichen Literatischen Beziehungen. hrsg.* C.H. van Schoonveld. The Hague, 1956.

CLIFFORD, A.C., *Atonement and Justification: English Evangelical Theology, 1640-1790: An Evaluation*. Oxford, 1990.

COCHRANE, C.N., *Christianity and Classical Culture: A Study of Thought and Actions from Augustus to Augustine*. New York, 1957.

COHN, N., *The Pursuit of the Millennium*. New York, 1970.

COLLINGWOOD, R.G., *The Idea of History*. New York, 1956.

CONGAR, M.J., *Chretiens Desunis*. Paris, 1937.

CONGAR, Y., *Vraie et fausse reforme dans l'Église*. Paris, 1950.

COPELSTON, F., *A History of Philosophy* (8 vols.). Garden City (NY). 1962-1966.

COULTON, G.G., *Art and the Reformation*. Oxford, 1928.

COX, H., *The Secular City: Secularization and Urbanization in Theological Perspective*. New York, 1966.

CULLMANN, O., *La Tradition: Problème exégétique, historique et théologique*. Paris, 1953.

CURTIS, G., *Paul Couturier and Unity in Christ*. Westminster (Md.), 1946.

D'ARCY, M.C., ED., *St Augustine: His Age, Life and Thought*. New York, 1957.

DANIELOU, J. (CARDINAL), *The Bible and the Liturgy*. Notre Dame, 1956.

———, *From Shadow to Reality: Studies in the Biblical Typology of the Fathers*. Trans. by W. Hibberd. London, 1960.

———, *The Lord of History: Reflections on the Inner Meaning of History*. Trans. by N. Abercombie. London, 1958.

DAVIE, J.G., *The Spirit of the Church and the Sacraments*. London, 1954.

DEGYANSKY, D. (FR.), *Orthodox Christianity and the Spirit of Contemporary Ecumenism*. Etna (Cal.), 1992.

D'HERBIGNY, M. & DEUBNER, A., *Évêques Russes en Exil: Douze ans D'épreuves* (1918-1930), *Orientalia Christiana* XXI, 67 (1931).

DELUBAC, H., *The Splendour of the Church*. Trans. by M. Mason. New York, 1956.

DEMAISTRE, J., *The Pope*. Trans. by A. McD. Dawson. New York, 1957.

D'ENTREVES, A.P., *The Medieval Contribution to Political Thought: Thomas Aquinas, Marsilius of Padua, Richard Hooker*. Oxford, 1959.

DILLSTONE, F.W., ED., *Scripture and Tradition in the Early Church*. Greenwich, 1955.

DOELLINGER, I. ("JANUS"), *Papst und das Concil*. Leipzig, 1869.

————, *Lectures on the Renunion of the Churches*. Trans. by H.N. Oxenham. New York, 1972.

DUCKETT, E.S., *The Gateway to the Middle Ages: Monasticism*. Ann Arbor, 1961.

DVORAK, M., *Idealism and Naturalism in Gothic Art*. Trans. by R.J. Klawiter. Notre Dame (Ind.), 1967.

DVORNIK, F., *The Idea of Apostolicity in Byzantium and the Legend of the Apostle Andrew*. Cambridge (MA), 1959.

DYOBOUNIOTES, K., *The Mysteries of the Eastern Orthodox Church from a Dogmatic Point of View*. Athens, 1912 (in Greek).

EMPIE, P.C. & MCCORD, J.I., ED., *A Reexamination of Luther and the Reformed Traditions* III. New York, 1965.

ENGELS, F., *Principles of the Philosophy of the Future*. Trans. by M.H. Vogel. New York, 1966.

EPHRAIM (METROPOLITAN), ED., *The Struggle Against Ecumenism*. Boston, 1998.

FAIRWEATHER, E.R., ED., *The Oxford Movement*. New York, 1964.

FERGUSON, E., ED. *Encyclopedia of Early Christianity*. New York, 1990.

FESTUGIERE, A.J., *Contemplation et vie selon Platon*. Paris, 1957.

————, *L'Enfant d'Agrigente*. Paris, 1941.

FLOROVSKY, G., *Collected Works: Bible, Church, Tradition: An Eastern Orthodox View* (3 vols.). Trans. by R.L. Nicholas, Belmont (Mass.), 1972.

————, *Ways of Russian Theology* (vol. 5, pt.). Trans. by R.L. Nichols. Belmont (Mass.), 1979.

FRANK, E., *Philosophical Understanding and Religious Truth*. New York, 1956.

FRAZEE, C.A., *The Orthodox Church and Independent Greece, 1821-1852*. Cambridge (Eng.), 1969.

GALAVARIS, C., *The Icon in the Life of the Church*. Leiden, 1981.

GARRIGOU-LAGRANGE, P., *Predestination*. Trans. by B. Rose. St Louis, 1953.

GAVIN, F., *Some Aspects of Contemporary Greek Orthodox Thought*. Milwaukee, 1936.

GIAKALIS, A., *Images of the Divine: The Theology of the Icons at the Seventh Ecumenical Council*. New York, 1994.

GIERKE, O., *Political Theories of the Middle Age*. Trans. with Intro by F.W. Maitland. Cambridge, 1927.

GIET, S., *Les idées et l'action sociales de saint Basile le Grand*. Paris, 1955.

GILSON, E., *Reason and Revelation in the Middle Ages*. New York, 1938.

———-, *The Elements of Christian Philosophy*. New York, 1960.

———-, *The Spirit of Medieval Philosophy*. Trans. by A.H.C. Downes. New York, 1940.

GRABAR, A., *Christian Iconography: A Study of Its Origin*. Princeton, 1968.

GRAEF, H., *The Devotion to Our Lady*. New York, 1963.

GRANFIELD, P., *The Papacy in Transition*. Garden City (NY), 1980.

GRATIEUX, A., *A.S. Khomiakov et le Mouvement Slavophile* (vol. 1). Paris, 1939.

GRILLMEIER, A., *Christ in the Christian Tradition*. Trans. by J.S. Bowden. New York, 1965.

GRILLMEIER, A. & BACHT, H., *Das Konzil von Chalkedon: Geschichte und Gegenwart (bd. 3)*. Wuerzburg, 1961.

GUETTE, V., *The Papacy*. Trans. by A.C. Coxe. n.d.

HALLER, J., *Das Papsttum* (bd. 2). Basel, 1953.

HAMPE, K., *Deutsche Kaisergeschichte in der Zeit Salier und Staufer*. Leipzig, 1912.

———-, *Feudal Society*. Trans. by L.A. Manyon. London, 1961.

HANSON, R.P.C., *Tradition in the Early Church*. London, 1962.

HARE, A., *Pioneers of Russian Social Thought*. London, 1956.

HARNACK, A. VON, *History of Dogma* (vol. 1). Trans. by J. Millar. London, 1905.

———-, *Lehrbuch der Dogmengeschichte (bds. 1-2)*. Leipzig, 1910.

HAZARD, P., *La crise de la conscience, 1680-1715*. Paris, 1962.

HEADLEY, J.M., *Luther's View of Church History*. New Haven, 1963.

HEER, F., *The Intellectual History of Europe*. Trans. by J. Steinberg. Cleveland, 1966.

———-, *The Medieval World*. Trans. by J. Sondheimer. New York, 1961.

HEFELE, C.J., *A History of the Councils of the Church*. Trans. by W.R. Clark. Edinburgh, 1883-1896.

HENRY, P., ED., *Schools of Thought*. Philadelphia, 1984.

HERON, A.I.C., *A Century of Protestant Theology*. Philadelphia, 1980.

HEUSSI, K., *Der Ursprung des Moenchtums*. Tuebingen, 1936.

HICKS, J. & McGILL, A.C., ED., *The Many-Faced Argument: Recent Studies on the Ontological Argument for the Existence of God*. New York, 1967.

HOPKINS, J. & RICHARDSON, H., ED., *St Anselm and His Critics: A Reinterpretation of the Cur Deus Homo*. Edinburgh, 1954.

HUBBEN, W., *Dostoyevsky, Kierkegaard, Nietzsche, and Kafka: Four Prophets of our Destiny*. New York, 1968.

HUIZINGA, J., *The Autumn of the Middle Ages*. Trans. by R.J. Payton & U. Mammitzsch. Chicago, 1996.

HUSSEY, J., *Church and Learning in the Byzantine Empire*. London, 1963.

JALLAND, T.G., *The Life and Times of St Leo the Great*. New York, 1941.

JONES, C., ETC., ED., *The Study of Spirituality*. Oxford, 1986.

KALOMIROS, A., *Against False Union*. Trans. by G. Gabriel. Boston, 1967.

KANTORWICZ, E.H., *Frederick the Second, 1194-1250*. Trans. by E.O. Lorimer. New York, 1957.

——-, *The King's Two Bodies: A Study in Medieval Political Theology*. Princeton, 1957.

KEE, A., *The Way of Transcendence: The Christian Faith without Belief in God*. Hammondsworth, 1971.

KNOWLES, D., *The Evolution of Medieval Thought*. New York, 1962.

KOCH, H., *Quellen zur Geschichtes der Ascese und des Moenchtums in der alten Kirche*. Tuebingen, 1931.

KONTOGLOU, P., The Expression of Orthodox Iconography (vol. 1). Athens, 1979 (in Greek).

KOYRÉ, A., *L'ideé de Dieu dans la Philosophie de S. anselme*. Paris, 1923.

——-, *La Philosophie de Jacob Boehme*. Paris, 1968.

——-, *La Philosophie et la Problème National en Russie au début du XIX siècle*. Paris, 1929.

KRAMER, F., TRANS., *Examination of the Council of Trent*. St Louis, 1971.

KRIVOSHEINE, B., *The Ascetical and Theological Teaching of Gregory Palamas*. London, 1938 (Reprint from *The Eastern Churches* Quarterly, 4).

KUENG, H., & KASPER, W. ED., *The Plurality of Ministries*. New York, 1972.

——-, *Christianity: Essence, History and Future*. New York, 1995.

KURGANSKY, T. (HIEROMONK), *Sacraments or Holy Mysteries? The Orthodox Christian Doctrine of the Holy Mysteries and Divine Grace*. Dewdney (BC), n.d.

LADNER, G., *The Idea of Reform: Its Impact in the Age of the Fathers*. Cambridge (Mass.), 1959.

LAGE, D., *Martin Luther's Ethics and Christology*. Lewiston (NY), 1990.

LAMPING, A.J., *Ulrichus Velenus and His Treatise Against the Papacy*. Leiden, 1976.

LAISTNER, M.L.W., *Thought and Letters in Western Europe: A.D. 500-900*. Ithaca (NY), 1976.

LAMPRYLLOS, C., *La Mystification fatale: Étude Orthodoxe sur le Filioque*. Lausanne, 1987.

LANGEN, J., *Das Vatikanische Dogma von dem Universal-Episcopal und deer Unfehlbarkeit des Papstes (bd. 3)*. Bonn, 1873.

LAWLESS, G., *Augustine of Hippo and the Monastic Rule*. Oxford, 1987.

LENGSFELD, A., *Adam und Christus*. Essen, 1965.

LEROUX, D., *Peter, Lovest Thou Me? John Paul II: Pope of Tradition or Pope of Revolution*. Gladysdale, Victory (Aus.), 1990.

LOEWITH, K., *From Hegel to Nietzsche: The Revolution in Nineteenth Century Thought*. Trans. by D. E. Green. London, 1965.

––––, *Meaning in History*. Chicago, 1949.

LONEGRAN, B.J.F., *Grace and Freedom: Operative Grace in the Thought of Thomas Aquinas*. New York, 1971.

LOSSKY, V., *In the Image and Likeness of God*. Ed. by J.H. Erickson & T.E. Bird. New York, 1974.

––––, *The Mystical Theology of the Eastern Church*. Trans. by Fellowship of St Alban & St Sergius Fellowship. London, 1957.

––––, *The Vision of God*. Trans. by A. Moorhouse. Clayton (Wis.), 1963.

LOT-BORODINE, M., *Le Deification de l'homme*. Paris, 1970.

LOUTH, A., *Discerning the Mystery: An Essay on the Nature of Theology*. Oxford, 1983.

LYONNET, S. SABOURIN, L., *Sin, Redemption and Sacrifice: A Biblical And Patristic Study*. Rome, 1970.

MALONEY, G.A., *A History of Orthodox Theology Since 1453*. Belmont (MA), 1976.

MANUEL, F.E., *Shapes of Philosophical History*. Stanford (Cal.), 1965.

MANNING, H.E., *The Oecumenical Council and the Infallibility of the Roman Pontiff*. London,1869.

MARKUS, R.A., *Augustine: A Collection of Critical Essays*. Garden City, New York, 1972.

MARGERIE, B., *The Christian Trinity in History*. Trans. by E.J. Fortman. Hill River (MA), 1982.

MARITAIN, J., *Three Reformers: Luther-Descartes-Rousseau*. London, 1950.

MASARYK, G., *Die Philosophischen und Sociologische Grundlage des Marxismus*. Vienna, 1889.

MAZOUR, A., *The First Russian Revolution, 1825: The Decembrist Movement, Its Origin, Development and Significance*. Berkeley (Cal.), 1937.

McGINN, B., *The Foundations of Mysticism (vol. 1): The Presence of God*. New York, 1991.

––––, *The Calabrian Abbot: Joachim of Fiore in Western Thought*. New York, 1985.

McGRATH, A.E., *Justitia Dei: A History of the Christian Doctrine of Justification* (2 vols.). Cambridge (Eng.), 1986.

McINTIRE, C.T., ED., *God, History and Historians: Modern Christian Views of History*. New York, 1977.

McINTYRE, J., *St Anselm and His Critics: A Reinterpretation of the* Cur Deus Homo. Edinburg, 1954.

McNEILL, J.T., *The History and Character of Calvinism*. New York, 1954.

MELAND, P.E., *The Secularization of Modern Culture*. New York, 1960.

MERSCH, E., *The Whole Christ: The Historical Development of the Doctrine of the Mystical Body in Scripture and Tradition*. Trans. by J.R. Kelly. London, 1956.

METALLINOS, G. D., *I Confess One Baptism. . . Interpretation and Application of Canon VII of the Second Ecumenical Council by the Kollyvades and Constantine Oikonomos*. Trans. by Priestmonk Seraphim. St Paul's Monastery (Holy Mountain), 1994.

Meyendorff, J., *Introduction to the Study of Gregory Palamas*. Trans. by T. Lawrence. New York, 1963.

------, & McLelland, J., ed., *The New Man: An Orthodox and Reformed Dialogue*. New Brunswick (NJ), 1973.

Meyer, H., *The Philosophy of Thomas Aquinas*. Trans. by F. Eickhoff. St Louis, 1944.

Meyer, R.W., *Leibnitz and the Seventeenth Century Revolution*. Trans. by J. P. Stern. Cambridge (Eng.), 1952.

Misner, P., *Papacy and Development*. Leiden, 1976.

Moss., C.B., *The Christian Faith: An Introduction to Dogmatic Theology*. London, 1954.

Moss, H. St. L.B., *The Birth of the Middle Ages, 395-814*. New York, 1964.

Murray, R.H., *The Political Consequences of the Reformation: Studies in Sixteenth Century Political Thought*. Boston, 1926.

Niehbuhr, R., *The Nature and Destiny of Man: A Christian Interpretation*. New York, 1943.

Norris, R.A., *Manhood and Christ: A Study in the Christology of Theodore of Mopsuestia*. Oxford, 1963.

Oberman, H. O., *The Harvest of Mediaeval Theology: Gabriel Biel and Late Medieval Nominalism*. Cambridge (Mass.), 1963.

O'Connor, E.D., *The Dogma of the Immaculate Conception*. Notre Dame, 1958.

Ohnsorge, W., *Konstantinopel und der Okzident: Gesammelte Aufsaetze zur Geschichte der Byzantinisch-Abendlaendischen Beziehungen und des Kaisertums*. Darmstadt, 1966.

Oulton, J.E.L., *The Mystery of the Cross*. Greenwich (Conn.), 1957.

Ouspensky, L., *Theology of the Icon*. Crestwood, 1987.

------, & Lossky, V., *The Meaning of Icons*. Trans. by G.E.H. Palmer & E. Kadloubovsky. Crestwwod (NY), 1989.

Ostroumoff, I.N., *The History of the Council of Florence*. Trans. by B. Popov. Boston, 1971.

Pegis, A. ed., *A Gilson Reader: Selected Writings of Etienne Gilson*. Garden City (NY). 1957.

Pelikan, J., *Christianity and Classical Culture; The Metamorphosis of Natural Theology in the Christ Encounter with Hellenism* (The Gifford Lectures, 1992-1993). New Haven, 1993.

------, *Jesus Through the centuries: His Place in History and Culture*. New Haven, 1985.

------, *Mary Through the Centuries: Her Place in History and Culture*. New Haven, 1996.

------, *The Christian Tradition: A History of the Development of Doctrine* (4 vols.). 1971-1989.

PESCH, O.H., *The God Question in Thomas Aquinas and Martin Luther*. Philadelphia, 1972.

PETERSON, E., *Der Monotheismus als politischen Problem: Breitrag zur Geschichte der poli tischen Theologie im Imperium*. Leibzig, 1935.

PHILARET (Voznesensky), Metropolitan, *A Second Sorrowful Epistle to Their Holinesses and Their Beatitutes, the Primates of the Holy Orthodox Churches, the Most Reverend Metropolitans, Archbishops and Bishops*. The Synod of Bishops of the Russian Orthodox Church Outside of Russia. New York, 1972.

PIEPER, J., *Scholasticism: Personalities and Problems of Medieval Philosophy*. Trans. by R & C. Winston.New York, 1960.

PLACHER, W.C., *The Domestication of Transcendence*. Louisville, 1996.

POHLE, J. & PREUSS, A., *Christology: A Dogmatic Treatise on the Incarnation*. St Louis, 1952.

POMAZANSKY, M., *Orthodox Dogmatic Theology: A Concise Exposition*. Trans. by Hiero-monk S. Rose. Platina (Cal.), 1984.

POPOV, I.V., *The Personality and Teaching of Blessed Augustine* (vol. I). Trans. by A. Lisenko. Sergiev Posad, 1916.

PREUSS, E., *The Romanish Doctrine of the Immaculate Conception*. Edinburgh, 1867.

RANSON, P., ED., *Saint Augustine*. Paris, 1973.

RASHDALL, H., *The Idea of Atonement in Christian Theology*. London, 1925.

REUTER, H., *Augustinische Studien*. Aalen, 1967.

RICHARDS, J., *The Popes and the Papacy in the Early Middle Ages: 476-752*. London, 1979.

RITSCHL, A.B., *A Critical History of the Christian Doctrine of Justification and Reconcilia-tion*. Trans. by J.S. Black. Edinburgh, 1872.

------, *Three Essays*. trans. by P. Hefner. Philadelphia, 1972.

ROBINSON, I.S., *Authority and Resistance in the Investiture Contest: The Polemical Litera-ture of the Late Eleventh Century*. New York, 1978.

ROYCE, J., *The Spirit of Modern Philosophy*. New York, 1983.

RUNCIMAN, S., *The Great Church in Captivity*. Cambridge (Eng.), 1968.

RUNZE, A., *Der ontologische Gottesbeweis: Kritische Darstellung seiner Geschichte seit Anselm bis auf die Gegenwart*. Halle, 1882.

SARTORY, T., *Die oekumenische Bewegung und die Einheit der Kirche*. Augsburg, 1955.

SERAPHIM, (METROPOLITAN), *Die Ostkirche*. Stuttgart, 1950.

Schaefer, F., *Dancing Alone: The Quest for Orthodox Faith in the Age of False Religion*. Brookline (MA), 1994.

SCHRAMM, P.E., *Kaiser, Rom und Renovatio*. Darmstadt, 1957.

SCHUTZ, H.J., ED., *Tendenzen der Theologie im 20 Jahrhundret: Ein Geschichte in Portraets*. Stuttgart, 1966.

SIGGINS, I.D.K., *Martin Luther's Doctrine of Christ*. New Haven, 1970.

Smith, B., *The Fraudulent Gospel: Politics and the World Council of Churches*. Richmond (Eng.), 1977.

Southern, R.W., *Saint Anselm: A Portrait in a Lanscape*. Cambridge (Eng.), 1990.

———, *Western Society and the Church in the Middle Ages*. Hamondsworth (Eng.), 1975.

Spector, I., *An Introduction to Russian History and Culture*. New York, 1951.

Spinka, M., ed. & trans., M., *John Hus at the Council of Constance*. New York, 1965.

Stoudt, J.J., *Jacob Boehme: His Life and Thought*. New York, 1968.

Strauss, F.D., *The Life of Jesus Critically Examined*. Trans. by G. Eliot. Philadelphia, 1972.

Strauss, L. & Cropsey, J., *History of Political Philosophy*. Chicago, 1987.

Tavard, G.H., *Two Centuries of Ecumenism: The Search for Unity*. Notre Dame, 1962.

Tellenbach, G., *God, Church, State and Christian Society at the Time of the Investiture Controversy*. Oxford, 1940.

Tierney, B., *Foundations of the Councilor Theory: The Contributions of the Medieval Canonists from Gratian to the Great Schism*. Cambridge (Eng.), 1963.

———, *Origins of Papal Infallibility, 1150-1350: A Study of the Concepts of Infallibility, Sovereignty and Tradition in the Middle Ages*. Leiden, 1972.

Tillich, P., *A History of Christian Thought*. Ed. by C. E. Braaten. New York, 1968.

———, *The Theology of Culture*. New York, 1959.

Todd, J.M., ed., *Problems of Authority: Anglo-French Symposium*. London, 1962.

Tsirpanlis, C.N., *Introduction to Eastern Patristic Thought and Orthodox Theology*. Collegeville (Minn). 1991.

Ullmann, W., *Principles of Government and Politics in the Middle Ages*. New York, 1961.

Underhill, E., *Mysticism: A Study in the Nature and Development of Man's Spiritual Consciousness*. New York, 1955.

Van der Meer, F., *Augustine the Bishop: the Life and Work of a Father*. Trans. by Waltershaw. London, 1961.

Vasiliev, A.A., *History of the Byzantine Empire* (2 vols.). Madison (Wis.), 1964.

Vignaux, P., *Luther: Commentatur des Sentences*. Paris, 1935.

———, *Philosophy in the Middle Ages: An Introduction*. Trans. by E. C. Hall. New York, 1959.

Vischer, L., ed., *A Documentary History of the Faith and Order Movement*. St Louis, 1963.

Ware, T. (Archb.), *Eustratios Argenti*. Oxford, 1946.

———, *The Orthodox Church*. Baltimore, 1964.

WATHEN, A., *Silence: The Meaning of Silence in the Rule of St Benedict*. Washington, DC, 1973.

WATTS., A., *The Way of Zen*. New York, 1957.

WEIGEL, G., *Faustus of Riez*. Philadelphia, 1938.

WHITEHEAD, A.N., *Science and the Modern World*. New York, 1953.

WHITFIELD, J.H., *Machiavelli*. Oxford, 1947.

WIDMERT, G-P., *Gloire au Père, au Fils, au Saint Esprit*. Neuchatel, 1963.

WILKS, M., *The Problems of Sovereignty in the Later Middle Ages*. Cambridge (Eng.), 1963.

WILLIAMS, P.E., *The Moral Philosophy of Peter Abelard*. Lanham (Md.), 1980.

WINTER, M., *Saint Peter and the Popes*. London, 1968.

WOLF, E., *Peregrinatio: Studien zur reformatischen Theologie und kirchen Problem*. Muenchen, 1962.

WOLFSON, H.A., *The Philosophy of the Church Fathers* (vol. 1): *Faith, Trinity, Incarnation*. Cambridge (Mass.), 1956.

WOOD, D., ED., *The Church and Sovereignty, C. 590-1918: Essays in Honor of Michael Wilks*. London, 1991.

WORKMAN, H.B., *The Evolution of the Monastic Ideal*. Boston, 1930.

Yannaras, C., *Elements of Faith: An Introduction to Orthodox Theology*. Trans. by K. Schram. Edinburgh, 1991.

ZENKOVSKY, V.V., *A History of Russian Philosophy* (vol. 2). New York, 1953.

ZERNOV, N., *The Russian Religious Renaissance of the Twentieth Century*. New York, 1963.

2. ARTICLES:

ALTANER, B., "Augustinus und Origenes," in *Historisches Jahrbuch* LXX (1951), 5-41.

AZKOUL, M., "The Greek Fathers: *Polis* and *Paideia*," *St Vladimir's Theological Quarterly* XXIII, 1 (1979), 3-21; and XXIII, 2 (1979), 67-86.

———, "*Sacerdotium et Imperium*: The Constantinian Renovation According to the Greek Fathers," *Theological Studies* XXXII, 3 (1971), 431-464

———, BEBIS, G.S., "The Concept of Tradition in the Fathers of the Church," *The Greek Orthodox Theological Review* XV, 1 (1970), 22-55.

BENZ, E., "*Creator Spiritus*: Die Geistelehre des Joachim von Fiore," in *Eranos Jahrbuch* XXV (1957), 285-355.

BOCKMAN, J., "The Faith: Understanding Orthodox Christianity," by Clark Carlton (Salisbury, Mass., 1997, 286 pages)," *The Struggler* (VII, 3), 1998, 11-14.

BOLSHAKOFF, S., "Patristic Foundations of Khomyakov's Theology," *The Eastern Churches Quarterly* X, 5 (1954), 235-245.

------, "Le Metropolite Antoine de Kiev, President du Synod des Évêques Russes L'Étranger," *Irenikon* 5 (1935-1936), 558-577.

BONNER, G., "Augustine's Conception of Deification," *The Journal of Theological Studies* XXXVIII, 2 (1986), 369-386.

BULGAKOV, S., "Does Orthodoxy Possess an Outward Authority of Infallibility?" (Trans. by R.M. French), *The Christian East* (1926), 10-16.

------, "Vekhi (Signposts): A Collection of Articles on the Russian Intelligentsia (II): Heroism and Asceticism," *Canadian Slavic Studies* II, 4 (1968), 447-463.

CAVARNOS, C., "The Nature and Uses of Reason According to the Greek Orthodox Tradition," *The Greek Orthodox Theological Review* I, 1 (1954), 30-37.

CONSTANTELOS, J., ETC. ED., "The Bristol Consultation: Papers and Discussions" (25-29 July 1967), *The Greek Orthodox Theological Review* XIII, 2 (1968).

CHRYSOSTOMOS (of Etna), "A Tragedy of Orthodox Theology," *The Orthodox Word* XVI, 5 (1980), 237-242.

COTSONIS, J., "The Validity of the Anglican Orders According to the Canon Law of the Orthodox Church," *The Greek Orthodox Theological Review* III, 2 (1957), 182-196.

DOWNEY, G., "From Pagan City to the Christian City," *The Greek Orthodox Theological Review* X, 1 (1964), 121-139.

ENGLES, J., "La doctrine du signe chez Saint Augustine," in *Studia Patristica* IV, 4. Ed. F.L. Cross. Berlin, 1962, 366-373.

ERICKSON, J., "G.O. Metallinos, 'I Confess One Baptism. . .' Interpretation and Applications of Canon VII of the Second Ecumenical Council by the Kollyvades and Constantine Oikonomos'," *St Vladimir's Theological Quarterly* XLI, 1 (1997), 77-81.

FITZER, J., "The Augustinian Roots of Calvin's Eucharistic Thought," *Augustinian Studies* VII (1976), 69-98.

FLOROVSKY, G., "Die Krise des deutschen Idealismus (I): Der Hellenismus des deutschen Idealismus," *Orient und Occident*, heft 11 (1931), 1-8; "Die Krise des Idealismus als die Krise der Reformation" (II), heft 12 (1932), 2-12.

------, "Confessional Loyalty in the Ecumenical Movement," *The Student World* XLIII (1950), 200-205.

------, "Empire and the Desert: Antinomies of Christian History," *The Greek Orthodox Theological Review* III, 2 (1957), 133-159.

------, "Eschatology in the Patristic Age: An Introduction," *The Greek Orthodox Theological Review* II, 1 (1956), 27-40.

------, "Origen, Eusebius and the Iconoclastic Controversy," *Church History* XIX (1950), 68-79.

——--, "Orthodox Ecumenism in the 19th Century," *St Vladimir's Seminary Quarterly* IV, 3-4 (1956), 2-53.

——--, "Patristics and Modern Theology," *Proces-Verbeaux du premier Congress de théologie Orthdoxe* (29 Nov -6 Dec 1936). Ed. by H. Alivizatos, 1939, 238-242.

——--, "St Gregory Palamas and the Tradition of the Fathers," *The Greek Orthodox Theological Review* V, 2 (1960), 119-131.

——--, "The Ascetic Ideal and the New Testament: Reflections on the Critique of the Theology of the Reformation," *The Collected Works of Georges Florovsky* (vol. X): *The Byzantine Ascetical and Spiritual Fathers*. Vaduz, 1987, 17-59.

——--, "The Challenge of Disunity," *St Vladimir's Seminary Quarterly* III, 1-2 (1954-1955), 31-36.

——--, "The Eastern Orthodox Church and the Ecumenical Movement," *Theology Today* VII, 1 (1950), 68-79.

——--, "The Function of Tradition in the Ancient Church," *The Greek Orthodox Theological Review* IX, 2 (1963-1964), 181-200.

FREEMAN, A., "Theodulf of Orleans and the *Libri Carolini*," *Speculum* XXXIII, 4 (1957), 663-705.

FRITSCH-OPPERMANN, S., "Trikaya and Trinity: Reflecting on Some Aspects of Christian-Buddhist Dialogue," *Journal of Ecumenical Studies* XXX, 3-4 (1994), 47-54.

GREER, R.A., The Analogy of Grace in Theodore of Mopsuestia's Christology," *The Journal of Theological Studies* XXXIV, 1 (1983), 1-23.

GRABBE, G.,(Bishop) "The Betrayal of Orthodoxy Through the Calendar," *Orthodox Life* XXXIII, 6 (1983), 34-46.

GULOVICH, S.C., "The Immaculate Conception in the Eastern Churches," *Marian Studies* V (1945), 146-185.

HEIN, L., "Franz von Baader und Seine Liebe zur Russichen Orthodoxen Kirche," *Kyrios* XII, 1-2 (1972), 31-59.

HENRY, P., "The *Adversus Arium* of Marius Victorinus: The First Systematic Exposition of the Trinity," *Journal of Theological Studies* 1 (1950), 42-55.

ISTAVRIDIS, V.T., "Orthodoxy and Anglicanism in the Twentieth Century," *The Greek Orthodox Theological Review* V, 1 (1959), 9-26.

——--, "The Ecumenical Patriarchate," *The Greek Orthodox Theological Review* XIV, 2 (1969), 198-225.

JOHNSON, S., *"Becoming Orthodox."* by Fr. Peter E. Gillquist. Brentwood, Tenn.,1989, 189 pages," *The True Vine* V (1990), 64-76.

JUGIE, M., "Saint Augustine dans la litérataure Théologique de l'Église russe," *Echos d'Orient* XXXIII, 160 (1930), 385-395.

KALOKYRIS, C.O., "The Essence of Orthodox Iconography," *The Greek Orthodox Theological Review* XIII, 1 (1968), 65-102; XVI, 1 (1969), 42-64.

KALOMIROS, A., "The River of Fire," in *St Nectarios Orthodox Conference* (22-25 July 1980), 103-134.

KARMIRIS, J., "The Ecclesiology of the Three Hierarchs" (trans. by C. Cavarnos), *The Greek Orthodox Theological Review* VI, 2 (1960-1961), 135-185.

KESICH, V., "The Problem of Peter's Primacy in the New Testament and the Early Christian Exegesis," *St Vladimir's Seminary Quarterly* IV, 2-3 (1960). 2-25.

KLOGG, R., "The Correspondence of Adhamantios Korais with the British and Foreign Bible Society (1808)," *The Greek Orthodox Theological Review* XIV, 1 (1969), 65-84.

KOENKER, E.B., "Potentiality in God, *Grund* und *Ungrund* in Jacob Boehme," *Philosophy Today* X, 1/4 (1971),44-51.

KOTSONIS, J., "Impressions of Evanston," *St Vladimir's Seminary Quarterly* III, 1-2 (1954-1955), 53-54.

LIMOURIS, G., "The WCC and the Ecumenical Movement: Theological Contribution and Orthodox Witness," *The Greek Orthodox Theological Review* XLIV, 2-3 (1996), 166-177.

LOSSKY, N. O., "The Successors of Vladimir Solovyov," *The Slavonic Review* III, 7 (1924), 92-109.

LOSSKY, V., "The Procession of the Holy Spirit in Orthodox Triadology" (trans. by E. Every), *Eastern Churches Quarterly* VII, 2 (1948 Supplementary Issue), 31-53.

McGUCKIN, J.A., "The Christology of Nestorius of Constantinople," *The Patristic and Byzantine Review* VII, 2-3 (1988), 93-129.

McWILLIAM-DEWART, J., "The Influence of Theodore Mospsuestia on Augustine's Letter 187," *Augustinian Studies* X (1979), 113-136.

MEYENDORFF, J., "Ecclesiastical Organization in the History of Orthodoxy," *St Vladimir's Seminary Quarterly* IV, 1 (1960), 2-22.

———-, "St Peter in Byzantine Theology," *St Vladimir's Seminary Quarterly* IV, 2-3 (1960), 26-48.

———-, "Vatican II and the Orthodox in America: An Interfaith Appraisal," in *International Theological Conference* (University of Notre Dame, 22-26 March 1966). Notre Dame, 1966, 611-612.

PETERSEN, R.L., "Local Ecumenism and the Neo-Patristic Synthesis of Father Georges Florovsky," *The Greek Orthodox Theological Review* XLIV, 2-3 (1196), 217-242.

PHISEW, K., "Our Task in Iconography," trans. by G. Lardas. *Orthodox Life* XXX, 1 (1983), 33-38.

PSOMIADES, H.J., ""The Ecumenical Patriarchate Under the Turkish Republic: the First Ten Years," *The Greek Orthodox Theological Review* VI, 1 (1960), 56-80.

RANSON, P., "*Les Péres etaient-lis patristiques?*" *La Lumiere du Thabor* XXXVIII (1993), 1-8.

———-, "The Filioque: the Vital Orthodox Understanding of the Holy Spirit," *Orthodox Light* VII, 1 (1995), 1-16.

REDMANN, B.J., "One God: Toward a Rapprochement of Orthodox Judaism and Christianity," *Journal of Ecumenical Studies* XXXI, 3-4 (1944), 307-331.

RODZIANKO, V., "Filioque in Patristic Thought," in *Studia Patristica* (vol. II, 2). Ed. by K. Aland & F.L. Cross. Oxford, 1955, 295-308.

ROMANIDES, J., "Highlights in the Debate over Theodore of Mopsuestia and Some Suggestions for a Fresh Approach," *The Greek Orthodox Theological Review* IV, 2 (1959-1960), 140-185.

———-, "Notes on the Palamite Controversy and Related Topics," *The Greek Orthodox Theological Review* VI, 2 (1960-1961), 186-205; IX, 2 (1963-1964), 225-270.

———-, "Original Sin According to St Paul," *St Vladimir's Seminary Quarterly* IV 1-2 (1955-1956), 5-28.

———-, ED., "Aarhus: Unofficial Consultation Between Theologians of the Eastern Orthodox and Oriental Orthodox Churches" (11-15 August 1964), *The Greek Orthodox Theological Review* X, 2 (1964-1965).

SABANEFF, L., "Religious and Mystical Trends in Russia at the Turn of the Century," *Russian Review* XXIV, 4 (1956), 354-368.

SAKKAS, B., "The Calendar Question: the Festal Calendar as a Tradition of the Church," *Orthodox Life* XXII, 2 (1972), 18-34.

SCHAPIRO, L., "The *Vekhi* Group and the Mystique of Revolution," *The Slavonic Review* XXXIV, 8 (1955), 56-77.

SCHEMMANN, A., "The Idea of Primacy in Orthodox Ecclesiology," *St Vladimir's Seminary Quarterly* IV, 2-3 (1960), 49-75.

SCHULTZE, B., "Philosophie, Theologie und Mystik der Ostkirche," *Stimme der Zeit* CXXXVI, 3 (1936), 139-150.

SIOTES, M., "Constantine Oikonomos of the House of Oikonomos and the Operations of the British Bible Society in Greece (1780-1857)," *The Greek Orthodox Theological Review* VI, 1 (1960), 7-55.

TIMIADES, E., "Neglected Factors Influence Unity," *The Greek Orthodox Theological Review* XIV, 2 (1969), 111-137.

WALTON, L, "The Sophianic Lure: A Study in the Sources of Soloyov's Philosophy," *Dublin Review* CCXXXV, 2 (1951), 27-51.

WILLIAMS, G.H., "Fr Georges Florovsky's Vision of Ecumenism," *The Greek Orthodox Theological Review* XLIV, 2-3 (1196), 137-158.

———-, "Georges Vasilievich Florovsky: His American Career 1948-1965)," *The Greek Orthodox Theological Review* XI, 1 (1965), 7-107.

ZANDER, L., "Die Westliche Orthodoxie," in *Theologische Existenz Heute* LXXIII (Muenchen, 1959), 3-30.

————, "The Ecumenical Movement and the Orthodox Church," *The Ecumenical Review* I, 3 (1949), 269-278.

Zernov, N., "The Significance of the Russian Orthodox Diaspora and Its Effect on the Christian West," in *The Orthodox Churches and the West*. Ed. by D. Baker. Oxford, 1976, pp. 315-327.

INDEX

A

Abelard, P.   38, 131, *n.53*; 137*ff.*
Abelson, J.   167, *n.16*
Abgar, King of Edessa   251, *n.71*
Abgrund (*Ungrund*)   107
abscondita ecclesia   152 (*see* Charismatic church 274)
Academy, St. Sergius   271, 273, 301-302
Adam (Eve)   121, 214, 226, *n.26*
   Cain   214
Adams, H.   259
Adelmann of Liege   16
Aeterni Patris 49
Age (Day)   211
   Eighth   212
   History   121, 207*ff* (Ch. 8)
Aiken, H.D.   111, *n.19*
Alcuin of York   36, *n.11*; 52, 57, *n.2*
Alexander I   289
   Holy Alliance   290, *n.50*
Alexander, P.J.   250, *n.71*
Alger of Liege   18
Allen, J.J.   5, *n.1*
Ambrose, Hieromonk   267, *n.9*
anathema   154, 264
Anderson, H.   137, *n.70*
Anglican Orders   284, 288
Anselm of Canterbury   38, 58,102, 131, *n.53*; 150
Anselm of Havelberg   245
Anthimos VI   281
Anthimos VII   282
Anthony (Khrapovitsky) Met.   143 *ff.*; 156, 157, *n.3*; 271,*n.14*; 273, 288, *n.47*; 292, *n.* 55; 293, 298, 300
Antichrist   209
apatheia   242, *n.57*

apophatic theology   307
Apostolic Constitutions 177
Aquinas, T.   8, 39, 53, 102, 138*ff.*, 170, 195, 219, 230
   God   56, 61, *n.13*; 67*ff.*
   original sin   231, 256
   On Kingship: to the King of Cyprus 231, *n.37*
   ontology   256
   Sacraments   16, 176, *n.26*
   "the Greeks"   195, *n.67*
   Tradition   8, 40
Aristotle   8, 85, *n.39;* 213, 227, 231
Arnold, Bishop of Lisieux   171
Athenagoras Kokkinakis   268
Atonement   171
   Anselm of Canterbury   133*ff.*, 142
Augustine of Hippo   13; 36, *n.11*; 37*f.*, 40, 52, 53, 56, 61, *n.13*; 62, *n.16*; 112, 142, *n.78*; 147, *n.88*; 148-9, 158, 170, 219, 248, 273, 291, *n.54*; 307
   City of God   52, *n.7*; 178, *n.30*; 192, 214
   christology   19, 162, *n.8*
   Church   180, 181, *n.34*; 196, 299
   cosmology   252
   deification   135-137; 249, *n.70*
   dualism   8, 19, *n.16*; 224, *n.230*
   filioque   44, *n.25*; 52, 78-90
   freedom   244, *n.61*
   Grace   37, 73-8; 135-137
   history   211, *n.5*; 229, *n.30*
   homoousion   91, *n.43*
   Incarnation   102 *ff.*
   knowledge   63
   Knowledge of God   65 *ff.*, 70, 248
   monergism   19, *n.16*
   One Man   196
   Original Sin   37, 48, 122, 170*ff.*; 226, *n.26*
   Predestination   37, 74, 132, *n.55*; 181, *n.34*

Sacrament 16, 37, 178*ff*, 180, 181, *n*.32
Scripture 292, *n*.56; 295
soul 18, 37; 62, *n*.16
state 233
triadology 52
una persona Ecclesia 196
validity of heretical baptism 274
Augustinus Triumphus 196, *n*.70
Aulen, G. 128, *n*.47; 130, *n*.52; 143, *n*.79; 146, *n*.86; 150, *n*.89
authority 22
Averroes 7
Azkoul, M. 27, *n*.3; 59, *n*.7; 146, *n*.89; 226, *n*.25; 228, *n*.28; 302, *n*.78

Baader, Franz von 289, *n*.49
Bainton, R.H. 182, *n*.34; 260, *n*.89
Baptism (*see* Mysteries)
Barlaam of Calabria 73
Barraclough, G. 261, *n*.91
Barth, K. 59, *n*.8; 80, n.31; 102, 113
Bashier, A. 293, *n*.59
Baur, F.C. 49
Beatific Vision 96, 97, *n*.51, *n*.53; 100
Beaudin, Dom Lambert 264, *n*.2
Bebis, G.S. 13, *n*.7; 26, *n*.2
Belting, H. 248, *n*.59
Benz, E. 248, *n*.67
Berengar of Tours 17
Berdyaev, N. 73, 107, *n*.11; 209, *n*.4; 241, *n*.55; 264, *n*.2; 272, *n*.17; 302, *n*.78
Berman, H.J. 41, 131, *n*.54; 132, *n*.56; 193, *nn*.60, 61; 315, *n*.9
Bernard of Clairvaux 38, 137, *n*.73; 150, 245
Billington, J.H. 229, *n*.29
Birkbeck, W.J. 295, *n*.62
Blaine, A. 270, *n*.12; 274, *n*.19
Blankmore, R.W. 293, *n*.59
Bloch, M. 193, 236 and *n*.46
Boehme, J. 73, 106, *n*.9; 106-111
Bogolepov, A. 226, *n*.25
Bolshakoff, S. 292, *n*.55; 294, *n*.61; 296, *n*.66; 297; *n*.69; 298, *n*.70; 302, *n*.78
Bonaventura of Bagnorea 171, 19
Bonhoffer, D. 237
Bonner, G. 137, *n*.70
Borovy, V. 115, *nn*.29, 30
Bouyer, L. 62, *n*.16; 238, *n*.48; 243, *n*.59;

244, *n*.60
Brinton, J.J. 108, *n*.14
British/English and Foreign Bible Society 279, *nn*.26, 27, 28; 291
Brooke, Z.M. 193, *n*.93
Brunner, E. 42
Bulgakov, S. 73, 113, *n*.25; 189, *n*.49; 201, *n*.76; 202, *n*.77; 203, *n*.78; 204, *n*.81; 264, *n*.2; 271, 272, *nn*.16; 301, *n*.75; 302, *n*.78; 302, *n*.79
Bulgaria 192
Burke, E. 236
Burnaby, J. 136
Bury 207
Buckley, M. 95, 312, *n*.6

Cajetan, Tommaso Cardinal 194, *n*.65
Calvin, J. 102, 235
    Augustine 140
    Eucharist 178, *n*.30
    Predestination 140, 158
    "Word of God" 94, 259
Camus, A. 209, 262, *n*.93
Canons 270, 275, *n*.22
Canonists, Medival 194, 200, *n*.75
Carlival 194, 200, *n*.75
Carlyle, R.W. 220, 221, *n*.16
Cassirer, E. 229, *n*.30
Cavarnos, C. 251, *n*.74
Cerularius, Michael 22
Chemnitz, M. 26, *n*.2
Chadwick, O. 34, *n*.9; 44, *n*.22, 24; 216, *n*. 13
Charlemange 52, *n*.7; 191
Charles V of France 200
Chenu, M-D. 39, *n*.13; 245, *n*. 62
chiliasm 303
Christ
    Chalcedon 19, *n*.16; 114-120
    economy (dispensation) 101, 117, *n*.32; 172
    gnome 118
    Incarnation 117, 168
    Monophysites 115*f*.; 307
    Nestorianism 116*f*., 119, 146, *n*.86; 307
    "non-Chalcedonian" 114, *n*.28
    Recapitulation 121, *n*.38; 123, 156
    synapheia 119

"theandric", theandropic 156, 159
"theanthropos", theanthropic 178
Chrysostomos of Etna 270, *n*.12; 271
Church
    Apostles 153, 160
    Body of Christ 154
    Canons 154, 226, *n*.25; 275, *n*.22
    canonical/charismatic 274-276
    charismata 274
    "Christian race"
    Doctrine 53, 298–300
    economy 285
    episcopacy 204, *f.*
    hagios (sanctus) 159
    Holy Spirit 159, 298–300
    Intercommunion 268, 286, *n*.40; 296, 297
    Judaism 153
    katholikos 296, *n*.64
    koinonoia 43, *n*.21
    Mysteries 174*ff.*, 285
    Prophets 153, 160
Cizevsky, D. 289, *n*.49
Clifford, A.C. 139, *n*.71
Colleran, J.M. 103, *n*.1
Collingwood, R.G. 229, *n*.30
Conferences
    Aarhus 114, *n*.28, 115, *n*.29; 116, *n*.31
    Amsterdam 268
    Assisi 265*f.*
    Dehli 265
    Evanston 268
    Harare 266
    Lambeth 286
    Niarabi 265
    Oberlin 268, 270, 276
    Vancouver 26
coincidenta oppositorum 108
Colleran, J.M. 103, *n*.1
Congar, M.J. 188, *n*.48
Congar, Y. 146, *n*.86; 193, *n*.63
Conrad of Gelnhausen 200
consensus patrum 10
consubstantiation 18
Copelston, F. 151, *n*.93
Corrigan, K. 11, *n*.5
Councils
    Basel 172, 201*f.*
    Bologna 201
    Constance 201*f.*
    Florence 194, *n*.65; 201, 229, *n*.30
    Lyons 1274

    Orange II 106
    Pisa 200
    Trent 44, 188, *n*.49; 260,*n*.90
    Vatican I 202, 204
    Vatican II 174, 185, 202, 203, *n*.30; 264
Councils, Ecumenical 204
    FIRST: Nicea I 325 A.D. 51, 52, 282, 288, 308
    SECOND: Constantinople I 381 A.D. 51, 297
    THIRD: Ephesus 431 A.D. 176-77, *n*.27; 308
    FOURTH: Chalcedon 451 A.D. 114-120, 218, 223, *n*.20, 307*f.*
        Canons 28, 189, *n*.50; 251, 253, 257
    FIFTH: Constantinople II 553 A.D. 178, *n*.30; 308
    SIXTH: 680-681 A.D. 118-120, 308
    SEVENTH: Nicea II 787 A.D. 252; 308
Conciliar Movement 199-202
Cox, H. 262, *n*.92
Crum, W.F. 273, *n*.16
Cur Deus Homo 67; 257, *n*.85; 259, *n*.88
Curtis, G. 301, *n*.74
Cyprian, Archimandrite 251, *n*.74

D

Daniel the Prophet 208, 217, 229
    Four Kingdoms 228
    Roman Empire 208
Danielou, J. 211, *n*.5; 212, *n*.6; 216, *n*.14
Dasyupta, S. 312, *n*.7
Davies, J.G. 176, *n*.27
Dawson, C. 214, *n*.9; 215, *nn*.10,11
D'Entreves 230, *n*.33, 231, *nn*.35, 36
de Coulanges, F. 226, *n*.27
de Unamuno, M. 68, 311, *n*.4
DeChanac, W. 171, 172, *n*.20
DeMaistre, J. 194, *n*.65
Defensor pacis 232, *nn*.38, 39; 234, *n*.42
Degyansky, D. 265, *n*.4; 287, *n*.42
Descartes, R. 236
deification *(theosis)* 23, 65, 75, 77; 135-137
democracy 199, 227
Deus Absconditus 69
Dispensation (*see* Economy)
docetic, docetism 157, 308
Documentary History of the Faith and Order Movement: 1927-1963 268, *n*.11

Doellinger, I. von   194, 195, *n.67*; 283, *n.36*
Donati Constantini (Donation of Constan-
    tine)   191, *n.54*; 192, 193, *n.63*
Dorotheus of Brussa   286, *n.41*
Downey, G.   p.223, 242; *nn.21, 22*
dualism   8, 18
Duerer, A.   260
Dun Scotus   139*f.*, 151
Dvornik, F.   188, *n.45*
dyarchy   222
Dyobounites, K.   284, *n.38*

Easter (*see* Pascha)
Economy (*see* Christ)
Ecumenical Movement   263-276
"ecumenical" Orthodox   2
ecumenism   263, *n.1*; 298, 302
Encyclical of 1920   263, 286
Engles, J.   178, *n.30*
Ensslin, W.   221, *n.17*
Epistola Concordiae (1379)   200
Erickson, J.   302, *n.80*
Eucharist (*see* Mysteries)
eschatology
    eschaton, eschatos   168, *n.7*; 209, 228
    hell (*gehenna*)   124, *n.42*
    history   211, 229, 253, 295
    Judgment   124, *n.42*
    last day   176
    "realized"   307
Eunomius   65
Eusebius of Caesarea   214
    Conciliar Movement   199-202
evangelical Orthodox   2

Fairweather, E.R.   47, *n.35*
faith and reason   295
Fallow, T.M.   127, *n.46*
Fathers   8-15, 40
    St Ambrose of Milan   61, *n.3*; 66, 74,
        n.20; 100, 135, *n.66*; 165, 166, 174, 177,
        n.27, 198
    St. Andrew of Caesarea   167, *n.15*
    St Anthony the Great   294
    St Aphrahat   130

St Athanasius the Great   28; 135, *n.66*
St Basil the Great   26, 27*ff.*; 62, 70-1, 100,
    175*ff.*, 182, 211*ff.*, 215, *n.10*; 239, 255,
    300, 316
St Bede the Venerable   167, *n.15*; 214
St Benedict of Nursia   244, *ff.*
St Berenguard   167, *n.15*
St Celestine of Rome   34
St Cyprian of Carthage   165, 180, *n.31*;
    187, *n.44*; 299
St Cyril of Alexandria   93, 101, 115, 116,
    n.31; 122, *n.40*; 129; 135, *n.66*; 158, 165,
    226, *n.26*
St Cyril of Jerusalem   30, 69, *n.20*; 160,
    209, *n.2*
St Dionysius the Areopagite   27, *n.4*; 30,
    69, *n.70*; 71, 81, 86, *n.41*; 175, 241
St Ephraim the Syrian   166
St Faustus of Riez   176, *n.27*; 216
St Flavian of Constantinople   116
St Germanus   251, *n.73*
St Gregory of Nyssa   11, *n.5*; 17, *n.14*;
    69, *n.20*; 71; 135, *n.66*; 155
St Gregory of Sinai   10
St Gregory the Great   69, *n.20*; 73, *n.20*;
    155, 189*f.*, *nn.51-53*; 221, 251, *n.73*
St Gregory Palamas   65, 69, *n.20*; 73, 173,
    174, *n.23*; 178
St Gregory the Theologian   9, 11, 51, 61,
    69, 70, 81, 99, 135, *n.66*; 220, 238, 104,
    n.6; 125, *n.42*; 129, 156, 227, 312
St Geregory of Tours   214
St Hilarion (Troitsky)   162, *n.8*; 180*f.*; 293,
    298-300
St Hilary of Poitiers   74, *n.20*; 101; 135,
    n.66; 315*f.*
St Hippolytus of Rome   1, 66, 135, *n.66*;
    183, *n.37*, 228
St Hosios of Cordova   222
St Ignatius of Antioch   69, 183, *n.37*; 153,
    178
St Irenaeus of Lyons   32; 77, 121, 123;
    135, *n.66*; 158, 219, 180, 183, *n.37*
St Isaac the Syrian   62*ff.*; 294
St John Cassian   148, 216, 243*ff.*
St Isaac the Syrian   62*ff.*
St John Climacus   239
St John Chrysostom   61, *n.13*; 100, 122,
    130; 135, *n.66*; 187, *n.44*; 155*f.*; 214,
    220, 226, *n.26*; 238, 250

St John of Damascus   61, 74, *n.23*; 90,
     93, 104, *n.6*; 118, 166, *n.13*; 176
St John Maximovitch   168, *n.17*
St Justin Martyr   9, 127
St Justinian   220, 221, *n.16*; 222; 223, *n.*
     21; 223, *n.20*
St Linus   187, *n.4*
St Leo I the Great   15, 61, *n.13*; 69, *n.20*;
     100, 115, 129, 135, *n.66*; 174, 182, 189
St Marcarius the Great   126
St Marcian the Emperor   114
St Maxim of Turin   135, *n.66*
St Maximus the Confessor   12*f.*, 69, *n.20*;
     70, 118
St Methodius of Olympus   175
St Nectarios of Aegina   288, *n.47*
St Neketas Remesiana   159, *n.7*; 177, *n.27*
St Nicephorus of Constantinople   250, *n.*
     71
St Pachomius of Constantinople 250, *n.71*
St Nikodemos of Mt Athos   238
St Pachomius   243
St Paisius Velichovsky   239, 293, *n.60*
St Peter Chrysologus   122; 135, *n.66*;
St Photius the Great   22, 78, 82-90, 192
St. Seraphim of Sarov   158, *n.5*; 154, 183,
     293
St Sophronius of Jerusalem   119
St Symeon of Thessalonica   187, *n.44*
St Symeon the New Theologian   127, 239
St Theodore the Studite   168, *n.17*
St Tikon Confessor   301, *n.73*
St Valerian of Cimiez   123, 183
St Vincent of Lerins   26, 30*ff.*; 216
Fellowship of St Alban and St Sergius   301
Festurgiere, A.J.   240, *n.50*; 241, *nn.52, 53*
Feuerbach, L.   111*ff.*
Fitzer, J.   178, *n.30*
filioque   78-90
Florovsky, G.   19, *n.16*; 26, *n.2*; 27, *n.2*; 32;
     43, *n.20*; 155, *n.2*; 213, *nn.7, 8*; 229, 30,
     n.32; 268, 270-276, 284, *n.37*; 289, *n.*
     48; 290, *n.51*; 292, *n.56*; 295; 298, *n.*
     71; 304, *n.80*; 306
   Augustine, endorsement of   273, 274
   canonical church   74
   charismatic church   274
   ecumenism   271
   hellenism   273

   heresy, attitude towards   275, 276, 292,
        n.56
   Iconoclastic controversy   251, *n.74*
        "neo-patristic synthesis"   272, 273
        "Paris Theologians"   271, 301-302, 309
        "pseudomorphosis"   273, 276
        St Sergius Academy   271, 301
        St Vincent of Lerins, criticism of   273
Francis of Assisi   247-248
Frank, E.   45, *n.26*
Frazee, C.A.   280, *n.29*; 281, *n.32*; 282, *n.34*
Freemasonry   264, 278, 289, 291, *n.53*
Fritsch-Oppermann, S.   265, *n.4*

G

Galavaris, C.   251, *n.74*
Galileo   310
Garrigou-Lagrange, R.   74, *n.23*
Garvin, F.   272, *n.16*; 285, *n.39*
Geanakoplos, D.J.   223, *n.20*
Gerson, Jean   200
Giakalis, A.   251, *n.74*
Gilson, E.   6, 7, 58, *n.4*; 103, *n.3*; 311
Glossa Ordinaria   194, *n.66*
Glukarev, M.   293, *n.58*
God
   existence of, arguments for   59, *n.7*
   filioque   157, 283
   Uncreated Energies   5, n.;1; 55, 57, 188,
        n.49; 220, *n.15*
Golytsin, A.   289
Gottschalk of Obrais   147
Grabar, A.   251, *n.74*; 257, *n.84*
Graef, H.   172, *n.20*
Granfield, P.   194, *n.65*
Gratian   193, 194, *n.66*
Gratieux, A.S.   277, *n.24*
Greece
   Constitution of 1843
Gregorios VI 283
Gregory (Grabbe)   288, *nn.45, 46, 47*
Grillmeier, A.   104, *n.7*
Greer, R.A.   104, *n.6*
Grotius   236
Guette, Abbée   192, *n.57*
Gulovich, S.C.   172, 173, *n.21*

H

Hale, J.   258, *n.87*
Haller, J.   191, *n.55*; 193, *n.59*
Hampe, K.   162, *n.8*; 193
Hanson, R.P.C.   28, *n.5*
Hare, A.   289, *n.49*
Harnack, A. von   46, 49, 80, *n.30*; 103, 134, *n.64*; 181, *n.34*
Heer, F.   18, *n.15*; 19, *n.17*; 302, *n.78*
Headly, J.M.   42, *n.18*; 43, *n.21*
Hefele, C.J.   119, *n.34*
Hegel, G.   12, 45, 46, *n.29*; 81, *n.32*; 219, 236
Hein, L.   289, *n.49*
Hergenrother, J.   21, *n.18*
heresy   275, 276, 292, *n.56*; 295, 296, 297
hesychia   242, *n.57*
Hesychast controversy   242, *n.57*
    Uncreated Energies, Grace   253
Heussi, K.   243, *n.59*
Hildebertus of Lavardin   16
Hugh of St. Victor   39
Hume, D.   236
Hobbes, T.   235
Holy Cross Greek Orthodox Seminary   270, *n.12*
Homer   225
Hooker, R.   235
Hopkins, J.   134, *n.65*
Huizinga, J.   258, *n.86*
Huss, John   200

I

Iconography   11, *n.5*; 250-262
    archeiropoietos   251
    archetype   254, *n.79*
    blasphemy   258
    Franciscan   248, *n.67*
    Laetenur coeli "icon"   98
    mandylion   251
    nimbus crucifixus   255
    Western halo   256
Ideas, theory of   71
Immaculate Conception   169, 174
Islam   37
Istavridis, V.T.   286, *n.40*

J

Jaeger, W.   224
Jalland, T. G.   189
James of Viterbo   196, *n.71*
Janus   194, *n.66*
Jean Gerson   200
Jerome   215, *n.10*
Joachim III   284
Joachim of Fiore   53, 246
John of the Cross   249, *n.70*
John of Paris   199
John of Smolensk   275, *n.22*
Joannes Teutonicus   200, *n.75*
Jugie, M.   76; 291, *n.54*

K

Kalokyris, C.D.   251, *n.74*; 254; 255, *n.80*
Kalomiros, A.   136, *n.67*
Kant, I.   12, 58, 60, 236, 252
Kantorwicz, E.   86, *n.41*; 195, *n.68*; 228, *n.28*
Karlovci Synod   271, *n.13*; 273
Karmiris, J.   116, n.31; 164, *n.11*
Kesich, V.   187, *n.44*
Kierkegaard, S.   111, *n.21*
Kireevsky, I.   294, 295
Kittel, G.   145, *n.84*; 146, *n.87*
Klee, H.   36
Knowles, D.   17, *n.13*; 39, *n.14*; 42, *n.17*; 138, *n.76*
Koch, H.   238, *n.48*
Koenker, E.B.   106, *n.10*, 107, 12
Kokkinakis, Athenagoras   268
Komiakov, A.   36, *n.11*; 239, 274, 293, 294
    Augustine, 274
    heresy 275, 295
    The Church is One 295
    Slavophilism 277, 289, *n.49*
Kontoglou, P.   251, *n.74*; 253
Kontogones, K.   280, *n.31*, 281
Koraes, A.   278, 279, n.27
Koyre, A.   108, *n.17*; 291, *n.53*
Krivosheine, B.   126, *n.45*
Kueng. H.   316, *n.10*
Kurgansky, T.   175, *n.25*

L

Labzin, A.F.   291
Ladner, G.   34, *n*.9
Lampe, G.W.H.   26, *n*.2
Lampryllos, C.   44, *n*.25
Lanfranc of Bec   17
Latourette, K.S.   161
Langen, J.   195, *n*.67
Lawless, G.   244, *n*.61
League of Nations   287
Leibnitz, G.   72
Lengsfeld, P.   120, *n*.37
Leo I, Emperor   221, *n*.16
LeRoux, D.   265, 139, *n*.77
Lessius, L.   95
Locke, J.   235
Lonergan, B.J.F.   40, *n*.15
Loewith, K.   111, *n*.20; 111, *n*.21; 215, *n*.12
L'Osservatore Romano   264
Lossky, N.O.   302, *n*.78
Lossky, V.   31, *n*.6; 74, 86, *n*.41; 123, *n*.41;
      133, *n*.60; 172, *n*.21; 174, *n*.22; 242, *n*.56;
      256, *n*.82
Lowenthall   236, *n*.45
Louth, A.   244, *n*.60
Luther, M.   61, *n*.13; 80, *n*.31; 183, *n*.37
      Augustine   44, *n*.23
      Church   43, *n*.21
      elect   142, 157, 158
      Eucharist   18
      images   260
      justification   140, 145
      Scriptura sola   253
      consubstantion   178, *n*.29
      Wrath of God   129

M

Machiavelli, N.   218, 232, 235, *n*.44; 310
Maloney, G.A.   280, *n*.29
Mango, C.   251, *n*.74
Manning, H.E.   197, *n*.73
Marsilius of Padua   232
Marius Victorinus   90*ff*.
Margarie, B.   81, *n*.32; 82, *n*.34; 84, *n*.38

Markus, R.A.   178, *n*.30
Marx, K.   113, *n*.25; 219, 235, 237, 289, *n*.48
Mazour, A.   291, *n*.53
Masaryk, G.   113, *n*.25
McGinn, B.   14, *n*.10; 209, *n*.3; 136, *n*.68
McGrath, A.E.   134, *n*.61; 144, *n*.83; 145,
      n.85; 146, *n*.86; 147, *n*.88; 150, *nn*.91, 92
McKenna, S.   91, *n*.43
McIntire, C.T.   207, *n*.l
McIntyre, J.   134, *n*.63
McLaughlin, T.P.   197, *n*.73
McWilliam-Dewart, J.   103, *nn*.5, 6
Meister Eckhart   73, 102, 248, 249, *n*.68
Meland, P.E.   252, *n*.75
Meliton, Metropolitan   264
Meletios Metaxakis   287
Mersch, E.   17, *n*.12; 54, 55, *n*.l
Metallinos, G.D.   302, *n*.80
Meyendorff, J.   103, *n*.5; 163, *n*.10; 187, *n*.44;
      188, *n*.47
Montesquieu   236
Megale Idea   276; 287, *n*.43
monasticism   237-250
      anchoretic   238
      Augustinian   246, *n*.63
      Benedictine   244
      Cistercian   247
      Dominicans   247
      coenobetic   238
      female   238, 246, *n*.63; 245
      Franciscans   247*f*.
      "model christian"   175
monothelites, monothelitism   119, 157
Motovilov, N.A.   158, *n*.5
Moss, C.B.   201
Muratori, A.   172, *n*.20
Murray, A.V.   138, *n*.76
Mysteries (sacraments)   174, 225
      Baptism   154, 174, 177, *n*.27; 182, 183,
            198, 302, *n*.80
      Baptism by desire   163, *n*.9
      heretical baptism   274, 299
      Eucharist   175, 176, 254
      epiklesis   176, *n*.27
      sacramenta futuri   177
      transubstantiation   16, 17, 176, *n*.26

N

New Calendarists   268, 288
Newman, J.H.   37, 47*ff.*, 93, 174
Nichol, D.M.   191, *n.54*
Nicholas of Cusa   73
Nichomachean Ethics   225
Nietzsche, F.   219, 277, *n.23*
noetic contemplation   10
Nominalism   199
Norman Anonymous of York   196
Norris, R.A.   105, *n.7*

O

Obermann, H.O.   169*f.*
O'Connor, E.D.   170*f.*, 171, *n.19*
Oikonomos, K.   278*f.*, 279, *nn.26, 28*
Old Catholics   282*f.*
Optina monastery   293, *n.60*
Origen of Alexandria   10, 14 *n.10*; 33,
   178, *n.30*
Orthodox ecclesiology   202, 270, 274, 282*f.*
Ouspensky, L.   251, *nn.72, 74*; 254, *n.79*; 256
Outler, A.C.   42, 45, *n.28*
Oxford Movement   47, 283

P

Pacem in Terris   264
Palmer, W.   296, 297, *n.67*
Papacy
   Alexander   45, *n.28*
   Avignon   199
   Canonists   198
   De Potestate ecclesiae   198, 199
   Boniface VII   195, *n.68*; 198, 199
   Boniface VIII   261, *n.91*
   Clement VII   199
   Donation of Constantine   191, *n.54*; 232,
      261, *n.91*
   Eugenius IV   201
   Felix V   201
   Gregory VII   192*f.*, 194, 199, 203
   Gregory XIII   288, *n.45*
   Innocent III   195, *n.68*
   Pseudo-Isidorian Decrentals   191, *n.54*;
      193, *n.63*; 194, *n.66*
   John XXIII   99, 264, *n.2*

   John-Paul II   266
   Julius II   194, *n.65*
   "keys of the Kingdom"   195
   Leo III   191
   Leo IX   149
   Martin V   201
   Nicholas I   22, 192*f.*; 245
   Paul IV   203, *n.80*
   Paul VI   264
   Pius IX   p.171, *n.19*; 277, *n.23*; 281
      Syllabus of Errors   219, 305
   Steven II   191
   Urban VI   199
   Vicarius Christi   196
   Papal infallibility   203, *n.79*
Papastephanou, E.   268
Particular Judgement   99
   "Abraham's Bosom"   99
   hades   99, 128
Pascha   127
Patelos, C.   265, *n.3*
Patriarch of Antioch   115, *n.28*
Patriarchal Encyclicals
   of 1848   25, 281
   of 1895   282, *n.35*
Pedalion   278, 281, *n.33*
Pelagius   147*f.*
Pelagius II, Pope   221
Pelikan, J.   11, *n.5*; 12, *n.6*; 49*ff.*; 56, 62,
   n.14; 168, *n.18*; 172, 73, *n.21*
Peter Damian   196
Peter the Great   229, 30, *n.32*; 303
Peter the Lombard   18, 39, 171
Peterson, E.   228, *n.56*; 28
Philaret of Moscow   274, 291-3; *n.56*; 299
   longer catechism   293, *n.59*
Philaret of New York   303
Philokalia   10, 278, *n.25*
philosophy
   Greek   308
   medieval   20
phronema   15, 297
Photios of Triaditsa   288, *n.45*
Pieper, J.   39, *n.13*
Pierre D'Ailly   200
Placher, W.C.   94
Plato   70, 101, 224, 227, 248, 252, 253, 272
Plotinus   12, 90, 213, 252, 312
Platon of Moscow   285, *n.39*
Pohle, J.   120, *nn.35, 37*
Polybius   213

Pomazansky, M.   168, *n.17*
Popov, I.V.   91, *n.43*
Popovich, J.   118, *n.33*; 268, *n.11*; 277, *n.23*; 289, *n.47*
Prince, The   235, n.44
Prokopovich, T.   229, 30, *n.31*; 291, n.51
Prospor of Aquitane   146
Protestantism   248, 278, 295*f.*
"Pseudo-Dionysius" (*see* St Dionysius the Areopagite under Fathers)
Psomiades, H.J.   287, *n.43*
Puhalo, L.   124, *n.42*; 162, *n.8*

Radbertus of Corbie   16*f.*
Rahner, K.   74, 96, *n.50*; 137, *n.71*
Ranson, P.   44, *n.25*; 85, *n.40*, 92, *n.45*
Raphael Hawaweeny, Bishop   286, *n.40*
Rashdall, H.   123, *n.41*; 130, *n.52*; 133, *n.59*; 138, *n.74*; 139, *n.77*
Ratramnus   16*f.*
recapitulation   121, *n.38*; 123, *n.41*
Redman, B.J.   265, *n.4*
Renouvier, C.   271, *n.15*
Richards, J.   187, *n.44*
Ritschl, A.B.   49, 50, 132, *n.57*; 152, *n.95*
River of Fire, The   136, *n.67*
Robinson, I.S.   192, *n.58*
Rodzianko, V.   88, *n.42*
romanum imperium christiana   208, 226
    Nicholas I   277, *n.24*
    Third Rome   228, 277, *n.24*
Romandies, J.S.   66, *n.19*; 122, *n.40*; 125, *n.44*
Rousseau, J.J.   236
Runze, A.   59, *n.9*
Russia and the Universal Church   264, *n.2*

Sabaneff, L.   289, *n.49*
Sabellius, Sabellians   92, *n.45*
St Pulcheria   251, *n.73*
St Patriarch Tikon   271, *n.13*
St Peter   202
St Nicholas II   208
Sakkas, B.   288, *n.45*
salvation (see deification)
Samuel, V.C.   115
Sartory, T.   146, *n.86*

Schaff, P.   190, *n.51*
Schapiro, L.   302, *n.78*
Scheler, M.   208
Schelling   109, *n.18*; 290, *n.49*
Schmemann, A.   184, n.40; 188, *n.49*; 239, *n.49*; 273, *n.18*
Scholasticism   6
Schultze, B.   289, *n.49*
Scotus Eriugena   15
scripture   16, 291-293, 292, *n.56*; 295
Sevcenko, I.   229, *n.31*
shekinah   167
Sherlock, W.   94
Siggins   142, *n.78*
Siotes, M.   279, *n.26*
sobornost'   296, *n.64*
Socrates   90, 224
Southern, R.W.   57, *n.2*; 13, *n.54*; 134, *n.63*; 193, *n.63*; 246, *n.64*; 249, *n.68*
Soloviev, V.   216, *n.14*; 264, *n.2*; 271, 289, *n.49*; 296, *n.64*
sophiology   271, *n.15*; 289, *n.49*
soteriology   135-137
Sozomen   214
Spector, I.   290, *n.50*
Spengler   207
Spinoza, B.   235
Stone, D.   304, *n.80*
Stoudt, J.J.   108, *n.15*
Stremoouukhoff, D.   229, *n.30*
Sylianopolis, T.   280, *nn.30, 31*
synapheia   119
Synod of Hatfield   44, *n.5*
Synod of Laodicia   7, *n.4*
Synodicon of Orthodoxy   p. 66

Tavard, G   263, *n.1*
telos (teleology)   129, *n.50*; 210
Tellenbach, G.   192, *n.58*
Teresa of Avila   249, 50, *n.249*
Ternus, J.   105, *n.8*
Tertullian   7, 25, 34, 135, *n.66*; 188, *n.46*
theandrically   118, *n.33*
Theodore of Mopsusestia   19
Theodoret   214
theology   292
theology of history   214
theoria   64

theosis (see deification)
theosophy 249, 271, *n.*15
Tierney, B. 194, *n.*65; 197, *n.*73; 199, 200, *n.*75
Tillich, P. 60 131, *n.*53
time 213
Timiadis, E. 267, *n.*10
Tradition
    Apostolic 12
    "development of doctrine" 172, 73, *n.*21
    paradosis 176
transubstantiation
Tsirpanlis, C. 164, *n.*11
Tsonievsky, P.C. 116, *n.*31

Ullmann, W. 192, *n.*56
Una Sancta 270, 274, 283
Unam Sanctam 195, *n.*68; 199
Uncreated Energies 55, 57, 65, 71*ff.*
Underbill, E. 241, *n.*54; 307, *n.*2
Unfading Light 271, *n.*15
United Nations 263
Unity of the Church and the World Conference of Christian Communities 180, *n.*31; 181, *n.*33; 298

Valla, L. 191, *n.*54
Vamvas, N. 279, *n.*28
Van der Meer, F. 181, *n.*32
Vatican Dogma, The 201, *n.*76
Venerable Bede 167, *n.*15
Venizelos, E. 287
Vincentian Canon 30*ff.* (*see* St Vincent of Lerins)
Virgin Mary
    Ever Virgin 167
    Immaculate Conception 170-173
    Mother of God 167
    "New Eve," "Second Eve" 166, 173
    Theotokos 168, *n.*17; 169, 173, 174
Voltaire 207*f.*

Walafridus of Strabo 192
Walker, W. 199, *n.*74
Walton, L. 289, *n.*49
Ware, Timothy 22, *n.*19; 172, 73, *n.*21
Watts, A. 57, *n.*3; 312, *n.*7
Ways of Russian Theology 272
Weigel, G. 34, 73, *n.*21
Wilks, M. 194, *n.*65; 197
Williams of Ockham 199
Williams, G.H. 19, *n.*16; 228, *n.*28; 271, *n.*14; 274
Williams, N.P. 148, *n.*90; 313, *n.*8
Williams, P.L. 136, *n.*68
Winter, M. 187, *n.*44
Witfield, J.H. 235, *n.*44
Wolf, E. 43, *n.*21
Wolfson, H.A. 14, *n.*8
Wolters, A.B. 172, *n.*20
Workman, H.B. 238, *n.*47; 240, *n.*51
World Council of Churches 263, 314
Wycliff, J. 42, 200, 218

Yannaris, C. 18, *n.*15
Ypsilantis, A. 278

Zander, Lev 301, *nn.*76, 77
Zelinsky, A.N. 288, *n.*47
Zenkovsky, V.V. 302, *n.*78
Zernicavius, A. 44, *n.*25
Zernov, N. 228, 264, *n.*2; 301, *n.*75
Zizioulas, J. 175, *n.*24